THE ROUTLEDGE COM
CULTURAL INI

The Routledge Companion to the Cultural Industries is a collection of contemporary scholarship that seeks to re-assert the importance of cultural production and consumption against the purely economic imperatives of the 'creative industries'.

Across 43 chapters drawn from a wide range of geographic and disciplinary perspectives, this comprehensive volume offers a critical and empirically informed examination of the contemporary cultural industries.

A range of industries are explored, from video games to art galleries, all the time focusing on the culture that is being produced and its wider symbolic and socio-cultural meaning. Individual chapters consider their industrial structure, the policy that governs them, their geography, the labour that produces them, and the meaning they offer to consumers and participants.

The collection also explores the historical dimension of cultural industry debates, providing context for new readers, as well as critical orientation for those more familiar with the subject. Questions of industry structure, labour, place, international development, consumption, and regulation are all explored in terms of their historical trajectory and potential future direction.

By assessing the current challenges facing the cultural industries, this collection provides students and researchers with an essential guide to key ideas, issues, concepts, and debates in the field.

Kate Oakley is Professor and Head of the School of Culture and Creative Arts at the University of Glasgow. Her research interests include the politics of cultural policy, labour in the cultural industries, and inequality.

Justin O'Connor is Professor in the School of Creative Industries, University of South Australia, and is visiting Professor in the School of Media and Design, Shanghai Jiaotong University.

Contributors: Mark Banks, David Bell, Chris Bilton, Scott Brook, Sarah Brouillette, Chantel Carr, Nicole S. Cohen, Christopher Doody, Gillian Doyle, Kingsley Edney, Lee Edwards, Scott Fitzgerald, Des Freedman, Anthony Fung, Chris Gibson, Nitin Govil, Xin Gu, Shane Homan, Yudhishthir Raj Isar, Helen Kennedy, Brendan Keogh, Bastian Lange, RichardMaxwell, LeslieM. Meier, Steven Miles, KatieMilestone, Toby Miller, Catherine Murray, Caitriona Noonan, Kate Oakley, Dave O'Brien, Justin O'Connor, Laikwan Pang, Matt Patterson, Greig de Peuter, Keith Randle, Steve Redhead, David Rowe, Andy Ruddock, Anamik Saha, Cornel Sandvoss, Philip Schlesinger, Daniel Silver, John Sinclair, John Tebbutt, David Throsby, Graeme Turner, Andrew Warren, David Wright.

THE ROUTLEDGE COMPANION TO THE CULTURAL INDUSTRIES

Edited by
Kate Oakley and Justin O'Connor

Routledge
Taylor & Francis Group

LONDON AND NEW YORK

First published in paperback 2019

First published 2015
by Routledge
2 Park Square, Milton Park, Abingdon, Oxon OX14 4RN

and by Routledge
52 Vanderbilt Avenue, New York, NY 10017

Routledge is an imprint of the Taylor & Francis Group, an informa business

British Library Cataloguing-in-Publication Data
A catalogue record for this book is available from the British Library

Library of Congress Cataloging-in-Publication Data
The Routledge companion to the cultural industries / edited by Kate Oakley and Justin O'Connor.
pages cm
Includes bibliographical references and index.
ISBN 978-0-415-70620-9 (hbk) ~ ISBN 978-1-315-72543-7 (ebk) 1. Cultural industries. 2. Cultural policy. 3. Arts--Economic aspects. I. Oakley, Kate. II. O'Connor, Justin.
HD9999.C9472R68 2015
338.4'77--dc23
2014043229

ISBN: 978-0-415-70620-9 (hbk)
ISBN: 978-1-138-39187-1 (pbk)
ISBN: 978-1-315-72543-7 (ebk)

Typeset in Goudy
by Taylor & Francis Books

Printed and bound in Great Britain by
TJ International Ltd, Padstow, Cornwall

CONTENTS

CONTENTS

FIGURES AND TABLES

Figures

Tables

ACKNOWLEDGEMENTS

We would like to thank all those who contributed their work to this volume. Special thanks to Joanne Hollows for getting the chapters into shape. And thanks to Natalie Foster and Sheni Kruger at Routledge for commissioning the volume and all working with us on its production.

Kate and Justin

CONTRIBUTORS

Mark Banks is Professor in the Department of Media and Communication at the University of Leicester, UK. He writes about work and policy in the cultural industries, and most recently on music, money and the new intensities of cultural labour.

David Bell is a Senior Lecturer in Critical Human Geography and Head of School at the University of Leeds, UK. His most recent book, co-authored with Kate Oakley, is *Cultural Policy* (Routledge, 2015).

Chris Bilton teaches management and creativity at the Centre for Cultural Policy Studies, University of Warwick, UK. Recent publications include the *Handbook of Management and Creativity* (Edward Elgar, 2014) and *Creativity and Cultural Policy* (Routledge, 2011). He is currently working with Stephen Cummings and dt Ogilvie on a new research project entitled 'Creativities'.

Scott Brook is Assistant Professor at the Centre for Creative and Cultural Research, University of Canberra, Australia. His research focuses on creative labour and cultural policy studies.

Sarah Brouillette is an Associate Professor in the Department of English at Carleton University in Ottawa, Canada, where she teaches contemporary literature and topics in print culture and media studies.

Chantel Carr is a Ph.D. candidate in the Department of Geography and Sustainable Communities at the University of Wollongong, Australia. Her research examines maker cultures, material skill and ways of making do in the context of climate change adaptation.

Nicole S. Cohen is an Assistant Professor at the Institute of Communication, Culture, Information and Technology at the University of Toronto, Canada. She is currently collaborating with Greig de Peuter and Enda Brophy on a project tracking cultural workers' collective organising efforts: culturalworkersorganize.org.

Christopher Doody is a Ph.D. candidate in the Department of English Language and Literature at Carleton University, Canada.

Gillian Doyle is Professor of Media Economics and Director of the Centre for Cultural Policy Research at the University of Glasgow, UK, where she directs Glasgow's M.Sc.

in Media Management and leads a number of research projects on economic and policy aspects of media.

Kingsley Edney is Lecturer in Politics and International Relations of China in the School of Politics and International Studies at the University of Leeds, UK. He is the author of *The Globalization of Chinese Propaganda: International Power and Domestic Political Cohesion* (Palgrave Macmillan, 2014).

Lee Edwards is Associate Professor in Communication Studies and PR, School of Media and Communication at the University of Leeds, UK. She is author of *Power, Diversity and Public Relations* (Routledge, 2014), *Understanding Copyright* (with Dr Bethany Klein and Dr Giles Moss, Sage, 2015) and editor, with Dr Caroline Hodges, of *Public Relations, Society and Culture: Theoretical and Empirical Explorations* (Routledge, 2011).

Scott Fitzgerald is Senior Lecturer in the Curtin Business School, Curtin University, Perth, Australia. His research interests cover cultural industry corporations, creative work, public services and new public management. He is the author of *Corporations and Cultural Industries: Time Warner, Bertelsmann, and News Corporation* (Lexington Books, 2012).

Des Freedman is Professor of Media and Communications at Goldsmiths, University of London, UK. He is the author of *The Contradictions of Media Power* (Bloomsbury, 2014) and *The Politics of Media Policy* (Polity, 2008), and co-author (with James Curran and Natalie Fenton) of *Misunderstanding the Internet* (Routledge, 2012).

Anthony Fung is Professor in the School of Journalism and Communication at the Chinese University of Hong Kong. He is also the Pearl River Chair Professor at Jinan University in China. His research interests include the political economy of media, culture and communication, Hong Kong cultural identity, popular culture and cultural studies.

Chris Gibson is Professor of Human Geography at the University of Wollongong, Australia, and Director of the interdisciplinary research programme Global Challenges: Transforming Lives and Regions. His books include *Surfing Places, Surfboard Makers: Craft, Creativity and Cultural Heritage in Hawai'i, California and Australia*, with Andrew Warren (University of Hawaii Press, 2014), and *Sound Tracks: Popular Music, Identity and Place*, with John Connell (Psychology Press, 2003).

Nitin Govil is Assistant Professor of Critical Studies at the School of Cinematic Arts, University of Southern California, USA. He is the co-author of *Global Hollywood* (British Film Institute, 2001) and *Global Hollywood 2* (British Film Institute, 2005). His latest book is *Orienting Hollywood: A Century of Film Culture Between Los Angeles and Bombay* (New York University Press, 2015).

Xin Gu is a native Shanghainese living in Melbourne. Xin teaches media studies at Monash University, Australia. She is working on the book *Culture and Economy in the New Shanghai* (Routledge, forthcoming).

Shane Homan teaches in the Communications and Media Studies programme at Monash University, Australia. He has written widely on the popular music industries and music policy.

Yudhishthir Raj Isar is Professor of Cultural Policy Studies at The American University of Paris and Adjunct Professor at the Institute for Culture and Society, University of Western Sydney, Australia. He is founding co-editor of the Cultures and Globalization Series (Sage). Earlier, at UNESCO, he was inter alia Executive Secretary of the World Commission on Culture and Development.

Helen Kennedy is Professor of Digital Society at the University of Sheffield, UK. She has extensive experience of researching, writing about and working in the digital media industries. She is author of *Net Work: Ethics and values in web design* (Palgrave, 2011), amongst other things.

Brendan Keogh is a Ph.D. candidate in Media and Communications at RMIT University, Australia and a freelance video game critic for a variety of publications.

Bastian Lange is an urban and economic geographer. He spearheads the research and strategic consultancy office Multiplicities-Berlin and was Guest Professor at the Humboldt University, Germany from 2011 to 2012. He is a Fellow of the Georg Simmel Centre for Metropolitan Research at the Humboldt University.

Richard Maxwell is Professor of Media Studies at the City University New York, USA. He has published widely on a range of topics, from television in Spain's democratic transition to Hollywood's international dominance, from media politics in the post 9–11 era to how big political economic forces work in the mundane routines of daily life and culture.

Leslie M. Meier is Lecturer in Media and Communication at the University of Leeds, UK. Her research interests include the music industries, advertising and promotional culture, and cultural labour. Her work has appeared in the *Journal of Popular Music Studies*, *Popular Music and Society* and the *Canadian Journal of Communication*.

Steven Miles is Professor of Sociology at Manchester Metropolitan University, UK. His research interests include consumption, identity and youth. He is the author of *Spaces for Consumption: Pleasure and Placelessness in the Post-Industrial City* and he is about to publish *Retail and Social Change*.

Katie Milestone is Senior Lecturer in Sociology and Cultural Studies in the Department of Sociology at Manchester Metropolitan University, UK. Katie has a longstanding interest in popular culture and is currently completing a book about nightclubs and a research project about 'intensive' parenting and social media.

Toby Miller is Emeritus Distinguished Professor at the University of California, Riverside, USA, the Sir Walter Murdoch Professor of Cultural Policy Studies at Murdoch University, Australia, and Professor of Journalism, Media and Cultural Studies at Cardiff University/Prifysgol Caerdydd, UK.

Catherine Murray is Professor in the School of Communication at Simon Fraser University, Canada. Her research interests include cultural policy and governance; political communication and democratic renewal; and research design for policy evaluation.

Caitriona Noonan is Lecturer in Media, Culture and Communication at the University of South Wales, UK. Her research interests include cultural policy decisionmaking and media production. She co-edited *Cultural Work and Higher Education* (Palgrave, 2013) and her work has appeared in a number of journals.

Kate Oakley is Professor and Head of the School of Culture and Creative Arts at the University of Glasgow. Her research interests include the politics of cultural policy, labour in the cultural industries, and inequality. Her books include *Cultural Policy*, with David Bell, (Routledge, 2015) and *Culture, Economy and Politics: The Case of New Labour*, with David Hesmondhalgh, David Lee, and Melissa Nisbett (Palgrave, 2015). She is currently researching the role of arts and culture in sustainable prosperity as part of the CUSP Project (www.cusp.ac.uk/) and working on inequality and cultural work with https://culturalworkersorganize.org.

Dave O'Brien is a senior lecturer in cultural policy at Goldsmiths College, University of London, UK.

Justin O'Connor is Professor in the School of Creative Industries, University of South Australia. Until the end of 2018 he was Professor of Communications and Cultural Economy at Monash University, where he headed the Culture Media Economy research unit and was program leader for the Master of Cultural and Creative Industries. He is part of the UNESCO 'Expert Facility', supporting the 2005 Convention on the Protection and Promotion of Cultural Diversity, and is visiting Professor in the School of Media and Design, Shanghai Jiaotong University. He has written cultural policy papers for a number of cities, states, and countries. He is the author of the 2016 Platform Paper *After the Creative Industries: Why We Need a Cultural Economy*, and is finalising the book *Cultural Economy in the New Shanghai*. He is co-editor, with Rong Yueming, of *Cultural Industries in Shanghai: Policy and Planning Inside a Global City* (Intellect, 2018).

Laikwan Pang is Professor of Cultural Studies in the Department of Cultural and Religious Studies at the Chinese University of Hong Kong. She is the author of a number of books, including *Creativity and Its Discontents: China's Creative Industries and Intellectual Property Rights Offenses* (Duke University Press, 2012).

Matt Patterson is a Ph.D. candidate in Sociology at the University of Toronto, Canada. His research focuses on the relationship between culture, identity, and the urban form. He is interested in how people invest meaning in buildings, parks, and other physical features of the city.

Greig de Peuter is Assistant Professor in the Department of Communication Studies at Wilfrid Laurier University in Waterloo, Canada. He is co-author, with Nick Dyer-Witheford, of *Games of Empire: Global Capitalism and Video Games* (University of Minnesota Press, 2009).

Keith Randle is Professor of Work and Organisation at the University of Hertfordshire, UK. For the past 15 years he has been researching work and employment issues in the creative industries, especially film and television. He has a particular interest in how inequalities, for example around class, (dis)ability, ethnicity and gender are created and reproduced.

Steve Redhead is Professor of Jurisprudence in the Faculty of Arts at Charles Sturt University, Australia. He was previously Professor of Law and Popular Culture at Manchester Metropolitan University, UK, Professor of Sport and Media Cultures at University of Brighton, UK, and Professor of Interdisciplinary Legal Studies at University of Ontario Institute of Technology, Canada.

David Rowe is a Professor at the Institute for Culture and Society, University of Western Sydney, Australia. He has published extensively on media and popular culture, especially sport, television, journalism, music, and urban leisure. David's work has been translated into several languages, including Chinese, French, Turkish, Spanish, Italian, German and Arabic.

Andy Ruddock is based at Monash University, Australia. He is author of *Youth and Media* (Sage, 2013), *Investigating Audiences* (Sage, 2007) and *Understanding Audiences* (Sage, 2001). His work on violence, sport, celebrity and pornography has appeared in several anthologies and refereed journals. He is currently working on a fourth book, *Exploring Media Research*.

Anamik Saha is a Lecturer in the Department of Media and Communications at Goldsmiths, University of London, UK. Prior to this he worked in the Institute of Communications Studies at the University of Leeds, UK. His work has been published in journals such as *Media, Culture and Society*, *Ethnic and Racial Studies* and the *European Journal of Cultural Studies*.

Cornel Sandvoss is Professor of Media and Journalism at the University of Huddersfield, UK. He has published widely on the interplay between media use, identity and globalisation as well as on fans and fan cultures.

Philip Schlesinger is inaugural Chair in Cultural Policy at the University of Glasgow, UK. He is currently researching cultural crisis in Europe and is also working on a study of contemporary British film policy. His most recent, co-authored, books are *The Rise and Fall of the UK Film Council* (Edinburgh University Press, 2015) and *Curators of Cultural Enterprise* (Palgrave Macmillan, 2015).

Daniel Silver is an Associate Professor of Sociology at the University of Toronto, Canada.

John Sinclair is an Honorary Professorial Fellow in the School of Historical and Philosophical Studies at the University of Melbourne, Australia. His internationally published work covers various aspects of the globalisation of the media and communication industries, most recently *Advertising, the Media and Globalisation* (Routledge, 2012), and (with Joe Straubhaar) *Latin American Television Industries* (British Film Institute, 2013).

John Tebbutt is in the School of Media, Film and Journalism, Monash University, Australia. His research includes Australian Research Council funded projects, The ABC in Asia and its Impact on Cultural Exchange, 1956–2006, and Cultural Conversations: A History of ABC Radio National.

David Throsby is Distinguished Professor of Economics at Macquarie University, Australia. His research areas include the economics of art and culture, creative industries, cultural policy, the economic role of artists and culture in sustainable development. His books include *Economics and Culture* (Cambridge University Press, 2001) and *The Economics of Cultural Policy* (Cambridge University Press, 2010).

Graeme Turner is Emeritus Professor of Cultural Studies, in the Centre for Critical and Cultural Studies, at the University of Queensland, Australia. His most recent publications include *What's Become of Cultural Studies?* (Sage, 2012) and (with Anna Cristina Pertierra) *Locating Television: Zones of Consumption* (Routledge, 2013).

Andrew Warren is Lecturer in Human Geography at the University of Wollongong. His research interests include cultural and political economic theory, industrial cities and labour geographies. Andrew's new book *Surfing Places, Surfboard Makers: Craft, Creativity and Cultural Heritage in Hawai'i, California and Australia* with Chris Gibson (University of Hawaii Press, 2014) explores the cultural heritage, industrialisation and labour practices of the surfboard making industry.

David Wright is an Associate Professor at the Centre for Cultural Policy Studies at the University of Warwick, UK. He has research interests in taste, popular culture and cultural work. His new book is *Understanding Cultural Taste* (Palgrave, 2015).

THE CULTURAL INDUSTRIES

An introduction

Kate Oakley and Justin O'Connor

From culture to creativity – and back again?

Twenty years ago publishing a book on the cultural industries would first, no doubt, demand some kind of reckoning with Adorno's monolithic Culture Industry. One might point to their pluralisation and fragmentation – into the cultural *industries* – alongside continuing processes of agglomeration and concentration. It would involve recognition of their more contradictory and ambiguous relationship to those wider processes of power and control articulated within and through their structures and products. This work of retrieval and complication, done under the broad rubric of the political economy of culture, communications and/or media, had been under way in North America, France and the United Kingdom (UK) since the 1970s (Mosco, 1996). Unlike other approaches – notably that of cultural studies – the political economy approach was less concerned with the high/low, art/commerce distinction than it was with the role of media and communications systems in the reproduction of a complex modern (capitalist) society. It wanted to know how, and on what grounds, might the modern democratic state organise or regulate such a system, and what complex social, economic and political considerations needed to be made in the light of this. It was very much engaged – not implacably opposed but engaged – in the heated debates about the de- or re-regulation of the broadcast media and new kinds of commercial and public sector channels coming into being across the 1990s (Hesmondhalgh, 2013a).

Elsewhere the reckoning with the Culture Industry took a local turn. A book on the cultural industries in the mid-1990s might evoke an eclectic new set of producers and intermediaries who mixed art, popular culture, technology and a kind of street-wise entrepreneurialism quite tangential to the formal structures of the arts funding system (Wynne and O'Connor, 1996; Leadbeater and Oakley, 1999). Community arts and new social movements combined with a contemporary popular culture (animated by the spirit of cultural studies) to embrace an urbanism re-emerging from under the rusted hulks of the Fordist city (Bianchini and Parkinson, 1993). These announced a new potential for local re-invention. By the mid-1990s consultancy and

1

local government reports in the UK were identifying this new breed of cultural producers as being in possession of the kind of qualities required for a transformed city – a city with the potential to take its future in its own hands, no longer determined by the accidents of geography and geology.

Autopoesis rather than autonomy was the watchword, as endogenous growth based on re-inventing and mobilising existing strengths became an alternative to the disempowering script of attracting mobile global capital. Though often thought of as some kind of economism or instrumentalism by which the arts sector attempted to protect its shrinking funding base, the cultural industries at local level tried to diffuse the structuring tension between culture and economy. As culture was becoming more important economically so too 'economics' (though the discipline was lagging behind the reality perhaps) was finally acknowledging the reality of culture. The cultural industries might not be the whole solution to the questions raised by the socio-economic transformation of the post-industrial city, but whatever the solution there was little doubt culture would be part of it. Nicholas Garnham – involved in the experiments of the Greater London Council 1979–86 (Garnham, 1990) – linked these political economy and urban development strands together: both contemporary democracy and democratic cultural policy at multiple scales demanded an engagement with the realities of the production, distribution and consumption of culture.

It is less likely that such a book – in the Anglophone world at least – would acknowledge that they were in the middle (1988–97) of the World Decade for Culture and Development (WCCD, 1996). Emerging out of a number of United Nations umbrella organisations – in particular the United Nations Educational, Scientific and Cultural Organization (UNESCO) – the 'culture and development' tradition emphasised both the cultural context in which development necessarily took place and the values articulated by this culture as a crucial benchmark of a qualitatively human rather than technocratic development process (Arizpe, 2004; De Beukelaer, 2015; Isar, this volume). In this the cultural industries, conceived as a modern cultural infrastructure of production, distribution and consumption, were crucial both to nation building and protecting local identity in the face of a globalising culture. Growing out of the failure of the New World Information and Communications Order (UNESCO, 1980; Mosco, 1996; Singh, 2011), the cultural turn in development studies (as generally in the social sciences) and post-colonial and post-development literatures, 'culture and development' combined both an anthropological and a political economy approach to cultural industries. However, in the metropolitan heartlands, worried by the domestic employment impact of the re-location of manufacturing to the 'developing world', the cultural industries appeared primarily as a developed world option.

Ten years on and the landscape had changed considerably. First the creative industries, and then creative economy, had either replaced or been bolted on to the cultural industries: cultural and creative, or cultural creative. Indeed there were other couplings such as art and cultural, art and creative, creative and digital; or various idiosyncratic terms such as 'copyright', 'attention' or 'experience' industries/ economies. Many at the time saw this as a purely pragmatic title change, or were 'what's in a name' agnostic; it was not immediately clear how the replacement of 'cultural' by 'creative' worked both to preserve and to expunge elements traditionally associated with 'culture'. 'Creativity' as an input (rather than culture as an output) allowed the imaginative, dynamic, transformative and glamorous aspects of culture to be pressed into the service of an innovation machine. Questions of value other than innovation and other economic impacts were dropped.

That this was not immediately apparent says a lot about the cultural industries 'imaginary'(s) of the mid-1990s, which should neither be reduced to a simple 'precursor' of the creative industries nor viewed as a radically distinct set of ideas and aspirations (O'Connor, 2013). In general, the kinds of loose coalitions that pursued the creative industries agenda grew out of those involved in the cultural industries. They were concerned with cultural small and medium size enterprises (SMEs) and entrepreneurs, regenerating cities and regions, programming new kinds of mixed use cultural spaces, setting up local development agencies, re-tooling higher and further education courses, developing training programmes and sometimes, via the relevant culture or trade ministries, trying to influence legislation or gain political legitimation.

Three developments altered this easy continuity. First came the explosion of the Internet and digital and computing technologies generally, with their reconfiguration of the established nature of, and connections between, cultural production, texts and audiences. The UK government's addition of computing and information and communication technology (ICT) to the 'creative industries' list in 1998 has been frequently commented on (Garnham, 2005; Tremblay, 2011). Not only did it boost the employment numbers, often by around 40 per cent, but it worked to subsume the cultural (now creative) sector under the rubric of the knowledge economy. Many promoting the cultural industries had already positioned culture as part of the knowledge economy but its imaginary had shifted from that of a city or region able to re-invent itself through resources of culture towards the capacity to release the heroic entrepreneurial energies eulogised by the Californian ideology.

It seemed incontrovertible that the 'digital revolution' was transforming the landscape of (what had been) the cultural industries, pulling the plug on their business models, bringing in new entrants, transforming the way audiences interacted, purchased and adapted cultural texts. In this light the creative industries, with their horizontal networks, co-creative practices, and open-ended texts providing digital affordances for the creative citizen-consumer, could be seen to incarnate (and make redundant) many of the transformative aspirations of the cultural industries (Hartley, 2005). The creative industries announced a new kind of economy that drew on culture-inflected creativity within a (transformed) commercial sector that was as far away from Adorno's Culture Industry as one could possibly imagine. At the same time – given the radical flattening of hierarchies and the infinite creativity of the consumer – it could simply sidestep the dour strictures of political economy.

Second came Richard Florida's creative class, which seemed to encapsulate – and indeed statistically *nail* – the broad connections between culture and the future of the post-industrial city that had emerged in the 1990s (Florida, 2002). The simplicity of the idea – build 'cool', 'edgy' places in the city as amenities to attract artists and cultural workers, scientists and technicians, senior management and professionals – has both been routinely denounced and phenomenally successful (Peck, 2010). Florida's opening out of arts-led regeneration to embrace hip, popular and everyday cultures (lifestyles) was welcomed as a democratic move. It also made the spaces of cool consumption – and of course local cities could insert almost any new development into this space – a synecdoche for the wider creativity of the city (even though the real economy might lie elsewhere). It was this unspecified – yet seemingly statistically demonstrable – catalytic connection between a trendy consumption infrastructure and the overall creativity of the city that proved irresistible to the elected officials – if not the cultural managers – of many otherwise sensible cities.

The third change was perhaps the most surprising – certainly for the agency that had come up with the term in the first place. Soon after the Department for Culture, Media and Sport (DCMS) launched the 'creative industries' idea in 1998, it was taken up by the very East Asian countries – or 'economies' as they had become known – from whose manufacturing prowess these new industries were meant to allow the post-industrial countries to escape. Singapore, South Korea, Hong Kong, Taiwan and eventually China enthusiastically embraced the creative industries as the next step up the value chain (Wang, 2004; O'Connor and Gu, 2006; Kong et al., 2006; Keane, 2007). Taking seriously the evolutionary schema that was mostly political rhetoric in the UK – from a manufacturing to a service to a creative economy – these East Asian nations, also unlike the UK, put their money where their mouths were. In so doing they took seriously the notion of creative industries as intellectual property (IP) intensive and thus included in their lists bio-tech, pharmaceuticals, software and computing, product design, consulting and other advanced business services. They split them off from culture – which (somewhat off message) they saw as involving non-economic values – and subjected them to the kinds of 'catch-up' strategies they had earlier applied to advanced manufacture and other high-value added industries.

This created unexpected opportunities for agents such as the British Council – the brand leader – as western know-how was sought for these emergent industries. What they got was not quite what they wanted. Creativity and entrepreneurialism was very much linked to the artistic persona – the maverick, the rebel, the non-wearing of a suit. It also depended on notions of open, loose but high trust networks of SMEs that – according to the rhetoric at least – marked the kind of creative economies emerging in the West. What East Asia wanted were industry strategies, foreign direct investment, value chain analysis, brand management, market structuring and so on. These were rarely available from western cultural agencies who masked the complete absence of any kind of capacity, or willingness, for an industry strategy in the rhetoric of unplanned, market-driven creativity, where the job of the state was to get out of the way. These kinds of cultural–creative initiatives continue to operate in East Asia out of the various offices of the British Council and similar agencies from Germany, the Low Countries and Scandinavia. But they were often symbolic inputs. The real learning was from direct contact with the people who really knew – the global cultural corporations and their attendant consultancy companies (O'Connor and Gu, forthcoming).

The least successful export was the creative class. Eagerly adopted in Hong Kong, it quickly ran into problems when the persona of the 'creative' and the kinds of cultural ambiance they required – ethnic diversity, gay (friendly) businesses, bohemian enclaves – were deemed to be less than desirable. The new creative economy was to be run by serious people in nice suits and dresses, not BoHos. More popular was the older 'high culture' or arts-led regeneration. This had its brand impact – but it also took culture out of direct generation of wealth in ways that suited the 'traditional' outlook of East Asia.

The availability of the creative industries agenda outside the metropolitan heartlands was also embraced by the international development agencies who saw its possibility for developing, and not just developed, countries. UNESCO, traditionally the lead agency in the cultural field, was dealing with its issues around the 2005 Convention on the Diversity of Cultural Expressions – a complex combination of political economy and culture and development strands set against the rampant globalisation agenda of the World Trade Organization and other agencies of the 'Washington Consensus' (De Beukelaer, 2014a; 2014b; Isar, this volume). The United Nations (UN) agencies concerned with international trade stole a march and embraced the creative industries as a new sector more available to developing countries than other sectors requiring capital-intensive investment. Two reports on the trade in global in cultural goods and services would soon be be published (UNCTAD, 2008; 2010), building on extensive statistical information showing how the balance of global trade was shifting away from the Global North to the Global South.[1] It was not yet completely apparent, but the signs were already there in 2005 that the creative economy was to be a global rather than a 'western' agenda.

In 2015 we are again in a different world. The global financial crisis was not the end of neo-liberalism but that programme is clearly no longer what it was. We go along with it because there is nothing else. There is an interregnum. In an age of austerity and economic uncertainty, mixed with a deepening cynicism about the political process, the optimistic threads that marked both cultural and creative industries have unravelled. Some might point to the resilience of the cultural industries or cultural economy in a post-global financial crisis world (Pratt and Hutton, 2013) but the optimistic vision of a creative economy set to replace the old in some evolutionary progression is gone. Not that iPhones won't continue to sell. It is simply that the creative economy is perfectly compatible with the most egregious forms of exploitation, inequality and economic disenfranchisement. If the creative economy is going somewhere it is not clear where to or who it is taking with it.

Rampant gentrification and persistent urban decay; the increasing (self-) exploitation and 'precarity' of cultural workers; the instrumental use of flagship cultural buildings, especially in the newly developed countries; new forms of global dominance by cultural aggregators outpacing the old corporate cultural industries; cultural funding drastically cut; all this against a collapse of public value into economic metrics leaving cultural policy in a vacuum. In this context creativity, innovation and entrepreneurialism have become, along with sustainability, merely empty signifiers (Davies, 2014).

Many of these tendencies are outlined in the chapters that follow. The situation is not to be characterised in Adorno-esque tones of pessimism. In fact, unlike the 1990s – the true decade of Adorno according to Frederick Jameson (2006) – there are gaps and fissures, signs of hope and pressures for change. As this book illustrates, the growth of activism and scholarship (and activist scholarship) in the cultural industries has given a new purchase on many of the questions raised in the 1980s and so often cast aside in the 'noughties' (2000–09). Many of these issues have been taken up in the very different circumstances of 'developing' countries, as these too are now being brought into the creative industries development script. The hopes and aspirations of both governments and cultural producers open up points of leverage for a more inclusive and locally grounded development agenda here (Pratt, 2014; De Beukelaer, 2015; Isar, this volume). Indeed, new connections are being made between 'developed' and 'developing' countries as places in both North and South grow to resemble each other. On the other hand, many of the concerns of the political economy school have been displaced almost entirely by a technocratic, market-driven set of rationalities. At the moment, it is rare to see these concerns for a democratic, diverse public media policy being aired as possibilities let alone implemented (see Freedman, this volume).

Creative industries

What purpose, then, a book on cultural industries? The object designated by this term has become elusive and the programme it might articulate uncertain. Located somewhere between the arts and the creative industries, does it include or exclude these two outliers? If it refers to a separate sector, what are its distinguishing characteristics? Are the cultural industries still at the cutting edge of economic and technological innovation – or have they become lumbering dinosaurs in a nimbler digital age? Do we expect from them employment growth or competitive flagship industries any more or is it more about global country branding, soft power or cultural diplomacy?

A trawl through various national and international policy documents won't get you very far towards an answer. The problem is not just a question of definitions and terminologies – which we discuss below. It is more that the broad agreement on the fundamental purpose of public policy for culture, media and communications has more or less collapsed, or at least fragmented. This makes the critical juxtaposition staged by the term 'cultural industries' no longer immediately available. In large part this is because the 'imaginary' of the cultural industries has been radically displaced by that of the creative industries (cf. O'Connor, 2013).

The creative industries, conjured up late at night in the offices of the DCMS, have remained notoriously difficult to define in terms of their taxonomic borders and distinct characteristics (DCMS, 1998). This is because they were designated by an input – creativity – and an objective – the production of intellectual property rights – that are so broad and vague as to defeat statistical precision.

'Creativity', when used outside of the cultural practices to which it has traditionally referred, can be applied to any professional activity that requires situated skills and intelligent judgement. As a consequence, the lines drawn between a 'creative sector' (media, design, marketing and so on) and other high skilled sectors can only be arbitrary – as the list of sectors frequently included by East Asian countries indicates. This is often glossed as the 'opening up' of creativity – mobilising bio-political resources for a knowledge economy and democratising a capacity previously locked up in art for art's sake. In fact it makes the identification and characterisation of a specific 'creative' sector very difficult without surreptitiously using the notion of 'culture' (O'Connor and Gibson, 2014).

The DCMS list included the arts as well as the cultural industries – only the addition of 'software and computing services' (distinct from 'interactive leisure software' i.e. video or computer games) was unusual. As was pointed out at the time, not only did this conveniently add 40 per cent to the employment figures but it also opportunistically linked the cultural sector to the emergent discourse of innovation and national competitiveness – encapsulated at that time by the word 'digital'. It sealed the homologies between the entrepreneurs of Silicon Valley and 'creatives' everywhere. However, the products of 'software and computing services' are platforms for cultural goods, not cultural goods in themselves.[2] In 2008 the DCMS dropped this sector from its statistics, as most European Union reports have done, but it persists elsewhere, causing immense confusion (O'Connor and Gibson, 2014).

The term 'creative industries' was on firmer ground in the field of advertising and marketing (Sinclair, this volume). Indeed the 'creative' tag – as opposed to 'account management' – in these industries was equally important for the new 'creative industries' moniker. The cultural industries' agenda had already set itself against the denigration of the market in the name of 'art' or 'culture' as a position both illegitimate and unrealistic. But when it is simply a question of 'creativity' any tension between cultural and economic logics disappears. So it did not matter if creatives applied themselves to selling products as old as tobacco or as cynical as a political scare campaign. Indeed, the more an industry employed creatives the more creative it became, whether mining, finance or manufacturing. Similarly, the exponential rise of investment in advertising from the 1980s onwards along with its growing profile as a distinct business service sector could only suggest that the economy itself was becoming more 'creative'. Any questions about the relationship between advertising and marketing and the wider communications systems of contemporary society were no longer of concern for creative industry programmes.

Similar things could be said about the third sector to which the distinctly 'creative' label is frequently applied, that voluminous catch-all known as 'design' – product, graphic, architecture, fashion, interiors and so on. Two arguments ran together here. On the one hand, design was about re-thinking the function of objects and systems through a process that involved some kind of suspension of the 'normal' functioning of both. Design thinking was clearly related to the kinds of 'creative thinking' commonly associated with artists but exemplary in the application of this capacity to functional, everyday uses. In the creative industries imaginary, the mark of that practical application was its commercial viability. On the other hand design exemplified the 'aestheticisation of everyday life', the increased role of aesthetic or symbolic consumption in the formation of individual identities. Function was no longer enough: the aesthetic form of the object or service was now a crucial part of that commercial viability.

Buried under the term 'design' then were the unravelled strands of what the early 20th century had anticipated as the unity of form and function, bringing together the decorative arts, architecture and new forms and techniques of production in a transformative project for a new mass industrial society. The persistent tensions between functionality and expressivity, and between individual and collective consumption exploded in the 1980s. Design in the creative industries imaginary came to be about developing products and services that might resonate with the aesthetics of niche commercial 'lifestyle choices'; the application of 'creative skills' (often explicitly artistic) to production and service design; and about 'sculpting' the vectors of consumer choice (whether of public or of private goods and services) to produce commercially viable 'affordances'.

In all these ways 'creativity' as input avoided any of the collective or shared values implied by 'culture' – it was an individual capacity to be harnessed by businesses or proto-businesses to commercial ends (NESTA, 2012; 2013). Yet the ability of creativity to designate a specific 'creative' sector (different from the skilled professional and technological practices of science, medicine, finance, advanced manufacture etc.) only makes sense if we see these 'creative' industries as about the communication of meaning through symbolic texts. The creative industries stripped these practices of any collective meaning other than that of aggregate consumer choice (revealed preferences) and of any overarching cultural or political values other than enhanced competitiveness. It thus undermined – sometimes explicitly (Cunningham, 2014) – the basic critical thrust of the political economy of culture approach and those strands of cultural studies that remained committed to some notion of culture as a collective value.

If the definitional shift to *creativity as input* was both arbitrary and debilitating, the concomitant emphasis on the production of intellectual property (IP) was equally misplaced. Clearly the cultural or creative industries as a whole produced IP, but many individual cultural businesses did not. Nor did they all receive the same (if any) share of the IP their labour created. The DCMS' easy equation of IP, individual wealth creation and talent was pure ideology to anyone who studied the sector in detail. More damagingly, this approach did not allow an informed understanding of how the cultural or creative industries actually worked. Though organisational creativity was emphasised over the individual 'romantic' genius (the bête noire of the last 40 years!) as an industry its growth could be best secured by ensuring a supply of creative individuals (increasingly defined in terms of problem solving within commercial constraints). For developed countries embracing the creative industries, the job of the state was to get out of the way. Indeed, as with many developing countries, that they did not need to fund or extensively support the sector was for many governments part of the attraction in the first place (De Beukelaer, 2015). This explains in part the paradox in which creative industries programmes are heavily promoted but chronically underfunded. Only research and development investment is allowed into the 'market failure' enclosure (Cunningham, 2013).

The shift around 2005, from creative industry to creative economy, was significant. Statistically it drops the notion of an industrial sector and focuses on occupations (NESTA, 2012; 2013). This allows it to count individuals in occupations outside the creative industries – which can often nearly double the numbers used for advocacy. It also transposed the definitional disputes around 'what is a creative industry?' to 'what is a creative occupation?' NESTA, for example, define creativity as 'the application of creative talent to commercial ends' and creative occupations as 'a role within the creative process that brings cognitive skills to bear about differentiation to yield either novel or significantly enhanced products whose final form is not fully specified in advance' (NESTA, 2012: 24).

This, of course, could apply to a broad range of skilled professionals and hence remains arbitrary. But there is also a deeper conceptual change. The creative economy is not a sector but the collective input of millions of creative individuals inside and outside the creative industries. It is a system of communication and culture that proceeds granularly through millions of small commercial innovations in the symbolic value of products and services (Hartley and Potts, 2014).

For some of its more wide-eyed proponents, a creative industry stops being creative the moment it settles into a fixed industrial pattern (Potts et al., 2008). It designates the pure cutting edge, the avant-garde, a kind of collective Schumpeterian entrepreneur hero.[3] The creative economy designates that part of the innovation system in which new technologies interface with new patterns of social communication and individual expressivity leading to new commercial applications. They acclimatise the population to new technological possibilities, therefore feeding further growth in new design products (Cunningham, 2014). The content of the creative economy is of no concern – that is for the consumer to decide – and the Internet makes distribution less and less of an issue. The creative society envisaged by some of its proponents is one in which all are both producers and consumers, activities mediated by the direct one-to-one communication of the Internet (Flew, 2012). This utopian combination of Rousseau and Schiller (with a bit of the Young Marx thrown in) was precisely the kind of simple-mindedness against which the political economy of media and communications had set itself – but against the romantic Left rather than the libertarian Right (Garnham, 2000).

The creative industries agenda has done more than simply reduce cultural value to the economic or instrumental, in the manner of Oscar Wilde's 'price of everything and the value of nothing'. Creativity allows cultural value to be put to work. 'Creative labour', 'social market networks', 'creative innovation systems' allow the transformative energies associated with cultural production and consumption to be uncoupled from any judgement of cultural or indeed political value. Any friction between culture and economy – a thread running through most of the cultural industries literature as we shall see – is removed. Indeed, any such friction can only be the result of a residual elitism, bohemian aloofness or the temporary gap between a new idea and its subsequent commercialisation.

William Davies (2014: 4) suggests neo-liberalism is 'the pursuit of the disenchantment of politics by economics'. Politics might be disenchanted but the dismal science is re-enchanted, and the creative economy directly partakes in this. Reversing the culture wars of the 1990s, in which cultural industries were opposed to the conservative values of the New Right, the libidinal energies of creativity were articulated to the neo-liberal imaginary. Their celebration of creativity involved a displacement of collective cultural values – of the very possibility of collective or public values – onto the heroism of the creative entrepreneur, of the self or of a business, themselves mapped onto the innovation economy of the competition state (Jessop, 2002).

Davies also suggests neo-liberalism has become a form of nihilism. In its absolute utilitarian positivity it can admit of no ground, other than 'efficiency', on which to decide what is legitimate, what is of common value. Creative industries is equally nihilistic, providing no grounds for deciding what should be valued or why, only what is innovative and productive of new commercial value. It rests on a kind of vitalism, creativity as a switching or nodal point in a fast-moving global circuit of signs and symbols, money and desire. In this way capitalism as a creative economy proves endlessly fascinating for many critical opponents who can't help but admire its protean adaptability (Thrift, 2005). The creative economy mobilises a kind of Nietzschean self-overcoming whose collective sign is the multitude. This is not the virtual potential of Hardt and Negri's *Commonwealth* (2011), nor (though we are getting warmer) John

Hartley's (1999: 162) global humanity united under the golden arches of McDonald's, but the virtual humanity constructed by big data (cf. Kennedy this volume) which has no need of any conscious collective will as big data alone is capable of revealing this from the analysis of billions of small (creative) decisions (Andrejevic, 2013).[4]

Cultural industries by default?

There are many good reasons for re-introducing the term 'cultural industries'. David Hesmondhalgh's definition in *The Cultural Industries* (2013a) gives a more precise focus on those industries primarily involved in the mass production, circulation and consumption of symbolic texts. This allows him to distinguish this sector from the 'arts' – whose products tend to be singular or limited, and/or presented in live formats – and from 'design' – whose products involve more functional rather than symbolic considerations. We think these distinctions can be problematic and not always necessary, as we discuss below (Pang, this volume), but we have broadly followed the rubric (though we include sport – see Redhead, Rowe, this volume) in this book both for reasons of space and in order to focus on three key aspects of the cultural industries we think are crucial.

First, the 'cultural industries' has the benefit of using the word 'culture'. However elusive this term might be it designates a collective space in which a certain set of values are at play that are distinct from the 'economic' (Banks, Bilton, this volume). This friction allows the possibility of critical intervention and a way of under-standing some of the specific dynamics of the sector. Second, culture/industry was a productive juxtaposition not just of culture and economy but more particularly the traditional artistic-centred mode of cultural production with that of mass indus-trialised production. It sought a focus on the specificity of mass cultural commodity production – what Miege (1987) called their 'social logic' (and see Edwards, this volume) – without cancelling either 'culture' or 'industry' through their opposition. Third, though the relationship of culture and economy, or the production of culture as commodity, was crucial, this was only part of a reconceptualisation of the role of (necessarily) mediated culture in modern (though not necessarily) capitalist society. These all allow us to ask questions unavailable within the creative industries imaginary: how is cultural production structured in contemporary society; how does this affect the kind of culture we get; and why does this matter?

The scholars assembled in this book are all concerned with changing aspects of the cultural industries – their production systems, their 'texts', their audiences and their regulation. They draw on what is now a solid body of scholarship going back to the 1970s in order to locate the developments of the last decade in that longer-term perspective of continuity and change evoked by Hesmondhalgh (2013a). As such they are not exclusively focused on the 'cutting edge' at the expense of the commonplace – the outer limits of social media rather than the everyday use of television, for example (Freedman, this volume). Nor do they allow the profound implications of the Internet to displace the structuring dynamics of the cultural industries with roots in previous centuries (Brouillette and Doody, Doyle, Tebbutt, this volume). The cultural industries corporations are not dinosaurs, having responded in a range of complex ways to the new landscape of the last decade, and neither are the new digital corporations free of these older constraints (Keogh, Fitzgerald, this volume). As such they represent a snapshot of active and engaged contemporary scholarship trying to chart the real dimensions of the cultural industries beneath the current creative hype.

Nevertheless, these questions are being addressed 'after' the creative industries. They return us to the question of the value of culture and why its modern industrial organisation needs to be clearly understood. They also return us to other aspects of culture that have become atrophied or distended in the creativity drive. The mutual accommodation between innovation, creative destruction, the tradition of the western avant-garde and the 'counter-culture' is clear. The creative industries have also margin-alised values of ritual, social bonding, communal ethos, preservation and tradition and so on. Indeed, it has often been cultural conservatives such as Roger Scruton who have pointed to the socially destructive currents in contemporary cultural production. This more critical appraisal of the free creative consumer can be seen in the work of Philip Blond and 'Red Toryism' (2009) and various currents of 'neo-communitarianism' (Davies, 2014). On the other hand, as Ruddock (this volume) shows, older concerns with the effects of cultural industries – often dismissed as 'mass culture' theory – have returned, as well as work showing just how deeply entrenched in ritual contemporary media has become (Couldry, 2003).

'Culture' – for reasons very different to those noted by Raymond Williams (1976) – is now a difficult word to use. After the creative industries it can be easily be positioned as heritage, or the arts, or the subsidised, or the kind of broad everyday context that structures the choices of consumers and the drives of entrepreneurs. It is not easily available for those who would set up its value distinct from – let alone over – the eco-nomic as capable of informing public policy. The discourse of culture does not command the same legitimacy in the public realm as it once did. Its distinctiveness from economic value is now purely residual. As a consequence the predominant tactic of the cultural sector over the last 20 years has been to position itself as contributing to the economy, or at least the social cohesion and creative dynamism required by competiveness and social order (Belfiore, 2012; Hesmondhalgh et al., 2014).

On the other hand, 'industry' itself is no longer what it was either. Evocations of the factory – central to Adorno's polemical intent – have gone and so too have images of large, faceless corporations (though a brief glance at Apple, for example, might bring second thoughts about both). It is not just that production and consumption now take place across extended and articulated networks, or that it assembles a range of different actors and practices across complex 'ecosystems' taking us beyond the delimited sense of 'industry'. We do not have to buy into the discourses of 'pro-sumption' and distributed co-creation, or indeed the notion of the 'social factory', to recognise that, despite the continuing presence of large and powerful corporate players, the production and consumption of culture is much more pervasive than it was. This was already implied by the notion of creative industries and ratified by the switch to creative economy. For these reasons many use the term 'cultural economy' to designate this implication of wide swathes of social and cultural life in the production and consumption of cultural commodities.

The juxtaposition of culture and industry, culture and economy no longer has polemical power, nor is it the preserve of 'cultural materialism'. We are all cultural materialists now. Indeed the (relative) autonomy of culture is more likely to be invoked by the Left than the Right, who have thoroughly pressed it into service. Thus any attempt to use cultural industry or cultural economy now operates in a more complex field in which the relations between culture and economy, and the concrete analysis of cultural production, have been taken up within a number of different perspectives.

Political economy – cultural studies

David Hesmondhalgh's book (2013a) – the most comprehensive overview of the literature and issues in this field – is structured around the twin perspectives of political economy and cultural studies. This is a very well-rehearsed debate though one that many suggest is now superseded. Political economy did a number of things. First, it opposed the liberal pluralist analysis of the media and tried to show how the media reflected and contributed to the reproduction of domination and inequality. Second, it opened out the narrow 'economic' focus of neo-classical economics to bring social and political factors into the picture (cf. Mosco, 1996). Third, it foregrounded cultural production over consumption, seeing this as key to understanding how power was distributed and used in society. Fourth, it developed an account of the role of the media in contemporary 'distanciated' mass societies marked by an extensive division of labour, with particular respect to questions of the public sphere. Fifth, it outlined the ways in which the commodification of culture constrained the industries that produced them and contributed to the shape and dynamics of the sector. In the ensuing debate with cultural studies not all of these aspects were in play at any one time.

In the Anglophone sphere the political economy approach to media and culture set itself as a corrective to prior cultural studies that, they argued, was too focused on textual analysis (Garnham, 1992; Murdock and Golding, 2005). This gave rise to a long-running debate in which various scholars in cultural studies accused the political economy school of being about structure not agency; economic reductionist; too determinist about the reception of texts with their fixed meanings; concerned with news and factual media rather than entertainment – information not pleasure – and so on (cf. Wasko and Meehan, 2013). For cultural studies, very much concerned with the (potentially) autonomous agency of the 'end user', there were two things at stake. They stressed, first, the ability of individuals and groups to 'decode' previously 'encoded' messages and second, the possibility for culture to bind together a popular-political block. These two were of course connected in the 'Birmingham School' tradition of cultural studies. However, in later cultural studies the 'active viewer' was uncoupled from the necessity of putting this creativity to use in the construction of counter-hegemony. In any event cultural studies disrupted the easy connection between the structures involved in production and the actual use made of these products by the people for whom they were (though not always) intended.

The evolution of the 'active viewer' into the 'creative consumer' is fundamental to much of the academic creative industries literature, and is specifically exemplified in the work of John Hartley (2005). The refusal to see the market as anything other than a free play of expressed creative preferences; the rejection of claims of manipulation or the prior coding of acts of consumption as intellectual elitism (the only elitism that matters) or Marxist; the use of Internet facilitated feedback to dissolve the hierarches between producers and consumers; and the evocation of a ubiquitous 'start-up' economy gradually eroding the powers of the corporate dinosaurs – all these are common tropes in the creative industries imaginary (Flew, 2012; O'Connor, 2012).

More critical strands of cultural studies have increasingly become concerned with the production of culture. Hesmondhalgh suggests that the opposition of the two schools is redundant and that they simply emphasise different aspects of the triad of production–text–audience. In recent years, for example, we have had a new 'critical media studies' (Holt and Perren, 2009) in which cultural studies has moved into production studies, claiming – against political economy – a more attuned ear for the micro- and meso-levels of this production and a concern with entertainment, not just news-centric media. The robust response of Janet Wasko and Eileen Meehan (2013) in their recent overview suggests the debate is alive and well, as they reject – as had Garnham and others before – the characterisation of political economy as about top-down, structure-led and information centred production systems. Indeed, they suggest that recent critical media studies often refuse to go beyond a certain level of analysis of media production and identify some of its more determining structures – suggesting that it is much less 'critical' of 'the industry' and capitalism than it likes to believe.

This shift towards production in cultural studies is paralleled by an increased interrogation of the kind of leeway claimed for consumers in their acts of decoding. If reception is not determined by the encoded message it is certainly manipulated by a range of techniques and 'affordances' (Edwards, Sinclair, Kennedy, this volume) – just as the social energies of 'fandom' have been integrated into the strategies of cultural industry corporations (Sandvoss, Fitzgerald, this volume). Equally there has been a concern with why this matters. As Andy Ruddock argues in this volume, there is a revisiting of the concerns with the effects of media on audiences that a decade ago was roundly dismissed as positivist, patronising, and the hand-wringing of disaffected intellectuals. Just what kinds of texts are being produced by the cultural industries and with what consequences for those constantly consuming them? What role do the cultural industries now play in social reproduction and control in societies marked by 30 years of neo-liberalism?

On the other hand, political economy – and social science in general – famously had its 'cultural turn' in the 1990s. Writers such as Bob Jessop have been concerned to integrate the 'cultural' into political economy. His work with Ngai-Ling Sum (Sum and Jessop, 2013) has a Gramscian concern with the moment of the political as crucial to the ways in which economic systems are reproduced, challenged and transformed. Their notion of the 'economic imaginary' draws on an anthropology in which any course of collective action necessarily demands that we select from a range of possibilities and develop these within a particular, simplifying narrative in order to become generally accepted. 'Cultural political economy' thus becomes aware of that symbolic and imaginary realm in which political and economic decisions are made and contested. However, unlike the political economy of communications and media, Jessop and others do not discuss how this media or cultural production system is organised or how the texts that it produces work to secure specific economic – or indeed other – imaginaries.

One of the strengths of the political economy approach applied to the media and cultural industries was that it attempted to show systematically how the commodification of culture actually worked and with what kinds of consequences for its organisation (Miege, 1979; 1987; 1989; Garnham, 2000). Like the wider school of political economy, it rejected the neo-classical model, bringing in historical, sociological and political aspects. At the same time it suggested that the cultural industries had their own distinct characteristics – they were a sector unlike the rest of the economy because of the nature of their product (an argument also made by Richard Caves (2000) within a more orthodox tradition). Cultural goods were uncertain in their appeal to volatile and fragmented markets; their tendency to become 'public goods' meant they were hedged around by all sorts of techniques to create artificial scarcity; they had high production and low reproduction costs; and they had to manage high levels of creative labour input in efficient ways.

Holding these 'social logics' (Miege, 1987) of production and distribution in focus whilst giving the complex relationship between texts and audience their full due, and accounting for the relationship between these and wider social reproduction and transformation was, and remains, the challenge for political economy and cultural studies. Cultural studies were very much marked – at least in those areas influenced by the Birmingham School – by an emancipatory notion of culture reaching back to those late 18th century and early 19th century traditions identified by Raymond Williams (1958a). So too the political economy school was deeply influenced by the concern with the public sphere outlined by Habermas (1989) and the role of the media within it. The tensions between cultural studies and political economy might in part be mapped onto these two traditions, even perhaps the two spheres – the political and the literary – identified by Habermas (cf. Garnham, 1992). Both of these traditions carved out a sphere for culture and communications that was distinct from the market and from the State, even though they were implicated in both.

Well into the 1980s 'culture' could act as a kind of unifying 'imaginary' around which a broad cultural politics could rally. This imaginary very much animated the cultural industries coalition of the 1990s and was still present in the early iterations of the creative industries. Culture was a material practice, an economy – but it was a different sort of economy involving non-utilitarian values and immaterial goods that made it refractive to orthodox economic analysis. However, across that same period the distinctiveness of culture was being eroded. On the one hand the growth of neo-liberalism in public policy eroded the very idea of a separate sphere for politics and – inevitably – culture (Davies, 2014; O'Brien, this volume). On the other, 'the economy' itself was becoming more like the cultural sector. As a consequence, the availability of 'culture' to act as a policy imaginary was severely attenuated. We can explore this a little more by looking at two other prominent approaches to the questions of cultural industries and economy that have become very influential in the last decade or so.

Cultural economy as actor network theory

Paul Du Gay's (1997) introduction to *Production of Culture/Cultures of Production* positioned 'cultural economy' as a kind of moderator or intermediary between political economy and cultural studies. 'Cultural economy' would focus on produc-tion *and* consumption, industries *and* texts, structure *and* agency and so on. The 'economics' of cultural production were embedded in specific social and cultural contexts that actors brought to bear on the production process, which in turn had a large influence on what texts were produced and how they were consumed, and thus the wider cultural context (cf. also Du Gay and Pryke, 2002).

However, Du Gay suggested two further things. First, that the economy itself was becoming more cultural. The aesthetic or symbolic dimensions of goods and services were now of growing importance, as were the kinds of skills required for their produc-tion. Similar arguments had been made by Scott Lash and John Urry in their 1994 *Economies of Signs and Space*. They had extended the claims around the information or knowledge economy to the specific activities of the cultural industries (as they were still known) – overnight turning their labour intensive, uncertain and highly reflexive production practices from those of pre-industrial handicraft to post-industrial cutting edge (see Gibson et al., this volume).

This 'aestheticisation of everyday life' (Featherstone, 1991), with new kinds of individualised identities resulting in the increasingly symbolic consumption of previously utilitarian goods and services, became a central theme of the creative industries. The democratising intent of Raymond Williams' 'culture as a whole way of life' (1958b) was transposed to lifestyle and the creative consumer, making design as well as advertising and marketing central to the imaginary of the creative economy.

The expansion of the 'cultural economy' outlined by Du Gay – echoed by many proselytising for increased policy attention to the cultural/creative industries – rapidly shaded into the broader claim that the economy itself was becoming more 'cultural'. This is not the same as suggesting high growth in cultural sector employment and income. It follows on from Lash and Urry's claim that culture – knowledge in general, aesthetic knowledge in particular – is now integrated into the manufacturing process at much deeper levels. Hence their claims about the 'cutting edge' – rather than exceptionalist – nature of the cultural industries (1994: 123). However, the pro-liferation of symbolic goods and their increasing impact on previously utilitarian sectors does not necessarily suggest that the line between culture and economy has dissolved. Or rather, it is not clear what this dissolution entails.

Andrew Sayer (2001) saw this dissolution as an erosion of the distinction between the 'system' and the 'lifeworld'. This is echoed generally in (cultural) political economy by its identifying processes and logics that go beyond the lived experience and immediately given meanings of individuals and communities. That is, one can identify the social and cultural embedding of the economic without thereby denying the specific and systemic efficacy of profit, accumulation, competition and so on.

In a telling exchange Ray and Sayer (1999) opposed culture to economics as the 'intrinsically meaningful' to the 'instrumental'. Cultural policy is concerned with substantive values as opposed to the instrumentality of economic means. In response Du Gay and Pryke not only pointed to the economic aspects of cultural production, but also suggested that any categorical distinction between 'intrinsically' and 'instrumentally' oriented activity is impossible; these judgements are 'contextually specific and historically contingent' (2002: 11). This exchange points us towards the idea that the economy is historically constructed – though not linguistically or discursively as the 'cultural turn' was often accused of arguing – an argument which was picked up in that tradition of 'cultural economy' closely linked to Actor Network Theory (ANT).

The association of culture with 'intrinsic' and 'economy' with 'instrumental' need not be a-historical or essentialist. Nevertheless, the growth in the volume and pervasiveness of cultural production and consumption within a highly commercialised system may very well have implications for what we understand by 'culture' as a set of values and practices that once stood distinct from the 'economic'. We return to this at the end of this section.

The relational or constructivist trajectory of Du Gay's version of 'cultural economy' intersected with work coming out of ANT and science studies – especially the work of Bruno Latour (1991; 2005) and Michel Callon (1998). Latour especially set out to 'deflate' social scientific notions such as 'the social' or 'the economy'. This approach does not proceed as if there is an economy operating as an autonomous system in some distinct social space that then 'impacts' in various ways on social actors. They want to show how such a 'system' is assembled and maintained by a variety of actors, institutions and things. The 'economic' is *this* set of actors operating in complex networks organised in such and such a way, using such and such instruments, on such and such sets of things, out of the offices using this transportation network and so on.

The ANT version of cultural economy – as noted by Anheier and Isar (2007) and Hesmondhalgh (2013a) – does not normally deal with 'culture' as a production/consumption system. As exemplified in the *Journal of Cultural Economy*, it has focused on 'real' economic practices such as finance, corporations, risk, market governance etc. It has thereby provided some extremely valuable insights into how 'economic laws' are in fact constructed and maintained as such by a definitive set of actors.[5] Latour and others have equally deflated 'culture'. Just as there is no economy (unless we can show how it is constructed and maintained through various actor networks), so equally there is no 'culture' that forms the 'context' for this economy, or stands over and against 'nature', or is the 'symbolic' or 'representative' dimension of 'society'.

> There isn't a reality on one hand, and a re-presentation of that reality on the other. Rather there are chains of translation. Chains of translation of varying lengths. And varying kinds. Chains which link things to texts, texts to people, and things to people. And so on.
>
> (Callon and Law, 1995: 501)

'Cultural economy' in this version then is not the mutual interpenetration of culture and economy but a radical de-ontologisation of both culture and economics.

In one sense then cultural economy as a mediating term ends up as a 'plague on both your houses' – political economy and cultural studies are both dismissed as clunky 19th century sociology. Positively we can see this approach as a call to 'do the work' of showing how 'culture' or 'economy' actually operate rather than resting on lazy nomenclature as a kind of *deus ex machina* to explain these processes. It asked us to show just *how* that which we call the 'financial market', or the 'social', or 'technology' and so on comes to be assembled and maintained in such and such a way in such and such a set of relations. It is an unabashed call to empirically grounded research (McFall, 2008).

Missing from much of this cultural economy project has been studies on the production of culture itself – the cultural economy of the cultural economy, so to speak. Joanne Entwistle and Don Slater (2014) have suggested that Latour never 'reassembles' the 'cultural' as he did the 'social' and the 'economy'. Thus, for example, though the economy does not exist as such, Callon and others show how it is constructed and thus directly operative, as a real category with performative implications. This, Entwistle and Slater suggest, has not been done for culture – something they set out to rectify by a brief study of the use of models in the fashion industry.

Entwistle and Slater's account of the use of fashion models is organised around the 'look'. They set out to show, first, that this look is constructed across a multiplicity of actors. But second, they suggest that in fact it does bring in a wider notion of culture – one that is not a sociological category explaining these processes but a concept actively brought to bear by the actors themselves. The first act of deflation involves the 'look' that has usually been seen as a 'self-evidently "cultural" good … framed as text, sign or representation' (Entwistle and Slater, 2014: 167).

> Against this backdrop, ANT provides a principled basis on which to contest the 'textualising' of cultural objects whereby they are treated as produced, circulated and consumed as representations in and through logics of signification. Instead of analysis positing models and looks as texts imbued with 'meanings' and 'symbolism', we follow models as materially assembled entities, whose identity and meaning is widely dispersed, both within the modelling world itself and beyond, to the eventual consumption of model images by readers.
>
> (167)

This is simply a straw man, written as if the last 30 years of debates in political economy and cultural studies had not existed. Nevertheless, thus identifying the ways the 'look' is constructed in the complex production–consumption complex with its various actors and intermediaries, Entwistle and Slater suggest, *pace* Callon and ANT, that 'culture' does come back in to play – not as 'a totalised social moment wheeled on as an explanation of the social' (171) but as a term invoked by the actors themselves as a way of understanding their own practices. The actors in the modelling industry see the 'look' as something to be produced but also as having objective form outside of their attempts to produce/control it – an existence that 'belongs to a wider network beyond them which is constantly evolving and transforming' (171). This 'beyond' is referred to by the actors as 'the 'zeitgeist' or contemporary taste or 'values' or simply 'Culture'.

> This context is treated as objective: as an environment to which they must adapt and respond. Knowledge of this context may take the form of market research and formal measurement (e.g., sales figures, gut instinct or embodied knowledge and experience).
>
> (171)

Welcome to the cultural industries!

The actual results of this 'reassembling' do not particularly stand out from – though they ignore – the work that has been done routinely around the cultural industries for three decades. Moreover, like much of the ANT literature, whatever new insights it might generate, the refusal of 'totalisation' means it fails to account for the systemic nature of the kinds of cultural production discussed here.[6] Equally, it makes the 'objective' dimension of culture difficult to specify. But the project of reassembling culture will, Entwistle and Slater suggest, require some very large-scale architectonic reconstruction:

> Finally, we can think about larger recognisable cultural objects such as 'western fashion', or overarching 'values' (equality, inclusiveness, empowerment) which form the invoked backdrops to interlinked practices. In all these cases, the analytical gains of de-textualising and deflating cultural goods – of returning them to the moving assemblages through which they are dispersed – must be weighed against the actors' 'realist' stance: their constitutive assumption that things like looks, brands, genres, fashion, values and culture are real entities or social facts in relation to which they may act.
>
> (170)

Ignoring the sense of disciplinary arrogance – we've deflated your categories whilst we set about reflating them in our terms – we are presented with the kind of 'behind the back of the actors' kind of reasoning against which ANT set itself in the first place (Latour, 2004). 'We' know it is a construct but the actors don't, so we need to tread carefully and take them seriously. Given this, any expectation that we might get a critical account of a cultural production system that might sustain a cultural (industries) policy or politics might have to wait some time.

In fact some of this larger architectonic work has been done by Tony Bennett. He brings to cultural economy that tradition of critical cultural policy studies which set out to dismantle the radical Marxist pretensions of cultural studies and sought to find a framework and a language (attuned to the ears of policy makers themselves) in which a reformist cultural policy could be effectively formulated (Bennett, 1998). His historical project has been to show just how the 'work of culturalisation' (Moor, 2012) was done. Recently (Bennett, 2013) has followed ANT in suggesting that 'culture' is not a distinct ontological realm or space manifesting the 'general properties of the symbolic or logics of representation'. However 'culture' does exist as a 'complex', that is:

> the public ordering of the relations between particular kinds of knowledges, texts, objects, techniques, technologies and humans arising from the deployment of the modern cultural disciplines (literature, aesthetics, art history, folk studies, drama, heritage studies, cultural and media studies) in a connected set of apparatuses (museums, libraries, cinema, broadcasting, heritage etc.). The historical and geographical distinctiveness of this complex consists in its organisation of specific forms of action whose exercise and development has been connected to those ways of intervening in the conduct of conduct that Foucault calls governmental.
>
> (Bennett, 2013: 14)

There is, we would suggest, no necessary connection between the first and second half of this statement. We might want to look at how culture has been constructed historically in this way – this is surely part of the ongoing work in understanding contemporary culture. However, the specific claim that this culture is brought into being exclusively or primarily by the governmental processes of the liberal state is not a corollary of this. Indeed (noting Entwistle and Slater above) historically the invocation by actors of an emancipatory (political or personal) and transformative potential for 'culture', one that is not reducible to either the logics of the market or the state, has been an extremely powerful motive force. 'Deflation' here might play the role of a recall to clear-eyed historical reassessment; equally it might also be a highly political intervention against those who would hold on to this emancipatory potential.

There is clearly a serious ethical and political gap between the deflationary analysis pursued by the social scientist and the belief by actors in the 'reality' of the values they pursue. The 'instrumentalisation' of culture, for example, has been a major stake in public debates around culture, certainly since the 1980s. The 'culture' here is not some eternal 'intrinsic' meaningfulness versus materialism and utilitarianism; nevertheless, historically this kind of opposition is what 'culture' in part had come to signify. Deflationary accounts of these as 'fictions' are certainly not a precondition for empirically grounded analysis of the cultural industries and have limited application to the question of why that culture is seen to matter.

The work of Boltanski and Chiapello (2005) around the emergence of a new cultural capitalism[7] shows how detailed historical and sociological work can inform these debates without adopting some 'value-free' *epoché*. Boltanski and Chiapello's work charts the ways in which in 1960s white collar workers' 'cultural critique' of capitalism was registered and then reworked by management to transform the capacities they could require from these workers (mobility, networking, creativity etc.), and thus the nature, conditions and remuneration of that work – along with the alliances they might form with non-white collar workers. Boltanski and Chiapello approach the issue of culture in a specific context in which the kinds of value articulated by culture (such as non-alienated labour) are subjected to 'test' – to contestation and negotiation based on a broadly shared sense that these values matter in some way (see also Boltanski and Thévenot, 2006; Davies, 2014). It is the nature of this 'test' around the value of culture and cultural production, and which way the values it articulates are being transformed, that is at stake across the current, multiple conflicts around cultural policy, cultural work, public broadcasting, urban cultures and so on – conflicts or 'tests' and their possible results that many of the essays in this volume try to elucidate.

Cultural economy as economic and urban policy

Informed and critical approaches to these issues have benefited enormously from another strand of cultural industries scholarship, one emerging from urban and regional economic geography and often directly linked to policy development at city, national and international levels (Gibson et al., this volume). It has been concerned with the cultural industries as a substantive, and substantial, economic sector, but has also retained a critical edge derived from its recognition of the value of the *cultural* in the cultural economy. As such it should not be confused with the kind of economic arguments used to promote the creative industries and concerned only with some general capacity of creativity, or innovation or IP generation. Nor is it about the 'economics' of culture as in the work of cultural economics, with which it is often linked (cf. Throsby, 2000; 2010; this volume). We would broadly distinguish these two approaches in that cultural economy does not separate the 'economics' and the 'culture' into two parallel value systems. Like political economy, it tries to show how the values of culture are intertwined with, and actively inform, the ways in which it is produced – and vice versa. In turn, if political economy tends to focus on the specific nature of the cultural commodity, and the consequences of this for its commercial production, cultural economy in this sense focuses on the locational factors and structuring dynamics that underpin the production of cultural commodities, what that production requires from its location and with what consequences.

This spatialisation of cultural production brought an important new critical dimension to the cultural industries literature. It has its complex provenance in economic and human geography that experienced a social (if not yet cultural) turn in the 1980s. As with political economy this school rejected the narrow focus of neo-classical economics, in particular its 'frictionless' modelling of industrial location and competitiveness. Economic activity was deeply embedded in networks of trust, knowledge and other 'shared externalities' including local 'cultures' (Scott and Storper, 1992). In the 1990s Allan Scott (2000) and others (cf. Christopherson and Storper, 1986; 1989) applied these insights to the cultural industries themselves, whose complex relation to the places in which they were located exemplified to a high degree these embedded firms working 'between hierarchies and markets'. As with Lash and Urry's (1994) re-ordering of the historical temporality of the cultural industries – from remnant of the past to cutting edge – the cultural industries were not exceptional but exemplary of locally embedded knowledge intensive economies, the kind of economies that were set to expand in the future.

The study of cultural industries was thus immediately locational and very much focused on the large metropolitan areas where this production and consumption was concentrated. This grounded empirical economic analysis coincided with the increasing interest of cities globally, which were beginning to see the cultural industries as a future growth sector. In this way the work in regional and urban economic geography in North America crossed with concerns in Europe to develop urban and regional economies as post-nation re-invention of municipal social democracy. In this European tradition local cultures were to be central to any kind of embedded, endogenous post-industrial economies. In this way local cultural industries' strategies flowed into a wider stream of culture-led urban regeneration and branding strategies (Bianchini and Parkinson, 1993).

Allen Scott's work characterises the cultural industries as intensively transactional, requiring face-to-face communications and demanding highly specialised skills in a complex place-based division of labour – conditions generally only met in urban agglomeration economies (Scott, 2000; 2004; 2006). The cultural industries are part of the wider knowledge economy but they are more particularly specified as 'cultural-cognitive' industries (Scott, 2007). They demand the kind of formal and informal cultural infrastructure and amenities, embedded tacit knowledge, and the dynamic clash and exchange of ideas that has long characterised urban life. This cultural aspect of production – they deal with a range of meanings, experiences and signs – is thus symbiotic with the culture of the place. Urban landscape and cultural production mutually inform one another, as the place of production is incorporated into the product, and vice versa (Scott, 2001).

In Europe Andy Pratt has also applied regional and urban economic geography concerns to the cultural industries, in addition linking the themes of embeddedness, networks and shared externalities to the specific 'social logics' of cultural production. This was done less in the sense of the specificity of the cultural commodity and more in the requirements such production makes of its locale. That is, he is concerned with the cultural industries' rootedness in a wider 'ecosystem' or 'cultural economy'. This approach has also been more closely connected with the tradition of the cultural industries going back to the Greater London Council (GLC). That is, as a new and complex set of cultural producers with strong links to the arts, popular culture and new social movements and as concerned with cultural values and making a living as much as rapid, profit-driven growth. These do not show up in standard neo-classical business analyses but are the preconditions that make the formal cultural business sector possible (Pratt and Jeffcut, 2009; Pratt, 2012). As such Pratt (again recalling the GLC experiment) is much more concerned with questions of (urban) governance and thus what the 'cultural' in cultural economy policies might entail.

Pratt suggests that the cultural economy – the production system of cultural goods and services (Pratt, 2008) – is not amenable to neo-classical economic analysis or the standard industrial policy that derives from it (Pratt, 2012). He uses the term cultural economy to refer specifically to this spatially located system of the production of culture – which includes a range of 'non-cultural' (professional services, manufacture etc.) as well as profit and not-for-profit, third sector and institutional inputs (Pratt, 2004). Though he has written about the national level (mostly in developing countries) his main focus is on the urban scale, where most cultural industries are located, though recognising their role as nodes in global networks (Pratt, 2000; 2002).

Both writers have spatialised cultural production in ways that have allowed a much more nuanced, location specific and non-dogmatic account of how cultural industries are embedded in a wider cultural economy. Rather than strict taxonomic borders, there are place-based ecosystems in which different values – social, cultural, economic – are in play. Thus the subsidised arts as well as design industries can be included as both contribute to the cultural economy of cities – providing a range of inputs and externalities (a thriving local cultural offer, for example, or local brand) – without which many 'mainstream' cultural industries could not work. In placed-based production and consumption ecosystems the role of arts, crafts and design – and indeed manufacture and other related 'non-creative' services – becomes a matter of empirical investigation rather than taxonomic rigour.

Focused on the urban level, they are also able to identify shared cultural values that directly inform production and consumption, rather than a generic capacity for 'creativity'. Unlike many locational studies of the creative economy – which tend to be 'value-neutral' econometric accounts with little sense that this is the production of anything other than a specific kind of service or knowledge-intensive product (contrast with, e.g. Cooke and Lazzeretti, 2008) – they are well aware of the exploitation, inequality, displacement and injustice involved in the cultural economies of cities (cf. Scott, 2008). As such they – Pratt especially (2000; 2002; 2009) – have intersected with critical urban studies. This latter tends to be more directly focused on questions of equity and participation – with 'gentrification' being a key term – and on the 'ownership' of urban brands. Those working in this area tend to be positive about small-scale cultural production and independently led consumption spaces – often providing detailed research and grounded local rationale for cultural economy and creative industry programmes (cf. Part III, this volume). They have been less sanguine about the use of such dynamics to promote urban regeneration and city branding. Sharon Zukin's work is a touchstone here (1982; 1991; 1995). It has been critical of Richard Florida's instrumental use of urban culture for exogenous growth programmes (attracting the creative class) and the 'creative city' rubric more generally. It has stressed the everyday production of culture, the connection between culture and social movements, and the wider connections between citizenship and the urban scale.

Recognition that this is a cultural economy does not necessarily mean a reduction of culture to economics. This urban and regional economic geography approach certainly emphasises the growing importance of this sector to employment and economic well-being. Pratt especially has been involved in a great range of policy related interventions on behalf of cities, states and international agencies trying to promote the cultural industries. In pursuing this policy agenda both Scott and Pratt have addressed the question not just of how the cultural economy can be promoted but why it matters. Indeed, they suggest that understanding the latter is key to pursuing the former.

For Scott and Pratt, the cultural economy matters not only because it brings the economic benefits expressible in aggregated gross domestic product terms but also because of the kind of employment and income it generates. The cultural economy is, on the whole, a more progressive, equitable economy, relying on high levels of skill and knowledge, and involving a myriad of small firms and entrepreneurs alongside the large corporations. They are rooted in place, thus more resilient, and they contribute positive externalities to the city, making it more liveable, which in turn increases the stock of shared cultural knowledge and personnel available for the cultural economy. In short, it is a benign economy and contributes to the quality of urban living for producers and consumers.

It is this potential – complexly juxtaposed to the innovation imaginary of the creative economy – that has tended to inform urban based cultural economy policies, concerned to link endogenous development to quality of life in ways, that national governments have found difficult to achieve. The city has become a central horizon of cultural economy thinking.

As noted above, this potential has also been crucial to the cultural or creative economy agendas of international development agencies. For those 'emergent economies' that see the IP intensive creative sector as leading their manufacturing and service bases to higher levels, the creative economy has been most appealing (O'Connor and Gu, 2014). For those who see limited possibilities for the growth of a creative industries sector, it has been the mobilisation of local cultural capacities and the requirements of local education, rather than spending on capital investment capacities, that has been key. In this sense the cultural economy agenda has crossed over into the 'culture and development' agenda (UNESCO, 2013; Isar, this volume; De Beukelaer, 2015). Here culture moves from being a context *for* development towards culture *in* development (Pratt, 2014) – the kind of investment in local skills, knowledge, micro-finance, access to markets, cultural infrastructure and so on not only helps generate new economic possibilities but does so in a way that empowers people and makes them resilient rather than providing yet another fleeting, low skilled, off-shoring initiative.

Thus an economic policy for the cultural industries is in many ways a de facto cultural policy. One of the key points of leverage within the uneven, contested, confused and expanding landscape of the global creative/cultural economy agenda is that the economic benefits of this sector can only be fully realised if it is governed in accordance with its particular requirements (cf. Isar, this volume). That is, cultural economies are embedded in, and mobilise, a range of local social and cultural capacities that require investment and nurturing (Pratt, 2012; 2014). They operate within dense transactional networks in which cultural, social, ethical values are at play alongside the economic. This cultural economy therefore intersects with those critical strands of development, feminist and ecological thinking that seek to re-embed and re-think economics in their wider socio-cultural and environmental context (Mosco, 1996; Gibson-Graham, 2006; Gibson, 2012). That is, to return to the tradition of 'political economy' in which the economic is approached from the perspective of the ways in which it generates and distributes wealth as part of a 'good' society (Mosco, 1996; Piketty, 2014).

Thus Pratt's approach to the governance of the cultural economy is one that breaks with traditional neo-classically informed business development strategies and recognises the range of different values being created and pursued. This requires far more complex and sophisticated forms of governance, building on high levels of networked intelligence and research, with varied quantitative and qualitative indicators linked to open and flexible forms of ongoing sectoral consultation (Pratt, 2012). We would suggest that this kind of thinking informs much of the pragmatic, day-to-day operations of cultural policy consultants and activists working in what is now a global field of cultural economy. It is often this approach that keeps culture in play in an otherwise purely innovation-driven Masters of Business Administration-dominated field of creative economy thinking. If you want a cultural economy you need to pay attention to the wider cultural infrastructure – education, facilities, spaces, micro-finance, arts, social and community enterprises and so on. That is, cultural economy puts into play a series of tests around the value of culture in which local negotiations and contestation take place.

However, we also suggest that there are a number of challenges.

First, this approach very much builds on the imperative to build up local cultural production connected with the agendas famously associated (first) with the GLC (Garnham, 1990) and other cities or regions. It is frequently sold as a solution to post-industrial challenges. Its focus on the requirements of production rather than consumption demand a level of strategic thinking from governments that set it apart from the quick fixes of Florida's 'creative city' (Peck, 2010). And, of course, Pratt, Scott and others are aware of the need to address issues of distribution and access to market, that not every place can build up a significant cultural economy – the global landscape is dominated by a few metropolitan nodes and this is not likely to change quickly. However, it is very hard for them to argue for an investment in a cultural economy if this is not likely to produce high levels of growth. On what grounds a cultural economy policy that delivers mainly cultural benefits?

Second, the call that a cultural economy requires a governance system that pays attention to the socio-cultural values at play in this economy frequently falls on deaf ears. The rampant gentrification consequent on (and sometimes pursued by) the rise of cultural activity in an area is frequently noted. The growing disaffection with the 'creative city' is one symptom of this (Oakley and O'Connor, this volume). Another is the way in which the cultural economy is easily transmuted into the high-growth, commercial-led focus on design, digital media and other 'innovative' sectors at the expense of long-term investment in more inclusive cultural economy growth. This applies in creative industry strategies in a developed country such as Australia (O'Connor and Gibson, 2014; Gibson et al., this volume) as much as in the very different economies of West Africa (De Beukelaer, 2013; 2015). That is, a de facto cultural policy only goes so far. Unless it acquires a more explicit narrative of cultural value it will constantly be sidelined by the current economic imaginary that recognises itself in the creative, rather than the cultural, economy.

Third, the localisation of the cultural economy approach in place-based development – one that is so much part of its strength – has its limits. The cultural economy agenda here has bifurcated from that of media and communications policy. This has been the case since the 1990s as nation-states willingly or unwillingly opened up their media and telecommunication spaces to new global companies. These have increasingly set out to undermine the rationale for public sector broadcasting or, indeed, any public rationale for media regulation other than consumer choice and 'free' competition, IP protection and ethical (defamation, explicit images and so on) standards (cf. Hesmondhalgh, 2013a). There is very little connection between these core concerns of the political economy of media and communications and the cultural economy school we are discussing here.

This is in part a question of scale – cities are not nation-states, nor do they control major media and communications systems. However, it also relates to the different emphases on production and consumption. Cultural economy sees production as rooted in the active, vernacular, placed-based view of the city (cf. Zukin, 1991 and her place/market distinction) whereas cultural consumption is viewed as external, abstracting, passive (Pratt and Hutton, 2013). Production-focused approaches recall the validation of the expansion of cultural activity celebrated in the GLC-style approaches. Garnham's ambiguous tribute to the GLC (1990) suggested not only the need to gain control of distribution mechanisms (a political economy concern) but also that production is elastic whilst consumption is relatively inelastic. That is, a cultural policy emphasis on production was limited without an understanding of consumption practices and structures. This is what the place-based cultural economy school tends to lack.

As the political economy school has reminded us, shared, collective cultural values are inevitably complex – they are established across a range of market, state and civil society actors and intermediaries in a context of a society that is inevitably mediated. As such, however benign localised cultural economies and their governance may be, unless they deal with this trans-mediasphere(s) they cannot fully address the issues of contemporary culture.

All of these suggest an expanded cultural (economic) policy would have to have an explicit set of cultural values. They cannot be smuggled in under the guise of a (benign) economic development agenda. This, however, is made somewhat problematic by the ways in which an older cultural policy – art centred, 'romantic', an unqualified public good – is often counter-posed to the solidly contemporary and materialist cultural industries (cf. Hesmondhalgh and Pratt, 2005; Pratt and Hutton, 2013). Acknowledging the limitations of traditional cultural policy and its failure to adequately recognise the cultural industries as anything other than 'commercialisation' does not necessarily imply a rejection of that prior tradition. How the two can be recombined is surely one of the key challenges of the next decade.

Making this connection would take us into the territory of the political economy of media and culture – which had its own difficult relationship to cultural policy, despite its promising start (Girard, 1982). Here the notion of citizenship and its relationship to 'culture' has become increasingly central (Stevenson, 2013). It is the decreasing availability of both 'citizen' and 'culture' that is concerning. Culture as a kind of mobilising rhetoric or 'resource' (Yudice, 2003) with which to alter or temper the dominance of economic value has been marginalised – not that it was ever central (Bell and Oakley, 2014; O'Brien, this volume). Any power claimed by culture as it announced its rapprochement with the economic has been attenuated by its rapid incorporation – mostly via 'creativity' – into the imaginary of neo-liberalism. Of course, any renewed agenda for citizenship faces formidable challenges, not least in the declining legitimacy and power of the nation-state before global cultural corporations operating more or less outside of anything but *Pax Americana* – tempered by the *real politick* of negotiating with powerful market territories such as China. This is why the emergence of a global cultural economy agenda becomes so essential – as a way of articulating cultural citizenship across the multiple sites in which it is being contested (UNESCO, 2013).

At the same time it has been difficult to establish what a cultural public sphere (McGuigan, 2005) might entail. How are the literary and the political dimensions to be reconciled (cf. Garnham, 1992)? This takes us back to the political economy/cultural studies dispute around the use of texts and the political moment of the cultural. This is less a question of the creativity of the audience than the establishment of shared value(s) through which culture is to be judged. Hesmondhalgh and Pratt (2005) note the challenge presented by questions of aesthetic judgement, explored later by Hesmondhalgh in some detail (2013b). Here is Stefano Harney on the 'unfinished business' of cultural studies:

> Art is closer to people than at any other time in history. People make and compile music. They design interiors and make-over their bodies. They watch more television and more movies. They think deeply about food and clothes. They write software and surf the net of music videos and play on-line games together. They encounter, study, lean and evaluate languages, diasporas and heritages. There is also a massive daily practice in the arts, from underground music, to making gardens, to creative writing camps. And with

this there is production of subjectivities which are literally fashioned, which are aesthetic, which are created. ... There is a massive daily register of judgment, critique, attention, and taste.

(Harney, 2012: 156)

On the other hand, Eric Hobsbawm, surveying culture and society in the 20th century, pointed also to the proliferation of culture, the erosion of the walls between art and life, work and leisure, body and spirit:

At the end of the twentieth century the work of art not only became lost in the spate of words, sounds and images in the universal environment that once would have been called 'art', but also vanished in this dissolution of aesthetic experience in the sphere where it is impossible to distinguish between feelings that have developed within us and those that have been brought in from outside. In these circumstances how can we speak of art?

(Hobsbawm, 2013: 19)

As both Bennett (2013) and Ranciere (2013) in their different ways have argued, culture is not anthropologically prior to art, something to which this elitist distillation must return as the democratic vernacular of everyday life is returned to its rightful place. The two concepts emerged at the same time, and with the demise of one as a distinct realm perhaps we will witness the demise of the other. Nevertheless, the problem of a complex society mediated by images, sounds and texts, in which the common good can be articulated over and above the utilitarian nihilism of neo-liberalism, remains central to the work of any critical study of the cultural industries.

Conclusion: Why cultural industries now?

As we hope the above has made clear, we believe it is crucial to retrieve the notion of cultural industries as a distinct and rich tradition rather than an interchangeable label with that of the 'creative industries'. We have tried to show in this introduction and in the pages that follow how characterisations of the cultural industries as some lumbering corporations linked to an outmoded nation-state centred policy framework (cf. Cunningham et al., 2008) are incorrect. We have suggested four reasons for asserting the relevance of cultural industries as a term.

First, it retains the distinct and critical 'cultural industries' approach to the subject of mass cultural production. This has a much longer established academic and policy literature than that of creative industries. The focus is not on the very broadly defined input of 'creativity' (which in many instances draws in computing, science and high-tech) but on the production and consumption of goods and services whose economic value is drawn primarily from their cultural or symbolic value. This allows us to focus on questions of industry and of policy from a perspective of cultural value as well as economic growth. Making this explicit and drawing on a longer history of writing on this subject allows this book to reframe the issues around this sector in new and progressive ways.

Second, this volume combines industry, policy and socio-cultural themes in a critical but also empirically up-to-date manner. Moving beyond outright condemnation and uncritical celebration, the book asks its contributors to assess the current challenges facing the cultural industries from a range of different perspectives. Questions of industry structure, labour, place, international development, consumption, regulation and so on are all explored in terms of their historical trajectory and potential future direction.

Third, this book assumes a longer historical context than the creative industries debate (which tends to start post-1997) and thus explores the historical dimension in a set of important essays. This will provide context for new readers as well as critical orientation for those more familiar with the subject.

Fourth, we retain a focus on the culture that is being produced and consumed by these industries, in addition to their wider economic and socio-cultural impacts. Whilst these will be addressed in the conceptual chapters, the emphasis will be on what is being produced, how, by whom, for whom and in what structural and dynamic circumstances. This will allow the book to reassert the role of cultural industries as precisely that – *cultural industries* with a distinct relation to wider areas of cultural and other public policy and to broader social and economic change.

The different parts will be introduced individually. Clearly some chapters could fit into other sections. We have not imposed any 'line' on the authors other than to mark or reflect on the terminological distinction between cultural and creative industries. Many talk about both, as we have done in this introduction. Our choice of authors inevitably reflects our own networks and reading and location. Nevertheless, we hope they reflect some of the extent and multiplicity of current negotiations and contestations within, around and about the 'cultural industries' and why they should matter to us.

Notes

1 That China accounted for most of this shift, and that it did so because 'cultural goods' covered a range of manufactured products such as toys, glassware, furniture and audio-visual hardware, did little to dampen the enthusiasm.

2 We might want to include them in the 'depth' account of the cultural sector – along with a range of manufacturing and ancillary services. But this is not what the list of 'creative industries' was attempting nor did it include any of these other sectors.

3 Giving rise to the rather gnostic claim that the creative industries (as a sector) are not really creative industries (Potts et al., 2008).

4 It is no coincidence that the doyen of the creative consumer has written a book on cultural evolution with a neo-liberal economist and member of Australia's far right Institute of Public Affairs (Hartley and Potts, 2014).

5 Timothy Mitchell's work, though not aligned with the JCE, exemplifies this critical work (Mitchell, 2008).

6 We might note the invocation of Bourdieu in this paper as precisely the kind of systematic field organisation that Latour lacks or refuses.

7 Also the work of Jacques Ranciere (2013) around the space of the aesthetic. His non-governmental account of the historical specificity of the 'aesthetic regime' has thereby attracted the ire of Tony Bennett (2013).

References

Andrejevic, M. (2013) *Infoglut: How Too Much Information Is Changing the Way We Think and Know*. London: Routledge.

Anheier, H. and Isar, Y.R. (2007) 'Introducing the Cultures and Globalization Series and the Cultural Economy', in Anheier, H. and Isar, Y.R., *The Cultural Economy*. London: Sage, 1–12.

Arizpe, L. (2004) 'The Intellectual History of Culture and Development Institutions', in Rao, V. and Walton, M., *Culture and Public Action*. Stanford: Stanford University Press, 163–84.

Belfiore, E. (2012) '"Defensive Instrumentalism" and the legacy of New Labour's cultural policies', *Cultural Trends*, 21 (2): 103–11.

Bell, D. and Oakley, K. (2014) *Cultural Policy*. London: Routledge.

Bennett, T. (1998) *Culture: A Reformer's Science*. London: Sage.

Bennett, T. (2013) *Making Culture, Changing Society*. London: Routledge.

Bianchini, F. and Parkinson, M. (1993) *Cultural Policy and Urban Regeneration: The West European Experience*. Manchester: Manchester University Press.

Blond, P. (2009) 'Rise of the Red Tories', *Prospect*, 29 February.

Boltanski, L. and Chiapello, E. (2005) *The New Spirit of Capitalism*. London: Verso.

Boltanski, L. and Thévenot, L. (2006) *On Justification: Economies of Worth*. Princeton: Princeton University Press.

Callon, M. (ed.) (1998) *Laws of the Markets*. London: Wiley-Blackwell.

Callon, M. and Law, J. (1995) 'Agency and the hybrid *collectif*', *South Atlantic Quarterly*, 94: 481–507.

Caves, R. (2000) *Creative Industries: Contracts Between Art and Commerce*. Cambridge, MA: Harvard University Press.

Christopherson, S. and Storper, M. (1986) 'The City as Studio; the World as Back Lot: The Impact of Vertical Disintegration on the Location of the Motion Picture Industry', *Environment and Planning D: Society and Space*, 4: 305–20.

Christopherson, S. and Storper, M. (1989) 'The Effects of Flexible Specialization on Industrial Politics and the Labour Market: The Motion Picture Industry', *Industrial and Labour Relations Review*, 42 (3): 331–47.

Cooke, P. and Lazzeretti, L. (2008) *Creative Cities, Cultural Clusters and Local Economic Development*. Cheltenham: Edward Elgar Publishing.

Couldry, N. (2003) *Media Rituals: A Critical Approach*. London: Routledge.

Cunningham, S. (2013) *Hidden Innovation: Policy, Industry and the Creative Sector*. Brisbane: University of Queensland Press.

Cunningham, S. (2014) 'Policy and Regulation', in Cunningham, S. and Turnbull, S. (eds), *The Media and Communications in Australia*. Crows Nest, NSW: Allen & Unwin.

Cunningham, S., Banks, J. and Potts, J. (2008) 'Cultural Economy: The Shape of the Field', in Anheier, H. and Isar, R., *The Cultural Economy*. London: Sage, 15–26.

Davies, W. (2014) *The Limits of Neo-Liberalism: Authority, Sovereignty and the Logic of Competition*. London: Sage.

DCMS (Department for Culture, Media and Sport) (1998) *Creative Industries Mapping Document*. London: DCMS.

De Beukelaer, C. (2013) 'Culture and Development in Burkina Faso: Social and Economic Impacts Explored.' *Cultural Trends*, 22 (3–4): 250–58.

De Beukelaer, C. (2014a) 'The UNESCO/UNDP 2013 Creative Economy Report: Perks and Perils of an Evolving Agenda', *The Journal of Arts Management, Law, and Society*, 44 (2): 90–100.

De Beukelaer, C. (2014b) 'Creative Industries in "Developing" Countries: Questioning Country Classifications in the UNCTAD Creative Economy Reports', *Cultural Trends* (in press).

De Beukelaer, C. (2015) *Developing Cultural Industries: Learning From the Palimpsest of Practice*. Amsterdam: European Cultural Foundation.

Du Gay, P. (1997) *Production of Culture/Cultures of Production*. Milton Keynes: Open University Press.

Du Gay, P. and Pryke, M. (2002) 'Cultural Economy: An Introduction', in Du Gay, P. and Pryke, M., *Cultural Economy: Cultural Analysis and Commercial Life*. London: Sage.

Entwistle, J. and Slater, D. (2014) 'Reassembling the Cultural', *Journal of Cultural Economy*, 7 (2): 161–77.

Featherstone, M. (1991) *Consumer Culture and Postmodernism*. London: Sage.

Flew, T. (2012) *Creative Industries: Culture and Policy*. London: Sage.

Florida, R. (2002) *The Rise of the Creative Class: And How It's Transforming Work, Leisure, Community and Everyday Life*. New York: Basic Books.

Garnham, N. (1990) 'Public Policy in the Cultural Industries', in *Capitalism and Communication: Global Culture and the Economics of Information*. London: Sage.

Garnham, N. (1992) 'The Media and the Public Sphere', in Calhoun, C., *Habermas and the Public Sphere*. Cambridge, MA: MIT Press, 359–76.

Garnham, N. (2000) *Emancipation, the Media, and Modernity: Arguments about the Media and Social Theory*. Oxford: Oxford University Press.

Garnham, N. (2005) 'From Cultural to Creative Industries', *International Journal of Cultural Policy*, 11 (1): 15–29.

Gibson, C. (2012) 'Cultural Economy: Achievements, Divergences, Future Prospects', *Geographical Research*, 50: 282–90.

Gibson-Graham, J. K. (2006) *Postcapitalist Politics*. Minneapolis: University of Minnesota Press.

Girard, A. (1982) 'Cultural Industries: A Handicap or a New Opportunity for Cultural Development?' in UNESCO (ed.), *Cultural Industries: A Challenge for the Future of Culture*. Paris: UNESCO, 24–39.

Habermas, J. (1989) *The Structural Transformation of the Public Sphere: An Inquiry into a Category of Bourgeois Society*. Cambridge, Mass.: MIT Press.

Hardt, M. and Negri, T. (2011) *Commonwealth*. New York: Belknap Press.

Harney, S. (2012) 'Unfinished Business: Labour, Management, and the Creative Industries', in Hayward, M. (ed.), *Cultural Studies and Finance Capitalism*. London: Routledge.

Hartley, J. (1999) *Uses of Television*. London: Routledge.

Hartley, J. (2005) 'Creative Industries', in Hartley, J. (ed.), *Creative Industries*. Oxford: Blackwell, 1–39.

Hartley, J. and Potts, J. (2014) *Cultural Science: A Natural History of Stories, Demes, Knowledge and Innovation*. London: Bloomsbury Press.

Hesmondhalgh, D. (2013a) *The Cultural Industries*. London: Sage.

Hesmondhalgh, D. (2013b) *Why Music Matters*. Oxford: Wiley-Blackwell.

Hesmondhalgh, D. and Pratt, A.C. (2005) 'Cultural Industries and Cultural Policy', *International Journal of Cultural Policy*, 11 (1): 1–13.

Hesmondhalgh, D., Nisbett, M., Oakley, K. and Lee, D.J. (2014) 'Were New Labour's Cultural Policies Neo-liberal?', *International Journal of Cultural Policy*. doi.org/10.1080/10286632.2013.879126

Hobsbawm, E. (2013) *Fractured Times: Culture and Society in the Twentieth Century*. London: Little Brown.

Holt, J. and Perren, A. (eds) (2009) *Media Industries: History, Theory, and Method*. Maiden, MA: Wiley-Blackwell.

Jameson, F. (2006) *Late Marxism: Adorno, Or, The Persistence of the Dialectic*. London: Verso.

Jessop, B. (2002) *The Future of the Capitalist State*. London: Polity.

Keane, M. (2007) *Created in China: The New Great Leap Forward*. London: Routledge.
Kong, L., Gibson, C., Khoo, L.-M. and Semple, A.-L. (2006) 'Knowledges of the Creative Economy: Towards a Relational Geography of Diffusion and Adaptation in Asia', *Asia Pacific Viewpoint*, 47: 173–94.
Lash, S. and Urry, J. (1994) *Economies of Signs and Space*. London: Sage.
Latour, B. (1991) *We Have Never Been Modern*. Hemel Hempstead: Harvester Wheatsheaf.
Latour, B. (2004) 'Why Has Critique Run Out of Steam? From Matters of Fact to Matters of Concern', *Critical Inquiry*, 30: 225–48.
Latour, B. (2005) *Reassembling the Social: An Introduction to Actor-Network Theory*. Oxford: Oxford University Press.
Leadbeater, C. and Oakley, K. (1999) *The Independents: Britain's New Cultural Entrepreneurs*. London: Demos.
McFall, L. (2008) 'Rethinking Cultural Economy: Pragmatics and Politics?' *Journal of Cultural Economy*, 1 (2): 233–37.
McGuigan, J. (2005) 'The Cultural Public Sphere', *European Journal of Cultural Studies*, 8: 427.
Miege, B. (1979) 'The Cultural Commodity', *Media, Culture and Society*, 1: 297–311.
Miege, B. (1987) 'The Logics at Work in the New Cultural Industries', *Media, Culture and Society*, 9: 273–89.
Miege, B. (1989) *The Capitalisation of Cultural Production*. New York: International General.
Mitchell, T. (2008) 'Rethinking Economy', *Geoforum*, 39: 1116–21.
Moor, L. (2012) 'Beyond Cultural Intermediaries? A Socio-technical Perspective on the Market for Social Interventions', *European Journal of Cultural Studies*, 15 (5): 563–80.
Mosco, V. (1996) *The Political Economy of Communication*. London: Sage.
Murdock, G. and Golding, P. (2005) 'Culture, Communications and Political Economy', in Curran, J. and Gurevitch, M., *Mass Media and Society*. London: Hodder Arnold.
NESTA (2012) *A Dynamic Mapping of the UK's Creative Industries*. London: NESTA. Online at www.nesta.org.uk/publications/dynamic-mapping-uks-creative-industries (accessed 9 October 2014).
NESTA (2013) *A Manifesto for the Creative Economy*. London: NESTA. Online at www.nesta.org.uk/sites/default/files/a-manifesto-for-the-creative-economy-april13.pdf (accessed 9 October 2014).
O'Connor, J. (2012) 'Surrender to the Void: Life after Creative Industries', *Cultural Studies Review*, 18 (3): 388–410.
O'Connor, J. (2013) 'Intermediaries and Imaginaries in the Cultural and Creative Industries'. *Regional Studies*, DOI: 10.1080/00343404.2012.748982
O'Connor, J. and Gibson, M. (2014) *Culture, Creativity, Cultural Economy: A Review*, Report for Australian College of Learned Academies. Online at www.academia.edu/8368925/Culture_Creativity_Cultural_Economy_A_Review (accessed 6 October 2014).
O'Connor, J. and Gu, X. (2006) 'A New Modernity? The Arrival of "Creative Industries" in China', *International Journal of Cultural Studies*, 9 (3): 271–83.
O'Connor, J. and Gu, X. (2014) 'Creative Industry Clusters in Shanghai: A Success Story?' *International Journal of Cultural Policy*, 20 (1):1–20.
O'Connor, J. and Gu, X. (forthcoming) *Cultural Economy in the New Shanghai*. London: Routledge.
Peck, J. (2010) *Constructions of Neo-liberal Reason*. Oxford: Oxford University Press.
Piketty, T. (2014) *Capital in the Twenty-First Century*. Cambridge, MA: Harvard University Press.
Potts, J., Cunningham, S., Hartley, J. and Ormerod, P. (2008) 'Social Network Markets: A New Definition of the Creative Industries', *Journal of Cultural Economics*, 32: 167–85.
Pratt, A. (2000) 'New Media, the New Economy and New Spaces', *Geoforum*, 31: 425–36.
Pratt, A. (2002) 'Hot Jobs in Cool Places: The Material Cultures of New Media Product Spaces: The Case of South of the Market, San Francisco', *Information, Communication and Society*, 5: 27–50.

Pratt, A. (2004) 'The Cultural Economy: A Call for Spatialised "Production of Culture" Perspectives', *International Journal of Cultural Studies*, 7: 117–28.

Pratt, A. (2008) 'Locating the Cultural Economy', in Anheier, H. and Isar, Y.R., *The Cultural Economy: Cultures and Globalisation Series*. London: Sage, 42–51.

Pratt, A. (2009) 'Urban Regeneration: From the Arts "Feel Good" Factor to the Cultural Economy. A Case Study of Hoxton, London', *Urban Studies*, 46 (5–6): 1041–61.

Pratt, A. (2012) 'The Cultural and Creative Industries: Organisational and Spatial Challenges to their Governance', *Die Erde*, 143(4): 317–34.

Pratt, A. (2014) 'Creative Industries and Development: Culture in Development, or the Cultures of Development?', in Jones, C., Lorenzen, M. and Sapsed, J. (eds), *Handbook of Creative Industries*. Oxford: Oxford University Press.

Pratt, A. and Hutton, T. (2013) 'Reconceptualising the Relationship Between the Creative Economy and the City: Learning from the Financial Crisis', *Cities* (33): 86–95.

Pratt, A. and Jeffcut, P. (2009) 'Creativity, Innovation and the Cultural Economy: Snake Oil for the 21st Century?' in Pratt, A. and Jeffcut, P. (eds), *Creativity, Innovation and the Cultural Economy*. London: Routledge, 1–19.

Ranciere, J. (2013) *Aisthesis. Scenes from the Aesthetic Regime of Art*. London: Verso.

Ray, L. and Sayer, A. (1999) *Culture and Economy after the Cultural Turn*. London: Sage.

Sayer, A. (2001) 'For a Critical Cultural Political Economy', *Antipode*, 33 (4): 687–708.

Scott, A.J. (2000) *The Cultural Economy of Cities*. London: Sage.

Scott, A.J. (2001) 'Capitalism, Cities and the Production of Symbolic Forms', *Transactions of the Institute of British Geographers*, 26: 11–23.

Scott, A.J. (2004) 'Cultural Products Industries and Urban Economic Development: Prospects for Growth and Market Contestation in Global Context', *Urban Affairs Review*, 39: 461–90.

Scott, A.J. (2006) 'Entrepreneurship, Innovation and Industrial Development: Geography and the Creative Field Revisited', *Small Business Economics*, 26: 1–24.

Scott, A.J. (2007) 'Capitalism and Urbanisation in a New Key? The Cognitive-Cultural Dimension', *Social Forces*, 85 (4): 1465–82.

Scott, A.J. (2008) 'Inside the City: On Urbanisation, Public Policy and Planning', *Urban Studies*, 45: 755–72.

Scott, A.J. and Storper, M. (eds) (1992) *Pathways to Industrialization and Regional Development*. Boston and London: Routledge.

Singh, J.P. (2011) *United Nations Educational Scientific and Cultural Organisation (UNESCO): Creating Norms for a Complex World*. London: Routledge.

Stevenson, D. (2013) 'Culture, Planning, Citizenship', in Young, G. and Stevenson, D. (eds), *The Ashgate Companion to Planning and Culture*. Farnham: Ashgate.

Sum, N.G. and Jessop, B. (2013) *Towards a Cultural Political Economy: Putting Culture in its Place in Political Economy*. Cheltenham: Edward Elgar.

Thrift, N. (2005) *Knowing Capitalism*. London: Sage.

Throsby, D. (2000) *Economics and Culture*. Cambridge: Cambridge University Press.

Throsby, D. (2010) *The Economics of Cultural Policy*. Cambridge: Cambridge University Press.

Tremblay, G. (2011) 'Creative Statistics to Support Creative Economy Politics', *Media, Culture and Society*, 33 (2): 289–98.

UNCTAD (United Nations Conference on Trade and Development) (2008) *Creative Economy Report – The Challenge of Assessing the Creative Economy: Towards Informed Policy-Making*. Geneva: United Nations Conference on Trade and Development. Online at unctad.org/en/Docs/ditc20082cer_en.pdf.

UNCTAD (2010) *Creative Economy Report*, Geneva: United Nations Conference on Trade and Development. Online at unctad.org/en/Docs/ditctab20103_en.pdf.

UNESCO (United Nations Educational, Scientific and Cultural Organization) (1980) *Many Voices, One World. Towards a New, More Just and More Efficient World*. Paris: UNESCO.

UNESCO (2013) *Creative Economy Report*. New York: United Nations Development Program (UNDP). Online at www.unesco.org/culture/pdf/creative-economy-report-2013.pdf.

Wang, J. (2004) 'The Global Reach of a New Discourse: How Far Can "Creative Industries" Travel?', *International Journal of Cultural Studies*, 7 (1): 9–19.

Wasko, J. and Meehan, E. (2013) 'Critical Crossroads or Parallel Routes? Political Economy and New Approaches to Studying Media Industries and Cultural Products', *Cinema Journal*, 52 (3): 150–56.

WCCD (World Commission on Culture and Development) (1996) *Our Creative Diversity: Report of the World Commission on Culture and Development*. Paris: UNESCO.

Williams, R. (1958a) *Culture and Society*. London: Chatto and Windus.

Williams, R. (1958b) 'Culture is Ordinary', in Gray, A. and McGuigan, J. (eds), *Studies in Culture: An Introductory Reader*. London: Arnold, 1997, 5–14.

Williams, R. (1976) *Keywords*. London: Fontana/Collins.

Williams, R. (1981) *Culture*. London: Fontana.

Wynne, D. and O'Connor, J. (1996) *From the Margins to the Centre: Cultural Production and Consumption in the Post-Industrial City*. Aldershot: Ashgate.

Yudice, G. (2003) *The Expediency of Culture: Uses of Culture in the Global Era*. Durham: Duke University Press.

Zukin, S. (1982) *Loft-Living: Culture and Capital in Urban Change*. London: The John Hopkins Press.

Zukin, S. (1991) *Landscapes of Power: From Detroit to Disney World*. Berkeley and Los Angeles: University of California Press.

Zukin, S. (1995) *The Cultures of Cities*. Oxford: Blackwell.

Part I

PERSPECTIVES ON THE CULTURAL INDUSTRIES

As we outlined in the introduction, scholarship around the cultural industries – what they are and why they matter – has developed extensively in the last decades. Rather than being outmoded by the creative industries agenda the critical questions they allow have persisted and grown. In this section we introduce a broad range of perspectives on the cultural industries.

Mark Banks addressed a central question of this volume – why do the cultural industries matter? Exploring the complex relationship between 'cultural' and 'economic' value the chapter tries to show how the very intractability or incommensurability of this opposition itself provides a value. The fact that 'creative industries' erases this opposition has made it more difficult to address the difficult questions of value, of why the cultural industries matter.

Many versions of the cultural industries agenda join that of the creative industries in marginalising 'art' as heritage, or some residual category of 18th century Romanticism. Laikwan Pang's essay shows us how aspects of the European tradition of art and aesthetics continues to operate within the cultural and creative industries. Pang outlines how autonomy, critical self-reflection, and freedom are still central stakes in current debates around cultural labour. Nevertheless, she takes this further into questions of community and connectivity – key terms of the cultural economy – which are still too tied to the discourse of the individual artist, especially in areas such as intellectual property rights. She ends by suggesting new ways in which communal creativity can be affirmed outside the confines of the 'creative economy'.

David Throsby has been central to the rise of cultural economics, which has asserted both the relevance of the work of the economist and its proper limits vis-à-vis cultural value. As such it is a welcome corrective to the focus on metrics and universal commensurability under the sign of the 'efficiency' that has marked neo-liberalism. Throsby shows how the cultural sector might be accommodated within standard economic national accounting systems in ways that would allow a more productive and open dialogue between questions of economic resources and cultural values.

Scott Fitzgerald's chapter gives us an overview of one of the key debates in the cultural industries – the relative weight of global corporations and the proliferation of small and medium size enterprises (SMEs). This has been central to the claims of the creative industries, that the distributed creativity associated with the Internet and other technologies has side-stepped the debates about corporations, power and control that marked the political economy school. Fitzgerald shows how the large corporations have responded in different ways to these challenges, and that many of the approaches of the cultural industries – such as Miege's 'social logics' – still provide a better explanation than theories of the 'prosumer' and so on.

Finally, Chris Gibson, Chantel Carr and Andrew Warren give a critical account of the positioning of the cultural and creative industries as post-industrial. Challenging the inevitability of the off-shoring of manufacture, they suggest this is much more of a deliberate strategy to kill it off. In this process 'creativity' as 'knowledge economy' played a central role. Challenging the characterisation of manufacture as unskilled, dirty and old-fashioned, they suggest that any future it might still have is not incompatible with the cultural industries. Indeed, its rootedness in craft skills and its connections to the materiality of production holds out the possibility for the re-invention of the cultural economy on more equitable and sustainable lines.

1
VALUING CULTURAL INDUSTRIES

Mark Banks

Why do cultural industries matter? I'll suggest two main reasons. First, they matter because they provide contexts for human beings to discover, disclose and distribute their creativity – in all its diversity and complexity of social and cultural meanings. In this way, cultural industries help make possible the examination of life. Second, they matter because they provide a means of economising, for generating and distributing resources – particularly for those who have a direct interest in processes of production, distribution and consumption. The cultural industries therefore concern us doubly – culturally and economically. Yet this duality begs a further question, one this chapter seeks specifically to address; namely, how should we appropriately *value* the cultural industries?

To value is to identify the worth of something, its standing or quality in a world of others. In respect of the cultural industries, we are presented with some obvious difficulties in establishing value or worth. For one, it is not immediately apparent what we ought to be evaluating – cultural or economic practices, or something of both? Neither is it obvious what scheme of evaluation we might best adopt – a monetary or aesthetic scheme? Or a measure attuned to 'cultural value', providing such a value can adequately be defined? And even if we conceive an effective means of evaluating, we might reasonably ask how extensive or applicable are its measures, across different times and territories? Clearly the problems of establishing value are legion – but few have been discouraged from tackling them. As the cultural industries have come to prominence, so the number of ways and means of evaluating them has proliferated in and between industry, government and academia. There is little doubt that cultural industries have been widely accounted for, appraised and assessed – their worldly worth scrutinised (e.g. DCMS, 2008; Throsby, 2010; UNESCO, 2013; Work Foundation, 2007).

In what follows I wish to outline some problems of value using the framing example of the United Kingdom and its particular efforts to (re)value the cultural industries as the 'creative industries'. In doing so the first aim is to stress the difficulties involved in valuing and to draw attention to the stakes involved in making an evaluation. It will then be argued that at the heart of valuing the cultural industries lies an intractable difficulty; a problem of incommensurability that precludes settlement on a singular measure of value, whether cultural or economic. Yet, while much energy has been expended in attempting to efface this problem, I will argue that it is a difficulty that has its *own* value, one that is vital to recognise and sustain, since the consequences of its resolution or disappearance would prevent us from fully understanding the cultural industries, and be less congenial – socially and politically – than we might be inclined to imagine.

Conceptions of value

How have the cultural industries been hitherto valued? The original use of the term 'culture industry' was resolutely unequivocal, and largely pejorative, reflecting Adorno and Horkheimer's (1944/1992) dismay at the expanding commodification of human creativity. Here the cultural industries were largely value*less* – at least in the aesthetico-idealist terms favoured by the Frankfurt School. Adorno argued that through industrial standardisation and mediation, all good culture came inevitably to a bad end. What value remained was only that lodged in capital accrued – the tainted profits of vulgarity and destruction.

The subsequent development of the 'mass' cultural industries has, of course, seen the concept gradually re-evaluated in more upbeat terms – not least by those industry actors, national governments and policy makers keen to nurture and reap the economic rewards provided by its component activities. Today, the cultural industries are understood somewhat less as manifestations of a corrupted Enlightenment and rather more as vanguard executants of post-industrial economic growth. Now, re-packaged as the 'creative industries', the cultural industries are most commonly regarded as hugely valuable contributors to the wider 'creative economy' of information, knowledge and symbolic commodities – vital sources of national wealth, as well as social innovation and cohesion (Work Foundation, 2007; DCMS 2008; NESTA, 2013; UNESCO, 2013).

Yet between these poles lies a somewhat turbulent history that reveals another vital and enduring value of the cultural industries – at least from the perspective of critical social science and the humanities, and many practitioners and consumers alike. This is the value of cultural industries as contexts for the cultivation of counter-vailing forms of political, social and cultural expression, association and critique. During the 20th century, a gradual shift towards understanding cultural industries as means for producing symbolic and expressive *life* – and not merely commodities – helped moved analysis beyond the petrifying austerity of Frankfurt critical theory, as well as frame the subsequent range of national and popular re-evaluations of the role and value of the commercial media, art and culture of high or late modernity. The re-evaluation of the cultural industries in post-Second World War European and United States contexts was marked by recognition of their increasingly important value economically, in the midst of developing consumer societies, *and* their role in enhancing the polity in liberal democracies, by helping to effect forms of public debate, popular representation and self-expression (see Miège, 1979; Hesmondhalgh, 2007; O'Connor, 2011).

In essence, then, we have three discrete values for cultural industries – three different, seemingly incommensurable, conceptions of their worth. Cultural industries as valueless, or as economically or culturally valued. These continue to be publicly rehearsed, in ways that solidify their enduring and singular status. But here I want to explore the intersections between them – or rather the latter two – by drawing attention to the durability of an interstitial order of value located between economic rationality and cultural critique.

This might seem curious given the current primacy afforded 'creative economy' policy and rhetoric. Indeed, it has become common to claim that the kind of rationality underpinning creative economy thinking has fatally damaged any other competing value, including those long-established components of culture and critique (McRobbie, 2002; Miller, 2009). I would suggest, however, that this is not entirely the case, and that while cultural value might well be degraded, it is far from destroyed. Indeed, I'll argue it would be hard for this to occur, since part of what defines cultural industries is the existence of an intrinsic space of possibility at the interface of culture and economy, foundationally generative of both commodification *and* forms of cultural representation, meaning and critique. As we'll see, while the economic and the cultural might exist as relatively discrete and free-standing values, in the cultural industries their production (and destruction) relies necessarily on their dialectical dependency.

Economic value – creating the creatives

The UK creative industries appeared as a specific instrument of government, expediently fashioned to help manage a given set of productive activities at a particular historical moment. They arose as a solution to an emergent problem of value – how to value appropriately a set of discrete but interwoven activities, interests and compulsions, sufficient that they might serve the purposes imagined for them.

Let us consider the issues in play at the time of their formation. Why were the creative industries regarded as a vital and necessary innovation and what value were they imagined to provide? Firstly, as Nicholas Garnham (2005) has convincingly argued, the emergence of the creative industries idea in the mid-1990s was linked to state and commercial desires to develop more fully post-industrial 'informational' or 'knowledge' economies based on the production and consumption of immaterial commodities and services, including the kinds of expressive, symbolic or meaning-laden goods usually associated with cultural industries. In the UK the drive to reap the benefits of knowledge and symbol production, and (especially) the intellectual properties that pertained to them demanded a means of classifying and evaluating the kinds of activities likely to generate the commodities identified as crucial to growth. The term 'creative industries' thereby emerged, providing a frame and context for manifesting and managing a set of objects that could be harnessed to deliver some demonstrable (new) economic outcomes. By the admission of some the principal architects and proponents this was an exercise in uncertainty, something of a tentative step into 'unchartered territory' (Newbigin, 2011: 232). In some ways, then, in the contingency of its genesis, 'creative industries' offered nothing more than a working grammar for codifying a set of existing and emergent objects that appeared to possess some kind of family resemblance – a means for a willing and responsive government to adjust itself to the contours of a rapidly shifting economic terrain.

Yet the choices made were not accidental. The primacy given to intellectual property exploitation was reflected in the chosen composition of the creative sector – which rather oddly included advertising and software production (hitherto not widely regarded as cultural industries per se) – inclusions that allowed the sector to be presented as more economically significant and more substantially geared to the 'new' economy than might have otherwise been assumed. For Garnham, the creative industries entailed the value ascribed to the cultural industries becoming more or less solely re-calculated in terms of the priority accorded to new, intellectual property driven media and technology businesses – where beefed-up estimates of productive activity could act as a magnet for UK Treasury support and also demonstrate the seriousness with which the UK was able to meet the kind of new economy challenges being identified internationally by the EU, UNESCO, the World Bank and other development agencies.

Garnham's analysis serves to explain some of the desire to bring cultural industries into the new economy fold. Clearly, however, other factors were in play, helping to usher in the *particular* idea of creative industries. While it might be suggested that the creative industries concept appeared as something of a speculative gambit, much was revealed in the deliberate (and value-laden) shift from the 'cultural' to the 'creative'.

Partly, the use of the creative industries was about avoiding accusations of 'elitism' and separating out public support for the creative industries from traditional patronage of the arts and culture – this was resolutely not about supporting 'market failure' but about encouraging returnable 'investment'. Indeed, as commercial success emerged as the principal arbiter of value – what sold was what mattered – the market's apparently liberating tendencies helped push aside other (non-economic) concerns and expressions of democracy. This included the idea of cultural industries that had reappeared in the UK in the early 1980s as an organising frame to describe the small, local, popular culture industries that were springing up in post-industrial inner cities. In this context, Garnham's own key position paper (see Garnham, 1990), written for the left-wing Greater London Council (GLC), articulated a vision of cultural industries as both commercial and popular, ideally geared towards providing ordinary people with the kinds of texts and experiences they valued. This assumed an important role for the market and the (local) state in enabling such culture to be made, relatively distinct from big business and the kinds of ostensibly 'elitist' or non-commercial 'high' culture conventionally supported by national government. Here culture was tied to economy, but mainly in the interests of enhancing the democratic polity. While the proposed cultural industry policies for the GLC were never fully implemented, there was enough piecemeal activity in London, and more concrete policy and self-organised developments in regional (predominantly 'Old' Labour) cities such as Sheffield, Liverpool and Manchester, to show that popular culture was becoming increasingly linked to both employment creation *and* forms of social cohesion, representation and renewal, linked often to a progressive politics (Hesmondhalgh, 2007). The idea that culture industries could provide employment and generate socio-cultural benefits for marginal groups had obvious appeal to the left, seduced by the egalitarian and integrative drives underpinning such innovations (Pratt, 2005).

In many of these industries, in idealised terms, economic potentials and material existences were clearly conjoined to practitioner's own valued capacities to express and articulate their lived cultural experience, including, often, the production of oppositional meanings and social critique. But as demonstrably *cultural* industries – with the duality of culture and economy finely balanced in productive tension – these activities obtained a less positive evaluation than the emergent and favoured kinds of 'new' creative entrepreneurialism that appeared to privilege commerce primarily, and culture secondarily, if at all.

We might also note that the arrival of the creative industries coincided with moves to deregulate and marketise the major cultural industries and their constituent labour markets (especially in state cultural institutions, such as the British Broadcasting Corporation (BBC) or in the state-licensed network of commercial television broadcasting companies; also the print newspaper industries). This process involved disintegrating existing socialities and cultures through 'flexible' contract and employment reform – as well as making attacks on perceived 'closed shops' and vested interests, on unions and perceived leftist blocs populating the more significant state and commercial cultural industries. The idea of thinking of such industries anew in 'creative' terms arguably helped draw attention away from some of their inherited 'cultural' baggage, and helped to focus light on the productive individual; the self-creative person, working within – but now more productively released from – organisation.

Arguably, then, evaluation migrated from a concern with the generative contradictions that had animated many previous advocates of cultural industries – namely, the productive interface of culture and economics, premised on appreciation of the intrinsic value ascribed to vernacular art and culture production, as a means of mobilising a plural set of possibilities, of which economic development was merely one – towards a more commercially directed initiative marked by a commitment to the kinds of enterprise culture underpinning (what has now become) the creative economy. This is not to say, of course, that culture (or even the idea of the social) entirely disappeared, rather to note that it became subordinate to, or was made to appear correspondent with, this purposeful re-evaluation of the role of cultural industry, amidst much broader transformations of society and economy. The shift to bland and individualistic notions of social 'access' and 'inclusion', and creative, competitive individualism, away from cultural collectivity (often hooked to innovations in gentrification and 'culture-led regeneration') became the binding mode of attribution for culture, as for those social and political realms deemed peripheral to the core purpose of effectively managing economic re-adjustment and growth.

The consummation of this shift now seems apparent in the positive value afforded UK 'creative economy' initiatives, where the idea of a tension or incommensurability between culture and economy has been more fully effaced. Indeed some of the more recent UK policy discussions and interventions (e.g. DCMS, 2008, 2014; NESTA, 2013; British Council, 2010; CBI, 2014) make little or no mention of the non-economic values or capacities of art and culture at all. Such ideas appear to have sunk without trace beneath the horizon of an apparently harmonious and generalised sociability that is valued only as the source of a vastly expanded repertoire of 'innovation', 'creative occupations' (including many lying beyond the creative industries) and 'creative' commodities (NESTA, 2013).

This critical narrative is well-rehearsed and highly credible – up to a point. What remains unclear is whether such shifts have now fully disabled the kinds of critical autonomy and cultural value argued to pre-date the creative industries moment (McRobbie, 2002). In fact, while it is tempting to reduce the present to a simple story of the triumph of individualism, economy and empirics over culture, politics and meaning, this would traduce a more complex reality (O'Connor, 2011). Certainly, the logic of the market has assumed a greater precedence, and in some quarters the possibilities of critique and cultural politics have been curtailed or forced into retreat; but equally, we should note, in others they have flourished – realised in the now intensified pursuit of various cultural alternatives, heterodoxies and forms of the common. This suggests less a pre-determined and straightforward displacement of cultural value by the economic, but instead a more complex and uncertain dialectic. So while the rise of the creative industries marks a significant advance for some instrumental, economic values, the negative impacts of which are rightly decried, in the next section I will outline why, in the cultural industries, the value of culture – as politics and critique – *must* remain both a durable and essential component of the cultural industries, even in the face of its current degradation.

Cultural value – an intrinsic good?

To some it might seem banal to note that cultural value lies at the heart of cultural industries. Yet it is also important to recognise that this is not an incidental facility but an abiding structural feature. Indeed, while the precise meaning or definition of 'cultural value' continues to provoke intense debate, this is of less concern here than acknowledging its pervasive durability as a focus for organising action and its valuation as an intrinsic good. First, the desire to pursue and maintain some specifically critical, cultural value in cultural (or even 'creative') work exists as a foundational organising principle, widely (if not universally) held by those engaged in the kinds of artistic, creative or aesthetic practices that underpin cultural industry production. Such desires are not just individually held, but are of course institutionally embedded in the various forms of state and community support for arts and culture, and (less markedly) in commercial endeavours. In such contexts, culture is generally regarded as an intrinsic good with 'transformative value', and a kind of 'meta-good' (as Russell Keat, 2000: 157 terms it), a good that endows people with the capacity to reflect on the quality and necessity of *other* kinds of goods. In generating symbolic meaning, cultural industries provide a context and resource for evaluating the prevailing order of life. This sense of culture has, of course, come under various forms of attack – but it has by no means disappeared.

Second, and less obviously, recognition and provision for cultural value *also* exists as structural precondition for effectively operating capitalism. This is because providing cultural workers with relative autonomy (or 'cultural freedom') to fashion demonstrably new goods remains the best guarantee of any future accumulation. How so? As Bill Ryan has deftly observed, the cultural industries are suspended on a tension between providing cultural workers with cultural and artistic freedom and curtailing and managing that freedom:

> The historical problem facing capitalists engaged in the production and circulation of cultural commodities has been how to devise a system of employment which enables artists to create genuine original and marketable works of art which are stamped with signs of genius, but which also disciplines the creative process and bring it under the control of the firm, such that management may set the standards, rate and timing of creation and keep labour costs to a minimum.
>
> (Ryan, 1992: 104)

The principal aim of capitalism is unfettered accumulation – to be guaranteed partly by the scientific management of the workforce. But cultural industries exist in contradiction to this managerial imperative. A crucial point here is that the demand from the public for original products – generated by concrete rather than abstract labour – tends to impair the ability of capital to fully depersonalise and standardise creative labour inputs. Or put another way, the common-sense idea that cultural value is intrinsic to the works of freely acting, autonomous authors and creators tends to allow (some) cultural workers an unusual degree of workplace freedom. It is in this zone of permissibility – between culture and economy, management and freedom – that cultural goods (of all kinds) are precisely made. Thus, the cultural (or creative) industries can never be entirely about a 'pure' or disembedded economy – and can never be fully divested of their cultural or non-economic components – since they would cease to be recognisable *as* cultural industries, either for workers *or* capitalists.

This does not, of course, per se guarantee any socially progressive outcomes, or negate any less desirable ones. It simply means that cultural industries, by definition, exist in an unruly space – where abiding desires for cultural or artistic value, or a transformative value that challenges the hegemony of political and economic arrangements, can co-exist, combine or clash with a commercially seated principle. As Ryan (1992: 14) notes, '[t]he culture industry is explicable not as purely capitalist but only in its combination with art'. This relation (the 'art–commerce relation' in Ryan's terms), regardless of *what* it generates, ought to be recognised as having an intrinsic productive value – a crucible that provides opportunities to shift the focus of cultural industries in any number of different ethical directions, for good or ill.

If this is given, the issue becomes less one of lamenting the *absolute* decline of culture, amidst a now totalising economy, and more about evaluating how culture is counter-posed, managed and arrayed in *relation* to the economic – and often against it – in particular empirical contexts. Here, neither the cultural nor economic 'order of worth' (Stark, 2009) can be assumed to exert a permanent primacy or dominance, rather each comes to the fore, or works co-effectively, at different times, according to the object, project or industry in question. Of course, economic priorities have a tendency to crowd out cultural ones, under conditions of market competition – but this will vary according to the industry, institutional context (say, between public or private organisations) and market in question. Evidence for this can be found in the now extensive set of researches into cultural industries work. Here, economic concerns interleave dynamically with non-economic commitments to aesthetics, artistic autonomy and self-actualisation, personal and social well-being, family, kinship and community and radical politics – demonstrated for example in work on new media workers (Kennedy, 2012), television workers (Hesmondhalgh and Baker, 2011), arts and craft workers (Luckman, 2012) and film-makers (Vail and Hollands, 2012) to name only a few recent examples that deal with the most ordinary workers and organisations. Beyond these mundane contexts, we might imagine all kinds of other arrangements are possible (Ray, 2004).

We can also see evidence of competing and colliding orders of worth even in those public and policy documents most fulsomely charged with ushering into being the social fact of the creative economy. While, as we have seen, the drive to economise creativity has dominated recent policy, some other policy commentaries continue to emphasise the value of culture, not just as economic opportunity, but also as a source of energising life. For example, recent work by the United Nations Educational, Scientific and Cultural Organization (UNESCO) identifies six globally competing models of classification of the cultural industries (including the UK Department for Culture, Media and Sport (DCMS) model), each emphasising different aspects of 'culture' or 'creativity', with a surprising amount of variability between them (UNESCO, 2013). To take one example, the now influential 'concentric circles' model developed by the cultural economist David Throsby (see Throsby, 2010) places cultural activity and value at its 'core' (as the principal source of value ascribed more widely to cultural and creative industries) and has since been widely adopted or adapted for use, not least by UNESCO itself, and in the UK by the influential Work Foundation, whose own model identified the primacy of 'expressive value' at the heart of cultural industry. Such a model not only brings further refinement to existing categories and imputed relationships, but also reaffirms the centrality of culture to a creative industry analysis. Writing the British Council's creative economy report of 2010, John Newbigin, one of the architects of the original DCMS classification of creative industries, felt able to affirm the Work Foundation's belief that 'expressions of cultural as much as of economic value' (British Council, 2010: 2) underpin the creative industries, and to draw attention to the plurality of values and citizen and community benefits potentially afforded through creative economy development.

In retaining a cultural problematic, such literature might well be paying only a lip service, but at least has the virtue of continuing to present the cultural industries publicly in complex terms – as sites of competing, co-operating, though ultimately incommensurable, orders of worth. Policy initiatives that disavow the value of culture, or imagine that commercial growth relies only on culture's deracination into an insipid and inoffensive commercial 'creativity', not only fail to take cultural values seriously, but also fail to understand that it is often culture's very intransigence and difficulty that contains the kernel of its commercial potential. Culture is not able to be simply absorbed into economy, since it is an independent and co-existent order of worth, capable of being both complementary and antithetical to an economic imperative – a contingency that remains vital to the cultural industries *as* the cultural (or indeed the creative) industries. The cultural industries, as containers of contradictory values, cannot be properly evaluated without some consideration of that difficulty and disjuncture which is irreducible. Pragmatically, one might argue that creative industries policy must retain the capacity to value and nurture (and not try to tame) the cultural values that (originally) underpinned it in order to be effective *as* a policy, since to wish away culture – and its claims to possessing intrinsic value, internal rewards and for generating the ineffable – is to wish away the cultural (or creative) industries altogether.

Conclusion

This chapter began by asking the question 'how should we value the cultural industries?' It introduced three orders of value, and then explored the rise of an economic value (carried by 'the creative industries'), at the seeming expense of a cultural value. It then argued that the cultural industries are not wholly defined by the prevailing 'creative economy' logic, powerful though this might be, since some intrinsic and productive tensions between cultural and economic values remain essential. A model of cultural decline, whereby economic value is argued to have fully disarmed the possibilities of culture and critique, is favoured less than a model that takes account of the constancy of each value, but advocates empirical inquiry into their particular unfolding and relative patterns of advance and retrocession. This is by no means meant to convey some sense of natural equilibrium or 'harmony of the spheres'. While this may well occur empirically, there is today plenty of evidence to suggest that the economic order appears eminently capable of overriding cultural concerns to suit its preferential pecuniary interests – and its negative impacts must be challenged. But whether it does, or does not, remains an open empirical question. And even if it does so, it must always (in the last instance) rely on the unruly logic of those cultural values that lie beyond its compass, and in doing so can't fail to provide opportunities for different and competing orders of worth, and value-arrangements to enter the field of cultural industries production. This is the space of possibility, the interstitial space of value, otherwise identified by David Harvey as the source of progressive 'transgressions' and 'oppositional movements' (Harvey, 2001: 409–10) in capitalism – not to mention the source of cultural opposition to the prevailing economic crisis.

So how, finally, should we value the cultural industries? While establishing economic value for the sector – and getting the categories 'right' – continues to (quite legitimately) preoccupy different interests, the pursuit of a robust economic analysis is only one part of the story of value. Indeed, establishing standardised economic categories, 'mapped' and measured with analytical precision, is not necessarily the most engaging or vital aspect of the debate over the value of cultural industries. Neither is promoting the 'creative economy' in its own right – divested of any sense of the necessary tensions between culture and economics – the best way forward. This is because such efforts not only serve to narrow the debate about value, they tend also to exfiltrate the political and cultural questions that must necessarily arise in the context of any cultural industry evaluation. In this respect, the question of 'what is the value of the cultural industries?' meets an equivalent in 'what is at stake in attempts to define and capture that particular value?' Or, 'how is value actually being defined and measured in an evaluation, and what other values are at stake?' The continued absence of any accepted clarity in answers to the first question suggests that we might need to focus more on the second and third. Only then might we establish more fully why the cultural industries really matter.

References

Adorno, T. and Horkheimer, M. (1992) *Dialectic of Enlightenment*, Verso, London.
British Council (2010) *The Creative Economy: An Introductory Guide*, British Council, London.
CBI (Confederation of British Industry) (2014) *The Creative Nation: A Growth Strategy for the UK's Creative Industries*, CBI, London.
DCMS (Department for Culture, Media and Sport) (2008) *Creative Britain: New Talents for the New Economy*, DCMS, London.
DCMS (2014) *Creative Industries Economic Estimates*, DCMS, London.
Garnham, N. (1990) *Capitalism and Communication*, Sage, London.
Garnham, N. (2005) 'From Cultural to Creative Industries', *International Journal of Cultural Policy*, 11 (11): 15–29.
Harvey, D. (2001) *Spaces of Capital*, Edinburgh University Press, Edinburgh.
Hesmondhalgh, D. (2007) *The Cultural Industries*, Sage, London.
Hesmondhalgh, D. and Baker, S. (2011) *Creative Labour*, Routledge, London.
Keat, R. (2000) *Cultural Goods and the Limits of the Market*, Palgrave, Basingstoke.
Kennedy, H. (2012) *Net-work: Ethics and Values in Web Design*, Palgrave, Basingstoke.
Luckman, S. (2012) *Locating Cultural Work*, Palgrave Macmillan, Basingstoke.
McRobbie, A. (2002) 'Clubs to Companies: Notes on the Decline of Political Culture in Speeded Up Creative Worlds', *Cultural Studies*, 16 (4): 516–31.
Miège, B. (1979) 'The Cultural Commodity', *Media, Culture and Society*, 1: 297–311.
Miller, T. (2009) 'From Creative to Cultural Industries', *Cultural Studies*, 23 (1): 88–99.
NESTA (2013) *A Manifesto for the Creative Economy*, NESTA, London.
Newbigin, J. (2011) 'A Golden Age for the Arts?' *Cultural Trends*, 20 (3–4): 231–34.
O'Connor, J. (2011) 'The Cultural and Creative Industries: A Critical History', *Ekonomiaz*, 78 (3): 25–45.
Pratt, A. (2005) 'Cultural Industries and Public Policy: An Oxymoron?' *International Journal of Cultural Policy*, 11 (1): 31–44.
Ray, G. (2004) 'Another Art World is Possible', *Third Text*, 18 (6): 565–72.
Ryan, B. (1992) *Making Capital from Culture: The Corporate Form of Capitalist Cultural Production*, Walter de Gruyter, Berlin.
Stark, D. (2009) *The Sense of Dissonance: Accounts of Worth in Economic Life*, Princeton University Press, New Jersey.
Throsby, D. (2010) *The Economics of Cultural Policy*, Cambridge University Press, Cambridge.
UNESCO (United Nations Educational, Scientific and Cultural Organization) (2013) *Creative Economy Report: Special Edition*, UNDP, Paris.
Vail, J. and Hollands, R. (2012) 'Cultural Work and a Transformative Arts: The Dilemmas of the Amber Collective', *Journal of Cultural Economy*, 5: 2.
Work Foundation (2007) *Staying Ahead: The Economic Performance of the UK's Creative Industries*, The Work Foundation, London.

2

ART AND CULTURAL INDUSTRIES

Autonomy and community

Laikwan Pang

The discourse of art and that of cultural industries does not overlap much in current scholarship, largely due to the latter's interest in articulating its methodology and concerns, as opposed to art history's entanglement with auteur studies and aesthetic transcendence. The cultural industries are supposedly made up of contractual relationships instead of individual talents, and cultural commodities are often based on fashions or quick utilities instead of timeless artistic ideals with constructed naïveté. Emphasizing late-capitalist production and an environment of consumption, cultural industries scholars, however, have perhaps underestimated the persisting relations between arts and cultural industries, and the extent to which traditional aesthetic concepts still directly inform the operation of cultural industries. Apple sells simplicity, Nike sells perseverance and solitude, and many tourist commodities claim to embody transcendence. The architecture of Zaha Hadid and that of Rem Koolhaas are as extravagant as they are shocking; so are their Lacoste and Prada products. The products of cultural industries are variously marked by the existing aesthetic vocabulary of the West. While it is true that certain cultural industries, such as tourism and culinary consumptions, do not so obviously manufacture cultural representations with aesthetic value, they all deploy aesthetic means to package their commodities so as to promote consumption.

Most importantly, concepts inherited from the European art tradition continue to define the identification and aspirations of many creative laborers around the world. Cultural industries are specifically defined by "new" modes of production and an environment of consumption in which products are still invested with "old" aesthetic values, particularly on the level of creative input. The sociology of art has richly demonstrated the ways that economic transactions relate to the production and consumption of art, and Pierre Bourdieu purposefully adopts the notion of capital to address the relation between art and people (Bourdieu 1993). But sociology does not deal with aesthetic value in itself, and it tends to see art in terms of personal capital that artists use to advance their careers or realize themselves, and that consumers use to showcase their class status. As such, it does not address the ways that art is fundamentally different from other social capital in the psychology and aspirations of many cultural workers. This chapter aims to reconnect the two discourses of art and of cultural industries in order to explore the tensions between autonomy and community that underlie many current debates concerning creative labor, including to what extent workers in the cultural industries should be protected from market coercions, and the ways that networks and creative communities can be built to facilitate their endeavors.

Simply put, the idea of the Romantic genius who creates art out of her own unique talent and private, interior journey continues to influence our conception of cultural workers. However, this fundamental faith in the artist-designer is also challenged, first, by industrial modes of production, which cannot afford the resources required for the cultivation of precious artistic moments, and, second, by a consumer society ruled by consumer demand. Many creative-labor scholars and critics, therefore, are concerned about the ability of workers to maintain their limited autonomy in the face of complete marketization. This tension between high valuation and the ultimate debasement of the artist remains a paradox of the cultural industries. By reintroducing the connection between art and cultural industries, this chapter not only deconstructs the fetishization of authorship and creativity, but also emphasizes the importance of intersubjectivity in all cultural activities, and maintains that cultural production and consumption are meant to connect people rather than isolate them.

The value of autonomy in the arts

Since the eighteenth century, European artists and philosophers have conceptualized the value of art in terms of artists' independence from social interference; art demonstrates truth not only because artists can choose their own subject matters and styles, but also because viewers and critics can judge arts independently from any other structures of meanings. Around this time we also observe the birth of aesthetics and its close link to the philosophical problematic of individuality. Elucidating Kant's idea of aesthetic judgment as independent from any doctrine in the *Critique of Judgment*, Jean-Marie Schaeffer observes that "The aesthetic sphere would thus be that of concrete, autonomous subjectivity: in artistic creation and in judgments of taste, the individual acts freely, without being subject to any heteronomy, whether theological, conceptual, or ethical" (Schaeffer 2000: 18). The notion of artistic autonomy in the modern age must be understood along with the unique and subjective perspective of the artist and that of the viewer in relation to the rapidly changing and alienating modern world. The self in modernist arts—the depicting, the depicted, and the watching self—is often the one who faces critically and helplessly the nameless masses, increasing tempo, and expanding space. The world is changing too fast, introducing too many sensory excitements and consumption desires, and one of the main duties of the aesthetic experience is to offer shelter from these alienating experiences. The helpless individual getting lost in the modern world is translated into the world of art to become the lone but genius artist capable of producing the most transcendental artwork by connecting with her inner, private self. Artistic production can be understood as the autonomous action of an individual who combats the passivity cultivated by the modern world.

In the nineteenth and twentieth centuries, this romanticist celebration of individual genius encountered new interests in artistic form in the West. The demand for formalistic innovation and the increasing abstraction of art from reality are prominent in many modernist art movements, and the avant-garde's urge to overthrow traditions and the status quo further accentuates the modernist indulgence in individual art forms. This interest in pure creativity effectively strengthens the discourse of the autonomy of arts, which refers both to artistic form and to artistic expression, as the highest principle in artistic creation. The slogan of "art for art's sake" first emerged in early nineteenth-century France, and the idea that the intrinsic value of art resides in itself, radically separated from any other ideological or utilitarian functions, gained wide currency not only among artists but also the general public well into the twenty-first century.

This European-based concept of art is heavily coded, assuming that art is the highest form of all cultural productions. Because of the privileges artists supposedly enjoyed, art works became class indicators as well as embodiments of national identities that had to be respected and protected. The discourse of artistic autonomy is part of this narrowly defined but globally circulating concept of art, which, of course, has also attracted much criticism. Feminist art critics, for example, argue that arts are not transcendental works but representations situated squarely in their own social conditions and projecting dominant ideologies, particularly that of the patriarchy. We find in all arts a systematic hierarchy of meanings and knowledge, whose ideological origins and impacts are both inside and beyond the artwork itself. In her study of the beautiful-woman faces so profuse in European art, Griselda Pollock reminds us that these faces are produced and secured by "the erasure of indices of real time and actual space, by an abstracted representation of faces as dissociated uninhabited spaces" (Pollock 2003: 170). The discourse of the autonomy of art is a fiction, in other words, one heavily invested with the patriarchy's attempt to appropriate women. Postcolonial scholars and cultural anthropologists also remind us that arts are communally based in many places in the world, and that the "autonomous" European arts were indeed invested with many racialized ways of looking at people (Mudimbe 1998).

The strongest critics of "art for art's sake" also include Marxist theorists, who condemn modernist art as naïve in claiming independence from society, and who accuse artists of failing to respect and uphold the organic relationship between life and art. Georg Lukács, for example, turned into a fierce critic of modernism when he became a Marxist, accusing modernist artists of dwelling in subjectivism and denying an explicable objective world (Lukács 1995: 187–209). For Lukács, the objective world is explicable to the extent that life is determined by ideological forces. And if the world is ideological, art, which faithfully reflects the world, should also be ideological and therefore political. Obviously, Lukács did not read arts and literature in a completely mechanical way:

> For the inter-relationships between the psychology of people and the economic
> and moral circumstances of their lives have grown so complex that it requires

a very broad portrayal of these circumstances and interactions if people are
to appear clearly as the concrete children of their age.

(Lukács 1983: 40)

But any idea that art could be independent from its social material reality had to be
condemned. It is primarily in opposition to "art for art's sake" that a Marxist theory
of art began to develop in the twentieth century, followed up by such prominent
artists and critics as Bertolt Brecht and Walter Benjamin, who describes art as an
epistemological tool for both the writer/artist and the reader/viewer to understand
the pervasiveness of capitalism and its influence on all social relationships (Benjamin
1978).

These criticisms should not be read simply as a blow to creative freedom. At
the same time, not all modernist artists are apolitical, and an indulgence in form can
also be socially engaging. It is well known that many modernist artists were highly
responsive to the world and critical of the increasing alienation resulting from modernity and capitalism. Not only were they concerned about the conditions of their own
artistic production, but they also explored the ways that art can comment on and
reflect the general social conditions of disciplined labor and exploitation, and many
were critical of capitalism in general (Gagnier 2000). Richard Brettell (1991) convincingly demonstrates that modernist concerns with alienation and dislocation amount to
critiques of capitalism. Matei Calinescu also reminds us of the fundamental appeal of
Marxism to many avant-garde artists, however much they were suspicious of ideologies
in general (Calinescu 1987: 128–29). Unless we want to be entirely conceptual, there
is no need to equate the autonomy of the art form with the artist's freedom of expression. A modernist artist could believe in the autonomy of art to assert a pronounced
political position, and a contemporary filmmaker or designer could denounce the
modernist pursuit of pure form while still striving for independence from market
and political coercions in his or her work. The latter is indeed a major dilemma
facing many creative workers in the current cultural industries. To properly respond
to actual social conditions, what we need are not slogans but a more sophisticated
understanding of the dialectics between autonomy and connectivity.

Creative labor and the discourse of protection

While most cultural industries are preoccupied with the production of aesthetic values,
these values are too abstract and unstable to be easily planned and manufactured. These
industries are therefore very much concerned with talent, and the successful creation
of "stars" continues to be a guarantee for profit. The aesthetic value invested in
cultural products is generally understood as the output of certain creative agents,
whose unique talents and sensitivities are in turn carved into the products. Many
people are attracted to work in the cultural and creative industries precisely because
of the self-actualization and self-expression that such industries promise (McRobbie
1998: 147–48). Some critics also argue that a degree of creative freedom is protected
by such industries because their products require creative input (Banks 2010). We
can say that the operation of the cultural and creative industries is still significantly

and intimately linked to the myth of the talented and quasi-independent artist who expresses his or her true self in a creation.

The notion of artistic freedom is, however, quickly absorbed by a certain industrial mode of cultural operation in order to support a pervasive neo-liberal logic. As many scholars have pointed out, the value of autonomy is often employed to isolate creative laborers from wider social and political networks, and myths of artistic freedom clandestinely legitimize the exploitation to which creative laborers are increasingly subjected—with the irony that modernist aestheticism emerged in the nineteenth century partly to combat the control of the rapidly developing market. Some kinds of freedom might be structured within cultural and creative industries, but this freedom is also highly ambivalent because workers are often not provided with financial safety nets and medical benefits, and creative workers are victimized by harsh and aggressive treatment related to working conditions and job security (Hesmondhalgh and Baker 2011). Neo-liberalism promotes the ideal of self-reliance, and the self is increasingly conceptualized as an isolated individual capable of solving all problems and taking all risks alone; in this way neo-liberalism empties out the meaning and importance of the social. Angela McRobbie further demonstrates that with this promotion of the isolated self, the concept of talent is aggressively deployed to dramatic effect, mediated by a new rhetoric of mobility and success. Those individuals who can be pushed to become inexhaustibly resourceful and entrepreneurial are idealized as the talent and ultimately as the winners (McRobbie 2002: 101–2). Under this set of social conditions, the autonomy of arts is doubly alienated: not only is it not practiced, but it is also resurrected only as a myth in order to create a fake private relationship between the consumer and the producer, both of whom are imagined in singular form.

In response to this capitalist appropriation of artistic autonomy, critics appeal to the ideal of autonomy all over again in an attempt to develop a protectionist discourse that would fend off the highly intrusive logic of capitalism. Along with the rise of the creative industries discourse scholars have realized the increasing domination of economic logic in the production of art and culture is highly problematic (Boorsma, van Hemel, and van der Wielen 1998). The revaluation of the modernist value of autonomy, which emphasized the artist's internal probing and the power of art, is thus not nostalgic but rather is symptomatic of the recognition that arts and culture are becoming resources for all kinds of interested parties to use. Cultural industries advocates urge their governments to formulate more protective cultural policies in the belief that arts are losing their autonomy and failing to survive under the hegemony of the market. This criticism of neo-liberalism also leads leftist critics to realign themselves in support of artistic autonomy, and to argue that art should not be controlled by the market.

But adopting the slogan of "autonomy" could never be an effective politics for combating the labor alienation increasingly found in cultural and creative industries, because pure autonomy is never possible, and it can easily become an empty signifier awaiting appropriation. I propose that only when the notion of autonomy is understood together with its dialectical other, connectivity, can the more complex face and propensity of art be discovered. Recourse to the notion of connection also enables us to revisit in more specific terms the freedom promised both by art as form and art as creative production.

Transcendence and embeddedness

Let me return to art as form. A prominent critic of the increasing inability of art to relate to the world is Jürgen Habermas, who demonstrates the modern tendency of aesthetics to separate from the discursive realms of the epistemological and the moral-political (Habermas 1984). Habermas develops Weber's idea of pre-modern society as characterized by a more coherent worldview according to which knowledge, justice, and taste were more unified and interconnected. Habermas argues that in modernity, knowledge, justice, and taste are increasingly differentiated into autonomous fields of reasoning, to the extent that they become mutually incompatible. Moral and aesthetic ideals are excluded from the political decision-making process, and policies are formulated based on scientific research only. Observing the marginalization of the arts, Habermas calls for intercommunication between the realms, which he believes would prevent the irreparable splitting of society into competitive value spheres, as posited by Weber. By inviting the arts to speak once more to the political and the epistemological, we can also fulfill the modern promise of critical self-reflexivity (Habermas 1997: 45). But this theory of intercommunication, which presupposes the possibility of equal and effective communication, does not respond to the fierce appropriation of arts and culture by powerful economic and political forces as observed today (Yúdice 2003). Thus it is widely contended that Habermas's idealization could only be a utopia.

From a completely different purview, Jacques Rancière also demonstrates the importance of making art relevant to politics, but instead of a model of communication, which probably never works in any actual power-structure situations, he advocates a model of dialectics, which brings us back to the nature of art. Rancière reminds us that art must retain a certain autonomy in order to relate to the world, and it is this dialectic of autonomy and connectivity that makes art politically powerful.

On the one hand, Rancière insists that there is a part of art that is by nature autonomous from politics—according to the broadest definition of the latter term. Rancière is highly critical of the traditional Marxist theory of fetishism for turning art into some positivist sociological evidence for people to investigate underlying political forces (Rancière 2004: 32–34). For Rancière, the political value of art can be located only if art is respected first and foremost as art, autonomous from the realm of the political; only through the dissensus between art and politics can each interrogate the other (Rancière 2010: 115–17). Being politically engaged, Rancière still maintains a certain Kantian understanding of the arts, and he endorses Kant's aesthetic judgment as a judgment without concepts—without the submission of the intuitive to conceptual determination. On the other hand, Rancière maintains that art is by nature political because it can redistribute time and space by the way that it orders its visibility. To him, art might be a Greek statue, manifesting its idleness and indifference but, due to its actual occupation of time and space, it also necessarily calls attention to its own distribution of the sensible; it thus questions its own separate reality, indirectly suggesting the possibility of constructing something different (Rancière 2009: 19–44).

Accordingly, Rancière points out two attributes of art: its autonomy, or independence from social reality, and its heteronomy, or dependence on social reality. He explains that while the two forces of autonomy and heteronomy bind each other together, they also call each other into crisis: all art is tied to a certain form of politics, and this attribution threatens the aesthetic regime (Rancière 2009: 44). But at the same time, the autonomy of the aesthetic regime accounts for the resistance to politics that inheres in the work of art. All artworks are bound to the dialectic between aesthetics and politics, between independence and dependence on other socio-political forces. "To say that art resists thus means that it is a perpetual game of hide-and-seek between the power of sensible manifestation of works and their power of signification" (Rancière 2010: 174). In other words, it is the simultaneous embodiment of and resistance to signification that defines art's political potential. For Rancière, art's most important function is to disrupt politics, but this ability is conferred by its own autonomy and plurality in contrast to the control and singularity of politics. While he is highly critical of the linear classic Western aesthetic regime, according to which art passively retains and transmits the artist's intention, the most distinguished dimension of Rancière's aesthetics is his belief in the active power of the artwork itself.

This dialectical theory of art might end up being entirely interpretive, implying that it is the critic's job to establish whether a certain artwork is effectively political, since all art has the potential to be both active and passive. But Rancière's insistence that art's value must not be detached from its "relationship" with social reality is helpful for reconceptualizing a politics of creative labor in the cultural industries that would be based on art's propensity to make connections. This innate ability of art and culture to order the world, to connect and reconnect things and humans, demonstrates not only their political nature but also their economic nature: interrelations between culture, politics, and economy result not from people's good will, but from these realms always already being part and parcel of each other. This realization leads us back to the freedom necessarily implied in creative labor.

Community and connectivity in cultural industries

The notion of the network is extremely important in cultural industries discourse, which addresses products that are no longer artworks as such and whose production and distribution demand inputs from different agents and institutional supports. Basically, all products of cultural industry are meant to be commodities for sale, to be advertisements of other commodities, or to create added values to yet other economic activities. As such, no cultural commodity is a lone product. Most importantly, present-day creative labor operates in a network society, where workers cannot be isolated from their peers. Even freelance workers face an accumulation of resources online, where agents and platforms are available to help self-employed or amateur artists produce and present their products.

Networks and connections are generally assumed to affect workers' career development. In this context we can identify two main types of networks. First, networking is essential for workers to survive within and gain access to existing institutions. Just like the old boys' clubs, networking facilitates the worker's climb of the career ladder. These networks represent the status quo, and they endorse built-in inequality—entrance presupposes exclusion. But there are also networks that are meant to facilitate mutual support and to offer alternative routes for creative laborers to produce and distribute their works. The two types of network seem to refer to completely different politics and values, but some cultural industry and creative labor studies tend to conflate them. A problematic result is the assumption that the networks are set up only for players to play along, instead of transcending the existing dominant structures to offer new possibilities for navigating them.

An example of this assumption is the "creative cluster," an emerging term in cultural industry and cultural policy studies. The geographical concept of the cluster is meant to encourage the agglomeration of specialized talents and institutions so as to enhance communication, competition, and innovation. In the last decade, governments and public policy organizations around the world have demonstrated clear interest in and commitment to the concept of creative clusters, which are considered capable of promoting local and regional growth in a post-industrial environment (Kong and O'Connor 2009). Proximity of related firms and workers is assumed to encourage a supportive network and collaboration in solving problems, accumulating knowledge, and developing further specialization. In China, many city governments pursue creative clusters. Old factories are re-occupied, communities are extricated, and significant real estate interests are mobilized to conjure up such clusters (Keane 2011: 37–56). The problem with many creative clusters, however, resides specifically in their inability to offer alternatives to the existing institutional restraints, and they fail to present new tensions and opportunities in the cultural industries in question. New networks do not necessarily lead to new conditions within the cultural industries; instead, many creative clusters are established by existing power structures for their own benefits.

Many network analyses also tend to see network size as a determinant variable of a successful cultural career: the wider the network, the more information and career opportunities a worker has, which would lead to more professional success. Helen Blair demonstrates, however, that size and density of networks does not necessarily lead to greater employment opportunity, partly because there are usually many redundant contacts providing the same information, and partly because the effort expended in maintaining a huge network often goes unrewarded by proportional information benefits. But most importantly, social institutions often precede the existence of any given individual or network of individuals, and networking often reinforces these pre-existing institutions instead of challenging them (Blair 2009). The basic structure of inclusion and exclusion is not always challenged by acts of networking or community building, so that someone from an ethnic minority, an underrepresented gender, or a certain class background who puts effort into establishing networks might only thereby be led back to those ghettoized jobs already prescribed for him or her.

It might be too much of a cliché to reiterate that both autonomy and connectivity are needed in creative labor, yet we must also realize that they are both quickly appropriated by the market and the industry to facilitate capitalist logic, making the two concepts vulnerable and their meanings unsteady. We can assume that the discourse of cultural industries, which emphasizes multiple sources of influence on cultural production, has the potential to offer new ideas for reconceptualizing the tensions and dynamics between autonomy and connectivity. Many cultural industries and their related discourse end up endorsing the existing structure and logic of capital, when arts and culture could be called upon to broaden the understanding of community that has been narrowed by the dominating logic of administration and possessive individualism. We are caught in an environment when even relationships are commodified, and a major business model of Web 2.0 is precisely to organize the rubric of relationships built up online to make them salable (Van Dijck 2013: 14–18). I maintain that there is a connective nature in art that can never be reduced by any simple claim to "autonomy," and that its inherent relationship with the material world always resists, however subtly, the prevalent attempts at privatizing works of creative labor (Adorno 2001: 107–17). The most important question for us is how to rediscover the active dimension of art that would make connections with and in the world possible again.

To link this discussion to creative labor, we should ask whether, and how, the communities built by creative workers actually facilitate and realize the connective potential of art. On the level of production, can cultural workers be encouraged to relate to the world beyond the utilitarian purposes of work itself? On the level of consumption, would the consumption of cultural pieces lead the viewer to transcend the work and be reminded of the social conditions in which he or she is embedded? In both cases, a true sense of autonomy could be achieved. If networks are constructed only to help workers fix the immediate purposes and restrictions of the work itself, then these networks betray and cancel out the rich potentiality of autonomy and heteronomy endowed in the art form. If the network is understood and employed in a merely utilitarian way that aims to match the flexible and adaptable nature of culture to comparable market mechanisms, then the creative and transformative potential of cultural works would only be repressed in order to strengthen and enrich existing institutions. Such communities would not offer new viewpoints and mechanisms to create new power structures.

Similarly, when we try to articulate the importance of autonomy and independence in creative labor, we need to make sure such arguments are not based on a fundamental fear of lending oneself and one's works to the foreignness of others, who might embrace and distort the integrity of the work into a different form. Most assertions of artistic autonomy are advanced under the presence of a controlling force against which art is trying to escape. If the autonomy of art that was promoted in eighteenth and nineteenth century Europe was based on the individual's fear of a rapidly changing world, this individual was also highly problematic, in that its insecurity was caused by a desire for knowledge and control of the world (Pang 2012: 224–26). Instead of simply maintaining the importance of artistic autonomy, cultural industries critics should campaign for creative workers not in order to isolate them in a discourse of rights, but in order to establish respect for such workers' unique embedding in and transcendence of the world, an embedding and transcendence that might be able to regenerate the energy of culture.

A discussion of community is urgent in current critical theory because Western modernity has overemphasized the value and the will of isolated individuals. But resurrecting community in the traditional egalitarian sense is not an option. Discussions of community, or relationality, as Jean-Luc Nancy puts it, should be geared toward the denial of any metaphysics of the absolute (Nancy 1991: 1–42), which also amounts to the denial of any political, economic, or social project that aims for a community of essence or immanence, such as Nazism (Nancy 1991: 12). Community, therefore, is not composed of individuals of shared identities pursuing a common goal, but it is characterized by the impossibility of such consensus and stable relationships. A community is not meant to be stable, and a community is always at risk, as are the individuals composing it. A true sense of community would refute any unifying principle that defines a community, because the matters making up a community are always relational, and finite. Connectivity is neither a rendition of a designed order, nor a development toward some final goal. If we use Nancy's concept of community to understand the potentiality of cultural industries, we can avoid questions of definition and modeling, and we can instead envision constantly mutating institutions that produce cultural products for the sake of building symbolic relationships.

References

Adorno, T. (2001), *The Culture Industry: Selected Essays on Mass Culture*, New York: Routledge.

Banks, M. (2010), "Autonomy Guaranteed? Cultural Work and the 'Art-Commerce Relation'," *Journal of Cultural Research* 14, no. 3: 251–59.

Benjamin, W. (1978), "The Author as Producer," in P. Demetz (ed.) *Reflections*, New York: Schocken Book.

Blair, H. (2009), "Active Networking: Action, Social Structure and the Process of Networking," in A. McKinlay and C. Smith (eds.) *Creative Labour: Working in the Creative Industries*, Basingstoke: Palgrave Macmillan.

Boorsma, P., A. van Hemel, and N. van der Wielen (1998), *Privatization and Culture: Experiences in the Arts, Heritage and Cultural Industries in Europe*, Boston: Kluwer.

Bourdieu, P. (1993), *The Field of Cultural Production*, New York: Columbia University Press.

Brettell, R. (1991), *Modern Art 1851–1929: Capitalism and Representation*, Oxford: Oxford University Press.

Calinescu, M. (1987), *Five Faces of Modernity: Modernism, Avant-Garde, Decadence, Kitsch, Postmodernism*, Durham, NC: Duke University Press.

Gagnier, R. (2000), *The Insatiability of Human Wants: Economics and Aesthetics in Market Society*, Chicago: University of Chicago Press.

Habermas, J. (1984), *The Theory of Communicative Action*, vol. 1, Boston: Beacon Press.

Habermas, J. (1997), "Modernity: An Unfinished Project," in M. d'Entrèves and S. Benhabib (ed.) *Habermas and the Unfinished Project of Modernity*, Cambridge, MA: The MIT Press.

Hesmondhalgh, D. and S. Baker (2011), "'A Very Complicated Version of Freedom': Conditions and Experiences of Creative Labour in Three Cultural Industries," *Variant*, issue 41 (Spring 2011); www.variant.org.uk/41texts/variant41.html#L10 (accessed August 29, 2013).

Keane, M. (2011), *China's New Creative Clusters: Governance, Human Capital and Investment*, Abingdon: Routledge.

Kong, L. and J. O'Connor (ed.) (2009), *Creative Economies, Creative Cities: Asian-European Perspectives*, Dordrecht: Springer.

Lukács, G. (1983), *The Historical Novel*, Lincoln: University of Nebraska Press.

Lukács, G. (1995), "The Ideology of Modernism," in A. Kadarkay (ed.) *The Lukács Reader*, Oxford, UK: Blackwell.

McRobbie, A. (1998), *British Fashion Design: Rag Trade or Image Industry?* London and New York: Routledge.

McRobbie, A. (2002), "From Holloway to Hollywood: Happiness at Work in the New Cultural Economy?" in P. du Gay and M. Pryke (ed.) *Cultural Economy: Cultural Analysis and Cultural Life*, London: Sage.

Mudimbe, V. (1998), *The Invention of Africa: Gnosis, Philosophy and the Order of Knowledge*, Bloomington: Indiana University Press.

Nancy, J. (1991), *The Inoperative Community*, Minneapolis: University of Minnesota Press.

Pang, L. (2012), *Creativity and Its Discontents: China's Creative Industries and Intellectual Property Right Offenses*, Durham, SC: Duke University Press.

Pollock, G. (2003), *Vision and Difference*, New York: Routledge.

Rancière, J. (2004), *The Politics of Aesthetics*, London: Continuum.

Rancière, J. (2009), *Aesthetics and Its Discontents*, Cambridge: Polity.

Rancière, J. (2010), *Dissensus: On Politics and Aesthetics*, London: Continuum.

Schaeffer, J. (2000), *Art of the Modern Age: Philosophy of Art from Kant to Heidegger*, Princeton, NJ: Princeton University Press.

Van Dijck, J. (2013), *The Culture of Connectivity: A Critical History of Social Media*, Oxford University Press.

Yúdice, G. (2003), *The Expediency of Culture: Uses of Culture in the Global Era*, Durham: Duke University Press.

3

THE CULTURAL INDUSTRIES AS A SECTOR OF THE ECONOMY

David Throsby

Introduction

Interest in the role of the cultural industries as a sector of the economy can be traced back at least to the 1980s. Although the term "industry" applied to the arts was not in widespread use at that time, it was beginning to be recognised that the arts sector generated output, incomes, employment and exports that were of some economic significance. Arts advocates in a number of countries, concerned at the tightening of public budgets and an increased questioning of the rationale for government funding of cultural activity, turned to the economic contribution of the arts industries as a justification for continued financial support. In fact, simply demonstrating the economic size of the sector provided no such justification, although numbers showing the extent of job creation or the proportion of GDP that the arts contributed at least served to indicate that the cultural industries were not some economic backwater but a significant component of the macroeconomy.[1]

During the 1990s the concept of arts-as-industry was widened to co-opt broader notions of culture, identity, heritage and creativity into an economic framework, laying the foundation for an expansion of cultural policy into the economic arena. An interpretation of cultural policy simply as arts policy began to be replaced with a more broad-ranging agenda, as synergies were increasingly recognised between the cultural industries and economic progress (Throsby 2010). The celebrated *Creative Nation* statement of the Australian Government in 1994 encapsulates this merging of artistic and economic purpose in its vision of the information and communications revolution, and its foretaste of the arts in the digital economy (Commonwealth of Australia 1994). Subsequently these ideas were picked up by the first Blair government in the United Kingdom (UK), setting the scene for the Creative Industries Taskforce of 1997 (Department for Culture, Media and Sport 2001). The agenda here, however, was shifted from culture to a focus on creativity; in this scenario, creative dynamism was seen as a source of innovation, and the intellectual property that creative output generates was looked to as the primary source of revenue. It was no accident, therefore, that the economic activities of interest in the UK policy initiative were called creative and not cultural industries (Garnham 2005).

As is well known, the designation of 13 creative industries in the UK was influential during the first decade of the twenty-first century in the formation of cultural policies in a number of countries, particularly in Europe. The concept of the creative and/or cultural industries that took shape during this period in academic and policy-making circles was consolidated into the collective term the "creative economy". This term was used to describe a subsector of the macroeconomy that was reputed to be a source of dynamism in creating output and employment growth in otherwise sluggish economies. Data showing that this sector was growing more rapidly than traditional sectors such as manufacturing persuaded politicians and their bureaucrats to take notice.[2]

Whether the creative economy was comprised only of the cultural industries or whether it embraced something more was a question that was answered in different ways in different countries, as discussed further below. But the role of the specifically cultural industries in the creative economy was strongly asserted in the influential *Creative Economy Report*, published by the United Nations Conference on Trade and Development (UNCTAD) in 2008 and updated in 2010. These reports were particularly oriented towards talking up the development potential of cultural industries in countries of the global South as a means towards the economic and cultural empowerment of the people and as a panacea for poverty alleviation. The reports had much to say about the scope for increased trade in cultural goods, although the lack of data on trade in cultural services such as audiovisual product meant that an important component of cultural exports and imports was not adequately covered. In 2013 responsibility for producing the report shifted from UNCTAD to the United Nations Educational, Scientific and Cultural Organization (UNESCO) (with the involvement of the United Nations Development Programme continuing); a new *Creative Economy Report* was produced in that year with a focus on local cultural development (UNESCO 2013). In this forum, and many others, debate about the role of cultural industries as an economic sector continues.

Why might economists, whether in the academy, in government, in international organisations or elsewhere, be interested in the cultural industries? One obvious reason has been the rapid increase in interest in the creative sector amongst policy-makers, as referred to above; the emergence of a group of industries not previously regarded as of any consequence in the policy hierarchy served to awaken economists to possibilities for applying their traditional tools of trade in a new arena. The tasks that economic analysts set themselves in addressing issues relating to these industries can be grouped under three headings, which reflect in turn the structure of this chapter.

First, notwithstanding the endless discussion as to whether or not culture can be or should be corralled into an industrial framework, economists have no difficulty in identifying cultural activities of all sorts as industries. Production, distribution and consumption of cultural goods and services take place in an orderly manner that readily fits the economic definitions of an industry, as we shall see in the next section. But beyond the broad industrial interpretation lies a host of definitional issues that must be addressed if the concept of a cultural industry as a sector of the economy is to be made operational.

Second, simply defining industries is by no means the whole story. The interesting analytical issues arise when attention is turned to the relationship amongst the cultural industries themselves and between them and the rest of the economic system. A discussion on how we might interpret the structure of the cultural sector of the economy follows.

Third, we consider measurement. What are the principal economic variables to be accounted for and how are they to be evaluated? Estimates of the economic contribution of the cultural industries require a sound statistical foundation and appropriate analytical methods. These issues are discussed in the light of recent developments in the estimation of a wide range of cultural statistics.

Finally in this chapter we draw some conclusions as to the uses and limitations of an economic approach to the cultural industries. It is argued that economic analysis of the cultural industries should not be seen as oppositional to other disciplinary approaches, but rather as complementary to alternative interpretations of the place of culture in society.

Definitional issues

The concept of an industry is an essential one in economics as a means of interpreting the structure of an economy on the basis of how production is organised. The most obvious way to group business firms in this system is in terms of the products they produce; industries are then defined as collections of firms that produce a similar product. This then leads to the standard analytical approach of industrial organisation theory, which addresses how industries function, looking at:

their *structure*, i.e. the level of concentration, the nature of product differentiation, and the extent of barriers to entry and exit of firms;

their *conduct*, i.e. the way firms compete through price setting and by other means; and

their *performance*, i.e. how efficiently they operate, what rates of return and levels of profit they achieve, and how effectively they service other non-profit-related objectives.

The application of these standard methods of industry economics to the cultural industries is apparently straightforward. *Structural* issues are of interest, for example, in the global music industry, where major transnational publishing and recording companies dominate the market, and smaller firms compete through a variety of price and product differentiation strategies. Similarly, assessment of industry *conduct* and *performance* can be applied, for example, to the operations of theatre companies or commercial art galleries in a particular city; these enterprises can be studied in terms of how they set their prices and how well they survive financially in a competitive market place.

Nevertheless there is a prior question that must be resolved before any analysis of the role of the cultural industries as an economic sector can proceed. This is the fundamental issue of how a cultural industry is to be distinguished from other industries.

One could adopt a pragmatic approach to this issue, accepting that for policy purposes the cultural or creative industries are whatever a particular government defines them to be. For example, the set of 13 industries designated as creative in the UK that we referred to above has remained the standard delineation of what is meant by the creative economy in that country, even though there may continue to be argument about which industries should have been included and which should have been left out. Other countries have reached different conclusions, as we shall see further below.

For our purposes, however, a principles-based approach is preferable. From the viewpoint of economic analysis, the product-group definition provides an appropriate starting point. Applying this concept to defining a cultural industry moves the definitional responsibility back one stage, requiring an unambiguous definition of cultural goods and services in order for it to become usable.

Two approaches to distinguishing cultural from other goods and services in the economy have emerged in recent times. The first is to identify the distinctive characteristics of such goods that relate in some way to the concept of culture. For example it can be suggested that cultural products that are derived from the creative arts share the following characteristics:

they require the input of human creativity in their production or presentation;
they carry some form of symbolic meaning that elevates them beyond a purely utilitarian function; and
they contain, at least potentially, some intellectual property that may possibly provide a source of revenue for those who produce them.

The second approach to defining a cultural good depends on an elaboration of the second characteristic noted above. The symbolic meaning or cultural content embodied in or conveyed by a cultural good or service such as a film, an artwork, a poem, a video game or a music performance, can be interpreted as a form of value that the good generates. This value is separate from whatever utilitarian value the good possesses. It can be referred to as the good's cultural value; if this concept can be identified in an objective and replicable manner, its presence could be used as a means of defining a cultural good.

Of course the definitional issues do not end there. Implicit in the set of three criteria noted above are two further difficulties: the identification of creativity and the recognition of the symbolic meaning upon which in turn the definition of cultural value rests. These difficulties exercise the minds of economists interested in art and culture just as much as they do those of practitioners in other disciplines. In addition, even if these problems are set aside there may be argument as to where the borders of the product group should be drawn; cases exist of cultural goods whose inclusion or otherwise continues to be problematical. Nevertheless, despite these various obstacles we can proceed, for the purposes of this chapter, on the assumption that either or both of the above definitions of a cultural good or service provides a workable basis to categorise a recognisable product group. Accepting this assumption then enables the identification of a set of cultural industries as being those industries concerned with the production and distribution of these goods and services. Defining the cultural industries in this way in turn allows an economically plausible delineation of the cultural sector of the economy.

The above definitions also facilitate a resolution of the tedious argument about whether the industries of interest should be referred to as creative or cultural industries. According to the approach outlined above, a creative industry emerges as one to which only the first of the three distinguishing criteria applies; a cultural industry, on the other hand, will be defined as one complying with all three characteristics. Thus the set of cultural industries in the economy can be seen as a subset of the more wide-ranging group of creative industries, and the ambit of the industrial content of cultural policy is accordingly more specific than that of creative industries policy generally. In other words, it is argued that the distinction between cultural and creative industries is not a matter of philosophical principle or disciplinary preference, but simply one related directly to the meaning of words used to describe the products of these industries.[3]

We noted at the beginning of this section that the cultural or creative industries could be defined de facto as those that happen to be accepted as such in any particular jurisdiction; it is readily observable that different countries have reached different conclusions in applying whatever criteria they regard as relevant to the definition of cultural or creative industries for their own policy purposes. Nevertheless, certain commonalities can be found in the resulting industrial mix. For example, in a comparison of the creative or cultural industries designated as such across 17 European countries, Mikić (2012) finds that film and video, radio and television, performing arts, music, architecture and publishing are included in all or most classifications. The next most prominent group includes visual arts, design and advertising, followed by museums, archives, libraries and heritage. Somewhat similar conclusions can be reached if a comparison of included industries is made across different models of the cultural sector as seen from various disciplinary perspectives (Throsby 2008a).

Structural relationships

As an economic sector, how do the cultural industries function and how do they relate to one another and to the economy at large? These questions can be addressed from several different directions. Here we consider four approaches to portraying and analysing the economic role of the cultural sector once a particular set of cultural industries has been determined.

The first interpretation is that depicting the sequential process whereby raw materials are transformed into a finished cultural product. The process can be seen as a supply chain or a value chain, with successive stages providing further services and adding value until the point of final demand is reached. The book industry is a good illustration. A novel, for example, begins life as an idea in an author's mind, transformed into words that may go through many iterations before landing on the desk of a publisher. A literary agent may assist along the way, and editorial input is likely once the book is accepted for publication. If it is to appear in hard copy, designers and then printers are brought in, followed by distributors, advertisers and the book stores which convey the final product to the consumer. Each stage can be seen as a transformative process, and the value-adding that occurs along the way is rewarded ultimately as a series of allocations from the retail price at which the book is sold; typically the share going to the original creator – the novelist – is likely to be relatively small, perhaps 10 per cent or less.

Within this sequential-production framework, the structural features of the cultural industries can be interpreted in terms of the contractual relationships existing between successive stages. Caves (2000) identifies the characteristics peculiar to cultural goods and services that give such contractual arrangements their distinctive nature. These include the "nobody knows" characteristic that encapsulates the radical uncertainty regarding the likely market success of a cultural product such as a movie – films unexpectedly become block-busters, and sure-fire hits turn out to be box-office failures. Contractual conditions also affect production because each unit of an original cultural good is unique – an extreme case of product differentiation – although copies are infinitely replicable.

The apparently inexorable linear sequence depicted in the supply-chain model does not necessarily mean that influences and interconnections flow in only one direction. In any production chain, feedback effects are likely whereby downstream players may influence what happens at an earlier stage in the process. For this reason it can be suggested that the term *value network* may be a more accurate description of cultural production processes than the value chain (Hearn et al. 2007; Keeble and Cavanagh 2008).

Although we can point to the product group as defining a single industry producing a given product type (the visual arts industry, the fashion industry, and so on), the supply-chain sequence relating to the creation, manufacture and distribution of a particular cultural good or service is likely in fact to traverse a number of different industries. For example, the stages comprising the music industry's operations include the separate "sub-industries" containing song-writers, publishers, record companies, agents, promoters of live concerts, music retailers, and so on. Each of these sub-industries can be analysed in terms of its own organisational and operational characteristics, and each may have its own value-chain sequence that is a component of the larger music value chain covering the entire production and distribution process. It is apparent, therefore, that economic analysis of the cultural industries according to the supply/value-chain model can become quite complex as finer levels of detail are sought.

The second approach to portraying the role of the cultural industries in the economy takes the supply chain or cultural production cycle model and elaborates it to interpret the interrelationships between components of the cultural sector. This approach was adopted as the basis for a model of the cultural sector proposed by the UNESCO Institute for Statistics (UIS) for use in the design of national cultural statistics collections (UNESCO Institute for Statistics 2009). The resulting Framework for Cultural Statistics groups cultural activities into several "domains", comprising six "core" domains:

- cultural and natural heritage;
- performance and celebration;
- visual arts and crafts;

- book and press;
- audiovisual and interactive media;
- design and creative services;

together with two "related" domains:

- tourism;
- sport and recreation;

and three "transversal" domains:

- education and training;
- archiving and preserving;
- equipment and supporting materials.

The rationale for this approach was articulated by the UIS as being to meet "the challenge for a robust and sustainable cultural statistical framework ... to cover the contributory processes that enable culture to not only be created, but distributed, received, used, critiqued (*sic*), understood and preserved" (UNESCO Institute for Statistics 2007: 25).

The cultural cycle concept as represented in the UIS Framework enables the specification of product-based, industry-based and employment-based depictions of cultural production, and extends the simple supply-chain model to include consumption of cultural goods and services. It thus has the capacity to provide a comprehensive view of the structure of the cultural sector and its place in the economy.

The third approach to interpreting the structure of the cultural industries focuses on the dynamics of cultural transmission within a cultural production system. An illustration of this approach is the so-called "concentric circles model" which interprets cultural transmission as a process whereby original ideas move from a creative core to successive layers of industries in the cultural sector and beyond (Throsby 2008b). The circles are arranged in descending order of the cultural content of the industries' output, or equivalently in increasing order of the industries' degree of commercialisation. Thus the core comprises the primary creative arts, other core industries include film, galleries, etc., wider cultural industries include media, publishing and so on, and there is a group of related cultural industries in which production is primarily commercial, such as advertising and fashion.

The concentric circles model is an approach to conceptualising the structural features of the cultural industries that incorporates both the economic and cultural value of cultural goods and services, outlined as follows:

> The model assumes that cultural content springs from the incorporation of creative ideas into the production and/or presentation of sound, text and image and that these ideas originate in the arenas of primary artistic creativity. This is an assumption that accords primacy to the processes of artistic (as distinct from scientific) creativity, and is the reason why the creative arts – music, drama, dance, visual art, literature – lie at the centre of the

model, with successive layers of the concentric circles defined as the ideas and influences of these creative activities diffuse outwards. The economic content of the model is represented by the market and non-market value of the goods and services produced as either intermediate or final products in the various layers of the system.

(Throsby 2010: 91)

The diffusion of ideas and influences in this model can be interpreted as operating through the processes of knowledge transfer that are familiar to economists studying the generation and adoption of innovation in the economy at large. But it is not only ideas that move, it is also creative workers themselves. Thus some part of the diffusion process depicted in the concentric circles model occurs through the fact that workers who gain their training or experience in the core may find employment in the wider cultural industries or outside the cultural sector altogether, applying their creative skills in often innovative ways.[4]

A final approach to portraying the economic role of the cultural industries is one that focuses on economic power, interpreting the dynamics of cultural transmission within a broader societal system relating to both the production and the consumption of cultural products. In such models the exercise of economic power is the motivating force used (whether deliberately or otherwise) to influence consumer attitudes and behaviour, and to shape cultural preferences. A number of chapters in this volume are based in one way or another on this perspective, providing an alternative view of the economic role of the cultural industries.

To conclude this section it is worth noting that the above discussion of alternative models of the cultural industries contains several mentions of the word "core". The concept of a core in some system implies centrality or a heightened degree of importance attributable to some elements of a system. Thus the core cultural industries would be those regarded for some reason as being of greater significance than the rest. Given that ideas as to what constitutes significance vary widely depending on purpose, discipline and/or ideological orientation, it is not surprising that designations of the cultural core will differ from one analyst to the next. Some writers focus on the mass media and products such as film, music and video games that are important in popular cultural consumption, relegating the so-called "high arts" to peripheral status (Hesmondhalgh 2007). Others look to a "creative core" that sees the production of primary cultural content as the guiding principle (KEA European Affairs 2006; Work Foundation 2007; DeNatale and Wassall 2007; Throsby 2008b). A more neutral designation of the core cultural industries might see them simply as those most often included in cultural industry sectors across countries, as described above.

Measurement

We turn now to aspects of the cultural industries that economists are interested in measuring and how they go about it. The answers to these questions depend on the purpose of the analysis. The most straightforward approach is to evaluate the contribution that a particular cultural industry, or the cultural sector as a whole, makes to the macroeconomy, measured in terms of variables such as gross value of production, value added, employment, exports and so on. From such data are derived the popular national indicators of the cultural sector's contribution to GDP, or the share of creative workers in the country's labour force. These statistics are generally collected on a regular basis over the long term, enabling trends over time in major variables to be identified.

The concept of an industry's contribution to the economy can be contrasted with the assessment of economic impact. The latter term relates to the short-term once-over effects of some intervention such as a festival or a cultural investment project. In such cases measurement focuses on the direct and indirect impacts of the intervention, including flow-on and multiplier effects. Impact studies have been widely used to assess the economic benefits to local or regional communities generated by cultural institutions, arts events and so on (Madden 2001; Throsby 2004; Seaman 2011). Such studies are less applicable to the cultural industries as a whole. Thus the rest of this section deals only with measuring the cultural sector's economic contribution, as defined above.

The two most important variables to be measured in assessing the economic contribution of a cultural industry are output and employment. The value of the output produced by industries in the economy is measured in the national accounts in various ways, including as the gross value of production and gross value added. With appropriate agreement as to which industries are included in the cultural sector, it is possible to use the data in these accounts to identify the value of the sector's contribution to the economy. The data refer to marketed output, i.e. production that is transacted through markets and that ultimately serves the final demand of consumers. Production sold or exchanged through the informal economy is not counted.

The first point of reference in considering data collection at the whole-economy level is the national accounts. In most countries these are based on the System of National Accounts (SNA), an internationally agreed framework for the collection of statistics relating to output, incomes, employment etc. within the economy. The SNA covers industries at various levels of disaggregation, and identifies various sectors such as the household sector, the government sector, and so on. Although these accounts have been invaluable over many years in providing a consistent basis for the collection of data concerning the economy, they do not cover several important areas, such as household production, the input of volunteer labour, etc. Moreover, when consulted for data on a specific sector of the economy such as the cultural sector, the categorisation of industries can be somewhat rigid, making it difficult to specify a group that exactly coincides with a priori notions of what the sector contains.

Some of the limitations of the SNA as a basis for estimating the contribution of the cultural industries to the economy can be addressed through the development of a set of satellite accounts for culture. A satellite accounts model for a given sector allows for an expansion of information contained in the national accounts by providing for a more finely articulated classification system for the industries of concern, and through the introduction of additional data, alternative concepts and greater descriptive detail. Such accounts have been prepared in the past for sectors such as tourism and the environment, but have only recently begun to be developed for culture. Initial work in Colombia (Convenio Andrés Bello 2009) and Finland

(Finnish Ministry of Education 2009) has been followed by several empirical studies, including projects in Spain (Spanish Ministry of Culture 2011), the United States (Bureau of Economic Analysis/National Endowment for the Arts 2013), Australia (Australian Bureau of Statistics 2014) and Uruguay (Asuaga et al. 2013).

To illustrate the sorts of data that a set of satellite accounts for culture can generate, the following statistics are drawn from results for the year 2011 arising from the US project referred to above:

- the production of arts and cultural goods added more than $504 billion to the US economy, representing about 3.25 per cent of gross domestic product (GDP) in that year;
- these industries employed nearly 2 million workers and generated $289.5 billion in wages, salaries and supplements for these workers;
- multipliers calculated from the satellite accounts indicate that every $1 increase in the demand for arts and culture generates $1.67 in output of all US commodities, and every $1 million increase creates approximately 1,750 new jobs; and
- the US experienced a trade surplus for cultural goods and services in 2011, with $39.4 billion in exports and $28.9 billion in imports.

These data are more reliable than previous estimates because they are based on a more precise and carefully controlled group of included cultural industries.

Satellite accounts for cultural production measure the market value of commercially provided cultural goods and services and also contain an estimate for the value of cultural output provided at reduced or zero price by non-profit organisations.[5] In addition, however, it is generally thought that the arts and culture provide significant public benefits that escape the market. The value of such benefits, to the extent that they exist, is reflected in the willingness of the community to pay for supporting the arts and culture through compulsory taxation or through voluntary contributions to cultural institutions, foundations, appeals, etc. This value can be measured using techniques such as contingent valuation, implemented via a sample survey of the relevant population (Cuccia 2011). Any overall assessment of the aggregate economic value generated by culture in the economy will fall short of providing a complete evaluation measurable in monetary terms if it does not include an estimate of the value attributable to these non-market effects.

We turn now to the other major variable to be measured, namely employment. Here again definitional problems arise. For example, is a cultural worker someone who produces direct cultural output or simply someone who happens to work in a cultural industry? Likewise, how are "creative occupations" distinguished from other jobs? Different countries use different definitions, and as a result international comparisons of the contribution of the cultural industries to aggregate employment are difficult to draw.

A particular group of cultural workers that has engaged the attention of economists is creative artists (Throsby 2012). These workers generally do not conform to conventional economic models of labour market behaviour, being motivated importantly by non-pecuniary considerations in their labour supply decisions. They typically face a choice between working at their artistic practice for relatively little monetary reward, or taking on less satisfying work outside the arts that is more remunerative. The choice has to be made subject to a minimum income constraint. Such decisions exemplify one of the many ways in which economic considerations may influence the qualitative nature of an artist's work.

Other aspects of creative labour that have been addressed by economists include the determinants of artistic earnings, the unemployment experience of artists and the career trajectories of new entrants onto the artistic labour market. Given that in most countries there is typically an oversupply of potential artists relative to the labour market's capacity to absorb them, questions are raised about the outcomes of education and training programmes in the visual and performing arts. It has been found that although many graduates from such programmes do not end up working as artists, they are nevertheless able to apply the creative skills they have acquired in fulfilling ways in other occupations.[6]

Finally, cultural economists have been increasingly interested in expanding the understanding of value in the economics of art and culture, extending the concept to recognise cultural value, considered as those aspects of the value of cultural phenomena that are not expressible using the standard economic metric of monetary value. Questions of measurement abound here, with no settled methodology or assessment procedures yet. Nevertheless, some progress is being made in collaboration with other disciplines concerned with the same sorts of problems, for example in the evaluation of cultural heritage.[7]

Conclusions

This chapter began by pointing to the continually increasing interest in the role of the cultural industries as a sector of the economy over the three decades since the mid-1980s. We noted the more wide-ranging interpretation of these industries that grew up in the 1990s; this expanded view informs debate today about how the cultural industries can be brought into the cultural policy discourse. A field of particular interest in this respect is the role of culture in economic development and the potential for the cultural industries in promoting equitable and sustainable growth in the developing world. Although these issues have been a matter of central concern in international cultural policy-making since the days of the World Commission on Culture and Development (World Commission on Culture and Development 1995), it has taken on new significance in the lead-up to the proposed reformulation of the United Nations' (UN) Millennium Development Goals, scheduled for 2015. Since it is likely that any set of revised development objectives to be adopted by the UN system will have a strong focus on sustainability, considerable effort has gone into articulating more clearly the role of culture as both a facilitator and a driver of development (United Nations Educational, Scientific and Cultural Organization 2013). In this rapidly evolving environment the contribution of the cultural industries to the economies of developing countries is emerging as a key component of arguments to give culture a stronger profile in international policy-making. The UN General Assembly has passed several resolutions to this effect. In due course these efforts may lead to a more effective integration of cultural and economic policy-making in advancing sustainable development across the world.

To return finally to the contribution that economics can make to studying the cultural industries, it can be observed that questions remain in the minds of some about the intrusion of economists into any area concerned with culture and the arts. Many cultural analysts from disciplines outside economics continue to be critical of what they see as the commodification of culture implied by the application of standard methods of economic analysis to the cultural industries. When such applications ignore cultural dimensions entirely, treat cultural goods and services as if they are no different from any other products, and see economic outcomes as the only ones that matter – as is inherent in standard neo-classical economic models – the criticism would seem to be well founded. However, the contribution of economics to debates about culture is moving from the narrow confines of the neo-classical paradigm to embrace heterodox theory and interactions with other disciplines.[8] These trends are likely to continue. Ultimately, it can be argued that economic analysis of the cultural industries should not be seen as oppositional to other disciplinary approaches to studying culture in the economy and society, but complementary to them.

Notes

1 See, for example, Myerscough (1988).
2 For some recent data demonstrating this growth performance for the UK, see Department for Culture, Media and Sport (2014).
3 For further discussion see, for example, O'Connor (2011).
4 The latter are described as "embedded" workers in the so-called "creative trident" model (Cunningham and Higgs 2009).
5 The latter is sometimes referred to in accounting terminology as "non-market output", although in economics this term is reserved for externalities or public goods, i.e. instances of market failure.
6 See, for example, Oakley et al. (2008); for a response, see McRobbie and Forke (2009).
7 Heritage specialists have used rating systems for some time in the assessment of the cultural significance of historic buildings and sites; see, for example, Marquis-Kyle and Walker (2004). Methods for assessment of the cultural value of heritage are reviewed in Throsby (2013).
8 As exemplified, for example, in contributions to Hutter and Throsby (2008) and Ginsburgh and Throsby (2014).

References

Asuaga, C., Trylesinski, F. and Medeiros, G. (2013), *Satellite Culture Account for Uruguay: Visual and Plastic Arts Sector*, Association for Cultural Economics International Working Paper no. AWP-08-2013.

Australian Bureau of Statistics (2014), *Australian National Accounts: Cultural and Creative Activity Satellite Accounts 2008–2009*, Cat. No. 5271.0, Canberra: ABS.

Bureau of Economic Analysis/National Endowment for the Arts, US (2013), *Arts and Culture Production Satellite Account*, Issue Briefs Nos. 1–6, Washington DC: BEA/NEA.

Caves, R.E. (2000), *Creative Industries: Contracts Between Art and Commerce*, Cambridge, MA: Harvard University Press.

Commonwealth of Australia (1994), *Creative Nation: Commonwealth Cultural Policy*, Canberra: Department of Communications and the Arts.

Convenio Andrés Bello (2009), *Consolidación de un Manual Metodológico para la Implementación de Cuentas Satélites de Cultura en Latinoamérica [Consolidation of a Methodological Manual for the Implementation of Culture Satellite Accounts in Latin America]*, Bogotà: CAB and Inter-American Development Bank.

Cuccia, T. (2011), 'Contingent valuation', in R. Towse (ed.), *A Handbook of Cultural Economics*, 2nd edn, Cheltenham, UK: Edward Elgar, 90–99.

Cunningham, S. and Higgs, P. (2009), 'Measuring creative employment: Implications for innovation policy', *Innovation: Management, Policy and Practice*, 11: 190–200.

DeNatale, D. and Wassall, G.H. (2007), *The Creative Economy: A New Definition*, Boston: New England Foundation for the Arts.

Department for Culture, Media and Sport, UK (2001), *Creative Industries Mapping Document 2001*, London: DCMS.

Department for Culture, Media and Sport, UK (2014), *Creative Industries Economic Estimates: Statistical Release, January*, London: DCMS.

Finnish Ministry of Education (2009), *Culture Satellite Account: Final Report of Pilot Project*, Helsinki: Department for Cultural, Sport and Youth.

Garnham, N. (2005), 'From cultural to creative industries', *International Journal of Cultural Policy*, 11: 15–29.

Ginsburgh, V. and Throsby, D. (eds) (2014), *Handbook of the Economics of Art and Culture*, Vol. 2, Amsterdam: Elsevier/North-Holland.

Hearn, G., Roodhouse, S. and Blakey, J. (2007), 'From value chain to value creating ecology', *International Journal of Cultural Policy*, 13: 419–36.

Hesmondhalgh, D. (2007), *The Cultural Industries*, 2nd edn, London: Sage.

Hutter, M. and Throsby, D. (eds) (2008), *Beyond Price: Value in Culture, Economics, and the Arts*, New York: Cambridge University Press.

KEA European Affairs (2006), *Economy of Culture in Europe*, Brussels: European Commission, Directorate-General for Education and Culture.

Keeble, D. and Cavanagh, R. (2008), 'Concepts in value chain analysis and their utility in understanding cultural industries', in Conference Board of Canada (ed.), *Compendium of Research Papers from the International Forum on the Creative Economy*, Ottawa: Conference Board of Canada, 161–70.

Madden, C. (2001), 'Using "economic" impact studies in arts and cultural advocacy: a cautionary note', *Media International Australia*, 98: 161–78.

Marquis-Kyle, M. and Walker, P. (2004), *The Illustrated Burra Charter: Good Practice for Heritage Places*, Burwood, Australia ICOMOS.

McRobbie, A. and Forke, K. (2009), 'Artists and art schools: For or against innovation? A reply to NESTA', *Variant*, 34: 22–24.

Mikić, H. (2012), *Measuring the Economic Contribution of the Cultural Industries: A Review and Assessment of Current Methodological Approaches*, Montreal: UNESCO Institute of Statistics.

Myerscough, J. (1988), *The Economic Importance of the Arts in Britain*, London: Policy Studies Institute.

Oakley, K., Sperry, B. and Pratt, A.C. (2008), *The Art of Innovation: How Fine Arts Graduates Contribute to Innovation*, London: NESTA.

O'Connor, J. (2011), *Arts and Creative Industries: A Historical Overview and an Australian Conversation*, Sydney: Australia Council for the Arts.

Seaman, B. (2011), 'Economic impact of the arts', in R. Towse (ed.), *A Handbook of Cultural Economics*, 2nd edn, Cheltenham: Edward Elgar, 201–10.

Spanish Ministry of Culture (2011), *Satellite Account on Culture in Spain: Advance of 2000–2009 Results*, Madrid: Ministerio de Cultura.

Throsby, D. (2004), 'Assessing the impacts of a cultural industry', *Journal of Arts Management, Law and Society*, 34: 188–204.

Throsby, D. (2008a), 'Modelling the cultural industries', *International Journal of Cultural Policy*, 14 (3): 217–32.

Throsby, D. (2008b), 'The concentric circles model of the cultural industries', *Cultural Trends*, 17 (3):147–64.

Throsby, D. (2010), *The Economics of Cultural Policy*, Cambridge: Cambridge University Press.

Throsby, D. (2012), 'Artistic labour markets: Why are they of interest to labour economists?' *Economia della Cultura*, 22 (1): 7–16.

Throsby, D. (2013), 'Assessment of value in heritage regulation', in I. Rizzo and A. Mignosa, (eds), *Handbook on the Economics of Cultural Heritage*, Cheltenham: Edward Elgar: 456–69.

UNESCO Institute for Statistics (2007), *The UNESCO Framework for Cultural Statistics: Draft*, Montreal: UIS.

UNESCO Institute for Statistics (2009), *The 2009 UNESCO Framework for Cultural Statistics*, Montreal: UIS.

UNESCO (2013), *The Creative Economy Report: Widening Local Development Pathways*, New York: UNESCO.

United Nations Conference on Trade and Development (2008, 2010), *Creative Economy Report*, Geneva: UNCTAD.

United Nations Educational, Scientific and Cultural Organization (2013), *Creative Economy Report*, Paris: UNESCO.

Work Foundation (2007), *Staying Ahead: the Economic Performance of the UK's Creative Industries*, London: Department for Culture, Media and Sport.

World Commission on Culture and Development (1995), *Our Common Future*, Oxford: Oxford University Press.

4

THE STRUCTURE OF THE CULTURAL INDUSTRIES
Global corporations to SMEs

Scott Fitzgerald

Introduction

The cultural industries have long been characterised by complex connections between large corporations and a swarm of small and medium enterprises (SMEs). Critical analysis of these connections has emphasised that control of distribution and finance has been central to governance and value capture in networks of cultural production. SMEs, connected through a myriad of horizontal relationships in specific locations, remain an essential aspect of cultural production; yet in the last three decades the position of a few large corporations across a range of cultural industries has been reinforced via horizontal and vertical integration, ostensibly at the behest of 'convergence' and 'synergy' in the related fields of media, telecommunications and ICT. Conglomerate firms have increasingly gained control of access to cultural markets.

Notwithstanding this trend, in the first decade of the 21st century, corporations combining different communication and cultural industries within larger corporate structures have undergone unpredictable and often seemingly contradictory processes of restructuring. Not surprisingly, these developments have often been associated with changes in patterns of distribution and finance. Accounts of change have most commonly centred on a new phase of media *convergence* and the destabilising effects of new technical capabilities on the tight corporate control of cultural commodity distribution. Others have emphasised *de-convergence* and the splintering of cultural industry conglomerates as corporate investors lost patience with low profits, minor revenue increases and depressed stock prices, prompting a shift to new business models. However, such broad accounts do not adequately encapsulate the complex manner in which large companies, such as Google, Apple, Bertelsmann or Comcast-NBC Universal have sought to retain or capture power within the value chains of *specific* cultural industries. Such peculiarities have often been neglected in the shift 'back to work' in the studies of the creative economy. These studies have focused on small and micro businesses and removed cultural workers from the context of different cultural industries and the strategies of larger corporations; indeed, some accounts of convergence challenge the continuing relevance of the category of *industry* in the analysis of cultural production.

This chapter provides an overview of the structure and industry dynamics of the cultural industries, from 'global' corporations to SMEs. First, it provides an empirically up-to-date overview of large conglomerates and charts differences in their size and degree of diversification across different sectors. In doing so, it highlights how diversification involves several forms of control and corporate integration. Building on this, the chapter examines the continuing role of small firms in the cultural industries and assesses the possibly changing relationship between these firms and large corporations in light of the above-described processes of convergence or de-convergence. In analysing and critiquing such accounts of shifting value chains, the chapter draws upon the distinct cultural industries approach and identifies how specific socioeconomic logics of diverse industries shape the changing aspects of these relationships.

Dynamic corporate structures in the cultural industries

Industrial concentration based on economies of scale and scope has been the standard mode of organisation for the communication and cultural industries. A principal reason is that it provides a means of managing the chronic uncertainty and endemic commercial failure associated with cultural commodities. From the late 1970s corporations in the cultural industries were facilitated in taking full advantage of this fact by shifts in patterns of investment and regulation which were marked by complex transformations of capitalism and often glossed by the terms globalisation and neo-liberalisation (Fitzgerald 2012; Hesmondhalgh 2013). The role of the state, and in particular the United States, has been fundamental in this regard.

As corporations such as Time Warner, Disney and News Corp assembled different operations under their management and control, their competitiveness was argued to be a result of their structure and not simply their size. They sought both to achieve critical mass through the merger and acquisition of businesses in the same field (*horizontal integration*) and to gain control of the central points of the production, distribution and exchange processes (*vertical integration*). These strategies sought to reduce external market uncertainties produced by, for instance, several strong competitors in the circuit of production, and increase overall rates of return. Increased control and profitability were also pursued via integration across cultural industries (*conglomeration*). It was argued that this strategy would enable firms to engage in cost savings, achieve synergies and capture a greater proportion of audience attention and media expenditure. Moreover, the administered systems of financial flow would further significantly reduce market risk via cross-subsidisation and permit greater competition among product line divisions.

The result was that by the late 1990s a small group of vertically integrated conglomerates played a conspicuously powerful role in international cultural markets: Time Warner, Walt Disney, News Corporation, Sony and Bertelsmann. By early 2000, this group had been joined by Vivendi-Universal, and Time Warner had reinforced its leading position through its combination with America Online (AOL). These corporations further strengthened their ostensible ability to control their environment through alliances and inter-firm linkages with each other and other large national media players. This 'march of the behemoths' narrative was always a simplification: it presented an 'ideal type' form of corporate consolidation which in actuality covered corporate entities differentiated by their degrees of diversification and ownership; and it concealed the degree to which the corporate histories continued to involve failure and crisis within particular cultural industry divisions and across entire corporations.

These realities became more evident during the first decade of the 21st century and the aftermath of the dot.com bubble, as the Vivendi-Universal and AOL-Time Warner conglomeration deals collapsed under the weight of debt and engendered massive corporate write-downs. During this period, the changing influence of two processes, conspicuous since the 1980s, affected the cultural industries' organisational structure: convergence and financialisation. The communication industries' development always had an influence on cultural industries; yet in the 21st century, communication industry actors (telecommunication firms, Internet service providers, software manufacturers and Web companies) have noticeably expanded their operations as, in particular, the articulation between cultural content and the digital devices they control has become more economically viable. The strategies of new types of actors, Google, Amazon and Apple, have had a destabilising effect, especially on distribution networks. Financialisation has been associated with constant restructuring of a corporation's 'portfolio' of business units to maximise profit rates and share price performance. Although this initially drove corporate consolidation, the sentiment of the investors, lenders and analysts has shifted away from vertically integrated conglomerates (although bondholders more than shareholders remain attracted to the fixed assets associated with vertical integration). By the middle of the 2000s the crisis induced process of de-conglomeration, epitomised by AOL-Time Warner and Vivendi-Universal, had achieved a more considered form, epitomised by Sumner Redstone's 2005 decision to split Viacom-CBS in two. The global financial crisis (GFC) (2007–9) does not appear to have altered the course of reorganisation in the cultural industries: 'Media valuations are [now] back to pre-crisis levels and as News Corp, Time Warner and Bertelsmann attest, portfolio shuffling is fashionable again in media' (Edgecliffe-Johnson 2013). In 2013 some of the largest conglomerates (see Tables 4.1 and 4.2) initiated or completed wide-ranging restructuring processes involving de-merger and de-conglomeration (including Time Warner, Vivendi and News Corp).

Analysing forms of control and corporate integration: Models and chains

The cultural industries tradition of analysis provides a useful framework to examine the uneven and combined development within such corporate forms, where competition drives organisational transformation and the stratification of capitals. A characteristic quality of this tradition is an emphasis 'on the unique and specific attributes of the media economy *and* the persistent *barriers* that impede the wholesale commodification of culture' (Winseck 2011: 29–30). The barriers to commodification and industrialisation reflect the reliance on creative labour and the high initial costs of production relative to reproduction and distribution; the constant need for superficially 'new'

Table 4.1 International media conglomerates compared, 2006–13 (US$ billion)

Company	Revenues				Net income					Market capitalisation				
Year	2012	2010	2008	2006	2013	2012	2010	2008	2006	2013	2012	2010	2008	2006
1. Comcast	62.57	37.94	34.25	24.96		6.20	3.63	2.547	2.53	89.08	67.61	46.5	56.90	57.59
2. Walt Disney	42.28	38.06	37.84	33.747		5.68	3.96	4.427	3.374	113.72	86.69	55.9	58.37	55.16
3. Time Warner	28.73	26.89	46.98	43.69		3.02	2.58	-13.40	6.552	53.90	32.95	33.3	49.60	75.9
4. Viacom/CBS	27.98	22.8	28.57	25.68		3.56	1.58	-10.42	3.253	29.51/ 27.95	23.0/ 19.82	18.02/ 8.9	24.9/ 14.93	30.13/ 19.02
5. News Corp.	25.05	32.78	32.99	25.32		1.18	2.54	5.387	2.314	49.39	36.18	35.24	58.6	56.65
6. Bertelsmann	21.80	21.75	23.23	26.23		0.64	0.64	0.198	2.813	N/A				
7. Sony	22.27 (28.17%)	22.51 (29.1%)	21.4 (24.15%)	14.52 (22.8%)		-5.56	-0.437	-0.203	0.315	18.03	26.73	26.25	44.48	45.46
8. NBC Universal	N/A	16.90 (11.25%)	17.06 (9.35%)	16.24 (10.7%)		N/A	2.261	3.13	2.92	N/A	166.5	365.5	359.7	
9. Vivendi	13.325 (45.96%)	12.49 (43.25%)	15.719 (44.5%)	12.365 (46.8%)		0.22	2.938	3.623	5.311	25.43	23.65	28.22	43.73	40.01

Sources: Orbis Database; Company Reports
Figures in brackets for Sony, NBC Universal and Vivendi are the percentage of revenue derived from media operations.

Table 4.2 Major areas of operation of international media conglomerates, 2013

Corporation			Industry sectors										
Name	Headquarters	N° of employees	TV broadcasting	Radio broadcasting	Cable channels	Film or TV production	Press	Books	Music	Video games	Cable or satellite system	Web content or social networking	E-commerce
Time Warner	New York, USA	38,000			◀	◀	◀ *						◀
Disney	Burbank, USA	144,000	◀		◀	◀							◀
Comcast	Philadelphia, USA	107,000	◀		◀	◀						◀	◁
News Corp	New York, USA	24,000			◁	◀	◀	◀					
21st Century Fox	New York, USA	25,600	◀		◀	◀							
Sony	Tokyo, Japan	170,200	◀		◁	◀			◀	◀			◀
Bertelsmann	Gutersloh, Germany	102,983		◀	◀	◀		◀	◁				
Viacom	New York, USA	11,200	◀		◁	◀							
CBS	New York, USA	25,580		◀	◀			◀				◁	
Vivendi	Paris, France	58,500			◀				◀		◁		

◀ = significant operations

* Time Warner's presence in the area of the press will end in 2014

symbolic goods; and the high level of uncertainty of valorisation based upon symbolic goods whose use-value, first, is established in part through cultural 'distinction' and, second, is not destroyed through consumption (Miège 1989; Garnham 1990; Hesmondhalgh 2013). The organisational responses such issues engender mean that there are specific limits to which cultural industries can be treated like any other sector.

In seeking to analyse the complexity of the diverse and segmented structure of the cultural industries, Bouquillion, Miège and Mœglin (2013: 76–82) argue that two concepts are particularly valuable: *models* and *value chains* (filières). Looking at models first, within the cultural industries tradition they have been used to provide ideal type frameworks to capture the different *socioeconomic logics* that shape the prevailing institutional forms assumed by the commodification and industrialisation. These forms reflect different 'content' types, a mode of organising the production, selection and delivery of content and financing modes associated with direct commodification based upon intellectual property rights and indirect commodification via advertising or state subsidy systems. Two dominant models (publishing and flow) and three intermediate models (the club, the metered economy and information brokerage) are commonly identified (for a further elaboration see Fitzgerald 2012: 72–92). In the publishing model (e.g. books, music, DVDs) an editor/producer uses a catalogue of cultural artefacts as a means of mediating between various creative/artistic submissions, industrial production and the uncertainty of market demand. Here the final consumer contributes *directly* to the financing of the content they consume (a book through Amazon or a music track on iTunes) by purchasing a *copy* that they can own (the purchasing of a cinema ticket is still a notable exception). The flow model (e.g. broadcasting) responds to uncertainty by producing 'a constant flow of products as a packaged service and where speed and range of distribution is critical' (Garnham 2000: 53). Consumers neither possess nor directly pay for this continuous programming; rather, a third party, usually advertisers, provides funding *indirectly*. Table 4.3 summarises these models.

These models, and the logics on which they are based, serve to distinguish industrial concentration trends under 'general market' conditions from trends towards scale and scope economies that are specific to the cultural industries. As Table 4.3 makes clear, the market and industry structure of the flow model – in which uncertainty is partially offset via demand for a steady flow of programmes/content – has historically differed from the publishing model – where control of diverse contributions to a catalogue permits a relatively small number of commercially successful commodities to underwrite a larger 'publishing' enterprise. Nonetheless, it is unusual for any cultural industry, whether new over-the-top Internet television or 'mature' areas of book publishing, to reflect an unadulterated version of these models. To help determine the processes of change in operation and organisational structure we need to analyse, at a more concrete level, the segments of the value chain that connect finance, design, production, distribution and consumption in specific industries.

These value chains can be traced within both large conglomerates and the intra-industry sequences between firms of different sizes in production and distribution that have long characterised the cultural industries. Thus, while independent production companies became prevalent in Hollywood in the 1950s, apparently giving

Table 4.3 Distinction between flow and publishing model

Model characteristics	Flow	Publishing
1. Sectors	Broadcast TV and radio	Books, music and film
2. Dominant payment method	Indirect adverting revenue and state subsidies	Direct sales to consumer
3. Content	Continuous provision of ephemeral prototypes	Discontinuous provision of durable, individual copies
4. Central coordination function	Editorial maintenance of catalogue	Programmer construction of schedule
5. Creative labour remuneration	Steady employment based on contracts and salaries: broadcast workers, technicians, journalists, hosts, etc.	Small core workforce flanked by large pool of writers, directors, composers, artists, etc. remunerated through royalties
6. Industrial structure	Quasi-industrial, vertical integration and central planning. Managerial control of all elements in the value chain	Oligopoly with a competitive fringe – few large companies, shared infrastructure (printing, studios, etc.), project-based networks and small firms
7. Market structure	Tight oligopoly, vertical integration	Oligopolistic core surrounded by small firms

Source: Winseck 2011: 32 (adapted from Lacroix and Tremblay (1997: 56–65)).

rise to vertically disintegrated, post-Fordist/flexibly specialised production, analysis of the industry's global value chains revealed how Hollywood studios had effectively created de facto vertical integration or 'virtual integration' with these small firms through complex licensing, financing and distribution contracts (Christopherson 1996). The film industry thus took on aspects of industrial organisation that had long characterised the book and music industries. In the 1980s arrangements involving interdependent networks between small and large companies became prevalent across new areas of the cultural industries, most significantly in European broadcasting: the value chain elongated to comprise independent production companies and a multitude of small ancillary and technical support firms (Hesmondhalgh 2013: 211–12). Such changes were in line with wider transformations of the 'organised capitalism' of large corporations that gave rise to 'subsidiary and subcontractor modes of inter-corporate relations' (Wayne 2003), a process associated with the drive to increase 'shareholder value' through the reorganisation of international divisions in labour and commodity markets.

The handful of international media conglomerates, discussed earlier, have developed on this basis: the industry structures of the cultural industries have been characterised by large national and transnational corporations (TNCs) which link (regionally embedded) networks of SMEs to national and international markets. International media conglomerates have attempted to combine 'global' reach with a responsiveness to local markets by granting affiliates enlarged autonomy and increasing their specialisation and connectedness with local inter-firm networks. As 'runaway' production in audio-visual industries attests, this also permits the competitive search for a balance between skill sets and costs. The outcome is global production networks (GPNs) that 'combine concentrated dispersion of the value chain across firm and national boundaries, with a parallel process of integration of hierarchical layers of network participants' (Ernst and Kim 2002: 1418). Because the development of cultural commodities, though comparatively expensive, can usually be undertaken on a relatively small scale, multi-divisional conglomerates within such GPNs can finance and distribute production 'in-house' through their own semi-autonomous divisions or finance and distribute productions that have been subcontracted to smaller companies. By controlling distribution on a national and international scale, a small number of these large firms are thus able to collect a significant portion of the income of a sector as a whole. While this may underpin the production of the most expensive yet lucrative content (blockbuster content and ubiquitous marketing campaigns), the majority of the costs and risks of production are borne by a myriad of relatively smaller, and more 'flexible'/expendable, firms. In exchange for greater access to markets, these small firms support the economies of scale on which the large firm's distribution systems are built. Moreover, at the cost of bearing the risk of innovative, or different and untested, products for uncertain cultural markets, small companies can maintain the cachet of cultural 'independence' in the marketplace and hence attract talented employees who want greater 'creative autonomy' from commercial pressures. This is 'especially [important] in those cultural industries and genres where there is a mistrust of corporate bureaucracies, such as rock or indie film making or certain kinds of games' (Hesmondhalgh 2013: 212).

Since the 1990s a range of approaches has emerged to examine how complex and dynamic economic networks, made up of inter-firm and intra-firm linkages (Dicken 2011), have changed the relationships:

- between management over immediate production processes (*operational control* over labour power/physical means of production) and the ability to set overall policy and strategy (*allocative control*); and
- between the ability to control the flow of resources in and across firms (*economic ownership*, i.e. investment, profit distribution and share issue) and various forms of legal title to property (*legal ownership*, e.g. stock ownership) (Murdock 1982: 118–19).

As the corporate economy has developed, there has been a tendency for *dissociation* between economic and legal ownership and a *functional differentiation* between operational and allocative control and these processes have only become more complicated with the shift to forms of 'subsidiary and subcontractor capitalism'. However, in analysing organisational forms between hierarchies and markets, some analyses have both underplayed the extent to which legal ownership constrains interfirm 'project' relationships and the extent to which forms of hierarchical control and power inequality shape the organisation of value chains/networks in supposedly collaborative value networks in which value is co-created and revenues are shared amongst all participants (Arsenault 2011).

Here Gereffi, Humphrey and Sturgeon (2005) have offered a highly influential and heuristically useful model of types of network coordination mechanisms and the changing relationship between lead firms and suppliers from a high degree of explicit coordination and power asymmetry (hierarchy and captive coordination), a moderate degree (relational coordination), to a low degree (modular and market coordination). These ideal types of governance arise from transaction cost analysis and economic sociology: governance patterns are influenced by the capabilities of the suppliers; the complexity of the transactions; and the ability to codify complex information. All affect the ability to lock suppliers into unfavourable contractual relationships. However, Parker, Cox and Thompson (2014) argue that further essential factors affecting governance arrangements and power asymmetries are market concentration and limited competition in key segments of the chain(s), which give rise to 'bottlenecks'. Such arguments have long been central to the analysis of the cultural industries' tradition of political economic analysis: significant assets – ownership of distribution systems and copyrighted cultural catalogues (Garnham 2000: 52) – allow large capitals to establish 'virtual integration' or 'captive value chains'. Nonetheless, it has been argued that a confluence of technological, cultural and economic change has altered these arrangements and produced more relational or modular coordination patterns. This in turn has had an impact upon the place of small and medium size firms within lengthening and increasingly complex value chains of the new 'creative economy'. Indeed, Rainnie, Herod and McGrath-Champ (2013) argue that it should not be assumed that small firms are always dominated in global production networks and draw on Rainnie's work to categorise the role of small firms in the strategies of large firms and the state (as either dependent, dominated, isolated or innovative).

A new phase of media convergence: Arm's length economic coordination

The established value chain patterns in the cultural industries have been argued to be disrupted by a new stage of media *convergence*. As noted, central here is the destabilising effects on the oligopolistic control of cultural commodity distribution. In turn, it is argued that this is leading to the radical reshaping of the global communications landscape (Jin 2013) and the expansion of the entrepreneurial role of small firms and creative individuals in an enlarged cultural market. While digital technologies and the Internet figure prominently in such accounts, these formulations emphasise the multifaceted nature of convergence so as to escape the (warranted) charge of technological determinism. That the term 'convergence' is used in many different ways also importantly reflects that it has been renewed and reshaped for over 30 years as central to different mobilising projects that promote and legitimate corporate strategies and accompanying state policies.

From the 1980s the notion of convergence was regularly used to justify the formation and expansion of 'multi-media' conglomerates: digitisation would link not only data processing, telecommunications and (cable) television (as envisaged in the 1970s), but all cultural and communications industries in a unified sector whose expanded levels of global competition would require corresponding levels of corporate consolidation. Convergence was therefore used to warrant a range of regulatory liberalisations in order to expand and respond to inter-sectoral competition. By the early 1990s, an initial focus on the merger between hardware manufactures and software producers (e.g. Sony) was replaced with corporate strategies centred on conquering the emergent Internet. Competitive advantage would arise from the delivery of a diverse array of cultural content and information services that the consumer would select through one-off payments or better still via subscriptions to 'walled gardens'. This more 'active' form of consumption would break the (flow) logic of programming to a 'passive' audience; however, advertisers and marketeers would be provided with ever-greater surveillance and data-monitoring potential. Propelled by processes of financialisation, the convergence paradigm legitimised a range of merger and acqui-sition activity, based upon debt and stock market capitalisation, which for the most part has turned out to be spectacularly unsuccessful (except for speculative investors and a cadre of corporate managers). We will return to the unfulfilled promises of synergy and the process 'deconvergence' shortly.

As Bouquillion, Miège and Mœglin (2013) note, in the last decade the mobilising project of convergence has not disappeared but has been revived and combined with the themes of participatory collaboration (e.g. Jenkins 2006) and creative industries (e.g. Flew 2012, 2013). The collaboration paradigm, as proselytised by self-proclaimed 'public intellectuals' such as Jenkins, envisages a new emancipatory era of active audiences seeking to explore the potential of an array of online communication tools (vaguely defined as Web 2.0). The resulting 'convergence culture', where a 'work-as-play' occupational culture of digital cultural sectors is mirrored by the 'serious leisure' of amateur participation (in the form of the *prosumer*), is also a space, we are told, in which these bottom-up creative initiatives increasingly intersect with top-down decisions taken in company boardrooms. Such boardroom decisions are, however, primarily reactive as audiences gain control over content circulation via methods legal or not. Existing cultural industry corporations' control over distribution and the economic logics that this reflects (established practices of advertising and sales) are threatened by the emergence of an ecology of 'spreadable media' built upon people selecting and sharing media content (Jenkins, Ford and Green 2013). While emphasising the crisis of existing media, Jenkins, Ford and Green acknowledge that corporate interests have driven the data-mining architecture (information brokerage) of Web 2.0. What is not acknowledged, though, is that in challenging copyright regimes and conflating user-generated or 'curated' content with commodities produced by cultural industries, the collaborative paradigm provides legitimation for the predacious strategies of major communication players such as Google, Apple or Facebook and their reliance on cultural and information content produced by other industrial actors (Levine 2011).

Bouquillion, Miège and Mœglin (2013) argue that if the convergence paradigm focuses on corporate integration of the cultural industries and the collaboration paradigm foresees the dissolution of the cultural industries, the creative industry's paradigm sees the prime role of the cultural industries, including digital content, games and interactive media, as being innovative service providers to other segments of a wider, more 'service based, design led and ideas driven' economy (Flew 2013: 32). Digitisation would induce a modular industry structure necessitating vertical specia-lisation as opposed to vertical integration. The apparent 'importance of the Internet for the rise to economic prominence of the [creative industries] sectors' (Flew 2013: 32) allows creative industry advocates, such as Flew, to argue these sectors are now 'dynamic, open, self organising networks' at the centre of a wider networked informa-tion economy. If the economic success of the 20th century 'information, knowledge and creative industries' is acknowledged prior to the Internet (as surely it must be), it is premised on bygone network economics and distribution bottlenecks producing an 'hourglass' industry structure. Things are now very different, argues Flew, who cites Castells and Benkler:

> With the radical dispersal of creative capabilities and the ability to distribute creative products enabled by digital media technologies and the networked infrastructure of the Internet, it is the information, knowledge and creative industries that are the harbingers of … a new era of social production [that] entails the rise of models of production that are loosely collaborative, not typically 'owned' by a single individual or group, and often not primarily driven by pecuniary motivations.
>
> (Flew 2013: 32)

According to the creative industries paradigm, the Internet now supports 'loosely configured, emergent networks of cultural producers – that increasingly involve the consumers as well – which remain the mainspring of innovation in the arts, media and cultural sectors' (Flew 2012: 191). In Rainnie, Herod and McGrath-Champ's (2013) terminology, these sole traders and small firms are innovative and, while complimenting and servicing the interests of other large firms, can potentially avoid dependency by the generation of new forms of intellectual property and copyrighted content. Flew (2013: 91) concedes that Noam (2009) has provided evidence of growing concentration in Internet related industries and growing importance of integrator firms which include Apple, Google and Microsoft. Given that this might complicate the new era of social production, he argues, however, that if Noam's analysis is in fact correct it should be remembered that concentration strategies do not always prove successful. More directly, Flew argues that the digital content industries are marked by a greater level of Schumpeterian innovation and creative destruction than the oligopolistic world of the traditional large media players; indeed, these traditional, industrialised players would themselves soon be overwhelmed by creative individuals and SMEs if it was not for the lobbying clout and political power they wield to maintain regulatory protection (Flew, 2012: 171, 191; see Fitzgerald 2012: 69–70 for a critique of such neo-Schumpeterian arguments).

Here advocates of the creative industry paradigm ignore both the specific organisational characteristics that have supported large media firms' 'oligopolistic world' and the recent history of large Internet-related industries (O'Connor 2012). Citing contributory factors such as network economics that support massive demand-side economies of scale, the lock-in effects of technical standards and the protective and offensive use of patents, McChesney (2013: 130) argues that the Internet 'has become one of the greatest generators of monopoly in economic history'. He concludes that given the extent of consolidation in the sector, there is little evidence to support claims of continuing Schumpeterian waves of creative destruction: 'the profitability of the digital giants is centered on establishing propriety systems in which they control access and the terms of the relationship, not the idea of Internet as open as possible' (McChesney 2013: 135). Once more, we see the emergence of 'walled gardens' as the basis for the Internet but ones marked by different forms of corporate integration as envisaged in earlier convergence predictions. The resultant top-down corporate controlled ecosystems of Amazon, Apple, Google and Microsoft are shaping the form and extent of the bottom-up ecosystems of spreadable media.

These points can be made more concrete if we briefly examine the digital games industry, which is marked by both rapid technological change and corporate consolidation; today it is subdivided into console-based and online games sectors (cf. Keogh in this volume). The Triple A, console-based sector has developed on a publishing model in which large publishers, and ultimately the three major console manufacturers (Sony, Nintendo and Microsoft), are able to direct production networks through a mixture of captive and relational (i.e. reputational and trust-based) coordination of a multitude of software producers. Control of distribution and finance permits publishers and console manufacturers to shape the creative output of software firms. In the online games sector, the emergence of new mobile devices such as smartphones and tablets provide access to consumer markets outside of the control of publishers or console manufacturers. For lower levels of capital investment, small developers can retain the intellectual property of these 'casual games' and control the production process. However, in exchange for reduced barriers to entry and a higher degree of creative autonomy, these app-based game developers assume all the development costs and risks in an intensively competitive environment that is dominated by two standardised distribution interfaces, Apple's App store for iOS devices and the Google Play store for Android powered devices. In contrast to the extended interaction between publishers and developers in the console market, the relationship between the major distributor, Apple, and developers is limited: Apple charges a flat fee for uploading games to its App store and takes a 30 per cent commission on games sales, in-app purchases and advertising via an 'agency model' agreement. Apple maintains control via language coding requirements for the games and standardisation of the interface, ensuring that game developers cannot easily swap between platforms: as one games developer remarked 'Apple is trying to make its own ecosystem in which developers become Apple developers. We are "Apple developers", rather than we are "developers" – we are "game developers" and suddenly we are "Apple developers"' (Parker, Cox and Thompson 2014: 180). Even if the number of games platforms increases via Facebook and Microsoft, Parker, Cox and Thompson (2014: 181) argue that 'a small number of large corporations will control the retail end of the games market while access to games development remains open with low barriers to entry in the production of mobile games'. 'Casual game' development is consistent to the market or modular model of governance put forward by Gereffi, Humphrey and Sturgeon (2005) and may more readily match the description of open, dynamic networks suggested by Flew (2013); however, the control that platform providers/online retailers exert belies the notion that these are self-organising networks. To accept this depiction would be to neglect what Thompson, Parker and Cox (2010) refer to as the distribution bottlenecks of 'actually existing capital'.

The strategic position of console and mobile device manufacturers within global digital games value chains is argued to foreshadow the experience of the majority of cultural industries, as telecommunication firms, Internet service providers, software manufacturers and Web companies expand their interests with regards to cultural content distribution (Perticoz 2011, cited in Bouquillion, Miège and Mœglin 2013).

The communication actors do not constitute a homogeneous category and their position within their main field of operations ensures that their strategies are differentiated. Nonetheless, they are all set to benefit from the further displacement of traditional bottlenecks at the expense of traditional physical distributors, who normally enjoyed oligopolistic positions (the bankruptcy of the book retail channel Borders in 2011 provided a clear example). Such changes reproduce the form of relationship between large capitals and small capitals long characteristic of the cultural industries but one whose logic of risk management is now shaped by the increasing dominance (rather than control) of large communication actors. Bouquillion, Miège and Mœglin (2013: 127) note that what remains highly uncertain are the conditions of viability for the network of small, dependent firms contributing to an enlarged, and potentially more diverse, level of production. They argue that the number of such firms is expanding (particularly in sectors with publishing logics: music, books and digital games (Bouquillion 2011)) but with even less economic security. Moreover, now the future of such cultural enterprises is increasingly influenced by a handful of powerful communication companies that, with the exception of Sony, have a more arm's length relation to cultural production and whose strategies are not driven primarily by a concern to develop the cultural industries per se. This is beginning to alter somewhat with, for example, Amazon establishing its own publishing arm and imprints and Google, via YouTube, financing and distributing via subscriptions its own professional content with a variety of niche partners. Nonetheless, rapid market consolidation (in which loss leading content is used, for example by Apple and Amazon, as a means to drive hardware sales) and maintaining their exceptional financial markets support have been the primary concern of communication actors' strategies (Bouquillion 2012).

De-convergence: Lumbering dinosaurs to small or mid-sized companies?

The production of content in the cultural industries remains crucial to the profitability of different distribution networks, be they of established media or wider communication firms. Cultural industry corporations, such as News Corporation, Bertelsmann and Vivendi, have been challenged in a number of areas by communication actors' more effective adoption of specific revenue modes that have developed with the deployment of digital media (publishing club, metering and information brokerage). However, the migration of advertising expenditure and the disruption of distribution systems have occurred while processes of financialisation have also driven reorganisation involving de-conglomeration and consolidation (Winseck 2011; Fitzgerald 2012; Hesmondhalgh 2013). Corporations increasingly focus on reducing debt and repurchasing shares (to support share prices and increase the earnings per share and the dividend per share). Financial agents have pushed for the 'unlocking of value' of separately traded corporate entities and argued that strategic alliances are a more effective option. Conglomeration is still perceptible, yet it has become more limited.

Jin (2011, 2013) has mapped these trends at the macro-level and emphasises that 'deconvergence' has emerged as the new 'golden strategy' or dominant business model. Jin notes that this has involved both a shift away from more diversified and unfocused forms of horizontal integration and ambitious vertical integration strategies (e.g. Time Warner). However, although Jin (2011: 178) initially suggested that through deconvergence 'lumbering dinosaurs' like Disney, Time Warner, and Viacom 'tried to morph into small or mid-sized companies', he argues that in the short term a shift towards 'de-concentration' does not foreshadow a fundamental change in the ownership structure in the media sector (Jin 2013: 124). Rather, deconvergence entails a renewed focus on a few core content areas via horizontal consolidation. Following Jenkins (2006), Jin surmises that 'content is king' because audiences are more concerned with access to quality content rather than maintaining an allegiance to a particular medium.

There are significant recent examples of international media corporations engaging in forms of horizontal integration to amass larger scale in content. Instances here include the break-up and acquisition of EMI, which reduced the 'big four' music majors to the 'big three' (Universal, Warner and Sony), or the merger of the Pearson-owned Penguin with the Bertelsmann-owned Random House to create the world's largest trade publishing house. Such focus on horizontal acquisitions has been argued to be a response to 'digital Darwinism' unleashed by the power of new distributors like Apple and Amazon (Budden 2012). However, as J.B. Thompson (2013: 370) makes clear in his account of the trade book publishing industry, the Bertelsmann-Pearson venture needs to be viewed in a wider context than the challenge of Amazon's e-books. It also needs to be placed within the evolution of publishing's concentrated corporate structure and large corporations' 'absolute priority … to protect bottom line profitability, which they have to report to their corporate bosses'. This commitment to year-on-year growth has taken place, moreover, in conglomerate forms in which financialised management strategies foreground intra-sectional and intra-corporate rivalries. That is, prevailing rates of return on capital have set the benchmark for the performance of book, music or film and TV divisions against each other within larger corporate forms, as well as against rival firms in specific cultural market segments.

The value of the cultural industries tradition is that it highlights the specific and uneven development of diverse cultural industries (including their rates of profitability) and thus unpacks an undifferentiated focus on deconvergence as standard 'business model'. This differentiation is revealed in the patterns of de-merger and de-conglomeration amongst the international media conglomerates referred to earlier: faced with difficulties in adjusting to digital distribution and declining advertising rates, book, newspaper and magazine operations have been consolidated, divested or split off. To raise rates of return on investment, some entities such as Bertelsmann or Lagardère, the world's second largest trade book publisher, have pursued horizontal consolidation in some of these areas. Yet as Table 4.2 indicates, TV networks, film studios, and broadcasting operations retain a favoured position amongst the diversified holdings of the largest media conglomerates. Here the recent large-scale acquisitions in the United States' broadcasting and cable industry, for example, underscore that corporate consolidation is not limited to the control of copyrighted cultural catalogues. Moreover, such developments require that we question broad ranging claims that digital media technologies have substantially eliminated traditional distribution bottlenecks, leading to a shift towards vertical specialisation in value networks and the end of vertical or 'virtual' integration in value chains. Rather than a simple zero-sum transference of power to content holders and new communication actors such as Google in all cultural industries, analysis of context-specific and dynamic value chains is required. Models of convergence or deconvergence do not advance analysis far in this regard.

Conclusion

Large-scale corporate strategies to assemble and manage the organisational structures of the cultural industries have clearly altered. The financial difficulties of the largest cultural industry conglomerates highlighted the failure of promised industrial synergies between their operations. In part, these difficulties arose from the fact that the specific logics of different cultural industries have remained distinct, if not unchanging, and they continue to reflect different patterns of interrelation between finance, design, production, distribution and consumption. The strategies of communication actors and their attempts to inter-link consumers' access to cultural commodities into their own value chains have also increasingly posed operational difficulties for established industries. In response, international conglomerates such as Time Warner or News Corp have reduced the scope and diversity of their operations. At the same time, a lowering of entry barriers (largely associated with digitisation) in some industries have increased the number of small and medium-sized companies (or indeed prosumers) participating in the value chain; yet forms of rationalisation, processes of concentration and bottlenecks based on distribution or content remain defining characterises of the overall industry and market structure. Despite the growing presence of communication actors, the basic organisational form of an 'oligopoly with a competitive fringe' (Miège 2011: 93) continues to define the culture industries.

References

Arsenault, A. 2011. 'Mapping the global networks of the information business'. In: Winseck, D. and Jin, D.Y. (eds) *The Political Economies of Media: The Transformation of the Global Media Industries*, London: Bloomsbury.

Bouquillion, P. 2011. 'Les mutations des filières et leurs enjeux pour la diversité culturelle'. In: Bouquillion, P. and Combès, Y. (eds) *Diversité et industries culturelles*, Paris: L'Harmattan.

Bouquillion, P. 2012. 'Concentration, financiarisation et relations entre les industries de la culture et industries de la communication'. *Revue française des sciences de l'information et de la communication*.

Bouquillion, P., Miège, B. and Mœglin, P. 2013. *L'industrialisation des biens symboliques. Les industries créatives en regard des industries culturelles*, Grenoble, Presses universitaire de Grenoble.

Budden, R. 2012. 'Dealing with digital Darwinism'. *Financial Times*, 4 December.

Christopherson, S. 1996. 'Flexibility and adaptation in industrial relations: The exceptional case of the U.S. media entertainment industries'. In: Gray, L.S. and Seeber, R.L. (eds) *Under the Stars: Essays on Labour Relations in Arts and Entertainment*, Ithaca: Cornell University Press.

Dicken, P. 2011.*Global Shift: Mapping the Changing Contours of the World Economy*, 6th ed., New York: Guilford Press.

Edgecliffe-Johnson, A. 2013. 'Flattering letter gives Hirai chance to save Sony'. *Financial Times*, 16 May.

Ernst, D. and Kim, L. 2002. 'Global production networks, knowledge diffusion, and local capability formation'.*Research Policy*, 31, 1417–29.

Fitzgerald, S.W. 2012. *Corporations and Cultural Industries: Time Warner, Bertelsmann, and News Corporation*, New York: Rowman & Littlefield.

Flew, T. 2012. *The Creative Industries: Culture and Policy*, London: Sage.

Flew, T. 2013. *Global Creative Industries*, Cambridge: Polity.

Garnham, N. 1990. *Capitalism and Communication: Global Culture and the Economics of Information*, London: Sage.

Garnham, N. 2000. *Emancipation, the Media, and Modernity: Arguments about the Media and Social Theory*, Oxford: Oxford University Press.

Gereffi, G., Humphrey, J. and Sturgeon, T. 2005. 'The governance of global value chains'. *Review of International Political Economy*, 12, 78–104.

Hesmondhalgh, D. 2013. *The Cultural Industries*, London: Sage.

Jenkins, H. 2006. *Convergence Culture: Where Old and New Media Collide*, New York: NYU Press.

Jenkins, H., Ford, S. and Green, J. 2013. *Spreadable Media: Creating Value and Meaning in a Networked Culture*, New York: NYU Press.

Jin, D.Y. 2011. 'Deconvergence and deconsolidation in the global media industries'. In: Winseck, D. and Jin, D.Y. (eds) *The Political Economies of Media: The Transformation of the Global Media Industries*, London: Bloomsbury.

Jin, D.Y. 2013. *De-Convergence of Global Media Industries*, New York: Routledge.

Levine, R. 2011. *Free Ride: How the Internet is Destroying the Culture Business, and How the Culture Business Can Fight Back*, London: Bodley Head.

McChesney, R.W. 2013. *Digital Disconnect: How Capitalism is Turning the Internet Against Democracy*, New York: New Press.

Miège, B. 1989. *The Capitalization of Cultural Production*, New York: International General.

Miège, B. 2011. 'Theorizing the cultural industries: Persistent specificities and reconsiderations'. In: Wasko, J., Murdock, G. and Souza, H. (eds) *The Handbook of Political Economy of Communications*, Malden, MA: Blackwell.

Murdock, G. 1982. 'Large corporations and the control of the communications industries'. In: Gurevitch, M., Bennett, T., Curran, J. and Woollacott, J. (eds) *Culture, Society and the Media*, London: Routledge.

Noam, E. 2009. *Media Ownership and Concentration in America*, New York: Oxford University Press.

O'Connor, J. 2012. 'Surrender to the void: Life after creative industries'. *Cultural Studies Review*, 18, 388–410.

Parker, R., Cox, S. and Thompson, P. 2014. 'How technological change affects power relations in global markets: Remote developers in the console and mobile games industry'. *Environment and Planning A*, 46, 168–85.

Rainnie, A., Herod, A. and McGrath-Champ, S. 2013. 'Global production networks, labour and small firms'. *Capital and Class*, 37, 177–95.

Thompson, J.B. 2013. *Merchants of Culture: The Publishing Business in the Twenty-First Century*, London: Polity.

Thompson, P., Parker, R. and Cox, S. (2010). 'Re-visualising creative labour', *Paper to 28th International Labour Process Conference, March 2010*, Rutgers University, New Jersey.

Wayne, M. 2003. 'Post-fordism, monopoly capitalism, and Hollywood's media industrial complex'. *International Journal of Cultural Studies*, 6, 82–103.

Winseck, D. 2011. 'The political economies of media and the transformation of the global media industries'. In: Winseck, D. and Jin, D.Y. (eds) *The Political Economies of Media: The Transformation of the Global Media Industries*, London: Bloomsbury.

5

MAKING THINGS

Beyond the binary of manufacturing and creativity

Chris Gibson, Chantel Carr and Andrew Warren

In December 2013 US auto giant General Motors announced it would wind up production in Australia. It signalled the end of domestic production of the iconic "Australian" Holden motor car, and subjected thousands of workers and their families in Adelaide and Melbourne, where their plants and components suppliers were located, to the spectre of unemployment. Along with similar announcements from Mitsubishi, Toyota and Ford, as well as major retrenchments in the steel, clothing and textiles industries since the global financial crisis (GFC) in 2008, the announcement fuelled a growing sense of crisis about the future viability of manufacturing industries in the face of seemingly hegemonic overseas competition from cheap labour-cost countries.

The assumption in Australia – as in other advanced economies such as the United Kingdom and the United States – has been that the decline of manufacturing is inevitable, exemplified in commentaries by "experts" in metropolitan broadsheets who have depicted recent crises as part of an inevitable and permanent transition, a "historic shift in the structure of the global economy as the Industrial Revolution finally reaches the developing countries," as Ross Gittins (2011), economics editor at the *Sydney Morning Herald*, put it. According to this argument, de-industrializing western countries such as Australia must now find other things to do to replace manufacturing: dig up resources to supply manufacturers in China or India; become tourist destinations; export services ("know-how") rather than physical commodities; or focus on the so-called "knowledge" and "creative" industries, where the greatest proportion of the value of a product is said to be in its intellectual or design content, not its material fabrication.

At the very same time, proponents of the creative industries have claimed prominence in economic policy debates by presenting such sectors as design, film and advertising as alternatives or "replacements" for heavy industry and manufacturing. Much of the emphasis has been on intellectual property or immaterial design processes rather than on the physical crafting and manufacture of goods. The assumption among many creative industries proponents is that the physical manufacture of products is by and large an uncreative, repetitive task undertaken elsewhere. Accepted as "normal" is an international division of labour that posits creative genius with "creatives" in the affluent West, and deskilled factory production with "blue collar" workers elsewhere in the world, wherever labour costs can be most effectively minimized.

In this chapter we critique this state of affairs and ask, what are the deleterious effects of falsely distancing manufacturing workers and cities from the creative industries debate? We discuss a range of such effects, from setting up novelty and innovation as superior to creative repair and re-use of physical things, to divorcing design processes from physical production and haptic, bodily skills. Dematerializing conceptions of the creative industries also eschews consideration of deeper questions of the social injustices of low-waged labour, and the environmental imprint of forms of cultural production.

We thus seek to broaden the debate, in two ways: first, by questioning the onto-logical and political premises underpinning the false distinction between making material things and creative labour processes. We respond to recent calls for analysis to look beyond the artistic and creative subjects that have been privileged in creative economy thinking (Banks 2010; Christopherson 2008), to bring into frame the labour of those who sit apart from the "rewards of authorship" (Lovink and Ross 2007: 231). Second, we argue that a broader cultural economic frame, rather than a narrow focus on creative industries, enables a different kind of debate in which the social or moral dimensions of economic activities are foregrounded (Gibson 2012). Put differently, what things do we make, or do we need to make, given the spectre of economic and environmental crisis? Under what conditions are they made? And what role might culture and creativity play in refocusing forms of material work and production? Re-connecting cultural production, creativity and the way we make (and re-make) physical things is an urgent task – lest the cultural and creative industries become marginalized as mere "entertainment" or "content" amidst socio-economic and environmental volatility.

Creative economy: Wither material production?

Where did the idea that culture and creativity were separate from material production come from? Arguably, proponents of creative industries never consciously jettisoned material production from concepts of cultural production and creativity, but rather, material manufacture came to assume an antonymic positionality vis-à-vis creativity through a series of overlapping conflations, assumptions and, in some cases, political and definitional manoeuvrings.

Our view here rests on seeing the economy not as an entity or construct separate from politics, but rather as a socio-technical system literally built through the actions, ideas, and opinions of "experts" – inventors, technocrats and, especially, economists who "claimed only to describe this object [economics], but in fact ... participated in producing it" (Mitchell 2008: 1116). In this kind of analysis, "the economy" is not a separate entity but a "project" that particular actors with vested interests work towards. Ideas about creativity and the economy, as well as manufacturing and its character, have circulated through knowledge-policy-advocacy assemblages, the "project" mutated in different regional and national jurisdictions (Kong et al. 2006) – what Brett Christophers has described as capitalism's "territorial fix." Such ideas are *made* to work – given meaning and operationalized across different policy terrains and in the service of different interest groups" (O'Connor 2004: 39). It is therefore critical to evaluate "truth claims" about the evolving nature of the economy, a task of teasing apart multiple and often intertwining flows of knowledge and ideas that have had the cumulative effect of dematerializing cultural production.

One place to start is with the normative script of creative economy in market-based development thinking (Gibson and Kong 2005). This script has become increasingly viral in the past decade along with the popularity of "celebrity urbanologists" such as Richard Florida, Michael Porter and Charles Landry, key "thought leaders" who purport to be promoting radically new visions for the economy, but who do little to budge the status quo (Davidson and Gleeson 2013). According to this normative creative economy script, contemporary capitalism is characterized by more recently dominant forms of accumulation based on the commodification of culture and the injection of aesthetic "content" into all commodity production. Also influential here was Lash and Urry's (1994: 123) thesis of the shift to symbolic forms of production: cultural industries, it was argued, provided the blueprint for the economy, not manufacturing – while "ordinary manufacturing industry is becoming more and more like the production of culture. It is not that commodity manufacture provides the template, and culture follows, but that the culture industries themselves have provided the template."

In the normative creative economy script some places were said to do better than others from this shift: those that have highly skilled, creative, innovative, adaptive workforces, sophisticated telecommunications infrastructures, interesting and diverse populations and relatively low levels of government interference in regulating access to markets, as well as lifestyle attractions, restaurants and arts institutions to attract the new "creative class." In order to compete in the new cultural economy, it is said, places should seek to implement particular policy initiatives: encourage cultural industry clusters, incubate learning and knowledge economies, maximize networks with other successful places and companies, value and reward innovation and aggressively campaign to attract the "creative class" as residents.

What is often forgotten is that this current orthodoxy of creative industries-as-economic development thinking had its genesis in a particular school of urban and regional economic geography that had rather different antecedent aspirations. American scholars such as Allen J. Scott (1988), Susan Christopherson and Michael Storper (Christopherson and Storper 1986) and, in the United Kingdom, Andy Pratt (1997) were prominent early figures. The intent was not to give birth to a new "brand" of neoliberal, proto-capitalist policy-making. Indeed, some years later, Allen Scott countered the increasing "fad" for creative economy promotion with a frank discussion of the "darker dimensions" of creative city strategies, while Susan Christopherson, increasingly critical of issues such as the exploitation of cultural workers, urged that we move beyond a focus on the figure of the self-expressive creative genius (see Christopherson 2008; Scott 2006).

Rather, such economic geographers had come to be interested in cultural production from a specific antecedent intellectual space: they had spent the better part of the 1980s and 1990s debating the rise of post-Fordism and so-called "flexible accumulation" and were seeking to capture analytical insights that explained the cultural embeddedness of capitalist activities, and the simultaneous emergence of new spatial configurations in production (there was, for instance, a conscious disposition towards examining "new spaces of production" in regions other than the fading rust belts, such as the "third Italy," and southern California).

Hence for Scott (1996), the structure and dynamics of modern production systems fuelled massive agglomerations of capital and labour – effectively the basic building blocks of the large metropolises that were in turn the motors of the global economy. The city-region became "a nexus of production relationships and associated social infrastructures" (Scott 2004: 486). Expanding on this thesis were empirical projects examining specific industries such as printed circuits, garments and film animation, allowing extension into related questions of the interrelationships between regions, trade flows, competition and globalization (Scott 1997).

Early proponents were interested in the entirety and complexity of production chains across geographic space – rather than just the design or "immaterial" stages or aspects (see, for example, Pratt 2008). Indeed, even the earlier, pre-"creative class" work of Richard Florida focused on innovation among automotive manufacturers (see Florida and Kenney 1991). Rather, the task was to update knowledge of the urban and regional dynamics of capitalism more generally – within an overarching paradigm that sought to disentangle the dynamics of uneven development.

Nevertheless, when the more neoliberalized policy fashion for creative economy gained momentum in the late 1990s and early 2000s (see Gibson and Klocker 2005 for critique), this kind of regional economic geography model provided it with an unintended scholarly knowledge base, such as it was, offering an explanation for the growth dynamics underpinning previously ignored "cultural" and "creative" industries. Via a loose and decentralized knowledge-policy-advocacy assemblage the production of culture was shorn of much of its political economic grounding, and mutated in such a way as to weld creative industries much more firmly to a wider political agenda of looking to "market forces" to "replace" older industries with culture and creativity. A policy fad had been unleashed, and academics with an early track record in examining creative industries found new opportunities to exploit the grey area between research and advocacy, promoting catchy neologisms and consultancy services. For a prime example, see http://creativebusiness.org.

Political economy: Wither manufacturing?

Of course, such circulations and mutations of ideas about industries, material manufacture and creativity have taken place within wider political landscapes, well beyond the academy. Indeed, any history of creativity involves fraught relations between material manufacture and imagination, between creativity and production and between creation and re-creation (Pope 2005). Such tensions frequently find expression in reconfigurations of the relations between capitalists and labour. The beginnings of a division of labour between thinking and making arguably emerged with the early industrialists, who complained that the guild system (which connected the design process directly with manufacture) was counter-intuitive to innovation, with its stronghold over intellectual property bound up in the oral and haptic methods of skills transfer. In the late 1990s and 2000s there was similarly a peculiar context in which an imagined separation of manufacture and creativity served convenient political ends. In the United Kingdom this was the rise of a cultural and creative industries policy agenda, providing Blairite Labour an alternative "Third Way" narrative, following on from Thatcher's onslaught on traditional unions. That agenda jettisoned the earlier, more democratic, cultural policy elements of the former Greater London Council, and sidestepped more difficult and entrenched questions of class and inequality (O'Connor 2004; Oakley 2004). Splitting design from manufacture was also necessary to allow capitalists to seek lowest-cost labour overseas for costly elements of production or for those stages in production processes that could be most easily deskilled. The political fallout from the collapse of British manufacturing could be offset so long as a monopoly could be established over the higher-value, higher-profit parts of the value chain.

Here in Australia, the relevant political landscape grew out of the experiences of recession in the early 1980s, and attempts by the then Federal Labor Government to deregulate the Australian economy. National banks, airlines, and insurance agencies were privatized; barriers to entry by foreign banks were lifted; and the national currency was floated. The Australian Labor Party (ALP) developed and implemented an international competitiveness strategy, after negotiating a delicate industrial relations accord between business and unions. It unleashed a "programme of dramatic restructuring across the nation's protected industry sectors" (O'Neill and Weller 2013: 74), targeting manufacturing. Meanwhile right-wing factions of the ALP aligned themselves more closely with business interests, corporate lobby groups and the finance sector, linked to the growth of banking and finance in Sydney, and a conscious attempt to shift the party's support base from the traditional unions to the business-suited end of town. As O'Neill and Weller (2013: 75) described, "Sydney emerged as Australia's global entrepot and financial services centre, while many regions languished."

Those regions that languished were especially orientated towards manufacturing and heavy industry, sectors that in turn became increasingly positioned as burdensome and inefficient. Manufacturing became a prime target for restructuring, and "the worst recession in Australia's post-war history" in the early 1980s "both forced the pace of the restructure and disguised it" (Schultz 1985: ix). Government abandoned trade barrier support for manufacturing in textiles and clothing and in steelmaking, and the free-floating dollar (unleashed from the Bretton Woods currency pegging system in false anticipation of a permanently lower Australian dollar) put exporters at the whim of fluctuating currency speculations on the open financial markets (Webber and Weller 2001). Many thousands of factory workers lost jobs and livelihoods in hard-hit regions such as Adelaide, the western suburbs of both Melbourne and Sydney, and the smaller cities of Newcastle and Wollongong (Haughton 1990). The pace and depth of restructuring amplified existing socio-economic hardships in those regions, and cast a dark cloud over the remaining parts of the manufacturing sector that those regions have arguably never since been able to evade.

Revisiting this era in light of the current debate, manufacturing didn't "naturally" die as some kind of outcome of distant market forces, but was effectively handed a death sentence by policy moves that were masked by global recession and the synchronous deregulation and growth of the financial sector. Media and public discourses constructed manufacturing as old fashioned in comparison with rapid growth in seemingly more glamorous sectors such as banking, tourism and the cultural industries. When the much-celebrated *Creative Nation* (1994) report came out from the Keating Labor Government it was thus arguably less a ground-breaking statement of a future vision for creative industries than the congealment of a particular "project" that had a metanarrative to replace "old" industries with "new" and to mask the political fallout of deindustrialization and trade liberalization (Commonwealth of Australia 1994).

Creative industries advocates and scholars with backgrounds in design, music and media studies were often complicit in this "project," becoming creative industries "experts" (Prince 2010). The potential economic benefits of culture and creativity to struggling deindustrializing regions were used as arguments to secure research funding; professional education for creative and cultural sectors was becoming more industry-focused (Bill 2008). Meanwhile, supply chain managers within the private sector were actively divorcing design and thinking stages of the production process (where the true genius of creativity was said to lie) from increasingly repetitive, automated and deskilled material fabrication. Manufacturers such as Pacific Brands (whose Bonds lines of underwear and apparel had been iconic in Australia) retained design teams in Australia but shifted all production offshore, predominantly to China. So-called convergence of information, digital technologies and cultural production – all the rage in the late 1990s – rested on corporate rhetoric of the eschewing of material production in favour of the generation, trade and accumulation of intellectual property.

Since then, the normative, neoliberalized script of creative economy and development has found traction in diverse quarters of academia, in government and in policy-making – especially in cities and regions where the effects of deindustrialization were most intensely felt. Melbourne sought to re-invent itself as an indie/cultural tourism destination of alleyway cafés and boutiques; Parramatta in western Sydney followed suit, developing a night-time economy focused on converting laneways and previously boring office districts into creative hubs with public exhibitions and events, eat-streets and small funky bars. Adelaide hosted Charles Landry as a Thinker in Residence; and Marcus Westbury's Renew Newcastle scheme sought to revamp abandoned inner-city buildings as hubs of creativity and cultural expression in the wake of that city's own steelworks closures. Of these various creative city strategies and visions, Westbury's Renew Newcastle has probably come closest to a whole-of-production/whole-of-process approach – with many of its grassroots creative arts initiatives encompassing the crafting/making of physical things. Otherwise, across these examples, the emphasis has been largely on consumption, performance and design. Material manufacture is, by and large, nowhere to be seen.

Material transformations: Revising manufacturing

The irony is that in the intervening years manufacturing has itself undergone significant changes in structure and character. Notwithstanding continuing layoffs and closures, manufacturing has persisted in Australia, as in the United Kingdom and United States, though with different form and function. Some products (paint, bricks) continue to be made domestically because they are heavy and expensive or tricky to transport; others (mining equipment, air ambulances, medical devices) are made by specialist local firms because clients want customized products and on-going support and therefore seek manufacturers who respond quickly, can visit in person and who speak the same language.

Often smuggled into the debate is the presumption that manufacturing is dominated by large firms using mostly repetitive methods, low-skilled labour within Fordist assembly lines. Despite the headlines of job losses in large firms, small and medium enterprises with fewer than 50 employees make up a majority of Australian manufacturing firms (OECD 2013). Contra the assumption that manufacturing is somehow moribund, it remains the most significant investor in research and development of any Australian industry sector, measured on a per-employee basis (Department of Industry, Innovation, Climate Change, Science, Research and Tertiary Education 2013). Those investments have increased at a rate faster than in the remainder of the Australian economy – even during the recent post-GFC period. And yet in academic research on manufacturing as well as in creative industries the connection between making and creativity is rarely acknowledged or explored.

Meanwhile, highly specialist niche cultural products – hand-wired guitar pedals, analogue synth circuits, indie fashion, snowboards, leather products – have become boutique, hybrid creative/manufacturing sectors linked to specialist user groups, communities of aficionados through online retailing and bulletin board cultures, weekend festivals and markets, as well as local urban and regional cultural scenes. The purported binary between manufacturing and creative industries is constantly blurred by craft practices and the acquisition of haptic skills, as in trades, and by creativity as incrementally expressed through the manipulation of materials (Sennett 2008). Nevertheless, craft-based forms of manufacturing creativity bring with them distinctive (and not unproblematic) reconfigurations of labour-capital-technology relations.

An illustrative example that has been part of our research is the surfboard industry. As a sector dominated by small independent workshops that cater to niche user groups, it typifies newer forms of manufacturing. By contrast, the "major" surf labels, Billabong, Rip Curl and Quiksilver, trade mostly in apparel, not in surfing hardware – and indeed consider themselves intellectual property companies trading in branding rather than physical goods (the latter they produce via subcontractors in low-cost labour countries – see Warren and Gibson 2014). Surfboards are still made by hand, by expert "shapers" who plane and sand foam "blanks," and "glassers" who seal them against the elements. Because they are customized to local waves and body size, most Australian surfers ride boards made locally – even when cheaper imported boards are available.

In craft-based forms of manufacturing such as surfboard-making, creativity is expressed by producers through a combination of manual skills with tools, technical knowledge and aesthetic design flair. Meanwhile, embeddedness in local and online social and cultural scenes is critical, in ways reminiscent of an earlier era of thinking about music as cultural industry (see Brown et al. 2000). Such craft-based manufacturing forms involve diverse and diverging network topologies (Thomas et al. 2013), and industrial landscapes, from reinvigorated guild traditions and reconfigured relationships with downstream suppliers (who often have divergent philosophies from crafters – see Jakobs 2013), to more precarious employment conditions and a culture of individualism as opposed to collective bargaining (Warren 2014). The point is not to promote niche manufacturing of cultural/creative products as a superior alternative to Fordist manufacturing, but rather to suggest that manufacturing has itself changed and fused with cultural industries logics in diverse ways that require further academic attention.

Manipulating materials: Rethinking "redundant" skills

Finally, what kinds of problems emerge when the manual skills of manufacturing workers are assumed to be "redundant" in the creative age? Here we are especially mindful of the broader ecological crisis and that carbon-sensitive futures will rely heavily on the creativity and abilities of those who can make things and re-purpose materials with minimal energy and resource requirements. Material commodity production is at the forefront of a necessary move away from high volume, low quality production, towards a productive capacity built on creativity, longevity and stewardship (Lane and Watson 2012). Shifting the creative economy agenda to a dialogue of production ought to be a key part of this. And that shift inevitably involves questions of manual skill with materials.

The knowledge and skills of maligned production workers enables them to delve deeper into the assemblage of things – to look beyond the "thing-power" encountered by Jane Bennett (2010) in her pursuit of "Vibrant Matter" – to the very materials that compose objects, and to exercise creativity in manipulating them. The hand-drill, for example, is a consumer object, a "thing," yet under repair it becomes a collection of diverse elements: copper wire, metal brushes, nickel cadmium, magnetic force, momentum, heat, friction. The tradesperson with the skill to both use and repair the hand-drill is engaging with the agency of the thing in undertaking work tasks, but also engages with the agency of the matter within, uniquely understanding (to paraphrase Bennett) the clustering, affiliation, proximity and co-ordination required of each constituent element, to the agency of the thing. This has important implications for repair (and the reduction in resource consumption), but also in putting materials to new uses if, for example, the drill can't be repaired.

Part of the debate therefore needs to be not just what manual skills might support new manufacturing or creative niches, but what capacities there are among seemingly "redundant" workers to make and re-make objects in various city spaces, including at home, through the manipulation of physical materials (Carr and Gibson, forthcoming). Rather than the normative characterization of industrial cities and workers relentlessly engaged in the production of "stuff," placing grave strains on our commons, the manual workers, tradespeople and technicians that make up the bulk of the manufacturing workforce possess haptic skills and ingenuity, and are deeply embedded in local manufacturing cultures that respect materials and their re-use.

Conclusions

In the minds of many policy-makers as well as creative industry academics, manufacturing remains antonymic with creativity. In tying the creative industries to the production of intellectual property, founding definitions in the United Kingdom and Australia drove a division between creativity and the process of physical production at the outset. And yet arguably at no time in recent memory has the task of making things creatively (for instance, through innovation for low-carbon goods) been more important. We need smarter material goods that use fewer finite resources, last longer, that take advantage of and fairly reward already-present human skills and resources, and that capitalize on existing regional specializations (Bryson et al. 2008). The picture of manufacturing therefore needs to be made more complex in public policy debate, and its sectoral diversity, and existing and potential connections to innovation and creativity as well as the carbon reduction agenda duly acknowledged.

At the same time, just as cultural studies scholars have been making arguments for the moral economy of media and cultural industries to be brought back into the creative economy agenda (Hesmondhalgh 2013; Banks, this volume), so too ought we to think about forms of material manufacture in terms of both their creative input and their broader role in creating a better kind of society and economy. Against a backdrop that casts industrial city workers as "lacking" capacities to cope with deindustrializing futures, creativity in manufacturing regions and workers draws on and builds people's qualities and skills (embodied experimentation, adaptability, innovation, resourcefulness). These are qualities and skills that enable work, social networks and meaning to come into existence in everyday life in the industrial city. Our point is, therefore, not so much to push manufacturing as a creative sector – to simply "throw" manufacturing into the already bulging "bucket" of what might constitute creative industries – than to find, through examples of the material making of things, qualities and skills in people that ought to be better conceptualized within discussions about the future of seemingly "imperilled" cities and regions.

References

Banks, M. (2010) "Craft Labour and Creative Industries," *International Journal of Cultural Policy*, 16: 305–21.

Bennett, J. (2010) *Vibrant Matter: A political ecology of things*, Durham, NC: Duke University Press.

Bill, A. (2008) *Creative Girls: Fashion design education and governmentality* [Ph.D. thesis], University of Auckland.

Brown, A., O'Connor, J. and Cohen, S. (2000) "Local Music Policies Within a Global Music Industry: Cultural quarters in Manchester and Sheffield," *Geoforum*, 31: 437–51.

Bryson, J. R., Taylor, M. and Cooper, R. (2008) "Competing by Design, Specialization and Customization: Manufacturing locks in the West Midlands," *Geografiska Annaler: Series B, Human Geography*, 90: 173–86.

Carr, C. and Gibson, C. (forthcoming) "Geographies of making: rethinking materials and skills for volatile futures," *Progress in Human Geography*.

Christophers, B. (2014) "The Territorial Fix: Price, power and profit in the geographies of markets," *Progress in Human Geography*, 38: 754–70.

Christopherson, S. (2008) "Beyond the Self-expressive Creative Worker," *Theory, Culture and Society*, 25: 73–95.

Christopherson, S. and Storper, M. (1986) "The City as Studio; the World as Back Lot: The impact of vertical disintegration on the location of the motion picture industry," *Environment and Planning D: Society and Space*, 4: 305–20.

Commonwealth of Australia (1994) *Creative Nation*, Canberra: AGPS.

Davidson, K. and Gleeson, B. (2013) "The Urban Revolution that Isn't: The political ecology of the new 'urbanology'," *Journal of Australian Political Economy*, 72: 52–79.

Department of Industry, Innovation, Climate Change, Science, Research and Tertiary Education (2013) *Manufacturing Data Card* (accessed 23 August 2013: www.innovation.gov.au/industry/manufacturing/Pages/ManufacturingDataCard.aspx).

Florida, R. and Kenney, M. (1991) "Organization vs. Culture: Japanese automotive transplants in the US," *Industrial Relations Journal*, 22: 181–96.

Gibson, C. (2012) "Cultural Economy: Achievements, divergences, future prospects," *Geographical Research*, 50: 282–90.

Gibson, C. and Klocker, N. (2005) "The 'Cultural Turn' in Australian Regional Economic Development Discourse: Neoliberalizing creativity?" *Geographical Research*, 43: 93–102.

Gibson, C. and Kong, L. (2005) "Cultural Economy: A critical review," *Progress in Human Geography*, 29: 541–61.

Gittins, R. (2011) "Invest in Children of Knowledge Revolution," *Sydney Morning Herald*, August 31 (accessed 10 October 2013: www.smh.com.au/federal-politics/political-opinion/invest-in-children-of-knowledge-revolution-20110830-1jk02.html).

Haughton, G. (1990) "Manufacturing Recession? BHP and the recession in Wollongong," *International Journal of Urban and Regional Research*, 14: 70–88.

Hesmondhalgh, D. (2013) *Why Music Matters*, Chichester: Wiley.

Jakobs, D. (2013) "Crafting Your Way out of the Recession? New craft entrepreneurs and the global economic downturn," *Cambridge Journal of Regions, Economy and Society*, 6: 127–40.

Kong, L., Gibson, C., Khoo, L.-M. and Semple, A.-L. (2006) "Knowledges of the Creative Economy: Towards a relational geography of diffusion and adaptation in Asia," *Asia Pacific Viewpoint*, 47: 173–94.

Lane, R. and Watson, M. (2012) "Stewardship of Things: The radical potential of product stewardship for re-framing responsibilities and relationships to products and materials," *Geoforum*, 43: 1254–65.

Lash, S. and Urry, J. (1994) *Economies of Signs and Space*, London: Sage.

Lovink, G. and Ross, A. (2007) "Organic Intellectual Work: Interview with Andrew Ross," in G. Lovink and N. Rossiter (eds), *MyCreativity Reader: A critique of creative industries*, Amsterdam: Institute of Network Cultures.

Mitchell, T. (2008) "Rethinking Economy," *Geoforum*, 39: 1116–21.

O'Connor, J. (2004) "Cities, Culture and 'Transitional Economics'," in D. Power and A. J. Scott (eds), *Cultural Industries and the Production of Culture*, New York: Routledge.

O'Neill, P. and Weller, S. (2013) "To what Extent has Australia's Development Trajectory been Neoliberalist?" *Human Geography*, 6: 69–84.

Oakley, K. (2004) "Not so Cool Britannia: The role of the creative industries in economic development," *International Journal of Cultural Studies*, 7: 67–77.

OECD (2013) *Entrepreneurship at a Glance* (accessed 23 August 2013: www.oecd.org/industry/entrepreneurshipataglance.htm).

Pope, R. (2005) *Creativity: Theory, history, practice*, London: Routledge.

Pratt, A. C. (1997) "The Cultural Industries Production System: A case study of employment change in Britain 1984–91," *Environment and Planning A*, 29: 1953–74.

Pratt, A. C. (2008) "Cultural Commodity Chains, Cultural Clusters, or Cultural Production Chains?" *Growth and Change*, 39: 95–103.

Prince, R. (2010) "Fleshing Out Expertise: The making of creative industries experts in the United Kingdom," *Geoforum*, 41: 875–84.

Schultz, J. (1985) *Steel City Blues: The human cost of industrial crisis*, Sydney: Penguin.

Scott, A.J. (1988) *New Industrial Spaces*, London: Pion.

Scott, A.J. (1996) "Regional Motors of the Global Economy," *Futures*, 28: 291–411.

Scott, A.J. (1997) "The Cultural Economy of Cities," *International Journal of Urban and Regional Research*, 21: 323–39.

Scott, A.J. (2004) "A Perspective of Economic Geography," *Journal of Economic Geography*, 4: 479–99.

Scott, A.J. (2006) "Creative Cities: Conceptual issues and policy questions," *Journal of Urban Affairs*, 28: 1–17.

Sennett, R. (2008) *The Craftsman*, New Haven and London: Yale University Press.

Thomas, N., Harvey, D. C. and Hawkins, H. (2013) "Crafting the Region: Creative industries and practices of regional space," *Regional Studies*, 47: 75–88.

Warren, A. (2014) "Working Culture: The agency and employment experiences of non-unionized workers in the surfboard industry," *Environment and Planning A*, 46: 2300–16.

Warren, A. and Gibson, C. (2014) *Surfing Places, Surfboard Makers: Craft, creativity and cultural heritage in Hawai'i, California and Australia*, Honolulu: University of Hawaii Press.

Webber, M. J. and Weller, S. A. (2001) *Re-fashioning the Rag Trade: The internationalisation of the TCF industries in Australia*, Sydney: University of New South Wales Press.

Part II

CORE CULTURAL INDUSTRIES

In this section we look at some of the current challenges facing some old, new and frequently marginalised cultural industries. These individual industries – characterised by specific historical social logics, technologies, regulatory structures and cultural dynamics – have faced new challenges in the last decade and their paths have increasingly crossed and intertwined. However, despite 'convergence' and the all-purpose descriptor of 'the digital', there are many aspects of these that remain rooted in older forms of production, distribution and 'monetisation'. On the other hand, there are many changes that are not so visible, such as the erosion of the public realm, the homogenisation of content, the marginalisation of less powerful social groups that is barely registered in discourses of ubiquitous media and consumer choice.

Some of the chapters in this section introduce a whole industry (games, advertising) or make claims for its inclusion under that rubric (sport). Others focus on industries or aspects of the industry that have often been overlooked (radio, literary publishing). Finally, we have chapters that take a specific perspective on very well-known industries – television and music. Film, a notable absence, is covered in sections concerned with *space and place* and *policy* below.

Sarah Brouillette and Christopher Doody look at literary publishing and how it operates within what is one of the largest and most concentrated branches of the cultural industries. They look at how the values of the 'literary' – its aesthetic and intellectual pleasures – are positioned across the industry in various ways. Gillian Doyle looks at one of the foundations of the public sphere and one of the first cultural industries in the post-Gutenberg age – newspapers. Seriously challenged by Internet technologies, they have responded in various ways, suggesting that they will certainly survive in some form. Questions as to what kind of content they deliver, to whom and in what form are not yet clear, but indications suggest a reduction in diversity and depth.

Des Freedman picks up these themes in his chapter on television. He shows how 'choice' has become distributed to audience segments willing and able to pay, with 'residual' audiences increasingly marginalised. Investment in content has shifted away from news and local content, and drama has become more targeted at global audiences. Sport has seen funding increases across the board. Freedman ends by suggesting that policy has become focused on technologies and markets and has moved away from concern with the content of television. The absence of this interest, one that marked the State's concerns with the industry in the last century, is a major challenge for those concerned with contemporary cultural (industry) policy. Anthony Fung takes some of these themes up from a global industry perspective, showing how television formats have become major drivers in the industry – and especially in East Asia. Fung's is a critical examination of the interaction between state and policy, media, content and local adaptation, audience and the market in the development of global television.

Shane Homan explores the challenges faced by the music industry in the wake of the Internet and MP3 files. He charts the radical challenges to the business models of the major music industry players, as well as the rise of new players such as iTunes and Spotify. However, Homan finds that the brunt of these changes has fallen on musicians themselves, who are now expected to promote themselves across multiple platforms with little access to the resources that record companies once supplied. Homan's chapter ends with a sense of 'plus ca change'.

Brendan Keogh picks up one of the music industry's key distinctions – between mainstream and indie – in his account of the video-games industry. The appearance of this distinction in this new industry suggests that many of the tensions associated with cultural industries – their interlinked economic and cultural values – apply just as much here. However, Keogh shows how the possibility of such a tension has only recently been recognised, as video games have been positioned by industry and non-industry media alike as technology driven entertainment for nerds. The emergence of this tension and its role in the structuring of the industry are central concerns of this chapter.

Steve Redhead explores another industry whose 'cultural' credentials have long been doubted – sport. Coming from a localised cultural industry policy perspective, Redhead looks at the different dimensions of the question of sport as a cultural industry. Though clearly coming from a different trajectory, where entertainment has less connection to 'symbolic goods', the ways in which sports audiences and media have been brought together in global networks of value suggest that we exclude them from our cultural policy concerns at our peril (see also Rowe, Part V).

John Sinclair introduces us to a branch of the cultural industries long associated with their overt and damaging commerciality, and often marginalised in scholarly work for this reason. His chapter shows how central this branch has been to the overall argumentation around cultural and creative industries, and how it has also been subject to extensive changes in recent years. Finally, John Tebbutt looks at a branch of the cultural industries that has frequently been ignored in both scholarship and policy literature: radio. Moving between communications and broadcasting, culture and technology, radio has been around for over a century and remains a central – if overlooked – aspect of our cultural consumption practices. This chapter provides an account of how the audio form that is radio has been constructed and reconstructed over the years. It concludes by suggesting there are long-term changes around the shift to digital that concern diversity and access which we cannot afford to ignore.

6

THE LITERARY AS A CULTURAL INDUSTRY

Sarah Brouillette and Christopher Doody

Book publishing is often absent from or treated cursorily in cultural industries research. The little research that does consider publishing does not discuss what characterizes and informs the production, circulation and reception of particularly *literary* titles. At first glance we might explain this lacuna as a matter of disciplines. Cultural industries researchers are mainly working in sociology and in cultural and media studies, whereas those concerned with the specificity of literature work in English faculties. Our chapter questions this divide.

In Part I, we note the interrelation between the literary and the cultural industries in the influential oeuvres of Pierre Bourdieu and Theodor Adorno. Ruthless in his critique of the deadening effects of mass culture, Adorno preserved the possibility that the literary might remain a space apart, where autonomous artistic activity could foster social and political transformation. In Bourdieu's work there is a comparable desire to set the literary against the reduction of all cultural expression to what he called the "heteronomous field," where making money and reaching a wide audience trump all other concerns.

Their work has unfortunately tended to be read in ways that affirm division rather than interrelation. Literary scholarship has embraced Adorno's aesthetic theory, whereas research on the cultural industries has tended to critique Adorno's whole approach as elitist and inimical to its own goals. Cultural industries research has found value in Bourdieu's models because he treats all culture as a means to acquire and control some kind of capital, while literary scholars have embraced Bourdieu's work because of the tribute it pays to literature as the lynchpin of the "autonomous field," where value and wealth are accrued almost despite themselves.

In Part II, we stress that these divisions make less sense now than ever before. Most major publishers exist within enormous media conglomerates eager to see the literary endlessly repurposed. For them literature is not necessarily a shelf of thick books, although such an image has its uses. Instead the literary is a set of ideas about cultural value—associated with meaning, agency, inquiry, exploration, self-discovery, and interpretation, for example—that circulate well beyond the publishing industry, permeating film, television, radio, and digital media. The literary is increasingly shorthand for a set of generative values and experiences that are produced to be accessed across all media. It is only by thinking about literature as itself a cultural industry that we can understand the attractiveness and marketability of its ostensibly unique and particular pleasures.

Part I

While literature scholars almost never reference cultural industries research, they have for some time now thought about literature as having an industrial context and dimension (English and Felski 2010), to the point that commentators have recently lamented "too much sociology" in the study of literature (*N+1* Editors 2013). You would in fact be hard pressed to find a scholar of literature who would maintain that the literary is a transcendent space of pure imagination, expression, creativity and feeling, unfettered by the constraints of corporate enterprise. They are more likely to stress readily the impact that the material realities of book production, distribution and consumption have on what and how we read.

Pierre Bourdieu's work on the pull between autonomous or "elite" work and heteronomous or "popular" production has been particularly influential. Bourdieu has been at times caricatured as insisting that all cultural expression can be explained as the product of a highly structured field or game in which people compete to secure their personal interests and accrue cultural, social and economic capital. But we notice in his electrifying essay "The Field of Cultural Capital" (1983) the suggestion that the literary represents exactly that part of the cultural economy that cannot be entirely reduced to economic incentive. This aspect of his thinking—this tendency to trumpet autonomous culture—became only more prominent in his later years.

In Bourdieu's work the literary is consistently associated with the delimited but nonetheless significant freedom that enables new ideas and forms to come to exist within the field and slowly change its boundaries and presumptions. He writes that the "literary or artistic field is a *field of forces*, but it is also a *field of struggles* tending to transform or conserve this field of forces" (1983: 311–12, emphasis in original). He conceives literature as primary amongst those forms of expression that are able to struggle against the field of forces to which they belong. The literary could even be defined, for Bourdieu, as the transformative potential latent within any field of forces and struggles. He writes that "when a new literary or artistic group makes its presence felt in the field of literary or artistic production, the whole problem is transformed, since its coming into being, i.e. into difference, modifies and displaces the universe of possible options" (1983: 314). This is not a rigid model. It assumes a dynamic system in which permanent conflict and thus permanent change are standard: "the generative, unifying principle of this 'system' is the struggle" (1983: 316), he writes. Literature is given a privileged combatant's role within this aversive space.

A key feature of Bourdieu's theoretical project is his insistence that the objective conditions of the "literary and artistic field" include our subjective belief that the culture in our field is uniquely prestigious and worthy of celebration, uniquely respectful of art's superiority to other kinds of culture. He will call these beliefs "deceptive certainties," but caution that in calling them deceptive we must nevertheless recognize that adherence to them is a crucial part of the objective reality at hand (1983: 317). They are not truths that Bourdieu himself patiently escapes by illumi-nating their determination by material factors. It was Bourdieu after all who insisted upon a relentlessly reflexive sociology. He is not outside the system. He too invests in a realm of superior expression that can transform the constraints of the existing field. The field wouldn't be operative if knowledge of its workings magically made one immune to its pressures.

Bourdieu of course claims that faith in uniquely aesthetic merit is a product of the rise of commercial culture, as that rise was accompanied by an ideology of artistic separation from market concerns. That ideology contributes to the field of restricted cultural production, which exists only anxiously within a larger marketplace reliant on large-scale production as a means of capitalist accumulation. To be sure, Bourdieu's analysis of the development of a belief in artistic autonomy in a sense debunks the notion of artistic disinterest, and shows that those who try to separate themselves from socio-economics are, by the very gesture of separation, in fact determined by them. However, Bourdieu was worried about the corporatization of culture, in which he saw a disappearance of the division between elite and mass production. He thought it threatened what autonomization had achieved in creating the conditions for "the full creative process proper to each field" and for some "resistance to the 'symbolic violence'" exerted by the dominant system that made economic rather than cultural capital its lodestar (Benson 1999: 465). Bourdieu thus offers a critical historical account of the forms that autonomy has taken, while asserting strongly that this autonomy has positive dimensions worth preserving. Not least, the power of intellectual intervention in the political sphere would continue to depend upon social validation of the values of disinterestedness and expertise associated with them (Bourdieu 1996: 340).

Bourdieu has little to say about large-scale commercial cultural production, except insofar as its operations matter to the way the restricted sub-field's participants imagine themselves: for instance, that they are autonomous while commercial culture is heteronomous, or that their culture is the product of artists' own intellectual impulses rather than a response to external demand. Throughout his oeuvre, it is literature that exemplifies the upside-down economic world his theory of autonomy depends upon, in which there is an interest in distinterestedness, and participants in the field only feel comfortable symbolically consecrating that which does not seek consecration.

"The Field of Cultural Production" concludes with discussion of some writing by Stéphane Mallarmé, in which he seems to reduce beauty "to no more than the pro-jection into a metaphysical beyond of what is lacking in the here-and-now of literary life" (1983: 354). According to Bourdieu, Mallarmé presents beauty as a fantasy that disguises the ugliness of daily struggle. Bourdieu cites it here because it would imply that, like his own analysis, there is no transcendent realm of aesthetic bliss truly unanchored from what it tries to escape. This is clear enough. However, he goes on to state that "if the pleasure of the love of art has its source in unawareness … then it is understandable that one might, by another willing suspension of disbelief, choose to 'venerate' the authorless trickery which places the fragile fetish beyond the reach of critical lucidity" (1983: 354). We find here a nice summation of Bourdieu's conception of culture's economic entanglement. Critical lucidity means letting go of the "fragile fetish" of aesthetic beauty; yet when we know that pleasure might be tied to lack of awareness of the industrial aspects of culture, we are not then stuck in the position of mocking those who don't share our superior knowledge. Instead we can choose to suspend our own disbelief and engage in the veneration of the art that pleases us. Pleasing art is not, thus, reducible to its economic entanglements. Describing it in relation to them does not traduce its value. In a dialectical fashion, art's resistance to being traduced is what makes it superior.

Adorno's approach to the aesthetic of course has a different inflection. Whereas Bourdieu sees class distinctions emerging in and solidified by cultural consumption, Adorno tends to emphasize the class relations disguised in the fiction of democratic access to a proliferating mass culture. In their work on the culture industry, Horkheimer and Adorno conceive it as an "iron system" of mass standardized production. They argue that the expansion and consolidation of large cultural corporations hinged on the idea that to meet the needs of countless consumers in many disparate places "standard products" were required (2007: 95). The result was inducement of a "pseudo individuality" in which people are enjoined to express their ostensibly unique identities and values through their consumption of indistinct mass goods. They write that in the culture industry, "not only do hit songs, stars, and soap operas conform to types recurring cyclically as rigid invariants, but the specific content of productions, the seemingly variable element, is itself derived from those types. The details become interchangeable" (2007: 98).

Those who charge this foundational essay with elitism imply that its primary target is passive consumers addicted to substandard culture. But this is untrue. What they attack, rather, is the idea that the culture industry is simply the fruit of superior technical systems for monitoring and responding to consumers' needs. It is the industry's presumption to know its audience, and the excuse that it is responding to audience demand, that troubles the authors, because control over the industry is in the hands of economic elites. This elite in fact works to create the public that approves of its efforts, and justifies its own domination by claiming it has a handle on the technology that allows it to be responsive to common people.

Nor is the essay a lament about the ideal of "pure expression" existing no longer. In fact this precise lament is faulted. What Adorno and Horkheimer do say about the notion of "pure expression" is not unlike Mallarmé's perspective as Bourdieu represents it: obsession with purity reflects the desire of the privileged to inhabit a realm separate from the daily struggles of people whose disadvantages serve the elite. It is difficult to see how one might level the charge of elitism against the contrast they draw between the elite's faith in "pure expression" and "the real universality" of an art that aligns itself with society's least privileged. In their words: "while all needs [are] presented to individuals as capable of fulfillment by the culture industry, they [are] so set up in advance that individuals experience themselves through their needs only as eternal consumers, as the culture industry's object" (2007: 113). There is no superior disdain here, but rather attentiveness to the hardships that entertainment pretends it can remedy. Leisure, and the culture consumed as part of it, become as routinized and mechanized as assembly-line work. It offers no authentic relief, but rather promises to divert via temporary amusements that do nothing to remedy an absence of substantive freedom.

In "Commitment" (1974) Adorno envisions the culture industry's countermeasure. He praises artworks whose formal innovations produce in their audiences a desire for the change that the works cannot themselves enact. "It is not the office of art to spotlight alternatives, but to resist by its form alone the course of the world, which permanently puts a pistol to men's heads" (1974: 78), he famously states. Avowedly critical forms like social realism threaten to become saleable images of suffering. The moral condemnation that the committed work means to express thus "slithers into the abyss of its opposite" (1974: 85), permitting amoral consumption of others' hardships. Indeed the sheer act of representing something in art threatens to make it more palatable and more meaningful, and meaning itself is a property we might want to withhold from some horrors. "Even the sound of despair pays its tribute to a hideous affirmation" (1974: 85), he writes.

Thus, the work that Adorno singles out for praise avoids any affirmation of a direct commitment. Instead it critiques empirical reality itself. Franz Kafka and Samuel Beckett, for example, write in ways that "arouse the fear" that more discursive works might explore as their explicit content (1974: 86). Writing like theirs "compels the change of attitude which committed works merely demand" (1974: 86–87). He elaborates:

> He over whom Kafka's wheels have passed has lost forever both any peace with the world and any chance of consoling himself with the judgment that the way of the world is bad; the element of ratification which lurks in resigned admission of the dominance of evil is burnt away.
>
> (Adorno 1974: 87)

The highest literature thus disavows the empirical demands of more evidently committed writing. The best works "point to a practice from which they abstain: the creation of a just life" (1974: 89). They promise a better world even as they refuse to please their readers or provide any reconciling consolation about a bad reality. Even though they may never read it, this superior art is on the side of the oppressed precisely because it can stimulate—rather than directly representing—social change.

Returning to the comparison with Bourdieu, now, we see that the superiority of the art Adorno admires is dialectically tied to the inferiority of the culture industry and the iniquitous world that the culture industry is designed to make us accept or forget. Every bit of content and every literary form originates, he writes, "in the empirical reality from which it breaks free" (1974: 86). There is no pure distinction between the literary and culture industry. They exist together and develop together is aversive lockstep. It is in *Aesthetic Theory* (1970) that Adorno makes this point at greatest length. Art achieves its autonomous status not by denying that it has any kind of relation to the culture industry, but by wrestling within itself—at the level of formal technique—with the contradictions of its own status as a commodity.

Part II

The last few years have seen an increase in scholarly work from a cultural studies perspective that includes a serious consideration of the literary as an important cultural industry in itself. These studies tend to affirm—though to quite different ends—Adorno's perspective on the contradictory relation between literary expression and its industrial production. These include, among others, Simone Murray's *The Adaptation Industry* (2012), Ted Striphas's *The Late Age of Print* (2009), Shuyu Kong's *Consuming Literature* (2005), and Jim Collins's *Bring on the Books for Everybody* (2010). Taken as a whole, these works demonstrate why now more than ever the literary and other culture industries need to be studied together.

The desire or impulse to separate literature off from other cultural industries is hardly unique to academic cultural studies. As Ted Striphas argues:

> [T]he notion that books belong at a significant remove from the realm of economic necessity is one of the most entrenched myths of contemporary book culture. ... People buy and sell books all the time. ... Still, conventional wisdom says there's something more to them—something that sets books apart from, say, light bulbs, DVDs, automobiles, and other mass merchandise for which people pay good money. ... What makes a 'good' book good—or, rather, what makes *books* good—is their purported ability to transcend vulgar economic considerations for the sake of ... loftier goals.
>
> (Striphas 2009: 6)

Striphas argues that this myth exists, at least in part, because of the "everydayness" of books—books have become such common, mass-produced commodities that "certain economic realities of the book trade have come to be seen as so customary, so banal, as to be overlooked entirely today" (2009: 6). Striphas's work is an attempt to dismantle this myth, by examining the various ways in which books, and the literature industry at large, are intricately connected to, and have helped produce, the current state of consumer capitalism.

Striphas's work looks at five unique aspects of contemporary book culture—e-books, big-box stores, online stores, Oprah's book club, and the Harry Potter phenomenon—arguing that to understand them we need to understand their particular histories as well as book culture's broader interconnectedness with consumer capitalism. In his chapter on e-books, for example, Striphas traces the current problem of ownership and distribution of books as a commodity back to the 1930s. The fear that readers reselling and sharing their books would undermine the industry was so great that publishers tried to market the term "book sneak" to denote "a pejorative word for the book borrower, the wretch who ... deprived authors of earned royalties" (2009: 35). This fear re-emerged in the 1980s with widespread access to photocopiers. Today's attempts by publishers to "lock" e-books with digital encryption are a simple extension of these concerns. Striphas notes that "e-book technologies constitute the end result of more than fifty years' worth of effort to render problematic people's accumulation and circulation of printed books, as well as those of other mass-produced goods" (2009: 45). The rest of Striphas's work follows a similar pattern of explaining why, in practical terms, it is essential for a proper understanding of the literature industry to consider books as mass-produced goods, with similar economic, social, and political restrictions as any other cultural product. While Striphas successfully disproves the myth that the literary industry is autonomous from economic concerns, and in fact shares many similarities with other cultural industries at large, his focus is not on the way in which the production of literature is intertwined with other cultural industries.

Simone Murray's work on the literary adaptation industry does provide this focus. Murray argues that critics of adaptions have a "distorted understanding" of it because they lack knowledge of the industry (2012: 12). Segregating the production of literature from other cultural industries has actually hampered the development of adaptation studies as a field. The solution, Murray argues, is in dispelling some "myths" held by adaptation critics, one of which is "the claim that books are the product of individualized, isolated authorial creation, whereas film and television result from collaborative, industrialised processes" (2012: 12). Book historians have shown that the production of literature is a social process in which many agents, influenced by political, social, and economic concerns, work to produce a given book. To treat the literature industry as separate is to ignore basic features of its contemporary production. For example, Murray notes that "adaption for the screen is not merely an add-on or after-thought of this complex [literary] economy, but is now factored in and avidly pursued from the earliest phase of book production" (2012: 13). Adaptation studies, and by extension other areas of cultural studies research, will "only be fully able to comprehend its object of study once it conceptualises book and screen media as components of a single, converged 'global entertainment industry'" (2012: 14).

One of Murray's key interests is the changing role of authors in what she terms the "adaptation economy." This economy is the result of the contemporary age in which publishing companies are housed within an "oligopoly" of media conglomerates and "multi-sectoral transnational media corporations" (2012: 34). These massive transnational media corporations own a variety of companies that produce cultural content: publishing houses, newspapers, television shows, film studios, radio programs, digital platforms, etc. As a result, these corporations are keen for cultural products that can be endlessly repurposed. In this adaptation economy, the format of the book is "increasingly envisaged as only a temporary vessel for 'liquid' content, which may be decanted and reconstituted across the full gamut of contemporary media platforms" (2012: 38). The metaphorical liquid that Murray describes here is the *literary*—a property in and of itself, a creative commodity that is repurposed and refashioned into as many different mediums as the economy will allow for.

Murray argues that contemporary authors are already well aware of the mutability of their product, and have had to respond in kind: "Twenty-first-century authorship is no longer a single-medium (or even print-specific) role" (2012: 41). The changing role of authorship in the adaptation economy has a profound impact on the cultural industry as a whole. Murray notes:

> The contextual pressures upon authors to conceive of their creative work as incipiently multiformat are present from the earliest phases of content creation: pre-empted by the conglomerate owners of much of the book publishing industry, itemized in the minutely detailed rights clauses bulking out publishing contracts, and foremost in the business strategies of their agent advisers.
>
> (Murray 2012: 36)

Authors themselves, aware of the numerous ways that their literary work can be adapted and resold, are beginning to "understand their work as 'a branded property,'" and their contracts are following suit. These "itemise the exact division between author and publisher of rights to book content in every conceivable form" (2012: 37). While authors are changing along with the broader literary industry, accustoming themselves to the interconnectedness and interdependence of the adaptation economy, the adaptation industry itself actually benefits from the widespread belief in the socially autonomous author and literary industry. Using the presence of the author at a film premier as her example, Murray explains how the adaptation industry relies on the literary cultural capital of authors. Noting that "waves of Arnoldian, Leavisite and New Critical approaches to the teaching of literary fiction have deeply embedded (albeit often covertly) Romantic conceptions of author-genius and inculcated ignorance of the commercial realities of the book trade" (2012: 27), she argues that these approaches ultimately serve the adaptation industry. How else to explain "the ritual appearance of the author at the adapted film's premier" than as an "authorial imprimatur and creative blessing" (2012: 27) bestowed upon the adaptation? Even when the author figure has had no impact on the production of a film adapted from their work, their blessing upon the film sanctifies it with the aura of literature. The process only works because the author figure is widely perceived as socially autonomous and therefore untainted by economic and political concerns. Murray thus argues that, contradictorily, the "revival of the (never entirely dispelled) Romantic sanctification of authorship" is now cultivated by the same industry "whose very existence would—at first glance—seem to disprove it" (2012: 28). This example suggests that the relation between the literary industry and other cultural industries is far more complex than normally imagined. While the current state of multi-national media conglomerates ensures that the literary industry is necessarily intertwined with all other cultural industries, these other industries also benefit, to varying degrees, from the Romantic notion of the literary as autonomous, because this (false) separation is what endows the literary with its value.

Richard Nash has recently discussed how publishers are trying to find new ways to capture and profit from this value. Nash argues that "the business of literature," which translates cultural prestige into commercial value, is in and of itself not limited to books. "You begin to realize that the business of literature is *the business of making culture*, not just the business of manufacturing bound books," he writes (Nash 2013: n.p., emphasis added). Like Murray, Nash acknowledges that the contemporary literature industry is relying more and more on the value of literature's aura to make a profit, as opposed to selling actual material books. "Selling a book, print or digital, turns out to be far from the only way to generate revenue from all the remarkable cultural activity that goes into the creation and dissemination of literature and ideas," Nash observes (2013: n.p.). For example,

> Several larger US publishers now offer speakers bureau services, which, for poets and for management consultants alike, are far more remunerative than the book. (Even though the book undergirds the value of the talk, it is not the vehicle through which the actual revenue is conveyed.) O'Reilly, the computer-book publisher, earns more from the conferences it orchestrates

than from selling books, although its intellectual reputation and network of connections as a publisher positioned it to create the conference.

(Nash 2013: n.p.)

As the literature industry begins fully to realize its economic imbrication with other cultural industries, these types of non-typical publisher activities will become more common. Nash, only slightly tongue-in-cheek, imagines some of the possibilities:

> [I]f Marc Jacobs can sell books, why can't publishers in turn partner with designers to create shoes inspired by a particular character? Publishers could partner with wine wholesalers to offer wine clubs, with caterers providing literary-themed events, with boutique travel agencies to offer tours.
>
> (Nash 2013: n.p.)

Although they have yet to go this far, some publishers are beginning to create literary material that is explicitly meant to be outsourced to other cultural industries.

Shuyu Kong explains that since the 1990s the literature industry in China has had to negotiate its role in relation to the growth of other cultural industries, specifically television and movies. Writers began writing television and movie scripts because the pay was better and it required less work than writing a short story or novella. "Instead of being wiped out by the competing new media," however, "the Chinese literary industry … learned to exploit these new media for its own purposes—namely, to promote and market literature" (2005: 171). Publishers succeeded because they began to view their products as "multidimensional literary products (*duo wei chanpin*)" and to embrace the idea that a "single piece of writing can be repackaged and adapted to appeal to many different markets through a variety of media" (2005: 171). What Murray describes as happening in the adaptation economy is, in Kong's account, commonplace in China. The recycling of literary works into other media is so common that it has spawned a new genre, "'television and film literature' (*yingshi wenxue*)", which is created specifically by publishers to "help package, advertise, and promote books" for these visual mediums (2005: 175). These Chinese publishers, along with Murray and Nash, all understand that the literary is no longer confined to the literature industry, and that to segregate it from the industries in which it now emerges and circulates makes little sense. As Kong writes, "No longer separate entities with their own independent existence, literary works are now written and read as simply a part or stage in a multimedia and multidimensional production process" (2012: 182–83).

We see, then, that a conception of the literary and the broader cultural economy as involved in close and contradictory relation, as literature's aura of distinction from commerce is thoroughly branded and marketed, is more pressing now than ever. The two parts of Bourdieu's and Adorno's respective concerns—the faith in the restricted production of autonomous artworks and the attention to heteronomous production of culture for mass consumption—must necessarily collapse into one another, since the idea of restricted culture sells on a mass scale, and the ideal of the autonomous artwork is more a saleable anti-autonomous image than a substantial reality.

References

Adorno, T. (1970; English trans. 1984) *Aesthetic Theory*, ed. Gretel Adorno and Rolf Tiedemann, trans. Christian Lenhardt, London and Boston: Routledge and Kegan Paul, 1984.

——(1974) "Commitment," *New Left Review* I, 87–88: 75–89.

Benson, R. (1999) "Field Theory in Comparative Context: A New Paradigm for Media Studies," *Theory and Society*, 28: 463–98.

Bourdieu, P. (1983) "The Field of Cultural Capital," *Poetics*, 12: 311–56.

——(1996) *The Rules of Art: Genesis and Structure of the Literary Field*, Stanford, CA: Stanford University Press.

Collins, J. (2010) *Bring on the Books for Everybody: How Literary Culture Became Popular Culture*, Durham: Duke University Press.

English, J. and Felski, R. (eds.) (2010) "New Sociologies of Literature," Spec. issue of *New Literary History*, 41.2.

Horkheimer, M. and Adorno, T. (2007) *Dialectic of Enlightenment: Philosophical Fragments*, ed. G.S. Noerr, trans. E. Jephcott, Stanford, CA: Stanford University Press.

Kong, S. (2005) *Consuming Literature: Best Sellers and the Commercialization of Literary Production in Contemporary China*, Stanford: Stanford University Press.

Murray, S. (2012) *The Adaptation Industry: The Cultural Economy of Contemporary Literary Adaptation*, New York: Routledge.

N+1 Editors (2013) "Too Much Sociology," *N+1*, 8 April. Online. Available at: nplusonemag.com/too-much-sociology.

Nash, R. (2013) "What is the Business of Literature?" *Virginia Quarterly Review*, 89.2: n.p. Online. Available at: www.vqronline.org/articles/2013/spring/nash-business-literature/.

Striphas, T. (2009) *The Late Age of Print: Everyday Book Culture from Consumerism to Control*, New York: Columbia University Press.

7

MULTI-PLATFORM MEDIA

How newspapers are adapting to the digital era

Gillian Doyle

Introduction

The role played by newspapers in supplying the interpretations of events that shape our viewpoints, ideas and many of our cultural attitudes is well recognized. But newspaper publishing has been profoundly affected in recent years by changing technologies and by forces of globalization and recession which, for some, have posed a serious threat to survival.

Much recent academic work has focused attention on the perceived "crisis" in the economics of newspaper publishing (Siles and Boczkowski 2012). Many studies have focused especially on the ways in which journalism and news production have been affected (Brock 2013; Erdal 2011; Fenton 2010; Bressers 2009). Digital convergence and growth of the Internet, and accompanying changes in patterns of media consumption and advertising, have placed unprecedented financial pressures on newspaper publishing organizations (Mitchelstein and Boczkowski 2009; Picard 2011). The effects of such pressures have been acutely felt, particularly in the United States where "[i]n the past year, seven major newspaper chains have declared bankruptcy, several big city papers have shut down, and many have laid off reporters and editors, imposed pay reductions, cut the size of the physical newspaper, or turned to Web-only publication" (Kirchhoff 2010: 1).

Declining circulations for print media have impacted adversely on the revenues of newspaper publishers throughout the developed world and this reflects a wider pattern whereby digital media and digital products of all sorts are displacing physical goods from the value chain (Graham and Smart 2010). Thus, in the United Kingdom as elsewhere across Europe, newspaper groups are struggling to develop suitable strategic responses to the Internet and related technological developments that have disrupted their long-standing successful business models (Holm et al. 2013).

The newspaper sector is by no means alone within industries devoted to creating and supplying culture and cultural content in finding itself at the epicentre of what is sometimes seen as a period of "creative destruction" precipitated by digital convergence, growth of the Internet and associated changes in consumption patterns. Other sectors including film and music, book and magazine publishing have encountered considerable challenges in adjusting production practices, distribution strategies and/or business models to the contingencies of the digital era. But the pivotal role of newspapers (as other mass media) within the infrastructure of daily cultural exchange has meant that questions about the ability of newspaper publishers to successfully adjust and renew in the face of technological change have received plentiful attention.

This chapter examines and analyses a strategic response commonly adopted by newspapers in response to the impact of digital convergence and growth of the Internet – that of transforming from a single platform to a multi-platform supplier of media. It provides an empirically based analysis of how players in the UK newspaper sector have gradually re-invented themselves as multi-platform entities in order to address environmental adversities and at the same time to harness the perceived advantages of digital expansion. Although the focus here is on newspapers, the prevalence of adopting a multi-platform corporate configuration reflects a much wider pattern across the whole of the media industry over recent years of companies responding to digital convergence by adopting an approach that entails re-conceptualizing the business of supplying media as an activity involving multiple distribution platforms.

The evidence presented and summarized in this chapter was collected as part of an ongoing Economic and Social Research Council funded study on how media organizations are adapting to digital convergence.[1] Research involved interviews with leading UK newspaper publishers including News International (publisher of *The Times*), the Telegraph Media Group (*Telegraph*), Associated Newspapers (*Daily Mail*) and the FT Group (*Financial Times*). Interviews with senior management at these organizations and analysis of each company's financial data were carried out by the author in 2012 and 2013.

Focusing particularly on the experience of UK newspaper groups, this chapter considers how the adoption of a multi-platform strategy is affecting operational and production practices and how it is impacting on consumption, content and business models. A central theme is how the imperative of finding ways of engaging with and catering effectively for digital audiences is forcing ongoing adaptation in the organization of production activities in contemporary newsrooms. This chapter also considers how newspaper publishers are using digital expansion to diversify their revenues and change the nature of their businesses. Finally, some preliminary reflections are offered on the implications for public policy of newspaper publishers moving steadily from purely print towards digital multi-platform status.

Why are media firms shifting to a multi-platform approach?

Adoption of a multi-platform approach has been a common response among media companies to digitization and growth of the Internet. What are the perceived advantages that have encouraged this approach? In what ways, if any, is a converged multi-platform approach to production and distribution improving the management and exploitation of resources involved in supplying news content? How are multi-platform approaches to content production, assembly and distribution affecting the ability of media suppliers to exploit their resources and serve audience demands more effectively?

Broadly speaking, digital technology has made sharing and recycling of content easier than before and multi-platform re-purposing is therefore common practice (Doyle 2013). Techniques of "windowing" (Owen and Wildman 1992) to fully exploit intellectual property long pre-date digitization and, in principle, are now more relevant than ever for media suppliers, albeit that the range of distributive outlets and the factors likely to dictate their sequencing is more complex in a digital context and policing copyright effectively has become much more difficult. However, migration towards a multi-platform outlook is not solely motivated by the desire to exploit content more effectively. The re-envisaging of corporate missions in a more multi-platform way also reflects a widespread recognition that major changes in consumption patterns and in the appetites of (especially younger) audiences have taken place (Ofcom 2013). At the same time as offering opportunities to innovate, these changes threaten to leave behind media organizations that fail to adapt to the contingencies of the digital environment.

Opportunities for innovation and improved efficiency stem from the ways digital technology is reshaping relationships between media suppliers and audiences (Storsul and Krumsvik 2013). New technology is allowing suppliers unprecedented opportunities to get to know their audiences and to match up content more closely to their needs and desires (Turow 2012). Because of improved signalling of audience preferences, the ability of content suppliers to trace, analyse, monitor and cater more effectively to shifting and specific tastes and interests amongst audiences has vastly increased. In addition, digital platforms allow for a much more engaged and intensive relationship between content suppliers and audiences, thus providing both creative and commercial opportunities (Napoli 2011).

Evidence gathered through interviews with senior personnel at the case study organizations suggests that, despite the continued importance for revenue generation of print versions of newspapers, all leading national newspapers in the United Kingdom now regard and present themselves as digital multi-platform entities. The Managing Editor of FT.com describes the *Financial Times* as "a multi-platform business" albeit one that has gradually more and more emphasis on digital (Carter 2012). According to a senior executive at Telegraph Media Group (TMG): "We are not a newspaper company. We are not a digital news company. We are both. And our goal is make them work lock step with one another which is not an easy task but at its best it works unbelievably well."

The requirements of being a digital multi-platform publisher differ from those of print newspaper publishing and so this journey has had a significant impact on the nature and the mix of resources (production skills, equipment, etc.) needed to successfully run a newspaper business. Thus, a process of renewal through re-allocation of resources is in progress right across the industry (Doyle 2014). This process can be dissected by examining in close detail how patterns of, for example, employment and staff usage within specific newspaper firms have changed over time. For instance at the TMG, the total number of employees in the newsroom remained relatively stable in the period from 2007 to 2012. However, during this time a pronounced re-direction in the activity of employees has been achieved through investment in developing and acquiring the specialist skills needed to ensure digital in addition to print delivery. The Digital Editor at TMG indicates that an estimated 25 per cent of staff effort was devoted to digital distribution at the end of 2012, versus less than 10 per cent five years earlier. The process of renewal through factor reallocation is ongoing at TMG and this is a fairly common sort of trend.

Although the exact extent and pace of change has varied across UK press groups, dynamic capability or the capacity to evolve and reconfigure in the face of changing environmental conditions (Helfat and Peteraf 2003; Teece et al. 1997) is clearly a source of potential advantage for individual firms. Looking across the UK's national newspapers as a whole, the general pattern of recent years has involved: (a) a progressive strengthening of digital skills, achieved partly through re-training but also new recruitment (in areas such as digital page editing, video production, interactive graphics, etc.); and (b) more investment in *equipment* to support digital multi-platform production and distribution, especially in content management systems (CMSs). These are the software systems that allow journalists to do a lot of the work on assembly, headlines, pictures, layout and so on that used to involve separate specialists; and new CMSs also make it easier to publish and distribute across multiple digital as well as the traditional print formats.

The effect of multi-platform publishing on news production and content

As well as transforming the nature of and the mix of resources needed to be a newspaper publisher, the journey towards digital multi-platform publishing has impacted heavily on the daily routines and workflows and on decisions about how to produce and present news content. Awareness of the multi-platform dimension and a desire to exploit digital distribution opportunities can affect the sort of news stories that are selected and how they are covered. Across the UK national newspaper sector, many managing editors agree that video, pictures and graphics are especially important in conveying a story on digital platforms and so the potential availability of, for example, an appealing video clip will in some cases affect the perceived newsworthiness of a content item under consideration.

Thus, distribution across digital platforms will to some extent shape the sort of news content that is selected and produced. According to the Digital Editor at TMG, digital distribution works especially well for high-profile stories with a strong visual element and immediacy. The Commercial Director of Times Newspapers agrees that, on account of digital distribution, immediacy is an imperative. When a story breaks journalists must now get something onto the website within fifteen minutes, whereas in the past they would have until the deadline for print production in the evening. The Managing Editor at the *Financial Times* concurs that the way in which stories need to be written up has changed, with more emphasis on blogs and on providing a "two paragraph quick news take" as opposed to lengthy analytical pieces.

Another way in which content is being re-shaped in response to delivery across digital platforms stems from the two-way data flows facilitated by digital technology. At the same time as news content is supplied on digital platforms, the availability of data coming back to the supplier along the return path about the ways in which that content is being used ensures that editorial teams are provided with much increased and improved information about what readers like and dislike (Turow 2012).

Tagging of digital data means that editors and journalists now know which elements of content are particularly appealing and this intelligence can impress itself over what is supplied in numerous ways.

In the newsrooms of most major UK newspaper groups, screens that convey web analytics in real time are an increasingly prominent presence, providing vast volumes of information in a constant feedback loop. So, as well as monitoring a range of potential sources of news stories (now including social media), journalists and editors are now also monitoring and responding to real time data on screens telling them which stories are trending and receiving most attention on social media. Such feedback often has an immediate effect on the positioning and prominence given to news items and on how much coverage they receive. At the *Telegraph* for example, daily news conferences for print and digital are chaired by the same overall editor and, according to the Digital Editor, selection of stories is strongly informed by data "on what is doing well on Google, on Twitter, on Facebook, on our own site".

Analysis of return path data at an aggregate level (that is, across the full readership for any title) currently provides valuable information that can help editors to broadly re-shape and improve their content offerings. However, for the Digital Editor of TMG, the future will involve greater use of more granular and individualized return path data to tailor the product more effectively. The view that figuring out how best to use return path data to provide individually tailored content services will be vital in future is not confined to newspapers but is shared by senior executives in the UK television sector, including at the British Broadcasting Corporation (BBC). Looking beyond the UK media industry, some online content providers such as Yahoo are already proficient in using the digital return path to gather signals about tastes and preferences and to target and shape delivery at the levels of individual consumers, for example by varying what is displayed on the home page from one receiving device to the next, based on historic consumption behaviours (Doyle 2013).

While digital delivery makes automated customization entirely feasible in technological terms, it is questionable to what extent a move towards fuller reliance on algorithm-driven tailoring of content makes sound business sense. A number of senior managers at UK national newspapers interviewed in 2013 were adamant that part of the ongoing value and appeal of newspapers and of newspaper brands stems from the editorializing function carried out by editors and journalists that give each title its distinctive voice. Therefore, while the additional data about audience preferences collected via the return path is regarded as being of significant value, in the words of one *FT* executive, "editing by numbers" is something that most newspapers want to avoid.

An additional concern about moving towards catering to individual rather than mass audiences is that, as the Commercial Manager of News International put it, producing high-quality, professionally crafted news content is expensive and so, irrespective of technological advances, the newspaper business remains reliant on being able to spread costs over a large number of readers/users. In essence, a potential danger is that strategies of personalization may cut across publishers' ability to harvest the scale economies that have long been integral to the business of news publishing.

The migration to a multi-platform approach has entailed a need not only for new sorts of resources in newsrooms and new thinking about news content but also for changes in patterns of work. For most national UK titles (although not the *Daily Mail*), the transition from print to print plus digital distribution has been accompanied by a restructuring of news production operations to facilitate converged content creation for both print and digital editions. Earlier newsroom studies have highlighted challenges surrounding embedding a fully converged multiplatform and/or "digital first" approach to news content creation (Bressers 2009; Erdal 2011). Our research into the United Kingdom's national newspaper sector confirms that, despite the economic imperatives that favour a joint or converged approach to news production, achieving this is beset by many challenges, not least amongst which is the tendency for the traditional routines and values associated with print to continue to reign supreme notwithstanding the progressive ascendancy of the needs of the digital end user.

For an emerging web-connected generation, the means and habits by which content is consumed in an online context – involving short and frequent visits to news sources – is very different from traditional approaches to consumption of print newspapers. Subscribers to a digital news content service generally expect to make multiple visits per day to the service in question so the need, on digital delivery platforms, for engaging content that is frequently refreshed and updated is great. However, achieving a news production culture in which journalists post fresh content around the clock is somewhat at odds with the eleven hour daily window within which most journalists typically work and with the twenty-four hour print cycle with a deadline every evening that has traditionally dominated in print newspaper publishing.

Achieving a fully converged or integrated approach to print/digital news production is, according to the Digital Editor at TMG, an ongoing process with several stages still to go through. It involves a change of mindset amongst journalists with more orientation towards "the digital side, because that's where the growth is in terms of audience and revenues". For example, the section head for motoring should be using digital platforms to gauge and engage the interests of readers via blogs and email alerts and "from waking up in the morning [should be] thinking about what is obsessing petrol heads and commissioning stories about that; writing about it and living and breathing the web".

On account of the large volume of feedback about user preferences available to newspaper publishers via the return path, it is now possible for editors to assess not only which sorts of news stories and other content items are popular, and with whom, but also what periods in the day the peaks and troughs occur in online consumption of digital content. At the *Financial Times* for example, managers have at their disposal large volumes of return path data indicating when the peak periods occur in terms of subscriber engagement with FT.com content. They know the times of day when the FT's online content service is being most heavily used by its subscribers and typically these are in the early morning and at lunch time in the United Kingdom and in the United States. So in order to cater effectively to the appetites of digital subscribers it would make sense to refresh online content at times that fit with these consumption patterns. Yet, as one senior manager interviewed in November 2012 conceded, it remained the case at that time that, typically, an analysis of the number of stories published every hour at FT.com throughout a twenty-four hour period would show a very marked increase in the early evening when the print edition of the newspaper is approaching its production deadline (Doyle 2014).

Despite the availability of copious return path data, a misalignment still occurs between spikes in usage of online versions of newspapers and the daily publication cycle. This was a key concern addressed in an open memo from the *Financial Times'* Editor Lionel Barber to the newspaper's staff in October 2013 calling for greater flexibility in work practices and for journalists to "publish stories to meet peak viewing times on the web rather than old print deadlines" (Barber 2013b). This misalignment reflects a stubborn adherence within newspaper publishing to the traditional routines and practices of print production. Many staff are still working to the deadlines that were right for the print era but this does not suit the needs of the digital era and this tendency is widespread right across the newspaper industry and overseas, including at leading titles such as the *Wall Street Journal* (Romenesko 2013).

Earlier work examining transition to a multi-platform approach within the UK television industry has identified how, in television as well as in print publishing, overcoming a prevailing orthodoxy in which traditional production cultures continue to hold sway represents a particular challenging aspect of adjustment to a digitized world (Bennett and Strange 2012). Amongst newspapers, the strength of traditional print routines continues to restrain recalibration of workflows. The supremacy of traditional print journalistic culture can impact on processes of business innovation too since, according to interviewees, one of the conditions required to foster successful experimentation is close integration between information technology specialists and journalistic staff (Doyle 2014).

Reflections on implications for policy

Despite the challenges involved, a key motive driving newspapers to become digital multi-platform publishers is in order to diversify revenues and reduce reliance on print sales (Picard 2011). Many are experimenting with the use of interactivity as a means of building new income streams, for example through deploying data-driven marketing techniques to increase digital subscriber levels (as *FT.com* does) and through use of return path data to sell behavioural advertising (as *Mail Online* and most other titles do). However, newspapers are faced with some very serious competitive threats in the digital arena from, for example, social networking services such as Facebook that generally are much better placed to gather detailed consumer data and to sell targeted behavioural advertising and from the rise of automated advertising sales (Goldfarb 2013; Fuchs 2012).

Thus, many have sought to move beyond the traditional mainstays of reader payments plus advertising by developing a range of online income generating activities such as retailing, membership clubs and online gaming that capitalize on high volumes of consumer traffic surrounding news content on digital platforms. The cultivation of new streams of income in some instances involves full-scale downstream diversification into online activities and markets that are in fact quite distinct from the core business of news provision. Newspapers such as the *Telegraph*, *The Times* and the *Daily Mail* have developed new websites that function as separate standalone businesses, for instance selling holidays or cars or offering e-recruitment services or last-minute deals. While some of these distinct new businesses areas involve elements that are complementary to news publishing (for example, because they allow for re-use of editorial content or data sharing with the newspaper or cross-marketing), the new ventures are not necessarily functionally interdependent with news publishing (Doyle 2014).

Diversification away from news publishing raises questions about strategic coherence given that, in the words of one senior UK newspaper executive, the specialist skills involved in operating shopping and gaming businesses "are not [necessarily] native to newspaper publishing". However, an additional concern relates to the potential for blurring of the lines between editorial and commercially driven content. The inter-viewees spoken with in the course of our research were alert to this concern and to the need for transparency and for editors to vigorously maintain the independence and integrity of news content. However, the more that newspaper groups gather within their ambit new and unrelated commercial activities that feed off the traction around online news, the greater the potential for a clash between the commercial and editorial aims invested in provision of that content.

Another issue of likely interest for policymakers stemming from the migration to multi-platform delivery relates to the increasing propensity amongst newspapers and other media suppliers to collect data via digital return paths about the behaviours and habits of consumers. Amongst leading UK newspaper groups, it is now common practice to use return path data at least at an aggregate level – but where feasible at an individual level too – partly in order to tailor and improve content delivery but also in order to sell behavioural advertising. Publishers of newspapers and magazines and also television broadcasters are increasingly alert to the advantages of registration systems that enable the collection and use of data at a granular level about the pre-ferences, tastes and habits of readers and users. As Turow (2012: 89) notes, "[t]he quiet use of databases that combine demographic information about individuals with widely circulated conclusions about what their clicks say about them presents to advertisers personalized views of hundreds of millions of Americans every day without their knowledge". The increasing use of personal data raises concerns not only in relation to intrusions against the privacy of individuals but also about the potential for undisclosed profiling and related risks of social discrimination (Goldfarb and Tucker 2011).

At a time when pluralism is a recurrent theme on national and international policy agendas, another potential concern is how the adoption of a multi-platform outlook is affecting diversity of content. One aspect of the transition to distribution across digital platforms that raises questions for pluralism is that of personalized products. To the extent that use of return path data by news media to tailor and individualize services so that they contain only those stories deemed to be of relevance to any particular reader (thus assisting targeted advertising) is on the increase, from the individual reader's point of view such filtering comes at the cost of a progressive diminution in the range and diversity of content to which s/he is exposed.

Another concern is how the advent of multi-platform distribution is affecting diversity within the composition of output supplied by such major national UK title brands as *The Times*, the *Telegraph* and the *Guardian*. It is clear that the transition to multi-platform distribution has multiplied the overall volume of news output pub-lished under the auspices of each of these brands since, instead of constituting just a print product, the "newspaper" is now supplied simultaneously in digital versions. Our research findings suggest that the number of staff involved in leading UK newspaper groups has in some cases decreased and in others grown but overall levels of newsroom staffing generally remained relatively stable over the period 2007–12 (Doyle 2014). During this same period, the volume of outputs produced by newspapers has multiplied enormously – readers are now supplied with online, tablet and mobile versions of newspapers and with a plethora of accompanying outputs from leading journalists across social media. At first glance, it seems fair to conclude that cost-efficiency within news production has improved dramatically. But how is the composition of news output changing? To what extent is multi-platform publishing contributing to a widening of content diversity and choice or, conversely, in what ways is it encouraging recycling of the same content across multiple platforms and greater emphasis on a narrow range of high impact?

According to the Digital Editor at TMG, the transition to multi-platform distribution has vastly increased the volume of output of the *Telegraph* and, to some extent, has increased diversity with more blogs, video content and picture galleries and with many more stories published online than appear in the paper. On the other hand more "papers are slowly recognizing the need to attach their brands to a smaller number of areas of expertise" in order to reinforce and sustain their own clear identity. He argues that producing a larger number of stories is not necessarily advantageous to the strategic positioning and profitability of a newspaper:

> if you said to a journalist five years ago, "by the way for your information we are going to double the outputs of content" they would have been up in arms saying we would destroy standards and all the rest of it. And actually no one asked them to do that – no one said "double your outputs". But they did it anyway. [But] that may not be a good thing. There is no compelling evidence that producing an ever-greater number of stories is good for your business. You could certainly argue the reverse – that it is about *quality* not volume. About having a distinctive brand built around a smaller number of stories.

Likewise at the *Financial Times* the volume of news output has multiplied massively from twenty years ago when all that existed was a single print version. The Managing Editor confirms that there are more stories and a greater diversity of content on the web version than in the print newspaper but he questions whether having such a "long tail" is ideal and says it exists partly because they are still working to establish "what works on the web". As integration across digital and print has progressed, a redirection of resource in favour of digital has resulted in the print newspaper becoming more "simplified". The Managing Editor explains that whereas in the past four different regional editions plus different time editions were published, efforts are now being made to cut back to a more common global edition. This was confirmed in a memo from *Financial Times* Editor Lionel Barber to staff in January 2013 that spoke of the need to "sharpen" commissioning in order to produce content for a more selective, common paper with emphasis on priority stories (Barber 2013a). A subsequent open memo confirmed that the transition to a single print edition of the *Financial Times* will go ahead in the first half of 2014 (Barber 2013b).

In general, a converged approach to content production has facilitated and encouraged an emphasis on potentially high-impact stories, stories that reinforce distinctive brands and the re-use of content across platforms. According to the Commercial Director of News International, the additional resource involved in creating each digital version of *The Times* is "the equivalent of producing another edition – it is no more or less than that … because your basic content is already prepared". The view that digital output is largely a recycled version of print news content tends to support conclusions from an earlier empirical study carried out at Goldsmith's College in London into how digitization is affecting news production. This study found that the Internet has not, in fact, expanded the news we read or hear nor changed mainstream news values and formats but rather has contributed to a relentless recycling of content across platforms which, while making it easier to access news at all times, may at the same time be harmful to quality and diversity (Fenton 2010). And similar findings emerge in earlier research about how migration in the television industry towards a multi-platform approach is affecting content: a common response amongst broadcasters is to focus on producing fewer and bigger programme ideas across several platforms (as opposed to several smaller productions) and to place more emphasis on high-profile projects with extended life spans (Doyle 2010). Thus, as the question of how best to promote pluralism and diversity in an era of technological change is under consideration by policymakers both in the UK and Europe, it is worth remembering that the media industry's migration to a multi-platform approach to distribution, while unquestionably extending opportunities for consumption of content, is also propelling strategies of brand extension, content recycling and the relentless market presence of a limited number of high-profile content properties.

Note

1 This is a UK Economic and Social Research Council funded project titled "Multi-platform media and the digital challenge: Strategy, distribution and policy", which runs from July 2012–June 2015. Principal Investigator: Gillian Doyle; Co-Investigator: Philip Schlesinger; Research Associate: Katherine Champion.

References

Barber, L. (2013a) "Lionel Barber's Email to FT Staff Outlining Digital-first Strategy", *Guardian*, 21 January (accessed 13 December 2013: www.theguardian.com/media/2013/jan/21/lionel-barber-email-financial-times).

Barber, L. (2013b) "Lionel Barber Memo to Staff on Reshaping the Newspaper for the Digital Age", *Financial Times*, 9 October (accessed 13 December 2013: aboutus.ft.com/2013/10/09/lionel-barber-memo-to-staff-on-reshaping-the-newspaper-for-the-digital-age/#axzz2nLqtkmY3).

Bennett, J. and Strange, N. (2012) "Linear Legacies: Managing the Multiplatform Production Process", in D. Kompare, D. Johnson and A. Santo (eds), *Intermediaries: Cultures of Management/Management of Culture*, New York: NYU Press.

Bressers, B. (2009) "Promise and Reality: The Integration of Print and Online Versions of Major Metropolitan Newspapers", *International Journal on Media Management*, 8 (3): 134–45.

Brock, G. (2013) *Out of Print: Newspapers, Journalism and the Business of News in the Digital Age*, London: Kogan Page.

Carter, M. (2012) "Rob Grimshaw – Interview", *InPublishing Magazine* (accessed 13 December 2013: www.inpublishing.co.uk/kb/articles/rob_grimshaw_interview.aspx).

Doyle, G. (2010) "From Television to Multi-Platform: More For Less or Less From More?" *Convergence*, 16 (4): 1–19.

Doyle, G. (2013) *Understanding Media Economics*, 2nd edition, London: Sage.

Doyle, G. (2014) "Re-invention and Survival: Newspapers in the Era of Digital Multi-platform Delivery", *Journal of Media Business Studies*, 10(4): 1–20.

Erdal, I. (2011), "Coming to Terms with Convergence Journalism: Cross-media as a Theoretical and Analytical Concept", *Convergence*, 17 (2): 213–23.

Fenton, N. (ed.) (2010) *New Media, Old News: Journalism and Democracy in the Digital Age*, London: Sage.

Fuchs, C. (2012) "The Political Economy of Privacy on Facebook", *Television New Media*, 13 (2): 139–59.

Goldfarb, A. (2013) "What is Different About Online Advertising?" *Review of Industrial Organization*, 42: 63–83.

Goldfarb, A. and Tucker, C. (2011) "Privacy Regulation and Online Advertising", *Management Science*, 57 (1): 57–71.

Graham, G. and Smart, A. (2010) "The Regional-Newspaper Industry Supply Chain and the Internet", *Supply Chain Management: An International Journal*, 15 (3): 196–206.

Helfat, C. and Peteraf, M. (2003) "The Dynamic Resource-based View: Capability Lifecycles", *Strategic Management Journal*, 24 (10): 997–1010.

Holm, A., Günzel, F. and Ulhøi, J. (2013) "Openness in Innovation and Business Models: Lessons from the Newspaper Industry", *International Journal of Technology Management*, 61 (3/4): 324–48.

Kirchhoff, S. (2010) "The US Newspaper Industry in Transition", *Congressional Research Service*, Ref 7–5700 R40700 (accessed 13 December 2013: www.fas.org/sgp/crs/misc/R40700.pdf).

Mitchelstein, E. and Boczkowski, P. (2009) "Between Tradition and Change", *Journalism*, 10 (5): 562–86.

Napoli, P. (2011) *Audience Evolution: New Technologies and the Transformation of Media Audiences*, New York: Columbia University Press.

Ofcom (2013) *Communications Market Report*, London: Ofcom.

Owen, S. and Wildman, S. (1992) *Video Economics*, Cambridge, MA: Harvard University Press.

Picard, R. (2011) *Mapping Digital Media: Digitization and Media Business Models*, London: Open Society Foundation.

Romenesko, J. (2013) "WSJ Staffers Told to 'Stay the Course – and Accelerate'", Jimromenesko.com (accessed 13 December 2013: jimromenesko.com/2013/03/10/wsj-staffers-told-to-stay-the-course-and-accelerate/).

Siles, I. and Boczkowski, P. (2012) "Making Sense of the Newspaper Crisis: A Critical Assessment of Existing Research and an Agenda for Future Work", *New Media and Society*, 14 (8): 1375–94.

Storsul, T. and Krumsvik, A. (eds) (2013) *Media Innovations: A Multidisciplinary Study of Change*, Gothenburg: Nordicom.

Teece, D., Pisano, G. and Shuen, A. (1997) "Dynamic Capabilities and Strategic Management", *Strategic Management Journal*, 18 (7): 509–33.

Turow, J. (2012) *The Daily You: How the New Advertising Industry is Defining Your Identity and Your Worth*, Newhaven, CT: Yale University Press.

8

THE RESILIENCE OF TV AND ITS IMPLICATIONS FOR MEDIA POLICY

Des Freedman

Introduction

Watching television continues to dominate a large part of our waking hours and yet it occupies a bafflingly small part of the media policy agenda in places like the United Kingdom and the United States. Why might this be the case? Perhaps because it represents a declining passion and a fading industry that has been overtaken by digital pursuits? Not according to the data presented in this chapter that suggests the opposite: that television is stubbornly popular and set to play a decisive role in the new online media ecology. Perhaps then because of a reluctance to get involved in questions of "content" for fear of undermining First Amendment and media freedom principles. This might be more persuasive if it were not for the very decisive interventions curbing freedom of expression that we have seen in recent years from the use of the Espionage Act by the Obama administration to intimidate journalists (CPJ 2013) to prime minister David Cameron's warning to British journalists to show "social responsibility" in the reporting of state secrets (Watt 2013). When pressed, few administrations show that much fear in calling for content controls.

More likely, it is simply because contemporary policymaking is far more comfortable when dealing with questions of technology and infrastructure than it is when engaging with purposeful or progressive interventions into media structures. Yet these policy initiatives have often been at the heart of our media systems – from an institution like the British Broadcasting Corporation (BBC), itself nothing more than a creature of public policy, to instruments like the Fairness Doctrine and the "Fin-Syn" rules in the United States that sought to promote more marginal voices and to prevent the monopolization of the airwaves by only a handful of companies. In neoliberal times, however, it is market logic rather than the public interest that is deemed to drive innovation and to satisfy consumers and therefore there is significant pressure on all parts of the media to deliver economic efficiency, brand value and export potential as the most desirable public policy objectives. In this context, markets have been liberalized, public service broadcasters disciplined and technology fetishized (Freedman 2008).

Recent communications policy in the United Kingdom epitomizes this approach. The policy agenda is overwhelmingly focused on building and securing the digital economy and has therefore prioritized questions of broadband connectivity, intellectual property, consumer safety and affordability (DCMS 2013) above the need to nurture a creative infrastructure that is capable of delivering quality content to diverse audiences about a range of issues and in a variety of registers. Policymakers' attention is focused less on the resources and institutions necessary to make the broadcast content that audiences continue to consume in their millions than on stimulating broadband roll-out and updating regulatory structures to meet the demands of an evolving digital environment. Yet broadcast audiences keep growing and demonstrate a resilience that seems more than a little surprising given the predictions made by George Gilder nearly twenty-five years ago of a "life after television" (Gilder 1994).

This chapter reflects on why UK policymakers are not directing public resources towards and focusing attention on television, despite the vital role it plays in the daily lives of citizens and provides us with such a crucial framework through which to make sense of the world. It also highlights the need to challenge the increasing enclosure of free-to-air programmes, given the fact that "inclusion" and "connectivity" are such policy buzzwords. The current "hands off" approach to policy means that television is largely at the mercy of a market sensibility (not just in commercial but also in public service broadcasting) that is not able to distribute cultural resources on an equitable basis. I want to argue instead for a commitment to the redistribution of resources and a paradigm shift inside policy debates to ensure that there is a more democratic institutional arrangement inside the broadcast media so that citizens are more adequately represented and private interests are more effectively regulated in the public interest.

Television is not dead

Television viewing is increasing. The measurement of TV consumption is far from perfect and different surveys tend to produce different results. However, one conclusion remains clear: television viewing is far from disappearing and, indeed, we appear to be watching *more* rather than less TV. In the United States, average daily consumption of TV has increased nearly 20 per cent, from 264 minutes in 2010 to 311 minutes in 2013 (Statistic Brain 2013). Even in studies that show slightly different figures, viewers still manage to spend some 271 minutes per day with television, in contrast to the 309 minutes they spent with digital platforms (Steel 2013). Of course, given that it is not clear how much of this latter figure is accounted for by online viewing of television or television-like content, it would be premature to suggest here that broadcast consumption is declining.

In the United Kingdom, the communications regulator Ofcom (2013a: 127) reports that average viewing has increased from 218 minutes per day in 2007 to 240 minutes in 2012, a 10 per cent rise. The figure varies across different demographics so while it is true that those aged above 65 are by far the heaviest consumers of TV, "digital natives" – those aged between 16 and 24 who were predicted to lead the exodus from a supposedly obsolete technology – watch exactly the same amount of TV as the same age group did back in 2004: two hours and thirty-six minutes a day (Ofcom 2013a: 182).

The grip of television on our cultural habits is even more pronounced when we compare TV viewing to time spent, for example, with Facebook or Twitter. While those in the United Kingdom watch TV for some 7,000 minutes per month, they spend a mere 484 minutes a month on Facebook or a paltry thirty-three minutes a month using Twitter (Ofcom 2013a: 299). In the United States, average monthly use of Facebook was higher at 1,105 minutes per month (Statista 2013), but nevertheless marginal in comparison to the more than 9,000 minutes spent in front of the TV. In fact, far from undermining the appeal of TV, social media innovations have merely extended its allure, offering audiences new possibilities to converse, comment and interact with each other and with the programmes. It is widely acknowledged that Twitter, for example, has improved the viewing experience of everything from the BBC's politics panel show *Question Time* to the international format behemoth *X Factor*. Partnering with, not squashing, social media is now the accepted corporate strategy, particularly in relation to "media events" like the Superbowl in the United States or the Christmas period in the United Kingdom when hugely expensive advertisements are aired to lucrative mass audiences who have already been "warmed up" with campaigns run on social media channels. The 2013 Christmas commercial for retail giant John Lewis involved a "film-style 'premiere'" that took up an entire ad break during the programme *X Factor*, having already been "teased" on social media. The company spent £6 million on buying the television airtime and a further £1 million on social media and other channels (Butler 2013).

Not surprisingly, therefore, television's continuing popularity means that advertisers are still willing to invest a vast amount of money in TV, an amount that is expected to grow in the next few years. The influential Magna Global report revealed that in 2013 television accounted for 40 per cent of all US advertising, a higher proportion than that directed online (Magna Global 2013). Even in the United Kingdom, where online advertising is now the dominant form, TV advertising revenue is expected to reach record levels, nearly £4 billion, in 2014 (Deans 2013). This, along with growth in subscription payments, has contributed to a 10 per cent growth in overall television revenue in the UK in the last five years, rising from £11 billion in 2007 to £12.3 billion in 2012 (Ofcom 2013a: 21). Money is flowing *into* and not *out of* television.

So despite predictions that TV would lose viewers and interest when faced with the enormity of the challenge from digital developments and social media, it appears that it has continued to make itself relevant to a range of audiences across different demographics. Indeed, despite the challenges from a range of new devices, television remains by far the most ingrained and popular activity: while 20 per cent of the public would miss their mobile phones the most, some 43 per cent would miss watching TV (Ofcom 2013a: 27). Despite the challenge from online sources, TV remains easily "the most important and frequently-used mode of news consumption" (Ofcom 2013a: 105) with 78 per cent of the UK population relying on television news compared to 40 per cent for newspapers, 35 per cent for radio and only 32 per cent for online platforms (Ofcom 2013a: 105).

It is not the case that nothing has changed – television has undergone a huge transformation in the last generation, shifting from analogue to digital, low to high resolution, "stupid" to "smart", live at the point of consumption to asynchronous and, of course, from a handful of channels to multichannel – but that these changes also involve a significant continuity of experience. As one business report notes, "Television today is little changed from a decade ago and yet at the same time profoundly different. The ways in which we consume television have altered relatively little, but supply has evolved markedly" (Deloitte 2012: 1) with the emergence of new content providers, distribution mechanisms and funding streams. To understand television today is to appreciate both the continuity of its appeal as a creative form and the transformation of how this form is delivered to audiences.

Public service channels still have most of the audience. Television viewing in the United Kingdom is still largely dominated by the five free-to-air public service broadcasting (PSB) channels operated by the BBC, ITV, Channel 4 and 5. Recent figures show that these channels had an audience share of 52 per cent of all households (Ofcom 2013a: 188), a significant decline since 2004 when they accounted for nearly three-quarters of all viewing. However, this is more than compensated for by the growth in viewing of their "portfolio" channels like BBC3, ITV2, More4 and E4. The success of these channels has meant that audiences for the total output of the PSB operators in multichannel homes have actually stayed pretty constant, with a 72.9 per cent share in 2012. Despite the view that multichannel television has fragmented the audience and diminished the appeal of the traditional broadcasters, the share of PSB viewing in multichannel homes has actually increased. Viewing of non-PSB channels, on the other hand, has actually declined – from 35 per cent of viewing in 2004 to 27 per cent in 2012 (Ofcom 2013a: 193).

Of course, it is true that BBC1 and ITV1 do not have the stranglehold over audiences that they used to exert, falling from a combined 53.5 per cent share in 2004 to only 36 per cent in 2012, but their influence is qualitatively greater than any other non-PSB channel. For example, the most popular pay TV channel, Sky Sports 1, attracts a mere 1.2 per cent of the multichannel audience (Ofcom 2013a: 200) while the *total* share for Sky programmes (including all of its sports, movies, news and entertainment channels) has actually fallen from 10.4 per cent in 2004 to 8.3 per cent in 2012 (Ofcom 2013a: 194). Let us make this clear: in the midst of a decisive shift from analogue to digital television and given the growth of multichannel television, the share of both the BBC and ITV in multichannel homes has *increased* since 2004 while that of the largest pay TV company, BSkyB, has *decreased*. This is probably not the headline you will see in any news bulletin, nor are you likely to discover that, while trust in the British press is amongst the lowest in Europe, over three-quarters of the British public are either "quite" or "very satisfied" with public service broadcasting (Ofcom 2013b: 12).

Changes in viewing and consumption habits are often overstated. We need carefully to consider discourses about the inevitability of the digital "revolution" that underpin the thinking of leading policy actors about whether the popularization of digital technologies may make traditional media regulation obsolete. For example, many have long predicted the radical impact of digital video recorders (DVRs) on the viewing experience, with the former BBC director general Greg Dyke describing them at the turn of this century as "the real revolution" (BBC 2000). Yet most recent figures themselves show something rather different: that while 67 per cent of households now have a DVR, some 90 per cent of viewing even in these homes remains live (Ofcom 2013a: 202). If we break this down more, we find that of the 10 per cent that is "time shifted", just under half is watched on the same day with the remainder consumed within a week of the original broadcast. Research by Enders Analysis reveals higher levels of timeshift viewing with some 19 per cent of viewing taking place "after the event", but even here, Enders admit that, since 2007 the share of timeshift viewing "has remained very stable, underlining its importance as a second line of choice after an initial search through the main broadcast channels" (Enders Analysis 2013: 7). Indeed, personal recording technology has not displaced but instead "reinforced the appeal of the live linear schedule" (2013: 8). Despite the increasing popularity of catch-up TV, and in particular the BBC's iPlayer, the viewing experience remains overwhelmingly a live one. This is also the case in the United States, where, despite many predictions of an on-demand environment, more than 90 per cent of TV viewing remained live in 2012, with 278 minutes consumed every day in traditional linear fashion as opposed to twenty-four minutes that were time shifted (Poggi 2012).

PSB channels dominate investment in UK programming. Public service channels account for a majority of spending on UK television – £2.9 billion out of £5.6 billion in total (Ofcom 2013a: 166–67), and certainly make up by far the biggest proportion of investment in original UK programming. The £2.6 billion spent on original output in 2012 was only slightly less than the *total* spend on all programming by commercial multichannels of £2.7billion, 65 per cent of which is taken up by buying rights for sport and films alone (Ofcom 2013a: 176). Indeed, BSkyB's promise to invest £600 million per year on original homegrown content by the end of 2014 seems a rather paltry one in relation to its enormous revenue and healthy profits: £7.2 billion and £1.33 billion respectively in 2013 (BSkyB 2013: 30), far exceeding those of its rivals. This disjuncture between revenue and the commissioning of original output is rarely commented on and certainly not seen as an issue for public policy. Sylvia Harvey is right to describe this reluctance to confront pay TV's priorities as "one of neoliberalism's blindspots": that "there is an inability or unwillingness to see that it is the lauded and arguably most competitive television that invests the least in original production" (Harvey 2006: 105).

The enclosure of television

Given the fact that television viewing remains incredibly important in the midst of a digital "revolution", we ought to be asking what resources are necessary to secure a television service that fully serves and reflects the population. The problem is that the dominant policy and regulatory responses to existing habits and emerging platforms is failing to secure these resources on behalf of the public. We are instead in the grip of a commitment to market forces and an uncritical celebration of technological innovation that threatens radically to disrupt the shared public spaces historically offered by broadcasting and that ought to be offered by social media platforms in the future. It is now a truism to say that the citizen inside media policy has been displaced by the consumer (Livingstone et al. 2007).

The result is that while more money is now being invested in TV content, it is not being shared out evenly and is systematically skewed towards certain genres and channels. Much more money is being spent on film and sport channels whose budgets have shot up up by just over 50 per cent since 2007. This compares to a small rise of 6 per cent for BBC1 and falls in spending for the other main channels: 18 per cent for BBC2, 4 per cent for ITV1 and 7 per cent for Channel 4, the home of independent production (Ofcom 2011: 121; 2013a: 167). Spending on PSB output has fallen in total by 17 per cent in the last five years (Ofcom 2013b: 17). While the total hours of first-run originated peak-time output on PSB channels is pretty much the same as it was in 2007, it has substantially decreased outside of peak hours and by some 7 per cent in terms of regional output. Spend on original material, however, has been really squeezed: down by 7 per cent on BBC1 since 2007, 28 per cent on BBC2, 13 per cent on ITV1, 13 per cent on Channel Four and 4 per cent on Channel 5 (Ofcom 2013b: 22) making up a total decrease in investment in original programming on PSB channels of just under 25 per cent since a high point between 2002–4 (Ofcom 2013b: 18).

Some genres have been especially affected by this redistribution of PSB spend. Despite the emergence of new digital platforms, news budgets in 2012 were down by 13 per cent since 2007, arts by a huge 40 per cent, education by 41 per cent and children's programmes by 23 per cent (Ofcom 2013b: 26). Spend on factual programming has decreased by 22 per cent in the last five years despite a significant increase in the number of hours, which points to a redefinition of "factual programming" towards lower cost, lifestyle output. To put it simply, those genres that have long been at the heart of the public service project have been hit the hardest, while only one genre has had spending increased: sports, where investment has risen by 16 per cent (2013b: 26). Of course, this is all relative and public service broadcasters still managed to spend over half a billion pounds on original drama in 2012 but the direction of travel is, nevertheless, a warning. Spending is being directed towards those genres that are likely to be most profitable – or rather removed from those genres with little obvious commercial viability.

What is the response from viewers? As I have already pointed out, consumption continues to rise but substantially more people think that TV is getting worse than getting better (31 per cent in contrast to 13 per cent), although for the over 65s a near majority (48 per cent) think it is deteriorating while only 8 per cent think it is improving. What accounts for this perception of decline? Overwhelmingly, it is *not* because of concerns with bad language, violence or sex but simply because of "more repeats", a "lack of variety" and "more reality shows" (Ofcom 2011: 154). This is a question of funding priorities and not of moral decline.

We should also be concerned about the wider implications of a shift to subscription-based viewing and, especially, about the grip of Sky on pay TV. Subscription is now by far the dominant source of revenue in UK television and has risen from 34 per cent in 2004 to 43 per cent of total broadcast revenue in 2012, well above that of advertising (less than 30 per cent) and licence fee income (only 22 per cent). What this means is that, adding together subscription revenue and the proportion of advertising that goes to pay channels, more than 50 per cent of all revenue is generated from only 27 per cent of the viewing audience (Ofcom 2013a: 179) – a section of the population that is super-exploited and under-served in the provision of UK originated content.

The significance of subscription as the dominant form of television revenue has an added impact in that increasing amounts of content are now being hidden behind rather expensive paywalls. We are seeing, therefore, the simultaneous driving down of investment in original content in key genres at the same time as the *enclosure* of other forms of content. While 59 per cent of regular sports viewers see Premier League football as "must have content" (OECD 2013: 4), they are forced to pay premium prices for it, in part to cover the enormous costs of acquiring football rights – most recently the £3 billion paid by Sky and BT in 2012 for three years of live coverage. Sky also signed an exclusive deal with HBO in 2010, worth around £150 million over five years, to have exclusive access to both first-run and archive HBO programmes including *Boardwalk Empire*, *Treme*, *Entourage* and *Curb Your Enthusiasm*. As we have already noted, Sky's promised to spend £600 million on original UK material by the end of 2014 is aimed at channels including Sky One, with a 0.9 per cent audience share, and the two Sky Arts channels, each of which currently have an average weekly viewing of one minute, with Sky Arts 1 registering a 0.1 per cent share and Sky Arts 2 registering *nothing at all* (BARB 2013). Of course, we should welcome any new investment in original programming, but what if it is going into gated communities aimed thus far at a tiny minority of people who happen to get the channels because, by and large, they are sports fans who have little choice except to subscribe if they are to watch their favourite football teams? Public money aimed at mass audiences is being replaced by private money aimed at lucrative subscription audiences in a twenty-first century iteration of the vision of Alan Peacock who was commissioned by Margaret Thatcher in 1985 to develop proposals for a more market-friendly TV structure (Goodwin 1998).

The saturation of market logic in the policy process

Should the near-disappearance of programmes like *Mad Men* and *Boardwalk Empire* be seen as a public policy question, or is this simply how the market operates? This is a moot question as, despite its popularity, it is not television that provides the organizing logic for contemporary media policy but the internet as part of a more general transition to a digital environment. This has obvious implications for how, and whether, we can continue to regulate the broadcast media in the public interest given a stated preference, particularly in relation to digital platforms, to pursue self- and co-regulation. The previous UK government's *Digital Britain* white paper argued that we are now at a "tipping point" (BIS/DCMS 2009: 11) in relation to the transformative impact of the internet on our media environments and insisted that, when it comes to public service broadcasting, we need "to address the place for intervention and the transition in the type of intervention as we move from the analogue to the fully digital world" (2009: 18). The message here is clear: in an on-demand world characterized by abundance and consumer choice, there is little scope for purposeful interventions to address inequalities in representation and access, such as the marginalization of women on screen and in the industry (Doherty 2012) and the stereotyping of working class people (Jones 2013).

Instead, there is a focus on consumer rights and questions of efficiency and affordability. The UK government's latest media policy statement is called *Connectivity*,

Content and Consumers (DCMS 2013) and subordinates content issues to those of broadband development, spectrum management and consumer safety in the context of the overall need to achieve economic growth. Its proposals to support "world-beating content", in other words content that is easily exportable and thus valuable, is almost entirely economically or technologically determined: to maintain the prominence of public service broadcasters at the top of the Electronic Programme Guide, to provide tax breaks for digital media content and to target intellectual property crime (DCMS 2013: 24–30). Where it does mention proactive regulation, it is only to minimize it by reducing Ofcom's duties in relation to public service broadcasters in order "to reduce unnecessary burdens" (2013: 9). The only recognition of an imbalance in the programme supply market is its wish to see the end of payments made by PSBs to pay TV operators to carry their programmes – a scandal that ought to have been terminated some time ago. Overall, while it is entirely legitimate to reflect on the impact of digital technologies on market and consumer behaviour, there is an incredibly narrow focus on competition and absolutely no conception of how best to produce and sustain content that is not privileged by the market.

More disturbing, however, is the UK government's assessment that everything is rosy in the world of British television. Far from identifying any problems in terms of content production and distribution, the government insists that "[o]ur discussions with industry and others demonstrated that the present framework is broadly working well, supporting economic growth and innovation, and the things that we value as a society: high-quality news, radio and TV programmes" (DCMS 2013: 6). As I have already attempted to show, this is not the case and budgets for key areas and genres enjoyed by millions are either declining or being siphoned off and segregated behind exclusive cordons. The government's positive assessment also ignores the more troubling reviews into the pay television market that have been carried out by regulators over the last few years. For example, Ofcom's Pay TV market review (Ofcom 2010) concluded that the UK market was not genuinely competitive because of the stranglehold exercised by Sky on key genres. This was followed by the Competition Commission's own investigation into pay television, which noted "the very high and stable levels of concentration, the low level of switching between suppliers, the difficulty of large-scale entry/expansion as a traditional pay-TV retailer and the absence of countervailing buyer power in pay TV" (Competition Commission 2012: 8). Yet, despite the facts – that while the appetite for television is increasing, public service budgets are under pressure in a marketized environment; that pay TV operators already account for a majority of broadcast revenue while underserving and overexploiting their audiences – the government is wedded to an ideological view of the innovative and liberalizing dynamics of digital markets and refuses to act.

Conclusion

In his short book *On Television*, Pierre Bourdieu rails against the fetishization of audience ratings and the saturation of market principles inside television as fundamentally anti-democratic. According to him:

Submission to the requirements of this marketing instrument is the exact equivalent for culture of what poll-based demagogy is for politics. Enslaved by audience ratings, television imposes market pressures on the supposedly free and enlightened consumer. These pressures have nothing to do with the democratic expression of enlightened collective opinion or public rationality.

(Bourdieu 2011: 66–67)

We face a similar battle to ensure that the market fundamentalism currently enshrined inside the policy process does not further distort the provision of a suitable range of programmes aimed at multiple audiences on topics that are of relevance to ordinary viewers. Bourdieu is right that we need a public, not a private, rationality, which involves opening up and democratizing emerging platforms and technologies as well as protecting older popular spaces from underfunding and enclosure. This will involve a redistribution not just of policy focus but of resources to make sure that our media does not bow down to a narrow market logic. In order to foster equality, our media system ought to be restructured along lines that do not privilege simply those with the largest pockets and most powerful friends but one that has a commitment to equitable forms of provision and distribution. UK broadcasting has historically operated with regulated, public spaces at its heart; its engine, if not its soul, is now serviced by private capital within far less regulated structures. We need, finally, a vision of equality and not of market efficiency to guide us if we want a broadcast system that will deliver the kinds of programmes that so many people continue to demand and that society so urgently requires.

References

BARB (2013) "Total Viewing Summary, 11–17 November", *Broadcasters Audience Research Board* (accessed 2 December 2013: www.barb.co.uk/viewing/weekly-total-viewing-summary).

BBC (2000) "10 Ways TIVO Will Change Your Life", *BBC Online*, 28 September (accessed 30 November 2013: news.bbc.co.uk/1/hi/uk/945275.stm).

BIS/DCMS (2009) *Digital Britain: Final Report*, June, London: BIS/DCMS.

Bourdieu, P. (2011) *On Television*, Cambridge: Polity.

BSkyB (2013) 'Annual Report 2013' (accessed 29 April 2014: annualreview.sky.com/downloads/BSkyB_Annual_Report_2013.pdf).

Butler, S. (2013) 'Jingle Tills: Stores Bet Big on Festive Ads', *Guardian*, 8 November, p. 27.

Committee to Protect Journalists (CPJ) (2013) 'The Obama Administration and the Press: Leak Investigations and Surveillance in post-9/11 America', 10 June (accessed 29 April 2014: cpj.org/reports/2013/10/obama-and-the-press-us-leaks-surveillance-post-911.php).

Competition Commission (2012) *Movies on Pay TV Market Investigation*, London: Competition Commission (accessed 2 December 2013: www.competition-commission.org.uk/our-work/movies-on-pay-tv).

DCMS (2013) *Connectivity, Content and Consumes: Britain's Digital Platform for Growth*, July, London: DCMS.

Deans, J. (2013) "UK Ad Spend Set to Hit Record £14bn", *Guardian*, 25 November accessed 30 November 2013: www.theguardian.com/media/2013/nov/25/uk-advertising-spend-hit-pre-crash-high).

Deloitte (2012) "TV: Why?" London: Deloitte (accessed 30 November 2013: www.deloitte. com/assets/Dcom-UnitedKingdom/Local%20Assets/Documents/Industries/TMT/uk-tmt-tv-why-perspectives-on-uk-tv.pdf).

Doherty, R. (2012) "Women on TV: Too Few And Far Between", *Huffington Post*, 16 June (accessed 2 December 2013: www.huffingtonpost.co.uk/rosa-doherty/women-on-tv-too-few-and-f_b_1589471.html).

Enders Analysis (2013) *General and PSB Viewing Trends*, London: Enders.

Freedman, D. (2008) *The Politics of Media Policy*, Cambridge: Polity.

Gilder, G. (1994) *Life After Television*, New York: Norton.

Goodwin, P. (1998) *Television Under the Tories*, London: British Film Institute.

Harvey, S. (2006) "Ofcom's First Year and Neoliberalism's Blindspot: Attacking the Culture of Production", *Screen*, 47 (1): 91–105.

Jones, O. (2013) *Totally Shameless: How TV Portrays the Working Class*, BBC Four, transmitted 24 November 2013.

Livingstone, S., Lunt, P. and Miller, L. (2007) "Citizens, Consumers and the Citizen-Consumer: Articulating the Interests at Stake in Media and Communications Regulation", *Discourse and Communication*, 1 (1): 85–111.

Magna Global (2013) "Advertising Forecasts", *Magna Global*, 14 June (accessed 30 November 2013: news.magnaglobal.com/article_display.cfm?article_id = 1463).

OECD (2013) "Competition Issues in Television and Broadcasting", *Global Forum on Competition*, Paris: OECD (accessed 2 December 2013: search.oecd.org/officialdocuments/publicdisplay documentpdf/?cote=DAF/COMP/GF/WD(2013)39&docLanguage=En).

Ofcom (2010) "Pay TV Statement", *Ofcom*, 31 March (accessed 2 December 2013: stakeholders. ofcom.org.uk/consultations/third_paytv/statement/).

Ofcom (2011) *Communications Market Report 2011*, London: Ofcom.

Ofcom (2013a) *Communications Market Report 2013*, London: Ofcom.

Ofcom (2013b) *Public Service Broadcasting Annual Report 2013*, London: Ofcom.

Poggi, J. (2012) "Live Viewing Still Overwhelmingly Dominates TV", *Ad Age*, 11 September (accessed 30 November 2013: adage.com/article/media/live-viewing-overwhelmingly-dominates-tv/237130/).

Statista (2013) "Average Monthly Time Spent on Facebook per Unique User in the United States as of February 2013", *statista.com* (accessed 30 November 2013: www.statista.com/ statistics/256343/monthly-minutes-spent-on-facebook-by-us-users-by-channel/).

Statistic Brain (2013) "Television Watching Statistics", 7 September (accessed 30 November 2013: www.statisticbrain.com/television-watching-statistics/).

Steel, E. (2013) "Tipping Point for Media Viewing as Couch Potatoes Go Digital", *Financial Times*, 1 August (accessed 30 November 2013: www.ft.com/cms/s/0/a0fbb2ca-fa9d-11e2-87b9-00144feabdc0.html).

Watt, D. (2013) "David Cameron Makes Veiled Threat to Media over NSA and GCHQ Leaks", *Guardian*, 28 October (accessed 30 November 2013: www.theguardian.com/world/ 2013/oct/28/david-cameron-nsa-threat-newspapers-guardian-snowden).

9
THE GLOBALIZATION OF TV FORMATS

Anthony Fung

Cultural industry produces cultural products that are sold globally on a massive scale. There is a very unique – perhaps a more advanced form of – cultural industry that, however, does not produce and reproduce cultural products, but sells and transfers know-how and idea: it is the global trade and franchising of production and circulation of television formats. Television format business is the trading of a package of copyrighted calculated formula and well-planned concept for a television programme that is readily adapted to different cultures. In other words, quite different from our traditional understanding of cultural industries such as film, animation or music industries, the core business of which rests on its creativity, production and then its distribution, the television format trade is a secondary level of (re)production. It starts out with a source of knowledge and creative production of the original televised format, which is then ensued by a more complex and long process of cultural adaptation and localization of the knowledge in different locales under different contexts. As it has shown, while many adapted television formats largely follow the structure and flow of the original format design, there are some television formats that are vastly modified to cater for local taste, advertisers and political context.

In the last ten years the trade in television, or TV, formats has become extremely active, partly because of the proven popularity of the formats, and partly because television stations across the world are in extreme need of quickly produced television content that fills up the air time, in particular in Asia where the number of channels has increased exorbitantly as the economy has risen. With the ever-increasing popularity of TV formats that travel globally, there is a concomitantly growing number of publications on TV formats. Among them, most studies have conceived and classified TV formats as an emerging and popular genre of television that creates local and global impact by various means of local adaptation, and hence it becomes a cultural form of globalization. While such descriptions are in general correct, globalization of TV formats is relatively a new phenomenon in the history of television, and therefore a more accurate trajectory of approach and framework of studying TV format is still under exploration.

The study of TV formats has undergone two decades of change. In retrospect, it was common to see that the studies of television formats were mainly case analyses or examination of a particular television format (e.g. reality TV) that is prevalent worldwide. Initially, it was usually singled out as an individual phenomenon; it was usually incorporated into the field of the television studies, which are customarily textual and qualitative analysis of the specific genre, and sometimes broadly include discourse study of the television programme, its production and distribution processes, and the connection between television and society, culture and politics. In a professional journalism school, the study of television formats is also of practical concern in terms of the skills and techniques of television production and so on.

Later, as TV formats, in particular reality TV, have become more prominent, their study is not just confined to a detailed analysis of their nature and content. Cultural theories were being applied to the study of reality TV: a broader perspective about how TV formats are being connected to the social and cultural context can be seen, probably, in a second stage of development. The sort of mediated construction in which actors are arranged and subjected to perform precisely in reality TV becomes what cultural theories have to deconstruct. From a political economy perspective, studies (e.g. Pozner, 2010) offer a critical dimension to the so-called communicative capitalism: is the programme accountable to the consumers? Does TV evolve into a new form that effectively deludes audience? Is it simply a new and extended capitalist way to manipulate reception? Jodi Dean (2009) defined "communicative capitalism" as "a political-economic formation in which there is talk without response, in which the very practices associated with governance by the people consolidate and support the most brutal iniquities of corporate-controlled capitalism" (p. 24). Compared with "industrial capitalism", which "relied on the exploitation of labor", "communicative capitalism" extends the exploitation to viewers and thus maximumizes capitalists' business interest. Meanwhile, Dean pointed out that despite the proliferation and commodification of digital technologies, which has created new platforms for audiences to express their view, the communication facilitated is often "unresponsive" and "non-inclusive". In other words, communications technology is more about creating a "fantasy of participation" than serving democractic functions. The political aspect of media is overtaken by the commercial side. On the other hand, from a cultural studies perspective, studies question the programme's accountability to the consumers: reality TV reassembles the dominant narratives and social discourses of comical showbiz, and in turn it constitutes another form of panoptic surveillance for the audience to abide with (Andrejevic, 2003). Besides, the constructed reality in reality TV that fits the consumerist demand could perpetuate and reinforce cultural biases about gender, race and class (Pozner, 2010).

Television formats have received more attention in academia perhaps because of the globalization of the reality TV format. The trend of studying reality TV (e.g. Murray and Ouelette, 2008; Pozner, 2010) has in fact become one of the rejuvenating drives of television studies in this post broadcast era (Turner and Tay, 2009), and this trend has continued, matching reality TV's ongoing popularity. Turner and Tay (2009) studied how the role of television changed and they identified its shift from "broadcast era" to "post broadcast era". In "broadcast era", television had an education role in advocating democracy, cultivating national identity and highlighting important information to the public. And yet, as the commercial interest of media carries more weight, the television industries face an increasingly complex environment driven by audience fragmentation, programme diversification, rise of new media and multi-platform television. As the audience segments in the "post broadcast era" are fragmenting and content is distributed across channels, independent production companies are also given a chance to find their niche market. In TV format pro-ductions, most of the popular ones are produced by media giants in the United States and Europe. Besides academic work, trade books on reality TV also proliferate. Author Michael Keneski even published a guide, *Survivor: The Unofficial Bible of the Greatest Reality Show Ever Made* (2011), which summarized how finalists won different seasons of the reality TV show *Survivor*. Participants of some reality shows, *The Bachelor* for example, have also published books based on their experiences. For instance, Courtney Robertson, who joined the sixteenth season of *The Bachelor*, wrote *I Didn't Come Here to Make Friends: Confessions of a Reality Show Villain* (2015) in which she documented her psychological journey of joining a reality show, in which women are expected to compete for the chance to win the heart of America's most ideal man. In addition to trade books, the study of reality show has become an area of research interest. Take feminist journalist Jennifer L. Pozner's *Reality Bites Back: The Troubling Truth About Guilty Pleasure TV* (2010) for example: Pozner observed a pattern in reality television, which attracts audiences by playing around with mis-conceptions and sterotypes such as sexism, racisim and homophobia. Susan Murray and Laurie Ouellette's *Reality TV: Remaking Television Culture* (2008) is another example. Murray and Ouellette pointed out that the represetation on reality TV, which appears "real" and "authentic", is a socially constructed situation. And the birth of this TV genre has changed the dynamics among producers, participants and viewers. The study of the globalization of television format has emerged as the second stage of systematic study.

It is only recently that we have seen TV formats treated as a globalized cultural form under the operation and production of cultural industries, in which the entire circuit of culture, content adaptation, ideological control, market potentials and the expression of cultural identity can be examined with critical reflection. In terms of geopolitical concern, the study of globalization of format initially focused on the UK or US produced formats in Asia (Iwabuchi, 2003 in Japan; Khalil, 2004 in the Middle East) and other non-Anglo-Saxon countries (Hetsroni, 2004; Jensen, 2007 in northern Europe), in which these formats are locally adapted and modified, and making local impacts. Roughly around 2010, studies of television formats have gradu-ally entered into an epoch of synthesis and crystallization in which the structure, production and output are studied within a framework of globalization (Keane et al., 2007; Cooper-Chen, 2005; Moran, 2009). For example, Keane et al. (2007) examined the flow and circulation of television in Asia and described how some television "ideas" were directly cloned and copied in this immature format trade in Asia, and yet still were immensely popular. These studies detail the adaptation process of television formats, which in turn reflects how the issue of dialectics between localization and globalization, contradiction of the television content and the indigenous values, or the global and the local are resolved. In sum, this phase of study of the globalization of TV formats starts to explicitly or implicitly consider it within a framework of cultural industry in which the interaction between state and policy, media, content and local adaptation, audience and market are examined (Chalaby, 2010, 2012; Gutiérrez Lozano, 2010). With a more comprehensive approach to the study of media, both the regulatory role of the state and the connection between television content and local identity are further explored.

What is a television format?

Until now, television formats have been loosely defined or widely misunderstood. Some media and production houses package and design formats and sell the ideas as a "blue book", and additionally, and seemingly more commonly, ideas for programmes are copied and imitated illicitly. But from a cultural industries point of view, a television format is basically a commercial and global strategy for designing, producing and distributing a copyrighted concept and branding of a television programme or show. The globalization of television formats involves their adaptation in different parts of the worlds, with formats converted and modified to suit the local context and language.

Across the world, major production companies include the Italian-based Mediaset's Endemol, Bertelsmann's FremantleMedia, Mexican multimedia company Grupo Televisa, Germany's Red Arrow Entertainment Group, to name but a few. The more renowned and successful formats include reality TV, dating shows, other competition-based formats and some specific TV drama formats (including the comedy drama *Yo Soy Betty, La Fea*, firstly produced in Colombia). With the ever-increasing expansion of global capitalism, and in different nation-states, with the increased privatization of media service and even with the commercialization of state-owned media in authoritarian regimes, the adaptation of existing packaged TV format has slowly become a regular and popular way of television programming and production routines. What we have seen are different national versions and variations of *Big Brother* and *Pop Idol*, and internationally, the adapted format of *Australian Survivor*, the Chinese version of *Ugly Betty*, Korea's own version of *Take Me Out!* and *Love Switch!*, Japan's production of *The Weakest Link* and Indonesian remakes of *Who Wants To Be A Millionaire?*, amongst others. Apart from the legally acquired franchised formats, there are numerous cloned version of the format or television programme using similar ideas, ranging from the make-over of China's *Supergirl* (a combination of the *Big Brother* and *Pop Idol* format) to dating show like Singapore's *Angel Gate* (which uses a similar format to *Dragon's Den* and *Shark Tank*); such cloned formats are found not only across Europe and the United Kingdom but also reaching Asia in the current era of globalization.

In fact, TV format adaptations are also popular in the European market. Take *The Voice of Holland*, for example: it is a reality show featuring a singing contest, which seeks to identify aspiring singers with musical talents. The United States revised the concept and developed *The Voice*. Interestingly, this TV format returned to Europe again and became one of Europe's top five formats in 2012, creating $126.9 million (Kemp, 2013) in value across the region. *The Million Pound Drop Live*, a game show first developed in the United Kingdom, is another example. In the United States several changes were made to this concept and *Million Dollar Money Drop* was developed. This TV format generated $213.4 million and was the top format in Europe in 2012. Apart from reality TV shows, there are several TV dramas with the same TV format. For example, *Queer as Folk* was a British television series featuring the life of three gay men in Manchester. The series was broadcasted in the United Kingdom in 1999 and 2000. This concept was revised and incorporated into a co-production between the United States and Canada. The US–Canadian version of *Queer as Folk* was set in Pittsburgh and featured more characters, and the series was broadcasted from 2000 to 2005.

The adaptation of programme formats in television systems across the world has become a regular media trade and a common strategy for media stations. The trend is most likely precipitated by the new communication technologies (e.g. digitalization of television) that drive programme and market needs, the trend of the privatization of services and the blooming of television broadcasting in Asia and in developing countries. The study of the phenomenon of global television format is thus conceived as the analysis of the stages and processes – efficiently or contradictorily – in which this specific mediated form of cultural globalization or commodity is created, marketed and distributed by the operation of global capitals and distributors and transnational production companies in global trade and markets, and finally how the format knowledge, design or ideas are being (re)produced by and broadcast on local media. In addition to the process of localization, the issues examined may include the policy of the state, the strategy and position of the media that localize the format, regulation of and contracts for remaking the format, the concept of copyright and intellectual property, and piracy (Moran and Malbon, 2006). The issues may cover political, cultural, economic, organizational and legal dimensions of the television format.

Globalizing formats and global culture

The globalization of television formats not only represents this increasing global trade business. The globalizing of television formats results in cultural globalization, to some extent homogenizing culture and values, namely capitalism, liberalism, gender values, consumerism and cosmopolitanism across the globe. García Canclini (1995) points to cultural hybridity as a key dimension of cultural globalization. The terminology "hybridity" highlights globalization as an ongoing process of mediation between global culture and local cultures. To apply this concept to media studies, the underlying question is how transnational media serves as a key engine to facilitate the process and to bring foreign cultural elements in different local contexts and vice versa. Empirical studies in global television studies actually have provided strong evidence of the globalizing trend. For example, in a study of the US television schedules from the 2007–8 broadcast season, Andrea Esser (2010) revealed a high share of formatted programming in primetime schedules (which accounts for 33 per cent of broadcast time). Inevitably, the enormous volume of the television format also signifies the increasing drive for media and production companies to create formats. On the one hand, this trend of producing and franchising its intellectual property contributes to the convergence of television globally, not just structurally but also in terms of concrete, albeit locally modified content (Esser, 2010). On the other, when formats are well-received, it sparks the production and selling of the formats in a larger industrial scale, which enables television formatting to evolve into a form of cultural industries.

In this global circulation of television format, beyond the cultural product itself, their concern on global trade and operation has slowly converged with studies on cultural industries.

Besides this global trend – meaning that the global format production houses manufactured formats and exported them overseas – cloning, circulation and franchising of television formats is also at works, which constitutes somewhat the so-called Inter-Asia cultural flow. *Meteor Garden* is an example. It is a comic story that originated in Japan, written and illustrated by Yoko Kamio, describing the love story happening among the four boys from well-off families and a girl from a humble background in an elite high school. The comedy was adapted into four versions of TV dramas: Taiwan, Japan, South Korea and China. The comedy was first adapted into drama by Taiwan, named *Meteor Garden*, which created and guided the fashion of *Youth Idol Drama* as the pioneer of Taiwan to broaden their overseas market. The TV drama achieved a huge commercial success with a minimum of 500 million viewers across Asia, according to the producer. F4, the four casts in the drama, also gained popularity and created a trend of Young-Boy-Idol group in Taiwan. This TV format was later adapted by South Korea (named *Boys Over Flowers*), Japan (also named *Boys Over Flowers*) and China (named *Let's Watch the Meteor Shower*). All versions not only achieved economic viability but also reshaped the idol star market across the region.

Currently the study of global TV formats focuses on reality television formats, which are more prevalent worldwide. Therefore, probably what is not emphasized is the initial creation of the franchised format that might come out of a small production company. While transnational production companies dominate the market, it is also true that the globalization of information flows within the TV industry is as important as the independent production sector in sustaining this value chain of the globalization of the TV format business (Chalaby, 2010).

Emerging concepts in creative industries

Under the framework of creative industries, new issues and concerns over the globalization of television formats emerge.

Interactivity

Interactivity used to refer only to the interaction between the audience and the actor in the reality or game show in formatted programmes. Now the framework of creative industries opens up discussion on institutional connection or interconnectivity on a structural level. It emphasizes the institutional linkages of television stations to related industries, including global distributors, marketers or producers worldwide, and the formation of an integrated business or industries that operated on media content and format production (Waisbord, 2004). As illustrated by the Latin American media cases, Waisbord (2004) stresses the inseparability between the local television system and the global system. In other words, television is now simultaneously global and local, or international and national, and the local media environment is constantly shaped by the pull and push of local and national cultures (Waisbord, 2004).

Moreover, as TV format trading facilitates cooperation between global media and local media amidst competition, the study of TV format's interactivity provides a perspective on how economy and culture are closely linked in the context of globalization.

Labour

As reality TV gains tremendous popularity, television stations start having a dedicated team for this genre. While reality TV production emerges as an expertise, the globalization of TV formats has cultivated an international community of professionals sharing the expertise. Troy Devolld, in *Reality TV: An Insider's Guide to TV's Hottest Market* (2011), outlines the pattern of programme development, storytelling and marketing of reality TV. The book is regarded as one of the industry guides for reality TV professionals. Apart from content and promotion, the globalization of TV formats also creates a new profession that is dedicated to the international trading of TV formats. Furthermore, given the increasing interaction within the television industry across the globe, along with some predominant video sites (e.g. YouTube) that indicate the number of video views, the way information and insights are disseminated has changed and industry professionals across the globe have more interactions than before. Still, although TV formats in the United States are no longer guaranteed best sellers with the highest hits, industry professionals tend to take television in the United States as a key reference (Waisbord, 2004).

Intellectual property

As many industry professionals tend to draw reference from those TV programmes proven to be successful in other markets, these programmes are exposed to the risk of being copied by other media without paying for permission. As such, producers and government are increasingly aware of the importance of intellectual property protection. Chalaby (2010) found that Britain, as the second largest exporter of TV formats, has been very proactive in creating a favourable environment with advanced intellectual property protection for content producers. In the meantime, producers and distributors have become more active in monitoring copyright violations. The legal dispute between a London-based format distribution company ECM and Shenzhen Cable (Waller, 2002) is an example: ECM sold the TV format of *Go Bingo* to Shenzhen Cable in 1998 but the Chinese company refused to pay the amount indicated in the contracts. After four years of legal disputes, a Chinese court forced the Chinese company to pay ECM $200,000 for the licensing rights. And yet, in some cases, the line to define whether a show is a copy or not is not clear. In 2012, Telpa Distribution, the producer of *The Voice of Holland*, accused China's *The Voice of China* of copyright violation. This case appeared controversial as the Chinese version has a couple of differences from the Dutch version. White and Brenner (2004) argued that concepts of reality TV shows are quite difficult to protect. In the context of China, for example, any phrases that contain the word "China" could not be part of the registered trademark. In other words, if *The Voice of China* seeks trademark protection, the producer can only register *The Voice*. Still, there are only a few studies dedicated to the intellectual property protection of TV formats. As such, it has become a new academic focus that requires further research.

The impact on local markets

While the United States and some European countries (especially the United Kingdom) are taking the lead on TV format production, countries in Scandinavia and Asia Pacific (including Australia) are regarded as localizers. Jensen (2007) compared the use of format adaptations between the public broadcasters in Denmark and Australia. The research unveiled that Danish public broadcasters tend to adapt TV formats more frequently than Australian public broadcasters. This could be explained by how public broadcasting is seen differently in Denmark and Australia. In fact, some countries even adapt the TV format of news and documentaries in order to build an authoritative voice in global discourse and thus extend the country's soft power overseas. For example, Russia Today, a Russian TV network founded in 2005, has adapted various formats from leading international media (e.g. CNN) in its news programmes and documentaries. Meanwhile, given the foreign influence that might be brought by an imported TV format, some countries, China for example, have limited the number of foreign TV formats. Since 2014, China's TV stations can only have one foreign TV format per year and one music talent show per quarter (Kemp, 2013). Illustrated by the examples above, the cultural industries perspective enables us to analyse how a TV format is being adopted in a certain region and critically examine this international flow and adaptation.

The publics, politics and identity

Although theories of cultural industries often focus on economy more than politics, there is a research niche area in how TV formats are closely linked to the publics, politics and identity. Beeden and de Bruin (2009) compared the original British version and the American adaption of *The Office*. The research revealed that the success of TV format adaptation significantly depends on its capacity to reflect the national culture and the articulation of national identity. Take Punathambekar's concept of "mobile publics" (2010) for example: some reality TV shows use digital technologies as a way to engage their viewers and this becomes a platform for audiences to express their identity. For example, in a reality show featuring Indian idols in 2007, the two finalists, Amit Paul and Prashant Tamang, who came from a a Northeast India cast, leveraged public support from their region. The reality TV format opens another door for the public to reflect on what is possible despite social construction and political circumstances. In fact, the image of idols carries certain weight in entertainment, and the study of idols also emerges as an area of research interest. For instance, Kjus (2009) studied how idols are produced in Norway and the research unveiled that given the participatory nature of reality TV and the use of digital technologies, reality TV actually provides a channel to recreate the society's value chains instead of simply advocating the existing state of affairs.

ANTHONY FUNG

Cultural industries as an approach to TV format studies

The rendezvous between global TV formats and cultural industries opens up new arenas for exploring the nature of TV formats, apart from the localization process of these global formats that are deemed essential. The approach of cultural industry to the study of TV formats elevates the production, marketing and distribution of TV formats from a media product on a macro "industry" level on which this unique media commodity is seen as reflecting the complex relationship with the audience, identity and politics, regulation for a specific culture and society where they adapt or clone the format. The focus on the cultural industries becomes more legitimate as the entire industries have started to develop the flow and chain of production, adaptation and purchase of television format maturely, and operate the commercial trade at a global scale (Havens, 2006; Jensen, 2007). Thus, from a macro perspective, the flow and then the adoption of television formats worldwide by television stations could cast a broad picture of the entire global political economy of culture.

An academic discussion of conceptualizing the production of TV format as a domain of cultural industries also necessitates theorizing TV format as a mass-produced "transnational" commodity (Mikos and Perrotta, 2012: 84). In more recent studies of the global adaptation of Colombian telenovela *Yo Soy Betty, La Fea*, Mikos and Perrotta (2012) compares local adaptations of the Colombian telenovela in different continents, and discovered that in the case of these adaptation, genre proximity – which is a more differentiated concept of cultural proximity (Straubhaar, 2007) – gradually becomes an obsolete concept if, simply, hybrid television formats are being produced to cater to the diversified audiences in different geographic locales. The arguments based on the cultural industries would imply that so long as the format is produced and distributed in such a way that it inherently meets the needs of the global television market by hybridizing different genre conventions and media experiences of the audiences in the production and eventually it is being adapted and localized, the explanation of the popularity of a television format should be explained in terms of, not the audience needs or taste, but the industrial and internal logic of the cultural production.

Such an argument shifts the entire discussion of television formats to a framework of cultural industries studies in which the local adaptation of television formats by the television stations matters when we explain the format's success. Take the TV format of the reality show, for example: its success is not a random coincidence but an extension and application of the industrial logic. First, there are certain formats of reality shows (e.g. competition) that are proven to be economically viable. Second, producers of these reality shows often have some successful formulas in term of content development, storytelling and marketing based on their past experiences. Third, while localizers draw reference to how popular some reality shows are, especially those from the United States and Europe, producers monitor the adaptations of their TV formats and ensure there are no violations of their own intellectual property. Last but not least, the reality TV business cultivates an international community of professionals with expertise in the production of reality shows, TV format trading and so on.

To a certain extent, the cultural industries perspective is a theoretical turn or a "turn back" to the industries, which in practice puts together the production on a routine

138

basis, rather than lopsidedly bestowing too much power to the audience or the genre as such. Audience and market size are advertisers' indicator for sponsoring the television programme, and the genre and the content still matter when it comes to viewership. But on the whole, the expected feedback of the audience and the previous proven popularity of the format if genre itself are just contingent factors among the multiple considerations of the television industries for adopting the television format. In the study of Danish and Australian adaptation of TV formats, Jensen (2007) considered their differences and similarities of patterns and schedules of TV formatted programme in terms of industry factor and structure. From the perspective of the industry, the television stations decided the genres, the schedule and the number of local adaptation based on market size, the notion and ideology of public service, the existing television programmes, media ecology and competition. This is also an indication that the industrial or structural aspect of the study of television formats has gradually taken place in addition to the concrete content modification and ideology of the representations in the new formats.

References

Andrejevic, M. (2003) *Reality TV: The Work of Being Watched*, Maryland: Rowman & Littlefield Publishers.

Beeden, A. and de Bruin, J. (2009) "The Office: Articulations of National Identity in Television Format Adaptation", *Television and New Media*, 11 (3): 3–19.

Chalaby, J.K. (2010) "The Rise of Britain's Super-Indies: Policy-Making in the Age of the Global Media Market", *The International Communication Gazette*, 72 (8): 675–93.

Chalaby, J.K. (2012) "At the Origin of a Global Industry: The TV Format Trade as an Anglo-American Invention", *Media, Culture and Society*, 34 (1): 36–52.

Cooper-Chen, A. (2005) "A world of 'millionaires': Global, local, and 'glocal' TV game shows", in A. Cooper-Chen (ed.), *Global Entertainment Media: Content, Audiences, Issues*, London: Lawrence Erlbaum, pp. 237–51.

Dean, J. (2009) *Democracy and Other Neoliberal Fantasies: Communicative Capitalism and Left Politics*, Durham: Duke University Press.

Devolld, T. (2011) *Reality TV: An Insider's Guide to TV's Hottest Market*, Los Angeles, CA: Michael Wiese Productions.

Esser, A. (2010) "Television Formats: Primetime Staple, Global Market", *Popular Communication: The International Journal of Media and Culture*, 8 (4): 273–92.

García Canclini, N. (1995) *Hybrid Cultures*, Minneapolis: University of Minnesota Press.

Gutiérrez Lozano, J.F. (2010) "Public TV and Regional Cultural Policy in Spain as Reflected Through the Experience of Andalusian Regional Television", *Cultural Trends*, 19 (1–2): 53–63.

Havens, T. (2006) *Global Television Marketplace*, London: British Film Institute.

Hetsroni, A. (2004) "The Millionnaire Project: A Cross-Cultural Analysis of Quiz Shows from the United States, Russia, Poland, Norway, Finland, Israel, and Saudi Arabia", *Mass Communication and Society*, 7 (2): 133–56.

Iwabuchi, K. (2003) "Feeling Glocal: Japan in the Global Television Format Business," in A. Moran and M. Keane (eds), *Television Across Asia: TV Industries, Program Formats and Globalisation*, London: ReoutledgeCurzon, pp. 21–35.

Jensen, P. (2007) "Danish and Australian Television: The Impact of Format Adaptation", *Media International Australia, Incorporating Culture and Policy*, 124: 119–33.

Keane, M., Fung, A.Y. and Moran, A. (2007) *New Television: Globalization and the Asian Cultural Imagination*, Hong Kong: Hong Kong University Press.

Kemp, S. (2013) "'The Voice's' TV Format Sings its Way to Euro Success", 20 March (accessed 9 December 2013: www.hollywoodreporter.com/news/voices-tv-format-sings-way-430011).

Keneski, M. (2011) *Survivor: The Unofficial Bible Of The Greatest Reality Show Ever Made*, Los Angeles, CA: CreateSpace Independent Publishing Platform.

Khalil, J. (2004) "Blending In: Arab Television and the Search for Programming Ideas", *Transnational Broadcasting Studies*, 13.

Kjus, Y. (2009) "Everyone Needs Idols:. Reality Television and Transformations in Media Structure, Production and Output", European Journal of Communication, 24 (3): 287–304.

Mikos, L. and Perrotta, M. (2012) "Travelling Style: Aesthetic Differences and Similarities in National Adaptations of *Yo Soy Betty, La Fea*", International Journal of Cultural Studies, 15 (1): 81–97.

Moran, A. (2009) "Global Franchising, Local Customizing: The Cultural Economy of TV Program Formats", *Continuum*, 23 (2): 115–25.

Moran, A. and Malbon, J. (2006) *Understanding the Global TV Format*, Bristol: Intellect Ltd.

Murray, S. and Ouellette, L. (2008) *Reality TV: Remaking Television Culture*, New York: NYU Press.

Pozner, J. (2010) *Reality Bites Back: The Troubling Truth About Guilty Pleasure TV*, New York: Seal Press.

Punathambekar, A. (2010) "Reality TV and Participatory Culture in India", *Popular Communication: The International Journal of Media and Culture*, 8 (4): 241–55.

Robertson, C. (2015) *I Didn't Come Here to Make Friends: Confessions of a Reality Show Villain*, New York: HarperCollins Publishers.

Straubhaar, J. (2007) *World Television: From Global to Local*, Thousand Oaks, CA: Sage Publications.

Turner, G. and Tay, J. (2009) *Television Studies After TV: Understanding Television in the Post-Broadcast Era*, London: Routledge.

Waisbord, S. (2004) "McTV: Understanding the Global Popularity McTV: Understanding the Global Popularity of Television Formats", *Television and New Media*, 5 (4): 359–83.

Waller, E. (2002) "ECM wins landmark format case in China", 4 February (accessed 9 December 2013: www.c21media.net/ecm-wins-landmark-format-case-in-china/).

White, A.M. and Brenner, L.S. (2004) "Reality TV Shows Difficult Concepts to Protect", *Law Journal Newsletters*.

10

THE POPULAR MUSIC INDUSTRIES

Shane Homan

Introduction

In 2013 thirty-four Michael Jackson fans sued the King of Pop's doctor, Conrad Murray, for "emotional damages" derived from the singer's death. Satisfied that five of the plaintiffs had indeed suffered, a court in Orleans awarded "symbolic damages" of one euro each in February 2014 (*Guardian* 2014). Beyond its novelty value, the ruling says much about popular music's trajectories in contemporary cultures. It reinforces how both the performer and their music speak to and for fans, underlining the deeply subjective modes of our choices and connections. Yet it also says something, perhaps, about the extent to which music fans have adopted the juridical and administrative discourses of industry, that our affective interactions with the star and their music are never far away from being transposed into their base commodity and legal forms (especially if threatened).

Music remains at the centre of popular cultural experience for many; at the same time, "much music is overheard in states of distraction, barely registered consciously, or just the noise of someone else annoying us" (Zuberi 2004: 214). The diversity of popular music experiences (digital game/film soundtrack, shopping centre noise, mobile phone ringtone, on-hold telephone distraction, tribute band pub performance, gym soundtrack, karaoke video or superstar concert) underlines the need to assess popular music as part of a cultural economy of "amusement, ornamentation, self-affirmation, social display" (Scott 1999: 807). Music has been at the forefront of debates about the interplay (and display) of "cultural capital" (Bourdieu 1993) and the commodified cultural form. It is also increasingly visible in cultural/urban policy as cities and towns readily display their own cultural capital to attract tourists, workers and economic capital. It is for these reasons that music is more ubiquitous than other cultural forms in its individual and community uses. As an industry involved in symbolic creation and consumption (Hesmondhalgh 2013; Throsby 2001), the exchange value of its commodified forms resonates historically and aesthetically: "pop was about buying a dream, rock was about buying an experience" (Harron 1990: 180).

The popular music industries share many of the characteristics evident in the broader development of the cultural industries.[1] Often leading industrial change within audio-visual sectors, recording, publishing and live music companies have also shaped the emergence of the corporate multi-national. The contemporary popular music industries consist of five sectors: live performance; the production and sale of sound recordings; the administration of copyright in compositions and sound recordings; the manufacture and distribution of music instruments, recording and amplification equipment; and education and training (Dane et al. 1996). These industries have always been highly dynamic (even within monopolistic markets). They can also effect change in the regulation of culture. The particular conditions and uses of technology and labour in popular music also throw light more generally upon the histories and contemporary conditions of the cultural industries in terms of how pleasure is organized and distributed. The music industries, then, have some claim as the "canary in the coalmine," announcing cultural and economic shifts in the cultural industries (Baym 2010) and as the "most advanced media model" (Cvetkovski 2013: 67).

Organization: Market to social models?

Economies of scale are important in a set of industries where investment entails high risk: for example, in 2000 only 19 per cent of British single releases achieved chart success (Burke 2011: 298). "Major" recording companies have existed since the 1940s by exploiting economies of scale in manufacturing, marketing and distribution. Five multinational companies dominated global recording in the 1990s. Subsequent mergers (Sony and the Bertelsmann Group in 2004) and acquisitions (Universal's purchase of EMI in 2012) have resulted in a concentration of three: Sony Music Entertainment, Universal Music Group and Warner Music. Majors in the 1970s and 1980s such as EMI and Polygram (and earlier companies such as RCA/Victor) were successful for several reasons. First, they relentlessly pursued vertical and/or horizontal integration to overcome deficiencies in either content or hardware (for example, Sony's purchase of CBS Records in 1991; and the CBS acquisition of Last.fm in 2007). Second, they were able to exert reasonable control over technological innovations (from multi-track recording to the Sony Walkman to the emergence of the compact disc) in ways that did not fundamentally change their production and publishing models. Third, this also entailed good control of the value chains of supply (A&R, manufacturing, retail). All these factors ensured, fourth, that oligopolistic conditions transposed to the relative stability of global and national markets (Tschmuck 2006).

The recording sector, of course, does not solely comprise the major companies. "Indies" (independent recording labels) have played an important role since the 1930s. Similar to other broadcasting sectors such as television and radio, independents have often been most effective in locating scenes and musicians, "acting as the research and development departments" for the majors (Wikstrom 2009: 128). The (often binary) debates about the merits of smaller independents (managerial synchronicity with creative aims; closer attention to a smaller artist roster) and the larger majors (access to global distribution, promotional, rights chains) for the artist remain.

The decline in the physical/analogue product has been profound since vinyl recording sales peaked in the 1970s, followed by the brief rise associated with the shift to CD formats. The recording sector has been slow to recover from the losses sustained by downloading since the 1990s. In 2010 global digital sales revenue increased by 5.3 per cent, while CD sales revenue continued to decrease by 14.2 per cent (Smirke 2011). In 2012 digital download sales increased by 12 per cent, with sub-scription services increasing by 44 per cent (IFPI 2013), driving renewed industry confidence, with global recording industry revenue in 2012 estimated to be $16.5 billion (IFPI 2013). This confidence is partly derived from additional vertical integration through investment in the range of digital cloud and streaming companies. For artists, the reduced scope of the majors in terms of national branch staffing and resources, combined with the increased amount of music available, has perversely reduced the recording sector's patience with new artists. Increased marketing costs have also meant that the older model of two to three albums for new signings has been replaced with the expectation of immediate hits (Wikstrom 2009: 129). It has also driven greater cross-pollination of genres, with artists more willing to collaborate to explore new markets.

How badly the majors handled digital evolution is evident in the inverted business model of the past twenty years, where live performances have subsidized recording. Accurate revenue statistics – and a consensus of definitions of "live music" – are rare, but performance revenues have overtaken those of the recording sector in some nations (Laing 2012). Live performance has also assisted in the longevity of older pop and rock heritage acts: the top three grossing performers of 2012 were Madonna, Bruce Springsteen and the E Street Band, and Pink Floyd's Roger Waters (IFPI 2013: 23). Reconfigurations of the stadium experience have added new layers of profit, offering more dedicated fans "exclusive" packages comprising VIP passes, privileged concert seating and backstage access. As the leading concert promoter, Live Nation Entertainment has booking rights/equity in 155 venues worldwide (Wikstrom 2009: 60) with ownership of key festivals and sports events in Europe and the United States. It has exercised its financial power by entering into artist management, with various deals struck with Madonna, Jay-Z, Shakira and U2. Its 2010 merger with Ticket-master now means it is possibly the largest music company in the world. Apart from concerns of duopoly arrangements in national markets such as the United Kingdom (Live Nation and AEG), the influence of the multi-national promoter upon smaller city venue and festival circuits is considerable (Brennan 2011: 70–71).

The "digital crisis" has also seen a belated interest in increasing other public per-formance rights income (broadcasting, bars, nightclubs, gyms, restaurants, shops); these revenues grew by 9.3 per cent in 2012, accounting for 6 per cent of total industry revenues globally (IFPI 2013: 9). For example, Australian collection societies have won substantial royalty increases for the use of sound recordings in hotels, nightclubs and gyms in recent years (Homan 2010). Gaming is increasingly lucrative; music content within global games (e.g. RUN-DMC and Ozzy Osbourne in *Grand Theft Auto*) and licensed music games such as *Rock Band* and *Guitar Hero* are profit-able through initial purchases and subsequent song downloads (Preston and Rogers 2011: 388).

The majors have been accused of collusion in setting retail prices in some markets (Prices Surveillance Authority 1990) and excused of this in others (Monopolies and Mergers Commission 1994). Over the past two decades the recording industry has attempted to forestall twenty-first-century technological innovation through resort to nineteenth-century legal rights even while this "time-consuming and exhaustive rearguard action provides the innovative competitors with valuable technological advantages" (Tschmuck 2003: 130). An equally defensive strategy has been one of co-option through purchasing of the newer distribution rivals (for example, Bertelsmann's purchase of Napster's assets in 2002), including the majors' purchase of equity in Spotify; "the fact remains that the creators and cultural industries that play a role in capturing the audience on behalf of the many free service providers do not appropriate the associated financial benefits" (Farchy 2011: 250). This has led to key hardware (Apple) and content aggregator (Yahoo, Google) firms deploying recording industry content in the name of related cultural experiences and sales.

It is why "the new cultural paradigm (music as service) will replace the old one (music as product)" (Tschmuck 2003: 139). This entails, partly, the rise of music companies that perform the entire range of promotional and service work required in the new global smorgasboard of consumer activities (Baym 2010: 178). Music search "app" Shazam has transformed the haphazard listening of everyday experience (what was that song in the shopping centre or on TV last night?) into both a commodity and predictive data; fifteen million song searches each day is enormously useful in predicting global shifts in popularity (Datoo 2013). The twentieth-century practice of priming chart success through management purchases or "cooking the books" of retail sales has its twenty-first-century equivalent in buying plays and fake comments on key music web sites (Matthew 2013). This speaks to the enormous amount of work now required in brokering and monitoring both the artist narrative and exposure of the digital release to ensure a modicum of web visibility. New industry jobs have been created in the streaming/online radio sites; consultancy/research work on finding audiences (for example, ReverbNation) and other social media management work (Baym 2010: 179).

Labour, rights and revenues

In Australia, a recent Arts Victoria/Australasian Performing Rights Association survey estimated the mean annual income for musicians to be $12,000 to $15,000, below the national poverty line of $18,616 per year (Graham 2013). This reinforces the mundane reality for the majority of performers: semi-professional circuits shaped by cash-in-hand gig payments, recording company disinterest, and increasing competition for gigs among tertiary-educated songwriters and musicians (Gibson 2003). It is cultural labour that is often precarious and part-time, that deploys a mix of artistic, cultural and technical expertise (Ellmeier 2010). Indeed, the connected DIY musician is urged to think of themselves akin to "tech startups" in terms of entrepreneurial strategies (Darker 2014).

At a 2013 public debate in Melbourne, one of the defenders of the existing system proposed that copyright "was a human right ... the foundation of our society ... necessary for freedom of expression" (Fraser 2013). We see here a contemporary expression of modern liberalism that equated property laws with an essential freedom within Western democracies (see Cvetkovski 2013: 10–25). Despite the lack of evidence that the strengthening of copyright laws increases creative output (Towse 2011: 129), intellectual property law has always spectacularly lagged behind industrial and technological change. "As the first cultural industry to make use of both digital processes and the new forms of communication, exchange and distribution of the internet" (Laing 2003: 252), music was also the first to contend with the broader social and economic implications of the digital commodity.

The ninety-nine cents set by Apple for individual iTunes songs – the "global psychological price ceiling for downloads" (Farchy 2011: 251) – has inevitably influenced internet royalty rates, which remain low across webcast radio, digital stores and streaming services. This has not prevented internet music companies seeking lower royalty rates (Pandora's legal action against ASCAP, the American Society of Composers, Authors and Publishers in 2012) while collection societies take to the courts in the name of higher rates (Broadcast Music Inc. against Pandora). Spotify's arguments that they have eroded illegal downloading in key markets and are overtaking royalty rates paid by traditional broadcasters are weakened by their low royalty rates: an average of \$0.006 to \$0.0084 per stream (Spotify 2013).[2] Despite a consumer base of twenty-four million listeners, Spotify lost \$60million in 2013 (McDuling 2013); it is an important test case in whether streaming services can simultaneously satisfy fans, musicians, recording companies and advertisers.

The "music copyright debate has observed one of the key Foucaultian tenets of governance: that a failure in regulation and policing inevitably leads to greater regulation and policing" (Homan 2014: 236). "Graduate response" ("three strike") laws have become crucial in this governmental cycle. New Zealand, South Korea, France and Britain have passed laws where internet service provider (ISP) users are warned of downloading infringements and ultimately disconnected from servers. The latest failure of legislatures and the courts to enforce rights in an era of abundance – and a global test case – is found in the 2010 Australian Federal Court hearing *Roadshow Films Pty Ltd v iiNet Pty Ltd*. With thirty-three other appellants including multinational music and film companies, Roadshow hoped to provide certainty for all audio-visual content providers in arguing that the host company's knowledge of the existence of copying amounted to authorization. Both the Federal Court ruling (2011) and High Court appeal (2012) found that iiNet did not sanction downloading, was not required to act upon infringers and that knowledge of BitTorrent activity did not amount to illegal behaviour. This was an important affirmation that "there is no compulsion (under liberalism) on any person to protect the copyright of another" (Cvetkovski 2013: 34).

At the same time the recording sector has constantly sought public approval for a system whereby the costs are socialized, while the profits are substantially privatized; it remains one of the few industries where all production costs must be recouped before the creator shares in the profits.[3] The rise of crowdfunding (for example, Pledge, Kickstarter) offers an alternative to the standard recording contract on more favourable terms. Collective fan financing of albums enables the artist to retain rights to the master recording, involve their fans in production, and to pursue projects that that have no major company interest. Problems remain with distribution and promotion against major and indie releases, but it is an intriguing new mixture of social and economic capital.

Globalization and governance

The often asserted globalization of cultural trade, production and consumption has to be treated with caution. Popular music practice is part of "new concentrations of power and 'legitimacy' that attach to global firms and markets" (Sassen 2008: 89) amidst a growing interdependence of technologies, institutions and communities. Yet this observation must also incorporate the many national and regional differences in the governance of cultural products and industries. Quota provisions for local music on national broadcasting systems, varying taxation regimes for audio-visual products, state censorship policies: all reveal the continuing role of the nation-state within "global" music cultures. While supra-national bodies such as the World Intellectual Property Organization (WIPO) engage in attempts to enforce global intellectual property standards, the ongoing battles by internet music services such as Pandora for a share of national territories further emphasizes the mixed nature of "borderless" theories.

The industry's past exploitation of "world music" – the selective success of "exotic" non-Western pop acts in Anglo-American and European markets – is a further indicator that claims to global frameworks are inevitably complicated. Substantial parts of the world market (Germany, Sweden, France, Italy, Spain, Japan) rely upon national repertoire for domestic sales. The truly global pop star (Adele, Psy, Pink) can still be produced in synchronization with media platforms. Boy band One Direction are a study in contemporary stardom: appearances in the UK's *The X Factor* programme in 2010 led to a record number of hits across social media by fans and 8.1 million followers on Twitter by 2012 (IFPI 2013: 19).

As Western markets continue to recoup lost sales through digital platforms it is clear that the recording sector is turning its attention to developing nations for future growth. Brazil, Russia and India are targets as nations with emerging middle-class consumer populations (IFPI 2013: 24–26). The International Federation of the Phonographic Industry (IFPI)'s conditions for such growth are revealing: the establishment of favourable copyright enforcement and the introduction of global digital/streaming platforms (IFPI 2013: 24–26). Others contend that more realistic price settings, attuned to local wages and cultural value, are a more appropriate means of reducing illegal sales in developing markets (Karaganis 2011). This signals the new discursive terrain of imperialist/global practice, less concerned with how the few non-Western acts to extend beyond their home territories are consumed and interpreted, and more interested in how profits are established and dispersed. Evidence has emerged of increasing pressure placed upon developing countries to align with the global vision of intellectual property rights of the dominant copyright exporters (Robinson and Gibson 2011).[4] Proposals for Burma to become a member state of the WIPO, and adhere to Western copyright norms, for instance, would considerably change the domestic culture. The ability of "copy thachin" composers to match Burmese lyrics to Western hits would be eliminated by the moral and economic rights of the original publishers and composers (MacLachlan 2011: 129–34).

The ability to win intellectual property reform has been accompanied by other governmental change. Less defined boundaries between low and high culture have affected the foundational premises of subsidy, although high music forms (opera, classical) continue to receive the bulk of support through different combinations of "excellence" and market failure discourses. Established frameworks have become unsettled: classical music borrowing pop culture strategies (symphony orchestras performing *Dr Who* soundtracks); regulatory intervention in previously commercial domains (government strategies to stem market failure in live venue sectors). While this has not eliminated the discursive shorthand of the funding of "excellence" which is only ever defined against itself, it has opened new debates about aesthetic value.

Promises to deliver employment as part of growing creative and copyright industries have seen popular music sectors gain increasing attention from local and national governments in the past two decades. This is particularly evident in the blizzard of urban regeneration schemes to either enhance or completely revitalize "downtown" areas. Cities as diverse as Toronto, Glasgow, Berlin, Austin and Liverpool have constructed policies to direct music industry *and* city growth, as often as not building on specific cultural heritage as the foundational sites for particular music genres or acts. The preponderance of city music strategies is partly a testament to the success of the Florida (2002) thesis emphasizing the need for cities to attract creative talent to retain competitive advantage.

As some cities have realized, it is difficult to impose a singular template upon cities with diverse and unique cultural histories and heritage. Yet a live music policy has resonated with city policymakers due to the visceral effects of live performance upon scenes, subcultures and identities. Several concerns have emerged as popular music becomes part of social amelioration or regeneration policies. First, the types of music privileged in city strategies can lead to a mainstream promotional effect that discounts or renders invisible some genres and music communities (O'Meara and Tretter 2013). Second, the competing pressures upon city managers to simultaneously deliver lively night-time cultures amidst residential and business community growth inevitably produces inequalities in terms of spaces and activities, most noticeable in noise law debates concerning music venues (Cohen 2013; Homan 2011). Third, the tendency of central business districts towards standardized/touristic fare (for example, music theatre, pubs with cover or tribute band entertainment) allows fewer spaces for alternative musics. Fourth, ongoing gentrification of central business districts and surrounding residential areas has led in some cases to more corporate, service-oriented venues as part of "more upscale leisure consumption" (Holt 2013: 153; Chevigny 1991). Such developments return us to some basic though urgent questions "about who the city is for, who controls it, and what a city is or should be" (Cohen 2013: 45).

Conclusion

The predominant economic model of the music industries shared many of the key features of the broadcasting industries from the 1940s to the 1970s: a scarcity of cultural goods carefully distributed by a few major production companies, reinforced by local/ regional regulations that protected existing chains of production and consumption. In this chapter I have attempted to explain some of the chief reasons why this model cannot be sustained. Music as a set of cultural industries cannot, of course, be simply or solely reduced to aspects of distribution, copyright and industry integration. The rise of political parties intent on copyright reform is instructive for just how far these debates have moved out of corporate–governmental axes and into social realms and new modes of popular culture consumption and communication as democratic discourse. Recording companies in this sense have wanted it both ways: continually emphasizing the special symbolic significance of music, while seeking legal protection as simply another commodity that has a price. The recording industry will continue to be successful in obtaining ever longer copyright terms for composers, but this is legal shadowboxing for a large number of "ghost" consumers who revel in shorter, everyday victories over what music means to them and how they use it. The prevalence of continual legislative and legal reform has to some extent masked how consumers have won the battle over how value is determined. For musicians, increasingly responsible for their own brand as "musicpreneurs" (Darker 2014), more flexible marketing strategies will require the genuine flowering of "networked audience engagement" (Baym 2010: 178) in very different ways to older arrangements between recording company, artist management and live booking agency.

Continual assurances that the "right" business model will surely fix relationships between fans, musicians and producers ignore the pace of change in the past three decades, and the inability of the interrelated industries to accommodate social and technological change. Recurring discourses of crisis ("the music industries have no future") or euphoria ("the internet will free composers, musicians and fans alike") are also not helpful. If music does indeed act as both carrier and predictor of political and cultural change (Attali 1985) then some tentative evaluations can be made. Popular music will lead other cultural industries in their use of big data to manage and predict increasingly complex relationships with consumers and advertisers. Secondary rights (the negotiation of film soundtrack, mobile phone or digital game uses) will increase in importance as recording sales become too piecemeal to sustain enduring revenues.

This is being accompanied by corporate realignment, as "traditional" companies seek to have a say in the digital levers of production and access as the default means of survival in the absence of innovation, with consequences for future meanings of diversity and cultural and economic power. New forms of monopoly capital are already emerging to disguise the loss of cultural authority of older music companies to harness and define the "authentic" music experience. The times are thus more suited to the independent (producer, recording company, critic, promoter) to convert the "analogue" pleasures of scenes, gigs and recordings to modes of digital authenticity. For musicians, the end products of their labour will be seen less as a commodity with a price that reflects a precise market value, and more as a process of mutable social exchange that allows global aggregators to ensure that they are simply one part of wider circuits of advertising and corporate sponsorship.

Notes

1 I focus here upon those music genres – such as rock, pop, country, blues, jazz, folk and hip hop – understood to be "popular" in the sense of their everyday consumption, modes of (mass) distribution and primarily commercial aesthetics. This definition excludes the industrial organization of classical and art musics that are consumed and produced by different means and in different contexts. After Cloonan and Williamson (2007), I avoid

the usual conflation of the "music industry" with the recording industry, to include the range of performance, publishing and related industry sectors.

2 Spotify insist that musicians' anger about royalty rates misunderstands their payment method by "market share" ("dividing an artist's streams by the total streams on Spotify") (Spotify 2013) rather than a fixed per-play calculation. As royalties are paid to the label, musicians' revenues are dependent upon their royalty arrangements with the company.

3 This is summarized well by one industry lawyer:

> the record company advances your production costs and that is an advance which is a pre-payment of royalties. Why they're so brutal, is that even when you've repaid the production costs, who owns the master? Who continues to own the copyright? The record company does. So when you repay the bank for your house, who owns the house? You. When you repay the record company for the master, who owns it? The record company. That's a fairly brutal thing to come to terms with. It doesn't really affect you for the first successful album, but by the time you get to the second and third, you're getting pissed off. You're never going to own the copyright.
>
> (Gibson 2003: 208)

4 At the time of writing, New Zealand, Brunei, Canada, Australia, Chile, Japan, Malaysia, Mexico, Singapore, Peru, Vietnam and the United States are negotiating a free trade agreement (the Trans-Pacific Partnership). Details are limited, although Wikileaks documents of the secret meetings have attracted criticism for intellectual property proposals that entrench US copyright frameworks including "graduated response" ISP mechanisms and laws that would remove national sovereignty and strengthen company resorts to international legal challenges (Loussikian 2013).

References

Attali, J. (1985) *Noise: The Political Economy of Music*, Minneapolis: University of Minnesota Press.

Baym, N. (2010) "Rethinking the Music Industry," *Popular Communication: The International Journal of Media and Culture*, 8 (3): 177–80.

Bourdieu, P. (1993) *The Field of Cultural Production*, Cambridge: Polity Press.

Brennan, M. (2011) "Understanding Live Nation and its Impact on Live Music in the UK," *Situating Popular Musics: IASPM 16th International Conference Proceedings*, IASPM, 69–75.

Burke, A. (2011) "The Music Industry," in R. Towse (ed.) *A Handbook of Cultural Economics*, 2nd edition, Cheltenham and Northampton: Edward Elgar Publishing, 297–303.

Chevigny, P. (1991) *Gigs: Jazz and the Cabaret Laws in New York City*, New York: Routledge.

Cloonan, M. and Williamson, J. (2007) "Rethinking the Music Industry," *Popular Music*, 26 (2): 305–22.

Cohen, S. (2013) "'From the Big Dig to the Big Gig': Live Music, Urban Regeneration and Social Change in the European Capital of Culture," in F. Holt and C. Wergin (eds) *Musical Performance and the Changing City: Post-Industrial Contexts in Europe and the United States*, New York and Abingdon: Routledge.

Cvetkovski, T. (2013) *Copyright and Popular Media: Liberal Villains and Technological Change*, Basingstoke and New York: Palgrave Macmillan.

Dane, C., Feist, A. and Laing, D. (1996) *The Value of Music: A National Music Council Report into the Value of Music*, London: University of Westminster.

Darker, T. (2014) "How to Prepare for the Musicpreneur Era," *Midem.com*, January 27 (accessed February 8, 2014: blog.midem.com/2014/01/tommy-darker-how-to-prepare-for-the-musicpreneur-era/#.UutTyRzM38N).

Datoo, S. (2013) "How Shazan uses Big Data to Predict Music's Next Big Artists," *Guardian*, December 10 (accessed February 8, 2014: www.theguardian.com/technology/datablog/2013/dec/10/shazam-big-data-prediction-breakthrough-music-artists).

Ellmeier, A. (2010) "Cultural Entrepreneurialism: On the Changing Relationship Between the Arts, Culture and Employment," *International Journal of Cultural Policy*, 9 (1): 3–16.

Farchy, J. (2011) "The Internet: Culture for Free," in R. Towse (ed.) *A Handbook of Cultural Economics*, Cheltenham, UK and Northampton, MA: Edward Elgar.

Florida, R. (2002) *The Rise of the Creative Class*, New York: Basic Books.

Fraser, M. (2013) "Forum Presentation," Copyright is Dead, Long Live the Pirates: IQ-2 Debate, Wheeler Centre, Melbourne, September 24.

Gibson, C. (2003) "Cultures at Work: Why 'Culture' Matters in Research on the 'Cultural' Industries," *Social and Cultural Geography*, 4 (2): 201–15.

Graham, P. (2013) "The Cost of the Uncollective Unconsciousness," *Music in Australia Knowledge Base*, May 21 (accessed February 8, 2014: musicinaustralia.org.au/index.php?title=The_Cost_of_the_Uncollective_Unconsciousness).

Guardian (2014) "Michael Jackson Fans Win Damages for 'Emotional Suffering' from Star's Death," *Guardian*, February 12 (accessed February 13, 2014: www.theguardian.com/music/2014/feb/11/french-court-awards-damages-emotional-suffering-fans-death-michael-jackson).

Harron, M. (1990) "McRock: Pop as a Commodity," in S. Frith (ed.) *Facing the Music: Essays on Pop, Rock and Culture*, London: Mandarin.

Hesmondhalgh, D. (2013) *The Cultural Industries*, London: Sage.

Holt, F. (2013) "The Advent of Rock Clubs for the Gentry: Berlin, Copenhagen and New York," in F. Holt and C. Wergin (eds) *Musical Performance and the Changing City: Post-industrial Contexts in Europe and the United States*, New York and Abingdon: Routledge.

Homan, S. (2010) "Dancing Without Music: Copyright and Australian Nightclubs," *Popular Music and Society*, 33 (3): 377–93.

Homan, S. (2011) "'I Tote and I Vote': Australian Live Music and Cultural Policy," *Arts Marketing: An International Journal*, 1 (2): 96–107.

Homan, S. (2014) "Popular Music," in S. Cunningham and S. Turnbull (eds) *The Media and Communications in Australia*, 4th edition, Sydney: Allen and Unwin.

IFPI (2013) *Digital Music Report 2012: Engine of a Digital World*, International Federation of the Phonographic Industry (accessed February 8, 2014: www.ifpi.org/content/library/DMR2013.pdf).

Karaganis, J. (ed.) (2011) *Media Piracy in Emerging Economies*, New York: Social Science Research Council.

Laing, D. (2003) "Industrialization," in D. Horn, D. Laing, P. Oliver, P. Wicke and J. Shepherd (eds) *Continuum Encyclopedia of Popular Music of the World, Volume 1: Media, Industry and Society*, New York: Continuum.

Laing, D. (2012) "What's it Worth? Calculating the Economic Value of Live Music," *Live Music Exchange* (accessed June 6, 2013: livemusicexchange.org/blog/whats-it-worth-calculating-the-economic-value-of-live-music-dave-laing/).

Loussikian, K. (2013) "Regional Trade Pact Puts Australia in 'Absurd' Position, Say Experts," *The Conversation*, November 14 (accessed Decemeber 10, 2013: theconversation.com/regional-trade-pact-puts-australia-in-absurd-position-say-experts-20299).

MacLachlan, H. (2011) *Burma's Pop Industry: Creators, Distributors, Censors*, Rochester, New York: University of Rochester Press.

Mathew, T. (2013) "How to Become a Soundcloud Superstar, One Fake Fan at a Time," *5 Magazine*, April 10 (accessed September 20, 2013: www.5chicago.com/features/april2013/how-to-become-a-fake-soundcloud-superstar/).

McDuling, J. (2013) "Music Streamers Fail to Hit Profitable Note," *Australian Financial Review*, May 29 (accessed June 6, 2013: www.afr.com/p/national/music_streamers_fail_to_hit_profitable_Mx5NGidfa8xj62k8qZgkqN).

Monopolies and Mergers Commission (1994) *The Supply of Recorded Music*, London: HMSO, Cm 2599.

O'Meara, C. and Tretter, E. (2013) "Sounding Austin: Live Music, Race, and the Selling of a City," in F. Holt and C. Wergin (eds) *Musical Performance and the Changing City*, New York and Abingdon: Routledge, 52–76.

Preston, P. and Rogers, J. (2011) "The Three Cs of Key Music Sectors Today: Commodification, Concentration and Convergence," in D.Y. Jin (ed.) *Global Media Convergence and Cultural Transformation: Emerging Social Patterns and Characteristics*, Pennsylvania: Hershey.

Prices Surveillance Authority (1990) *Inquiry into the Price of Sound Recordings*, Canberra: Commonwealth Government of Australia.

Robinson, D. and Gibson, C. (2011) "Governing Knowledge: Discourses and Tactics of the European Union in Trade-related Intellectual Property Negotiations," *Antipode*, 43 (5): 1883–910.

Sassen, S. (2008) "The Repositioning of Citizenship and Alienage: Emergent Subjects and Spaces For Politics," in B.K. Gillis (ed.) *The Global Politics of Globalization: "Empire" vs "Cosmopolis,"* London and New York: Routledge.

Scott, A.J. (1999) "The Cultural Economy: Geography and the Creative Field," *Media, Culture and Society*, 21: 807–17.

Smirke, R. (2011) "IFPI 2011 Report: Global Recorded Music Sales Fall 8.4%," *Billboard* (accessed February 8, 2014: www.billboard.biz/bbbiz/industry/global/ifpi-2011-report-global-recorded-music-sales-1005100902.story).

Spotify (2013) "Spotify Explained," February 6 (https://www.spotifyartists.com/spotify-explained/).

Throsby, D. (2001) *Economics and Culture*, Cambridge: Cambridge University Press.

Towse, R. (2011) "Creative Industries," in R. Towse (ed.) *A Handbook of Cultural Economics*, Cheltenham, UK and Northampton, MA: Edward Elgar.

Tschmuck, P. (2003) "How Creative are the Creative Industries? A Case of the Music Industry," *The Journal of Arts Management, Law, and Society*, 33 (2): 127–41.

Tschmuck, P. (2006) *Creativity and Innovation in the Music Industry*, Dordrecht: Springer.

Wikstrom, P. (2009) *The Music Industry: Music in the Cloud*, Cambridge: Polity Press.

Zuberi, N. (2004) "Music Media: Mobile Sounds in Networked Places," in L. Goode and N. Zuberi (eds) *Media Studies in Aotearoa/New Zealand*, Auckland: Pearson Education.

11

BETWEEN TRIPLE-A, INDIE, CASUAL, AND DIY

Sites of tension in the videogames cultural industries

Brendan Keogh

The contemporary videogame industry is popularly imagined as a homogenous site where large, international studios pour millions of publishers' dollars into technologically advanced blockbuster experiences. The sheer amount of money these Hollywood-like games return to their investors through sales is held up in countless scholarly and journalistic articles as both arguments for the cultural legitimacy of the medium and its complicity in neoliberal capitalism. Of this straightforward imagining, the videogames most visible in broader culture are, inevitably, those with the highest budgets and the most advertising—such as the juggernaut franchises of *Call of Duty* or *Grand Theft Auto*—and those online games with significant online communities such as massively-multiplayer online (MMO) games like *World of Warcraft* or competitive e-sports like *League of Legends* (see Taylor 2006; Taylor 2012 respectively). Much has been written about these most visible sectors: the games they produce (Deuze et al. 2007); the labour practices they cultivate (de Peuter and Dyer-Witheford 2005); the cultures they perpetuate (Kirkpatrick 2013). However, a far more diverse range of creators, audiences, and modes of videogame production and consumption has emerged with the rise of digital distribution and a proliferation of platforms. International corporate publishers now compete with—and draw influence from—smaller teams or individuals that are finding their own critical and commercial success in vibrant independent scenes. While a hobbyist, core, male-dominated "gamer" audience continues to prioritise technological progressivism and virtuosic control, more ubiquitous platforms such as smartphones and social network sites challenge these traditional values by broadening the reach of videogames to a more diverse and casual audience that has an everyday relationship to videogames. A lower barrier of entry to the tools of videogame production, meanwhile, has seen an emergence of DIY developers from marginalised backgrounds creating and distributing experimental and personal "zine" games. Across this diverse network of creators, nascent critical discourses are emerging both publicly and within the academy, in tandem with the enthusiast press, to discuss and debate the values and meanings of the videogame form.

This chapter traces an outline of this complex assemblage that is the videogame cultural industries. It explores major tensions that emerge from the intersect of these various actors to understand how the cultural value of videogames is established and judged between enjoyment and technological advancement, between accessibility and complexity, between commercial viability and artistic merit. While any one of these tensions could be (and has been) explored by entire books, this chapter is concerned with capturing the complexity of the whole. It hopes to instil an appreciation for the true breadth and heterogeneity of the videogames cultural industry beyond the blockbuster and multiplayer titles that form the visible tip of the iceberg, and will allow videogames to be better contextualised within the broader ecology of the core cultural industries.

Three sections explore the defining sites of these tensions in the contemporary videogame industry. First, the relationship between "Triple-A" and "indie" development will contrast the risk-adverse, conservative design of the blockbuster studios that, ironically, comes hand-in-hand with technological innovation, with the rise of "indie" games that set up a fruitful antagonism with the large studios. The rise of "indie" challenges many of the Triple-A industry's core values, with individual developers making names for themselves by refusing to look "forward" but instead aiming to replicate a "golden age" of videogame nostalgia. Second, I turn to the parallel rise of casual games across social and mobile media, and the tension between increased normalisation of videogames with questionable monetisation practices such as free-to-play. Third, I turn to the rise of hobbyist and DIY game production where genderqueer, economically disadvantaged, and non-white developers are challenging long-held, fundamental understandings of the videogame form. These creators are not primarily focused on producing economically viable products, but instead create videogames like one would create a zine, and this different approach drastically changes how videogames are imagined and designed. To conclude, I turn my attention to the rise of critical discourses in tension with traditional, consumer-orientated games journalism that has emerged in recent years alongside a maturing cultural form. Ultimately, this paper is less concerned with the impossible task of exhaustively mapping contemporary videogames than it is in demanding an appreciation for the impossibility of that task. Researchers of the videogame cultural industries must acknowledge the complexity of the form and the interdependency of its many scenes. To appreciate "videogames" is to appreciate a great many things.

Triple-A and indie

That most visible section of the videogame cultural industries—the studios and publishers pouring millions of dollars into the development and marketing of technologically spectacular franchises for home console machines—is commonly known as "Triple-A." As has been extensively explored by other authors (de Peuter and Dyer-Witheford 2005; Izushi and Aoyama 2006; Deuze et al. 2007; Kirkpatrick 2013), studios typically work under the oversight of a publisher (and with the publisher's investment) to produce a game that the publisher will market and distribute. The game will be released on personal computers (PCs) and the consoles of the day (at present the Xbox One and Playstation 4); or, they will enter exclusive contracts with the developers of just one platform. While development studios are many, publishers are few, multinational, and hold vast sways of power over what games do and do not get developed. Often, these large publishers—such as EA, Activision, and Rockstar—produce their own campus-sized development studios (such as EA Vancouver, or Ubisoft Montreal) or purchase ownership of independently started studios to gain exclusive rights over the labour and creative output of that studio.

Historically, videogames have always been a technologically driven medium. Huhtamo (2005) traces a fascinating prehistory of videogames through Industrial Age moving image cultures and Kirkpatrick (2013) notes important social pressures that influenced the medium's evolution. However, videogames have always been caught up with hacker ideologies of technological advancement and a "passion in virtuosity" (Turkle 2005, 187) ever since Massachusetts Institute of Technology (MIT) students hacked a PDP-1 computer to run *Spacewar!* in 1961. The spectacle of cutting-edge technology has been persistent throughout videogames' commercial history. Jason Wilson notes this in his study of videogame aesthetics through the 1970s and 1980s. On a flyer promoting Atari's 1976 arcade game *Night Driver*, "the backlight technology, sound effects, and on-screen display are all advertised as offering a heightened form of 'realism' and are all foregrounded as pleasurable aspects of the game" (Wilson 2007, 12).

A fixation on the power of advanced technologies to produce "realism" remains central to the trajectory of videogame development. The myth marketed to and pervasively believed by gaming audiences is that once technology allows videogames to be "realistic" enough, players will be able to step into the virtual world and not have to think about the technology at all (Kirkpatrick 2013, 85). The significance of constantly improving technology to the quality of videogames is carefully cultivated by the Triple-A industry, as is transparently clear in the notion of console "generations," each seen as superior to their predecessors (Dyer-Witheford and de Peuter 2009, 71). Throughout 2013, as Microsoft and Sony moved to launch their new consoles, this harking of technology as caught up with quality was explicitly clear. Talking on stage at Sony's Playstation 4 announcement event, game developer David Cage made the curious claim that "Getting the player emotionally involved is the holy grail of all game creators ... with the Playstation 4, games have now finally reached that stage." The promise of realism through more powerful technology is dangled like a carrot on a stick to ensure consumers regularly purchase new hardware or incrementally different titles in the same franchise (Deuze et al. 2007, 339).

This requires increasingly large teams and development cycles to produce "realistic" games, and inevitably takes its toll on the labour of game production, as has been the subject of several journalistic investigations in recent years (McMillen 2011; Zacny 2012). It is not rare for one game to be worked on by several geographically distant studios all owned by the one publisher, or for elements of a game to be outsourced to a third party (Deuze et al. 2007, 342). As explored in depth by de Peuter and Dyer-Witheford (2005) and touched on by Deuze et al. (2007, 345), the environment of these studios becomes increasingly hostile and unsustainable to employees. With a systemically de-unionised workforce (Williams 2013), hours are long and overtime pay is nearly nonexistent as developers "crunch" to meet milestones. Employees are lured by the promise of a "playful" working environment to turn them into "passionate pay slaves" (de Peuter and Dyer-Witheford 2005), made to believe that rather than overtime, they should be happy to be doing their "dream" job. These studios consequentially promote a fraternity culture, where employees feel like they are not working for "the man" even while corporate overlords insist they work 18-hour days with no overtime pay (de Peuter and Dyer-Witherford 2005). Such conditions, alongside gamer culture's ongoing cultivation of a "core" adolescent male audience (Kirkpatrick 2013, 89) leads to Triple-A studios being populated by a very particular demographic: young, no dependant family, and overwhelmingly male (Deuze et al. 2007, 345). Combined, these factors lead to a homogenised cultural workforce with high turnover and low experience.

Driven by the need to return a profit, publishers become increasingly risk adverse as the amount of money spent on a single title increases. When Crystal Dynamic's *Tomb Raider* (2013) sold 3.4 million copies in four weeks after its release, publisher Square Enix lamented that it had not reached its sales target (Phillips 2013). The focus shifts to making an incrementally better-looking version of what sold last time, and Triple-A games fall into narrower and narrower categories and franchises, such as the first-person shooter or the open-world driving game. "Middleware" such as game engines becomes increasingly important to streamline development cycles and, consequentially, further funnels the potentials for future games—games produced using the Unreal Engine, for instance, are constrained by what the Unreal Engine is capable of (Kirkpatrick 2013, 104). The Triple-A arm of videogames is thus dominated by games that must fit into known thematic and mechanical genres (fantasy, sci-fi, military; first-person shooter, role-playing game, action game); must be "difficult," "realistic," and "complex" in the conventional ways; must be appealing to a particular "core" audience of young men; and must also be technologically innovative.

The contemporary indie scene—where individuals or small teams can feasibly hope to return a profit—emerges through the 2000s in response to this increasingly homogenised and corporatised product-based industry. In the introduction to a special issue of *Loading* journal focused on the culture of indie games, Simon notes that to talk of indie games is "not to speak only of the games themselves or of the experiences of gameplay but rather of the cultures of game development from whence they came" (Simon 2013, 2). Much as indie music and film genres emerged in response to the industrialised status-quo of mainstream production (Lipkin 2013, 10), indie game developers cultivate a persona of care-free creativity and innovation. While there is a long and significant history of hobbyist developers and "modding" communities (Banks and Humphreys 2008; de Peuter and Dyer-Witheford 2005; Anthropy 2012), the contemporary and commercially viable indie developers emerge alongside a normalisation of digital distribution channels. No longer dependent on physical stores to distribute games, indie developers take full advantage of the internet to deliver cheaper and smaller games directly to users through their own websites.

Indie games have also become a significant presence on major digital distribution storefronts such as Valve's Steam, Microsoft's Xbox Live, Sony's Playstation Store and, as explored in the next section, Apple's App Store. Such a presence reveals a core contention with the indie label: that its stated antagonism with Triple-A leads to an inevitably symbiotic relationship. Those games most commonly thought of as the flag-bearers of "indie," such as Jonathan Blow's *Braid*, 2D Boy's *World of Goo*, and Team Meat's *Super Meat Boy*, are available on the same corporate platforms as Triple-A titles. Meanwhile, Mojang's *Minecraft*, while produced and developed independently, has sold tens of millions of copies and allowed the originally one-man studio to grow to such a size to be publishing other developers' games, while still holding onto the "indie" persona. Indie, then, is not simply every amateur developer (although many amateur developers will identify themselves as "indie"), but a carefully cultivated antagonism against the status quo of the mainstream industry.

The rise of indie studios, with their lower overhead costs, has created new genres and design directions (and resurrected old ones) outside of that central trajectory of technological upgrade culture that Triple-A publishers deem safe investments. The pixel art, sidescrolling platformers, and low-fi music of indie games are in part a deliberate attempt to return to a "golden age" of game development (ie. the games the developer played as a kid) and in part an economic necessity as, working as individuals or in small teams, 2D games are easier to produce. These indie aesthetics, as they become normalised, reflexively influence broader aesthetic values across the industry and are inevitably coopted by the mainstream industry as a new status quo (Lipkin 2013, 15). Further, as indie developers explore new ways to fund themselves, these monetisation practices feed back into the industry. For instance, *Minecraft* popularised paying for "alpha" access, effectively creating a player base that both provides free testing labour and funds further development of the game, and this has been formalised through the normalisation of "beta access" to larger games, as well as Steam's "Early Access" program. The Humble Indie Bundle, which introduced a pay-what-you-want model for a bundle of indie games, has also seen Triple-A publishers follow the same route. Crowdsourcing websites, meanwhile, such as Kickstarter or Indiegogo have seen both indie developers and Triple-A studios turn to crowd investment for productions that traditional publishers would not invest in. Through how they are developed, the atmosphere and culture they project, and through how they are distributed, indie game are a significant intervening factor when considering the values and strategies of the videogame cultural industries and what they produce, existing in a symbiotic tension with Triple-A development——both opposing and entangled in the narratives and values of the Triple-A industry.

Casual and mobile games: Videogames become normal

If the rise of the indie scene is about videogames being legitimised as more than "mere" entertainment products (Parker 2013), then the rise of casual games, as Juul notes in his preliminary but extensive study of the field, is about videogames becoming normal (2010, 1). As social and mobile media such as Facebook and smartphones become increasingly ubiquitous in many contemporary cultures, videogame developers have access to an increasingly broad audience beyond the core "gamer" culture. Instead of targeting adolescent male audiences through certain masculine genres and performances, casual videogames attract a broader audience through more accessible style and design.

Juul notes five key design concerns that differentiate casual games from the traditional "hardcore" games of the Triple-A industry: inoffensive fiction; usability
through an intuitive or mimetic interface (such as the Wii-mote or a touchscreen); a
balanced difficulty; excessive audiovisual feedback; and, significantly, interruptibility
(Juul 2010, 30–55). Combined, these concerns allow casual games to be incorporated
into the everyday life of people who do not have a lifetime experience of playing
videogames, such as a quick game of *Candy Crush Saga* while checking Facebook, or
a couple of stages of *Angry Birds* on the train. While the term "casual" immediately
connotes ideas of a less committed or less serious player, and has been critiqued for
obscuring the amount of labour players regularly devote to casual games (Taylor
2012, 241), the strength of the term is in its connotations of flexibility, as casual
games are often played by a "body-in-waiting" (Hjorth and Richardson 2009, 29).
Just as a casual employee may still work extensive hours but on a more flexible
roster, players of casual games may—and often do, as Juul's interviews show—play
games with as much commitment as players of non-casual games, but in brief
moments here and there, through social network sites or mobile platforms.

Much like indie games, then, casual games often focus on rejuvenating older game
genres and designs, especially the intermittent-play design of arcade games. Many casual
games focus on short, point-scoring bouts, such as Halfbrick's *Fruit Ninja* or Wonder-
land's *Stickets*. Indeed, many developers of casual games do consider themselves "indie,"
as many casual game studios are similarly startups trying to design games outside the
traditional publisher model. But casual games have heralded a new corporate side of
games separate from but related to the traditional Triple-A industry, with large publisher/
developer houses emerging, such as Zynga. The rise of casual games as a legitimate business venture sent ripples through the games industry, as was clear from various heated
discussions at the 2010 and 2011 Game Developers Conferences (GDC) in San Francisco,
with many traditional developers seeing casual games as venture capitalism hiding
under the thinnest veil of game design. In particular, the rise of cheap or free mobile
games functioning under a "free-to-play" model led to claims such as Nintendo of
America President Regie Fils-Aime dismissing mobile games as "disposable" in a GDC
2011 keynote (Kohler 2011), while at the same conference, critic and developer Ian
Bogost called out Zynga's social game model as "high fructose slot machines" and further
critiqued them with a satirical Facebook game, *Cow Clicker* (Brown 2011). Free-to-play
alters game design to, in the worse scenario, create a "pay-to-win" scenario where a game
is deliberately broken until the player pays money to fix it.[1] Concerns have been
raised of the similarities between free-to-play games and gambling machines such as
slot machines to lure players in and then ask for money, often in fake currencies to
obscure how much money they are actually spending (Woodford 2013).

While these concerns are valid, they also highlight an anxiety in established game
development and consumption practices towards a new form of games that does not
conform to known values—casual games are neither the technologically advanced
"realism" of Triple-A games, nor the ambivalence of financial success important to
indie. What is ultimately at stake in the "casualisation" of videogame cultures is an
identity: what it means to be someone who plays videogames. Traditionally an out-
sider identity held by geeks and hackers as a badge of honour, videogames are now
mainstream and ubiquitous, played on trains by businessmen and on computers by

parents and on airplanes by small children. There is no longer anything unique about being into videogames. However, a fascinating survey by Adrienne Shaw (2011) shows that, despite this ubiquity of videogames, very few videogame players identify as "gamers." Indeed, it is only those (predominately male) players of core games that identify as such. Most people who play videogames do not consider it a defining part of their identity but as "an integral part of everyday [social network site] communication" (Hjorth and Arnold 2012, 105). Just like watching commercial TV or listening to pop music, videogames are now just something people do, and their design has changed—for better and for worse—to adapt to this.

The DIY and amateur scenes: Videogames become personal

If the casualisation of videogames sees them being produced for wider audiences, then the nascent DIY scenes related to but excluded from "indie" are about videogames being *produced by* wider audiences. As a medium that emerged from science departments that privileges programming and technological virtuosity, videogame development has been traditionally dominated by those middle-to-upper-class (mostly white) men that can afford to and are encouraged to enter science, technology, engineering and maths (STEM) university courses. This is no less true of the supposedly more democratic indie scene as for corporate Triple-A studios, as most revealingly shown in the conspicuous lack of non-male or non-white developers in the documentary film *Indie Game: The Movie*. "Indie" sees influence on game design distributed beyond more than the Triple-A publishers, but continues to privilege the same demographic of creators.

Game developer Anna Anthropy—perhaps the most recognisable developer in the DIY scenes—succinctly notes this issue as a "culture of alienation":

> Limiting the creation of games to a small, exclusive group leads not only to creative stagnation, but also to the alienation of anyone outside that group ... games are designed by a small, male-dominated culture and marketed to a small, male-dominated audience, which in turn produced the next small, male-dominated generation of game designers. It's a bubble, and it largely produces work that has no meaning to those outside that bubble, those not already entrenched in the culture of games.
>
> (Anthropy 2012, 12–13)

This echoes Kirkpatrick's observations that those who make the previous successful games get to determine what it means to be a "good" game (2013, 80), and can be seen in all facets of mainstream videogame culture, from the utter dominance of male playable characters (Bee 2013), to sexist advertising (Walker 2013b), to heteronormative and white-washed narratives (Walker 2013a). Anthropy's call to rectify this is not to make games for more kinds of people, as casual games do, but to have more kinds of people making games.

While the commercial indie scene remains entangled with economic concerns to produce a sustainable living from their games (as is explicit in the closing scenes of *Indie Game: The Movie*, concluding by mentioning how many sales each game has made), the DIY scene is more interested in making games for the sake of making. This is most visible in Anthropy's call for people to produce games like one would create a zine: personal, trashy, distributed through personal channels. She calls for people to "sketch" videogames like one might sketch out a poem or a doodle (2012, 112), less focused on realism or immersion or even quality than in trying to say something through the medium of games. This has become increasingly possible with the rise of affordable game development software like GameMaker, RPG Maker, and Unity. These programs make it increasingly easy for people with no practical experience to put a rough game together and, inevitably, this is leading to the production of new kinds of games, such as Mattie Brice's *Mainichi* (produced in RPGMaker) or Merritt Kopas's *Lim* (produced in Construct 2.0), both of which have been critically acclaimed and shown at various shows and conferences since their releases.

Most significant is Twine, a hypertext fiction editor that has been picked up by amateur game creators to spark a renaissance of text-orientated videogames. Through basic HTML code, Twine has allowed various developers to make and distribute successful games, such as Porpentine with *Howling Dogs*, Zoë Quinn with *Depression Quest*, and Kopas with *Conversations With My Mother*. While many Twine games are distributed for free, Quinn's *Depression Quest* and, more recently, Anthropy's *A Very Very VERY Scary House*, and Kopas's *Consensual Torture Simulator* have begun to experiment with selling their games directly to players through online portals such as Gumroad.

When considering the cultural industries of videogames, it would be tempting to dismiss these DIY developers as mere hobbyists working off to the side of the "industry," but to do so is to greatly misunderstand their significance. The contemporary DIY scenes represent, according to industry commentator Leigh Alexander, "the road to a healthy culture and a genuinely mature, artistically legitimate games industry" (2013, 48). They represent the first time game design *and* distribution has been in the hands of a more diverse crowd, and this greatly affects what videogames are popularly imagined to be by both creators and audiences. Such games as those above have already drastically impacted mainstream videogame culture. They are often discussed and written about on game journalism outlets such as *Kotaku* alongside Triple-A and indie releases. They spark extensive (and occasionally vicious) formalist debates among veteran developers and critics about just what a videogame "is" as these new developers ignore the standards imposed by a hegemonic culture that marginalised them.[2] At 2013's GDC, Anna Anthropy and Porpentine took central roles, such as Anna's reading of a version of game critic Cara Ellison's poem "Romero's Wives" to a predominately male audience, extensively listing moments of systemic sexism in the videogame industries (Anthropy 2012). The DIY scenes challenge entrenched powers and investments, and show new meanings and values videogames could have beyond the narrow "culture of alienation." To ignore these scenes in a discussion of the videogame cultural industries is to ignore a significant intervention in a traditionally and systemically hegemonic and patriarchal medium.

Conclusion

Across the intersections of Triple-A, indie, casual, and DIY game design, a diverse rang of values emerge and clash that mediate the games that are created and distributed. Triple-A games value technological power and virtuosic performances, the ability to depict a certain "realism" to be "immersed" in, and a certain level of challenge to feel powerful over. Indie games antagonise the values of Triple-A, prioritising out-dated realisms from previous eras of Triple-A development and producing a style that evokes a sense of nostalgia. Casual games, meanwhile, value accessibility and flexibility, removing the dense difficulty and incoherent control schemes that "core" gamers pride themselves on mastering, and reduce the time and attention demanded of players to instead be incorporated into their everyday lives through social and mobile media platforms. The emergent and influential DIY scenes counter the predominately commercial concerns to demonstrate that while games are increasingly created by larger teams for larger audiences, it is also possible to communicate personal, authored experiences through games.

Tracing the intersections and tensions between these different videogame scenes are nascent discourses of videogame criticism. While the consumer-orientated enthusiast press has existed for decades (Kirkpatrick 2013, 75; Carlson 2009), the past decade has seen a more critically focused discourse emerge between bloggers, essayists, and developers in what Abraham has observed as a "critical videogame blogosphere." Centred around websites like *Critical Distance*, these critics are more interested in discussing textual meaning than graphical power, gender representation than plot points. Such discourses hold the traditional cultural ambivalence of games to account, as has recently been seen in the past year in critical essays around blockbuster releases, such as Daniel Golding taking issue with *Bioshock: Infinite*'s "veneer of intelligence" (2013), or Cameron Kunzelman critiquing the flaccid satire of *Grand Theft Auto: V* (2013). Much like the DIY scenes, this maturing of critical discourses around the videogame medium reflects maturing and diversifying cultural industries not adequately represented by any one branch.

While this chapter has outlined some of the key tensions and debates currently shaping the videogame cultural industries, it has of course not acknowledged everything. There is an increased excitement around videogames as "tools" for social change and education, such as the "Games For Change" movement and the notion of a "ludic century" ahead of us (Zimmerman and Chaplin 2013). Further, there is the increasingly lucrative e-sports industry and the coinciding rise in online streaming and "Let's Play" videos (Taylor 2012). Also on the rise is an increased focus on regional game development to complement those of a global game industry, such as Daniel Joseph's observations on the "assemblage" of the Toronto indie scene (2013), Hjorth and Chan's focus on *Gaming Cultures and Place in Asia-Pacific* (2009), and Izushi and Aoyama's comparative analysis of UK, US, and Japanese industrial sectors (2006).

Videogames are more than the Triple-A experiences that dominate the media's attention and the popular imagining. These games exist in a complicated relationship with indie, casual, and DIY development cultures that each have some say in what is valued as good videogame design. While any one of these relationships could be explored in far greater depth than has been done here, this outline provides a starting point to appreciate the true complexity of the videogames cultural industries.

Notes

1 See Rogers's (2011) scathing assessment of *The Sims Social* as an example.
2 For this debate, see Anthropy 2013, Street 2013, and Kopas 2012.

References

Alexander, Leigh. 2013. "Playing Outside." *The New Inquiry* 17: 42–48.

Anthropy, Anna. 2012. *Rise of the Videogame Zinesters*. New York: Seven Stories Press.

Anthropy, Anna. 2013. "Well Played." *Auntie Pixelante*, August 10 (auntiepixelante.com/?p=2159).

Banks, John and Sal Humphreys. 2008. "The Labour of User Co-Creators: Emergent Social Network Markets?" *Convergence* 14 (4): 401–18.

Bee, Aevee. 2013. "No Women Bingo." *Mammon Machine*, September 10 (www.mammon machine.com/mammon-machine-central-routing/2014/9/27/no-women-bingo).

Brown, Nathan. 2011. "GDC 2011: Are Social Games Legitimate?" *Edge*, March 2 (www.edge-online.com/news/gdc-2011-are-social-games-legitimate/).

Carlson, Rebecca. 2009. "'Too Human' Versus the Enthusiast Press: Video Game Journalists as Mediators of Commodity Value." *Transformative Works and Cultures* 2.

De Peuter, Greig, and Nick Dyer-Witheford. 2005. "A Playful Multitude? Mobilising and Counter-Mobilising Immaterial Game Labour." *Fibreculture* 5.

Deuze, Mark, Chase Bowen Martin, and Christian Allen. 2007. "The Professional Identity of Gameworkers." *Convergence* 13: 335–53.

Dyer-Witheford, Nick, and Greig de Peuter. 2009. *Games of Empire: Global Capitalism and Video Games*. Minneapolis: University of Minnesota Press.

Ellison, Cara. 2012. "Romero's Wives." *Nightmare Mode*, November 30 (nightmaremode.thegamerstrust.com/2012/11/30/romeros-wives).

Golding, Daniel. 2013. "*Bioshock Infinite*: An Intelligent, Violent Videogame?" *ABC Arts*, April 9 (www.abc.net.au/arts/stories/s3733057.htm).

Hjorth, Larissa, and Dean Chan. 2009. *Gaming Cultures and Place in Asia-Pacific*. New York: Routledge.

Hjorth, Larissa, and Ingrid Richardson. 2009. "The Waiting Game: Complicating Notions of (Tele)presence and Gendered DIstraction in Casual Mobile Gaming." *Australian Journal of Communication* 36 (1): 23–35.

Hjorth, Larissa, and Michael Arnold. 2012. "Playing at Being Social: A Cross-Generational Case Study of Social Gaming in Shanghai." In *Global Gaming*, edited by Nina Huntemann and Ben Aslinger, 101–17. New York: Routledge.

Huhtamo, Erkki. 2005. "Slots of Fun, Slots of Trouble: An Archaeology of Arcade Gaming." In *Handbook of Computer Game Studies*, edited by Joost Raessens and Jeffrey Goldstein, 3–22. Cambridge: MIT Press.

Izushi, Hiro, and Yuko Aoyama. 2006. "Industry Evolution and Cross-Sectoral Skill Transfers: A Comparative Analysis of the Video Game Industry in Japan, the United States, and the United Kingdom." *Environment and Planning A* 38: 1843–61.

Joseph, Daniel. 2013. "The Toronto Indies: Some Assemblage Required." *Loading …* 7 (11): 92–105.

Juul, Jesper. 2010. *A Casual Revolution: Reinventing Video Games and Their Players*. Cambridge: MIT Press.

Kirkpatrick, Graeme. 2013. *Computer Games and the Social Imaginary*. Cambridge: Polity Press.

Kohler, Chris. 2011. "Apple, Nintendo Slug It Out for Gaming Supremacy at GDC." *Wired*, March 1 (www.wired.com/gamelife/2011/03/apple-nintendo-gdc-ipad-3ds/).

Kopas, Merritt. 2012. "On the 'Non-Game'." July 18 (mkopas.net/2012/07/on-the-non-game/).

Kunzelman, Cameron. 2013. "'An Immature and Outrageous Satire': on *Grand Theft Auto 5*, Satire, and Irony." *This Cage Is Worms*, October 15 (thiscageisworms.com/2013/10/15/an-immature-and-outrageous-satire-on-grand-theft-auto-5-satire-and-irony/).

Lipkin, Nadav. 2013. "Examining Indie's Independence: The Meaning of 'Indie' Games, the Politics of Production, and Mainstream Co-Optation." *Loading …* 7 (11): 8–24.

McMillen, Andrew. 2011. "Why Did *L.A. Noire* Take Seven Years to Make? Examining the Troubled Development of Team Bondi's Opus." *IGN*, 24 June (au.ign.com/articles/2011/06/24/why-did-la-noire-take-seven-years-to-make).

Parker, Felan. 2013. "An Art World for Artgames." *Loading …* 7 (11): 41–60.

Phillips, Tom. 2013. "*Tomb Raider* has sold 3.4 million copies, failed to hit expectations." *Eurogamer*, March 26 (www.eurogamer.net/articles/2013-03-26-tomb-raider-has-sold-3-4-million-copies-failed-to-hit-expectations).

Rogers, Tim. 2011. "*The Sims Social*" *Action Button*, September 23 (www.actionbutton.net/?p=1076).

Shaw, Adrienne. 2011. "Do You Identify as a Gamer? Gender, Race, Sexuality, and Gamer Identity." *New Media Society* 14 (1): 28–44.

Simon, Bart. 2013. "Indie Eh? Some Kind of Game Studies." *Loading …* 7 (11): 1–7.

Street, Zoya. 2013. "What is a Game? It Depends Who's Playing." *Zoya Street*, January 9 (zoyastreet.com/2013/01/09/what-is-a-game-it-depends-whos-playing/).

Taylor, T.L. 2006. *Play Between Worlds: Exploring Online Game Culture*. Cambridge: MIT Press.

Taylor, T.L. 2012. *Raising the Stakes: E-Sports and the Professionalization of Computer Gaming*. Cambridge: MIT Press.

Turkle, Sherry. 2005. *The Second Self: Computers and the Human Spirit*. 20th Anniversary Ed. Cambridge: MIT.

Walker, Austin. 2013a. "Me, on the Screen: Race in *Animal Crossing: New Leaf*." *Clockwork Worlds*, June 17 (clockworkworlds.com/post/53240010750/me-on-the-screen-race-in-animal-crossing-new-leaf).

Walker, John. 2013b. "Deep Silver Promote *Dead Island* with Appalling Statue." *RockPaperShotgun*, 15 January (www.rockpapershotgun.com/2013/01/15/deep-silver-promote-dead-island-with-appalling-statue/).

Williams, Ian. 2013. "'You Can Sleep Here All Night': Video Games and Labor." *Jacobin*, November 8 (jacobinmag.com/2013/11/video-game-industry/).

Wilson, Jason Anthony. 2007. "Gameplay and the Aesthetics of Intimacy." Ph.D. dissertation. Brisbane: Griffith University.

Woodford, Darryl. 2013. "Governance Challenges in the Global Games Industry." *New Directions in the Development of Creative and Media Industries Conference*. Chinese University of Hong Kong: June 7–8.

Zacny, Rob. 2012. "Death March: The Long, Tortured Journey of *Homefront*." *Polygon*, November 1 (www.polygon.com/2012/11/1/3560318/homefront-kaos-studios-thq).

Zimmerman, Eric, and Heather Chaplin. 2013. "Manifesto: The 21st Century Will Be Defined By Games." *Kotaku*, September 9 (kotaku.com/manifesto-the-21st-century-will-be-defined-by-games-1275355204).

12

'THIS SPORTING LIFE IS GOING TO BE THE DEATH OF ME'

Sport as a cultural industry

Steve Redhead

This chapter draws on the author's experience as Chair of Premier Geoff Gallop Creative Industries Taskforce in Western Australia, as well as advising various Ministers in other governments, including Tony Banks in the New Labour government in the United Kingdom, to tease out some of the connections between sport and cultural industries as global society becomes more "accelerated" (Redhead 2004) and "claustropolitan" (Redhead 2011). In some ways, the new watershed for "theory" is the global financial crisis (GFC) of 2007/2008 (Tett 2009) which was followed by a brief "global Keynesianism" (Blyth 2013) before a return to a more generalized, brutish neoliberalism. Many of the works on new directions in theory have been published since the watershed, though much of the work was bubbling under in the early years of the new century. More generally in academic life globally, discipline after discipline has agonized over whether the tenets of yesteryear still hold good, and whether or not we need to return to the beginning or origin of such disciplines (Douzinas and Zizek 2010: 209–26; Lacan 2008). For example, after cultural studies has, in the view of some participants, lost its way (Turner, G. 2012), other founding fathers have asked, anxiously, "what is the future of cultural studies?" (Grossberg 2010). Economists have asked what is there left of economics after the (economic) crisis (Turner, A. 2012). Legal studies has renewed its call for new critical legal theory and for "law and critique" as never before (Douzinas 2009). Critical criminology, including sub-disciplines such as cultural criminology, has found something of a new post-crash international direction (Hall 2012; Hall and Winlow 2012; Winlow and Atkinson 2012a, 2012b). In critical social policy, books like *Rethinking Social Exclusion: The end of the social?* (Hall and Winlow 2013) are compulsory reading for anyone interested in the "reproletarianization" of the West and global twenty-first-century capitalism's rush to the cliff edge of "post-catastrophe" (Redhead 2011). Philosophy has mused about whether it still has the power to explain events like the riots in the

United Kingdom in 2011 (Hall and Winlow 2013; Hall 2012) and the ongoing Arab Spring in the way that, say, Karl Marx analysed the revolutions in Europe in 1848 and provided ethical and political intervention (Badiou 2012a, 2012b, 2012c, 2012d, 2011, 2009, 2007; Zizek 2012a, 2012b; Badiou and Zizek 2009), reviving, for a new century, the question of the "idea of communism" (Zizek 2013; Douzinas and Zizek 2010) and the "communist hypothesis" (Zizek 2009: 87–157; Badiou 2010).

This sporting life will be the death of me

The film of David Storey's *This Sporting Life* (1963) remains, half a century after its release as a black and white film classic, an authenticated tale of violence, men and sport in the North of England. It is a 'realist' picture steeped in observations of a specific era of northern working class rugby league, using Wakefield Trinity's facilities for some of the shoot. The movie was made in 1963 from David Storey's 1960 novel of the same name (Storey 1960), part of a wider so-called "kitchen sink" portrayal of British working class culture. *This Sporting Life* starred Richard Harris and Rachel Roberts and involved 1950s New Wave protagonists Karel Reisz as producer and Lindsay Anderson as director. Anderson's anguish at his own hidden homosexuality, which was illegal in the England of the 1950s and early 1960s, and the sheer obsessiveness of his pursuit of Richard Harris, the leading man in *This Sporting Life*, pervade the film's images (Sutton 2005). David Storey, a working-class Wakefield boy who later studied at the Slade School of Art in London, was a prolific author and playwright but is still best known today for the novel that spawned the film. In his ordinary life in a northern town David Storey was a rugby league player who played professionally for Leeds for a while. Storey at age 72, interviewed by the *Observer Sport Monthly*, recollected that:

> At the age of 18 I signed a contract to play rugby league for Leeds. My father had been a miner and he was outraged when I told him what I really wanted to do was go to art school. Taking the contract was going to be the only way I could pay for my education. Being perceived as an effete art student often made the dressing room a very uncomfortable place for me ... I used to write the book on the train when I was coming back from art school to play for Leeds. The title came from something I heard on the radio one night: "This sporting life is going to be the death of me: I'm going to settle down." I know it's a cliché but the idea of sport as a metaphor for life was what interested me most. Fifteen publishers rejected the book; one told me they would consider it if I took out all the "fucks." Eventually Longmans agreed to publish the book – fucks and all. And then a few years later, Lindsay Anderson made it into a film, with Richard Harris in the lead, which gave it a tremendous boost.
>
> (Storey 2005: 3)

David Storey's book was voted number eight in the top fifty sports books of all time in a poll organized by the *Observer Sport Monthly* in 2005. There are many other examples of sports films and books, all of which would be easily classifiable as products of a specific cultural industry. Steven Patrick Morrissey (once of The Smiths), an incorrigible fan of the New Wave and its legacy, "came out" in his *Autobiography* (Morrissey 2013: 28) as a Manchester United football fan and, even more specifically, a George Best devotee. In a passage that could have come from the pen of David Storey himself (the book was, controversially, published in the Penguin Classics series in 2013 after all) he says:

> Best is the shocking new against Charlton's 1950s pipe-smoking discipline. It is the physical and facial glamour that gains him so much love and hate, for everybody wants what he has. My father takes me to see George Best play at Old Trafford, and as I see the apocalyptic disturber of the peace swirl across the pitch, I faint. I am eight years old. Squinting in the sun it is all too much for me, and I remember my father's rasp as he dragged my twisted body through the crowd and out into the street, causing him to miss the rest of the match. Another form of church, football was all that stood between earth and God.

Strangely, George Best seems to have been the "quarry" for the young Morrissey in 1967, almost as much as Richard Harris was for Lindsay Anderson. The decade David Storey first started writing was the 1950s, though he had considerable literary longevity for decades. It was the period of the dominance of "creative arts" as a concept and an organizing principle of cultural production. It predated concepts of cultural industries and creative industries by many years. It was also the period that Morrissey looks back on with fondness and longing in his Smiths and post-Smiths lyrics and "autobiographical" writing. It still overlaps with cultural industries and creative industries debates today.

A sporting future for all?

However, whether or not sport is, as David Storey proclaims, a "metaphor for life", the question before us remains – is sport itself a cultural industry? Or, even, more questionably, is sport a creative industry? In many countries, sporting industries are not regularly included in lists of creative or cultural industries when cultural mapping exercises are carried out. A review of the *Creative Industries Journal*, begun in 2008, reveals no articles on sport in any of the numbers published up to October 2013, issues which range widely and globally across creative and cultural industries. Equally, journals such as *Soccer and Society* and *Sport in Society* in the same period do not feature work on cultural or creative industries either. One area of connection has, however, been the field of fandom, particularly in the areas of sport and popular music and their crossover. Sport as a realm was seen as an anathema in many cultural industries' policy initiatives, such as the Greater London Council (GLC) in the 1980s in Britain, frequently because of its perceived connections to reactionary social and political practices such as hooliganism, homophobia, sexism and racism. Going further back into recent history the "creative arts" were seen as completely separate from "sports" at all levels. Ironically both were seen as intrinsically "good for you" and worthwhile in modern society in their own right: art for art's sake and sport for sport's sake. Sport, and sporting life, though, was not as often seen as regenerative for cities in the way that cultural or creative industries have been justified. For at least two decades, the notion of cultural industries has sat side by side with city cultures and urban regeneration, which in turn has included the problematic idea of the cultural regeneration of cities (Flew 2011; Kong and O'Connor 2009; O'Connor 2002, 2004), with cultural and leisure precincts or quarters becoming the major focus for boosterism and economic impact, dragging more diverse cultural pursuits – such as sporting industries, galleries and museums and gardens – in their wake in a very uneven manner. Cities throughout the world have begun to "brand" themselves through culture as the notion of the "creative city" has emerged and expanded globally (Kong and O'Connor 2009; O'Connor 2004).

However, the "creative industries" as a term emerged in the United Kingdom in the first Tony Blair/New Labour government, in part from the bowels of the Department for Culture, Media and Sport (DCMS) at Cockspur Street in London, and, in some territories around the world, sport and creative industries do distinctly overlap. The cultural production of sport globally is inclusive of image rights for players and media sports rights for clubs and other significant intellectual property. The knowledge economy approach within cultural and creative industries would suggest that sport should be routinely included as a cultural or creative industry.

But there are as many problems as possibilities with this kind of taxonomy. If we classify sport as *outside* cultural or creative industries, does it follow that sport is not an important consideration for cultural or creative industries debates? If it questions the basis of creative or cultural industries approaches then the answer is "yes". Partly the issue is a fraught debate over definitions of creative or cultural industries themselves. It is not "two cultures" of sporting industries and cultural industries that Stuart Cunningham refers to in his book on the "creative sector" but the age-old division between science and the creative sector, first identified by C. P. Snow fifty years ago. Definitions of "cultural" and "creative" industries vary widely (Cunningham 2013; Flew 2011; Bilton 2007; Hartley 2004; O'Connor 2002, 2004) but "culture" in this sense, at the very least, means industries and practices like design, architecture, multimedia, music, film, broadcasting, publishing and fashion, as well as information software and video games, but rarely sport and sporting industries. As some leading international academic commentators have pointed out (Andersen and Oakley 2008; Cunningham 2002), cultural industries as a phrase is essentially an older notion or definitional apparatus, with "creative industries" emerging as an international label in the mid-1990s, essentially through the preparations of the Tony Blair and Gordon Brown led Labour Party in the United Kingdom, first in opposition after the death of John Smith and then in government from 1997 to 2010 (Kong and O'Connor 2009; Andersen and Oakley 2008). As Justin O'Connor (2012) has pointed out, the origin of the label "creative industries" was never an academic or policy oriented one as was the case with the genesis of cultural industries. It was formed in the white heat of struggle between UK Treasury and the DCMS in its transition from the Department of National Heritage (DNH, lampooned as "the Department of No-One Home"!). Major academic and policy arguments have taken place over the area covered by the two seemingly similar labels, cultural and creative industries, frequently without any discussion of sport. The development of creative industries policy

(Andersen and Oakley 2008), especially in the DCMS in the thirteen-year-long New Labour government, was first local, then national, then global. Brown and Blair conducted an innovative experiment that is often cited approvingly in the creative industries and creative cities debates around the world, especially in Oceania and Asia (Kong and O'Connor 2009; Leo and Lee 2004), yet sport was problematic within this formation from the beginning. Sport in the 1990s and 2000s, most of the time, was dependent on policy formation based on fandom, or what I labelled, somewhat ironically, as "post-fandom" (Redhead 1997). It became de rigeur in this period for politicians and policy makers in Britain to claim allegiance to a particular football club, for instance, embarrassing as it may seem to recall. The inaugural Secretary of State for Culture, Media and Sport, Chris Smith, had no interest in sport or sporting industries. *Creative Britain* (Smith 1998), his book of speeches as New Labour Secretary of State in the late 1990s, ignored sport and sporting industries and their potentially progressive links with New Labour concepts of cultural politics and "cultural capitalism" (Bewes and Gilbert 2000), instead reflecting the overdetermination on first term New Labour thinking of the "Brit Art" and pop culture of the Damien Hirst painting on its cover. It was left to former GLC acolyte and Chelsea fan, Minister of Sport Tony Banks, to wave the flag, or, rather, carry the can when the old sporting life of hooliganism, homophobia, sexism and racism raised its ugly head in New Labour cosmopolitanism. The New Labour policy *A Sporting Future For All* was produced under Tony Banks' Sports Ministerial gaze but those of us who worked on it felt that it would have benefited from input from the earlier incarnation of Banks as a proponent of a radical cultural industries policy at the GLC when he was working alongside Ken Livingstone. Tony Blair, despite his media-led Newcastle United sports fandom, was only marginally interested in sport, though Gordon Brown was a keen and knowledgeable global football fan and Raith Rovers devotee. Essentially, sport was an add-on for New Labour – it was not part of any notion of creative labour or creative sector (Cunningham 2013; McKinlay and Smith 2009). My own personal experience as Chair of the Creative Industries Taskforce of Western Australia in 2004 was very similar; Geoff Gallop, the Premier, had been a long time friend of Tony Blair and the outlook for the "Creative WA" policy was essentially "Blairite". Some of "Creative WA" was implemented in Western Australia in the mid-2000s by Form – formerly Craft West – which took up the thrust of the "creative capital" ideas at its heart. But the Taskforce developed was strictly within the parameters of the first term New Labour government in the UK; sport as a cultural or creative industry was never on the agenda. It is argued here in the final section of this chapter that debates about cultural and creative industries should be resituated within the wider framework of the agenda of a claustropolitan sociology critique of cosmopolitan sociology and its (still problematic) analyses of sporting industries relying on theorists such as Zygmunt Bauman (Dixon 2013) and Norbert Elias (Gibbons 2014).

Claustropolitanism and the end of creative industries

It has started to be suggested in cultural and creative industries literature that the current period is one defined by getting used to "life after creative industries"

(O'Connor 2012). Academics who once branded themselves with the "creative industries" label have moved back to "cultural industries" or on to more traditional sounding epithets like "cultural science" or "cultural economy" or "creative economy", and around the world whole university faculties that transformed themselves into creative industries schools or faculties in the early twenty-first century have started to look elsewhere for branding and labelling for at least the rest of the decade. The positing of the "end of creative industries" involves two possible scenarios. One is the widespread imagining of the end of a pregnant concept, "the creative industries", which perhaps always had the trajectory of a relatively short shelf-life compared to the longevity of a concept such as cultural industries. Second, there is the scenario of a global move away from "cosmopolitanism", which has embraced concepts like creative industries and knowledge economy, in times of economic and political insecurity. Some writers have indeed talked of times "after cosmopolitanism" (Braidotti et al. 2013) but also of the need for a "cosmopolitics". I want to argue here that both sport and cultural industries, as fields, are underpinned by a sociology of "cosmopolitanism" that is now more and more questionable as we move from conditions associated with "cosmopolis" to those of "claustropolis" (Redhead 2011), and even a future claustropolitan society. I have argued in my recent work that, since the global financial crisis of 2007, a greater shift in global social relations is taking place than concepts and practices around cosmopolitanism have thus far imagined. With the regeneration of neoliberalism since the global financial crisis, it has been a case of business as usual for many commenators. But this is unlikely to remain the case for very long as more aftershocks take the global condition on a very different, and dangerous "post-catastrophic" road (Redhead 2011). We saw at the beginning of this essay the extent to which many disciplines are searching for renewal "after the crash", but the speed of the move into claustropolitan waters is so rapid that simple renewal may not be enough. What is required, in my view, at a minimum, is a more thorough-going "claustropolitan sociology" (Redhead 2011); but contemporary theoretical resources are scarce, and often prone to being what I call "over-apocalyptic", predicting too much of "the end times" in a quasi-theological theoretical rush for the cliff edge (Virilio 2012; Zizek and Gunjevic 2012; Zizek 2011; Feltham 2008). One of these contemporary theorists, Paul Virilio, the French theorist of the bunker and speed, and exponent of what I have labelled "bunker anthropology" (Redhead 2011), has noted in conversation with Sylvere Lotringer, "What I called claustropolis has replaced cosmopolis, where I'm from, since I'm the son of an illegal Italian immigrant in France. On the other hand in Shanghai, in China, they're the avant-garde of modernity, in terms of claustropolis" (Virilio and Lotringer 2008: 211).

Virilio has had all kinds of impossible conceptual demands made on his work (Armitage 2001, 2011, 2012, 2013; Armitage and Bishop 2013) from postmodernism and critical cultural theory, but quite aside from such milieu his specific insights are sharp and relevant as singular "post-theory" (Redhead 2011), especially in terms of the consequences of global sporting industries becoming part of what Virilio terms the "city of the instant" or "futurism of the moment", events broadcast live and watched all over the globe at the same time (give or take a little digital delay). As Virilio told Sylvere Lotringer in the early 1980s (Virilio and Lotringer 2008: 99–100), musing about the Maracana Stadium in Brazil (recently renovated and privatized for the 2014 soccer World Cup and which once held 200,000 people), the World Cup in Argentina in 1978 and the Moscow 1980 Olympics, live mega-events extraordinaire:

> The production of speed is a recent event: it goes back to the beginning of the nineteeenth century … the serious problem is that those present, those who participate, those for example who attend an auto race are disqualified by the absentees. The billion people who watch the Olympic Games in Moscow, or the soccer championship in Argentina, impose their power at the expense of those present, who are already superfluous. The latter are practically no more than bodies filling the stadium so that it won't look empty. But their physical presence is completely alienated by the absence of the television viewer, and that's what interests me in this situation. Once, the stadiums were full. It was a magnificent popular explosion. There were 200,000 people in the grandstands, singing and shouting. It was a vision from an ancient society, from the agora, from paganism. Now when you watch the Olympics or the soccer championship on television, you notice there aren't that many people. And even they, in a certain way, aren't the ones who make the World Cup. The ones who make the World Cup are the radios and televisions that buy and – by favouring a billion and a half television viewers – "produce" the championship. Those absent from the stadium are always right, economically and massively. They have the power. The participants are always wrong.

When we contemplate the mega sporting events of the next decade, we should remember Virilio's enigmatic phrase – "those absent from the stadium are always right." Think of the future events to come in an increasingly claustropolitan environment globally – after the Winter Olympics in Sochi, Russia 2014 and the soccer World Cup in 2014 in Brazil, there are potentially fraught mega-events such as the Olympics in Brazil in 2016, the soccer World Cup in Russia 2018, and the soccer World Cup in Qatar 2022, for example. But this scenario painted by Virilio also connotes a more apocalyptic, claustropolitan place for sport and sporting industries more generally: the world, for instance, of ubiquitous illegal betting dominated scandals in international cricket and the corrupt practices of financial incentives for sport media event bids like the World Cup within FIFA, the governing body of world soccer, from the 1990s onwards, and the "live" global sport media coverage of such events. For crotchety *Guardian* columnist Simon Jenkins (2010: 25),

> the truth is that international sport has become so bloated by national pride and celebrity as to lose all sense of proportion. The Geneva centre of housing rights and evictions reckons sport to be one of the biggest displacers of humanity, perhaps second only to war. In two decades some two million people have had to make way for Olympic stadiums and villages.

Paul Virilio (Virilio and Depardon 2008a: 184), too, has warned that, officially, it is being estimated that "the future environmental migrant" numbers will be "one billion"; moreover that "six hundred and forty five million people will be displaced from their homes over the next forty years" and that "two hundred and fifty million will be displaced by phenomena related to climate change", all part of a "demographic resettlement" of the globe on a massive scale as exodus from cities (and also, even, for Virilio, the planet) gathers pace in the next fifty years (Virilio 2010a, 2010b, 2009; Virilio and Depardon 2008b). Sport mega events, in various cities around the world will, far from regenerating the urban environment as has been the orthodoxy in the past in cultural industries and creative industries literature, be a cause of part of this resettlement.

This chapter has explored some of the questions inherent in thinking about classifying sport as a cultural industry. In many countries, sporting industries are not regularly included in lists of cultural industries when cultural mapping exercises are carried out. Sport as a field or a realm was seen as an anathema in many cultural industries policy initiatives but even as the question raises itself again in policy debates, the end of creative industries itself as a viable field of inquiry threatens to make these questions redundant in a coming era of claustropolitanism.

References

Andersen, L. and Oakley, K. (eds) (2008) *Making Meaning, Making Money: Directions for the arts and cultural industries in the creative age*, Newcastle: Cambridge Scholars.
Armitage, J. (2001) *Virilio Live: Selected interviews*, London: Sage.
Armitage, J. (2011) *Virilio Now: Current perspectives in Virilio studies*, Cambridge: Polity.
Armitage, J. (2012) *Virilio and the Media*, Cambridge: Polity.
Armitage, J. (ed.) (2013) *The Virilio Dictionary*, Edinburgh: Edinburgh University Press.
Armitage, J. and Bishop, R. (eds) (2013) *Virilio and Visual Culture*, Edinburgh: Edinburgh University Press.
Badiou, A. (2007) *The Meaning of Sarkozy*, London: Verso.
Badiou, A. (2009) *Pocket Pantheon: Figures of post-war philosophy*, London: Verso.
Badiou, A. (2010) *The Communist Hypothesis*, London: Verso.
Badiou, A. (2011) *Wittgenstein's Antiphilosophy*, London: Verso.
Badiou, A. (2012a) *The Rebirth of History: The times of rebellions and uprisings*, London: Verso.
Badiou, A. (2012b) *In Praise of Love*, London: Serpent's Tail.
Badiou, A. (2012c) *The Adventure of French Philosophy*, London: Verso.
Badiou, A. (2012d) *Philosophy for Militants*, London: Verso.
Badiou, A. and Zizek, S. (2009) *Philosophy in the Present*, Cambridge: Polity.
Bewes, T. and Gilbert, J. (2000) *Cultural Capitalism: Politics after New Labour*, London: Lawrence and Wishart.
Bilton, C. (2007) *Management and Creativity: From creative industries to creative management*, Oxford: Blackwell.
Blyth, S. (2013) *Austerity: The history of a dangerous idea*, Oxford and New York: Oxford University Press.
Braidotti, R., Hanafin, P. and Blaagaard, B. (eds) (2013) *After Cosmopolitanism*, London: Routledge.
Cunningham, S. (2002) "From Cultural to Creative Industries: Theory, industry and policy implications", *Media International Australia incorporating Culture and Policy*, 102: 54–65.
Cunningham, S. (2013) *Hidden Innovation: Policy, industry and the creative sector*, Brisbane: University of Queensland Press.
Dixon, K. (2013) *Consuming Football in Late Modern Life*, Aldershot: Ashgate.

Douzinas, C. (2009) "Law and Critique, Twentieth Anniversary: Editor's introduction", *Law and Critique*, 20 (1): 1–2.

Douzinas, C. and Zizek, S. (eds) (2010) *The Idea of Communism*, London: Verso.

Feltham, O. (2008) *Alain Badiou: Live theory*, London: Continuum.

Flew, T. (2011) *The Creative Industries: Culture and policy*, London: Sage.

Gibbons, T. (2014) *English National Identity And Football Fan Culture: Who are ya?* Aldershot: Ashgate.

Grossberg, L. (2010) *Cultural Studies in the Future Tense*, Durham: Duke University Press.

Hall, S. (2012) *Theorising Crime and Deviance: A new perspective*, London: Sage.

Hall, S. and Winlow, S. (eds) (2012) *New Directions in Criminological Theory*, London: Routledge.

Hall, S. and Winlow, S. (2013) *Rethinking Social Exclusion: The end of the social?* London: Sage.

Hartley, J. (ed.) (2004) *Creative Industries*, London: Wiley-Blackwell.

Jenkins, S. (2010) "Compared to a Lootfest like London or Beijing, Delhi is just an Also-Ran", *Guardian*, 24 September: 16.

Kong, L. and O'Connor, J. (eds) (2009) *Creative Economies, Creative Cities: Asian-European perspectives*, London: Springer.

Lacan, J. (2008) *My Teaching*, London: Verso.

Leo, P. and Lee, T. (2004) "The New Singapore: Mediating culture and creativity", *Continuum: Journal of Media and Cultural Studies*, 18 (2): 205–18.

McKinlay, A. and Smith, C. (eds) (2009) *Creative Labour: Working in the creative industries*, Houndmills: Palgrave.

Morrissey, S. (2013) *Morrissey: Autobiography*, London: Penguin.

O'Connor, J. (2002) "Public and Private in the Cultural Industries", in T. Johansson and O. Sernhede (eds), *Lifestyle, Desire and Politics: Contemporary identities*, Gothenburg: Daidalos.

O'Connor, J. (2004) "Cities, Culture and Transitional Economies: Developing cultural industries in St Petersburg", in D. Power and A. Scott (eds), *Cultural Industries and the Production of Culture*, London: Routledge.

O'Connor, J. (2012) "Surrender to the Void: Life after creative industries", *Cultural Studies Review*, 8 (3): 388–410.

Redhead, S. (1997) *Post-Fandom and The Millennial Blues: The transformation of soccer culture*, London and New York: Routledge.

Redhead, S. (2004) *The Paul Virilio Reader*, Edinburgh: Edinburgh University Press/New York: Columbia University Press.

Redhead, S. (2011) *We Have Never Been Postmodern: Theory at the speed of light*, Edinburgh: Edinburgh University Press.

Smith, C. (1998) *Creative Britain*, London: Faber and Faber.

Storey, D. (1960) *This Sporting Life*, London: Longmans.

Storey, D. (2005) "This Sporting Life", *Observer* [*Sport Monthy* magazine], May: 1–8.

Sutton, P. (ed.) (2005) *Lindsay Anderson: The diaries*, London: Methuen.

Tett,G. (2009) *Fool's Gold*, London: Little, Brown.

Turner, A. (2012) *Economics After The Crisis: Objectives and means*, Cambridge, MA: MIT Press.

Turner, G. (2012) *What's Become of Cultural Studies?* London: Sage.

Virilio, P. (2009) *Grey Ecology*, New York: Atropos.

Virilio, P. (2010a) *The Futurism of the Instant: Stop-eject*, Cambridge: Polity.

Virilio, P. (2010b) *The University of Disaster*, Cambridge: Polity.

Virilio, P. (2012) *The Great Accelerator*. Cambridge: Polity

Virilio, P. and Depardon, R. (2008a) *Manhattan Out*, Gottingen: Steidl.

Virilio, P. and Depardon, R. (2008b) *Native Land/Stop Eject*, Paris: Fondation Pour l'Art Contemporain.

Virilio, P. and Lotringer, S. (2008) *Pure War*, 3rd edition, Los Angeles: Semiotext(e).

Winlow, S. and Atkinson, R. (eds) (2012a) *New Directions in Crime and Deviancy*, London: Routledge.

Winlow, S. and Atkinson, R. (2012b) "York Deviancy Conference 2011", *Crime, Media, Society: An International Journal*, 8 (2): 119–27.

Zizek, S. (2009) *First As Tragedy, Then As Farce*, London: Verso.

Zizek, S. (2011) *Living in The End Times*, 2nd edition, London: Verso.

Zizek, S (2012a) *The Year of Dreaming Dangerously*, London: Verso.

Zizek, S. (2012b) *Less Than Nothing: Hegel and the shadow of dialectical materialism*, London: Verso.

Zizek, S. (ed.) (2013) *The Idea of Communism 2: The New York Conference*, London: Verso.

Zizek, S. and Gunjevic, B. (2012) *God In Pain: Inversions of apocalypse*, New York: Seven Stories Press.

13

ADVERTISING AS A CULTURAL INDUSTRY

John Sinclair

Occupying the common territory between economy and culture, advertising is a core cultural industry, unapologetically and *par excellence*. While we may think of advertising first and foremost as the creative product of advertising agencies – the images, slogans and jingles in TV commercials and on billboards, for example – that is only the most visible and public form of what the business schools call "integrated marketing communications", a broader set of cultural practices intent upon harnessing our ways of life to commercial purposes. From an economic perspective, advertising serves to connect advertisers, the producers of consumer goods and services, with their potential markets, and in fact, to bring those markets into being. Furthermore, it is those advertisers who are the source of the revenue that is the life-blood of the media business, by way of them paying advertising agencies to buy media time and space, as well as to devise their advertising campaigns for them. Thus, advertising is best thought of not as a single cultural industry, but as an integrated though shifting set of relations between advertisers, media and agencies: a "manufacturing/marketing/media complex" (Sinclair 2012).

Advertising is cultural in various respects. Its brands and logos pervade everyday life and social communication, as well as the fabric of material culture surrounding us in our homes and the streets of our cities – it gives capitalist modernity its very look and feel. Advertising draws upon, and feeds back into, popular culture, amplifying trends in subcultural activities, fashion and language, for example, and thus giving advertising agency personnel a particular role as cultural intermediaries. Even in the social critique that it attracts, advertising stands as a kind of proxy for consumer culture as a whole.

Advertising and the "cultural turn"

The 1980s marked a high point in the study of cultural meanings in advertisements, using neoMarxist theory and semiological methods to show how ads were structured so as to invoke common cultural meanings familiar to readers, and associate them with a given product (Williamson 1978). However, the focus of all this work was on advertisements, the products of the advertising industry, rather than the industry as such. By the end of that decade, a paradigm shift was taking place, in that the study of advertising was being eclipsed by the more inclusive analysis of "consumer culture". One of the most useful and influential formulations of this shift came from Mike Featherstone, who argued for "a dual focus: firstly on the cultural dimension of the economy; ... and secondly, on the economy of cultural goods, ... the market principles which operate within the sphere of lifestyles, cultural goods and commodities" (1987: 57). This kind of thinking set the stage for the 1990s to become known as the decade of the "cultural turn", defined as a broad movement away from political economy in favour of "an increasing concern with symbolic systems, systems of meaning and the self-reflexive"(Miller 2002: 172–73). Thus, even if the advertising industry was now to be subsumed into a larger context, the concept of consumer culture gave recognition to the unique position that it occupies, between economy and culture.

Notably, Scott Lash and John Urry argued that the economy and culture were becoming ever more integrated: "the economy is increasingly culturally inflected and ... culture is more and more economically inflected" (1994: 64). This could be seen in an "aestheticization" of economic production, meaning that goods, and services, had come to be designed to attract certain kinds of consumers and to fit with their lifestyles. Whereas once it had been enough to "get a life", advertising, and marketing more generally, promoted the idea that we each needed a lifestyle, a way of defining ourselves in terms of a distinctive pattern of consumption that we would assemble for ourselves. In their postmodernist perspective, Lash and Urry named this relationship between individuals and their consumption as "aesthetic reflexivity", or "the semiotization of consumption whose increasingly symbolic nature is ever more involved in self-constructions of identity" (1994: 61). Instead of Featherstone's "dual focus" on economy and culture, Lash and Urry tended to push the balance until culture outweighed economy, such that advertising in their view became a model for all of the culture industries, defined by a common function in achieving "the transfer of value through images" (1994: 138).

Branding and culture

In the 2000s, this capacity of advertising to create value for goods and services by endowing them with cultural meanings has been consciously hitched to the process of branding. This shift in advertising towards marketing and branding, as distinct from mere selling, in conjunction with the emergence of more streetwise and self-expressive consumers with access to social media, has produced "a distinctively postmodern mode of sociality in which consumers claim to be doing their own thing while doing it with thousands of like-minded others" (Holt 2002: 83). Correspondingly, the analysis and critique of branding has been the focus of some of the best academic work on advertising. In particular, Adam Arvidsson argues that common meanings created collectively by people (whether at the level of a subculture or a nation) is one of the main things we mean when we talk about "culture", but what brand marketers do is to pick up on these meanings and exploit them by associating them with particular products and services. Just as Lash and Urry see consumers as now more reflexive in understanding their responses to advertised goods, Arvidsson sees brand marketers as reflexive in the sense that they recognize the rise of an independent popular culture, but seek to bring it under control to serve their interests. However, they find consumer perceptions are "generally beyond the direct control of capital" (Arvidsson 2005: 242), so, particularly in the age of social media, advertisers risk exposing themselves to ridicule when their attempts to appropriate cultural meanings for their brand are perceived as cynical and inauthentic. The interactive properties of the internet work to an advertiser's advantage when their ad "goes viral", but very much against them when "culture jammers" put out a humiliating parody of it (Klein 2001).

Thus, the new forms of cultural expression enabled by the internet have set new limits upon the credibility and standing that advertisers can claim for their brands. Both social networking and "user-generated content" have become "touchpoints" at which brands can engage with popular culture, but it is a challenge for brand managers to ensure that it occurs on their own terms. Rather than the mass of manipulated "cultural dopes" that consumers were assumed to be in the neoMarxist critique of advertising influence, the coming of the internet has shifted the balance so that consumers, particularly young ones, are now seen to use brands in their own way, "to construct social relations, shared emotions, personal identity or forms of community" (Arvidsson 2006: 18).

One further contemporary theoretical perspective on advertising, and a particularly appropriate conceptual framework for the analysis of branding, is cultural economy. Cultural economy radically repudiates the commonsense distinction between culture and economy, arguing instead that advertising is "a constituent material practice in which the 'cultural' and the 'economic' are inextricably entangled" (McFall 2004: 7). Thus, the relation between production and consumption is seen as mutually constitutive, rejecting the one-way economic determinism of the cultural Marxism so influential in past decades, and the "cultural authority model" derived from it, the critical orthodoxy in which omnipotent advertisers were seen to control "how people think and feel through branded commercial products" (Holt 2002: 71).

"Cultural intermediaries" in advertising

The diffusion of the concept of "lifestyle" since the late 1980s as the foundation of postmodern brand marketing has already been alluded to in connection with the work of Featherstone (1987) and Lash and Urry (1994). More particularly, Featherstone cites the thesis of "cultural intermediaries" that the influential French sociologist Pierre Bourdieu put forward in his classic work, *Distinction* (1984). Bourdieu was referring to a new class, a petite bourgeoisie "who provide symbolic goods and services" in an emergent economy of consumption (1984: 310). He saw them as leaders of taste and style who on the one hand maintained affinities with the intellectuals and acted as a vanguard of the traditional, production-based industrial bourgeoisie, while on the other they performed the role of cultural entrepreneurs, propagating their "expressive and liberated lifestyles" amongst society at large (Featherstone 1987: 90–91). Bourdieu specifically identifies, as members of this class, managers in advertising and the media, which he sees as key "creative industries" that bring "the art of living" into everyday life (1984: 310), not unlike the "aestheticization" process later conceptualized by Lash and Urry (1994).

The concept of cultural intermediaries may have intuitive appeal at first sight, but it has been subject to certain lines of criticism. On the basis of his first-hand research with advertising personnel in London, Sean Nixon argues that when one looks beyond advertising managers alone to advertising as an occupation and as an institution, Featherstone's interpretation of the cultural intermediaries concept is seen to lack an empirical basis, and to neglect the actual differences that exist within the whole category of advertising workers (2003). Yet, even if not all advertising personnel are cultural intermediaries in Bourdieu's sense, other observers point to "the rise of a 'brand-managerial' class of cultural experts, entrepreneurs, and intermediaries" (Aronczyk and Powers 2010: 3). For the rest, advertising workers are by no means an "aristocracy of labour", but, like "creative" workers in general, are still workers, and have to survive in an environment of uncertainty. In the context of a broader critique of the "precarity" of labour in the era of neoliberalism, younger workers in particular have been characterized as "the precarious generation", obliged to constantly prove themselves in highly competitive and insecure circumstances of employment (Ross 2009: 6).

Advertising as a "creative industry"

Since the 1990s, "creativity" has become "something of a cant word" (Nixon 2003: 9), as various governments around the world have sought to manage a transition to "an increasingly culturalised economy" (McFall 2004: 131). Advertising has been identified, along with the other "creative industries", as cultural activities that have economic value, and therefore as national resources to be fostered (Yúdice 2003). In Britain, knighthoods have been bestowed upon prominent advertising industry figures such as Martin Sorrell, the CEO of British-based global WPP, and both Nigel Bogle and John Hegarty, of the successful creative agency Bartle Bogle Hegarty. Less formally, in the United States, the advertising industry has continued to pay homage to the key figures of their "creative revolution" since the 1960s (Frank 1997). Advertising is a creative industry with an explicit stake in creativity. Agencies have a very considerable investment in talking up creativity, and in their own mediating role between advertiser clients and their consumer targets. From the agencies' point of view, creativity is their product, understood in this context as the capacity to invest goods and services with cultural associations that give them meaning and value. In dealing with their advertiser clients, agencies must maintain the clients' faith that they can do this, making creativity something of a necessarily self-serving ideology. When the client's faith falters, they will go to another agency, a possibility that introduces a constant dimension of instability and risk into the agencies' performance of creativity, and thus sustains an eternal tension between management and creative staff.

There is a longstanding and ubiquitous distinction amongst advertising personnel between the "creatives" and the "suits", those responsible for the management side of the industry. In recent decades this has even led to a structural separation between the traditional creative and the specialist media-buying functions of advertising agencies, a manifestation of the peculiar fusion of culture and economy that is advertising. Yet even if agency executives see their creative staff as an unruly problem to be managed, they also have to recognize that creativity is the asset that attracts and holds clients. Anne Cronin's interviews with UK agency practitioners, for example, make it evident that they see their business as "a very unstable and competitive field" in which their agencies themselves are brands (and they are often referred to as such in the trade press). Part of their job therefore becomes "continually pitching their agency's creative and commercial talents to existing clients and potential clients in a reflexive self-promotional strategy" (2004: 342).

Advertising management personnel are uniquely positioned then as "promotional intermediaries" (Aronczyk and Powers 2010: 9) because the institution of advertising as such mediates between production and consumption. Creative personnel fit more closely to the "cultural intermediaries" concept of Bourdieu, because they are, as individuals, consumers as well as producers. While advertising creatives are pleased to distinguish themselves as such professionally, they are still "punters", that is, consumers and inhabitants of the world of popular culture from which they derive the "cultural capital" that is their stock-in-trade. The convergence of production and consumption thus works both ways. For example, Dick Pountain and David Robins argue that advertising "is not merely a cynical manoeuvre perpetrated by manipulated outsiders whose real interests lie elsewhere", but, they say, in their study of "Cool", "this mediocracy [of advertising and media personnel] knows how to employ Cool as a selling tool, how to manipulate its icons, precisely because it makes sense to them, it reflects their own values" (2000: 169). An apposite empirical example is Nixon's landmark study of advertising practitioners in London agencies in the 1990s, which found that the "new lad" style of marketing fashionable in the United Kingdom at that time was derived from the close identification that the young male creative workers themselves had with "laddish" forms of consumer behaviour and lifestyle (2003: 165–66).

So, creatives can indeed be seen as cultural intermediaries, not only in the sense that they pick up and popularize new styles of consumption, but also in that they themselves are committed performers of the self-branding practices that global corporations seek to foster in all of our subjective identities, as workers and consumers alike. Douglas Rushkoff has argued that "turning into a recognizable brand icon oneself" has become an adaptive strategy in a world of production and consumption defined by brands and corporations (Rushkoff 2009: 142). Just like the suits, the creatives have a vested interest in fostering the perception of creativity as an agency's greatest asset, and this in turn motivates self-branding and an "obsession" with creativity as "a strategy of distinction" in "an intensely competitive world of work" (Nixon 2003: 162). Advertising creative personnel evidently retain a clear understanding of the value of having a paid job, especially in a volatile industry, and the branding of their identity as creatives as an essential means to that. Equally, it is because there are so many young people who are outside the industry but who aspire to securing paid creative employment, a reserve army of creative labour, that self-branding pressures make them vulnerable to exploitation (Carah 2011). For those who do have a job, career advancement usually involves moving from one agency to another, rather than being promoted within the same one, and their capacity to do this will depend on self-branding performances such as their ability to garner awards, and generally to make themselves known on "the industry circuit of award ceremonies, launches and the wider social networks of the industry" (Nixon 2003: 72). The industry's trade journals clearly reflect such a preoccupation with peer recognition, providing reports from a complex world of creative awards that extends from the local to the global, along with details of the movement of personnel from one agency to another, and the all-important news of the latest changes in client–agency pairings.

Advertising in the era of social media

The relatively comfortable relationship that existed between advertisers, agencies and the media throughout the golden age of mass media in decades past is a business model that has been put under severe pressure by the advent of the more interactive and individualized social media on the internet. "Old" media are realigning themselves with the "new", while, on the internet itself, emergent business models compete for hegemony. The new social media companies, with their playfully childish names concealing their overblown stockmarket valuations, are built on ways of commercializing the internet that involve advertising, but not as we have known it. Although we can find internet versions of the traditional business models that have grown out of broadcasting history – sponsorship, delivering audiences and subscription – the advent of the internet has presented one more, in the form of search advertising. Instead of attracting an audience with the offer of information or entertainment content, as with traditional media, search engines – notably Google, Yahoo! and Bing – attract users to the service itself. As for the wildly popular social media, notably Facebook and Twitter, they capture and hold attention through their offer of interactive personal involvement.

The rapid rise of the global internet-based corporations and the diverse range of business models through which they have achieved it demonstrate how the internet is so much more than a new medium for advertising, and also can be taken as a measure of the exceptional extent of socio-cultural and economic change that the internet has wrought. The capacity of the internet to be accessed by mobile telephones and other devices, its ability to give access in turn to other media, such as video on YouTube, and its unique affordances to allow users' responses and input and engage in online social interaction are major technological features underlying a fundamental shift in the character of what we still call, from radio days, "audiences". The cornucopia of choice and the interactive ease and immediacy of the internet has transformed social communication in a way that rebalances the power relations between senders and receivers, and heightens interaction amongst receivers themselves – indeed, the internet has in a sense rendered obsolete conventional binarisms such as sender/receiver, or producer/consumer.

However, the significance of this transformation and rebalancing is much contested. It was noted above how brand owners now find that they have to worry about how their target consumers will react to advertising messages and marketing tactics in general. This new accountability that advertisers now find themselves having towards their consumers, and the capacity of consumers to react on the internet, whether in negative or positive ways, has led many observers to celebrate what they see as the "empowerment" of consumers in the form of the "produser": the user or consumer who, individually or collectively, is able to participate in content creation (Bruns 2008). On the other hand, advertisers have recognized the power of such "user-generated content", and sought to exploit it for their own purposes, such as with competitions to encourage consumers to produce their own commercials, or crowdsourcing, which is looking for idea generation or feedback from audiences for prospective new products. This is what can be referred to as the "empowerment–exploitation paradox" of social media (Sinclair 2012).

Furthermore, it is not only the creativity and social networking activities of users that can be taken advantage of by advertisers, but also the information about themselves that users offer up whether knowingly or unknowingly in the course of their everyday internet use. Just as we pay the true price of "free" television in terms of the time we spend watching commercials, and the hidden costs of advertising are passed on to us when we consume goods and services, the true price of using internet services such as Google or Facebook is in how we, in the course of using them, necessarily give over information about ourselves that they are able to monetize. Companies thus gain freely given information about consumers without them knowing how it might be used (Turow 2011). For instance, with their information on users' browsing history, Google and the other search engines can offer advertisers "interest-based" advertising, that is, ads that are matched to a user's track record, while Facebook makes it possible for advertisers to target ads in accordance with information that users have included in their profile. In contrast to television's golden age, in which the ratings system could only yield a broad demographic breakdown of the mass audience, the internet age is distinguished by "behavioural targeting" – unobtrusive electronic means of following users' online trails as the basis for cultivating niche markets and even pursuing individual consumers.

The advent of the internet and other new media have most certainly put into play a much more fluid set of relations than has existed for decades within the constellation of institutional associations between advertisers, their agencies and the media. It is not a simple question of whether a medium is "old" or "new", but whether and how it is able to give sellers access to buyers in a given market. Nor is it about the technologies as such, but how the technologies can be embedded commercially and socially via business models that the target audiences find attractive in an environment of ever more choice and social differentiation. However, the interactive qualities of new media also bring audiences into new relationships, of both empowerment and exploitation.

Advertising and globalization

In the context of globalization, the advertising industry is best seen as a service industry that supports the investment of global advertisers and stimulates global media development. Yet it is also evident that the advertising agency business itself is highly globalized in its organization, as well as being a force for globalization in national media and consumer markets. To understand this globalization of the advertising industry it is essential to take account of the shifting three-way relationship between advertisers, agencies and the media. The advertisers can be seen as the prime movers, at least since the 1960s and 1970s, which saw the ground being laid for the globalization era. Advertising agencies facilitated the process, and in the 1980s, radically reorganized themselves as global corporations in their own right. There were three dimensions of this reorganization. First, the international advertising agency networks were incorporated into "mega-groups". These are overarching global financial and management structures, fuelled by international capital, and often based outside of the United States, challenging that country's former supremacy in the business. Second, the traditional advertising functions were divided into separate "creative" and "media-buying" agencies, and third, these were then gathered together with other marketing "disciplines" under the umbrella of "integrated marketing communications".

The 1960s and 1970s was an era in which the world's cities became illuminated with the logos of globalizing corporations on the electric signs across their skylines. Reference to corporate histories of these companies shows that, typically, they had their origins in the late nineteenth or early twentieth century, often beginning from quite modest local enterprises in the United States or Western Europe (and later in the case of the Japanese companies), then building themselves, usually through mergers and takeovers, into major national corporations in their country of origin, and subsequently branching out into the rest of the world as "multinational" corporations. Coca-Cola is the paradigm case. The massive overseas expansion of these companies in that era was accompanied by a corresponding expansion in service industries, notably advertising.

The US agencies entered the new markets with the comparative advantages of perceived "American know-how", for at this stage Madison Avenue was still the epicentre of the world advertising industry, and they also had experience with television, the new medium that was then opening up in countries around the globe. But, above all, they came with capital, and had established relationships with the most desirable clients – the largely US-based multinational corporations. Generally, if an agency held a client's national account in the United States, it was mutually advantageous for the agency to open up an office, or merge with a foreign agency, in every country that the client did business.

However, the 1980s saw the beginning of true globalization, in the sense that the national origin of agencies, and clients, became less important than the combined interpenetration of capital from different national sources, and furthermore, that a completely new level of ownership and management was created in the form of the global advertising group, or "megagroup". As explained, these are not global advertising agencies in themselves, but corporations or holding companies that are composed of global advertising agencies, or "a network of networks" (Mattelart 1991: ix). What happened in the 1980s was that UK, French and Japanese-based agencies rose to challenge US domination of the industry at a global level. Although the United Kingdom and Western Europe also experienced the influx of US agencies in the 1960s, by the 1980s certain British agencies, cashed up by stock market speculation, led a counter-flow that resulted in several major US agencies being brought under

UK ownership by the end of the decade, in an intense period of mergers and acquisitions. One of the main factors impelling agencies to open up the new level of management above themselves was the need to manage "client conflicts". Basically, this refers to the principle, maintained in the Western world at least, that an agency must not hold the accounts of competing products or services. Megagroup-level management means that, for example, although Colgate and Unilever are competing global clients, the megagroup WPP can cater for them both, with the Young & Rubicam global network handling Colgate, while Ogilvy & Mather takes care of competing brands for Unilever.

As noted above, the second structural change in how the advertising industry organized itself was the "unbundling" of advertising's basic functions, with the traditional business of purchasing media space and time for clients being institutionally separated from the creative business of devising and executing advertising campaigns. "Media-buying" was thus organized into quite separate agencies, though usually integrated under the one holding group, along with the creative agencies, and companies offering other kinds of marketing services. This was the third dimension of the megagroup arrangement: to continue with the WPP example, if clients need public relations services, they can be referred to different companies in that field too, notably Burson-Marsteller or Hill & Knowlton, also available on a global basis. Other companies in the group can provide a range of services to support advertising, such as market research from Millward Brown or TNS, as well as non-advertising services in branding and design, direct marketing and promotions, and specialist areas such as healthcare and multicultural marketing.

The UK-based WPP remains the largest of the megagroups, while there are two US-based ones, Omnicom and Interpublic, and two French ones, namely Publicis and Havas. A list of six is rounded out by Dentsu-Aegis Network, which includes the UK-based Aegis, a media-buying group, now wholly owned by the huge Japanese marketing communications conglomerate Dentsu.

Between them, these groups control the international advertising industry, but always subject to pressures from advertisers, and trends from within the media, the other two members of the manufacturing/marketing/media complex. As a final note on advertising as a cultural industry, however, it is worth noting that in spite of critics' fears of global cultural homogenization, more striking has been the widespread "glocalization" of campaigns, evidencing their necessary adaptation to the deeply embedded realities of local, national, and regional cultures (Sinclair and Wilken 2009).

Further reading

Arvidsson, A. (2006) *Brands: Meaning and value in media culture*, London and New York: Routledge. (An excellent introduction to critical thinking on branding.)

Sinclair, J. (2012) *Advertising, the Media and Globalisation: A world in motion*, London and New York: Routledge. (A comprehensive account of advertising in the era of social media and globalization.)

Turow, J. (2011) *The Daily You: How the new advertising industry is defining your identity and your worth*, New Haven: Yale University Press. (Critical analysis of behavioural targeting.)

References

Aronczyk, M. and Powers, D. (eds) (2010) *Blowing Up the Brand*, New York: Peter Lang.

Arvidsson, A. (2005) "Brands: A critical perspective", *Journal of Consumer Culture*, 5: 235–58.

Arvidsson, A. (2006) *Brands: Meaning and value in media culture*, London and New York: Routledge.

Bourdieu, P. (1984) *Distinction: A social critique of the judgement of taste*, trans. Richard Nice, London: Routledge and Kegan Paul.

Bruns, A. (2008) *Blogs, Wikipedia, Second Life, and Beyond: From production to produsage*, New York: Peter Lang.

Carah, N. (2011) "Breaking into the Bubble: Brand-building labour and 'getting in' to the culture industry", *Continuum: Journal of Media and Cultural Studies*, 25(3): 427–38.

Cronin, A.M. (2004) *Advertising Myths: The strange half-lives of images and commodities*, London and New York: Routledge.

Featherstone, M. (1987) "Lifestyle and Consumer Culture", *Theory, Culture and Society*, 4: 55–70.

Frank, T. (1997) *The Conquest of Cool*, Chicago: University of Chicago Press.

Holt, D.B. (2002) "Why Do Brands Cause Trouble? A dialectical theory of consumer culture and branding", *Journal of Consumer Research*, 29: 70–90.

Klein, N. (2001) *No Logo*, London: Flamingo.

Lash, S. and Urry, J. (1994) *Economies of Signs and Space*, London and Thousand Oaks, CA: Sage.

Mattelart, A. (1991) *Advertising International: The privatisation of public space*, London and New York: Routledge.

McFall, L. (2004) *Advertising: A cultural economy*, London: Sage.

Miller, D. (2002) "The Unintended Political Economy", in P. du Gay and M. Pryke (eds) *Cultural Economy: Cultural analysis and commercial life*, London: Sage.

Nixon, S. (2003) *Advertising Cultures: Gender, commerce, creativity*, London: Sage.

Pountain, D. and Robins, D. (2000) *Cool Rules: Anatomy of an attitude*, London: Reaction Books.

Ross, A. (2009) *Nice Work if You Can Get It: Life and labor in precarious times*, New York: New York University Press.

Rushkoff, D. (2009) *Life Inc.: How the world became a corporation and how to take it back*, New York: Random House.

Sinclair, J. (2012) *Advertising, the Media and Globalisation: A world in motion*, London and New York: Routledge.

Sinclair, J. and Wilken, R. (2009) "Strategic Regionalization in Marketing Campaigns: Beyond the Standardization/Glocalization Debate", *Continuum, A Journal of Media and Cultural Studies*, 23: 147–56.

Turow, J. (2011) *The Daily You: How the new advertising industry is defining your identity and your worth*, New Haven: Yale University Press.

Williamson, J. (1978) *Decoding Advertisements*, London: Marion Boyars.

Yúdice, G. (2003) *The Expediency of Culture: Uses of culture in the global era*, Durham: Duke University Press.

14
A CULTURAL ECONOMY OF AUDIO AND RADIO TECHNOLOGIES

John Tebbutt

Sound, due to what Jonathan Sterne (2003) has described as its "plasticity," has been material to the cultural economy of number of technologies, including music, telephony and radio.

"Radio" does not exist in a single form but works as both messaging and mass media. Following its invention it was deployed in the early twentieth century as a point-to-point communication system that assisted transport and trade and emerged as an early global structure. As a messaging system, radio undermined existing imperial cable communications while assisting in the consolidation national cultures and the expansion of markets for modern technological products. Later, after its first few decades, it was shaped by commerce and culture into a one-to-many broadcasting system that allowed for the local distribution of cultural products and subsequently spread to all parts of the world. The popularity of broadcast listening may become an historical aberration as radio, in its digital iterations, morphs into podcasting – a public, peer-to-peer distribution form – and personalized, subscriber-based, internet delivered audio that expands the post-broadcast future of listening. All the while radio's various forms – including one-to-one communication, broadcast and subscriber delivered audio – remain vital, if attenuated. For now, radio broadcasting is the crucial cultural and economic formation derived from the properties of sound as it has incorporated the related formations of telephony and music in a distribution structure that has been robust, durable and geographically extensive. Lately it has been adapted to the internet as a distribution mechanism to form digital audio streaming of music and talk programming.

Radio transmission: Disruption, constraint and competition

Transmission by radiation, initiated by Heinrich Rudolf Hertz's discovery of wave properties in electromagnetism in 1887, was a technology that had the potential to disrupt existing economies. When Guglielmo Marconi invented a superior system to distribute electronic Morse code messages via waves rather than telegraph wires in 1894, existing economic interests sought to constrain the new system. In Europe Marconi was prevented from distributing terrestrial messages by laws that provided monopolies for message delivery to European government-run postal services. This encouraged Marconi's experiments with long distance message delivery across water. These experiments provided new services in ship-to-shore radio and demonstrated the potential for international broadcasting, a crucial signal of deep cultural change to follow. A few years earlier, American Thomas Edison had patented a system for delivering and decoding electric signals through electromagnetic waves, which he sold to the Marconi company. In America the postal services were privatized and the new technology could be implemented more readily. An emerging radio message industry, however, faced the problems of security. Radio messages were less expensive but not as private as those sent via telegraph and post. Still, the British-based Marconi company founded a viable business in America, especially in establishing crucial ship-to-shore services.

Initially, then, radio was largely a message delivery system that facilitated efficient dialogue. At the time of radio's inception in the 1880s, telephony was the emerging broadcast media, supported by subscriber-based public distribution. "Telephone concerts," where listeners wore headphones and dialed into a cable service providing live concert relays, had been established in Europe (especially France) in the 1880s. In America in 1895 telephony provided a dial-up service delivering news on political conventions, and in 1896 "long-distance telephone lines were plentiful enough for telephone companies to organize a national network for gathering and distributing election returns" (Marvin 1988: 219). Newspapers incorporated the existing sound technology into news distribution by printing late breaking news delivered to newsrooms by telephone. Perhaps more importantly, in 1893 subscribers in the Hungarian capital, Budapest, could dial up what may have been the world's first broadcasting service. With the help of the telephone network and headphones, a 14-hour-long, edited programme was transmitted to subscribers in the Magyar language. The programme consisted of news, recorded music and live transmissions from theatres and concert halls. This "diffusion" system lasted for over twenty years in Hungary, until the end of the First World War in 1918. In the meantime, similar systems were deployed in Italy, Sweden and Britain and became the precursors of a wired broadcasting system.

A new radio era: International communication and war

International message communication at this time was expensive and slow; it relied on underwater cable systems and relay stations. Radio's major economic advantage over telephony and cable systems was its ability to send messages overseas cheaply and instantly. Regulatory constraints on radio communication encouraged Marconi to experiment with transmitting across water, but the scientific convention at the time held that waves travel in straight lines and could not follow the curvature of the earth. Global electromagnetic communication was thought to be impossible. However,

Marconi's experiments demonstrated that shortwave signals could bounce off the lower ionosphere (upper atmosphere). This led to the development of an inexpensive, efficient international communication system that ushered in revolutionary cultural and economic change. It undermined existing imperial global communication systems. News and trade information had previously been managed along imperial lines, with the major European nations – Britain, Germany and France – each maintaining their own secure cable and wire networks (run by supportive companies Reuters, Wolff and Havas respectively). During the First World War European communication companies made enormous profits as they refused to constrain charges for war communications. Due to the disruption of the Atlantic cable by German sabotage, communication traffic between America and Europe was transferred to radio. After the war, radio technology became economically and culturally important in national and international communication strategies.

With the establishment of radio as a viable industrial technology with important strategic value, the issue of constraining the technology's impact on existing commercial and cultural systems shifted to how it could be controlled. This was particularly difficult because radio provided a relatively simple form of technological communication. Experimenters and amateur radio communicators, sometimes associated with new electrical trade schools, led the development of the technology in its early forms (Hilmes 1997). Listeners could use home-made receiving sets that ranged from easy-to-construct crystal sets (which used metallic elements to receive sound) to larger valve radios that catered for international shortwave communication. With such a diverse community involved in radio at a local level, centralization of equipment production and of formatted programming were, historically, institutional responses to radio as an industrial technology. Diverse cultural economies emerged around ways of organizing this response. In the United States there was a centralization of technical production and a proliferation of technical innovation and listening forms. In Europe the centralizing movement was more around the listening subject, as the state moved to impose and maintain broadcast standards that focused on the provision of appropriate formats for cultural programming. These differences in kinds of economies were informed by concepts such as that of a static public, which underpinned national radio broadcast systems, and that was often counterposed to the idea of a dispersed audience, which commercial broadcasters tended to address.

The early radio industry in the United States was characterized by small start-up stations and individual amateur broadcasters, but at a technological and industrial level it quickly became highly centralized. Prior to the First World War, British-owned Marconi companies dominated the radio industry. Marconi's two-way communication technology was installed in ships and US coastal monitoring stations as well as in other crucial communication services. After the war the US Navy approached General Electric (GE) and proposed that a company be formed to buy out Marconi's North American patents and other business interests. Subsequently the Radio Corporation of America (RCA) was founded in 1919 as a monopoly that pooled patents from its contributing companies including GE, American Telephone and Telegraph, the United Fruit Company and Westinghouse Electric Corporation. RCA initially produced radio technology for domestic and military use but also purchased radio stations, founding the National Broadcasting Corporation (NBC) in 1926. The monopoly on the industrial production of radio technology led to secure, highly controlled manufacturing processes that suited the US military and provided research and development infrastructure for a domestic commercial broadcast industry. RCA also engaged in the emerging popular music and film industries, providing high-quality recording equipment and domestic consumer goods.

Diverse cultural economies of radio

Gradually, radio broadcasting began to establish itself over wired telephony systems. American experimenters produced intermittent voice and music broadcasts until in 1920 Marconi demonstrated a quality broadcast by Australian soprano, Dame Nellie Melba. Soon after, licensed and unlicensed stations with ongoing broadcasts were established across the United States by experimenters and institutions. In Argentina enthusiasts established the first ongoing broadcasts of live programmes from a refurbished theatre. In Europe national radio systems emerged throughout the 1920s and 1930s. The British Broadcasting Company (BBC) was formed in 1922, under manager John Reith. Radio broadcasting had been operating since 1920 in Britain, when Marconi established a station at Writtle, 30 miles north-east of London, that largely broadcast gramophone recordings. The state, however, was concerned to manage the new technology's impact. Following an inquiry in 1923 the government invited the BBC to form a Corporation that would be the sole national radio broadcaster. In Germany regional broadcast stations, managed by provincial governments, emerged from 1923. In 1925 a national organization, the Reichs-Rundfunk-Gesellschaft (RRG), was established to co-ordinate the nine regional public broadcasting companies. This was nationalized by the National Socialist government in 1934. Various Nordic nations also set up systems in 1925. The Union of Soviet Socialist Republics (USSR) made extensive use of wired systems, which were introduced in 1924, and "by 1959 there were 40,000 relay stations in industrial plants, collective farms and cities" (Paulu 1967: 31). In France a combination of public and private regional city-based radio stations developed, and by 1928 there were 13 private and 14 public sector radio broadcasters (Kuhn 1995: 84). While commercial broadcasters took sponsorships of various kinds, license fees levied against radio receiver sets largely funded national systems, although in Germany provincial broadcasters included advertising, at specific times, until they were nationalized.

Outside Europe and the United States, commercial and state-run systems often operated in the same markets. Australia set up a national system funded by license fees in 1932. It broadcast alongside a commercial system that had operated since 1927. The Canadian Broadcasting Corporation was state-owned but could accept advertising, reflecting the influence of the free market approach that had been adopted in the United States where there were no state-funded broadcasters. Radio in other European colonial possessions tended to be strictly controlled. Portugal allowed commercial broadcasting to emerge in Mozambique, but many other Asian and African colonial possessions did not develop radio systems until late in the colonial period. South Africa called on John Reith to advise them, resulting in a BBC-style South African

Broadcasting Corporation (SABC) that only broadcast in Afrikaans and English. Despite colonial concerns, the cultural importance of radio for information and education, and the relative ease with which audio broadcasting could be established, led to its broad use in social movements, particularly after the Second World War when technological developments facilitated a move to smaller, more mobile radio technology. Between 1946 and 1949 Bolivian unions and teachers in mining areas established two "miners' stations" to promote education and workers' welfare. In Algeria in 1954, the Front de Libération Nationale established a revolutionary radio station that challenged imperial control with French language broadcasts.

Publics and audiences

National radio broadcasting systems were developed for a number of reasons. As I indicated above, there were concerns to secure the airwaves for various nationalist cultural projects. In certain territories – notably Germany and South Africa – this led to overt government control as fascist and racist forces attempted to constrain dissent and implement highly divisive social policies. In many cases nation-states used technical arguments that a finite number of frequencies were available through the electromagnetic spectrum. Consequently, the argument goes, central management was crucial and commercial and community access should be limited. Such public interest arguments were generally combined with promises, sometimes in the form of charters, for specific national cultural programming that was often set against a threat of rampant commercialism for which the US system was held up as an example.

Certainly the free-wheeling dynamism of the North American radio scene could appear to be chaotic and counter-productive. From the early 1900s there had been an explosion of experimentation in radio broadcasting. The 1912 Radio Act in the United States meant all operators had to get licenses and required individual amateur radio enthusiasts to use the shortwave frequencies. By 1917 there were 13,581 amateur radio operators and numerous commercial broadcasters (Scott 2008: np). Often individual broadcasters were experimenting engineers, independent inventors or entrepreneurs interested in commercial success. However, public institutions, notably the University of Wisconsin, also developed systems that aimed to distribute educational programming to diverse and remote communities. The US Weather Bureau established one of the earliest services to broadcast Morse code weather reports and experimented with voice delivered reports. The diversity and enthusiasm for broadcasting, no doubt assisted by the protected industrial production of radio equipment enjoyed by RCA, meant that in dense population centres any number of stations could claim a frequency and depend on the power of their transmitters to secure an advantage over competitors' signals. Further legislation in 1927 attempted to regulate this issue. Licenses to broadcast were not priced, however, and the vibrant do-it-yourself approach to broadcasting facilitated an expansion of the commercial system.

Commercial systems were not immediately drawn to general product advertising. Broadcast stations were often owned by radio retailers or by businesses that promoted their own services. In Australia large department stores invested in radio stations and built theatres within their establishments. They entertained shoppers with sponsored programming that drew from burlesque and popular theatre productions. In the United States in 1922 "educational institutions, radio clubs, civic groups, churches, government and the military owned 40 percent of stations" (Scott 2008: np). This assisted in the development of a "civic paradigm" (Goodman 2011) where commercial radio broadcasters and diverse communities co-operated to produce relevant programming. As commercial forces began to dominate the US industry by the late 1930s this co-operation became more of a compromise on the part of civic organizations. By the Second World War it had largely broken down but the impetus for radio broadcasting to be more than a marketing vehicle remained. In the late 1940s the Federal Communications Commission (FCC) allotted the lower end of the new FM band exclusively to non-commercial, educational stations, and in 1949 the first listener-supported public radio broadcaster was established in Berkeley, California.

Early audience measurement

By the 1930s advertising in US broadcasting was more generally accepted. Radio developed as a domestic medium and women in the home were perceived as important targets for product marketing. In 1934 Procter and Gamble's soap-powder, Oxydol, was losing markets to Rinso (produced by the English firm Unilever) so they hired an advertising man, Glen Sample, who had been adapting newspaper serials for radio. Sample integrated their soap-powder with daytime serials broadcasts, prompting newspapers to refer to the genre as "soap operas." While this was not the first use of soap advertisements during radio serials, the success of the Proctor and Gamble campaign has provided a reference point for the emergence of soap operas as a cultural phenomenon.

As product marketing developed alongside radio listening American institutions and businesses began to ask: who was listening? As historian Susan Douglas described,

> Contradictions about national identity abounded ... In a segregated country [...] the most popular show on radio was about two black men in Harlem. In a country known for its periodic outburst against papacy and immigrants, the Irish-Catholic priest Father Coughlin was a national demagogue drawing an estimated 30–45 million listeners a week.
>
> (Douglas 2004:128)

The emergence of radio in the United States coincided with the development of social sciences, in particular psychology, and institutions for measuring public opinion. George Gallup founded the American Institute of Public Opinion in 1935. Early American rating surveys used telephones to check listener recall or "coincident" listening (what was on the radio at the time of the call) (Douglas 2004:136–37). Educational institutions, however, wanted to know how their programmes compared to other activities in terms of relevance, and academic researchers wanted a more systematic monitoring of listening than surveys that relied on telephone ownership. In 1937 the Princeton Radio Research Project was established, with funding from the Rockefeller Foundation, to determine the impact of radio listening on population habits. European émigré Paul Lazarsfeld was appointed to lead the project. Lazarsfeld had experience with listener surveys in Austria; on the Princeton project, as well as in subsequent research, he developed an approach to studying radio habits that was driven by listener motivations. Lazarsfeld's interest in how musical habits were changing, something that had emerged in the Austrian research, led him to employ Theodor Adorno as an assistant on the project (Fleck 2011: 176). Later with another collaborator on the radio project, Frank Stanton, Lazarsfeld developed the first "in-process" measure of audience response, where a two-button device was used for listeners to register approval and disapproval in programme content. These developments, driven by the cultural impact of radio, were the foundation of extensive, internationally deployed systems of audience surveillance that were used to determine media effects and impacts. These systems for formalizing and visualizing radio audiences were transferred to television when it began commercial broadcasting in the late 1940s.

Lazarsfeld and Adorno's European sensibilities came to bear on their North American research. In particular they felt that the dulling effect of popular music was more insidious than propaganda, a view that was out of step with liberal educators in the United States (Fleck 2011:182). The idea that more centralized control over radio programming could lead to cultural enlightenment was more in keeping with the state-sponsored systems that both Lazarsfeld (in Vienna) and Adorno (in Frankfurt) had had direct experience of prior to emigrating to the United States. The rise of National Socialism in Germany however prompted concerns about centralized media and manipulation of the public. Hitler's skilled oratory and use of radio to relay his mass rallies across the nation came to epitomize the dangers inherent in state-sponsored broadcasting. At the same time it served as a limit against which more democratic forms of public service broadcasting could be measured. As the Second World War developed, centralizing and monitoring radio broadcasts were considered essential security measures. At the end of the war public service broadcasting (PSB) systems in democratic and socialist countries remained strong cultural institutions funded directly by the state or through extensive levies and subscriptions.

Public service broadcasting compromised

PSB systems were initially developed around an Arnoldian philosophy that cultural refinement could alleviate social divisions and promote understanding. This cultural uplift thesis was crucially dependent on the appearance of political independence, where culture and, increasingly after the Second World War, information could be delivered without overt interference by government; only this could stop PSB systems slipping into propaganda. At the same time, as I indicated earlier, there was an economic imperative to provide traditional and modern cultural products that may be popular – for example concert performances – but could be costly and challenging for commercial sponsors attempting to engage mass audiences. Public service systems provided employment for artists and facilitated experimentation in cultural production in the emerging audio arts field that developed following the mass production of magnetic audio tape after the Second World War. Such performances were also to be found in the United States, notably Norman Corwin's work for CBS radio, but well-funded public service systems facilitated extensive programming in a range of media arts suitable for radio including, orchestras, radio plays, opera performances and speeches and talks programming as well as audio documentaries and features.

Single national broadcasting systems run by the state became increasing hard to maintain after the 1960s. The ongoing costs associated with television once it was launched in the late 1940s and early 1950s led to reconsideration of the costs associated with state control of media systems. In Britain, Independent Television (ITV) was licensed to compete with the BBC for audiences in 1954. However, the BBC monopoly on radio continued until 1973. With a post-war boom in births a young population was emerging that did not have the same connection with traditional cultural arts and media. In Britain this led to a constituency that was alienated by the BBC's patrician broadcasting policies. At the same time the connections between politicians and the state broadcaster, developed during the war, came under close scrutiny as post-war conflicts in the Suez and in Northern Ireland tested the crucial independence thesis of PSB in Britain. This combination of circumstances led to the development of a unique form of pirate radio emerging to challenge that country's state broadcasting policies and programming.

There was never a time, since the formation of the BBC in 1922, when state radio had complete control over the British airwaves. Radio's inherent advantage over territory was that it could always build listenership from outside geographic and political boundaries. In 1925 Selfridges department store sponsored broadcasts from Radio Paris with its transmitter on the Eifel Tower. Later, Leonard F. Plugge, who had been associated with Selfridges' broadcast, established the International Broadcasting Company (IBC), which resold leased time on the French transmitter to sponsored English language programming aimed at audiences in Britain and Ireland. In 1931 Plugge established Radio Normandy in France to broadcast sponsored programming to Britain. In 1929 the Grand Duchy of Luxembourg awarded a monopoly license to a commercial operator to broadcast English language radio. Despite the promulgation in 1934 of the Lucerne Convention, which aimed to manage European airwaves, Luxembourg continued with its commercial radio broadcasts to England and Ireland. The success of Radio Luxembourg and Radio Normandy inspired post-war broadcasters to establish extra-territorial "pirate stations" to overcome the lack of contemporary popular culture available through the BBC. This was of course the time of rock-and-roll, a musical form that spoke to the new post-war youth but which had no place on BBC airwaves. In 1964 two ships, *Caroline* and *Atlanta*, began broadcasting into Britain from just outside the nation's territorial waters. The pirate broadcaster services coincided with a significant shift in listening practices that developed with the transistor radio (Johns 2011: 143). Portable radio took the listening experience out of the shared family rooms into bedrooms, playgrounds and eventually cars, removing constraints of familial authority over appropriate listening.

The time of the British pirates was relatively short. The BBC attempted to coopt youth audiences by hiring popular "disc jockeys" and, in 1967, establishing popular music broadcasts. By 1970 the election of Edward Heath's government, partly on policies to relax the BBC monopoly, meant that the *raison d'être* of broadcast piracy was removed. However the example of the pirates, in presenting alternative popular cultural products to the British youth, in developing media personalities and styles and in forcing the revision of state policies, provided an alternative cultural economy framework for radio broadcasting. In many ways the example of broadcasting from outside the mainstream provided a template for other new forms of radio that developed through the 1960s and 1970s. In the United States listener-supported community broadcasters began to expand outside the existing stations in significant population centres that harboured alternative cultures, such as San Francisco and New York. In Australia a vibrant community radio movement developed, partly inspired by the diversity of radio in the United States.

Formats and ferment

Throughout the 1960s another impact of the development of television on popular radio broadcasting became clear. Radio had moved from presenting diverse theatrical and educational offerings to consist of targeted music programming. Radio stations developed presentation styles around specific genres of formatted music such as progressive rock, top 40, middle of the road (MOR) and, more recently, contemporary hits radio. In this context radio largely became a carrier of content developed by a powerful music industry. This confluence of interests allowed radio to play a crucial role in the emergence of worldwide youth cultures. Even in nations that remained closed to modern cultural shifts international broadcasts reached into local communities – as the example of pirate radio broadcast into Britain demonstrated. At the same time, music that had niche audiences, including some classical music, became increasingly difficult to hear on commercial stations and state-based national systems that by now had compromised traditional cultural forms with contemporary popular music.

In commercial terms, networking became the preferred mode of ownership, leading to the emergence of huge agglomerations of stations such as the Clear Channel network in the United States, which was formed in 1972 and by 1999 owned 830 radio stations. Networking tended to remove local input for radio programmers. Commercial rationalization in the radio industry has been facilitated more recently by the development of computer-managed playlists with pre-recorded announcer inserts. The loss of localism led to concerns in the United States about lessening competition. In Australia similar developments led to concerns that non-urban and regional communities were losing important local news and information services. While commercial radio remained incredibly popular, particularly with youth audiences, these issues encouraged some listeners to explore alternative radio services offered by community and listener supported programming stations.

Australia provides an interesting case study for the development of alternative radio broadcasting. The United States had developed frequency modulation (FM) broadcasts that allowed for a higher quality sound in the 1940s and a number of the frequencies were allocated to non-commercial, specialist broadcasters. In Australia the commercial radio industry guarded its access to the air and argued, with the collusion of government officials, that FM was technically impossible in Australia, due to the vast distances some radio signals were required to travel. This was challenged by independent technicians and engineers supported by "fine music" enthusiasts and educationalists who wanted to expand the offerings provided by the complacent commercial broadcasters and the conservative PSB, the Australian Broadcasting Commission. Many of these activists had been exposed to FM radio by travelling overseas, particularly to the United States but also Europe. With the election of a reformist Labour government in 1972, the first change of government in Australia for nearly 30 years, the FM band was opened up and 12 experimental community stations were licensed. They represented fine and specialist music broadcasters, students and universities, and religious broadcasters. Community radio eventually became a third tier of broadcasting in Australia after the commercial and public broadcasters. Largely relying on volunteer programmers and administrators and funded by listeners and local business sponsorships, the sector became a vibrant source of alternative news and music for populations that were not addressed previously, including immigrant communities, and producing specific programming for communities such as gay, lesbian and transgender listeners.

From early on Australia's indigenous population took an interest in the new broadcast opportunities. In Alice Springs the Central Australian Aboriginal Media Association (CAAMA) was formed to take advantage of the opening up of licenses. CAAMA developed a unique system consisting of a centralized hub in the regional centre of Alice Springs. Here one studio was for broadcasting while another produced cassette programmes that could be distributed to more remote communities. The CAAMA studios often recorded stories and songs in local languages for remote indigenous communities and language groups outside Alice Springs. When Australia launched a satellite in 1983 the Australian Broadcasting Corporation (as it was then known) established a programme of Broadcasting to Remote Area Communities (BRACS) to assist indigenous populations in central Australia set up independent community services that could relay local programming as well as pick up CAAMA and the ABC services. Meanwhile, urban centres were learning from the CAAMA experience. In Sydney a black station, Radio Redfern, was established after a group of indigenous activists visited Alice Springs for meetings sponsored by CAAMA. The principals of Radio Redfern eventually travelled north to Brisbane, in 1993, to establish the first metropolitan-wide indigenous broadcaster 4AAA, now 98.9FM First Nation Country. There is now a national indigenous broadcasting sector with Australia-wide television and radio services. First nation broadcasters including those in Canada and Nordic countries, along with community broadcasters worldwide, come together under the banner of the World Association of Community Radio Broadcasters (AMARC), which supports training and governance project and holds regular international conferences.

Policy, change and post-broadcast radio

From the 1970s the impact of increased costs, especially with television, emerging audiences and new technologies such as transistors had undermined state support for national broadcasting systems. Regulations supporting local and community radio became increasingly important in the US and Australia and "local radio" was licensed in Britain, although this was closely tied to the BBC initially. Later, through the 1990s, the rationale of spectrum limitation as a centralizing rhetoric began to lose its force with policy makers with the introduction of digital technology. Digital radio has been developed since the first Digital Audio Broadcasting format demonstrations at the World Administrative Radio Conference in Geneva in 1985. Other formats have since been developed as well, including a proprietary (privately owned) broadcast system called HD Radio. One of the major contemporary challenges facing all radio broadcasters is the shift to digital broadcasting and the impact that the internet has had as an audio delivery platform, leading to a post-broadcast era.

The shift from analogue broadcasting to digital technologies has been supported by national regulation policies, although often belatedly. In a number of countries commercial industries have been threatened by new digital audio technologies and delivery systems. Digital technology introduced profound change as broadcasting became just one mode that listeners could use to access distributed audio. Digitally distributed audio can be provided in four ways: as terrestrial broadcast radio using digital signals (digital radio); as internet-delivered audio "streams"; as archived programming on dedicated servers that provide "audio-on-demand" (often referred to as podcasting); finally as embedded audio accessed along with other "metatext" material (biographies, discographies, timelines) on dedicated websites. Increasingly digital services are seeing the collapsing of differences between telephony and other sound-based technologies as mobile phones become the primary device for accessing audio, including music playlists, radio (usually only FM broadcasts) and the internet.

There are a number of critical issues that impact on digital terrestrial radio. Listeners must invest in a new receiver. For broadcasters, the buy-in to digital terrestrial broadcasting has high initial costs so that some existing broadcasters, for example community media, find it difficult to make the digital transition. There is a potential for an "analogue ghetto" if stations cannot afford the changeover, and it is envisaged that the analogue system will be turned off completely at some stage, so these broadcasters may then be forced off air. In addition, digital terrestrial broadcasting requires a multiplex distribution system that combines programming from various stations in a central technology, rather than broadcasters having separate transmitters, as is the case in analogue broadcasting. Some commercial broadcasters have been reluctant to hand over transmission control and have resisted the shift to digital terrestrial broadcasting. Further, multiplex systems tend to shift the allocation of channels away from regulators toward private infrastructure providers.

At the same time, new services for digital "streaming" deliver programme content, particularly music, via the internet – including digital subscriber systems Spotify and Rdio – and have begun to impact on existing broadcast models. Rdio, for example, is an online advertiser-supported music service that provides advertiser-supported free streaming or an advertisement-free subscription service in 60 countries. Such services, sometimes called "social jukeboxes," allow listeners to choose their own music from a large range of licensed offerings. These systems provide highly tailored listening experiences that shift the cultural production of radio away from producers and presenters, toward listeners as curators of their own listening experience.

Finally, podcasting has allowed for "audio-on-demand." Offerings combine archived programming from existing broadcasters as well as programming made just for internet delivery. Podcasts include free and subscription services and can be scheduled to be delivered to a home computer. This has provided a profound shift away from centralized time-based scheduling in broadcasting; it removes radio's connection with daily routines and allows for expanded listening opportunities. In 2014 the podcast "Serial" became a worldwide phenomenon. Podcasting has been responsible for increasing the profile of public service broadcasters after a period of decline from the 1970s. PSB often provide rich dedicated web pages that allow free downloads of previous broadcast programming, extending the life of once ephemeral radio productions and providing an alternative data set to ratings systems to measure engagement. With publicly funded infrastructure and lacking commercial constraints, PSB outlets have been able to experiment with new digital formats and metatext programming to develop complex, deep listening experiences augmented by text and images.

The development of digital technologies for distributing audio-based cultural products, along with the collapsing of radio sets into telephones and other music devices and the increasing use of images and text with audio, have raised the question of whether "radio" is still a viable concept. Despite the fact that digital signals are still propagated by electromagnetic waves and delivery of internet services increasingly rely on wireless technology, there remains a contemporary sense that "radio" is increasingly competing with "telephony" (ironically, as it had done at its inception) to provide a technological form for the plasticity of sound in a cultural economy.

References

Douglas, S.J. (2004) *Listening In: Radio and the American Imagination*, Minneapolis: University of Minnesota Press.

Fleck, C. (2011) "The Radio, Adorno and The Panel," in *A Transatlantic History of the Social Sciences: Robber Barons, the Third Reich and the Invention of Empirical Social Research*, London: Bloomsbury Academic, 165–220.

Goodman, D. (2011). *Radio's Civic Ambition: American Broadcasting and Democracy in the 1930s*, Oxford: Oxford University Press.

Hilmes, M. (1997) *Radio Voices: American Broadcasting, 1922–1952*, Minneapolis: University of Minnesota Press.

Johns, A. (2011) *Death of a Pirate: British Radio and the Making of the Information Age*, London: W.W. Norton.

Kuhn, R. (1995) *The Media in France*, London: Routledge.

Marvin, C. (1988) *When Old Technologies Were New: Thinking About Electric Communication in the Late Nineteenth Century*, Oxford: Oxford University Press.

Paulu, B. (1967) *Radio and Television Broadcasting on the European Continent*, Minneapolis: University of Minnesota Press.

Scott, C. (2008) "The History of the Radio Industry in the United States to 1940," in EH.Net Encyclopedia, R. Whaples (ed.), Economic History Association (accessed June 8, 2014: eh.net/encyclopedia/the-history-of-the-radio-industry-in-the-united-states-to-1940/).

Sterne, J. (2003) *The Audible Past: Cultural Origins of Sound Reproduction*, Durham: Duke University Press.

Part III

SPACE AND PLACE

The idea of thinking spatially or geographically about the cultural industries is not a new one, and as a field it continues to produce some of the richest work in the cultural industries literature, whether in accounts of cultural production, policy, consumption or identity. As Patterson and Silver note in their chapter, while culture is shaped by the places in which it is produced, in turn it helps to shape them.

This connection, complex and poorly understood as it often is, lies behind significant policymaker interest in the development of the cultural industries and they have been mobilised to serve a variety of policy goals: place branding, economic development, 'soft power' and social or community development.

This is most notable perhaps in the case of the city, as Oakley and O'Connor's chapter discusses. High-profile cases such as Paris and fashion or Los Angeles and film-making are the exception rather than the rule, but developing the cultural industries, sometimes under the mantra of the 'creative city' has been taken up by urban policy-makers across the world. Patterson and Silver give the example of Toronto, a city not generally regarded as one of the world centres of cultural production, but one that has been through most phases of urban cultural policy from flagship building and waterfront developments to arts districts and festivals. They argue that the collapse of the industrial economy and other significant social changes in the late 20th century plunged Toronto into an identity crisis, a phenomenon replicated in other post-industrial cities. The 'creative class' idea popularised by (sometime Toronto resident) Richard Florida seemed to promise a benign, prosperous and cosmopolitan response to the loss of a traditional identity. As such, it appealed to certain segments of the population, which included some, but by no means all, cultural workers, and such a policy coalition had enough power to put it into practice. However, as the chapter by Patterson and Silver shows, the conflicts that have erupted over the waterfront, as well as the election of a new mayor on a low-tax, pro-car platform, highlight the fact that many Torontonians have different priorities when it comes to urban governance.

While in Toronto's case active policy played a major role, Bastian Lange reminds us that in some cases weak or fragmented policy environments can open up space for cultural experimentation. Leipzig in the early years of the 21st century provides just such a case study where the combination of empty and abandoned properties, cheap rent, the collapse of traditional manufacturing employment and a strong cultural tradition left over from the former German Democratic Republic, both allowed and forced cultural practitioners to develop their own networks, organisations and spaces. Traditional economic development thinking, while paying lip services to such organic development, often finds it hard to support it, particularly when the motivation of many cultural workers is not business growth, but a variety of personal, ethical and artistic concerns.

If Toronto is driven by policy coalition, and Leipzig is bottom up, Xin Gu's chapter on Shanghai reveals a very different approach. Much of the early work on developing the cultural industries within cities has used Michael Porter's notion of 'clusters' along with related ideas such as the 'industrial district' and 'innovative milieu' to try to develop the cultural sector, and this has proved popular in China where large urban property developments more akin to traditional business parks have been branded as creative clusters. While many scholars accept that the tendency for cultural producers to co-locate is driven by real needs to swap ideas and contacts, socialise together and trade industry gossip, this kind of official cluster appears ill suited to the cultural industries. In this case of Shanghai, Gu argues, formal clusters have developed alongside unofficial cultural spaces – cosmopolitan nightscapes, music venues, new media production and of course online spaces, all of which might hold out greater prospects not only of longer term sustainable production but also the ability to articulate some of the non-economic values that Lange discussed.

Steven Miles' chapter reminds us that opportunities for cultural consumption are generally greater in cities than elsewhere, and the link between production and consumption is often strong. Musicians are generally keen consumers of music, for example. Moreover, the exchange of ideas on which cultural production thrives is commonly found in an interpenetration of the formal and informal, commercial and non-commercial fields in which cities are rich: public art galleries combined with street art, subsidised theatre alongside commercial shows. Indeed, Miles argues that the 'creative city' is in fact the city of cultural consumption and wonders whether this has resulted in the serving of middle-class consumption preferences in a way that, as the Toronto case also suggests, is potentially divisive.

Aside from the development of the cultural industries themselves, the link between place and culture is routinely invoked in a host of work on place marketing and branding. Reputational effects, where places have become associated with certain 'scenes', can create a virtuous circle whereby people interested in a cultural practice are drawn to these places. Again, policymakers have often sought to associate themselves with such efforts.

Nitin Govil's chapter considers how culture shapes places, as well as being shaped by them, by looking at how one cultural industry – film – helps create 'India' as a location. The chapter considers the film industry's own production of place, focusing on Hollywood's real and imagined engagement with India, at how locations are produced and represented and at how this is linked to the spatial distribution of film industry labour.

David Bell's chapter moves us away from the urban, not to 'the countryside' but to the variety of 'ruralities,' non-urban, peripheral and occasionally remote places in which cultural production takes place. He argues that, just as in the city, cultural

SPACE AND PLACE

industries have been used to 'sell' the countryside and a particular version thereof, often framed as 'white', settled and cohesive and contrasted with the edgy, restless but more 'creative' inner city. As he details, empirical work that looks at cultural production away from the metropolis is allowing us to challenge these stereotypes while opening up possibilities of different political settlements and even improved working conditions for cultural workers.

199

15

CULTURE AND THE CITY

Kate Oakley and Justin O'Connor

When Peter Hall asked, 'Why should the creative flame burn so especially, so uniquely, in cities and not in the countryside?' (Hall, 1998: 3) he summed up a line of thinking about the relationship between culture and the city that is both ancient and full of contemporary political resonance. The continuing importance of cities as centres of cultural production, the use of culture in city branding, the reliance on developing the cultural industries as an economic panacea and the contest over the right to city spaces, all attest to the depth and resilience of these links. Though clearly *the* site for cultural policy development in the last thirty years, the city is also where many of the contradictions and conflicts of the cultural industries and wider cultural policy that this volume identifies, are made manifest.

The evidence suggests that most cultural industries are biased to the urban; that is, cultural industries are more likely to be found within cities. There are a variety of reasons for this. The tendency for cultural workers to co-locate, sometimes within a few city streets of one another, is driven by the need for cultural producers to swap ideas and contacts, socialise together and trade industry gossip (Currid, 2007; Lloyd, 2006). Communicating these ideas is best done face to face, even in activities such as advertising or videogames production that make much use of digital technology. Indeed research suggests that the higher up the value chain – and the closer to the creative elements of production – the more likely it is that face-to-face interaction will be important (Pratt 2006, 2009). While this is true of other 'knowledge based sectors' – the trading and investment activities of the financial services industry also tend to cluster, for example – the urban co-location of cultural activities also owes something to the urban environment itself.

Opportunities for cultural consumption are generally greater in cities than else-where, and the link between production and consumption is strong. Put simply, musicians are generally keen consumers of music, comedians hang out at comedy clubs and filmmakers go to the cinema a lot. Moreover, the exchange of ideas on which cultural production thrives is commonly found in an interpenetration of the formal and informal, commercial and non-commercial fields in which cities are rich: public art galleries combined with street art, subsidised theatre alongside commercial shows, branded arenas for rock concerts and clubs and bars for up-and-coming bands.

In some cities there are reputational effects by which they have become associated with certain 'scenes', as in the case of Austin, Bogota or Detroit and popular music, and this can create a virtuous circle whereby people interested in a cultural practice are drawn to these cities or to neighbourhoods within cities. For firms in the cultural industries, and for the associated leisure sectors from bars and clubs to coffee shops and independent retail, being located in certain areas can be invested with what is sometimes referred to as 'symbolic capital' (Currid, 2007; Harvey, 2000; Lloyd, 2006).

Despite the success of some cities in developing a strong cultural-industry base in one or more sectors, these developments often prove difficult for city authorities to understand, let alone control or support. This seemingly organic mix of conditions appears intensely difficult to replicate, leading to the common misunderstanding that public policy makes little difference, or the invisible hand of the market is at work. More likely the policies that make a difference, from higher education costs and cheap transport or workspace to licensing laws and immigration rules, have not been enacted with the cultural industries in mind, but have nonetheless provided a beneficial set of conditions.

The growth in importance of creative industry/creative economy policies and the rhetoric of urban competiveness means that cities have in recent decades sought to 'operationalise' these factors and they have done so in a way characteristic of this stage of neoliberalism (Hesmondhalgh et al., 2014; Davies, 2014; O'Connor, 2011). There has been a rise in 'active state' policies from the expansion of higher education, including in so-called 'creative' subjects, to public investments in workspaces, studios and incubators, publicly funded networks and intermediaries (O'Connor and Gu, 2013), and tax 'breaks' devised to lure firms, particularly in the media sectors, from one urban location to another. While under the guise of urban regeneration, 'flagship' cultural buildings, arts districts and waterfront developments have been promoted in cities from Bilbao to Abu Dhabi.

At the same time, these policies, as Grodach and Silver note (2013: 3), have been conducted within an overall framework of deregulation, privatisation and with a concurrent 'reframing of traditional progressive policy goals such as diversity, inclusion, quality of life and sustainability, as facets of urban growth'.

Governing culture in the city

Despite the continuing lure of the 'creative city' (Boren and Young, 2013; O'Connor and Shaw, 2014), developing successful policies remains highly problematic. The object of policy is not stable, nor does it fit into the neat silos of public policy. For this reason, it generally involves not simply local governments, but also non-governmental actors such as cultural industry employers, arts organisations, citizens' groups and property developers (O'Connor and Gu, 2014). However, the ability of 'cultural' policymakers – traditionally concerned with arts and leisure provision rather than economic development – to respond to increasing demands has been questioned (O'Connor and Gu, 2013). A particular concern is that planning legali-sation, which many would argue is the key to sustainable cultural development, is generally outside the remit of cultural policymakers (Grodach and Silver, 2013). Yet many of the most important decisions concerning culture – workspace for artists, rents, zoning and land use planning, licensing and regulation of the night time economy – are in the domain of planners.

Property developers have become the most important policy players, posing a particular challenge for cities where cultural policymaking capacity and legislation is often weak, or has been weakened by a deregulatory policy regime. The dom-inance of property developer interests often centred on the development of city centre spaces with strong retail and leisure interests has been studied in a number of cities (Markusen and Gadwa, 2010; Zukin, 1995). In a few cases, active mayors or arts and citizen groups have been able to resist or modify developer influence (Grodach and Silver, 2013), but the general trend has been toward a strong focus on city centres and particular neighbourhoods, a concentration of cultural facilities, and a series of public–private partnerships to fund what were once public urban spaces. One result of this has been the growth of privately owned, semi-public spaces, often around shopping malls or so-called public squares such as Canary Wharf in London. Members of the general public are allowed in such spaces, but only if they fulfil certain criteria and refrain from a host of normal-seeming activities such as cycling, rollerblading or even eating. Some categories of citizen, such as homeless people, drug users and (as the Occupy movement found out) protestors, are explicitly not wanted.

Despite the centrality of flagship cultural institutions to some of these efforts, it would be difficult to argue that arts organisations or cultural industry businesses had been similarly central to the policy regime and indeed, as the 'creative city' concept has become narrowly focussed on economic growth, arts organisations have come to form an explicit opposition in some cases (Novy and Colomb, 2013).

Nonetheless, cities have experimented with a variety of creative networks and industry associations, with varying success. Both Miles (2010) in the United Kingdom and Gerin and McLean in Canada (2011) use the example of artistic or performance-based interventions that have been used in planning processes to reveal different conceptions of what citizens might want from regeneration, while Lehtovuori and Havik (2009) detail cases in Amsterdam and Helsinki where local sub-cultural groups participated in the development of new, site-specific cultural scenes.

Particularly popular in the United Kingdom under the New Labour government, the development of cultural industry networks was influenced by understandings of the role the density of networks that exists within the cultural industries (see Randle, this volume) and the importance of intermediaries such as agents. But added to this was an understanding that, despite their role in international networks of capital and ideas, the cultural sector is very much rooted in particular places. Detailed knowledge of the local cultural scene is therefore important. Traditional arts agencies, used to offering grants to arts institutions within the framework of public subsidy, rarely had sufficient understanding of small cultural businesses, most of whom (whether in new media, popular music, comedy or magazine production) did not see themselves as being in 'the arts'. This was not because their aims were purely commercial; but often because their own identity, or the cultural form in which they work, such as a comedy club or a magazine, was not seen as part of the subsidised arts sector.

As O'Connor and Gu (2013) have written in their account of one such agency, Manchester's Creative Industries Development Service (CIDS), a crucial part of this intermediation was 'translating' not only the business needs but also the social, cultural and urbanistic concerns of cultural organisations into the language of economic development. Questions such as licensing laws (which govern bars and nightclubs), planning decisions, and policing or drugs policy were of interest to city centre cultural businesses. They were often concerned about maintaining a mixed economy of for-profit and voluntary organisations, or were tolerant of a wide range of users of the urban realm, including homeless people, drug users and sex workers. Traditional business support agencies were unlikely to reflect any of these concerns in their dealings with government, or at least not in the way that small cultural business may want them to be reflected. Yet 'economic development', in the narrower sense of growth in businesses, jobs and turnover, was exactly what the many specialist agencies set up in the United Kingdom and elsewhere were generally tasked with doing.

These agencies were measured by the number of businesses they helped establish, the growth in jobs, the number of training places offered and so on. While many of those who worked in such agencies tried hard to gain the trust of small cultural organisations, such trust was often undermined by the requirement to *measure* the effectives of such interactions. O'Connor and Gu's work suggests that CIDS in Manchester had aimed to traverse the ground between economic policy, urban planning and cultural policy, but that the requirement of funding, and indeed the way cultural policy is organised at national level – separating economic development from culture – meant that these splits were too deep.

Creative city conflicts

There are of course versions of this urban creative economy 'script' in circulation, with differing roles for culture, differing emphaseses on production and consumption and different spatial patterns. There is also active debate in the literature about what kind of cultural investments produces more socially balanced outcomes. But all such debates are carried out against a background of several decades of evidence on the link between major cultural investments and gentrification (Zukin, 1982; Hackworth and Smith, 2001; Edensor et al., 2010).

Grodach et al. (2014) have recently argued that this link will only be the case in certain neighbourhoods (inner city areas, that are likely subject to rapid demographic change) and that investment in different art forms, and different neighbourhoods, can achieve different outcomes. Their research, in common with work by Stern and Siefert (2002) and Markusen and Gadwa (2010) suggest that while commercial cultural industries may be part of gentrification, arts organisations, particularly a mix of non-profit and publicly funded ones, may instead be part of more positive change – regeneration without associated gentrification – or what Markusen (2006) has named the 'artistic dividend'.

Silver and Miller (2012) in their study of Canadian cities and towns argue that while there is a strong correlation between the presence of artists in the workforce and rising local wages, the opposite is true when 'creative professionals', managers, technicians and administrators move in. There are various ways of interpreting this finding, but a plausible one is while lively artistic 'scenes' are associated with a relatively healthy, broader-based economic development, by the time an area is regenerated enough for managers to move in, gentrification has already started and polarisation between higher paid workers and lower paid ones is accelerating. One problem with such work is of course the problem of robust cultural occupational data; 'technicians', for example, might find themselves surprised to be lumped in with managers and the pay and status of 'cultural administrators' differs widely depending on the kind of institution in which they work.

Outside the inner city, the suburbs are sometimes touted as offering the potential for a counter-narrative to that of cultural clustering and gentrification (Edensor et al., 2010). This work is particularly developed in an Australian context, where Collis et al. (2013) argue that despite having only one 'global' city – Sydney – and a population that overwhelming lives and works in suburbs, the urban bias of much work on culture and place is still largely unchallenged. By looking at where cultural workers live and work, however, they find significant concentrations in suburban areas, particularly the Gold Coast and Sunshine Coast (South East Queensland). The people in this research are not unwilling refugees from high urban house prices, but proffer positive reasons for their location, including better access to the beach or countryside, less stress and, pleasingly, a desire not to be identified with the cliché of the inner city 'creative class' (cf. Gibson, 2011). Bain (2010) finds similar drivers of suburban cultural production in her study of Toronto (see also Hracs, 2010) and argues that in fact the absence of traditional cultural spaces in such areas – theatres, museums and galleries – opens up a variety of improvisational spaces such as community centres, which she sees as 'a more inclusive alternative to the spectacular spaces of urban creativity' (2010: 74).

Shaw (2013) in her work on 'indie subcultures' also argues that the non-profit and low profit creative activities may well be associated with more balanced economic development. But examining time-series maps of inner Melbourne to look at where these sub-cultural 'scenes' operate suggests that they are being squeezed into tighter and tighter areas as the relatively cheap rents on which they depend disappear. As she notes, and other researchers have observed (Zukin, 1995; Lloyd, 2006), cultural workers, whether artists, musicians or actors, are rarely marginal in class terms as individuals (and are arguably becoming less likely to be so, see Oakley and Banks, forthcoming 2015). But in terms of work and performance space at least, they are often economically marginal, unable to afford 'market' rents, particularly in inner-city neighbourhoods. As Shaw argues, this leaves city councils with a stark choice. They can pursue regeneration strategies that create a more amenable environment for capital investment and high end residential space, risking the loss of sub cultural and non-profit activities altogether, or they can intervene directly – through provision of publicly owned or subsidised space or via zoning laws – to prevent housing developments on inner-city land. The parlous state of public finances, particularly in Europe and the United States, suggests that this choice is, in most cases, not a real one.

Perhaps the longest-established study of the role of the non-profit and small-scale arts scene in community development is the work of Susan Siefert and Mark Stern at the Social Impact of the Arts Project (SIAP), University of Pennsylvania. For over twenty years they have been studying the role of arts organisations in communities, developing indicators of economic, social and cultural improvement, and their findings have generally supported an argument that small-scale cultural investment and what is sometimes referred to as 'creative placemaking' can have beneficial effects in neighbourhoods, without the harmful effects of gentrification and displacement.

Mapping cultural assets of various sorts (profit and non-profit), they distinguish between what they call 'market' districts of a city, where a relatively wealthy and educated population means that cultural offerings can find a market, versus 'civic' districts, where other forms of cultural facilities may be based – particularly community and publicly supported arts, but in a much more precarious situation. As Stern and Siefert argue (2013), the market will not make poorer neighbourhoods sustainable as cultural hubs. Transport problems, distance from the city centre and lower income levels of both residents and arts workers means that public or other support is needed to maintain such facilities – even though, as their data demonstrates, such facilities can have beneficial effects in terms of a variety of social indicators.

Yet public policy, they note, is moving in the wrong direction. The correlation between the wealth of residents and the cultural facilities available has increased over the last decade (a finding spectacularly supported by Stark et al.'s 2013 work on the United Kingdom), while community arts organisations have become more precarious. And the United States' strong philanthropic tradition had made little difference to this; philanthropic money is also going into wealthier neighbourhoods where economic growth is possible, rather than to poorer neighbourhoods where the benefits are less likely to be measured in jobs and growth.

The policy message from this is clear. The evidence of gentrification effects from cultural investments is robust; and while smaller scale, more disaggregated investments and particular sorts of arts and cultural activities and businesses can have less polarising effects, the outcomes from these investments are unlikely to fit the requirements for economic gains that public policy has focused upon. The regeneration of poorer neighbourhoods will only be achieved when the notion of what 'regeneration' means is changed.

City governments of course are not unaware of the fact that 'success' in the urban cultural economy often has the effect of undermining the very conditions on which it depends. Yet the creative city imaginary organises institutions and actors, from state, civil society and the commercial sector, in ways that allow them to 'fail forwards' (Peck, 2005), recouping immediate benefits whilst displacing the conflicts and contradictions to some future date.

David Harvey's hope that the increased instrumentalisation of arts and culture would lead artists to 'side with a politics opposed to multinational capitalism and in favour of some more compelling alternative based on different kinds of social and ecological relations' (Harvey, 2001: 410) has often looked optimistic in the decade or more since he expressed it, particularly when increased cultural budgets were making instrumentalisation more palatable (Hesmondhalgh et al., 2014). But the global financial crisis and the subsequent conversion of private into public debt, the increasingly precarious nature of the cultural workforce – particularly recent entrants with high student loans – next to a seemingly untouched core of the global super rich has led to a rebirth of arts and cultural activism that, if not as prominent as its supporters sometimes suggest, has at least started to articulate a new urban politics of culture.

In a few cases active resistance, sometimes led by artists, against regeneration along conventional lines, has been explicitly recognised by public policy. Boren and Young (2013) provide examples from Hamburg, Toronto and Stockholm where artists and activists have worked with city authorities to reframe regeneration. Such examples are often modest in scale and sometimes sit alongside other, more conventional regeneration attempts, within the same city authority. More commonly, cultural activists have sat outside or in direct opposition to city councils, Novy and Colomb (2013) give examples of such movements in Hamburg and Berlin – the latter case succeeding in bringing together radical activists from Berlin's arts scene with bar owners and nightclub managers who were also threatened by displacements (see also Lange, 2005). In the case of Hamburg, they argue that creative workers – increasingly politicised by their own precarious economic state (also see De Peuter and Cohen, this volume) have joined forces with other young people – also highly educated but in insecure economic conditions. In this way, as they note, Florida's 'creative class' may indeed possess a sense of group identity, but it is one that is articulated not by pressing for more 'creative class' policies, but by protesting against them.

The possibility for truly cross-class alliances, however, remains problematic. One way through this, as Long (2013) argues, is to return to Doreen Massey's (1994) cry for a progressive sense of place, one that remained aware of it own character while recognising and interacting with the global forces shaping it. Long's argument is that cultural activism that is focused on specific locales can retain a sense of legitimacy even when it runs the risk of appealing to some members of a community more than others. In contrast to (though not *opposed* to) the sort of mobile cultural activism associated with demonstrations and occupations (e.g. Routledge, 2012), Long looks at the 'Keep Austin weird' campaign as an example of localised cultural activism. This grassroots movement, which began in Austin, Texas as a form of discursive resistance to chain stores and the loss of independent businesses, has since spread across the USA and elsewhere. Despite its support for a more localised economy, the very success of the campaign and its uses of mediated images, T-shirts, slogans and the like, has led to it being described as more of a 'bumper sticker than a movement', just as the New Economics Foundation's anti-clone town campaigns in the United Kingdom has been criticised for its 'toolkit' approach to revisiting local economies. Long recognises that place-based cultural activism often runs the risk of commodification and developing its own forms of conspicuous consumption – independent businesses are unlikely to be able to offer the discounts that larger ones can for example – and thus are often the preserve of the middle class. But he doesn't want to concede the ground of localism too easily. He argues that 'keeping it weird' retains legitimacy because it is predicated on local solidarity and that such campaigns are more than nostalgia for a local community, but are also indicative of 'social camaraderie, solidarity and economic resilience' (Long, 2013: 63).

A similar argument is made by Buser et al. (2013), who, drawing on the example of Stokes Croft in Bristol, suggest that cultural activism has an important role to play in constituting particular urban neighbourhoods as centres of what they call 'social activism'. This activism uses arts and creative practice to disrupt conventional social understandings and by bringing together a history of radicalism in a particular place, in this case a neighbourhood of Bristol, not only does the Stokes Croft campaign act as a sort of urban laboratory but its connection to place helps sustain that resistance beyond specific campaigns. In this case, the arts were a central part of the anti-corporate campaign, fought most famously (and unsuccessfully) against Tesco, its centrepiece being not a petition, or a social media campaign, but a large mural. However, Buser et al. admit that in their interviews of activists from two groups, the 'People's Republic of Stokes Croft' and the 'No Tesco in Stokes Croft' campaigns, all but one were white and middle-class and that the links between Stokes Croft and the nearby neighborhood of St Pauls with its large Afro-Caribbean and Somali communities are weak.

Such observations make clear the nature of the challenge. There is a growing literature that suggest that smaller-scale, place-based and committed arts organisations, together with broad-based local governance, can develop models of urban cultural development that are more than 'papering over urban decay, adding a glossy veneer that prepares the city for reinvestment', as Leslie and Rantisi put it (2013: 85). Capital-led projects are of course continuing in China, the Middle East and the richer parts of richer cities in the global north, but many cities and towns may need to consider this sort of finer-grained, smaller and more localised approach, where lifestyle businesses and not-for-profits are not seen as failed business models, as was the case under the 'creative industries' regime, but as ways of sustaining meaningful work in a steady state or low-growth economy. Capital-led and fine-grained approaches are not necessarily opposed; examples such as the Museum of Old and New Art (MONA) in Hobart, Tasmania suggest otherwise (O'Connor, 2014). However, without a 'progressive sense of place' and the kind of re-invented urban imaginary that could go with it (O'Connor and Shaw, 2014) these two models seem to be set in a pattern of mutual antagonism.

References

Bain, A. 2010. 'Creative Suburbs: Cultural "Popcorn" Pioneering in Multi-Purpose Spaces' in Edensor, T., Leslie, D., Millington, S. and Rantisi, N. (eds), *Spaces of Vernacular Creativity*, London: Routledge.

Bell, D. and Jayne, M. (eds) 2004. *City of Quarters: Urban Villages in the Contemporary City*, Aldershot: Ashgate.

Boren, T. and Young, C. 2013. 'Getting Creative with the "Creative City"? Towards New Perspectives on Creativity in Urban Policy', *International Journal of Urban and Regional Research*, 37 (5): 1799–815.

Buser, M., Bonura, C., Fannin, M. and Boyer, K. 2013. 'Cultural Activism and the Politics of Place-Making', *City: Analysis of Urban Trends, Culture, Theory, Policy, Action*, 17 (5): 606–27, DOI: 10.1080/13604813.2013.827840.

Collis, C., Freebody, S. and Flew, T. 2013. 'Seeing the Outer Suburb: Addressing the Urban Bias in Creative Place Thinking', *Regional Studies*, 47: 148–60.

Currid, E. 2007. *The Warhol Economy: How Fashion, Art, and Music Drive New York City*, Princeton, NJ: Princeton University Press.

Davies, W. 2014. *The Limits of Neoliberalism: Authority, Sovereignty and the Logic of Competition*, London: Sage.

Edensor, T., Leslie, D., Millington, S. and Rantisi, N. (eds) 2010. *Spaces of Vernacular Creativity*, London: Routledge.

Florida, R. 2002. *The Rise of the Creative Class, and How it's Transforming Work, Leisure, Community and Everyday Life*, New York: Basic Books.

Gerin, A. and McLean, L. (eds) 2011. *Public Art in Canada: Critical Perspectives*, Toronto: University of Toronto Press.

Gibson, M. 2011. 'The Schillers of the Suburbs: Creativity and Mediated Sociality', *International Journal of Cultural Policy*, 17 (5): 1–17.

Grodach, C. and Silver, D. (eds) 2013. *The Politics of Urban Cultural Policy: Global Perspectives*, London: Routledge.

Grodach, C., Foster, N. and Murdoch, J. 2014. 'Gentrification and the Artistic Dividend', *Journal of the American Planning Association*, 80 (1): 21–35.

Hackworth, J. and Smith, N. 2001. 'The Changing State of Gentrification', *Tijdschrift voor Economische en Sociale Geografie*, 92: 464–77.

Hall, P. 1998. *Cities and Civilisation: Culture, Technology and Urban Order*, London: Weidenfield and Nicolson.

Harvey, D. 2000. *Spaces of Hope*, Edinburgh: Edinburgh University Press.

Harvey, D. 2001. 'The Arts of Rent: Globalization and the Commodification of Culture', in Harvey, D. *Spaces of Capital*, London: Routledge.

Hesmondhalgh, D., Nisbett, M., Oakley, K. and Lee, D.J. 2014. 'Were New Labour's Cultural Policies Neo-Liberal?', *International Journal of Cultural Policy*, doi.org/10.1080/10286632. 2013.879126.

Hracs, B. 2010. 'Beyond Bohemia: Geographies of Everyday Creativity for Musicians in Toronto', in Edensor, T., Leslie, D. Millington, S. and Rantisi, N. (eds), *Spaces of Vernacular Creativity*, London: Routledge.

Lange, B. 2005. 'Socio-spatial Strategies of Culturepreneurs: The Example of Berlin and its New Professional Scenes', *Zeitschrift fur Wirtschaftsgeographie*, 49: 79–96.

Lehtovuori, P. and Havik, K. 2009. 'Alternative Politics in Urban Innovation', in Kong, L and O'Connor, J. (eds), *Creative Economies, Creative Cities: Asian–European Perspectives*, Berlin: Springer Verlag.

Leslie, D. and Rantisi, N. 2013. 'Creativity and Urban Regeneration', in Grodach, C. and Silver, D. (eds), *The Politics of Urban Cultural Policy: Global Perspectives*, London: Routledge.

Lloyd, R. 2006. *Neo-Bohemia: Arts and Commerce in the Post-Industrial City*, New York: Routledge.

Long, J. 2013. 'Sense of Place and Place-Based Activism in the Neoliberal City: The Case of "Weird" Resistance', *City*, 17 (1): 52–67.

Markusen, A. 2006. 'The Artistic Dividend: Urban Artistic Specialization and Economic Development Implications', *Urban Studies*, 43: 1661–86.

Markusen, A. and Gadwa, A. 2010. 'Arts and Culture in Urban or Regional Planning', in Verma, N. (ed.), *Institutions and Planning*, Oxford: Elsevier.

Massey, D. 1994. *Space, Place and Gender*, Cambridge: Polity Press.

Miles, S. 2010. *Spaces for Consumption: Pleasure and Placelessness in the Post-Industrial City*, London: Sage.

Novy, J. and Colomb, C. 2013. 'Struggling for the Right to the (Creative) City in Berlin and Hamburg: New Urban Social Movements, New "Spaces of Hope"?', *International Journal of Urban and Regional Research*, 37 (5): 1816–38.

Oakley, K. and Banks, M. Forthcoming 2015. 'Class, UK Art Workers and the Myth of Mobility', in Maxwell, R. (ed.) *The Routledge Companion to Labor and Media*, New York: Routledge.

O'Connor, J. 2004. 'A Special Kind of City Knowledge': Innovative Clusters, Tacit Knowledge and the "Creative City"', *Media International Australia*, 112: 131–49.

O'Connor, J. 2011. 'The Cultural and Creative Industries: A Critical History' *Economiaz*, 79: 24–47.

O'Connor, J. 2014. 'Regeneration Redux: Hobart and MONA', in Ashton, P., Gibson, C. and Gibson, R. (eds), *Bi-Roads and Hidden Treasures: Mapping Cultural Assets in Regional Australia*, Perth: University of Western Australia Press.

O'Connor, J. and Gu, X. 2013. 'Developing a Creative Cluster in a Post-Industrial City: CIDS and Manchester', in Flew, T. (ed.), *Creative Industries and Urban Development: Creative Cities in the 21st Century*, London: Routledge.

O'Connor, J. and Gu, X. 2014. 'Making Creative Spaces: China and Australia – An Introduction', *City, Culture and Society*, 5 (3): 111–14.

O'Connor, J. and Shaw, K. 2014. 'What Next for the Creative City?' *City, Culture and Society*, 5 (3): 165–70.

Peck, J. 2005. 'Struggling with the Creative Class', *International Journal of Urban and Regional Research*, 20 (4): 740–770.

Pratt, A. 2006. 'Advertising and Creativity, a Governance Approach: A Case Study of Creative Agencies in London', *Environment and Planning A*, 38: 1883–99.

Pratt, A. 2009. 'Urban Regeneration: From the Arts 'Feel Good' Factor to the Cultural Economy: A Case Study of Hoxton, London', *Urban Studies*, 46 (5–6): 1041–61.

Routledge, P. 2012. 'Sensuous Solidarities: Emotion, Politics and Performance in the Clandestine Insurgent Rebel Clown Army', *Antipode*, 44 (2): 428–52.

Shaw, K. 2013. 'Independent Creative Subcultures and Why They Matter', *International Journal of Cultural Policy*, 19 (3): 333–52.

Silver, D. and Miller, D. 2012. 'Contextualizing the Artistic Dividend', *Journal of Urban Affairs*, 35 (5): 591–606.

Stark, P., Gordon, P. and Powell, D. 2013. *Rebalancing Our Cultural Capital*. www.artsprofessional.co.uk/sites/artsprofessional.co.uk/files/rebalancing_our_cultural_capital.pdf (accessed 12 July 2014).

Stern, M. and Siefert, S. 2002. *Culture Builds Community: Evaluation Summary Report*, SIAP, University of Pennsylvania, www.sp2.upenn.edu/siap/docs/culture_builds_community/summary_report.pdf (accessed 21 July 2014).

Stern, M. and Siefert, S. 2013. *Cultural Ecology, Neighbourhood Vitality and Social Wellbeing: A Philadelphia Project*, www.sp2.upenn.edu/siap/docs/cultureblocks/e_Summary&Imps.v5.dec13.cover&citation.pdf (accessed 20 June 2014).

Zukin, S. 1982. *Loft Living: Culture and Capital in Urban Change*, Baltimore: Johns Hopkins University Press.

Zukin, S. 1995. *The Culture of Cities*, Oxford: Blackwell.

16
CONSUMPTION AND PLACE

Steven Miles

Debates over the creative city have come to play a dominant role in the discourse that has surrounded the cultural industries over the past twenty years. The notion of the creative city is, however, underpinned by an often unarticulated and/or assumed relationship: that between consumption and place. This chapter will consider the proposition that the creative city is effectively a proxy for the consumer city. The cultural industries play a key role in tying the economy to a particular neo-liberal vision of that economy. This represents another stage in the "culturalisation" of the economy, something that is part of a long history, not least within the context of classical political economy (Hudson, 2005). However, the current relationship between consumption and place is perhaps most remarkable for how it ties cultural industries to a symbolic vision of the urban. In this context it is suggested that consumption represents the economic means by which culture has come to play a key role in the regeneration of the de-industrialised city.

Consumption has become an increasingly high-profile issue in discussions around place as a result of the dual processes of de-industrialisation and globalisation. The impact of global economic decline has been particularly hard on cities. But such impact reflects a longer-term trend for industrial decline in Western Europe and beyond in which the certainties of the old economic model can no longer be relied upon. It was in this climate that culture emerged as a potential means of helping to plug the economic gap.

The value of culture is in a sense a symbolic value. It offers cities a sense of aspiration. It demonstrates a city's ability to compete on a global scale and as such the cultural offer has become part and parcel of what it means to be a competitive city at the beginning of the twenty-first century. As such, since the 1980s and 1990s, as O'Connor (2007) points out, the cultural industries became increasingly tied to debates around the art of city making, which took many forms including: cultural venues and quarters, street markets, alternative retail, new forms of public art, large scale architectural regeneration projects and campaigns such as the "24 hour city". As part of this process the visual and performing arts have, in turn, become key players in cities' leisure and entertainment offer, creating a clear tension between debates around what constitutes commercial and popular success and whether that success can genuinely be perceived to be democratic, or, indeed, "authentic" in nature (O'Connor, 2007). This puts culture firmly in the arena of consumption: it becomes less important for its own sake and more important as a means to an economic end. Consumption provides the means by which culture can attain economic value.

Has, in effect, the relationship between consumption and place reduced cultural democracy to nothing more than a spectacle? In what follows I will consider the role of culture in the construction of place and how, specifically, the commodification of place and the experience of place has not only intensified aspects of capitalist development, but in doing so has led to a revaluation of the consumer's role in this process.

The "creative" city

The relationship between consumption and place is very much a question of identity. In effect, culture provides a means of representing the city, and all the components that constitute the so-called creative city, in the international marketplace. A key issue here centres on whether such representations can ever be more than partial or indeed formulaic in nature.

Various authors have tried to pin down what the notion of creativity means for the contemporary city. Carta (2008), for example, proposes that we should think of the creative city as consisting of "the three Cs of the creative city", namely culture, communication and cooperation. For Carta the talent of a city very much lies in its identity. This identity provides the city with its competitive resource:

> The talent of a city must also generate value; it must be submerged in the virtuous circle of the culture economy, the geography of experience, the design of quality. Culture, therefore, plays a part in the field of resources, enabling the city to become more creative.
>
> (Carta, 2008: 12)

For Carta there is a danger that a declaration proclaiming a city's creative credentials runs the risk of amounting to little more than empty gestures of principle: slogans rather than realities. Authors such as Evans (2001) have thus bemoaned the "just add culture and stir" approach to regeneration. In this context, consumption provides a means to an end: a way of providing the city with at least the appearance of change. It is in this sense that the creative city is a proxy for the consumer city. The relationship between consumption and place is inevitably primarily symbolic in nature. The generation of value is most likely to be precipitated through the process of consumption or, to put this another way, by the commodification of creativity.

The relationship between consumption and place is very much the product of a broader policy discourse in which policymakers and government bodies such as the Department for Culture, Media and Sport (which of course has a vested interest in demonstrating as much) in the United Kingdom want to believe culture, and thus the cultural industries, can play a key role in a post-industrial society. However, it is notoriously difficult to establish the causal impact of culture in terms of how it

intervenes as a contributory factor in broader aspects of social and economic development. In this context various cities have played leading roles in investing heavily in culture
as a prime focus for the reinvention of the city. But the concern here is that the decision-
makers responsible for cities/places in a post-industrial context seek to apply such an
analyses without due regard for the specific circumstances in which place sits. For
many commentators, culture has therefore by default come to play an almost ornamental role. It is effectively the pornography of the post-industrial consumer society
(Miles, 2010). In this context, Meades (2011) refers to the "sightbite", an ornamental
modernism propping up the broader principles of regeneration in which appearance
is everything and in which everything must be instantly memorable. From this point
of view the Bilbao Guggenheim has played a very particular role in promoting a
particular thinking about the consumption of culture through regeneration:

> What we are looking at is an advertisement, a perpetual marketing
> campaign. Every time it is photographed or posted on the web or televised
> it is Bilbao that the world hears of ... What Bilbao has shown is that the
> word regeneration has to be made flesh, so to speak, has to be represented
> matertially. A faith requires material expression ... Not only architecture but
> the entire apparatus of regeneration is slavish in its adherence to fashion. For
> an endeavour whose alleged purpose is the improvement of post-industrial
> cities and the alleviation of deprivation, it is signally ingrown, a smooth-
> talking verruca. In the very words of someone called, without irony, an urban
> regeneration guru, "What we need are fashion incubators attached to art
> installations".
>
> (Meades, 2011: 34)

For Meades, the regeneration "solution" is nothing more than formulaic: a partial
solution that barely considers the particularities of place.

The consumption of Bilbao

The city that has perhaps best exemplified the economic potential of the relationship
between place and consumption, certainly in the context of the cultural industries, is
indeed Bilbao. Formerly a mercantile and industrial town, Bilbao is perhaps the ultimate
example of a city that has had to deal with the ravages of post-industrial decline. But
at least in some senses the locating of the Guggenheim in Bilbao radically reversed
this situation, and within the first year of its operation it attracted approaching one
and a half million visitors, injecting an estimated $160 million into the local economy
in the process. The Guggenheim was the culmination of a broader programme of
architecturally led regeneration that included a state-of-the-art subway and an
extended airport. Architecturally, the Guggenheim represents the ultimate in iconic
statements:

> The escape from functional form making resulted in a spectacular cadenza,
> which, against the odds, transcended the potential to be a bombastic exercise

in self-expression or an expensive publicity stunt. The by-now iconic and florid descriptions of the photogenic building, endlessly circulated in tourist brochures, the popular press and the critical literature, hardly convey its complex urban reality adequately, even if they have undoubtedly mediated its reception and contributed to the general mythography.

(Ockman, 2004: 231–2)

Clearly, however, the Guggenheim Bilbao is a brand, one that is synonymous with the impact cultural investment can have on post-industrial regeneration. The success of the Guggenheim is attributed at least in part by Ockman to the way it combines the mediascape of global architecture with the ethnoscape that comes out of Basque regionalism. In this sense the success of the Guggenheim Bilbao is at least partly due to its strong sense of its own place. However, the space is symbolically reproduced so that it effectively constructs an "imagined world" for symbolic consumption. For Ockman this represents the antithesis of the sort of commodified homogenisation that many commentators have condemned (Zukin, 1998). The argument Ockman presents is that architecture is adaptable, as is place, and can be incorporated as part of a broader and self-conscious ambition for social and cultural change. The Guggenheim Bilbao works because it is in Bilbao – in New York or Los Angeles it would be utterly crass. As Evans (2003) puts it, public culture has come to emulate the world of branded commercial entertainment products and leisure shopping that equates to what he calls a brand of karaoke architecture: an extension of branding into the cultural realm. Furthermore, the benefits to be had from this emphasis on the powerful messages that such elite sites of cultural consumption come at a cost. And of course, the needs of local cultural producers are different to those of cultural institutions (Gomez, 1998). There is a danger that this focus on the consumption of places like Bilbao as a brand may lead to an emphasis on some forms of institutionally defined culture at the expense of others.

The consumption of place

In reality, of course, places are the products of their history and their heritage. This issue is perhaps best expressed in some of the work of Lancaster, who is concerned with the history of the North of England, which, he points out, is very much tied up with a broader picture of national history and politics. As Lancaster notes:

A northern upbringing frequently involves the inculcation of an unusually powerful set of attachments to place; a deep rooting in a particular physical, social and cultural environment. At the same time, however, those loyalties are strongly inflected, almost from the outset, by awareness of a questionable place within the larger social and political geography of England.

(Lancaster, 1995: 29)

Of course, every place has a degree of geographical/historical particularity. The role of culture in regeneration stumbles when it fails to take this into account.

Arguably the result of the above process is regeneration in which consumption is prioritised for its own sake. Perhaps an exception in this respect is NewcastleGateshead, in the north-east of England, which is often lauded as an example of the potential benefits of culture-led regeneration. NewcastleGateshead Quayside underwent a remarkable transformation between the late 1990s and the early 2000s through millions of pounds of public and private investment. At the heart of this redevelopment were two cultural venues: the Baltic Centre for Contemporary Art (BALTIC) built for £46 million and the Sage Gateshead Music Centre designed by Foster and Partners at a cost of £70 million. These venues went some way to meeting a pronounced need to meet the cultural requirements of the people of the north-east. However, beyond that function the buildings also, significantly, contribute to a broader symbolic process in which NewcastleGateshead also presents itself as a forward-thinking city, able to compete on an international cultural platform. These are spaces for consumption insofar as they offer opportunities for consumers to spend money on tickets, in bookshops or cafes, but also in that they construct an intangible image of place to be consumed from afar. The Quayside is a focal point for both Newcastle and Gateshead and the BALTIC and the Sage along with the £22 million Millennium Bridge also form a space for consumption from which nearby bars, restaurants and hotels can also benefit.

Cities are places where people strive to overcome the negative effects of past and current circumstances and struggle to create meaning in the place that history has located them (Lancaster, 1995). The Quayside development appears to have engaged with this process in a meaningful way, notably through the redevelopment of the BALTIC as an industrial building and by enhancing a declining quayside with a new and complementary lease of cultural life. More importantly, although consumption opportunities are present they arguably do not engulf the development, they complement it.

The above is not a trick that is so easy to pull off. As much as the relationship between culture and place is formulaic it is a formula commodified. The assumption here is that culture is good, but only a particular kind of culture: a kind of culture that can be packaged, what Meades (2011) calls "the new, accessibly accessible, fun-style fun-arts". But the belief that culture can fulfil a regenerating role is, according to Meades, based on nothing more than an unsubstantiated belief. The relationship between consumption and place is in this sense illusory: the images we associate with such a relationship allow for a leap of faith in which anything becomes possible. This leap of faith is perhaps best demonstrated by the work of Richard Florida (2002), whose underpinning proposition was effectively that all cities could aspire to be "creative" and that, by promoting the notion of the creative city, a sort of self-fulfilling prophesy could be enacted through the choices made by the potential residents of these places.

In trying to understand the broader relationship between consumption and place, Wood (2009) discusses the omnitopic nature of the city, a process by which an apparently uniform enclave apparently approximates all of urbanity, so that places become defined by very little other than a sort of generic perception. For some authors the relationship between consumption and place is indeed defined through experience or through "experiencescapes", so that place has effectively become a well-produced entertainment show (Mikunda, 2004).

South Street Seaport, New York

The work of Boyer (1992), who discusses the regeneration of South Street Seaport in New York, provides a useful example of how culture can be appropriated through this process. Once a neglected "edge-space", South Street Seaport is now an upscale cultural marketplace, a simulated landscape of consumption, an imaginary historical museum that surrounds "the spectator with an artfully composed historic ambience" (p. 182). But, as suggested above, this process comes at a cost. As Boyer (1992) puts it, this part of the city is effectively reduced to a "map of tourist attractions, which suppresses the continuous order of reality, the connecting in-between places, and imposes instead an imaginary order of things" (p. 192). To take this argument to its logical conclusion, place becomes tangible only so far as it is productive, useful or consumable, reflecting a situation in which in a global environment a city can compete if its aspirations are global. "Imageability" becomes the way that city markets itself so that spaces of consumption become the city or at least they become the means by which the city is known. Prior to the 1930s South Street Seaport itself was a two-mile street of ships that later declined into a no-man's land. A regenerated South Street Seaport was opened in 1983 and the model of regeneration to which it adhered was one of an outdoor museum with consumption possibilities:

> In their desire to solidify the traces of the past into a unified image, to restore an intactness that never was, developers of historicized urban bazaars and storehouse of hetereogeneity like South Street Seaport, where consumers can buy anything from anywhere, have so conflated geographical space and historical time that the actual uniqueness of place and context have been completely erased. These environments of simulation provide the décor for our acts of consumption.
>
> (Boyer, 1992: 196)

For Boyer, then, in one sense this process is not about place at all, but rather it represents part of a system of values that gives additional meaning to the urban landscape; a system primarily designed to increase consumption by suggesting that a particular lifestyle requires that such consumption should take place. Such spaces provide a combination of the real and the fantastic that serves as a backdrop in which consumption becomes inevitable; in which the commodity is at its most seductive. Consumption is important to South Street Seaport in a number of ways, not least insofar as its share of revenues from the central street of shops contributes directly to the preservation of the area's historic structures so that South Street Seaport effectively operates as an outside advertisement that constructs an historical story designed to fulfil the nostalgic desires of the consumer (Boyer, 1992). And perhaps most importantly of all, the visitor to South Street Seaport is primed to engage with the environment as a space for consumption demands: they become consumers of leisure lifestyles. The culture and heritage of the area is the raw material through which this process is achieved. Indeed, the transition underpinning consumption in South Seaport has been one of small boutiques to more recently a situation in which chain stores have come to dominate. So for Boyer (1992: 204) such places that used to exist outside the framework of the marketplace have become dependent upon "an experience that increasingly comes down to the moment of association when private desires become linked to future promises offered by items for sale". The end result of all this is a shift in the relationship between public and private spheres in which, as Boyer argues, the city is turned inside out so that so-called "public" communal spaces are in fact highly designed private spaces in which the way to belong is to consume.

Authenticity

Debates around the relationship between consumption and place lead to an almost inevitable discussion of the notion of "authenticity". Peck (2005) pointedly argues in his critique of Florida's work that it is simply not feasible to produce authentic neighbourhood cultures through deliberate public, or for that matter private, interventions, and as such interventions constantly run the risk of creating a self-consciously "funky" city where the authentic, if such a thing exists, is nothing but an after-thought. In this respect, Miles and Miles' (2004) discussion of Bario Chino in Barcelona is worth considering. Bario Chino could be said to be an illustration of such a process in which art has effectively been packaged for the masses. The re-invention of Bario Chino as a cultural quarter, or indeed more critically as a cultural "stage set", could be said to constitute a commodification of art. The plan behind the regeneration of the area was to create a tourist attraction, but by doing so the subsequent process of gentrification undermined the more home-grown forms of cultural production that existed previously. What emerged was a Bario Chino defined by a veneer of art galleries, boutiques and designer bars: by opportunities to consume. In this context, culture becomes a means to an end rather than an end in itself. The relationship between consumption and place is no doubt economically necessary, but it may also serve to reinforce broader patterns of gentrification.

There are many examples of cities that have struggled to construct a narrative that sufficiently engages with what makes a place special in the first place. This may be to do with the fact that such places are appropriated by policymakers more for what they say about a place than what they actually *do* for a place (Colomb, 2012). As such, Colomb (2012) reflects upon a situation described by Harvey (2001) whereby in an increasingly global market the pressure is on to keep some commodities unique and particular enough to maintain an edge in the marketplace (Harvey, 2001). In Berlin's case, Colomb suggests this has involved the transformation of cultural consumption practices through the mainstreaming of what was previously considered to be "underground" or "sub-cultural". These sub-cultures become commodified and assimilated, they effectively become niche markets, the blurring of the line between high and low culture allowing more and more art forms to be adopted by the mainstream for actual and symbolic consumption. This is exemplified in Berlin by what Colomb calls the integration of the hedonistic techno and club culture and of gay culture in city marketing campaigns, a discourse that can similarly be identified in the marketing campaigns of cities including Amsterdam and Melbourne. What has emerged in Berlin, and in perceptions of Berlin, then, is a narrative: a narrtive of "coolness" and of tolerance. As such, during the 2000s, argues Colomb, spaces that might previously have been referred to as marginal urban wastelands have come to be presented as new "urban playgrounds" for artistic production and consumption: evidence of Berlin's uniqueness. Berlin's ethnically mixed (and previously "normal") neighbourhoods have also come to be portrayed as tourist attractions, as stage-sets or as settings for young creative entrepreneurs. One way of describing this process is as one of aestheticisation, the process by which places have increasingly been constructed in the form of a visual tableau to be consumed (Williams, 2004). Thus in discussing the culture-led regeneration of Albert Dock in Liverpool, Williams laments how the city more broadly has been reinvented as a spectacle for consumption by tourists. For Williams, as much as there has been a culture-led regeneration of the United Kingdom this has been a revolution of "bourgeois taste".

Cultural quarters

Not only cities are in a position to be aestheticised in this way. In other words, some cities are obliged to look to alternative solutions beyond high impact, architecturally-led regeneration. As far as the cultural industries are concerned this process is arguably most clearly reflected in the emergence of cultural quarters in UK cities. The UK government has seen the cultural industries as constituting key players in sustainable regeneration and one of the ways this policy has been manifested is through the designation of cultural quarters, which McCarthy (2007: 1) argues have been "designated where a 'critical mass' of culture-related activity is seen as providing the basis for anticipated sustainable regeneration outcomes based on a 'holistic' mix of social, economic and environmental effects". City marketeers and managers have been drawn to the consumption of cultural goods and experiences as a means of achieving this mix. Small-scale cultural industries play a crucial role in this respect insofar as they bring a certain creative flair and vitality and the perception of an economic alternative that is absolutely necessary for those cities that are simply unable to compete on the global scale (Miles and Miles, 2004). Furthermore, Jayne (2004) argues in his discussion of the role of cultural quarters in Stoke-on-Trent that some cities are rendered "illegible" to post-industrial business. That, in other words, not all cities have the appropriate spatial and economic conditions to allow for a thriving programme of cultural intervention.

Where cultural quarters have thrived it might well be argued that consumption has played a key role, for example the number of live music venues in Manchester was, according to McCarthy (2007), a driving force in development of Manchester's Northern Quarter. A study undertaken by Urbanisitics in 1994 recommended the area should be used for a variety of purposes with the aim of retaining this emphasis on cultural creation and consumption, not least through the fashion wholesale industry. The report encouraged the promotion of indigenous industries alongside the "cultural" use of buildings: through a process of "cultural animation" in which liveliness, identity and vibrancy would be encouraged and stimulated. The Northern Quarter was envisioned as a mixed use space that combined elements of production and consumption alongside a night-time economy, as well as a significant degree of physical gentrification, an emphasis on information networks alongside the provision of business support as well as sensitively assimilated residential development (McCarthy, 2007). McCarthy argues that the fact that the Northern Quarter did emerge as a focus for the creative industries, and not least those related to musical production, is not entirely due to the branding and funding that is associated with the area, and may have developed naturally in the context of the bohemian culture with which it is associated. Equally significant in the evolution of Manchester as a so-called creative city is the district of Castlefield, described by Miles and Miles (2004) as "an aestheticised post-industrial space", an area close to the centre of the city notable for its canals, and for the reinvention of industrial buildings alongside new residential builds, pubs, bars and restaurants. O'Connor and Wynne (1996) similarly note how cultural industries have effectively been defined through such areas of "conspicuous" consumption.

Concluding thoughts

Such interventions as those discussed above may, then, end up being characterised above all by serving middle-class consumption cultures, and such a process is potentially divisive. To be genuinely successful cultural investment needs to be self-conscious in its inclusiveness. Decision-makers also need to be realistic about the legibility of the places that they are investing in emotionally as well as economically. It's also important not to forget the role of the consumer in this process. In an increasingly digital world the experience of the prosumer (see Ritzer and Jurgenson, 2010) – the consumer who both produces and consumes simultaneously – is apparently increasingly prominent and arguably serves to create spaces where homogenised forms of consumption are more and more likely to be challenged. However, in conclusion, the suggestion here is that any kind of a vision of a more liberated consumer is in danger of being overly optimistic. The early years of the 2000s have witnessed a period of austerity in which the freedom of choice we associate with consumption has inevitably been constrained. This has meant that the resources available to invest in a wholesale commitment to culture-led regeneration has come more and more under threat so that large-scale projects such as many of those discussed above are less likely to happen than they were in the past. However, the consumer remains complicit. Those visiting the regenerated city gladly consume the city in the way it was intended to be consumed. They effectively give up some freedoms as individuals in order to access others. The relationship between consumption and place is such that cultural interventions of the city say as much about the individual's desire to consume as it does about policymakers' determination to reproduce the city of consumption.

References

Boyer, M. (1992) "Cities for sale: Merchandising history at South Street Seaport", in M. Sorkin (ed.) *Variations on a Theme Park: The New American City and the End of Public Space*, New York: Hill and Wagg, pp. 181–204.

Carta, M. (2008) *Creative City*, London: List – Laboratorio Internazionale Editoriale Sas.

Colomb, C. (2012) *Staging the New Berlin: Place Marketing and the Politics of Urban Reinvention*, London: Routledge.

Evans, G. (2001) *Cultural Planning: An Urban Renaissance*, London: Routledge.

Evans, G. (2003) "Hard-branding the cultural city: From Prado to Prada", *International Journal of Urban and Regional Research*, 27 (2): 417–40.

Florida, R. (2002) *The Rise of the Creative Class*, New York: Basic Books.

Gomez, M.V. (1998) "Reflective images: The case of urban regeneration in Glasgow and Bilbao", *International Journal of Urban and Regional Research*, 23 (3): 658–64.

Harvey, D. (2001) *Spaces of Capital*, Edinburgh: Edinburgh University Press.

Hudson, R. (2005) *Economic Geographies: Circuits, Flows and Spaces*, London: Sage.

Jayne, M. (2004) *Cities and Consumption*, London: Routledge.

Lancaster, B. (1995) "City cultures and the 'Parliament of Birds': A letter from Newcastle", *Northern Review*, 2: 1–11.

McCarthy, J. (2007) "Quick fix or sustainable solution? Cultural clustering for urban regeneration in the UK", in C. Aitchison, G. Richards and A. Tallon (eds) *Making Space: Leisure, Tourism and Renewal*, Brighton: Leisure Studies Association, No. 96, pp.1–18.

Meades, J. (2011) "On the brandwagon", in J. Harris and R. Williams (eds) *Regenerating Culture and Society*, Liverpool: Liverpool University Press.

Mikunda, C. (2004) *Brand Lands, Hot Spots and Cool Spaces: Welcome to the Third Place and the Total Marketing Experience*, London: Kogan.

Miles, S. (2010) *Spaces for Consumption: Pleasure and Placelessness in the Post-Industrial City*, London: Sage.

Miles, S. and Miles, M. (2004) *Consuming Cities*, Basingstoke: Palgrave Macmillan.

Ockman, J. (2004) "New politics of the spectacle: 'Bilbao' and the global imagination", in D. Medina Lasansky and B. McLaren (eds) *Architecture and Tourism: Perception, Performance and Place*, Oxford: Berg, pp. 227–40.

O'Connor, J. (2007) *The Cultural and Creative Industries: A Review of the Literature: A Report for Creative Partnerships*, London: Arts Council England.

O'Connor, J. and Wynne, D. (eds) (1996) *From the Margins to the Centre: Cultural Production and Consumption in the Post-Industrial City*, Aldershot: Ashgate.

Peck, J. (2005) "Struggling with the creative class", *International Journal of Urban and Regional Research*, 29 (4): 740–70.

Ritzer, G. and Jurgenson, N. (2010) "Production, consumption, prosumption: The nature of capitalism in the age of the digital 'prosumer'", *Journal of Consumer Culture*, 10 (1): 13–36.

Williams, R. (2004) *The Anxious City: English Urbanism in the Late Twentieth Century*, London: Routledge.

Wood, A. (2009) *City Ubiquitous: Place, Communication and the Rise of Omnitopia*, Cresskill, NJ: Hampton Press.

Zukin, S. (1998) "Urban lifestyles: Diversity and standardisation in spaces of consumption", *Urban Studies*, 35 (5/6): 825–40.

17
COTTAGE ECONOMY
The 'ruralness' of rural cultural industries

David Bell

Recent years have seen increasing attention paid to the geographies of cultural production and consumption. This work has emphasized issues of place and scale, and has reminded researchers and policymakers of 'the difference that space makes' – that analyses of and interventions in the workings of cultural industries must think carefully about where those industries are located, the spatial reach of their networks and markets and interactions with other geographical features (the urban landscape, place image, etc.) and phenomena (migration, gentrification, etc.), and so on. Among the emerging geographies being mapped and discussed, we have global, national and regional scale case studies and comparisons, analyses of policy transfer and policy tourism, explorations of agglomeration, and detailed explorations of site-specific (and industry/sector-specific) cases. This is arguably most apparent in the creative industries domain, although there are parallel tracks focused on issues such as cultural tourism and culture-led regeneration. Among the geographical registers used to think about creative and cultural industries, one key approach has been to explore urban–rural differences (and similarities). This approach often begins with a critique of the centring of metropolitan cultural work and life in accounts of creative industries and creative economies; it is true that, say, a decade ago the dominant 'script' concerning the creative industries tended to assume a particular inner-city location – that creative industries are quintessentially urban (Banks et al. 2000). However, more recently we have witnessed the emergence of a literature that uses that critique as a platform to look elsewhere for creative activities: to look to the small city or market town, the outer suburbs, to 'peripheral' regions, and to the countryside (see respectively Waitt and Gibson 2009; Lazzeroni et al. 2013; Collis et al. 2013; Thomas et al. 2013; Bell and Jayne 2010). It is the latter 'elsewhere' that is the focus of this chapter. Through a discussion of research and policy discussion on rural cultural industries, my aim is to examine in particular the framing of 'ruralness' used to account for cultural production (and consumption) beyond the metropolis. In so doing, I want to think about the different countrysides that are conjured in accounts of, to use Susan Luckman's (2012) subtitular phrase, 'rural, regional and remote creativity'.

Local cultural industry

As noted above, attention to the geographies of cultural industries operates at a range of spatial scales; attention to scale is implicit in Luckman's 'rural, regional and remote' – as are issues of distance/proximity, and imagined geographies. The common sense antinomies implied in this triad barely need spelling out, but let's spell them out anyway: rural (*not urban*), regional (*non-metro*, to use Melissa Gregg's (2010) term), remote (*not nearby*). Each term in the binary pair carries its own specific weight: the 'not-a' signifies a lack. Part of the work of the emerging literature on rural cultural industry has been to redress this (im)balance, to re-centre the marginal, bring the remote in from the cold, rethink the regional and the rural. One strength of the work in this field has been its attention to imagined geographies but also to real places: to think, if you like, about what remoteness, regionality and ruralness means for a potter in the English Cotswolds, or an artists' collective in Bega, Australia, or the 'creative class' in the Canadian North, or for policymaking in Western Ireland (see respectively Luckman 2012; Waitt and Gibson 2013; Petrov 2008; White 2010). Increasingly, emphasis is placed on relational geographies, too – this returns us to those binaries, but also reminds us of connectedness, of networks and linkages, producing accounts of cultural ecologies or *compages* (Scott 2010). Relational thinking also operates across spatial scales, and work exploring scalar connections reminds us that the rural does not equate solely with the local; global circuits do not hover above or skirt round the countryside. Scott's (2010) study of the English Lake District relocates the region (at least in part) in the context of global flows – of tourists but also of texts (such as the retelling of one well known story from the Lakes in the movie *Miss Potter*). So while the Lakes remain peripheral in some geographical senses, the iconicity of the region 'lifts' it (but crucially, without disembedding) out of the local. And, of course, the rural also relates to the national: what counts as the countryside, and what the countryside means, is nationally specific, despite the sometimes homogenizing effects of certain globalizing narratives about the rural (Bell 2006).[1]

The issue of the meaning(s) of the rural is a key consideration in unpacking how that meaning relates to cultural production and consumption. At one level, we need to explore how rural cultural industries are engaged in 'selling' the countryside – or particular variants of the countryside. And we need to think about what ruralness means to cultural industries, as a place to do business, as a potential base for 'good work'. Susan Luckman (2012) pursues these (and other) lines of enquiry in her detailed discussion of the motives and experiences of rural cultural workers. And she puts place centre stage in her account: cultural work involves multiple interactions with place, space and landscape, and these interactions affect both the content and the practices of cultural production. Mindful of the hazards of essentializing 'The Rural' and its affects and effects, she draws on empirical work to complicate this particular relation – between place and work – and in so doing opens up numerous new questions about, as she summarizes, 'the complex affordances and sensory relationships intersecting cultural work and place, particularly the multifaceted encounters with the natural environment: individual and collective, productive and restricting, detrimental and sympathetic' (167). (Luckman revisits numerous older questions, too – she is attentive to the histories of place–work relations in the rural.)

At the same time, she never loses focus on the *business* of cultural work: while the 'good life' in the country might hold out the promise of 'good work' too, she recounts the difficulties as well as the pleasures her respondents encountered. And she re-reminds us that by turning our attention to these lives lived and the works made, we gain new purchase on the very issue of creativity: what it means, the value it carries, and what happens when it turns into a job. Crucially, she keeps an eye on *where* creativity happens, also at different scales, from an entire region, to a particular landscape, to an individual studio or workshop.

The creative class and the country

In so doing, Luckman reframes the 'creative class' narrative that has, until recently, assumed a metropolitan context: edgy or buzzy neighbourhoods, urban lifestyles, dense networking, blurring of work and non-work activities, etc. (Florida 2002; Landry 2001). As such, she adds to debates that seek to relocate creativity – which is not quite collateral with cultural industry, but has become somewhat synonymous – and to write a new narrative. As Gordon Waitt and Chris Gibson (2013: 75) ask, 'what alternative conceptualisations of creativity are possible to those that focus on certain forms of urban, market-dominated activities?' In this reframing, an 'other' cultural economy is evident, less bound by (and driven by) those 'urban, market-dominated activities' that have until recently practically defined the creative industries, especially as a policy target. Waitt and Gibson focus on an artists' co-op and its foregrounding of 'non-market' creativity – in the Spiral Gallery, located in Bega in the Far South Coast New South Wales region of Australia, they witness 'fugitive energies' producing a different understanding of the role of creativity in place.

This discussion accords with a new wave of interest in forms of cultural production that have been sidelined in the dominant economically focused creative industries script – instances include 'craftivism' and the broader revival in the handmade, homemade and D-i-Y, vernacular creativity, process-based and collaborative arts practice, and of course forms of user-generated content (Luckman 2012; Edensor et al. 2009; Kester 2004; Gauntlett 2011). Terms well known from the urban-economic creative industries literature, such as creative clusters, take on a new meaning in rural contexts (Harvey et al. 2012), while the obsession with mapping and quantifying creative industries gets pushed to its limit in academic and policy studies that bring to light 'hot spots' of creative work in the 'unsexier' sectors of cultural production such as traditional crafts, printing and publishing, or postcard production (see respectively Thomas et al 2013; Burns Owens Partnership 2006; Mayes 2010). And a different blurring of work/non-work is evident in some such studies: Mayes' discussion of 'lay' postcard making in Ravensthorpe, Western Australia focuses on a local production milieu using both paid and volunteer labour, with strong 'community' motivations alongside the business of making and selling cards – a practice in itself stitched into the broader cultural economy of place and 'local' production (in two senses: locally based, but also producing the local through postcard imagery). Mayes' study highlights the importance of mapping cultural practices in rural places like Ravensthorpe, attending to 'the role of "the rural" in shaping cultural *work*, as opposed to content' (Mayes 2010: 9; emphasis added). A million miles away from the hipster cultural workers usually imagined as the archetypal 'creatives', these lay makers remind us that – not exclusively in the rural – 'other' forms of cultural work can be profoundly important, not least for their participants.

Cultural work is ordinary

Mayes' study is also useful for reminding us of the ordinariness of cultural work: contrary to the 'splashy' accounts of the creative class, here is a story of the day-to-day doings of cultural production, its rewards and its drawbacks. An important turn in the (normally urban based) literature on cultural production has been a focus on cultural work-as-work, as labour (Hesmondhalgh and Baker 2011; Banks 2007). Emerging themes such as precariousness have subsequently been explored in non-metropolitan locations. Felton et al. (2010), for example, discuss the potentially greater resilience of outer suburban cultural workers in the context of recession: cheaper living costs and forms of 'economic elasticity' were found to make the suburbs relatively storm-ready. And Luckman (2012) takes her lead from the cultural work-as-work literature, bringing its insights into contact with her empirical findings from Australia and the United Kingdom. A key issue raised by her respondents concerns 'balanced lives' – this doesn't only mean so-called work–life balance, but also relates to life course and the contentious issues of 'lifestyle migration' and 'lifestyle businesses'. The latter are contentious because the term 'lifestyle' assumes an almost pejorative sense in some contexts – though many incomers to rural areas admit that their relocation decisions have significant 'non-economic' dimensions (Hoey 2005).

Of course, creatives and cultural workers aren't the only people considering an escape to the country: the phenomenon of internal migration away from non-metropolitan locations is well known. The impulse to go 'back to the land' has a long history, and the push and pull factors at work have become common sense and a staple of lifestyle media (Halfacree 2007; Thomas 2008). But the assumed negative meaning of 'lifestyle' and the commonly used term 'downshifting' to describe a recalibrating of work–life balance has been contested in some accounts of rural cultural worker migration – neologisms such as 'cross-shifting' being preferred by some for not suggesting any kind of downscaling of work (in terms of productivity, quality, etc.). Anxieties about the 'cultural cringe', about loss of credibility and about being seen as 'dropping out' by moving from the inner city sometimes require constant repudiation – or the construction of alternative narratives that seek to emphasize instead the benefits and pleasures of new ways of working and living (Collis et al. 2013). In policymaking circles it has sometimes been hard to apply existing models of creative industries development in rural settings; even harder to suggest alternative models, especially slow- or no-growth ones (Bell and Jayne 2010).

In one sense, then, rural cultural work is extraordinary: it bucks the trends and refuses the models that normally apply. And in some academic accounts, this idea of a dominant and dominating norm based on inner city creative work-life that rural studies counter treads a fine line between redressing an imbalance and romanticizing this 'new' research object, the rural creative. Just as there is a danger of essentializing

'The Rural' as always and everywhere the same thing, so there is a danger here in overemphasizing the extraordinary and the unique in rural cultural work. This is not to deny the value of switching our attention away from the familiar milieux of the big cities; clearly, to not do so would be a great disservice to these '"other geographies" of cultural production' (Harvey et al. 2012: 537) or 'other creative geographies' (Collis et al. 2013: 149) – yet, in calling attention to their otherness, we fall back into the trap of seeing the rural as marginal, as other (Gregg 2010). As with the emerging 'ordinary cities' literature (Robinson 2005), which pulls the focus away from exceptional metropolitanism and metropolitan exceptionalism, a less othering perspective on the *ordinariness* of rural (and non-rural) cultural work is overdue.

Producing ruralities

Which brings us to the issue of place-in-product: inevitably, we do need some focus on the ways in which rurality (or plural ruralities) gets made through cultural work. In the era of the so-called post-productivist countryside, and with a seemingly ever-growing commodification of the rural (though both these notions are contested), it's important to consider how cultural producers give shape to understandings of the countryside – again, issues of ordinariness and extraordinariness matter here, as do issues of the 'aestheticization and semioticization of the rural' (Scott 2010: 1546). Mayes' (2010) account of the postcard makers of Ravensthorpe reminds us of one potential drawback of rural cultural industry: the requirement to enact and represent particular forms of rurality, especially those that are marketable. While her study emphasizes work over content, it is important to explore the role of rural cultural production in producing and circulating certain versions of the rural – and to follow these representations and the work that they do. There is a symbolic economy at work here, too.

This also returns us to the issue of the local, and to the selling of local distinctiveness. As a respondent in Gibson et al.'s (2010: 30) study of cultural production in Darwin, Australia, said, 'In Darwin they [benefactors commissioning work] like the work to be *about Darwin*' (emphasis added). The requirement of 'aboutness' was seen in this study to be peculiar to rural and remote locations, not demanded of urban artists. Moreover, respondents in countless other studies confess unease at having to produce and perform rurality in order to suit particular markets, notably tourists. As Scott (2010) notes, the familiar problems of tourist places – museumization and Disneyfication – are projected onto cultural producers who can feel that their creativity is being undermined by the requirements of lucrative markets. An interviewee in Kneafsey et al.'s (2001: 306) study of rural West Wales described a special section in her shop aimed at tourists as 'the craporama area', while respondents in Luckman's (2012: 100) research worried about their work being seen as 'folksy' or 'twee', and cultural producers operating open studios or 'studio shopfronts' similarly bemoaned having to perform rurality for customers.[2]

Localness in content is partly an issue to do with the type of cultural product: a postcard needs to be local almost by definition, whereas other forms of cultural product might be able to address location in more generic, even abstract ways. The example of local TV is a useful illustration. In the United Kingdom in 2012, the Department for Culture, Media and Sport (DCMS) offered digital broadcasting licences for production companies to produce local programming.[3] In some places where bids for a local TV station were worked up, this generated intense (sometimes wry) debate: in the small town of Malvern in Worcestershire, England, for example, the very idea of local TV production was largely met with bemusement: what on earth would be of sufficient interest to be shown on television, even just for a local audience? Who would really want to watch Malvern TV? In local press coverage and debate, there seemed to be something incompatible about local identity and televisuality: Malvern is too local to warrant TV coverage (even though locals bemoaned lack of coverage on current regional news broadcasting). The idea of a local newspaper – in this case the long-running *Malvern Gazette* – did not seem oxymoronic in the same way that Malvern TV did (Harris 2013). Even place-specific heritage can seem 'too local' if it does not fit the expectations of visitors (Lazzeroni et al. 2013).

Luckman (2012: 95–6) proposes a broad typology for market relationships in rural cultural production, which is worth reflecting on here:

marketing and selling to locals goods/services with a distinct local/rural character;
marketing and selling to visiting outsiders goods/services with a distinct local/rural character;
marketing and selling widely goods/services with a distinct local/rural character;
marketing and selling to locals goods/services that just happen to be made in a rural, regional or remote location;
marketing and selling to visitors goods/services that just happen to be made in a rural, regional or remote location;
marketing and selling widely goods/services that just happen to be made in a rural, regional or remote location.

We might want to focus for a second on the phrase 'local/rural character': in collapsing these two placeholders, Luckman misses a significant distinction, between the concrete specificities of the local and the (possibly) more generic rural. Even our earlier example of picture postcards, on closer inspection, can speak across spatial scales – generic rural images (and, indeed, national images) are marketable alongside highly localized depictions of place. The same can be said to be true of other forms of cultural production: a film 'about' a particular rural locale also speaks to more generic tropes of country life (Fish 2007). So, to return to another earlier example, while *Miss Potter* is deeply rooted in an imagined Lake District, its themes also work across scales (hence its global backing and box office success). The image of the Lake District, it might be argued, is resoundingly glocal. This does not mean that rural cultural producers are condemned to endlessly repeat certain representations of the countryside, of course: rural images, narratives and themes are constantly reinvented across cultural texts. Representations of the rural are also doing cultural work, including reworking the rural itself.

Back to Luckman's typology, and to another interesting phrase it contains: 'just happen to'. It seems strange to say that some cultural goods/service *just happen to* be made in the rural, as if their makers have had no say in where they are based. This phrase therefore hides a whole set of (past, current and also arguably future) locational decisions, plus external forces that shape those decisions (including those that limit them; Gregg 2010). Aside from the danger of glossing those decisions and forces, in demoting any notion of agency the 'just happen to' idea also obscures the implication of cultural producers in rural transformation too, and not always in positive terms. In common with narratives about gentrification in inner city neighbourhoods popular-ized by urban creatives, the phenomenon of rural gentrification or 'greentrification' is increasingly attracting academic and policy attention (Smith and Phillips 2001). While not solely laid at the feet of rural creatives, the current wave of relocations, second home buying and 'staycationing' is undoubtedly fuelled by the continued circulation of images and ideas about the rural good life, propagated and disseminated by the cultural industries. While positive policy accounts stress the benefits of rural cultural industries in transforming flagging economies in post-productivist localities, there's a fine line between regeneration and gentrification that is equally apparent in the country and the city.

Of course, there's another fine line to tread here: the danger of fossilizing the rural by holding back those forces of transformation. Scott's (2010) work on the Lake District traces this line very clearly, in seeing a familiar story playing out: tourists (and we might add incomers) search for forms of authentic rurality that their very presence eventually erodes. The pricing out of artists in inner city neighbourhoods (and now, increasingly, non-metro locales) plays out in a similar fashion. Hence the difficult policy question: *how should rural cultural industry be managed?*

A little bit country, a little bit rock'n'roll

That question runs through both the policy work and the academic literature I have reviewed in this chapter. In academic discussion, we are now witnessing the maturing of a sub-field that blends economic geography, rural studies, policy analysis and cultural studies. We can spot an emerging agenda taking shape, and soon hopefully it should be possible to begin a paper on rural cultural industries without repeating the spot-the-urban-bias mantra. In so doing, we might be able to see rural cultural industry as ordinary, in a positive sense: not an aberration or a misfit, but part-and-parcel of the cultural industries 'scene'. This does not mean denying the specificities of rural cultural production – including its ruralities or ruralnesses; it is still important to explore how different forms of rural are played with and parlayed in rural cultural production, to look at the interplay between old and new, tradition and innovation. It means no longer trying to shoehorn rural cultural industries into an urban script, but instead writing a new script attentive to both urban and rural, and to the con-nections between them. It means teasing apart different ruralities, at different scales (and it is important to acknowledge that the discussion in this chapter has not moved beyond the global north).

Certainly, it is important not to lose sight of the value of an explicitly territorial approach – creative industry *in place* – by flattening any distinctions across space and scale. But I do think that a focus less on places-in-isolation and more on places-in-relation is helpful, not least when studying places in isolation reinforces the assumed isolation of those places. Bringing places in from the periphery by looking relationally allows us, as Chris Gibson et al. (2010) put it, to rethink remoteness and proximity. In their work on Darwin, a relational approach allows their 'local' case study to go 'glocal': ideas of remoteness (in this case, to metropolitan Australia) and proximity (in this case, to Asia), are pulled in and out of focus as cultural producers manage networks, make connections and trade strategically on both proximity and remoteness.

Rethinking rural cultural industries relationally also gives us a chance to go beyond the rural, and to reflect on some of the shortcomings of our general approach to the cultural industries. This includes the thorny question of definition: while in the United Kingdom (and diffused fairly widely beyond) a focus on cultural industries has been partially eclipsed by the creative industries, one of the merits of using the term 'cultural' has been in widening our scope beyond what Andy Pratt (2013) has recently called 'the DCMS 13' – those creative sectors listed in UK policy. This has sometimes proved contentious, and one key faultline concerns 'traditional' cultural production. The so-called craft revival is illustrative here, with its 'post-Etsy' emphasis on the funkier forms of craft work – guerrilla knitting rather than corn dollies (Luckman 2012). The lingering whiff of the twee or the folksy – not to mention of tourist tat and craporama – keeps some forms of craft in the cold. While the UK Crafts Council nods once to 'traditional' techniques in its value statement, its repetitive emphasis on 'contemporary craft' seems to leave little room for those traditions (see www.craftscouncil.org.uk); its 2011 briefing report on craft and rural innovation, while acknowledging connections to the tourist economy, draws on creative industries discourse to stress economic impacts (it refers repeatedly to a 2007 Nesta report on rural innovation that explicitly focuses on the 'DCMS 13' (Mahroum et al. 2007; Yair 2011)).

That Nesta report does highlight a key issue I have alluded to in this chapter: the role of rural creative (cultural) industries in place-making, though Nesta's conclusion is somewhat ambivalent. Having established a Williamsian structure of feeling role for culture in the rural, it notes that 'In the case of the contemporary UK countryside, much of the ongoing cultural innovation is *to diffuse a set of essentially urban cultural practices, ideas and values to rural areas, and to re-shape and re-cast these in this new context'* (Mahroum et al. 2007: 42, emphasis added). So the rural becomes an import zone whose role is to re-shape and re-cast urban cultural practices. This seems so heavy-handedly one-way as to border on symbolic violence. Of course, part of the problem is the policy shift from 'creativity' to 'innovation', and the continued assumed connection between cities and innovation, the countryside and tradition.

Some of the case studies and discussions referred to in this chapter think of place-making in a very different way; they think about landscape and environment, about place-in-product *and* product-in-place. They think about *ecologies*. Maybe it's the felt presence of the natural landscape that suggests this kind of language (and yes, there is work that discusses creative ecologies in cities). The ecological approach lets us see a denser network of relationships – certainly more than a focus on clusters or agglomerations. Of course, this does not mean tethering product and place. A useful analogy might be country music, which has kept connection to its roots while constantly innovating; has stayed locally rooted while going global; has a porosity that lets it deal head-on with contemporary issues while also remembering the eternal and universal themes. It comes in and falls out of fashion regularly, but it keeps going. And it is generously accommodating of tradition *and* innovation.

Notes

1 In addition, there seems to be an emerging national geography of academic research on 'non-metro' cultural industry, with Australia currently leading the pack. This is in itself revealing of the ideas about the countryside that take hold in a particular national context, leading – among other things – to funding priorities for academic research.
2 Of course, rural studies has long insisted that rurality is performed by many different actors, including tourists (Edensor 2006).
3 See https://www.gov.uk/government/policies/making-it-easier-for-the-media-and-creative-industries-to-grow-while-protecting-the-interests-of-citizens/supporting-pages/creating-a-local-tv-framework-so-that-local-tv-services-can-be-set-up-across-the-uk.

References

Banks, M. (2007) *The Politics of Cultural Work* (Basingstoke: Palgrave Macmillan).
Banks, M., Lovatt, A., O'Connor, J. and Raffo, J. (2000) 'Risk and trust in the cultural industries', *Geoforum* 31: 453–64.
Bell, D. (2006) 'Variations on the rural idyll', in Cloke, P., Marsden, T. and Mooney, P. (eds) *The Handbook of Rural Studies* (London: Sage) 149–60.
Bell, D. and Jayne, M. (2010) 'The creative countryside: Policy and practice in the UK rural cultural economy', *Journal of Rural Studies* 26 (3): 209–18.
Burns Owens Partnership (2006) *York and North Yorkshire Creative Industries Network: Economic Impact Study and Needs Assessment* (London: BOP).
Collis, C., Freebody, S. and Flew, T. (2013) 'Seeing the outer suburb: Addressing the urban bias in creative place thinking', *Regional Studies* 47: 148–60.
Edensor, T. (2006) 'Performing rurality', in Cloke, P., Marsden, T. and Mooney, P. (eds) *The Handbook of Rural Studies* (London: Sage) 484–95.
Edensor, T., Leslie, D., Millington, S. and Rantisi, N. (eds) (2009) *Spaces of Vernacular Creativity: Rethinking the Cultural Economy* (London: Routledge).
Felton, E., Gibson, M., Flew, T., Graham, P. and Daniel, A. (2010) 'Resilient creative economies? Creative industries on the urban fringe', *Continuum: Journal of Media and Cultural Studies*, 24: 619–30.
Fish, R. (ed.) (2007) *Cinematic Countrysides* (Manchester: Manchester University Press).
Florida, R. (2002) *The Rise of the Creative Class, and How it's Transforming Work, Leisure, Community, and Everyday Life* (New York: Basic Books).
Gauntlett, D. (2011) *Making is Connecting: The Social Meaning of Creativity, from DIY to Knitting to YouTube and Web 2.0* (Cambridge: Polity Press).
Gibson, C., Luckman, S. and Willoughby-Smith, J. (2010) 'Creativity without borders? Rethinking remoteness and proximity', *Australian Geographer* 41: 25–38.
Gregg, M. (2010) 'Available in selected metros only: Rural melancholy and the promise of online connectivity', *Cultural Studies Review* 16: 155–69.
Halfacree, K. (2007) 'Back-to-the-land in the twenty-first century: Making connections with rurality', *Tijdschrift voor Economische en Sociale Geografie* 98: 3–8.
Harris, W. (2013) *The Hills are Alive with Local Media: Malvern, Media and Belonging*, unpublished dissertation, School of Geography, University of Leeds.

Harvey, D., Hawkins, H. and Thomas, N. (2012) 'Thinking creative clusters beyond the city: People, places and networks', *Geoforum* 43: 529–39.

Hesmondhalgh, D. and Baker, S. (2011) *Creative Labour: Media Work in Three Cultural Industries* (London: Routledge).

Hoey, B. (2005) 'From pi to pie: Moral narratives of noneconomic migration and starting over in the postindustrial Midwest', *Journal of Contemporary Ethnography* 34: 586–624.

Kester, G. (2004) *Conversation Pieces: Community + Communication in Modern Art* (Berkeley: University of California Press).

Kneafsey, M., Ilbery, B. and Jenkins, T. (2001) 'Exploring the dimensions of culture economies in rural West Wales', *Sociologica Ruralis* 41: 296–310.

Landry, C. (2001) *The Creative City: A Handbook for Urban Innovators* (London: Earthscan).

Lazzeroni, M., Bellini, N., Cortesi, G. and Loffredo, A. (2013) 'The territorial approach to cultural economy: New opportunities for the development of small towns', *European Planning Studies* 21: 452–72.

Luckman, S. (2012) *Locating Cultural Work: The Politics and Poetics of Rural, Regional and Remote Creativity* (Basingstoke: Palgrave Macmillan).

Mahroum, S., Atterton, J., Ward, N., Williams, A., Naylor, R., Hindle, R. and Rowe, F. (2007) *Rural Innovation* (London: NESTA).

Mayes, R. (2010) 'Doing cultural work: Local postcard production and place identity in a rural shire', *Journal of Rural Studies* 26: 1–11.

Petrov, A. (2008) 'Talent in from the cold? Creative capital and the economic future of the Canadian North', *Arctic* 61: 162–76.

Pratt, A. (2013) 'The spectre of the creative industries', paper presented at the Cultural Policy under New Labour Seminar, Institute of Communications Studies, University of Leeds, September.

Robinson, J. (2005) *Ordinary Cities: Between Modernity and Development* (London: Routledge).

Scott, A. (2010) 'The cultural economy of landscape and prospects for peripheral development in the twenty-first century: The case of the English Lake District', *European Planning Studies* 18: 1567–89.

Smith, D. and Phillips, D. (2001) 'Socio-cultural representations of greentrified Pennine rurality', *Journal of Rural Studies* 17: 457–69.

Thomas, L. (2008) 'Alternative realities: Downshifting narratives in contemporary lifestyle television', *Cultural Studies* 22: 680–99.

Thomas, N., Harvey, D. and Hawkins, H. (2013) 'Crafting the region: Creative industries and practices of regional space', *Regional Studies* 47: 75–88.

Waitt, G. and Gibson, C. (2009) 'Creative small cities: Rethinking the creative economy in place', *Urban Studies* 46: 1223–46.

Waitt, G. and Gibson, C. (2013) 'The Spiral Gallery: Non-market creativity and belonging in an Australian country town', *Journal of Rural Studies* 30: 75–85.

White, P. (2010) 'Creative industries in a rural region: *Creative West*, the creative sector in the Western Region of Ireland', *Creative Industries Journal* 3: 79–88.

Yair, K. (2011) *Craft and Rural Development* (London: Crafts Council).

18
PRODUCING "INDIA" AS LOCATION

Nitin Govil

Studies of international film production have often considered the importance of location shooting. Many such studies, particularly those focusing on Hollywood, have detailed the processes of "runaway production" that structure the global movement of screen capital. These movements facilitate links between a globalized network of production sites, with far-reaching consequences for labor, finance, and representation (see Elmer and Gasher 2005).

Hollywood's popular figuration underscores the importance of location in orienting the film industries. After all, "Hollywood" refers to practices dispersed across different places. The political economies organized by a desire to locate this geographic diversity in a singular geographic reference point have served to ground Hollywood within the spatial imagination. This grounding played a critical role in the location of Hollywood itself. Mark Shiel has described how the topography of Los Angeles and its surrounding landscapes, the spatial distribution of ethnic populations, the architecture of the studio and its integration into the built environment of the urban municipality, impacted the reality and representation of Hollywood during its early history (Shiel 2012). As an extension of this idea of placement, "industry" has come to refer to the agglomeration of production activities clustered and embedded in certain geographic formations (Scott 2005). Yet, from its initial grounding, Hollywood's spatial distribution has led to the fabrication of a conveniently absent center of production. Affirming this heterotopic conception of Hollywood as a simultaneously "real and imagined place," director John Ford famously claimed that, "Hollywood is a place you can't geographically define. We don't really know where it is" (quoted in Bordwell et al. 1985: xiii; on heterotopia, see Foucault 1986).

Location shooting has exacerbated this sense of spatial abstraction. The accepted wisdom is that, especially after World War 2, Hollywood diverted unrepatriable overseas profits or "blocked funds" towards location shooting. This budgetary rationalization was supposed to save production costs by avoiding large-scale on-set scenery construction and by hiring local labor at cheaper rates. However, as Aida Hozic notes, films produced on location often went over budget because of profligate local spending (Hozic 2001). In either case, location shooting articulates the global and the local across wide itineraries of connection.

Municipal, state, and regional commissions constantly work to recruit film and media investment in location, often in the interest of boosting tourism as a key aspect of the new international cultural division of labor (see Miller et al. 2005). While location can become part of a region's creative capital, in terms of cultural policy, location can stand in for the nation, linked to imperatives that position the national within the global. Since tourism ties into the auratic assumptions about location and a perceived irreproducible distinctiveness (Benjamin 1968), international film producers have been drawn to location shooting because unique local geographies provide the requisite authenticity to anchor a film's narrative. Increasingly, as locations are integrated into broader policy and economic frameworks where "location interest" must be cultivated and managed, the attraction of locations "has become dependent on their capacity to be "bent" or "reshaped" for a variety of creative or narrative purposes" (Goldsmith and O'Regan 2005: 8). As Goldsmith, Ward, and O'Regan note in their work on "local Hollywood," all locations are subject to creative decisions as part of a broader production design, resulting in all sorts of minor and major enhancements (Goldsmith et al. 2010).

This chapter considers Hollywood's production of place, focusing on American cinema's real and imagined engagement with India. I am particularly interested in how geographies of production narrativize place across histories of practice. Given that location is central to the conception of industry, place is both tenet and theme in the organization of production culture. Locations are produced through reality and representation, the built and the natural environment. Furthermore, location frames the axes of proximity and distance that territorialize screen labor. The spatial distribution of these labor activities takes place in relation to the social forces of dispersion and centralization in the media industries.

Locations are intensively scouted, managed, marketed, and packaged. They emerge as a product of negotiation between global and local agents, especially line producers, location managers, crowd control, and scenarists. The infrastructure created in and around any location links place to other spatial nodes in the production network. The durability of these infrastructures varies from location to location, from the high-investment, relatively permanent studio facility to the low-investment, hastily constructed crowd scene. Despite this variability, location refers reflexively to the place of place in screen practice.

While acknowledging location at the intersection of physical experience and imaginative construction, my intention is not to counter-pose location against the global as a bulwark against a spatially dis-embedded global capitalism. Instead, I hope to demonstrate how global screen flows "add to, as well as take away from, the intensive and implosive practices in which locality is produced" (Lash and Lury 2007: 150).

Locating "India" in early Hollywood

Framing its earliest imaginations of global expansion, Hollywood figured the tropes of transcultural contact with India through popular actuality, travelogue, and ethnographic genres. Early short films at the dawn of Hollywood were designed to demonstrate

the lengths to which American film companies would travel to secure filmed entertainment. These included Edison's *Dramatic Scenes in Delhi* (1912), *Views in Calcutta*
(1912), and *Curious Scenes in India* (1913). These "descriptive" or "scenic" films featured
banyan trees and royal palms, landmarks and ruined remnants of past conflict, and
natives at play and at work in the hustle-bustle of colonial urban life. In these and other
films, Western cameramen were depicted as intrepid "film explorers" bearing the
marks of their encounters with the savageries of the East.

Longer two-reel films, shot on location and in the studio, fixed India as a signifier
of danger and as a safari destination. Solax's *Beasts of the Jungle* (1913), where an
American engineer loses his daughter to the wild tropics, was full of wild animals
and an Indian "atmosphere" that helped to popularize the animal picture. Selig's *A
Wise Old Elephant* (1913) was also set in India, but was made on the Selig wild animal
farm in Los Angeles. To decorate his films, Selig hired a naturalist to tour India for
vegetation and animals for the farm. In addition to these animal stories, dramas of
anti-colonial uprising were also produced. Such was the popularity of these "sepoy
stories" that American film studios planned to construct permanent "India" sets in
California during the nineteen-teens (Jones 1914).

Early on, then, the American industry went on location to Indian to film short travel
films that required geographic validation. As the industry moved towards longer
features, "animal" films could be shot in the studio (some had their own zoos) and
"India" could be suggested by a tree, a tiger, and a well-placed turban or two. Producers
often used recycled stock scenic footage to buttress films shot in the studio. Since
Hollywood produced "India" in its own studios as well as by travelling to South Asia,
the fabrication of scenarist attraction was as critical to the representation of alterity
as travelogue footage filmed "on location."

From the beginning, Hollywood's engagement with India as a geographic index
combined fiction with reality. This meant that India was both a physical place to
"orient" early Hollywood and an imagined space of a fantastic, otherworldly realm
(see Govil 2015). While early Hollywood used the production of films in India to
demonstrate its global reach and legitimacy, "India" was also a transnational production, with many Indian scenes filmed in New Jersey, Connecticut, and right at
home on the West Coast. The imagination of India played a critical role in the
"worlding" of Hollywood as space and place.

For example, Mutual's *The Toast of Death* (1915) was set in India but filmed in
California. For reviewers, knowledge of this physical displacement somehow added
to the film's veracity. One reviewer noted that it was "notwithstanding the fact that
California was the locale of the production, a real Oriental atmosphere pervades the
film, and it seems doubtful if Director Ince could have staged a more convincing
picture in Bombay itself." The reviewer then listed the crucial details that made the
picture a convincing account of Indian life:

> Elephants, camels, long retinues of servants, Indian princes and potentates,
> English officers and troops of every color and variety, tropical vegetation,
> servants, thatched huts and regal palaces, are all there in profusion, each
> lending its bit toward the whole effect.
>
> (Caward 1915)

The piecemeal fabrication of India as a geographically mutable location was a fairly common aspect of Hollywood's production apparatus. This trend continued in many of the India scenes in Hollywood's landmark "Empire films" of the 1930s, like *Gunga Din* and *The Rains Came*, which were filmed in Utah. A 1935 article in *Popular Mechanics* assessed the ways in which Indian location was composed:

> sometimes the movie-made scenery is even better than the real thing, and now and then, when a company is sent half way around the world to film parts of a picture, the results may be thrown away because lighting and technical problems cannot be controlled as well as nearer the studio. Three years ago, one studio spent months in shooting atmosphere scenes in India for backgrounds but after 70,000 feet of expensive, authentic film had been brought back most of it was discarded because a sharp-eyed location hunter had found identical scenery within a day's drive where the same scenes could be photographed to better advantage.
>
> ("The World" 1935).

In other words, Hollywood's American productions of Indian location could realize cost advantages while preserving the requisite alterity to transport viewers to exotic realms.

Driven by a burgeoning Indomania, Hollywood attempted to suggest location through atmosphere and scenery. Yet, reconstructing India in Hollywood created something of an authenticity conundrum for Hollywood. One of the ways in which Hollywood buttressed common forms of physical connotation was through its recruitment of "authentic" Indians in early productions, focusing on hiring local Hindu actors, extras, and costumers during a climate of intense xenophobia and anti-immigrant sentiment in California.

Hinduism offered Hollywood a kind of exoticized attachment to the world of the Orient. In films from Edison's *Hindoo Fakir* (1902) to D.W. Griffith's *The Hindoo Dagger* (1909), the word "Hindoo" combined a general ethnological interest with a heightened sense of narrative tension that alterity was supposed to signify. Film after film referenced a fascination with Hindu spectacle. These stories were created by Hollywood studio production, where opportunities abounded, but they were also available to those intrepid enough to shoot overseas. For example, in 1913, *Motion Picture Story Magazine* told readers about shooting in India and "the Hindu charm" and "the spirit of the Orient" that was to be found there (Wade 1913).

For Hollywood, then, India functioned as both a real and a screen space. These permutations of site and scene constructed India in terms of Hollywood's early Indological fascination, part of a broader representational logic through which America "envisioned" Asia (Roan 2010).

At its inception, Hollywood was invested in strategies of meaning-making that constructed India as a backdrop to exoticism and a place of mystery. Representations of India helped to position an iconography of exoticism that "oriented" Hollywood in particular ways. At the same time that India represented the power of Hollywood to bring a distant and exotic land close to home, India also framed the spatial limit to Hollywood's ambition, stretching the reaches of its international distribution.

If we flash forward to the other end of the century of Indo-American screen encounter, it is clear that Hollywood's priorities remain aligned with fairly consistent indices of geographic resemblance. In its contemporary location practices, global Hollywood has turned to India again, but how and to what end?

Orienting the war on terror: *Zero Dark Thirty*'s Indian shooting

In the past few years, Hollywood has been particularly interested in Indian location shooting, particularly in Delhi, Agra, Mumbai, Goa, and Rajasthan. However, clearances, permissions, and technical and logistical problems have complicated international location projects. As recently as 2011 *The Dark Knight Rises'* four-day shoot in Jodhpur, resulting in 20 seconds of screen time, took two months to secure the requisite shooting permissions. Recognizing that international filmmakers need to procure around 70 licenses before starting an Indian shoot, the Indian Ministry of Information and Broadcasting is planning to implement a single-clearance policy to make it easier for foreign studios to shoot in India.

While documentary production has remained significant and foreign producers have been able to channel Indian release profits towards funding location shooting, India has been unable to compete with other countries' aggressive tax and labor subsidies. Problems in Indian location shooting have forced Hollywood to improvise. For example, a scene in *The Avengers* (2012) that introduced the Bruce Banner character was set in Kolkata but filmed in the United States. The film's producer Jeremy Latchman noted that, "the city of Kolkata with its crowded streets and bazaars was recreated in New Mexico. This was done in association with the local Indian community. The idea was to introduce the character of Hulk to the Indian audience in a manner they can relate to" (quoted in Srivastava 2012).

However, Hollywood has found a new use for India, casting it in the role of a location-proximate antagonist.

In 2010 Kathryn Bigelow won the Best Director Oscar for *The Hurt Locker*, which was shot in Jordan after the producers were denied permission to shoot in Iraq. The same year, she announced her next project, a modestly budgeted (eventually US$35 million) thriller on the US mission to kill Osama Bin Laden in the years leading up to his assassination by a team of Navy SEALs in a Pakistani suburb in May 2011. Eventually titled *Zero Dark Thirty* (ZD30), the film was partially financed by Megan Ellison's Annapurna Pictures (named for the Hindu goddess of nourishment), distributed by Sony Pictures, and set for a December 2012 release.

Conceived before Bin Laden's assassination, the SEAL raid became the film's ultimate focal point, presaged by the procedural and operational features of intelligence gathering. Bigelow and her team had originally planned on shooting the film in Pakistan. These plans were abandoned because of security concerns, through some have suggested that the Pakistani authorities had denied permission, still stinging after the Abbottabad raid where Bin Laden was killed. Bigelow quickly pivoted to an Indian shoot, retaining contacts in Pakistan to give direction to Indian location managers. Looking for similar topography to recreate Islamabad and Abbotabad scenes, ZD30 producers settled on the North Indian state of Punjab, hundreds of miles from the actual site, but similar in "look and feel."

The Punjab capital of Chandigarh was chosen as the central shooting location. After featuring in a number of successful Bombay film productions over the previous decade, the city set up a Bollywood Facilitation Centre in 2008, creating a single window clearance system to shoot in the city. More than a dozen films shot in the city that year. ZD30 producers took advantage of Chandigarh's municipal distinctiveness and recruited a Los Angeles and Delhi-based line producer called Take One Productions to facilitate the shoot. Over the past few years, Take One has emerged as a major line producer for foreign shoots in India, working on films including *Alexander*, *Mission Impossible – Ghost Protocol*, and *The Life of Pi*. Take One secures permissions and clearances from Indian government, state and local permits, "J" category visas for cast and crew, does script and budget breakdown, location scouting, local casting, local crew, union liaison, taxation and contracts, equipment rental, hotel and travel coordination, equipment clearance, and exposed stock shipment.

In addition to Take One Productions, Bigelow and her team worked with a local Chandigarh outfit called Darshan Aulakh Productions, whose owner noted that "the crew has hired production houses here, actors and other service providers and compensated them adequately. They also provided short-term employment to others including laborers, transporters, rickshaw-puller and hand-cart vendors" (quoted in Kahol 2012). Aulakh himself was awarded a small role as a Pakistani inter-services intelligence chief in the film. The ZD30 team also used Indian casting director Seher Latif to aid with the casting. Latif had also worked on *Eat, Pray, Love,* and would go onto work on *The Best Exotic Marigold Hotel* (shot on location in Rajasthan).

I turn to the process of recreating Pakistan in India below. Before that, it's important to note that ZD30 is a film that testifies to the reality of a series of events. The opening shots of the film make this clear, as inter-titles announce the film's authenticity: "The following motion picture is based on first hand accounts of actual events" followed by "September 11, 2001." Screened against snippets of audio from flight recorders, cell phones, air traffic control, and first responders, the inter-titles function as part of a multimedia orientation, played over screams, panic and dying requests.

This opening inaugurates a series of visual confirmations that follow. At the CIA black site, an operative removes a mask to reveal her identity (gasp! a woman!), a man is water-boarded as his interrogator yells, "LOOK AT ME, AHMAD!" and we witness the intensity of torture's effects. The CIA interrogator tells the woman, "you know, there's no shame if you want to watch from the monitor," but she refuses, and declines to put on the mask that hid her face. He tells the defeated Al-Qaeda money-man in his charge: "This is what defeat looks like, bro. Your jihad is over."

ZD30's early engagement of ocular intensity, foregrounding the evidentiary element of visuality, dovetails with the film's production design. As executive/line producer Colin Wilson notes, the challenge was to be "insanely authentic and really hard-core ... this is telling the truth, as much as we can" (quoted in Blair 2012). This well-documented "extreme" authenticity is part of the paratext that has come to surround ZD30, confirmed by most of its participants. Bigelow claims that the film's focus on aesthetic realism carries the weight of journalistic integrity and the production team "worked closely to find or create environments that were correct and respectful to story, reality and authenticity. To service the story and still maintain a kind of aesthetic coherence was a pretty tall order" (quoted in Goldman 2013).

After the intense series of visual stagings and confirmations that open the film, the audience is acclimated to the reality of the event when they see the next title that accompanies a change of scene (Figure 18.1). This shot is followed by others that flesh out the geographic atmosphere of the place (see Figure 18.2 for the first in the series).

The *ZD30* script clarifies the filmmaker's atmospheric intent: "CUT TO: EXT. Islamabad, Pakistan, Morning. SUPERIMPOSE: Islamabad, Pakistan. A colorful, dusty city. Busy markets. Poor children. Dense traffic" (Boal 2011: 6–7). Indeed, the

Figure 18.1 Setting the scene in *Zero Dark Thirty*.

Figure 18.2 Setting the scene in *Zero Dark Thirty*.

film is replete with these moments of orienting the viewer to a location through a series of visualizations, such as the map pinned on the wall of the US CIA station in Islamabad (Figure 18.3).

The most direct engagement with this kind of spectatorship takes place in a series of shots that mark *ZD30* as a kind of "cartographic film" (see Conley 2007), as the security apparatus is able to pin down a target through a series of mapped visualizations (see Figure 18.4 for the first in the series). Guiliana Bruno (2002: 271) notes

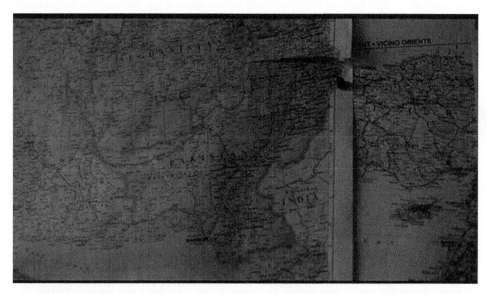

Figure 18.3 Orienting the viewer using maps in *Zero Dark Thirty*.

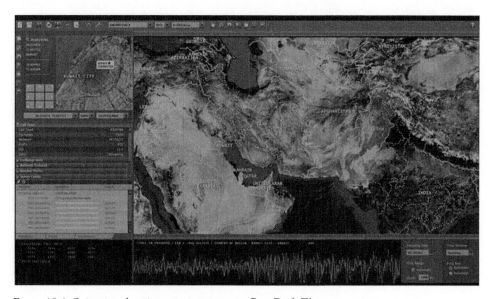

Figure 18.4 Orienting the viewer using maps in *Zero Dark Thirty*.

that such "reaffirmations of placement" are secured through conventions such as the establishing shot, "a way of securely mapping the viewer in space."

But of course, once we get in-country, we aren't really in Pakistan at all. *ZD30*'s location managers assiduously mocked up Sector 15 and Sector 26 market in Chandigarh. Auto rickshaws were painted blue, storefronts replaced with Urdu signage, license plates replaced with Lahore tags, buses brightly painted, women clad in burqas, men in skullcaps and pathani kurtas. Some of the set painting for the scenes was done in Delhi: Ramgarhia Hardware Store, named for its Sikh owner, became Shahzad Hardware and Paint Store, Regal Centre became Shahi Yunani Dawa Khana, Mahesh Garg's cloth store was made into "Hazoor Mutton and Chicken Shop" (Figure 18.5).

Internet cafes and call centers were renamed in Urdu (Kapoor 2012). Parmanan Sariya's sari shop was transformed into "Farhan Meat and Chicken Shop." Later the proprietor claimed surprise "to find the board of my shop changed and our entire market remained out of bounds for people, because of which we had no customers or business" (Bedi 2012). According to a local producer, auto-rickshaw owners were paid Rs. 2,000/day (US$40) to park their vehicles, and each fruit vendor was paid Rs. 1,500/day (US$30) in order to recreate a marketplace in Pakistan (Kahol 2012).

The film's editor, Dylan Tichenor, was planning to be on location in Chandigarh only for a short period of time, returning to the United States to cut the film. But Tichenor eventually stayed for the duration of the shoot, setting up a local cutting facility to move through the seven hours of footage captured through four to seven cameras. This prodigious gathering of footage was "almost like a documentary," notes Tichenor, adding that "the objective is to have a feeling of 'you are there'" (quoted in Peters 2013). This process, where footage was not only gathered but also assembled on location, deviated from the usual practice of principal editing back in the United States.

Figure 18.5 Recreating Pakistan through set painting in *Zero Dark Thirty*.

When *ZD30*'s producers turned to a suburb of Chandigarh, Mani Majra, to shoot the Abbotabad exteriors (Bin Laden's compound was meticulously reconstructed in Jordan), they ran into problems precipiated by the film's semiotic struggle between index and icon in the location of authenticity.

In early March, a few days into the shoot, right-wing Hindu activists disrupted the proceedings, protesting at the location site and shouting at cast and crew, removing Urdu signs and reportedly pushing around cameramen. A Vishwa Hindu Parishad (World Hindu Council) leader, Vijay Singh Bhardwaj, noted, "They are showing Chandigarh as Pakistan. This is unacceptable in any terms. Why should a place in India be converted to look like Pakistan? We will never allow Pakistan flags flying at places in the city" ("VHP Disrupts" 2012). Punjab VHP secretary Ramkrishna Srivastava added, "we don't want Pakistan flags on Indian soil and we don't agree that Indian markets should look like Pakistan" ("Hindu Protesters" 2012). The VHP claimed that Bigelow had been denied permission to shoot *ZD30* in eight countries, including Pakistan and Afghanistan, because of fears of repercussions. A local police officer named Rajesh Shukla helped disperse the crowd by assuring them that flags of Pakistan would not fly at Indian shooting locations, a point that Bigelow later confirmed.

As the VHP lodged a formal complaint against Bigelow at the local police station, the Indian line production company attempted to diffuse the situation, claiming that only background and establishing shots were being created with "a Pakistani feel." "No real sets have been built at all," claimed a representative, adding that "the actual recreation of Abbottabad will not even be in India. It's being done in Jordan … we explained that there is nothing here against Hinduism, nothing against Pakistan. It's just a movie" ("Hindu Protesters" 2012). The situation diffused, Bigelow proceeded with the shooting, prominently wearing her gifted garlands—a traditional marker of Hindu welcome—for part of the local filming.

After the shoot Colin Wilson, the producer of the film, along with writer and co-producer, Mark Boal, Jessica Chastain, and other members of the crew (notably not Kathryn Bigelow) hobnobbed with the Bollywood fraternity at the Chandigarh Golf Club. Wilson noted, "Chandigarh has been fabulous, and we will definitely return here to make another film, hopefully a romantic one … I love the attitude of the Indians" (quoted in Kapoor 2012a). Bollywood star Sanjay Dutt was one of the few to ask the obvious question – "Why would they shoot in Chandigarh? Why not Pakistan?" (quoted in Kapoor 2012a).

Later in March the shooting shifted to Punjab Engineering College in Chandigarh. In an earlier draft of the *ZD30* script Bin Laden is shown in college, studying civil engineering. The producers eventually used the school to stage the American Embassy in Islamabad. As the Engineering College ground to a halt during the shoot, the writer Mark Boal chatted with students, 20 of whom were selected to play security guards. The students were unpaid but the crew sent them gifts following the shoot. The staged Embassy is the site of a protest in the film, as Islamabad residents are shown to agitate against the American presence. Unlike the real Hindu activist protest, this staged protest was planned and went off without a hitch.

Later, Bigelow would note that "there was a very small, I would say, protest staged for the press that kind of got magnified in the news," adding that the producers "met with the Minister of Culture constantly and were very sensitive in handling this movie" ("'Zero' Script" 2012).

As publicity geared up for the film in the prelude to the 2013 Oscars, Subhash Saria, a local Mani Majra trade representative, said:

> it does not bother us that the film revolves around a dreaded terrorist and our locality is portrayed as Pakistan. We feel proud to be part of a Hollywood venture, that too by a well-known director. Though they changed the boards on our shops and our interiors, we can recognize our shops. And we will see many of our fellow shopkeepers in the film.
>
> (quoted in Sharma 2013)

It helped, of course, that the film's producers had paid Rs.700,000 (US$14,000) to the trade association in compensation.

After the shoot, the Indian Ministry of Tourism launched an "Incredible India" promotion that included footage of Mani Majra to showcase the town to foreign tourists. As the media advisor to the Tourism Ministry put it,

> places like Mani Majra that are several years old and have managed to maintain their original character and essence are much in demand. There are many filmmakers from Hollywood and other leading productions who want to capture these locales, but they are unaware of such places.
>
> (Sharma 2013a)

Others were not so sanguine in their appraisals of authenticity. Spotting errors in dialog (Arabic spoken where Urdu or Pashto would have been appropriate), the representation of the American embassy (located in a diplomatic enclave in Islamabad and inaccessible to protestors depicted in the film), and claiming that Peshawar looked more like 19th century Delhi, columnist Nadeem F. Paracha claimed that the film had become "a joke among Pakistanis" (quoted in "Pakistan" 2013). Film importers and distributors in Pakistan refused to import the film.

Hollywood remained undaunted, however. After ZD30 wrapped, Steven Spielberg arrived in Chandigarh to shoot an unnamed film, accompanied by a host of security guards, reportedly looking for a Punjabi woman to cast as the female lead in an upcoming film.

Terror-toriality and the securitization of location

ZD30's aggressive interest in authenticity is driven by an imperative to solemnize the recreation of national victory in the war on terror. This *spatial affect* is part of an emergent logic of orientation: locating contemporary geopolitical conflict through what we might call "terrortorialization" as a gesture to the new precariousness of cinematic placement. As Nicola Evans argues, part of the shock effect of the September 11, 2001 attacks was the palpable sense of spatial and temporal disorientation as many Americans struggled to place the attacks within history and geography. The trauma of the event was evidenced, she writes, in the way that "Americans sought to come to terms with the cartographic rearrangements in which the distant struggles of the Middle East had suddenly become a local problem, close to home" (Evans 2005: 132). ZD30's location-proximate authenticity and its determined geographic confirmations can be seen as an attempt to restabilize a comfortable visuality in the face of terror's fundamental spatial complexity (see Steyerl 2012).

But why bother to go to such extremes? What exactly is the function of location-proximate shooting given the predominance of special effects where places can be fabricated? For example, *Lone Survivor* (Peter Berg 2013) used multiple locations in New Mexico to recreate Afghanistan and Pakistan locations. The Sangre de Cristo mountains in the Santa Fe National Forest stood in for the Hindu Kush (a scale model of the HK mountain range was constructed by the film's LA-based art department), Chilili, a census-designated place in New Mexico, stood in for Afghan and Pashtun villages, and Kirtland Airforce Base in Albuquerque doubled for Bagram Airfield in Afghanistan. Furthermore, the films producers took advantage of New Mexico's 25 percent tax credit, preferring it to California's lottery system, which is hard to coordinate given the number of productions at any given time.

The American film industry's interest in Indian location shooting in films about the war on terror must be understood as part of a broader alignment between Hollywood and the security establishment. This manifestation of "para-Hollywood"—John Caldwell's reference to Hollywood's Blackwater-like subcontracting as a "profit-driven hermeneutical enterprise" (2013: 259)—was called into question by the controversy that erupted in the wake of ZD30's release.

As Simon Willmett (2013) notes, the Central Intelligence Agency was relatively absent from American screens after World War 2. During the height of the Cold War, through a combination of legal restraints and censorship, the American security establishment maintained a low public profile by a refusal to cooperate with Hollywood, despite filmmaker fascination. The political intrigue and controversy that surrounded the release of ZD30 indicate a fundamental transformation in the relationship between Hollywood and the American security establishment. In 2012 Republican senator and Chairman of the House Homeland Security Committee Peter King focused on possible unauthorized release of classified information, saying that leaked emails told a "damning story of extremely close, unprecedented, and potentially dangerous collaboration" between administration officials and ZD30 producers (quoted in Swaine 2012). When the film was released, a bipartisan group of senators from the Intelligence Committee wrote a letter to Sony denouncing the film's "suggestion" that torture helped secure the information that led to Bin Laden's assassination.

Wikileaks' recent release of secret US Embassy cables calls attention to an even more remarkable alignment between cinema and clandestine statecraft. In response to Washington's request for "specific, concrete ideas for India to use soft power in helping Afghanistan's reconstruction," a confidential March 2007 cable suggests that Bombay cinema engage the American cause (US Embassy Cable 2007). There were other ways for India to help the American war effort, noted the cable, like infrastructural aid in the areas of food aid, job training, telecommunication, and public works, but Bollywood presented a special opportunity: "We understand Bollywood movies are wildly popular in Afghanistan, so willing Indian celebrities could be asked to travel to Afghanistan to help bring attention to social issues there." These diplomatic entreaties are part of a now firm US strategic consensus, with closer military ties to India in the collapse of Pakistan's predictability as a stable American partner. The proposed Bollywood diplomacy has, to this point, not materialized, but *Zero Dark 30*'s "location-proximate" shooting suggests that the war on terror is being engaged on new—virtual and real—fields of battle.

References

"Hindu Protesters Disrupt Bin Laden Movie in India." (2012) *Daily News Egypt*, March 4.

"Pakistan: Little Audience for *Zero Dark Thirty* in Pakistan." (2013) *Right Vision News*, February 22.

"The World in Hollywood." (1935) *Popular Mechanics Magazine* (November), 128A.

"VHP Disrupts Shooting of Hollywood Film in Chandigarh." (2012) *The Pioneer*, March 2.

"'Zero' Script Scramble." (2012) *The New York Post*, December 5.

Bedi, R. (2012) "India Being Used for Pakistani Scenes in Film About Bin Laden," *The Irish Times*, March 3, 11.

Benjamin, W. (1968) "The Work of Art in the Age of Mechanical Reproduction," *Illuminations*, New York: Schocken, 217–52.

Blair, I. (2012) "Pros Restage Mideast Woes," *Variety*, December 17, 12.

Boal, M. (2011) *Zero Dark Thirty: An Original Screenplay*. Available at flash.sonypictures.com/shared/movies/zerodarkthirty/zdt_script.pdf (accessed October 15, 2014).

Bordwell, D., K. Thompson, & J. Staiger. (1985) *The Classical Hollywood Cinema: Film Style and Mode of Production*, New York: Routledge, 1985.

Bruno, G. (2002) *Atlas of Emotion: Journeys in Art, Architecture, and Film*, New York: Verso.

Caldwell, J. (2013) "Para-Industry: Researching Hollywood's Blackwaters," *Cinema Journal* 52, no. 3 (Spring).

Caward, N.G. (1915) "The Toast of Death," *Motography*, August 21, 366.

Conley, T. (2007) *Cartographic Cinema*, Minneapolis: University of Minnesota Press.

Elmer, G. & M. Gasher, eds. (2005) *Contracting Out Hollywood: Runaway Productions and Foreign Location Shooting*, Oxford: Rowman & Littlefield.

Evans, N. (2005) "Size Matters," *International Journal of Cultural Studies* 8, no. 2, 132.

Foucault, M. (1986) "Of Other Spaces," *Diacritics* 16 (Spring), 22–27.

Goldman, M. (2013) "The World's Most Wanted Man," *American Cinematographer* (February).

Goldsmith, B. & T. O'Regan. (2005) *The Film Studio: Film Production in the Global Economy*, New York: Rowman and Littlefield.

Goldsmith, B., S. Ward, & T. O'Regan. (2010) *Local Hollywood: Global Film Production and the Gold Coast*, Queensland: University of Queensland Press.

Govil, N. (2015) *Orienting Hollywood: A Century of Film Culture Between Los Angeles and Bombay*, New York: New York University Press.

Hozic, A. (2001) *Hollyworld: Space, Power, and Fantasy in the American Economy*, Ithaca: Cornell University Press.

Jones, M.E. (1914) "The Kalem Studios in California," *The Moving Picture World*, February 7, 671.

Kahol, V. (2012) "Bigelow's Osamabad Brings Smiles on Chandigarh Faces," *Mail Today*, March 5.

Kapoor, J. (2012) "From The Hurt Locker to ZD30: Bigelow Shoots Osama Film in Chandigarh," *Indian Express*, March 1.

Kapoor, J. (2012a) "Bigelow Team Thanks City as They Tee Off with Bollywood Stars," *Indian Express*, March 5.

Lash. S. & C. Lury. (2007) *Global Culture Industry: The Mediation of Things*, Cambridge: Polity.

Mendelson, D. (2006) "September 11 at the Movies," *The New York Review of Books*, September 21.

Miller, T., N. Govil, J. McMurria, R. Maxwell, & T. Wang (2005) *Global Hollywood 2*, London: British Film Institute.

Peters, O. (2013) "Editing *Zero Dark Thirty*," *Digital Video* (January), 23.

Roan, J. (2010) *Envisioning Asia: On Location, Travel, and the Cinematic Geography of U.S. Orientalism*, Ann Arbor: University of Michigan Press.

Scott, A. (2005) *On Hollywood: The Place, the Industry*, Princeton: Princeton University Press.

Sharma, A. (2013) "Manimajra Waits to See Itself in Bigelow Film," *Times of India*, January 11.

Sharma, A. (2013a) "Manimajra Forges Special Bond with Hollywood," *The Times of India*, February 10.

Shiel, M. (2012) *Hollywood Cinema and the Real Los Angeles*, London: Reaktion.

Srivastava, P. (2012) "(Re)Discovery of India," *Mail Today*, June 23.

Steyerl, H. (2012) "In Free Fall: A Thought Experiment on Vertical Perspective," *The Wretched of the Screen*, Berlin: Sternberg Press, 12–31.

Swaine, J. (2012) "Obama Gave Director Access to Secrets for Bin Laden Film," *The Daily Telegraph*, May 24.

US Embassy Cable EO 12958 (2007) Cable dated March 28. Available at www.guardian.co.uk/world/us-embassy-cables-documents/102286 (accessed September 22, 2014).

Wade, P. (1913) "A Girdle of Film Round the World," *The Motion Picture Story Magazine* (August), 105.

Willmett, S. (2013) "Quiet Americans: The CIA and Early Cold War Hollywood Cinema," *Journal of American Studies* 47, no. 1, 127–47.

19
CULTURAL ECONOMY AND URBAN DEVELOPMENT IN SHANGHAI

Xin Gu

Introduction

Cultural development is one of the most recent and distinctive models of Chinese modernization. In the West, cultural development entails a strong relationship between the regeneration of post-industrial cities and the development of cultural/ creative industries through place branding and local economic development. Central to the Chinese claim on this is the development of creative clusters. This includes the authorization of the use of inner city spaces by creative industries and to use this as a model to regenerate other parts of the city. As a result, in less than a decade, a city like Shanghai has gone from small-scale cultural production scattered in warehouses and factories to large, concentrated clusters of creative industries spread right across the city. However, the role of culture in rejuvenating urban decay in the context of Chinese socialist market reforms has to be mediated by the state. The transformation of creative clusters in Shanghai is metaphoric to a reconfiguration of the relationship between culture, market and policy in China.

The conceptual and empirical debates about culture and development in China have taken a distinctive form. In Shanghai, for instance, the change of term from 'cultural industries' to 'creative industries' has been justified in much more directly economic terms than has been the case in western cities. It has been explicitly linked to a range of economic outcomes and driven primarily by economic actors. The emergence of cultural economy in the form of the creative industries and creative clusters in Shanghai can thus be examined as a set of economic actions.

Such creative industries as economic process is highly contentious in the western context. This situation is exacerbated further when the discourses, institutions and practices involved encounter a context in which none of these can be taken for granted. When a city such as Shanghai begins to promote the 'cultural economy', it is faced with the question of aesthetics, cultural freedom, identity and individual creativity. At the same time, the relationships between the state, economy and everyday life have to be constantly negotiated at all levels. None of these conform to a 'Euro-centric' model of modernization.

Shanghai has used culture to propel itself to global city status. However, the results have been mixed. On the one hand there have been high-levels of return for real estate developers and for the city's global image capital; on the other the development of a 'cultural economy' in a socialist market has presented limited space for addressing cultural values that aren't part of the globalized circulation of capital. If Shanghai is going to represent a new global cultural capital, questions such as what kind of culture we are envisaging, and what kind of city, have to be answered.

Re-imagining the city

In the century before the 1949 revolution Shanghai functioned as an industrial and commercial base for western interests in China, as well as catalyzing a nascent Chinese capitalism and bourgeoisie. For the victorious Chinese Communist Party Shanghai represented imperialism, capitalism and decadence. Indeed, Shanghai has provided the space in which the currents of western and East Asia cultural modernities intermingled. For many the city seemed to have outlined a Chinese modernity very different from that of the communist modernization programme.

From the 1970s historians and writers attempted to reframe 1920s and 1930s Shanghai as China's lost cosmopolitan moment. Leo Ou-Fan Lee's highly influential *Shanghai Modern* (1999) outlined an 'urban cultural sensibility rooted in cosmopolitanism' (339), where for once China's self-sufficiency had opened up to the global flow of modernity. It was both nostalgia and a promise of return – a return of the modernity for which it stood, reversing the disasters brought by cultural revolution.

This emergent historical imaginary of a commercial, cosmopolitan Shanghai sat well with the 'reform and open' policy outlined in 1978. But such an historical narrative does not just float upwards to the urban imaginary, especially given the powerful ideological edifice of an imperialist, decadent Shanghai constructed over the preceding thirty years, the anti-urban strand within Maoism. The development of Shanghai modern in this sense is to produce a counter narrative making it available as the new urban imaginary. As Lee (1999: 349) noted, 'a new generation of Shanghai writers and poets have begun to explore … what they call a new "urban consciousness" – a subject of which they had previously known practically nothing.' But this re-imagining of Shanghai would position its cosmopolitan history as a central resource for becoming a global city.

This was going to be a programme for re-making the historical narrative in terms of a new urban imaginary of an entrepreneurial, innovative city ready to take what was necessary from the West. Akbar Abbas (2000) suggested that this urban cultural sensibility had, by the turn of the century, become fully integrated into Shanghai's development machine. And only in Shanghai, argued by Abbas, did rapid modernization not remove the past completely but instead engaged in its preservation.

Shanghai – like most western and many East Asia cities – quickly got wise to the cultural cachet of its colonial era buildings, which it started to preserve with the same fervour by which it set about demolishing every other remnant of the city's social and cultural fabric. Like those model 'global cities' Shanghai aspired to become, it embarked on a cultural facilities programme – concert halls, museums, galleries – that would provide its 'iconic' cultural and symbolic capital (O'Connor and Gu 2012). However, whilst European and North America cities sought arts and cultural industries as a replacement for declining manufacturing, Shanghai did so whilst actively removing its industry from the central areas to the outskirts and developing the central business district for advanced office-based business services. Indeed, it is as high-end occupants of such commercial real estate that the creative industries – positioned as a new kind of advanced business service – were initially received (Gu 2012).

This is the different contemporary context of 'cosmopolitanism' in an era of 'glocalization', that is, 'the need to adopt a global outlook to local conditions, a kind of "micromarketing" … encapsulated now in the corporate slogan "think globally, act locally"' (Abbas 2000: 784). Cultural mediation was no longer the job of the educated cosmopolitan artist-intellectual but of global corporations engaged in 'arbitrage', where global flows were calibrated to local needs and sensibilities in order to extract profit. In this account of the Shanghai urban imaginary, 'cultural intermediaries' were firmly under the control of the state (policy makers, state enterprises, developers, architects and so on) just as the process of mediating between the local and the global was parcelled out between the local state and transnational capital.

Yet it was another kind of urban cultural imaginary that Abbas aspired to, one that might invove different transnational flows with diverse actors. Such an imaginary will demand a new kind of 'cosmopolitanism', which would involve,

> not only the privileged transnational, at home in different places and cultures … [but] will have to include at least some of the less privileged men and women placed or displaced in the transnational space of the city and who are trying to make sense of its spatial and temporal contradictions.
>
> (Abbas 2000: 786)

This is an outline of a modernization project that is based not on 'maximizing profits' but on negotiating different values and dislocations caused by globalization. What later became known as creative clusters represented a kind of micro-site for such re-imaging of the city to take place. At the same time these micro-sites provided the platform whereby culture could gain a further grip on the development agenda.

Cultural economy and development

Creative industries are linked to the individual creativity that is embedded in local culture (Howkins 2001). Such understanding has led economic geographers to identify the clustering effect of local cultural industries (Scott 2000). Some went further to test policy transfer around 'creative cities' (Landry 2000). In particular, its effect has been discussed at the national and regional city level (Pratt 2005). By early 2000 the concept of a 'creative class' (Florida 2002) was familiar amongst policy makers across the world. Justin O'Connor (2011) provided useful analysis on how policy transfer around 'creative industries' resembles strong local preference because of the different political system at the local and national level. In China, 'creative industries' discourse arrived much later than 'cultural industries' and cities have varied feelings towards the adoption of creative industries.

The Shanghai municipal government adopted the UK-inspired term in 2005. Like its Asian neighbours, the 'creative industries' narrative in China was concerned with moving up the value chain – high value added 'design' associated with high tech industries. This general policy reform has met with a vast process of urban regeneration.

Shanghai had already started de-industrialization in the 1980s, relocating manufacturing industries to cheaper inland provinces to its west. This left behind an excessive amount of ex-industrial buildings and lands. But the question is whether the new creative industries are going to regenerate the city in the same way they did the western post-industrial cities. These questions arise as there are significant differences in the context within which such transfer takes place.

First, there is more pressure to assert the role of culture in development for Shanghai. Shanghai's post-industrial status was not a natural process of 'decline' but a suppression of existing industries. The centrality of 'culture' to the urban regeneration of many old post-industrial cities in the West has been strongly associated with securing inward investment. In Shanghai the attempt to attract investment was by no means a hard task. As Yeh (2007) documented, the 'derelict' inner city space of Shanghai was rebuilt into the financial capital of East Asia and equipped with high-quality housing and service infrastructures within a very short period of time, and with relatively little investment on the part of the local government. In this rapid achievement of redevelopment of inner city space, the cultural component of the urban narrative became less relevant and hard to implement.

Second, the emergence of creative industries in western cities is in most cases situated within local social and cultural context. For example, Britian's cultural economy has been largely associated with the notion of cultural democracy (Bianchini 1987). The idea owes much to the Greater London Council's attempt to install social democracy (Garnham 1990). In China, culture has just been allowed to operate in market terms. Creative industries in cities are industries that were only recently forced out of the state system. They are not very well integrated into the wider urban context. Artists and other cultural workers have just come out of the state system, and are still dispersed; they remain at the fringe of the city with limited access to capital. The 'creative class', or the bohemian value linking cultural production with cultural consumption, is emerging but there is a lack of understanding towards how this emergent cultural sector is related to the rest of the economy and to urban life.

These conflicting conditions in China suggest that the adoption of the cultural or creative industries narrative is going to face specific local challenges. To start with, cultural development is as much about modernization as about westernization. This was evident in Shanghai's attempt to embrace its decadent colonial past as a way of modernization. But how did Shanghai's cosmopolitan past allow for the organization of a contemporary urban cultural economy? Here 'development' as a process of westernization has become much more complex and contested. Most international agencies have tended to stress the importance of contextualizing development within local culture. In Shanghai, modernization received a radical dimension through its adoption of Soviet-inspired industrialization and socialist nation building.

Not only is the cultural context of development different, so is the cultural dimension of that development. In the West the work of Arjun Appadurai (1996) amongst others has stressed that measurement of development in gross domestic product is not enough – other values involving human dignity and 'capabilities' are required. There are three aspects of this that are particularly challenging to a Chinese policy discourse.

First, this forms the basis of an argument for human rights – the 'right to aspire', the right to dignity and free expression. In China the censorship of its citizens has increasingly been brought under human rights debate. Instead of separating culture and economic development, it intentionally obscures the two issues. As culture, the ethical-political questions are brushed off.

In creative industries development, a range of local and transnational cultural intermediaries might feature as grass-roots initiatives or global 'arbitrage'. Architects, policy exchange, development capital, heritage experts, international organizations, art world outriders, cultural entrepreneurs all began to circulate within and transform the local space. Their transformative power generates further conflicts between the official creative clusters and unofficial cultural spaces – cosmopolitan nightscapes, music venues, new media production and the proliferation of online spaces. This runs in conflict with the promotion of economic scale through state enterprises. The independent cultural spaces are increasingly attractive to the state but raise the question of how the state can be positioned in these establishments.

Second, they challenge the predominance of 'the economic' as the sole measure – in which case this may change the vectors of development. For economic growth, large corporations especially those run by the state, are privileged over small and medium sized enterprises (SMEs). It is not as straightforward as SMEs being excluded by all means (there is no evidence linking SMEs' failure to state intervention). What really happens is the lack of recognition of the cultural value in SMEs – the equation of market success to cultural success. This tends to exclude businesses that are not generating instant market hits.

Third, it raises the questions of the construction of cultural economy in very similar fashion to that of the rest of the economy. Continuing on the narrative of creative industries came the adoption of policies regarding the economy of culture in the form of socialist market reforms. This has seen the construction of big industries (such as the development of the China Central Television (CCTV) media group) in similar fashion to that of the rest of the economy. These become clearer in the development of creative clusters as the lines between culture as economic development and culture as state control were frequently drawn between the local and national actors. They also re-appeared within the local city as tensions between real estate development and the city's global cultural offer.

Creative clusters

In the light of the above, Shanghai adopted the creative clusters development policy. At first, it was similar to the science and technology park development model for animation and other new media industries. As Keane (2012) observed, this model is familiar to Chinese governments and has been used as a way of developing industrial scale by facilitating linkages across different sectors. The important aspect to draw from this 'boiled down' science park model is how the notion of culture was replaced with the notion of innovation in its attempt to access capital. Strictly speaking, these projects are not cultural developments because of the absence of any cultural value in the local development agenda.

Whilst the national governments are still subsidizing animation parks, the organically emerged artistic clusters pose real challenges to the local cities. From as early as the 1990s artists started to move into derelict warehouses and factories, setting up studios and social networks linking them to the awakening of Chinese contemporary art (Hee et al. 2008; Wang 2009; Zhong 2009). In Shanghai the famous M50 used to be a booming art village, home to many famous Chinese artists and galleries. It was amongst very few warehouses to survive the massive urban demolition that took place in the 1990s and early 2000s. A local activist group had campaigned for the survival of M50. What's unique in M50's urban regeneration story is how the local entrepreneurial state has learned to manage culture as assets.

M50 was administrated by Shanghai Spring Mill Factory, part of the large Shanghai Textile Group. The factory ceased production in the late 1980s and was left empty for decades. Artists moving into M50 caused unease to the state enterprise as to how to justify the unofficial use of industrial land by the then uncategorized creative industries and whether it is legitimate for a state enterprise to take 'commercial rent'. These were tricky problems but were protected by the local city authorities in their attempt to foster the new creative industries.

By 2005 creative clusters as an urban phenomenon had spread across the city. M50 and other successful clusters were designated 'official models' to be copied and re-adapted to other clusters. Policy makers from across China came to visit M50 and it became a key site for a Chinese model of creative industries development. Benefiting from the growing sector of the international art market, cultural heritage and cultural tourism, M50 has managed to survive. Shanghai Textile Group also thrived, rolling out the M50 model to over twenty factories that it owns. However, the driver behind the creative clusters was not culture, but economic development. Behind rapid cluster development are state-owned enterprises (SOEs) as major real estate developers. Not only are SOEs able to sell industrial land use for development, they are also shareholders in the new creative businesses protected by rules providing leverage to these SOEs.

During the process, the local entrepreneurial state is made increasingly powerful by being given the right to determine land use. This was soon put into play in 2005 when the Shanghai government officially announced the definition of 'creative industry cluster' and articulated rules for the repurposing of old industrial buildings for creative use. This has seen a resurgence of creative clusters developed by commercial real estate companies who would rent the land from SOEs and refurbish it to charge much higher commercial rents. It generates high tax returns for local district governments who usually act as deal broker between SOEs and developers.

Beneath the proliferation of creative clusters lie issues of sustainability. Creative clusters are generally not attractive to small-scale creative industries in the city as they are perceived as too commercial and too institutional. Most of the newly developed creative clusters find it hard to make ends meet in financial terms. Doubts have increasingly been cast on the success of creative clusters as economic developments.

The failure of creative clusters as profitable business ventures opened more opportunity of reconsidering the role of culture in all of these. Creative clusters certainly helped to define the cosmopolitan image of Shanghai as a global cultural capital showcasing refurbished warehouses alongside other cultural infrastructure, from museums and art galleries to cafes and bars. The urban spectacle generated by creative clusters cannot be underestimated in Shanghai's global branding (Greenspan 2012). But the real issue is how far did the development of creative clusters contribute to the wider urban economy and to local life? Or to what extent can we view creative clusters both as cultural outputs and as economic ones? The separation between culture and economy as a key process of Chinese modernity is increasingly challenged by its local development in China, as we will see below.

Cultural intermediary

Unlike most other cultural policy in China, the arrival of the creative industries agenda was not an entirely top-down implementation. It has attempted to work with cultural intermediaries both nationally and transnationally – practitioners, consultants, urban planners and academics alike. International agencies such as the British Council play a key role in helping to highlight international discourses that are suited to local aspirations. The British Council's cultural branch transported consultants from the United Kingdom to help formulate Shanghai's initial creative industries policy document. Multiple visits to Manchester, Liverpool and London led by Shanghai's senior policy makers, academics, architects and entrepreneurs have confirmed the creative clusters model.

Shanghai has not adopted the term 'creative clusters' unquestioningly. The local authority was fully aware of the potential risks in this direct policy transfer. They were concerned that the commercialization of culture could introduce counter-socialist ideology to the country (Pang 2012). A further problem that the Shanghai municipal government had with the British term was its promotion of individual creativity. This was associated with the promotion of SMEs, which was not something that the Chinese government was used to or wanted to engage with. SMEs were welcomed only when the government viewed them as 'epistemic nodes' of linking foreign companies with Chinese ones.

Shanghai Creative Industries Centre (SCIC) was set up by Shanghai Municipal government to solve the problem. Its first task in 2005 was to identify services critical for the growth of SMEs in creative industries. Various industrial associations, think tanks and expert groups were established, further boosting the 'SMEs theories' of creative industries. Although their suggestions still bear close resemblance to the western policy agenda, many started to claim the importance of SMEs in local practices. This first wave of cultural intermediaries through their experiments in Shanghai has been critical in pushing forward on the creative industries agenda across the nation.

Shanghai's explicit coupling of creative industries with creative industries centres (CICs) was one that kept certain elements of the 'industry park' model but increasingly linked to the re-use of local industrial infrastructure that would previously have been discarded as 'junk'. To meld the two together requires the re-invention of a Shanghainese 'urban cultural sensibility' through its various cultural intermediaries.

With most Chinese cities looking to classical music and the transnational performing arts as a source of international cultural capital, the meteoric rise in the profile of the international art world and its accelerating fêting of Chinese artists came as a surprise. In Shanghai, these early art warehouses were precarious places facing constant threat to be demolished. But the arrival of international art brokers, conservationists, cultural experts and tourists has helped to preserve and promote a burgeoning creative scene in Shanghai. A different imagery of the city has started to emerge.

Yet the reason for M50's increasing international profile was unclear to the authorities and mainstream developers. But M50 both persisted as a space and was made understandable to the policy world by the intermediation of its manager, Jin Wei Dong. As an employer of Shanghai Textile Group, he was charged with finding a source of revenue to cover the pensions of the redundant workers. The entry of artists into the empty textile factories was unplanned and the artists only paid low rent, but it was better than nothing. And through this close and increasingly sympathetic interaction with the artists Jin Wei Dong felt his way towards the specific challenges of managing a 'creative space'. Managers from SOEs like Jin were key players in formulating an understanding of this kind of model for older factories amongst policy makers. The latter started to register the viability of this model.

Overlapping with the emergent connectivity of local and global art worlds was that of architects and designers. Though architectural firms have long been global players, the 'transnational urbanism' they presented to China was directed towards large-scale projects in association with approved local partners (Ren 2011). The iconic manufacturing heartland of Suzhou Creek, with its rich industrial heritage, began to attract small-scale architect-led development, often in association with artist-led spaces. Taiwanese architect Teng Kun Yan setup his work studio in one of the warehouses in Shanghai in 1998 and others soon followed (Gu 2012). Increasingly these newly refurbished spaces began to attract design and media firms. Some smaller design firms even moved into older residential areas such as Taikang Road. This latter has many similar characteristics to the organic clusters in the West in its connectivity to local lifestyle and culture.

Both of these organic practices sought to retrieve an urban sensibility based on industrial heritage with the 'distressed' aesthetic value commonly found in the West. It was a different, somewhat vernacular urbanism, and one in which the production of art and design provided a micro-site for a different kind of transnational urbanism. It was within this milieu that the 'industrial aesthetic' and its application to creative industries became visible to the outside world.

The potential of the industrial aesthetic for real estate development had been officially recognized in 2004 with the opening of Xintiandi, an office, retail and bar/dining complex near a major shopping street. It was constructed from the elements of the old Shikumen housing blocks, but made fit for modern use. It was telling that the architecture company was from Hong Kong, to whom this kind of historical vernacular was highly visible and viable (Liang 2008).

If it took some time before local government recognized the potential of creative clusters, the bigger problem was with the unofficial nature of many clusters. What needed to happen in fact was an alternative real estate regulation policy. In this process intermediation took place within the administration. The lead body for the sector – Shanghai Creative Industries Centre – was therefore a hybrid of a Chinese-style industry association and the sorts of agencies that had developed in London, Manchester and other pro-creative industrial cities. It designed policy that allows creative businesses to occupy industrial spaces without their land use being re-designated as 'commercial'. It also allowed the owner of land to sell industrial land for commercial development without having to seek a formal land re-designation from the state government. SCIC's role was to certify these deals and provide consultancy services for them.

However, the growing coalition between the local government and developers in increasing the property market in old industrial areas was key to the displacement of artists and SMEs from industrial warehouses. Creative clusters stopped being the epicentre of Shanghai's urban cultural economy. It could be said that in Shanghai, creative clusters failed to secure further investment in culture as a result of its being too closely affiliated with urban development. The utilization of 'local culture' as symbolic value for development also caused the clusters to lose their authenticity. This was echoed by a recent trend of small businesses moving into the French Concession area (considered 'more authentic Shanghai') with the conversions of old residential buildings into galleries and workshops. This was soon followed by the re-use of office buildings outside of working hours for art salons, independent film screening, music gigs and art workshops. These new alternative cultural spaces have the tendency to bring with them strategic production procedures causing more and more cultural businesses to move out of official creative clusters. Artists and other cultural entrepreneurs alike in this sense act as 'epistemological intermediaries' in a global circulation of cultural capital. The inability to incorporate these epistemological intermediaries in policy discourse and to connect with their complex social networks are unlikely to deliver what Scott (2007) called 'cognitive-cultural economy' for Shanghai.

Conclusion

I have tried to trace a particular aspect of the cultural development project, that of the 'creative clusters' in refurbished industrial buildings, conceived as a re-imagining of the urban cultural economy. It shows how this model became part of a general adoption of culture as development in China. The selective and hybrid nature of this policy transfer in Shanghai raised issues about the limitation of a 'creative cities' policy agenda as constrained by local conditions. At the same time, it opens up the opportunity for a reimagined city that could go beyond the way that policy was framed.

These tensions around urban cultural policy have only increased in the last decade as different development interests have moved into the 'creative city' agenda. In China a cultural milieu has emerged alongside the market and the state-controlled sector. Whilst the latter becomes increasingly interested in economic development, the culture imaginary becomes progressively economically oriented and controlled by the (local) state. Artists have been increasingly pushed out of the creative clusters; other small cultural producers and entrepreneurs have also been marginalized in Shanghai. It is those who were closely linked to the local state that define the new urban cultural economy.

On the other hand, the global flow of cultural capital has looked elsewhere for aspirations and authenticity. International art dealers are now bypassing creative clusters to reach hidden places in the French Concession area; co-working spaces spur across the central business district, acting as a test space for a more flexible use of creative clusters – informed visitors to Shanghai can find music gigs in office blocks. These fast-moving, temporary uses of spaces create a more authentic feel of a Shanghai that was perhaps more celebrated by the process of globalization than by that of the linear model of Chinese modernization. The existence of this microcosm in parallel to the official cultural infrastructures is a real test of this imaginary as currently articulated by local cities.

References

Abbas, A. (2000) 'Cosmopolitan De-scriptions: Shanghai and Hong Kong', *Public Culture*, 12 (3): 769–86.

Appadurai, A. (1996) *Modernity at Large: Cultural Dimensions of Globalization*, Minneapolis: University of Minnesota Press.

Bianchini, F. (1987) 'GLC R.I.P. 1981–86', *New Formations*, 1: 103–17.

Florida, R. (2002) *The Rise of the Creative Class*, New York: Basic Books.

Garnham, N. (1990) *Capitalism and Communication: Global Culture and the Economics of Information*, London: Sage.

Greenspan, A. (2012) 'The Power of Spectacle', *Culture Unbound*, Special Issue on Shanghai Moderne, 4: 81–95.

Gu, X. (2012) 'The Art of Re-Industrialisation in Shanghai', *Culture Unbound*, 4: 193–211.

Hee, L., Schroepfer, T., Nanxi, S. and Ze, L. (2008) 'From Post-Industrial Landscape to Creative Precincts: Emergent Spaces in Chinese Cities', *International Development Planning Review*, 30 (3): 249–66.

Howkins, J. (2001) *The Creative Economy: How People Make Money From Ideas*, London: Allen Lane.

Keane, M. (2012) *China's New Creative Clusters: Governance, Human Capital and Regional Investment*, London: Routledge.

Landry, C. (2000) *The Creative City: A Toolkit For Urban Innovators*, London: Sterling.

Lee, L. (1999) *Shanghai Modern: The Flowering of a New Urban Culture in China, 1930–1945*, Cambridge, MA, London: Harvard University Press.

Liang, S. (2008) 'Amnesiac Monument, Nostalgic Fashion: Shanghai's New Heaven and Earth', *Wasafiri*, 23 (3): 47–55.

O'Connor, J. (2011) *Arts and Creative Industries*, Sydney: Australia Council for the Arts.

O'Connor, J. and Gu, X. (2012) 'Shanghai: Images of Modernity' in Isar, R. and Anheier, H. (eds) *Cultural Policy and Governance in a New Metropolitan Age*, Cultures and Globalization Series, Vol. 5, pp. 288–300, London: Sage.

Pang, L. (2012) *Creativity and its Discontents: China's Creative Industries and Intellectual Property Rights Offences*, Durham, NC: Duke University Press.

Pratt, A. (2005) 'Cultural Industries and Public Policy: An oxymoron? *International Journal of Cultural Policy*, 11 (1): 31–44.

Ren, X. (2011) *Building Globalization: Transnational Architecture Production in Urban China*, Chicago and London: University of Chicago Press.

Scott, A. J. (2000) *The Cultural Economy of the Cities*, London: Sage.

Scott, A. J. (2007) 'Capitalism and Urbanisation in a New Key? The Cognitive-Cultural Dimension', *Social Forces*, 85 (4): 1465–82.

Wang, J. (2009) '"Art in Capital": Shaping Distinctiveness in a Culture-Led Urban Regeneration Project in Red Town, Shanghai', *Cities*, 26: 318–30.

Yeh, W. (2007) *Shanghai Splendor – Economic Sentiments and the Making of Modern China, 1843–1949*, Berkeley and Los Angeles, CA: University of California Press.

Zhong, S. (2009) 'From Fabrics to Fine Arts: Urban Restructuring and the Formation of an Art District in Shanghai', *Critical Planning*, 16: 118–37.

20
CULTURAL INDUSTRIES IN TRANSITION ECONOMIES

Bastian Lange

Introduction

From the very beginning of the formulation of cultural industries in the last decades, many scholars in the field of cultural and creative industries (CCI) have emphasized the nexus of urban transformations to the spatial embedding of cultural industries as well as its transformation of work and production forms (e.g. Landry 2000; Hesse and Lange 2012). From the perspective of urban transition, cultural **industries** very often became manifest at abandoned and vacant locations, which allowed them to flourish and to develop over time. Various researchers have highlighted these very obvious observations when they were pointing to the role of metropolitan regions to accommodate these new cultural economies (Florida 2002, 2005; Hospers 2003; Scott 2006).

On the contrary, rather little attention has been shed on the very fact, if CCI are likely to develop much better, independently and self-sustaining, when they are confronted with culturally, economically as well as socially transitory spatial environments. Therefore, looking retrospectively at the political systemic changes that occurred in 1989 in East Germany, it can be stated that this particular societal situation poses a moment of significant difference to any other more silently on-going evolutionary transition phase that is infiltrating the everyday lives of human beings nowadays. As a consequence, in this particular systemic situation, its immediate unexpected structural shock might be considered as a special case of transition that allows us to relate the evolution of cultural industries retrospectively with the question, if a complex transitory context might propel cultural industries much better than a planned top-down branding, or classic economic development approach might have achieved.

Do cultural industries require transitory spatial contexts?

The following chapter starts with the assumption that this decisive moment in the history of the former East and West Europe 25 years ago has stimulated various creative practices in the strict and anthropological sense of the term. Various club, art and pop scenes dynamized the urban (e.g. Lugosi et al. 2010) and propelled a new age of urban based cultural experiences for a generation, that has been locked in the cage of either politically East vs. West oriented global policies. Roughly speaking, these creative practices started in the mid-1980s in various pop and art counter cultures. In the 1990s – as biographical and professional options – they served as blueprints for transitory possibilities when the national states started to dismantle the amenities of the former social welfare state. Infused by the rapidly rising technological changes, the ground for summarizing, systematizing and capitalizing these practices as CCI was paved.

In the following chapter I will expand on the assumptions and attributes that go along with the transitory notion of systemic changes in an East German case, the city of Leipzig. Other than, for example, in the former Soviet Union, the transitory phase in East Germany was framed by a rather stable state that – within a few years – installed democratically elected and transparent public and legal authorities. The city of Leipzig in the free state of Saxony is known worldwide as the seed plant of organized societal upheaval against the dictatorship of the state of German Democratic Republic (GDR). In doing so, I will connect the starting phase of the first 20 years of re-forming culture and cultural industries in the city of Leipzig as well as to the articulation of cultural industries in the city of Leipzig with the systemic transition conditions of the pre- and post-unification phases. Thereby, I will systematically shed light on the specific articulations of cultural industries and their embedded constitutional situatedness in a city that has been known since the industrial phase as a city of publishing, trade and music (Bathelt 2002, 2003, 2005; Lange 2010).

Following this evidence, I will merge lines of thinking to recent observation, that obviously demonstrate that global neo-liberal market conditions nowadays are silently aiming at implementing constant transitory instabilities in, for example, corporate organizations, welfare state conditions, education and the *projectification* of the everyday. Thereby, I will point out to parallel practices that are obviously referring to the very early transitory heyday of independent urban art and pop scenes in the 1980s and 1990s. These forms of flexibilization have been widely interpreted as an expression of late-capitalistic market formation (e.g. Crouch 2011). From the perspective of cultural industries and cultural policy making, appropriate public and state-run steering and governance measures for cultural industries are finding it difficult to be developed, for example when the local and regional state authorities are aiming at securing a minimum of state policy in the field of public, non-economic culture values for a broader public audience and users (Hesmondhalgh and Pratt 2005).

Following this line of thinking, I conclude with an obvious paradox that can be observed when looking at transitory conditions and their effects on cultural industries: a close relationship seems to exist between the depth and intensity of urban transition on the one hand and the (re-)formation of urban-based new creative markets on the other (Jarvis et al. 2009). As a consequence, CCI are considered to be a role model for presenting and enabling new "liberated" work modes as well as their subsequent lifestyles: for instance, one of the key urban and cultural developments in larger European cities is the emergence of a new hybrid of cultural as well as entrepreneurial agents, the so-called culturepreneurs (e.g., London: McRobbie 2002; Berlin:

Lange 2005; Vienna: Ellmeier 2003). This phenomenon has led to a reconsideration of entrepreneurial values in respect to urban values (Johnstone and Lionais 2004; Steyaert 2007). When understanding the role of new professions in CCI, it becomes obvious that labour is organized in a significantly different way in these emerging economies and that local social networks and projects play a crucial role (van Heur 2010).

Understanding and conceptualizing markets in cultural and creative industries

Rather disconnected from these transitional effects, another line of current research targets a better understanding of the formation of markets as a result of systemic transitions. To a large extent, CCI have been subjected to organizational changes within small and medium enterprises (Rae 2004; Wilson and Stokes 2005; Scott 2006; Neff et al. 2005; Lange 2007). These scholars vote for a paradigmatic shift in society and economy. Thereby, they take into account that new forms of "knowledge" are recombined and have thus restructured economy, public administration, entrepreneurship and as well as their socialities. It was Grabher in particular who focused on the inner-organizational dimension of the emergent network-based project ecologies and their entrepreneurial and socio-spatial practices in these industries (DeFillippi et al. 2007; Grabher 2002, 2004c). Rapidly changing project-based constellations within flexible network formations pose structural constraints not only on enhancing learning among temporary team members, but on sustaining what is understood as "traditional", long-standing learning cultures (Cameron and Quinn 1988: 8). Apart from such learning processes, several structural paradoxes are closely related to creative industries and their entrepreneurial agents. Major paradoxes include: a) the need to reconcile tensions between the work ethos and human resource practices in creative and more routinized activities; b) the need to balance the advantages of flexible and temporary organization with the advantages of tight integration. These researchers have shed light on the project-based character of these new businesses (Grabher 2004a, 2004b) epitomizing prototypical features of temporary systems in CCI (Lundin and Söderholm 1995).

When we apply these theoretical positions to the way markets in cultural industries are formed, we see that the very high dynamic in these markets goes along with highly informal and less institutionalized contexts. That makes it very difficult to apply common and standardized economic definitions to this field. Static concepts such as company, entrepreneur and product very often cannot grasp the very flexible nature of theses constantly shifting and moving markets (Bilton 1999; Lange et al. 2008; McRobbie 2002, 2003). Given that mainly 60 per cent of creative professionals operate as self-employed entrepreneurs, two major consequences have to be taken into account:

First, following for example McRobbie (2002), the very high professional mobility in these markets is accompanied with high demands of flexibility of these entrepreneurs and their practices to stay in these constantly moving and shifting markets.

Second, it can be assumed that the traditional understanding of entrepreneurial practices can not equally be adapted to the way creative entrepreneurs operate and describe themselves in the newly emerged markets within the wider field of creative industries (Hjorth 2004; Lange 2008; Rae 2002).

When we acknowledge this, a profound reconsideration of "entrepreneurship" in respect to space has to be taken into consideration in order to fully understand the complex nature of markets, as introduced by Steyaert and Katz (Steyaert and Katz 2004). Very often, it is of interest to find out how young entrepreneurs develop strategies to gain access to markets, to observe markets and subsequently establish a position in those markets when all the while they depend on social interaction, information on new trends, new products and production tools directly related to the same markets. When examining these perspectives, scholars address a specific problem that is rooted in the structural paradoxes of entrepreneurial, social as well as work practices in the field creative industries: when more than approximately 60 per cent of entrepreneurs act independently and solely in small, instable and insecure markets, how can a processes of professionalization be detected and what are the structural prerequisites for modes of acting professionally on the road to becoming an entrepreneur in the field of CCI?

Introducing Leipzig 1990–2011

Leipzig is situated in the Free State of Saxony in eastern Germany. It is the largest city in Saxony, closely followed by the state capital, Dresden. Leipzig is one of the core cities of the metropolitan region known as "Mitteldeutschland", consisting of the cities of Leipzig, Erfurt, Weimar, Magdeburg, Dessau, Dresden and Chemnitz/Zwickau. On a smaller scale, the axis linking the adjacent cities of Leipzig and Halle forms a conurbation with around 1.5 million inhabitants. The city of Leipzig itself has a population slightly exceeding 520,838 (31 December 2012).

In 2008, according to the German definition of creative industries (BMWi 2009), the city of Leipzig had 12,374 employees in the field of the CCI. Between 2005 and 2008, creative industries remained mainly equal. This situation could not compensate for the loss of 39,660 jobs between 2000 and 2008 in other economic segments of Leipzig; this was around 12.07 per cent of the workforce in 2000, similar to the losses of the state of Saxony or by 12.73 per cent. Creative industries take place mainly in the core area of the city, and a few quarters such as Plagwitz in western Leipzig. Among the professional fields with the highest job cuts between 2005 and 2007, we find the film industry, and radio and broadcasting. The highest growth rates can be found in the fields of the software and games industry, book marketing and design.

At the end of the 1980s, probably none of the GDR's major cities had such a down-at-heel appearance as Leipzig (Nuissl and Rink 2003). Leipzig, a centre of commerce for many centuries, concentrated its efforts on revitalizing the historical centre, as can be seen from the gentrification of the main railway station, the old merchants' warehouses and the shopping streets. Even though three-quarters of the old buildings were refurbished during the 1990s, the migration of people away from the city could not be halted. Of the 320,000 housing units, 55,000 are still unoccupied today (although fortunately this figure is slowly reducing).

From 1989 to 1993, Leipzig experienced a radical process of deindustrialization when the city's manufacturing workforce shrank from roughly 80,000 to below 17,000 (Nuissl and Rink 2003: 28). Apart from the harsh economic and social problems emerging, empty residential and industrial areas made the city's urban structure unstable. Some 800,000 square metres of newly built but unused office space as well as 60,000 empty flats in the mid-1990s led to Leipzig becoming the city with the highest vacancies in eastern Germany.

The combination of radical economic decline mostly in the first ring around the inner city and the growth of retail space in the second ring on the periphery of Leipzig led to what has been coined the "perforated city" structure of Leipzig (Lütke-Daldrup 2004).

Unintended formations of new creative and entrepreneurial agents

Apart from formally organized and politically induced crisis-solving policies, Leipzig's cultural scenes contain numerous modes of self-organizing formations. Even though the formal labour market has to be considered weak, inaccessible or unattractive, many cultural activists launched their own rather unusual entrepreneurial start-up businesses in the midst of a substantial structural crisis. Informal networks provided an important backbone in order to cope with minimal financial income, hardly any venture capital, or any other similar formal and "known" support structures (Bismarck and Koch 2005; Steets 2005).

In combination with existing cultural capital that had survived the GDR times (such as painting, photography, design, etc.), cultural scenes became more and more visible and so regained importance not only for the heterogeneity of cultural life and cultural consumption, but also as professional opportunities. In due course, architectural firms (such as L 21, KARO, URBIKOM, etc.), artistic collectives (such as NIKO 31), a gallery agglomeration in the former cotton mill in Plagwitz in west Leipzig, the leading cultural centre known as naTo in Südvorstadt, as well as a prospering media and film-related experimental creative scene emerged in the course of the harsh transformation processes in the mid-1990s (Bismarck and Koch 2005).

Prerequisites and criteria enabling the emergence of Leipzig's CCI

For a long time, Leipzig was viewed as the secret cultural capital of the GDR, being a melting pot of diverse subcultures and creative actors (Farin 2002: 154). The image and atmosphere of the city were shaped by writers, artists and punk bands (Bismarck and Koch 2005). In Leipzig, as elsewhere, the political changes of 1989 and the globalization that began in the 1990s led to a reorganization of the cultural creators' networks and scenes. Informal communication networks were crucial for coping with these changes. In 2006 over 1996 small and middle-sized companies operating in CCI had a turnover totalling over 1.5 billion euros. The CCI employed about 10,500 people, which makes them a relevant factor in the labour market. Leipzig is the centre of Saxony's CCI.

The field of CCI demonstrates – in respect to the complex economic changes, the failure of top-down planned growth expectations and large subsidizes economies – a very positive performance and positive growth rates in jobs in the city of Leipzig. Quantitatively, the media industries and their sub-segments contribute most to these growth rates. This situation is embedded in a broad institutionalized knowledge and educational landscape, with university, polytechnic college, several extra-university research centres and various art, music and technical schools. Attractive urban qualities, open-minded social milieus, active civil society and cultural facilities in various fields are able to stimulate economic competitiveness. Paradoxically, cultural industries in general have been identified as a strategic field of action by local government in the city of Leipzig only recently. Only recently, the existing Media Cluster has been extended by renaming it "Media and Creative Industries Cluster".

Institutional context

Apart from the media segment, almost all creative sub-branches evolved without explicit public funding or other direct creative policies in the last years. Leipzig demonstrates a large number of creative scenes (design, art, painting, fashion, film, music, architecture, photography, etc.) that play a crucial role in the everyday life as well as in the configuration of the city's economy (Lange and Ehrlich 2009). Furthermore, a dense network of art institutions, like the Gallery for Contemporary Art, the Academy of Fine Arts, art museums, and "bottom-up" cultural initiatives like the naTO as well as temporary thematic fairs (Designers' Open) and exhibitions serve as places for project-based communication and knowledge exchange.

Small-scale grass roots development

Numerous creative agents in Leipzig that are internationally renowned play an ever-increasing role in the public life of the city and work toward the formation of creative hot spots. They demonstrate a rather decentralized form of allocating temporally their entrepreneurial practices and their "collaboration in projects" in respect to traditionally more centralized placing of stable and durable "important" and representative economies.

In the course of recent creative entrepreneurial efforts, former industrial places like the Tapetenwerk, Werk II, Delikatessenhaus, and Westwerk offer possibilities for creative actors to enter the economic market, lowering their entrepreneurial and economic risk. Most of these flexible sites are located in the western part of Leipzig, with an ongoing increase of cultural and creative initiatives. Only recently, creative actors also discover the eastern districts of the city, because here they are even closer to the core of the city, and especially entrepreneurs at the very beginning of their career have an easier access to the market than they would have in the western part (e.g. Pöge-Haus: art-house and start-up centre; Des Geigers Rätsel: club/pub for cultural events and networking).

Spatial practices of the design and art scene – the case of the design fair Designers' Open

The micro-spatial practices of Leipzig's CCI have to be seen in the context of a "perforated city". Leipzig's cityscape is dominated by deterioration, housing vacancy and especially inner city modernization. The city no longer corresponds to the typical European image of a dense city structure (Steets 2008: 167). In the following, the micro-spatial practices of the Leipzig design scene can be described by referring to the design fair Designers' Open and the Baumwollspinnerei (a former cotton mill).

The actors of the design scene adopt a policy that also reacts to the city's unstable spatial situation. In 2007 the main exhibition spaces of the Designers' Open were vacant former department stores and exhibition houses in inner city and central areas. In 2008 they changed their decentralizing practice of space utilization by looking for new and smaller event locations spread over the inner city, turning the whole inner city into exhibition space. This closely interrelated conception of space represents the network-based cooperation that is essential for the scene. Furthermore, the acquisition of central areas of Leipzig represents a desire for a larger role in defining the city's image. By advertising in the city media as well as through flyers and mailings to the scene and beyond, the marketing measures for the Designers' Open aimed to attract a greater number of suitors, exhibitors and members of the general public so as to stimulate interest in the Leipzig design scene and increase demand for output.

In contrast to the recent and decentralizing trend within the Leipzig design scene, the art sector reacted early to the urban spatial situation, adopting a different policy with regard to the use of space and sites. Over the years, the Baumwollspinnerei, situated in Leipzig's west, became a model for the use of space, influencing other creative actors in Leipzig: low-cost purchase of former industrial areas for use as creative spaces was combined with the establishment of social networks. An essential starting point of the development of the Baumwollspinnerei area was the boom of the trend-setting New Leipzig School. Today, about 80 artists work on the site, which is now professionally managed. In 2005 Leipzig's most important art galleries moved to the area, and various enterprises have settled there (Steets 2008: 174–77).

Conclusion

Keeping in mind the question of the social-spatial condition of CCI, the situation in Eastern Germany and in Leipzig appears to be paradoxical. On the one hand, since 1990, de-industrialization, migration and demographic change led to a high vacancy rate. On the other hand, this opened new space for experiments: galleries, ateliers or temporary projects are locations that creative people use for their entrepreneurial actions and thus re-introduce them to the economic cycle (Steets 2005: 108–12). It is at those places where networks of creative people become socially relevant and spatially manifest: in times of a global crises of economy, of a shrinking in production, lack of ideas of established and administrative functionaries and increasing need of individualization, young creative people claim new forms of collaboration and collective (economic) actions (Friebe and Ramge 2008; Lange 2009, 2010). It is not the economic profit that is in focus, but the implementation of individual interests in collectives, thus furthermore gaining autonomy in regard to time, sociality and symbolic winnings.

These heterogeneous entrepreneurial scenes and creative milieus can be denominated as diverse cultural urban dimensions that contribute to the attractiveness of the cultural economy in Leipzig and its specific "bottom-up" articulation. Leipzig's relatively cheap rents and living costs as well as easily accessible workspace for creative agents have, over the course of time, driven forward and stimulated creativity more than any top-down planning procedures could have done.

Paradoxically, from an empirical situation, the absence of a strong cultural-economic development policy enabled these economies to flourish and to evolve much better than any top-down policy practice could have done so far (Lange et al. 2009). A deeper empirical view of Leipzig has shown that entrepreneurial scenes are generally based on socio-spatial differentiation practices. Yet, instead of following universal rules, they show an intrinsic logic of the city (Löw 2008). There are rules and certainties in the extraordinary nature of a city, in the way certain rituals, sociolects and ideologies work. Intrinsic logics can be described as the grammar of a city or place, determining what is possible in the city and where the specific within the usual is situated (Löw 2008: 43). This is especially true for the places and working contexts of the cultural and creative economy. Places reveal themselves through social and communicative processes. Social concentration and physical presence of the scene's members are thus necessary, because the discernible relation between the actors is necessary to make Leipzig collectively discernible as a significant place. Yet, for members of the scene, these places are seen as ways to get access to the market on the basis of cultural networks. Creative actors organize exhibitions, product presentations, vernissages, finissages and parties – in other words, short-term events that co-form social space by performativity. Dominating behavioural and language codes is crucial in order to get access to these social places and events. The "'look' and 'feel' of the location" (Helbrecht 2004: 200) determines visibility in social terms. Places thus have an intrinsic logic revealing itself in local-specific and not universally homogeneous forms of collectivization. They organize events displaying places as social fields on the urban map. These activities are aimed at obtaining social affiliation and certainty of action. They create social intensities and highly stimulating concentrations that attract attention and aim to introduce trends, styles, codes – in short: symbolic products – into social networks. As can be observed best in the fields of design, music, literature and fashion, these spatial policies are aimed at testing the products of CCI – sounds, pictures, texts, techniques, graphics – for performative effects. The social and performative testing process takes place inside the temporary and transitional rooms of these creative scenes.

References

Bathelt, Harald (2002): The Re-emergence of a Media Industry Cluster in Leipzig. In: *European Planning Studies* 10, Vol. 5: 583–611.

Bathelt, Harald (2003): Toward a Reconceptualization of Regional Development. Paths: Is Leipzig's Media Cluster a Continuation of or a Rupture with the Past? In: *Economic Geography* 79, Vol. 3: 265–93.

Bathelt, Harald (2005): Cluster Relations in the Media Industry: Exploring the "Distanced Neighbour" Paradox in Leipzig. In: *Regional Studies* 39, Vol. 1: 105–27.

Bilton, Chris (1999): Risky Business: The Independent Production Sector in Britain's Creative Industries. In: *The International Journal of Cultural Policy* 6, Vol. 1: 17–40.

Bismarck, Beatrice von and Koch, Alexander (2005): Beyond education. *Kunst, Ausbildung, Arbeit und Ökonomie.* Leipzig, Revolver – Archiv für aktuelle Kunst.

BMWi (eds) (2009): *Gesamtwirtschaftliche Perspektiven der Kultur-und Kreativwirtschaft in Deutschland.* Berlin: Bundesministerium für Wirtschaft, Forschungsbericht Nr. 577.

Cameron, Kim and Quinn, Robert (1988): Organizational Paradox and Transformation. In: Robert. E. Quinn/Kim Cameron (eds), *Paradox and Transformation.* Cambridge: Harper & Row, 1–18.

Crouch, Colin (2011): *The Strange Non-Death of Neo-Liberalism.* London: Wiley.

DeFillippi, Robert, Grabher, Gernot and Jones, Candace (2007): Introduction to Paradoxes of Creativity: Managerial and Organizational Challenges in the Cultural Economy. In: *Journal of Organizational Behavior* 28, Vol. 5: 511–21.

Ellmeier, Andrea (2003): Cultural Entrepreneurialism: On the Changing Relationship Between the Arts, Culture and Employment. In: *The International Journal of Cultural Policy* 9, Vol. 1: 3–16.

Farin, Klaus (2002): Generation-kick.de. *Jugendsubkulturen heute.* München: Beck.

Florida, Richard (2002): *The Rise of the Creative Class: And how it's Transforming Work, Leisure, Community and Everyday Life.* New York: Basic Books.

Florida, Richard (2005): *The Flight of the Creative Class.* New York: Routledge.

Friebe, Holm and Ramge, Thomas (2008): *Marke Eigenbau: der Aufstand der Massen gegen die Massenproduktion.* Frankfurt/Main: Campus-Verl.

Grabher, Gernot (2002): Cool Projects, Boring Institutions: Temporary Collaboration in Social Context. In: *Regional Studies* 36, Vol. 3: 205–14.

Grabher, Gernot (2004a): Learning in Projects, Remembering in Networks? Communality, Sociality, and Connectivity in Project Ecologies. In: *European Urban and Regional Studies* 11, Vol. 2: 103–23.

Grabher, Gernot (2004b): The Markets Are Back! In: *Progress in Human Geography.* 28, Vol. 4: 421–24.

Grabher, Gernot (2004c): Temporary Architectures of Learning: Knowledge Governance in Project Ecologies. In: *Organization Studies* 25, Vol. 9: 1491–514.

Helbrecht, Ilse (2004): Bare Geographies in Knowledge Societies – Creative Cities as Text and Piece of Art: Two Eyes, One Vision. In: *Built Environment* 30, Vol. 3: 194–203.

Hesmondhalgh, David and Pratt, Andy (2005): Cultural Industries and Cultural Policy. In: *International Journal of Cultural Policy* 11, Vol. 1: 1–15.

Hesse, Markus and Lange, Bastian (2012): Paradoxes of the Creative City: Contested Territories and Creative Upgrading – The Case of Berlin, Germany. In: *Die Erde* 143, Vol. 4: 241–61.

Hjorth, Daniel (2004): Creating Space for Play/Invention – Concepts of Space and Organizational Entrepreneurship. In: *Entrepreneurship and Regional Development* 16, Vol. 5: 413–32.

Hospers, Gert-Jan (2003): Creative City: Breeding Places in the Knowledge Economy. In: *Knowledge, Technology, and Policy* 16, Vol. 3: 143–62.

Jarvis, David, Lambie, Hannah and Berkeley, Nigel (2009): Creative Industries and Urban Regeneration. In: *Journal of Urban Regeneration and Renewal* 2, Vol. 4: 364 –74.

Johnstone, Harvey and Lionais, Doug (2004): Depleted Communities and Community Business Entrepreneurship: Revaluing Space Through Place. In: *Entrepreneurship and Regional Development: An International Journal* 16, Vol. 3: 217–33.

Landry, Charles (2000): *The Creative City: A Toolkit for Urban Innovators.* London: Earthscan.

Lange, Bastian (2005): Socio-Spatial Strategies of Culturepreneurs: The Example of Berlin and its New Professional Scenes. *Zeitschrift für Wirtschaftsgeographie* (Special Issue: Ökonomie und Kultur) 49, Vol. 2: 81–98.

Lange, Bastian (2007): *Die Räume der Kreativszenen. Culturepreneurs und ihre Orte in Berlin.* Bielefeld: Transcript Verlag.

Lange, Bastian (2008): Accessing Markets in Creative Industries: Professionalization and Social-Spatial Strategies of Culturepreneurs in Berlin. In: *Creative Industries Journal* 1, Vol. 2: 115–35.

Lange, Bastian (2009): Markets in Creative Industries: On the Role of Culturepreneurs, Professionalisation and their Social-Spatial Strategies. In: Harald Pechlaner/Dagmar Abfalter/Sandra Lange (eds), *Culture Meets Economy.* Bozen: Bozen University Press, 11–36.

Lange, Bastian (2010): Scene Formation in the Design Market: Comparing Berlin and Leipzig. In: *Regions Magazine* 1367–3882 277, Vol. 1, 01 Spring: 16–17.

Lange, Bastian and Ehrlich, Kornelia (2009): Geographien der Szenen – Begriffsklärungen und zwei Fallvergleiche im Feld der urbanen Kultur-und Kreativwirtschaft von Berlin und Leipzig. In: *Sociologia Internationalis*, Vol. 2: 1–25.

Lange, Bastian, Kalandides, Ares, Stöber, Birgit and Mieg, Harald A. (2008): Berlin's Creative Industries: Governing Creativity? In: *Industry and Innovation* 15, Vol. 5: 531–48.

Lange, Bastian, Kalandides, Ares, Stöber, Birgit and Wellmann, Inga (2009): Fragmentierte Ordnungen. In: Bastian Lange/Ares Kalandides/Birgit Stöber/Inga Wellmann (Hrsg.), *Governance der Kreativwirtschaft. Diagnosen und Handlungsoptionen.* Bielefeld: Transcript, 11–32.

Löw, Martina (2008): Eigenlogische Strukturen – Differenzen zwischen Städten als konzeptuelle Herausforderung. In: Helmuth Berking/Martina Löw (Hrsg.), *Die Eigenlogik der Städte. Neue Wege für die Stadtforschung.* Frankfurt am Main, Campus. 33–54.

Lugosi, Peter, Bell, David and Lugosi, Krisztina (2010): Hospitality, Culture and Regeneration: Urban Decay, Entrepreneurship and the "Ruin" Bars of Budapest. In: *Urban Studies* 47, Vol. 14: 3079–101.

Lundin, R. and Söderholm, A. (1995): A Theory of the Temporary Organization. In: *Scandinavian Journal of Management* 11, Vol. 4: 437–55.

Lütke-Daldrup, Engelbert (2004): Die perforierte Stadt. Eine Versuchsanordnung. In: *Bauwelt* 24: 40–42.

McRobbie, Angela (2002): Clubs to Companies: Notes on the Decline of Political Culture in Speeded Up Creative Worlds. In: *Cultural Studies* 16, Vol. 4: 516–31.

McRobbie, Angela (2003): I Was Knitting Away Day and Night: Die Bedeutung von Kunst und Handwerk im Modedesign In: Marion von Osten/Beatrice von Bismarck (Hrsg.), *Norm der Abweichung.* Zürich u.a., Edition Voldemeer, 99–118.

Neff, Gina, Wissinger, Elizabeth and Zukin, Sharon (2005): Entrepreneurial Labour Among Cultural Producers. "Cool" Jobs in "Hot" Industries. In: *Social Semiotics* 15, Vol. 3: 307–34.

Nuissl, Henning and Rink, Dieter (2003): *Urban Sprawl and Post-Socialist Transformation: The case of Leipzig (Germany).* Series of Working Papers (UFZ Berichte 4/03), Leipzig: UFZ Umweltforschungszentrum Leipzig-Halle GmbH.

Rae, David (2002): Entrepreneurial Emergence: A Narrative Study of Entrepreneurial Learning in Independently Owned Media Businesses. In: *The International Journal of Entrepreneurship and Innovation* 3, Vol. 1: 53–60.

Rae, David (2004): Entrepreneurial Learning: A Practical Model From the Creative Industries. In: *Education and Training* 46, Vol. 8/9: 492–500.

Scott, Allen J. (2006): Entrepreneurship, Innovation and Industrial Development: Geography and the Creative Field Revisited. In: *Small Business Economics* 26, Vol. 1: 1–24.

Steets, Silke (2005): Doing Leipzig. Räumliche Mikropolitiken des Dazwischen. In: Helmuth Berking/Martina Löw (Hrsg.), *Die Wirklichkeit der Städte.* Baden Baden, Nomos Verlagsgesellschaft, 107–22.

Steets, Silke (2008): *"Wir sind die Stadt!" Kulturelle Netzwerke und die Konstitution städtischer Räume in Leipzig*, Interdisziplinäre Stadtforschung. Frankfurt am Main: Campus.

Steyaert, Chris (2007): Life Worlds: "Entrepreneuring" as a Conceptual Attractor? A Review of Process Theories in 20 Years of Entrepreneurship Studies. In: *Entrepreneurship and Regional Development: An International Journal* 19, Vol. 6: 453–77.

Steyaert, Chris and Katz, Jerome (2004): Reclaiming the Space of Entrepreneurship in Society: Geographical, Discursive and Social Dimensions. In: *Entrepreneurship and Regional Development* 16, Vol. 3: 179–96.

van Heur, Bas (2010): *Creative Networks and the City. Towards a Cultural Politic Economy of Aesthetic Production*. Bielefeld: Transcript.

Wilson, Nicholas and Stokes, David (2005): Managing Creativity and Innovation: The Challenge for Cultural Entrepreneurs. In: *Journal of Small Business and Entreprise Development* 12, Vol. 3: 366–78.

21
TURNING THE POST-INDUSTRIAL CITY INTO THE CULTURAL CITY
The case of Toronto's waterfront

Matt Patterson and Daniel Silver

From films and Hollywood to paintings and Montmartre, the link between place and culture is well established in the popular imagination and in scholarly research (Lloyd 2004; Molotch 2003). The culture we consume often contains the trace of its geographic origins, which can be a valued part of the experience. Likewise, places are heavily shaped by the kinds of culture they produce. Just as Los Angeles makes films, the film industry "makes" Los Angeles by giving it an identity, contributing to the local economy, and drawing international attention to the city. The Louvre and the Musée d'Orsay do the same for Paris.

In the post-industrial era, regional policymakers have frequently turned to cultural production and consumption in order to create places that are economically and socially viable (Miles and Paddison 2005; Zukin 1995). Unique architecture and urban design (Julier 2005; Evans 2005), new museums (Shoval and Strom 2009), and arts districts (Mommaas 2004) are just some of the strategies that policymakers hope will create more vibrant, liveable, and productive cities. It is a perspective popularized in books such as Richard Florida's *The Rise of the Creative Class* (2002) and Charles Landry's *The Creative City* (2000).

However, cultural policies are far from an obvious choice. Their popularity is a relatively recent phenomenon, and it is still not clear how well they achieve their intended goals (e.g. Gómez 1998; Evans 2005; Markusen 2006). Additionally, critics have charged that such policies divert attention and money from more important social problems such as poverty and inequality (Peck 2005). Given these issues, how do we explain the rise and continued popularity of cultural policies?

In this chapter we address this question by examining the role of culture in the redevelopment of Toronto's central waterfront. Not traditionally known as an international centre of cultural production like Los Angeles or Paris, by the late-1990s Toronto's municipal government had embraced cultural policies with particular zeal.

The first decade of the 21st century saw a host of culture-related projects throughout the city from "starchitecture" (Patterson 2012), to "creative districts" (Catungal, Leslie, and Hii 2009), to arts festivals (Grundy and Boudreau 2008). Even Richard Florida relocated to Toronto to head a government-funded research institution. As a relative latecomer to the culture scene, Toronto offers an especially illuminating case for understanding the uptake of cultural urbanization strategies.

How did Toronto come to stake so much on cultural policy? We argue that the collapse of the industrial economy and other significant social changes in the late-20th century plunged Toronto into an "identity crisis." As old development policies and existing infrastructure appeared increasingly obsolete, policymakers were forced to grapple with the question of what kind of city Toronto should be in the 21st century. Amid this crisis, members of the cultural sector provided a convenient solution in the notion of the "cultural city." Steeped in "creative class" discourse (Florida 2002), this new urban planning model offered a vivid depiction of the urban good life characterized by artists' studios, public sculptures, and sidewalk cafes. It was also an image that resonated with a growing group of cultural organizations, knowledge workers, and downtown residents who had the capacity to put this vision into practice and codify it in municipal policy – a group that we call the "cultural city consensus."

Despite the success of this group, the cultural city has not received universal support or gone unchallenged. For others in the city, particularly those in the surrounding suburbs, different notions of the good life prevail. Thus, the rise of cultural policy is also a political phenomenon dependent not only on its appeal, but also on the support of actors with the power to implement it even against opposition stemming from alternative models.

These factors – the identity crisis, the cultural city model, and the consensus behind it – are particularly evident in the decades-long redevelopment of Toronto's central waterfront. Originally planned as an industrial port, by the 1990s the waterfront sat largely vacant. Today it is currently undergoing a dramatic transformation that has seen the rise of condominiums, office buildings serving the knowledge and "creative" economy, theatres, galleries, and even the largest soundstage in North America. Along the way, successive planning regimes cast about for ideas to revitalize the area, often without success or a clear notion of what revitalization would mean. Starting in the late-1990s, "culture" gained momentum as a potential answer, providing a legitimizing concept that could appeal to respected international authorities and forging effective links to some of the city's most dynamic organizations and influential actors. The story of culture's arrival on Toronto's waterfront provides a lens not only into the rise of cultural policy in Toronto more generally, but also into how post-industrial cities around the world are attempting to transform themselves into cultural cities.

Part I: Toronto's 21st century "identity crisis"

In the three decades leading up to the 21st century, two contradictory trends – rapid social change and stagnant urban development – disrupted existing notions of

Toronto's identity and plunged urban planning into a state of ambiguity. Among the social changes was the decline of the industrial sector and its replacement with a rising service- and knowledge-based economy (see Figures 21.1 and 21.2). By 2000 members of the "creative class" had eclipsed the traditional working class. However, this shift also came with increased inequality (Walks 2010), and wealth became geographically divided as gentrification in the core pushed poverty into the formerly middle-income suburbs (Hulchanski 2007).

Figure 21.1 Percentage of Toronto's labour market by employment sector as reported in the Canadian Census.

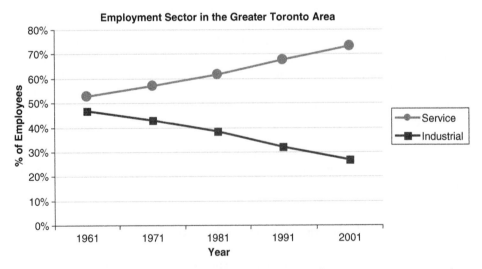

Figure 21.2 Occupations in Toronto area (creative class includes occupations in art, culture, and recreation, and the natural, social, and applied sciences).

Cultural changes were equally dramatic. In the mid-20th century Toronto was known as a conservative city dominated by White, Protestant Tories. Beginning in the late-1960s, successive waves of non-European immigration and the arrival of American war resisters transformed the city into a hotbed of social liberalism and one of the most ethnically diverse places on the continent (McIsaac 2003). Finally, capping off this period of change, Toronto's municipal government was dissolved in 1998 and amalgamated with its closest suburbs, quadrupling the city's population from 700,000 to 2.4 million and expanding its area from 97 to 630 km^2. Within the new "megacity" urbanites and suburbanites found themselves voting in the same mayoral elections, fighting over the same meagre municipal budget, and forced to decide whose lifestyle and interests should take priority.

In contrast to the dramatic changes occurring to its population, urban development in Toronto was stagnating. Twin recessions in the 1980s and government austerity measures imposed by the federal and provincial governments in the 1990s meant that Toronto's brand new population had inherited a cityscape built for a very different time. The municipal government, occupied by the complications of amalgamation, had neither the time nor the resources to undertake major city-building initiatives.

By the early-2000s the tide slowly began to turn. The new municipal government began to work out its most immediate funding and organizational problems, assisted by renewed investment from the federal and provincial governments. David Miller, a downtown city councillor, was elected mayor in 2003 and undertook an ambitious city-building agenda. Meanwhile, an unprecedented condominium boom drew billions of development dollars into the city.

However, reinvestment in Toronto's built form faced a major obstacle. Given how fast the city had changed and how long it had gone without major city-building projects, there were few obvious precedents to guide new development. The existing urban form, with its industrial waterfront, decaying brutalist buildings, and over-loaded transit system, was clearly designed for a city that no longer existed. But what exactly had Toronto become? This "identity crisis" opened up the possibility for new policy models to provide an updated account of the city's economic, cultural, and political characteristics and guidance for city-building in the 21st century.

Part II: The rise of cultural policy and the emergence of the "cultural city consensus"

During this period a more subtle transformation was occurring as culture moved from the margins to the centre of the city's policy portfolio. Throughout most of the 20th century what little municipal support existed for arts and culture in Toronto was largely the product of fierce lobbying by artists and their wealthy patrons. City Hall typically saw the arts as "a luxury and a frill which affected the lives of few people and were thought not to be widely available or desired by many" (Silcox 1974: 5). Things began to change in the 1960s as dedicated organizations and sustained funding were established, such as the Toronto Arts Council, which was founded in 1964 to distribute arts grants. The Canadian centennial celebrations of 1967 also set off a flurry of publicly-sponsored cultural activities. However, it was not until 1974 that Toronto adopted its first official plan for culture – the "Silcox Report" – which set out modest goals such as dedicating 0.25 percent of Toronto's budget to arts grants and having the city's Convention and Tourist Bureau promote local cultural services to visitors. Within the plan, culture was discursively constructed as a public good that enriched lives, and the primary purpose of cultural policy was to ensure this good was accessible to all Torontonians.

The late-1960s were also a time when culture was becoming a larger part of Toronto's private and non-governmental sector. As in other cities, new social movements emerged that were heavily tied to cultural and artistic expression. Assisted by the influx of American war resisters, Toronto's hippie movement spawned many associated scenes in music, visual arts, and theatre. Ethnic and sexual minority groups also turned to festivals and parades as a way of seeking recognition and asserting their rights. Though some of these movements were at first seen as threatening to Toronto's political establishment, they soon became entwined with mainstream institutions as artists and organizers began to take advantage of newly available grants.

By the 1980s, cultural policymakers were beginning to recognize the impact that the cultural sector was having on the local economy and arguing that cultural production was now a fundamental part of Toronto's identity (Hendry 1985).[1] Culture as a public service was still the dominant paradigm, but that would change by the late-1990s when it was recast as an economic development tool. Concepts like "liveability" and "creativity" now infused policy discourse not only as an end in themselves but also as a strategy for attracting foreign investment, skilled migrants and spurring local entrepreneurialism:

> [Toronto] needs to create an environment that nurtures and develops leading edge imagination and creativity. Arts and culture is not only a major industry within the city, but is also the epicentre of creativity that inspires ideas and innovation in many fields and is an important factor in retaining and attracting knowledge workers. ... Imagine what the city would be like without theatre, music, dance, museums, galleries, festivals, parades, poetry and story readings, and other activities that enrich our quality of life. Who would choose to live in such a place?
>
> (Toronto Economic Development 2000: 63)

In the era when public policy is increasingly conceived through the lens of global economic competition (Kipfer and Keil 2002), this new cultural city model seemed to provide the perfect solution for policymakers. Reflecting culture's discursive shift, Toronto merged its Cultural Services and Economic Development divisions in the early-2000s.

Culture's rise was further buoyed by the election of Miller, whose base support came from downtown and the cultural/knowledge sector. Miller became a personal champion of arts and culture and his tenure saw several reforms including a billboard tax that was earmarked specifically for arts funding. Additionally, the 2005/06 "Live With Culture" campaign provided several grants and programs designed to "spotlight Toronto's vibrant and diverse arts community and provide promotional opportunities for all of Toronto's cultural organizations" (City of Toronto 2005).

The new prominence of cultural policy had a reciprocal effect on the emerging networks of local artists and cultural organizations. As more public funding became available, the cultural sector became better organized and able to put the vision of a cultural city into practice. Soon organizations such as the Toronto Arts Council and Artscape (a non-profit organization dedicated to building and managing artist residences and studios) were participating in a variety of development projects from private condominiums, to public housing, to community parks, and (as we will see) waterfront redevelopment. Joining together artists, cultural organizations, city officials, real estate developers and others, this "cultural city consensus" took on characteristics akin to an urban regime (Mossberger and Stoker 2001).

Amidst Toronto's identity crisis, the cultural city model provided a useful answer to the question "what kind of city is this?" This new identity resonated with a growing segment of the population who were also willing and capable to put it into practice. Thus, culture was no longer some marginal municipal expense. It was now the all-purpose lens through which policymakers viewed and conceptualized issues as diverse as economic prosperity, urban design, and social welfare. As money began to flow back into the city in the 2000s, much of it was heavily guided by the cultural city model. Condominium developers traded public sculptures and gallery space for increased height allowances. The federal and provincial governments dedicated hundreds of millions of dollars to expand Toronto's largest cultural institutions in a project dubbed the "Cultural Renaissance" (Jenkins 2005). However, perhaps the clearest sign of culture's new dominance was its role in the ongoing $34-billion campaign to redevelop Toronto's waterfront.

Part III: Cultural policy in the remaking of Toronto's waterfront

Urban waterfronts have historically been important regional nodes of commerce, production, and public life and the subject of overlapping jurisdictions and intense political conflict. Their development or decline provides a window into how cities organize priorities, mediate competing interests, and define their collective identities. The regional importance of Toronto's waterfront was evident in 2001 when the federal, provincial, and municipal governments announced a joint campaign to redevelop 800 hectares of largely abandoned land in what was described as "one of the largest waterfront revitalization efforts ever undertaken in the world" (Waterfront Toronto n.d.). The guiding vision for the new waterfront was centred on cultural amenities and creative industries, which were expected to help draw visitors and residents to newly developed neighbourhoods and act as a sustainable source of employment.

Toronto Harbour Commission and the industrial waterfront (1911–67): The passing of an obsolescent image

What makes its place in the 2001 plan remarkable is that culture has not historically had any role in waterfront planning. Since the late-19th century, Toronto's central waterfront has been cut off from the rest of the downtown by a corridor of railways (with an expressway added in the early-1960s). Under the Toronto Harbour

Commission (THC) – a public corporation founded in 1911 to oversee Toronto's port – waterfront development in the first half of the 20th century was focused almost exclusively on the modernization of sanitation, transportation, and shipping infrastructure, as well as the filling in of marshland to create space for heavy industry (Reeves 1992). Creating landfill that could be sold or leased was the THC's economic lifeline and it continued to pursue this goal despite the absence of demand in Toronto's modest industrial sector (Desfor 1993). Waterfront recreation, which at the time was envisioned mostly as passive parkland and scenic boulevards rather than programmed cultural space, was also part of the discussion among Toronto's policy-makers, but it was inevitably pushed to the peripheries of the city in favour of industry.

A turning point came in 1967 when an updated waterfront report declared for the first time that the oldest section of Toronto's port be de-industrialized and opened to commercial and residential development. Outside this small section, however, the report renewed calls for more landfill to accommodate "the ever-increasing trade in the port" (Proctor, Redfern, Bousfield, and Bacon 1967: A10). In fact, port activity increased for only two more years before beginning a steep decline throughout the 1970s and 1980s (Desfor 1993:172). Though the THC attempted to pivot to real estate development, their efforts were limited to a few, partially-realized projects that faced significant opposition from City Hall. The city was changing around them, but they lacked the means to comprehend and guide those changes.

Harbourfront and the arrival of culture (1972–91):
From obsolescence to uncertainty

Culture first arrived on the waterfront in the mid-1970s; not as the result of any explicit plan, but as the unintended consequence of a vague promise made in the heat of the 1972 federal election. Fearing defeat, the governing Liberals announced a plan to convert 35 hectares of Toronto's industrial waterfront into open public space (Winsor 1974: 27). They would go on to win the election and then create the Harbourfront Corporation, tasked with acquiring and developing the land for the project. Right from the beginning, confusion reigned over what exactly Harbourfront was. News reports and even Toronto's own planning documents indicated that it would be a large urban park (e.g. see Baird 1974; *Globe and Mail* 1980). However, it soon became clear that the space would need to have other purposes as well. Harbourfront Corp. was required to become economically self-sufficient, which meant that some of the land would need to be leased to private developers. It was also feared that passive parkland would not be enough to draw the public past the expressway, rail yards, and still-operating industrial sites to get to the water's edge. Harbourfront needed landmark amenities, but what?

Early reports of Harbourfront Corp.'s public consultations reveal a diversity of suggestions. Some related to culture, but most suggestions were traditional recreational activities: playing fields, fitness centres, and even a rifle range (Miskian 1975; O'Malley 1976). However, being relatively simple to produce, cultural amenities soon dominated the early development of Harbourfront. When the first park was opened in the summer of 1974, a concert series was held to draw crowds (*Globe and*

Mail 1974). Soon after, an art gallery, studios, and a theatre were opened in some of the existing industrial buildings that Harbourfront Corp. had acquired. The ability to reuse these existing spaces made cultural amenities a relatively easy option early in the development phase. The amenities could also be run year round, which was a major goal of the project (Miskian 1975).

Despite these new cultural amenities, into the late-1980s Harbourfront was still struggling with what it called the "absence of a coherent character or vision" (Hack 1987: 7). For many in the press and at City Hall, Harbourfront Corp. seemed more interested in condominium development than public space (O'Malley 1976; *Globe and Mail* 1980). In fact, by 1987 only 7 hectares of parkland had been created while five high-rise condominiums had been built, with several more on the way (Nichols 1987). City Hall responded by placing a development freeze along the waterfront, effectively cutting off Harbourfront Corp.'s source of income. In 1991, the federal government (now under the Conservatives) dissolved Harbourfront Corp. and created a new non-profit organization, Harbourfront Centre, to maintain the collection of cultural amenities that had already been created. Harbourfront Centre proceeded to re-brand itself firmly as a cultural organization and distance its previous incarnation as the controversial land developer (Harris 1992; Hume 1995), eventually embracing the discourse of the cultural city.

While the THC suffered from an obsolete understanding of Toronto and its waterfront, Harbourfront Corp.'s problem was that it had no clear vision to begin with. In the three decades since the port began its decline, the THC and Harbourfront Corp. had succeeded in developing only a handful of offices and condominiums. What they did build was considered by many to be urban planning failures: bunker-like buildings that threatened to further block the waterfront from the rest of the city. Disapproval of these buildings led to a debate over whether or not the THC and Harbourfront Corp could be trusted with all of the vacant land (Reeves 1992: 125). This loss of trust, combined with the general decline in urban development throughout the 1980s and 1990s and the rapid disappearance of the city's industrial sector, meant that the waterfront sat in stasis; a material embodiment of Toronto's identity crisis. Describing it in 1994, architectural critic John Bentley Mays called the waterfront "a strange landscape [which,] if not picturesque, ... is graced with a subtle melancholy" (1994: 2–3).

Waterfront Toronto (2001–present): From stasis to action

Of all the projects that emerged as city-building returned in the early-2000s, waterfront revitalization was by far the largest and most ambitious. The project began with the founding of yet another public development corporation, Waterfront Toronto (WT). As the first stages got underway, initial public scepticism gave way to a mixture of enthusiasm and anxiety. Writing in 2006, journalist John Lornic laid out the stakes as seen by many policymakers:

> Post-industrial cities face two starkly different choices ... One leads to privatized waterfronts dominated by controlled-access view-oriented condo projects and theme-park-style uses such as casinos; the other produces

public waterfronts organized around generous open spaces and landmark heritage and cultural venues, supported by mixed-use neighbourhoods.

(Lornic 2008 [2006]: 296)

This characterization is noticeably influenced by the perceived failures of the THC and Harbourfront Corp. However, it also demonstrates how the cultural city provided a relatively clear, alternative vision that WT could embrace – a vision that was already achieving widespread legitimacy among many of the relevant agencies that would be involved in waterfront planning.

Reflecting this new civic identity, as well as policymakers' increased tendency to think in terms of global competition, the 2001 report on waterfront revitalization described Toronto as "one of an elite group of world cities which act as gateways to commerce, culture and tourism for their respective countries" (Fung 2001: 13). Unlike previous waterfront planning documents, this report was filled with references to other "world cities" such as Barcelona, London, and New York. What its authors found in these cities were clear precedents for culture-centred, post-industrial waterfronts. Images of the Sydney Opera House and the Museo Guggenheim Bilbao were contrasted with the vacant lots along Toronto's lakefront, providing evidence that the city was lagging behind and demonstrating what it could become.

Along with this new vision, WT benefited from the emerging networks of cultural organizations within the city. Unlike Harbourfront Corp., WT could focus exclusively on development and leave public programming to the specialists. Whenever an industrial heritage building needed to be preserved through reuse or when an empty lot was to be set aside for public space, WT could simply hand them over to a cultural organization. For example, Artscape took over several abandoned industrial buildings and turned them into studios and galleries in what is now called the "Distillery District." And when the City's Forestry Department moved its tree nursery out of the waterfront area, Toronto Cultural Services worked with a local record label to use the land for an annual music festival. Among the members of the "cultural city consensus," there appeared to be no shortage of players who had the knowledge and capacity to take on waterfront revitalization.

WT also embraced cultural and creative industries as a source of economic production and employment. Making room for what they called the "new economy" – tourism, technology, media, and professional services – was the primary justification behind the revitalization effort. Under the cultural city model there was widespread agreement among local policymakers that these industries now constituted the "core" of Toronto's economy. Thus, waterfront revitalization was not just a frill or election-time gift as it had been in 1972. Just as in the industrial era, the waterfront now seemed essential to the city's economic future. The existence of 800 hectares of largely vacant land so close to downtown was ideal to accommodate the new economy which, the report argued, would require a "technologically modern, flexible live/work space in an attractive and interesting context" (Fung 2001: 23).

Fulfilling this ideal meant pursuing businesses that embodied the new economy. Toronto's Economic Development division, with support from Mayor Miller, was particularly active in attracting two major developments: Corus Entertainment, a major Canadian media company, and Filmport, a film studio that features the largest soundstage in North America. Both businesses received tax breaks and other incentives as encouragement for relocating along the waterfront. Corus was particularly controversial because its headquarters was built on land that WT had designated for a major cultural amenity. City Hall, which owned the land, saw the opportunity to attract a major cultural business as a higher priority. Thus, overlapping jurisdictions and disagreements between public agencies have not been completely eliminated, even if they were eased by the unifying theme of culture.

Alternative visions for the waterfront

Conversely, realizing this new culture-centred waterfront has meant protecting it from incongruent uses. Despite culture's dominance in the official plan, it continues to compete with alternatives proposed by those outside the cultural city consensus. Among these outsiders is current mayor Rob Ford (elected 2010). Two alternative approaches in particular have produced some of the most heated political controversies along the waterfront.

First, heavy infrastructure has continued to survive, including power plants, an expressway, (much reduced) rail lines, and the Toronto Island Airport. Efforts by other public agencies to expand this infrastructure for the 21st century have been strongly opposed by Miller and his allies with only partial success. The Ontario government, ignoring the protests of Miller and WT, built a power plant along the waterfront in 2008. And though Miller was successful in opposing a new bridge connecting the airport to the mainland, the airport has continued to expand its capacity (with support from Ford). Finally, City Council has been deadlocked over whether to rehabilitate or remove the now-dilapidated waterfront expressway.

A second alternative is what Hannigan (1998) calls "fantasy city" development: self-contained, heavily-branded, consumer environments that attract visitors from much larger regions (typically by car), but are isolated from surrounding neighbourhoods. They often include casinos, convention centres, sports stadiums, and shopping centres. Though Toronto's waterfront has seen a few of these developments in the late-20th century, they have never been popular among the downtown residents or members of the cultural city consensus. Part of the motivation behind the 2001 WT plan was to prevent private developers from building "big box" and other large, regional retail outlets (Fung 2001: 20).

While virtually nonexistent under Miller, Ford has proposed or supported a variety of fantasy city projects including a casino, a 1.6 million-square-foot "megamall," a major sports facility, and a Ferris wheel, and has directly criticized WT's plans for taking too long to realize (Rider and Dale 2011). Despite his efforts, Ford's plans have consistently been rejected by City Council with strong, public encouragement from the same academics and urban planners who have been instrumental in popularizing the cultural city model (e.g. Cities Centre 2011).

Whatever their outcome, the conflicts between WT's plan and its alternatives remind us that culture is not the only way to develop the post-industrial city. Due to the vast amount of empty land so close to the core, Toronto's waterfront will continue to be a valuable resource over which a diversity of communities and interest groups project their own vision of urbanity.

Conclusion

While policymakers themselves often argue that the cultural city model is simply the most rational way to plan Toronto for the 21st century, we argue that rational planning alone does not explain the zeal by which this model has been embraced. In this chapter we have argued that three factors in particular have paved the way for the rise of the cultural city. First, rapid social change and the breakdown in conventional planning plunged Toronto into an "identity crisis," creating opportunity for new policy models to emerge at the turn of the millennium. Second, policymakers slowly developed the notion of Toronto as a "cultural city." Drawing on local and international discursive influences, they provided a new account of the urban good life in the 21st century and a relatively clear set of associated policy guidelines. Finally, the adoption of this model in major city-building initiatives such as waterfront redevelopment cannot be explained outside the coalition of downtown residents, knowledge workers, cultural organizations, and others in the cultural city consensus. For this group, the notion of a cultural city is both a desirable and realistic vision of urban life that fits with their own experiences. Furthermore, they had the power and capacity to put this vision into practice.

However, the conflicts that have erupted over the waterfront, as well as the election of Mayor Ford on a low-tax, pro-car platform, highlight the fact that many Torontonians have different priorities when it comes to urban governance. Ford's political base of suburban and lower-educated voters may find little appeal or real opportunity in the cultural city. Indeed, data show that the "creative" economy is much more likely to be situated downtown, whereas traditional blue-collar industries are more likely to be located in the suburbs.[2] These cultural and lifestyle differences compound the geographic divide in wealth. As inequality in Toronto becomes greater, it is reasonable to expect further conflict over the direction of urban planning and greater challenges to establishing models that achieve widespread consensus. Indeed, this is a trend that is occurring in cities across the world.

Though we cannot say for sure what the future will hold for the cultural city model, developing an empirically-grounded, social scientific understanding of where the model has come from (as opposed to relying on policymakers' or politicians' own justifications) will put us in a better position to grapple with new challenges, the possibility of future breakdowns, identity crises, and the formation of new policy models.

Notes

1 In its 1985 report on culture Toronto boldly declared itself the "arts/culture capital of English Canada" (Hendry 1985: 26).
2 These statements are based on an analysis of the North American Industry Classification System (NAICS) survey for 2006. Data available upon request.

References

Baird, George. 1974. *On Building Downtown*. Toronto: City of Toronto.

Catungal, John Paul, Deborah Leslie, and Yvonne Hii. 2009. "Geographies of Displacement in the Creative City: The Case of Liberty Village, Toronto." *Urban Studies* 46 (5/6): 1095–114.

Cities Centre, University of Toronto. 2011. "Letter to Toronto City Council." Retrieved November 20, 2013 from www.citiescentre.utoronto.ca/Assets/Cities+Centre+2013+Digital+Assets/Cities+Centre/Cities+Centre+Digital+Assets/pdfs/publications/Port+Lands+Letter+Sept19.pdf.

City of Toronto. 2005, June 13. "Mayor Miller Announces Major New Initiative for Toronto Arts and Culture – 'Live With Culture' Launched." Press release. Toronto.

Desfor, Gene. 1993. "Restructuring the Toronto Harbour Commission: Land Politics on the Toronto Waterfront." *Journal of Transport Geography* 1(3): 167–81.

Evans, Graeme. 2005. "Measure for Measure: Evaluating the Evidence of Culture's Contribution to Regeneration." *Urban Studies* 42(5/6): 959–83.

Florida, Richard. 2002. *The Rise of the Creative Class*. New York: Basic Books.

Fung, Robert. 2001. *Our Toronto Waterfront*. Toronto: Toronto Waterfront Revitalization Task Force.

Globe and Mail. 1974, July 2. "Music, Clowns, Actors Open Harbourfront '74." P. 27.

Globe and Mail. 1980, May 19. "Parkland Invaders." Editorial. P. 6.

Gómez, María V. 1998. "Reflective Images: The Case of Urban Regeneration in Glasgow and Bilbao." *International Journal of Urban and Regional Research* 22(1): 106–21.

Grundy, John and Julie-Anne Boudreau. 2008. "'Living With Culture': Creative Citizenship Practices in Toronto." *Citizenship Studies* 12(4): 347–63.

Hack, Gary. 1987. *Recharting a Course for Harbourfront*. Ottawa: Public Works Canada.

Hannigan, John. 1998. *Fantasy City*. London: Routledge.

Harris, Christopher. 1992, May 9. "What's in a Name? Harbourfront Centre Hopes to Retreat from Image as Developer." *Globe and Mail*. C14.

Hendry, Tom. 1985. *Cultural Capital*. Toronto: City of Toronto.

Hulchanski, J. David 2007. "The Three Cities Within Toronto: Income Polarization Among Toronto's Neighbourhoods, 1970–2005." *Research Bulletin 41*. Cities Centre, University of Toronto.

Hume, Christopher. 1995, April 8. "On the Rocks: Harbourfront Has Never Been a Happy Ship, But the Odds Are it Will Be Refloated and Sail Again." *Toronto Star* C1.

Jenkins, Barbara. 2005. "Toronto's Cultural Renaissance." *Canadian Journal of Communication* 30(2): 169–86.

Julier, Guy. 2005. "Urban Designscapes and the Production of Aesthetic Consent." *Urban Studies* 42(5): 869–87.

Kipfer, Stefan and Roger Keil. 2002. "Toronto Inc? Planning the Competitive City in the New Toronto." *Antipode* 34(2): 227–64.

Landry, Charles. 2000. *The Creative City*. London: Earthscan.

Lloyd, Richard. 2004. "The Neighbourhood in Cultural Production: Material and Symbolic Resources in the New Bohemia." *City and Community* 3(4): 343–71.

Lornic, John. 2008 [2006]. *The New City*. Toronto: Penguin Books.

Markusen, A. 2006. "Urban Development and the Politics of a Creative Class: Evidence from a Study of Artists". *Environment and Planning A* 38(10): 1921–40.

Mays, John Bentley. 1994. *Emerald City*. Toronto: Penguin Books.

McIsaac, Elizabeth. 2003. "Immigrants in Canadian Cities: Census 2001 – What Do the Data Tell Us?" *Policy Options*. May, 2003: 58–63.

Miles, Steven and Ronan Paddison. 2005. "The Rise and Rise of Culture-led Urban Regeneration." *Urban Studies* 42(5/6): 833–39.

Miskian, H. E. 1975. *Planning Harbourfront 1*. Ottawa: Ministry of State for Urban Affairs.

Molotch, Harvey. 2003. *Where Stuff Comes From*. New York: Routledge.

Mommaas, Hans. 2004. "Cultural Clusters and the Post-industrial City: Toward the Remapping of Urban Cultural Policy." *Urban Studies* 41(3): 507–32.

Mossberger, Karen and Gerry Stoker. 2001. "The Evolution of Urban Regime Theory: The Challenge of Conceptualization." *Urban Affairs Review* 36(6): 810–35.

Nichols, Mark. 1987, August 24. "Battles on the Waterfront." *Maclean's*. P. 20.

O'Malley, Martin. 1976, January 14. "What Happened to Waterfront for the People?" *Globe and Mail*. P. 7.

Patterson, Matt. 2012. "The Role of the Public Institution in Iconic Architectural Development." *Urban Studies* 49(15): 3289–305.

Peck, J. 2005. "Struggling with the Creative Class". *International Journal of Urban and Regional Research* 29(4): 740–70.

Proctor, Redfern, Bousfield and Bacon Consulting Engineers and Town Planners. 1967. *The Waterfront Plan for the Metropolitan Toronto Planning Area*. Toronto.

Reeves, Wayne C. 1992. *Visions for the Metropolitan Toronto Waterfront, Volume II*. Toronto: Centre for Urban and Community Studies, University of Toronto.

Rider, David and Daniel Dale. 2011, August 30. "Doug Ford's Dream Waterfront? Ferris Wheel, Monorail and Boat-In Hotel." *Toronto Star*. Retrieved 2013, November 1 from www. thestar.com/news/gta/2011/08/30/doug_fords_dream_waterfront_ferris_wheel_monorail_and_a_boatin_hotel.html.

Shoval, Noam and Elizabeth Strom. 2009. "Inscribing Universal Values into the Urban Landscape: New York, Jerusalem, and Winnipeg as Case Studies." *Urban Geography* 30(2): 143–61.

Silcox, David P. 1974. *Metropolitan Toronto's Support of the Arts*. Toronto: City of Metropolitan Toronto.

Toronto Economic Development. 2000. *Toronto Economic Development Strategy*. Toronto: City of Toronto.

Walks, Alan 2010. *Toronto Election 2010 Discussion Paper #11: Inequality in Toronto*. Toronto: Cities Centre, University of Toronto.

Waterfront Toronto. n.d. *Scope and Scale*. Retrieved March 25, 2013, from www.waterfron toronto.ca/about_us/scope_and_scale.

Winsor, Hugh. 1974, Jul 2. "A 1972 Liberal Election Promise Fulfilled." *Globe and Mail*. P. 27.

Zukin, Sharon. 1995. *The Cultures of Cities*. Malden, MA: Blackwell.

Part IV

CULTURAL INDUSTRIES AND LABOUR

That a volume on the cultural industries would be unthinkable without a separate section that looks at questions of labour is a mark of how significant this area of research has become in the last 20 years. Although questions of production have always been important to cultural industries research, the political question of labour – who gets to make culture and under what conditions – has sharpened enormously, as research from around the world reveals a consistent pattern of exclusion and exploitation that seems to be deteriorating rather than improving.

At the same time, traditional questions of cultural labour remain. What makes it different from other work? How is it to be managed, both by the self and by others? What are the pleasures that compel so many to continue to take the risks that this kind of precarious labour entails?

We have sought to avoid the traditional pairing of 'optimistic' and 'pessimistic' narratives of cultural work in this section. Very few serious researchers now wish to promote the millennial view of Dan Pink's (2002) *Free Agent Nation*, while at the same time detailed qualitative research reveals the complexities and nuances of workers' attitudes to the questions of inequality in their own labour markets. We have instead sought to approach the question of labour from a variety of angles (and labour appears elsewhere in this volume, see Murray and Banks for example) all of which offer an excellent introduction to the rich literature this area is now producing.

Brook looks at cultural labour in the wider context of underemployment and the so called 'hourglass economy', to try to unpick the values that are derived from such work, not simply in terms of what is sometimes referred to as intrinsic rewards, but as a way of negotiating the increasingly complex terrain of such an economy. This is not a simple story about 'transferable skills', but by looking beyond paid work to all forms of cultural production, and to wider notions such as that of 'vocation', Brook encourages us to see cultural work as a form of self-cultivation that goes beyond simply preparing oneself for the labour market.

Bilton looks at the management of cultural work and argues compellingly for an approach to it that recognises the distinctiveness of cultural labour and the need to avoid a generic, 'creative' approach to management that sees no difference between this and other forms of 'knowledge' work. He notes that while 'creativity' is by no means the preserve of the 'creative industries', there is still a need to 'protect the integrity of cultural products and the autonomy of cultural producers from the demands of the market', nicely making the distinction that this volume advocates. He also considers the educational implications of this (see also Noonan this volume), as higher education remains a principal supplier of both workers and managers in the cultural industries. In the sometimes unseemly rush to benefit from the growth of the creative sectors, higher education institutions have not only sometimes appeared to forget their traditional role as providers of artistic education but have also devalued the very competences that helped generations of cultural workers manage the very messy and complex business of work in these sectors, not by denying the twin drivers of creativity and commerce, but by wrestling with them.

Miller also looks at cultural work in the context of work more generally, arguing that it has become 'a shadow-setter' for conditions of labour, as consumers take on more of the productive work and the difficulty of getting payment for any sort of labour increases. He hints at the possibility for social movements linked to such precarious labour, a theme taken up by de Peuter and Cohen, whose chapter provides a rich and empirically detailed account of the emerging labour politics in this field. They take the traditional cultural industry concern with autonomy and reposition it as a political weapon that can be used collectively, as well as individually, to unlock questions about meaning, power and justice in the cultural workplace. By considering different forms of worker organisation and the wider policy context in which they take place, they challenge the myth of the self-interested or passive cultural worker and, while not denying the difficulties, provide some grounds for optimism about a rapidly changing, and politicising, field.

The scale of the problem of inequality in the sectors is brought home by Randle's piece, which provides a detailed account of the exclusions and inequalities that characterise cultural labour markets – in this case in the audiovisual sectors – in the United Kingdom and elsewhere. As Randle reminds us, there are differences in the class, gender and ethnic composition of the workforce between different cultural sectors and it is unwise to over-generalise – but the more glamorous the sector, the greater seems the exclusions; and the more central to our cultural life, the narrower the range of voices we are exposed to. These are questions of labour and of social justice, but as this section reminds us they are also profound questions of cultural value.

Reference

Pink, D. (2002) *Free Agent Nation*, New York: Warner Books.

22
MANAGEMENT IN THE CULTURAL INDUSTRIES

Chris Bilton

Over the past decade a number of books have explored new models of management in the cultural industries (e.g. Bilton 2007; Townley and Beech 2011; Parrish 2005; Bilton and Cummings 2010). At the same time, numerous universities and business schools, especially at postgraduate level, have begun to offer courses in creative enterprise, cultural entrepreneurship and cultural (or creative) industries.[1]

These developments have prompted criticism and scepticism amongst both arts and humanities scholars and business school academics. In cultural policy studies, there is growing concern about perceived 'managerialism' in the cultural sector; Jim McGuigan, for example, suggests that grouping 'creativity' with 'management' is a 'category error' (McGuigan 2009: 297). From the opposing wing, management scholars have meanwhile questioned the need for a 'creative' or 'cultural' approach to management. Chris Warhurst points out that there is no compelling evidence that a different model of 'creative' management is justified or effective (Warhurst 2011). If artists and musicians want to learn about management and entrepreneurship, why not acquire some basic skills at a business or management school?

Both these criticisms are vindicated by the nature of professional training offered to those entering the cultural and creative industries. Many of those undertaking arts and humanities degrees at UK universities (both academic and practical) are sheltered from management and business concerns. At the same time (and perhaps recognising a market opportunity), UK business schools are increasingly involved in delivering 'creative' management courses (for example the music business course recently launched by the Henley Management School, or Warwick Business School's 'Create' initiative). On the one hand, the old divide between arts or humanities based courses and management education persists, especially at undergraduate level; on the other hand, business and management schools are promoting a 'business as usual' approach to management in the cultural and creative industries, capitalising on a perception that the creative economy is growing faster than many traditional business sectors.

These two trends are of course to some extent self-fulfilling. As business schools and business skills become more implicated in 'creative' management courses, some traditional arts and humanities scholars and students will perceive business priorities encroaching onto the 'autonomy' of the arts and culture sector. Their discomfort is likely to become more acute as management scholars and business schools argue that cultural organisations will be better served not by a new approach to 'creative' management but by a better implementation of existing management techniques. So the divisions and mutual suspicions widen; cultural practitioners are alienated by a 'managerial' discourse and managers are unimpressed by the special pleading of the arts for a cultural exception from orthodox management rules and techniques.

In this chapter I will argue that management of the cultural industries is different, in degree if not in kind, from other forms of management. Moreover the autonomy of cultural producers and practitioners will depend to a large extent on their ability to develop and legitimise a distinctive approach to 'creative' management that is not 'business as usual'. I will begin by exploring the arguments for a distinctive approach to management in the cultural industries. I will then explore some of the difficulties in implementing such an approach in university courses. Finally I will consider the wider context, in which 'business as usual' as practised by large technology firms is increasingly marginalising 'creative management' in the cultural and creative industries, making the need for a model of autonomous creative management (or self-management) all the more pressing.

The cultural industries – not business as usual?

One of the first serious attempts to define a distinctive approach to management in the cultural industries was Dag Björkegren's *The Culture Business: Management Strategies for the Arts-Related Business*. One of Björkegren's key distinctions was between a 'cultural business strategy' and a 'commercial business strategy' (Björkegren 1996). The commercial business strategy, which Björkegren associated with the film industry's 'blockbuster' movies of the 1980s (Björkegren 1993), uses forceful marketing to manufacture 'hit' products that succeed on the market's terms. The cultural business strategy, which Björkegren associates with literary publishing, pursues success on the artist's terms, and is premised on the intrinsic value of cultural products. He gives the example of the work of Samuel Beckett (Björkegren 1993), eventually finding a market more than a decade after publication on terms set by the author and the publisher, not by the market.

Björkegren's distinction here is similar to the difference between 'arts marketing' and marketing (Bilton 2007: 142–44; Colbert 2007: 10–15). Ordinarily, marketing takes its cue from a customer's 'needs and wants' and adapts the product, and indeed the rest of the business, to delivering particular benefits to the customer. Arts marketing is more likely to be product-led, and will seek out customers on terms set by the producer and product (Colbert 2007: 8–10). Like Björkegren's cultural business strategy, the arts marketer trusts in the intrinsic value of a cultural product; such a 'product-led' approach would be disparaged by orthodox marketing, which prioritises the needs of the customer.

In reality most cultural producers employ a combination of 'commercial' and 'cultural' logics – they cannot afford to ignore their audiences and readers, but on the other hand simply attempting to give audiences 'what they want' is unlikely to be entirely successful either. As observed by Lord Reith, founding Director-General of the BBC, when it comes to cultural consumption, 'few know what they want, fewer what they need'. Cultural consumers may desire unprecedented experiences rather than familiar products; they may resist the marketer's predictive profiling because through cultural consumption they are attempting to reinvent and redefine themselves rather than simply reproducing and reinforcing their identity through consumption choices (Firat et al. 1995; Kellner 1992).

The idea that marketing of cultural products requires us to develop some different models and strategies could be applied across other aspects of management and strategy, from organisational structure to strategic planning. Listing all of these variations is beyond the scope of this chapter, but we can observe that cultural products and cultural consumers appear to behave differently from other products and consumers. For example, the cultural industries are characterised by high levels of risk and unpredictability at the point of production (Banks et al. 2000) meaning that emergent and experimental approaches may be more effective than deliberate 'top down' strategic planning (Mintzberg and Waters 1985). Cultural consumers may be motivated not only by satisfying needs and wants but also by challenging their needs and wants by engaging in 'difficult' aesthetic experiences (Boorsma 2005). They may seek pleasure through the experience of consumption rather than through the rational satisfaction of desired outcomes and goals (Hirschmann and Holbrook 1982). Leaders of cultural organisations may need to be more attuned to the way skills and creativity are distributed through the organisation, and allow space for 'leadership from below' rather than assuming that decision-making starts at the top with a 'heroic' model of leadership and creativity (Bilton 2010: 260–62). The defining characteristics of the cultural and creative industries – the unpredictable, value-laden nature of 'symbolic goods', the emotional and irrational aspects of cultural production and consumption, the need for creative processes and peoples to be governed by a light touch rather than by hierarchical structures – all point towards the need for a distinctive approach to cultural management.

However, these distinctions are not entirely clear-cut. As 'ordinary manufacturing industry' becomes more akin to the production of culture, the characteristics of the cultural and creative industries are becoming increasingly common in other sectors, from manufacturing and services to technology (Rifkin 2000; Lash and Urry 1994). In this context of convergence between industries and products, Warhurst's argument that cultural management is not so far removed from business as usual starts to make sense. 'Creativity' is not the exclusive preserve of the creative industries. Emergent strategy, distributed leadership, post-Fordist organisational structures and processes, team-based approaches to tasks, 'hedonic' and 'experiential' modes of consumption are found in almost every industry, and are a staple of mainstream management courses. The pragmatic argument that cultural organisations need a distinctive approach to cultural management based on their 'unique' characteristics appears rather tenuous.

But Björkegren's approach to cultural management is not purely pragmatic. He is also interested in the ethics of cultural production, in particular the extent to which managers can protect the integrity of cultural products and the autonomy of cultural producers from the demands of the market. Cultural organisations are not only governed by the logic of the market – the fact that Samuel Beckett's publishers adopted a 'cultural business strategy' cannot be explained simply as a business decision. Cultural producers and cultural consumers are driven by emotional, subjective values as much as 'rational' economic self-interest; paradoxically, emotional commitment rather than professional detachment may thus in the long run be a source of competitive advantage. Understanding this, and finding ways to deal with it through 'management', remains a distinctive challenge for people working in the cultural industries. Of course, non-financial measures, intangible benefits and emotional engagement are increasingly important in all aspects of our economy. But for the cultural industries, these aspects are not peripheral or optional, they are at the core of both the creative process and the experience of consumption; and these elements are filtered through individual experience, emotion and values. Which brings us to the question of how 'management in the cultural industries' can be communicated through education.

Management in the cultural industries – the educational challenge

Professional training of cultural managers is a comparatively recent phenomenon. The idea of generic management skills, competences or 'tools' that could be applied across any industry or sector only took hold with the invention of Taylorism and 'scientific' approaches to management approximately one hundred years ago. Most of our business schools and business studies degrees and management consultancies have an even younger history. And it was only in the latter part of the twentieth century that these management principles were imported into the cultural sector.

With the introduction of government funding for the arts following the end of the Second World War in 1945, Britain's transition from an amateur arts world to professional cultural bureaucracy was typical of developments across Western Europe, with paternalistic government policies replacing patronage and muddling through.

Through the nineteenth century many of the United Kingdom's leading cultural organisations were run by enthusiastic amateurs. Conversely, cultural practitioners from Dickens to Henry Irving were also cultural entrepreneurs, setting up magazines, running exhibitions or opening venues in order to promote their own work and that of their circle. Arts management was a natural extension of arts practice. That amateur spirit was clearly audible in the speech of the Arts Council's new director in 1945, the economist John Maynard Keynes, and his cheerfully laissez-faire exhortation to 'let every part of England be merry in its own way'.

The newly professionalised Council replaced two amateur organisations, the Council for the Encouragement of Music and the Arts (CEMA) and the Entertainments National Service Association (ENSA). The process of professionalisation accelerated as funding regimes became tighter and more accountable during the latter decades of the twentieth century.

From the mid-1980s the management of subsidised arts organisations in the United Kingdom became increasingly complex. With reductions in government funding came an increasing emphasis on accountability. Arts organisations were required to monitor quantitative and qualitative targets on audience composition and other funding priorities in order to meet the conditions for public funding. At the same time they were having to increase earned income as public funding became more constrained (and competitive). In the early 1990s the Arts Council of Great Britain encouraged arts organisations to invest in marketing, and 'arts marketing' emerged as a specialist field in its own right, with its own textbooks, training schemes and job titles. Arts education, previously a more or less idealistic attempt at cultural democratisation, became increasingly entangled with arts marketing in its new variants of 'audience development' or 'widening participation'. The neoliberal turn in arts policy was paralleled by a new managerialism in the arts sector. And whilst these changes have been much criticised (McGuigan 2005), we should conversely be wary of idealising the old amateur ethos.

Changes in policy and management were reflected in changes in recruitment. Whereas in the early 1980s many senior cultural managers had been internally promoted or recruited from within the cultural sector, much like the practitioner-managers of a century previously, during the 1990s the major cultural institutions – the Royal Opera House, the South Bank, the BBC, even the Arts Council itself – increasingly looked outwards, importing commercial management expertise from retail, the entertainment industry, law and finance. These new management professionals conferred a legitimacy on the cultural organisations that hired them. At a time when cultural organisations were viewed by some elements in the government and civil service as unmanageable, wasteful or unaccountable, the presence of mainstream business professionals on the board, however tokenistic or ineffective, was a reassuring symbol of probity and rigour.

Universities responded to this demand for a new 'cadre' of arts managers (Boltanski and Chiapello 2005: 57–62). The first arts management courses in the United Kingdom emerged in the early 1990s; what started as a handful of courses across the country now numbers in the hundreds, and what was once an exotic subsidiary of management studies is now a major source of revenue for UK higher education, recruiting students from across the world who are keen to learn from and work in the United Kingdom's apparently burgeoning creative and media industries. Graduates in arts and cultural management are trained to take up the demands of managing arts organisations without needing to be promoted from within. The new generation of cultural managers do not need to be former artists; and for those who are, the emphasis is on learning a new discipline rather than drawing on past experience. Just as cultural organisations sought legitimacy from the world of business, cultural management programmes have imported assumptions, models, methods, even entire modules and courses from schools of management and business.

One consequence of this new emphasis on business skills is a devaluing of cultural competences. In my own experience of teaching, students from an arts background (either a first degree in an arts-based subject, or a professional arts practice) are swift to dismiss their previous subject knowledge and expertise. Whilst students with some experience of commercial business are more sceptical towards the 'common sense' of management, younger students in particular are all too eager to reject cultural values and ideals in favour of the slick certainties of business, embracing this new faith with the passion of a convert.

No doubt some of the tools and models that have been developed in business schools can offer valuable insights to cultural managers; equally, creative processes and methods from the arts can add value to business. The key is a critical and selective approach rather than a wholesale embrace of one rationale over the other. This in turn might mean reconnecting with some aspects of the 'cultural business strategy' described by Björkegren and recognising that business schools do not have a monopoly on management wisdom.

Educational systems in the United Kingdom do not lend themselves to such an integrated approach. Specialisation in arts or sciences begins in secondary schools and is reinforced by the disciplinary boundaries of universities. Yet in the cultural industries especially, a more holistic approach is surely desirable.

One of the limitations of conventional approaches to management and strategy in the business school curriculum is that business schools have grown up with a model of Anglo-American big business, based on multiple business units, rigid structures and strategies, operating in stable economies and ever-expanding markets. That model looks increasingly out of date. It is not surprising, therefore, that today's business schools are seeking inspiration from alternative models and methods of management, including those of the cultural industries. It is ironic indeed that cultural management courses are still promoting a 'commercial business strategy', whilst business schools are increasingly drawn to a 'cultural business strategy' that values artistic experiences, 'creativity' and 'design thinking'.

The cultural industries are characterised by small, informal enterprises, project-based work, teams and individuals working in short bursts on prototypes and one-off innovations. Here the routines and roles of 'creative' and 'management' work converge. 'Cultural entrepreneurship' describes an attempt to reconcile and embody these two modes and, despite the well-documented tensions between 'creatives' and 'suits' in the commercial creative industries, there remains some residual mutual respect based on mutual dependency. University courses in cultural entrepreneurship and creative enterprise reflect the duality between 'cultural' and 'commercial' business strategies without setting them against each other. In the short run at least, most of our students will embody both sides of the creative business in one person; given the scale of many creative enterprises, there is no strict division between creative and managerial roles. This flexibility and complexity is precisely why business schools are interested in the cultural sector as a source of new ideas and methods.

Majors and independents

One of the difficulties in defining an approach to management in the cultural industries is the disparity in scale, ethos and structure that separates small and large cultural enterprises. If we consider the value chain of the cultural industries, from origination and development through to marketing, distribution and consumption, these differences become more understandable. In the following section I will consider how changes in the value chain have exacerbated these differences, widening the gap between 'cultural' and 'commercial' approaches to management.

It is a truism that the cultural industries are characterised by high levels of risk and unpredictability (Bilton 1999; Banks et al. 2000). This is traceable to the pressure to innovate and to the uncertain nature of prototype production and project-based enterprise. Above all, risk reflects the cultural industries' dependence on subjective judgements at the point of consumption in order to ascertain the value of symbolic goods; until and after cultural products have been experienced by audiences and consumers their meaning and value (both aesthetic and financial) remain uncertain.

Following from this, risk and uncertainty are unevenly distributed along the value chain, with most of the risky judgements taking place at the point of production; here, indeed, in the words of screenwriter William Goldman, 'Nobody knows anything'. As the product moves along the value chain, an accumulation of investments by other stakeholders (investors and intermediaries) as well as painstaking product and market testing have begun to legitimise the value of the prototype product and mitigate the risks of production. The closer the product comes to the customer and to the point of consumption, the more likely it is that cultural intermediaries can both predict and influence the end user's response. Of course distributors and marketers in the cultural industries are also taking risks – but often the challenge lies not so much in the degree of uncertainty as in the scale of investment required. Ideas are cheap, but marketing, packaging and distributing them can become expensive. Cultural producers are making relatively small investments in relatively unpredictable products and processes in conditions of extreme uncertainty; cultural distributors are making larger investments in products that have already been partially filtered by preceding decisions and investments, meaning that the initial high uncertainty has been some-what reduced. In terms of the value chain, their higher bargaining power has also allowed them to discard high-risk or failed prototypes in favour of those products most likely (in their admittedly fallible judgement) to succeed in the market.

The disparity in risk between cultural production and cultural distribution is reflected in the relative scale of cultural enterprises and the geography of the cultural industries. Cultural producers are typically small enterprises, with high levels of self-employment and with those enterprises which do not operate as sole traders typically employing fewer than ten people. Whilst there are of course significant variations, this picture is still remarkably similar across television, music, film and publishing. Cultural producers are embedded in local networks of co-dependency (Scott 1999) that help them to manage risks of cultural production (Banks et al. 2000).

Cultural distributors are typically global corporations that have solved the problem of risk by cross-subsidising hits and misses across product portfolios and markets. Whereas cultural producers are essentially micro-enterprises, cultural distributors (broadcasters, record labels, publishers) have typically consolidated their market position through mergers and acquisitions across media and territories. Convergent technologies have blurred the boundaries between media, allowing cultural distributors to take advantage of synergies across platforms, thereby facilitating the economic concentration that has seen an ever-diminishing number of major corporations commanding an ever-increasing share of a global market. And whereas cultural pro-duction might still be rooted in a particular time and place, cultural distribution operates globally, following the logic of the common denominator towards an offer of fewer standardised products to larger (globalised) markets (Levitt 1986).

Of course this is a broad brush picture of the cultural industries. Nevertheless, large sections of the cultural industries share this 'hollowed out' structure in which a large number of smaller 'independent' cultural production enterprises orbit larger global 'major' cultural distribution enterprises. Whereas the cultural producers are essentially concerned with the production of culture and more likely to gravitate towards the values and assumptions of Björkegren's 'cultural business' approach, cultural distributors are concerned with delivering products 'on the market's terms', with economies of scale and perceived market needs taking precedence – in line with Björkegren's 'commercial business strategy'. The 'long tail' (Anderson 2004) has only partially challenged this pattern. Democratisation of production has been offset by centralisation of distribution, with a new generation of intermediaries consolidating their grip on the cultural industries value chain.

The new intermediaries

The dominance of intermediaries or 'gatekeepers' in the cultural industries is well documented (Hirsch 1972; Burnett 1996; Hesmondhalgh 2007). More recently, though, the established gatekeepers – the Hollywood studios, the major record labels, the international media and entertainment conglomerates like Newscorp, Sony and Vivendi-Universal – are being challenged by a new generation of intermediaries drawn not from the cultural sector but from technology.

The new intermediaries, including telephone companies, internet service providers and search engines together with the 'Big Four' of Google, Amazon, Apple and Facebook, stand outside the cultural industries whilst playing a pivotal role within them. They do not meet traditional definitions of the cultural or creative industries as essentially 'copyright' industries set out by Caves and Howkins. Nor are the new intermediaries dealing primarily in 'symbolic goods' in the terms favoured by Hesmondhalgh and others to describe the cultural industries – they are dealing in information, in particular they are dealing in information about customers, which they can sell to advertisers. This gives them a competitive advantage over traditional publishers, distributors and retailers; their business model is less vulnerable to the threat of free content, both legal and illegal, whilst their access to consumers and consumer data allows them to dominate the cultural industries value chain.

Where these new gatekeepers differ from the old gatekeepers (record labels, publishers, broadcasters, newspapers, film studios) is in their relationship to content and content producers. A major record label or film studio depends to a large extent on the quality of its content, and hence on its relationships with content producers as well as the smaller intermediaries that make up the so-called independent sector. Consequently an uneasy synergy persists between the major distributors or publishers and the smaller cultural producers that orbit them. Both share an interest in 'content', albeit for a differing mix of cultural and commercial motives.

The new intermediaries like Google and Facebook are content agnostic. It does not greatly matter what kind of content they are hosting, provided that this content drives up traffic and delivers 'eyeballs' to advertisers. Their business model places them at the opposite end of the value chain from cultural production. Whereas the old intermediaries would invest in content and market that content to target consumers, the new intermediaries buy up content from multiple sources and aggregate it with other content to consumers who do not necessarily want it but will receive this as part of their subscription package. By being content agnostic and bundling multiple contents for their subscribers, they can appeal to an aggregate mass market rather than specific market segments. Content agnosticism thus reinforces the new intermediaries' bargaining position in the value chain. Content agnosticism also guides their attitude to copyright and content regulation. If the new intermediaries host pirate videos, pornography or terrorist manuals, blame can be shifted onto the producers and consumers who are circulating material on an open platform or 'common carrier', much as a telephone company can deny responsibility for a caller's conversation.

Why does this matter? By virtue of their value chain position and 'content agnostic' business model, the new intermediaries are far removed from Björkegren's 'cultural business strategy' of investing in and championing cultural products whose value they believe in, hopeful that the market will eventually fall into line. The familiar polarisation between cultural producers and cultural intermediaries has gone a step further, towards a scenario where the new intermediaries, in partnership with consumers, are effectively undermining the viability of content creators and content businesses by subverting copyright and backwards integrating their businesses to include the functions of traditional publishers, record labels and film producers.

Content creators meanwhile find themselves at the mercy of monopoly businesses that have little direct interest or expertise in content creation but a near monopoly on access to the market for content distribution.

The new intermediaries can point out that they are offering consumers more choice, reducing costs and bypassing some traditional gatekeepers that had their own interests in restricting and manipulating market access. By removing filters and providing an open platform, the new intermediaries have democratised production and distribution (Anderson 2004). Google's championing of free information also resonates with campaigners who, with some justification, argue that our current copyright laws are overly restrictive and reward established copyright holders (typically publishers and corporations) over those who are generating new intellectual property for the future (typically individual authors, artists and users).

Being 'content agnostic' does have a price. There is no longer any incentive or interest to make the new gatekeepers invest in new ideas and new talents. For every professional journalist, author, musician or artist there will always be somebody who thinks they can do the job better, and will do it without being paid. The new gatekeepers follow Björkegren's commercial business strategy of mass marketing and rapid turnover; Björkegren's cultural business strategy, requiring a patient investment in cultural products on cultural, not commercial, grounds does not fit with their business model. For all the talk of a 'long tail' that opens up a diversity of content beyond the reach of mainstream publishing, the new gatekeepers still seem to conduct the bulk of their business in mass market commodities, not niche cultural products (Wu 2006). Recent research from the music industry claims that just 1 per cent of artists account for 77 per cent of global music sales (Mulligan 2014).

Cultural producers are increasingly marginalised in this market environment. The uneasy détente that existed between majors and independents is replaced by a new indifference. Content is no longer valued in its own right. The truly valuable commodity is consumer relationships; content is the vehicle that allows these relationships to be tested, filtered and consolidated.

The price of content agnosticism is also borne by the consumer. In an increasingly monopolistic market that revolves around a continual recycling of the most popular themes and ideas, discovery of new ideas and content is increasingly problematic. The independent sector, which might have broken the repetitive cycle of hits and blockbusters, is marginalised to the point of invisibility; certainly it exists, but who can discover it in the white noise of unpublished, self-published, self-declared online content? Peterson describes the cycle of consolidation and reinvention in the music industry through the 1970s where the boredom of repetition sparked a new challenge from outside the mainstream (Peterson 1975). How can the new intermediaries initiate a new innovation cycle in symbolic production when they have no vested interest in the business of content creation?

The bargaining position of the new intermediaries is very strong. They do not invest in content creation because, ultimately, they do not need content or content creators in the traditional sense. Amazon does not need established authors to write novels when ordinary people are queuing up to self-publish through Amazon's open platform. Google is lobbying against copyright because – unlike a traditional inter-mediary such as a record label or publisher – its business model depends not on con-trolling supply but on promoting maximum access. Cultural production, the work of artists, authors and cultural practitioners, has accordingly been marginalised to the point where it is barely sustainable at a professional level. This has implications for the sustainability of the cultural industries, at least in their twentieth century form.

In this new creative economy the challenge for cultural producers is to devise some way of reconfiguring the value chain and reclaiming some of the bargaining power they have lost. This in turn takes us back to the challenge of management.

The new creative management?

In this chapter I have outlined two opposing approaches to management, following Björkegren's distinction between a 'cultural' and a 'commercial' business strategy. The cultural approach is essentially product-led and assumes that ultimate success depends on the intrinsic qualities of the product (and, by extension, the producer). The commercial approach is market-led and defines success on the market's terms. This division is reflected in the specialist education of 'artists' and 'managers' and in the distinctive management cultures of cultural producers and cultural intermediaries. In recent times the latter differences have been exacerbated by the growing influence of technology companies, acting as 'new gatekeepers' in the cultural industries. Because of their business models and value chain competences, these new cultural inter-mediaries have no direct investment in or knowledge of cultural production. Yet they are having a transformative effect on the ways in which culture is consumed and valued and on other businesses upstream of them in the cultural industries value chain.

Cultural producers face an increasingly precarious future as their bargaining position is further threatened by the dominant market position of technology companies and platforms like Google, YouTube, Facebook, Apple and Amazon. If they are to survive, they will need to take ownership of their own value chain and 'forwards integrate' elements of distribution and marketing (just as Amazon and Google have 'backwards integrated' some of the functions of publishers and editors for books and video). This in turn implies integrating some elements of the 'commercial business strategy' into a 'cultural' approach premised on faith in the product.

At a smaller, localised level, there are some indications that artists and content creators can begin to work with fans to take control of their value chain to a limited extent, and to shift from a 'product-led' approach towards a more 'customer-oriented' business model. In the music industry, artists like Trent Reznor, Radiohead and Beck have begun to experiment with new approaches to co-creation and marketing, working with fans to repackage and reconfigure music as customised experiences. Kevin Kelly has argued that it might be possible to sustain a viable business with '1,000 true fans' based on an annual revenue from each fan going direct to the artist without any intermediaries (Kelly 2008). Variations on this theme include crowd-funding sites like Kickstarter and self-publishing sites like Unbound – these platforms are not only raising money for new ventures, they are also building relationships between artists and consumers. Taking a cue from the online intermediaries like Google and Amazon, artists are learning not just to sell content but to commodify relationships (Rifkin 2000). A recent *Sunday Times* article provides some examples of emerging artists putting Kelly's model to work, selling gigs, exclusive releases, merchandising and a range of personalised interactions between artist and fans through an online platform to '5,000 loyal fans' (Eggar 2009). Artists are using digital platforms such as Pledge Music to 'forwards integrate' the value chain so that they take on much of the work (and the revenues) that would previously have fallen to an intermediary such as a record label, promoter or digital music service.

What is required here is a merging of attitudes and aptitudes, from 'cultural' to 'commercial' business strategies, combining the enthusiasm and energy of the amateur with professional knowledge and experience. The cultural business strategy is essentially product-driven, relying on the amateur's aesthetic sensibility rather than the professional's strategic control, and trusting in the audience to discover and share an interest in the product in that same spirit of amateur enthusiasm and engagement. The commercial business strategy is customer-driven and relies on strategic control of the value chain to match supply and demand. These two approaches are, respectively, concentrated at opposite ends of a value chain that is tilting inexorably in favour of the new intermediaries who control access to customers. Cultural producers need to find new ways of reconnecting directly with audiences and fans. This will require them to combine some of the professional, managerial competences of the intermediary with their own artistic abilities. This in turn points towards a more complementary model of arts and business education to equip future arts managers and cultural entrepreneurs, rather than the overspecialised (and mutually hostile) models of training and higher education described earlier in the chapter.

A creative approach to management is essentially bisociative (Bilton and Cummings 2010), requiring us to challenge the binary oppositions that separate 'creatives' and 'managers'. Such an approach requires educators to rethink what we mean by 'creative' and 'commercial' practices and the relationship between them (Negus

1995). It may mean rethinking the curriculum for cultural management in our universities and committing 'category errors' in the application of creative thinking models to management and vice versa. The alternative is to leave artists and cultural producers at the mercy of a new media infrastructure that has little interest in the old ways of rewarding content creators.

Note

1 For purposes of this chapter, I have not distinguished between the 'cultural industries' and 'creative industries'. In relation to my argument here, the term 'creative' industries lends itself more to the encroachment of management priorities into the cultural sector; 'cultural' industries is more likely to fit a defence of the autonomy of culture. I have therefore found it useful to refer to both terms in this chapter. The policy implications of the respective terminology, whilst undoubtedly important, lie outside the scope of my argument.

References

Anderson, C. (2004) 'The Long Tail', *Wired*, 12, 10 (available online at archive.wired.com/wired/archive/12.10/tail.html).

Banks, M., Lovatt, A., O'Connor, J. and Raffo, C. (2000) 'Risk and Trust in the Cultural Industries', *Geoforum*, 31 (4): 453–64.

Bilton, C. (1999) 'Risky Business: The Independent Production Sector in Britain's Creative Industries', *International Journal of Cultural Policy*, 6 (1): 17–39.

Bilton, C. (2007) *Management and Creativity: From Creative Industries to Creative Management*, Oxford: Blackwell.

Bilton, C. (2010) 'Manageable Creativity', *International Journal of Cultural Policy*, 16 (3): 255–69.

Bilton, C. and Cummings, S. (2010) *Creative Strategy: Reconnecting Business and Innovation*, Chichester: Wiley.

Björkegren, D. (1993) 'Arts Management', *Journal of Socio-Economics*, 22 (4, Winter): 379–95.

Björkegren, D. (1996) *The Culture Business: Management Strategies for the Arts-Related Business*, London: Routledge.

Boltanski, L. and Chiapello, E. (2005) *The New Spirit of Capitalism*, London: Verso.

Boorsma, M. (2005) 'A Strategic Logic for Arts Marketing: Integrating Customer Value and Artistic Objectives', *International Journal of Cultural Policy*, 12 (1): 73–92.

Burnett, R. (1996) *The Global Jukebox: The International Music Industry*, London: Routledge.

Colbert, F. (2007) *Marketing Culture and the Arts*, 3rd edition, Montreal: Les Editions de la Cheneliere.

Eggar, R. (2009) 'You Don't Need to Sell a Million to Make a Mint: How Web-Savvy Artists such as Kate Walsh and Tina Dico Can Do Nicely With Just 5,000 Loyal Fans', *Sunday Times*, 8 November.

Firat, A., Dholakia, N. and Venkatesh, A. (1995) 'Marketing in a Postmodern World', *European Journal of Marketing*, 29 (1): 40–56.

Hesmondhalgh, D. (2007) *The Cultural Industries* (2nd edition), London: Sage.

Hirsch, P.M. (1972) 'Processing Fads and Fashions: An Organization-Set Analysis of Cultural Industry Systems', *American Journal of Sociology*, 77 (4): 639–59.

Hirschman, E.C. and Holbrook, M.B. (1982) 'Hedonic Consumption: Emerging Concepts, Methods and Propositions', *Journal of Marketing*, 46 (Summer): 92–101.

Kellner, D. (1992) 'Popular Culture and the Construction of Postmodern Identities', in Scott Lash and Jonathan Friedman (eds), *Modernity and Identity*, Oxford: Blackwell, pp. 141–77.

Kelly, K. (2008) '1,000 True Fans' *The Technium*, March (available online at kk.org/thetechnium/2008/03/1000-true-fans/).

Lash, S. and Urry, J. (1994) *Economies of Signs and Space*, London: Sage.

Levitt, T. (1986) 'The Globalisation of Markets', in *The Marketing Imagination*, New York, London: Free Press, Macmillan.

McGuigan, J. (2005) 'Neoliberalism, Culture and Policy', *International Journal of Cultural Policy*, 11 (3): 229–41.

McGuigan, J. (2009) 'Doing a Florida Thing: The Creative Class Thesis and Cultural Policy', *International Journal of Cultural Policy*, 15 (3): 291–300.

Mintzberg, H. and Waters, J. (1985) 'Of Strategies, Deliberate and Emergent', *Strategic Management Journal*, 6: 257–62.

Mulligan, M. (2014) *The Death of the Long Tail: The Superstar Music Economy*, London: MIDIA Consulting.

Negus, K. (1995) 'When the Mystical Meets the Market: Creativity and Commerce in the Production of Popular Music', *Sociological Review*, 43 (2): 316–41.

Parrish, D. (2005) *T-Shirts and Suits: A Guide to the Business of Creativity*, Liverpool: Merseyside ACME.

Peterson, R. (1975) 'Cycles in Symbol Production: The Case of Popular Music', in Simon Frith and A. Goodwin (eds), *On Record: Rock, Pop and the Written Word*, London: Routledge, 1990, pp. 140–59.

Rifkin, J. (2000) 'Commodifying Human Relationships', in *The Age of Access*, Harmondsworth: Penguin, pp. 96–113.

Scott, A.J. (1999) 'The Cultural Economy: Geography and the Creative Field', *Media, Culture and Society* 21, pp. 807–17.

Townley, B. and Beech, N. (2011) *Managing Creativity: Exploring the Paradox*, Cambridge: Cambridge University Press.

Warhurst, C. (2011) 'The Missing Middle: Management in the Creative Industries', in B. Townley and N. Beech (eds), *Managing Creativity: Exploring the Paradox*, Cambridge: Cambridge University Press, pp. 217–36.

Wu, T. (2006), 'The Wrong Tail: How to Turn a Powerful Idea into a Dubious Theory of Everything', *Slate* 21 July (available online atwww.slate.com/id/2146225).

23
CREATIVE VOCATIONS AND CULTURAL VALUE

Scott Brook

The auteur thesis of cultural work

A key claim of creative labour studies is that cultural workers are defined by a primary value commitment to creative autonomy, one that we might describe as 'auteurist' in so far as it derives from the Modern figure of the literary author (Miège 2011: 87–88; Hesmondhalgh 2007: 67–70). The auteurist model highlights the cultural worker's commitment to both aesthetic and professional modes of autonomy, such as work routines that provide opportunities for self-expression, personal development and independence from supervision (Hesmondhalgh and Baker 2010: 62–67). While this thesis is widespread in the social sciences, in the context of cultural industries research it is distinctive as it serves a normative critical purpose. As such, it reflects a broadly Marxian critique of modern work as a source of worker alienation and a positive project of identifying those aspects of creative work that hold out the promise of a more authentic work relation. We might say that creative labour research in fact shares 'the artistic critique of work' that exists amongst the workers it studies, even as it supplements this critique with a social critique that highlights the distributional inequalities within a sector that has conspicuously low levels of collective organisation. (On the 'artistic critique', see Boltanski and Chiapello 2005.) At the same time, the thesis is also used to *explain* the existence of those 'vast reservoirs of under-employed artists' that are central to the functioning of the cultural economy (Miège 1989: 72). Quoting from David Hesmondhalgh, Bernard Miège writes that structural industry features – such as employment practices that favour growing a reserve of underemployed workers, or forms of intellectual property management that economically disadvantage content producers – are insufficient as explanations for why individuals would persist in such poorly renumerated labour markets, and that it is due to 'professional ideologies of authorship and creativity' that cultural workers are willing to 'trade in financial reward and security for creative autonomy' (Miège 2011: 88; see also Hesmondhalgh 2007: 207).

Leaving to one side the consequently vexed convergence of positive (Marxian) and regressive (neoliberal) manifestations of this ideology that then confronts creative labour studies (i.e. the contemporary valence of creativity reflecting both a viable

296

critique of work *and its recuperation* by a new disciplinary apparatus for inculcating flexible, personalised work relations), the casual reference to workers being willing to 'trade in' financial rewards and security is in fact entirely consistent with explanations in economic sociology, where notions of 'psychic income' or 'lifestyle benefits' add up to so many non-pecuniary rewards that account for career choices that would otherwise seem irrational. By 'psychic income', Pierre-Michel Menger refers to a range of social rewards, such as 'a high level of personal autonomy', 'opportunities to use a wide range of abilities and to feel self-actualized at work' and a 'high degree of social recognition for the successful artist' (Menger 1999: 555). The more-or-less rational calculations of agents who 'trade' employment conditions for non-pecuniary returns (poor working conditions becoming the 'shadow price' for such a vocation, as Menger suggests (555)) are grounded in a value commitment that, although possibly a product of either ideology or personal preference, isn't itself subject to economic interpretation. It seems that whether researchers come at the problem from backgrounds in cultural industries research, economic sociology or cultural economics, the explanation of what motivates cultural work falls back on a normative conception of social agency derived from classical economics; the worker is both a more-or-less 'rational' agent pursuing their specific interests *and* a normative value position on what those interests are.

The problem with positing a cultural value as the foundation of a set of economic relations it stands outside of is clear: it prevents understanding of why this value appeals to some more than others, at certain stages of life, is more highly valued in particular societies, or during certain historical periods. While this approach preserves the dignity of the cultural worker as one who is willing to make personal sacrifices in the name of culture, it fails to consider the specific practical circumstances in which such 'selfless' values are economically compelling. That is, it applies the Kantian conception of artistic value as 'purposive purposelessness' to the entire field of cultural work.

In this chapter I propose an alternative account of the current demand for cultural work, one that can consider the social trajectories for which the auteurist ideal becomes plausible; meaning believable *and* realistic due to its practical uses. Just as this approach looks away from value positions as a manifestation of higher commitments to the more mundane forms of economic reasoning, it similarly looks away from any normative conceptions of careers in the cultural sector and seeks to confront the reality of a loose field of vocational trajectories within *and across* the cultural field, the majority of which (as studies suggest) are conducted at some distance from formal employment or organised art markets. While the focus on professional work in the cultural industries and artists' labour markets has been important to empirically documenting the conditions of creative work, it has overshadowed attention to those 'vast reservoirs of under-employed artists', which are mostly composed, as Hesmondhalgh notes, of '*non*-professional cultural workers, who work occasionally and have to take other jobs to subsidise their artistic activities' (Hesmondhalgh 2007: 71, my emphasis). My approach hence decentres the role of the cultural industries in relation to the broader cultural field, and looks toward general changes in the relation between labour markets and education systems; in particular, the general phenomena of underemployment and the so-called 'hourglass economy' in demand for skilled labour.

In placing pressure on established interpretations of creative work, I'm not seeking to jettison the project of creative labour studies as a critique of work. My approach would, however, encourage us to distinguish between the explanatory and prescriptive role of discussion about creative autonomy, and hence situate such a value as value-*for* (specific groups or circumstances) rather than universal. Creative work is clearly a complex form of social exchange that is distinctive due to the unique and highly varied symbolic and social rewards that accrue to workers, rewards which are all the more conspicuous for being combined with poor employment conditions; the most conspicuous of which are key dimensions of underemployment, such as involuntary part-time work, 'overeducation', and low pay for the majority of creative workers who are multiple job holders (Feldman 1996). More specifically, to take this value claim for an explanation prevents us from understanding why creative vocations may in fact have a practical use for specific social trajectories confronted with under-employment, or for which a voluntary delay to entering the labour market may in fact be strategic. While my approach hence entertains the possibility of *reversing* the emphasis in the associated phenomena of underemployment and commitment to creative work, it does so not simply to negate the substantialist vision of the liberal economic subject in favour of a socially relational mode of explanation, but to open creative labour studies onto a number of important empirical questions about the specific and varied uses of cultural work. It is due this broader agenda that I do not invoke a distinction here between 'artists' and 'cultural workers' according to either the sectors of the field they are located in (e.g. the arts/cultural industries) or the different types of activity undertaken (e.g. 'cultural work'/'creative labour'). Although useful in other contexts of discussion, the methodological problem with the auteurist thesis concerns how we account for all forms of work that exhibit a value commitment to the cultural field, and would not be resolved by simply limiting its application to artists. Such differences are of course also problematic for researchers as they also partly reflect a set of symbolic distinctions at stake within the cultural field itself.

A further reason for this approach is that it enables creative labour studies to move beyond the simple negation of the 'knowledge economy' thesis as a keystone for the creative industries policy agenda, and situate the current moment of creative labour in terms of major changes in the relations between work and education. The study of creative labour inherits a strong and influential critique of the knowledge society/information economy thesis (see especially Garnham 2005 and 2010); however, this legacy has yet to get beyond the simple negation of these discourses as ideological, and move on to consider the ways in which labour markets in western developed countries have changed under the impact of increasingly massified tertiary education systems and the spread of information technologies. Such an economy is more use-fully described as a 'human capital economy' as this allows us to abandon the notion of some objective and absolute increase in demand for knowledge workers (as opposed to demand for 'knowledge *worked*', as Brown et al. suggest (2004: 55)), and focus instead on the strategies of those who must negotiate this changed terrain, including those strategies of 'self-appreciation' that Michel Feher has suggested define the neoliberal subject (2009). Such an approach enables creative labour studies to move beyond the auteur thesis in locating the specificity of creative work, and return to a founding conception of culture as a repertoire of activities for cultivating 'the person' as a particular type of social investment.

Creative vocations and the labour market

One of the noted problems with studies of artists' labour markets concerns how artists are to be defined. Using national employment data is always problematic, given that researchers are dealing with a population that is routinely unemployed. But the problem also hinges on the very notion that artists might constitute an 'occupational group', as the basis of this category is generally some nominated level of professional success. It is for this reason that such studies tend to focus on a very narrow range of institutionalised high art practices with strong levels of state subsidy. That there is an 'oversupply' relative to demand is hence partly an effect of framing artists as an occupational group oriented towards a single labour market.

However, if we take 'work' rather than 'occupation' as the base category, then it becomes possible to think about the relation between cultural practice and under-employment quite differently. A recent Australian Bureau of Statistics survey supports the notion that engagement in 'cultural work' is indeed increasing, and that the fastest growing pool of work is conducted outside paid employment. The 2007 survey of *Work in Selected Cultural and Leisure Activities* (ABS 2007) found that between 2004 and 2007 there had been a 30.2 per cent increase in the total number of Australians who had worked in the cultural activities surveyed (from approximately 2.7 to 3.5 million Australians). However, the percentage increase in the number involved in *unpaid* cultural work was more than three times that of those involved in 'some paid work' (38.3 per cent change as opposed to 11 per cent change) (see ABS 2007: Tables 2, 3 and 14). 'Work involvements' included all paid and unpaid work in the last 12 months, and crucially excluded 'hobbies', which were defined as 'activities undertaken solely for the person's own use or for the use of their family or friends' (ABS 2007: 36). While the survey covered an impressively broad range of practices and sites of cultural work, the most significant areas related to what would be conventionally regarded as strong examples of creative arts practice. The numerically most significant activities in 2007 were the visual and performing arts, design, writing, festival organising and music; and the largest percentage increases between 2004 and 2007 were for photography (638,600 persons, up from 300,100 in 2004), drawing (558,000, up from 288,700), computer artwork (552,500, up from 286,300), and painting (463,000, up from 262,400) (ABS 2007: 5).

Just as it would be implausible to interpret such numbers in terms of mass aspirations to careers in the arts or cultural industries, so too would it be implausible to posit any organic relation between creative work and groups whose interests it might express, such as a 'social class' or 'community'. One way around this problem is to suggest that we are not describing an occupational group whose choice of career is to be explained, so much as a field of 'creative vocations' that have highly varied relations to employment, both within and outside the cultural sector. It then becomes possible to ask why cultural work is becoming useful to more people without assuming that this constitutes an oversupply in relation to the cultural sector specifically.

More specifically, it becomes possible to inquire about the relation between cultural work and employment. Interestingly, the ABS survey found that those employed 'part time' (i.e. all employment beneath full-time employment) had a significantly higher involvement in cultural work (28 per cent) than those in full-time employment (23 per cent), the unemployed (21 per cent) and those outside the labour force (17 per cent) (ABS 2007: 4, 10–11). While those in part-time, casual and contract work are more likely to have time to undertake cultural work, this does not explain why they would invest this time in cultural work as opposed to recreation, nor why those with the most free time – those outside the labour force – are the *least* likely to use their time this way. We might ask what the relation between non-full-time employment and cultural work is, without automatically assuming that such work is 'preferable' to cultural workers as it provides a means of subsidising their cultural work.

One way of describing the relation between underemployment and creative work is in terms of what Bourdieu described as 'social inertia'. The social inertia hypothesis proposes that cultural work is attractive to those confronted with a delay in the process of converting their cultural capital (skills and qualifications) into satisfying careers (i.e. careers that reflect past conceptions of the value of these skills and qualifications), as it provides coherent vocational identities that are more or less independent of the formal labour market (Brook 2013). Based on Bourdieu's discussion of the 'broken' vocational trajectories of French graduates in the 1970s after the general decline in the value of degrees (Bourdieu 1984: 150), the social inertia hypthothesis suggests that having a creative vocation provides opportunities to exercise and enhance skills that may otherwise be unused in the workplace, as well as forms of social esteem appropriate to the cultural capital of workers which are not yet, and perhaps never will be, redeemed on the labour market.

This approach is appealing as it is consistent with two areas of labour market studies that have sought to document the effects of both massified tertiary education systems and rising information technologies in western developed countries; the first focuses on the increasing prominence of workplace 'overeducation' (or 'skills underutilisation', to frame the problem more optimistically), while the second focuses on the decline in demand for intermediate skilled jobs, or what has come to be described as the 'hourglass economy'. 'Overeducation' refers to the rising disjunction between the qualifications and skills held by employees and the qualifications and skills required to perform a job (Linsley 2008; Mavromaras et al. 2007). It is argued that overeducation results in increasing levels of employee dissatisfaction, as work increasingly fails to provide a level of social esteem and activity that is consistent with their qualifications or capacities. There are many theories of what drives overeducation, but the most plausible explanation would appear to be labour market competition (Linsley 2008), with employers being increasingly happy to employ workers with higher qualifications than required as such employees have 'desirable personal attributes' (Feldman and Maynard 2011: 235). A recent UK study shows increasing substitution of graduates for non-graduate labour in entry-level clerical, sales and administrative positions in the service industries (predominantly retailing, and transport and communications), leading to widening wage differentials in the graduate labour market (Mason 2002).

Since the late 1990s a range of studies seeking to track rising income inequality and the growth of knowledge work in the United Kingdom, United States and Australia have described reduced labour market demand for intermediate skilled occupations, with some growth in demand for workers at the very top and significant growth in demand at bottom of the skills hierarchy, leading to the hypothesis of an 'hourglass economy' (Fleming et al. 2004; Anderson 2009; Galbraith 1998). In the United States, where the evidence for a slowdown in labour market demand for graduates since the early 1990s is overwhelming, Claudia Goldin and Lawrence Katz conclude that new information technologies have simultaneously replaced many lower- and mid-level graduate jobs and complemented high-level graduate jobs (Goldin and Katz 2008: 302; on the slowdown in demand for college graduates independent of supply, see Table 3.2 on p. 101). However, the apparent growth in demand for high-skills jobs has been contested, with one UK study suggesting that this growth may be an effect of the credentialising of a number of intermediate-level occupations (Tomlinson 2008: 177), while an Australian study notes that the growing high-skills occupations are in fact at the bottom of the 'high-skills' scale, being in 'knowledge handling and service provision [...] with low levels of discretion and analytical skills' (Fleming et al. 2004: 735). That intermediate skilled positions are declining due to competition from information technologies would in fact complement the observation that many intermediately skilled occupations are moving up the skills scale ('jobs upgrading'), as professionalisation and credentialism via the university system are routine symptoms of increased labour market competition.

While the social inertia hypothesis might appear immediately relevant to those frustrated with the labour market returns on their investments in education or confronted with an involuntary delay in the process of redeeming their value, we might also consider how creative vocations might be actively sought in anticipation of the ways in which they augment current and/or future career trajectories. That is, intermittent involvements in cultural work might be quite purposeful and strategic in relation to careers that lie outside the cultural field.

In their study of the graduate recruitment processes for professional positions in major international companies, Phillip Brown, Anthony Hesketh and Sara Williams use the notion of 'personal capital' to refer to a range of personal skills, such as charisma, manner and self-presentation, that are necessary supplements to cultural capital, where the latter is regarded as a set of institutionally certified capacities. A key manifestation of 'personal capital' is the 'narratives of employability' that demonstrate a coherent professional identity that is independent of formal work and education history (Brown et al. 2004: 34–39). The basis of this proposition is the authors' observation of the declining ability of credentials to signal employee capacities (as opposed to screening interviewees), and the increased importance of professional applicants communicating 'an economy of experience' based on extracurricular activities (Brown et al. 2004: 36).

While many will consider the term 'personal capital' redundant, given that what it describes can properly be regarded as a subset of cultural capital concerned with interpersonal skills in managing symbolic and social capital,[1] the general argument and evidence the authors muster concerning the nature of competition for professional jobs is, I think, incontrovertible. (It is also supported by studies on student perceptions of the value of degrees; Tomlinson 2008.) Such an approach challenges creative labour studies to recall a very traditional definition of cultural practice as a form of self-cultivation, which we might describe as personal investment in human capital. That such investments are becoming prominent as *work* engagements (as opposed to private hobbies) would support Michel Feher's argument that societies governed by human capital theory increasingly delete the liberal distinction between spheres of market production (e.g. work) and non-market reproduction (e.g. recreation), as all domains of human practice become a basis for capital investment and appreciation (2009). Such an approach would further position creative labour studies to engage with important debates about the 'vocational' value of tertiary study for work in the cultural sector.

Conclusion

This chapter has sought to consider how cultural work, considered as a field of creative vocations and value commitments, may serve as a practical resource for augmenting, or remedying the effects of, increased competition in the labour market for skilled work. While it draws on the general sociological account of culture as a social resource developed by Bourdieu, it has also sought to situate this account as relevant to current historical conditions; i.e. the period in which the knowledge society thesis has prevailed. While Bourdieu's field theoretic account of mixed spaces of economic and symbolic value clearly provides a powerful model for analysing the practical economies of creative work, my choice of approach is partly expedient in that Bourdieu's lexicon of mid-level concepts seems to me an efficient means of describing creative vocations in a manner that can relate individual case studies to a broader process of complex social change. In any case, and before we develop an overly 'auteurist' account of Bourdieu's approach, it should be recalled that key phases of Bourdieu's early work on culture and social reproduction were developed in collaboration with others (Bourdieu and Passeron 1977; 1979 [1964]; Bourdieu and Boltanski 2000 [1978]; Bourdieu et al. 1990 [1965]), while Bourdieu's studies with Jean-Claude Passeron and Luc Boltanki were very much part of a generation of early critical receptions of human capital theory that would become increasingly prevalent across the social sciences. This is clear in the case of the sociology and economics of education, where other critics such as Randall Collins and Fred Hirsch highlighted the *relational* value of qualifications and skills as 'positional goods' (Hirsch 1977) that were, moreover, subject to a self-reinforcing 'credentialist' cycle of declining returns (Collins 1979). This was a period when the term 'overeducation' entered education studies in response to the phenomenon of graduate unemployment in the 1970s (Freeman 1976), a development that – the economic downturn notwithstanding – ran counter to the whole post-industrialist thesis of rising demand for knowledge work. So, while I would argue that Bourdieu's methodology offers a highly productive approach to the 'vast reservoirs' of underemployed cultural workers, the broader claim of this chapter – namely that we can interpret increases in creative work as in part an effect of general changes in labour markets – does not rest on or necessitate a Bourdieusian research agenda. Such an approach is also broadly consistent with Bernard Lahire's recent study on the 'double life' of French literary authors, one that faults Bourdieu's account of the literary field for reducing the study of writers to their membership of the literary field. Drawing on his sociology of the 'plural actor', Lahire suggests that for all but a few participants the literary field represents a 'game' or 'secondary field' in relation to a primary field of employment conducted elsewhere (Lahire 2010).

One of the reasons for the increased interest in the economics of creative labour is that cultural workers are seen as leading the way in terms of the skills required for engaging in flexible and enterprising work arrangements that will increasingly be required by the general workforce as it adapts to a 'new economy' (Throsby 2012). Such claims are of course part of a long tradition of essentially futurological writing that has sought to address contemporary changes in capitalism through reference to a new caste of symbolic workers, what Barbrook dubs (in an anthology of the same title) 'the class of the new' (Barbrook 2006). How creative labour studies therefore accounts for the vast reservoirs of cultural workers has consequences for how these changes can be understood.

Note

1 The concept's genesis and explanatory role is awkwardly identical to that of cultural capital; just as cultural capital was developed to explain the differences in attainments in students subject to the same schooling, the notion of 'personal capital' seeks to describe the different labour market outcomes for those with putatively equivalent levels of cultural capital. The problem with this proposition is that credentials are only one form of cultural capital, and that what Bourdieu classes as 'embodied' forms of cultural capital already communicate capacities cultivated in extracurricular contexts.

References

ABS (Australian Bureau of Statistics) (2007) *Work in Selected Culture and Leisure Activities*, Canberra: Commonwealth Government of Australia.
Anderson, P. (2009) 'Intermediate Occupations and the Conceptual and Empirical Limitations of the Hourglass Economy Thesis', *Work, Employment and Society* 23(1): 169–80.
Barbrook, R. (2006) *The Class of the New*, OpenMute. Online. Available at: theclassofthenew. net/ (accessed 8 December 2013).
Boltanski, L. and Chiapello, E. (2005) *The New Spirit of Capitalism*, trans. G. Elliott, New York: Verso.
Bourdieu, P. (1984) *Distinction: A Social Critique of the Judgment of Taste*, New York and London: Routledge.
Bourdieu, P. and Boltanski, L. (2000 [1978]) 'Changes in Social Structure and Changes in Demand for Education', in S.J. Ball (ed.) *Sociology of Education Volume II: Inequalities and Oppressions*, London and New York: Routledge.
Bourdieu, P. and Passeron, J.-C. (1977) *Reproduction in Education, Society and Culture*, trans. R. Nice, Sage: London and Beverley Hills.
Bourdieu, P. and Passeron, J.-C. (1979 [1964]) *The Inheritors: French Students and Their Relation to Culture*, trans. R. Nice, Chicago and London: University of Chicago Press.
Bourdieu, P., Boltanksi, L., Castel, R., Chamboredon, J.C. and Schnapper, D. (1990 [1965]) *Photography: A Middle-brow Art*, trans. S. Whiteside, Stanford, CA: Stanford University Press.

Brook, S. (2013) 'Social Inertia and the Field of Creative Labour', *Journal of Sociology* 49 (2–3): 309–24.

Brown, P., Hesketh, A. and Williams, S. (2004) *The Mismanagement of Talent: Employability and Jobs in the Knoweldge Economy*, Oxford and New York: Oxford University Press.

Collins, R. (1979) *The Credential Society: An Historical Sociology of Education and Stratification*, New York and London: Academic Press Orlando.

Feher, M. (2009) 'Self-Appreciation; or, The Aspirations of Human Capital', *Public Culture* 21(1): 21–41.

Feldman, D.C. (1996) 'The Nature, Antecedents and Consequences of Underemployment', *Journal of Management* 22 (3): 385–407.

Feldman, D.C. and Maynard, D.C. (2011) 'The Labour Economic Perspective on Overqualification', *Industrial and Organisational Psychology* 4: 233–35.

Fleming, P., Harley, B. and Sewell, G. (2004) 'A Little Knowledge is a Dangerous Thing: Getting Below the Surface of the Crowth of "Knowledge Work" in Australia', *Work, Employment and Society* 18 (4): 725–47.

Freeman, R. (1976) *The Overeducated American*, New York: Academic Press.

Galbraith, K. (1998) *Created Unequal*, New York: Free Press.

Garnham, N. (2005) 'From Cultural to Creative Industries: An Analysis of the Implications of the "Creative Industries" Approach to Arts and Media Policy Making in the United Kingdom', *International Journal of Cultural Policy* 11 (1): 15–29.

Garnham, N. (2010) '"Information Society" as Theory or Ideology: A Critical Perspective in Technology, Education and Employment in the Information Age', *Information, Communication and Society* 3 (2): 139–52.

Goldin, C.D. and Katz, L.F. (2008) *The Race Between Education and Technology*, Cambridge, MA: Harvard University Press.

Hesmondhalgh, D. (2007) *The Cultural Industries*, second edition, London: Sage.

Hesmondhalgh, D. and Baker, S. (2010) *Creative Labour: Media Work in Three Cultural Industries*, London and New York: Routledge.

Hirsch, F. (1977) *Social Limits to Growth*, London and Henley: Routledge and Kegan Paul.

Lahire, B. (2010) 'The Double Life of Writers', *New Literary History* 41 (2): 443–65.

Linsley, I. (2008) 'Causes of Overeducation in the Australian Labour Market', *Australian Journal of Labour Economics* 8 (2): 121–43.

Mason, G. (2002) 'High Skills Utilisation Under Mass Higher Education: Graduate Employment in Service Industries in Britain', *Journal of Education and Work* 15 (4): 427–56.

Mavromaras, K, McGuiness, S. and Wooden, M. (2007) 'Overskilling in the Australian Labour Market', *The Australian Economic Review* 40 (3): 307–12.

Menger, P.-M. (1999) 'Artistic Labour Markets and Careers', *Annual Review of Sociology* 25: 541–74.

Miège, B. (1989) *The Capitalization of Cultural Production*, New York: International General.

Miège, B. (2011) 'Theorizing the Cultural Industries: Persistent Specificities and Reconsiderations', in J. Wasko, G. Murdock and H. Sousa (eds) *The Handbook of the Political Economy of Communications*, first edition, Oxford: Blackwell Publishing.

Throsby, D. (2012) 'Artistic Labour Markets: Why Are They of Interest to Labour Economists?', *Economia Della Cultura* 22 (1): 7–16.

Tomlinson, M. (2008) '"The Degree is Not Enough": Students' Perceptions of the Role of Higher Education Credentials for Graduate Work and Employability', *British Journal of Sociology of Education* 29 (1): 49–61.

24
EMERGING LABOUR POLITICS IN CREATIVE INDUSTRIES

Greig de Peuter and Nicole S. Cohen

Concepts for resistant research on cultural work

Describing themselves as "the multitude of workers of the creative industries" (MACAO 2012), hundreds of cultural workers marched through the streets of Milan on May 5, 2012 to a 31-storey abandoned skyscraper and occupied it. In the ten days prior to their eviction, the occupiers transformed the space into a site for autonomous cultural production, a bold collective move taken in response to precarious employment and financial austerity in Italy (Cultural Workers Organize 2013). Across Europe and North America, cultural workers are responding to similarly strained conditions by experimenting with organizational forms and collective activities. Emergent organizations in New York City, such as The Model Alliance, the Retail Action Project, and W.A.G.E. (Working Artists and the Greater Economy), are presenting new ways to address the precarity faced by flexworkers in urban centres that valorize creative industries despite insecure and often poor working conditions (de Peuter 2014). Globally, interns and their allies are forming groups like the Canadian Intern Association, the Precarious Workers Brigade in London, and Génération Précaire in Paris, filing class action lawsuits, and waging social media campaigns to oppose the rapidly solidifying norm that unpaid labour is a young worker's ticket into the creative sector. These are just some examples of emerging labour politics in creative industries, where workers, often through new labour organizations that exist outside the bounds of traditional trade unions, are lobbying for social protections and higher pay and exerting collective pressure to reclaim autonomy over their crafts and their lives.

As these examples demonstrate, conflict and resistance mark the vaunted creative industries. Research on cultural labour tends, however, to conceptualize cultural workers as either model subjects of neoliberalism—enterprising selves adept at individual coping strategies and self-exploitation—or as victims of precarity. Recognizing cultural workers' roles as activists and agents of change calls for deeper engagement in communication and cultural studies of work with efforts to organize, agitate, and resist precarity. Our focus in this chapter is informed by a collaborative research project called Cultural Workers Organize, a four-country study that documents and examines some of the various ways flexworkers in the creative economy, including freelancers, part-timers, interns, casual, and contract workers, are collectively responding to precarity. To date, we have conducted interviews with sixty individuals active in cultural worker organizations and initiatives.

Cultural industries, especially newer creative industries sectors, are generally not unionized, which has sustained the spread of precautious employment that results in insecurity and presents new challenges to the already difficult task of unionization and collective bargaining. Despite this legal challenge, and in response to the inability of unions to address the needs of the precariously employed, our research observes that cultural workers are organizing in alternate constellations, including grassroots groups, virtual campaigns, in alliances with the labour movement, and in what Eidelson (2013) calls "alt-labour," non-union workers' organizations for those who cannot legally access a union. Attending to such instances of worker resistance, we propose, foregrounds alternative, worker-centred perspectives on how cultural production should be organized and supported.

A key concept in studies of cultural labour, and one animating our research, is autonomy. Autonomy appears in scholarship on cultural labour in two general iterations: creative or aesthetic autonomy, which describes workers' abilities to produce creative works independent of outside influences; and workplace or professional autonomy, which refers to workers' abilities to achieve self-determination in a workplace (Hesmondhalgh and Baker 2011; Banks 2010; Ryan 1992). Both conceptions of autonomy examine the possibility for, and limitations on, cultural workers' efforts to seek fulfilling, meaningful work and retain control over the creative content of their work in spite of the impulses of capitalist commodity production and market relations. Notwithstanding the insecurity that underpins contemporary cultural labour, and acknowledging its "negotiated" or "relative" nature (Banks 2010; Ryan 1992), autonomy has come to be understood as a defining characteristic of cultural work. We seek to widen and politicize the concept of autonomy beyond negotiating individual autonomy within workplace structures and seeking individual fulfillment through the content of work. Flowing from current efforts of activists, such a notion of autonomy would be expanded to include workers' efforts to collectively exert control over the terms under which their labour power is engaged, to question the dominant organization of cultural production, to seek ways to sustain independent work by de-linking social security from standard employment, and to produce alternative systems of meaning about work.

In this chapter, we propose three conceptual lenses for approaching research on cultural labour from worker resistance. These concepts hold potential for envisioning alternate routes to cultural labour autonomy, via *mutual aid*, or developing bottom-up infrastructures to support independent work; *policy from below*, or creating worker-centred policies to mitigate the precarity of non-standard work; and *counter-interpellation*, or building alternate vocabularies to define cultural labour that resist dominant ideological codes attached to visions of, for example, "creatives" and "free agents." A politicized concept of autonomy regards cultural workers as active in forging new ways to sustain their work and lives, going beyond workers' efforts to adapt or cope with precarity in ways that can reinforce self-exploitation. Our proposed conceptual entry points demonstrate that beginning from cultural workers' resistant practices opens new areas for inquiry and action in the field of cultural and communicative labour.

Mutual aid

It has become common for researchers to view cultural work through the conceptual lens of "enterprising individuals" (Rose 1996) or a cognate frame (Coulson 2012; McRobbie 2002). Deployed critically, enterprise designates a neoliberal regime of conduct in which self-reliance is a default disposition. Maintaining a self-reliant sensibility is necessary in creative labour economies, where self-employed, project-based workers are personally responsible for maintaining a steady flow of paid work, accessed through informal networks or assumed to hinge on possessing a distinctive personal brand. Enterprise overlays what Pasquinelli (2007: 80) starkly terms "immaterial civil war," whose frontlines include "the usual conflicts between cognitive workers," manifest in such keywords as "competition," "rivalries" and "envy." "Cooperation," Pasquinelli goes on to say, "is structurally difficult among creative workers, where a prestige economy operates the same way as in any star system ... and where new ideas have to confront each other, often involving their creators in a fight" (ibid.). Without underestimating the structural forces that amplify competitiveness, reinforce self-reliance, or otherwise inhibit labour solidarity in the creative industries, there is a need for progressive perspectives on cultural work that go beyond diagnosing the internalization of neoliberal priorities that can mute resistance (see Kennedy 2012: 23–51; Banks 2007: 156–87). We propose the concept of mutual aid as a useful entry point for researching (and inspiring) alternative social possibilities to competitive, self-reliant "culturepreneurs" (Davies and Ford 2000).

We were steered to the idea of mutual aid through the case of the Freelancers Union. Labelled "A Federation of the Unaffiliated," the Freelancers Union is a New York City-based non-profit organization whose 235,000-strong membership is skewed to a creative-class demographic. Its mission is to advance the "next safety net" for "independent workers," which it does primarily through providing health benefits and insurance services to members outside standard employment (Horowitz, personal comm., 4 October 2010). Founder Sara Horowitz (2013) locates the Freelancers Union within "the new mutualism" (see Birchall 2001), an umbrella covering diverse community-based social and economic activities through which workers and consumers satisfy their otherwise unmet needs by variously pooling, sharing, or collaboratively managing resources via organizations outside the purview of the state or investor-driven corporations. It is not necessary to dig too deep into the etymology of new mutualism to arrive at "mutual aid," a concept popularized by Russian anarchist Peter Kropotkin ([1902] 2006). Disputing the social Darwinist thinking of the late nineteenth century, Kropotkin argued that humans and non-human species are not exclusively engaged in, or condemned to, a competitive war of all against all. Kropotkin (2006: xiii) meticulously documented some of the myriad ways in which the survival and evolution of diverse species is enabled by forms of behaviour that do not corroborate a totalizing "law of mutual struggle," but instead demonstrate a countervailing "law of mutual aid" encompassing values and practices that range from support and cooperation to equity and solidarity.

For Kropotkin, practices of mutual aid do not arise from an a priori fellow feeling, but rather the recognition, conscious or otherwise, of the necessity of mutual aid to survive in the face of difficult material conditions or common adversaries. In our context, the research lens of mutual aid would zoom in on forms of cooperation that are not imposed on labour by capital in commodity production but instead spring from below. Examples of such "mutual aid amongst ourselves" (Kropotkin 2006: 184–241) include craft guilds and their successors, unions, which are rooted in a mutualist premise that, in the context of structurally unequal labour–capital relations, organizing collectively is essential to give workers bargaining power and, in turn, assert, protect, and advance their economic and occupational interests. Workers' organizations are rarely centre stage in the most prominent contemporary accounts of cultural work. But if research on cultural and creative industries is to contest individualization, then inquiry into trade unions, professional associations, and autonomous labour groups is necessary. By extending existing scholarship on the established unions in the commercial media and cultural industries (for example, Mosco and McKercher 2008; Amman 2002), our research identifies a new constellation of precarious workers' association emerging from the margins of the union movement, exemplified by such initiatives as the Canadian Intern Association, the Freelancers Union, Intern Aware, and the Model Alliance.

Fraternal societies are classic institutions of mutual aid. Here, too, as the historian David Beito (2000: 234) writes of the US case, "[m]utual aid was a creature of necessity." Historically, fraternal societies have pooled the resources of their frequently poor members so as to be able to extend economic support to members (or their families) at a time of need via, for example, sickness benefits or life insurance. Anticipating the centralized forms of universal social insurance administered by the welfare state (Birchall 2001), the model of the benefit societies is a staple of trade unionism, including in the cultural industries, where most workers are self-employed and thus unable to access workplace-based benefits. In Canada, ACTRA Fraternal Benefit Society serves members of the Writers Guild of Canada and the Alliance of Canadian Cinema, Television, and Radio Artists. The Freelancers Union began as Working Today, a non-profit provider of discounted health benefits for New York freelancers who could not access Medicaid or were not covered by an employer. Insurance may not be a glamorous topic for researchers of cultural work, yet access to insurance is often what draws independent workers to collective organizations. Mutual aid is prompted by other unmet needs among labour forces in creative industries. For example, dispersed workers are increasingly coming together in coworking spaces, where freelancers and others in non-standard employment share a common place to work, splitting the cost of rent and office services and reestablishing workplace community among disaggregated workers. Coworking spaces and benefits societies catering to independent workers demonstrate that, although the flexibilization of labour exacerbates competition and exploitation ("the law of mutual struggle"), it can also give rise to cooperation and association, confirming the persistence of the "law of mutual aid."

Mutual aid institutions strive to achieve more than enable cultural workers to better manage in precarious conditions. Practices of mutual aid in cultural production milieus encourage experiments in the construction of new relations of production to mitigate alienation and exploitation. Our research identifies three mutual aid institutions in the arts, media and cultural industries that create conditions for autonomous cultural work to be supported and sustained: first, artist-run centres, which are self-organized spaces where local artists come together to create, curate, and circulate work independently of commercial galleries and state-administered cultural institutions (Detterer and Nannucci 2012; Robertson 2006); second, worker cooperatives, member-owned and democratically-controlled businesses that intersect with creative industries (Boyle 2012), such as the coworking space Ecto in Montréal and the print-design shop Calverts in London; and third, occupied cultural spaces, which are more openly antagonistic to state and market power and governed via horizontal decision-making processes. These include MACAO in Milan and Teatro Valle in Rome, which are aligned with the Italian "common goods" movement (Bailey and Marcucci 2013). Artist-run centres, worker cooperatives, and occupied cultural spaces not only reflect but also help to cultivate the facility of mutual aid. These working institutions of mutual aid ought to be where we look to explore normative criteria of "good work" beyond the confines of the commercial cultural industries (Oakley 2014; Hesmondhalgh and Baker 2011).

Our point is not simply to observe that there are social alternatives to self-reliance but more broadly to advocate for the uptake of Kropotkin's approach in cultural labour studies. Kropotkin's inquiries into mutual aid, in the words of autonomist Harry Cleaver (1992), set out to discover "already existing activities which embody new, alternative forms of social cooperation and ways of being." Rather than draft blueprints, research on mutual aid would spotlight counter-capitalist experiments in the here and now. Investigating cultural work through the lens of mutual aid thus dovetails with the idea of "post-capitalist politics" developed by Gibson-Graham (2006) and applied to cultural work by Kennedy (2012) and Banks (2007). Fidelity to Kropotkin's method requires activist-oriented research that not only documents and examines "the desires and self-activity of the people," but also, adds Cleaver (1992), "articulate(s) them in ways which contribute both to their circulation and empowerment." While the task is that of tracking "emerging trends of mutual aid working at cross purposes to capitalist domination" (Cleaver 1992), what makes mutual aid a productive conceptual entry is its ambivalence. For although mutual aid among cultural workers points to possibilities beyond waged labour, the commodity form and state administration, the extent to which practices of mutual aid disrupt, co-exist with, or even bind workers to dominant political-economic logics requires situated analysis. Be that as it may, mutual aid establishes the social bonds necessary to contest labour precarity and affirms the self-organization necessary for alternative economies. The stakes, then, are not limited to cultural labour: on the contrary, the greatest significance of mutual aid among cultural workers is the formation of sensibilities that favour solidarity generally, including solidarity with segments of the working class outside the relatively privileged quarters of the creative industries. This takes us to what we call policy from below.

Policy from below

By many accounts, the growth and expansion of the creative industries has been fuelled by policy. Over the past few decades, governments the world over, policy-makers, consultants, and institutions all the way up to the United Nations have prioritized policies promoting arts, media, and culture as catalysts of jobs creation, economic growth, and urban "revitalization" (United Nations Development Pro-gramme 2013; Throsby 2010; Martin and Florida 2009; DCMS 2008). The ascendency of creative industries policy has been met with critique, particularly from scholars alert to the difficult conditions in which a growing number of cultural workers labour, including rising rents, low wages, and general precarity. Critically, many note a lack of attention in official policy discourse to issues of work and the quality of jobs that creative industries produce (Oakley 2013; Banks and Hesmondhalgh 2009; Ross 2009). Researchers "looking for work" in creative industries policy (Banks and Hesmondhalgh 2009) typically focus on the state and industry as the primary agents. Cultural workers in the arts, as Woddis (2013: 1) argues, are "rarely acknowledged by cultural policy researchers as being more than marginally involved in policy-making." Although Murray and Gollmitzer (2012) attend to policy fixes for precarity in creative industries, the efforts of workers themselves and their organizations to advocate for policy aimed at improving working conditions for the precariously employed are generally downplayed in the literature on labour and creative industries.

We propose zooming in on cultural workers' participation in policy processes by examining their role as generators of proposals attentive to labour issues (see Coles 2012). From this view, policy innovation lies not in the top-down designs of state and corporate actors, but in the bottom-up solutions proposed by workers and their collective organizations. Policy from below is targeted at remedying the gaps in creative industries and related labour policies, but could have farther-reaching effects in addressing precarious employment across the labour market.

Take, for example, the proposal for a basic guaranteed minimum income, which has resonance across the globe as a remedy for widespread precarity and economic inequality. In the 1980s, the Independent Artists Union (IAU), a grassroots group of artists based in the Canadian province of Ontario, organized, demonstrated and wrote policy briefs on the need for a form of basic income that would entitle working artists to receive an adequate living wage from the state. The IAU elevated a notion of art as labour and linked artistic autonomy to artists' material conditions. The IAU extended its call for material security in the form of a decent, guaranteed income to all workers (Independent Artists Union 1986).

Although the IAU disbanded by 1990, cultural workers in Canada continue to circulate policy proposals that could have mitigating effects on precarity, ranging from the narrowly focused bid to allow performers to average their fluctuating incomes for tax purposes, lobbied for by the Alliance of Canadian Cinema, Television and Radio Artists (ACTRA) (n.d.), to the sweeping purview of the national Urban Worker Strategy, a bill introduced in Canadian Parliament that responds to the plight of temps, freelancers, interns, part-timers and other flexworkers who flit from gig to gig, shift to shift, contract to contract, with no guarantee of income or of future work, let alone social protections (Cohen and de Peuter 2013). The Urban

Worker Strategy, developed by a member of parliament who himself worked for decades as a freelance musician and journalist, contains a patchwork of policies that could extend social protections typically reserved for those in standard employment: the bill includes expanding access to Employment Insurance and pensions, cracking down on employment misclassification, and better regulating temp work and unpaid internships. Notably developed through consultations with alt-labour and cultural worker organizations – including the Canadian Intern Association, the Workers' Action Centre, and ACTRA – the Urban Worker bill builds on the ongoing history of Canada serving as a test site for cultural-worker led policy development.

To date, the most significant Canadian policy that has resulted from art worker activism is the *Status of the Artist Act*, a unique piece of federal labour legislation enacted in 1995 – after extensive lobbying by artists and cultural worker organizations – that extends collective bargaining rights to self-employed cultural workers. The IAU, although short-lived, served as a critical venue for mobilizing artists around the notion that artists could secure decent material conditions only through collective bargaining (Condé and Beveridge forthcoming). Decades later, CARFAC, Canada's visual artists' union, is using *Status of the Artist* to pressure the National Gallery of Canada to bargain for artists' minimum fees and copyright protections, a labour dispute currently en route to the Supreme Court of Canada.

Beyond Canada, cultural workers and their emergent organizations are incubating policy proposals that fall under a framework of flexicurity, or security for workers in flexible working arrangements, which advocates note is key for supporting workers who seek out self-employment in a bid for autonomy (Murray and Gollmitzer 2012; Vosko 2010). The Freelancers Union, for example, has delved into policy development. After documenting over US$15 million in unpaid wages that freelancers have no legal recourse to collect, the organization drafted and lobbied for the Freelance Payment Protection Act, which would enable freelancers to use the state's resources to collect unpaid wages. The bill is currently in front of New York State's Labor Committee (Freelancers Union 2014). Other examples include artists lobbying for an artists' resale right; the Model Alliance mobilizing to pass a bill extending child labour protections for models under eighteen (Holpuch 2013); the fledgling intern advocacy movement pushing for the passage of bills to protect interns' labour rights in New York, Oregon, and Ontario (McKnight 2014; Gershman 2013); and Italian activists proposing new legal frameworks for conceiving of culture as a "common good" to protect cultural institutions from privatization (Mattei 2013).

Our research demonstrates that cultural workers' associations are not only documenting the scope of precarious employment but also proposing alternative visions for how cultural work should be supported and organized. In an era of declining union power and entrenched labour market precarity, as agents of policy development, cultural workers demonstrate the possibility of detaching social protections and security from an employment relationship. This is a significant step for cultural policy from below, which has shifted from focusing on the act of creating culture – requesting more state funding for the arts, for example – to demanding that work be sustainable and secure outside of traditional employment relationships. Such efforts point to a wider transformative vision of a model of social security that would go "beyond employment" (Vosko 2010: 219), one that has been proposed as part of rethinking labour under post-Fordist capitalism and the possibilities of delinking social protections from waged labour (Weeks 2011).

There is no guarantee that cultural worker policy proposals will benefit a broad swath of the labour market, however. Workers and their organizations must engage in the difficult task of cross-class, pan-sectoral organizing to broaden the reach of cultural policy from below. Inspiring, then, are instances such as the Urban Worker Strategy, which, although not without its problems, involves an effort to link cultural sector unions with other organizations such as Toronto's Workers' Action Centre, whose constituency includes migrant workers in low-wage service sector jobs. The struggles of art workers, interns, and freelancers to be compensated for their labour could, moreover, link up to broader anti-austerity struggles, including campaigns in North America to raise the minimum wage. In the meantime, cultural workers' proposals provide rich terrain for researchers looking for work in cultural policy, and provide pointers for what policy infrastructures might make independent livelihoods in art, culture, and beyond more sustainable. An important step in this process has been the efforts of cultural workers to redefine dominant labels offered to name and explain cultural labour, a process we consider through the lens of counter-interpellation.

Counter-interpellation

The labour turn in contemporary social theory is synonymous with a surge of concepts created to name ongoing transformations in the nature of work and capitalist valorization processes, including "immaterial labour" (Lazzarato 1996), "cognitive labour" (Berardi 2009), "affective labour" (Hardt 1999), and "digital labour" (Fuchs 2014). Cutting across these Marxian categories is the point that although the world of work is mutating in dramatic ways, it remains driven by familiar economic imperatives and power asymmetries. This is a key message of the pioneering critical studies of labour in creative industries that were carried out under such headings as the "no-collar" workplace (Ross 2004) and the "cybertariat" (Huws 2003), terms coined to tarnish the egalitarian gloss on high-tech work in the early twenty-first century. These reality-checking labels continue to provide a much-needed antidote to persistent neoliberal frames such as the "creative class" (Florida 2012) and the "free agent" (Pink 2002), entrepreneurial identities that neutralize class and power relations. Overall, these varied terms are volleys in a contest over the meaning of work, workers, and workplaces in contemporary creative industries.

While there are now rich empirical accounts of cultural production detailing experiences of labour and unpacking practitioners' understanding of their work (Hesmondhalgh and Baker 2011), less attention has been devoted to the diverse ways in which working people in creative industries, in the context of collective organizing, struggle over the meaning of their employment status, working identities, and the labour they perform. This gap can be addressed through our third concept, counter-interpellation. If interpellation designates the process through which ideology hails individuals to inhabit a subject-position simpatico with the priorities of the dominant order, counter-interpellation encompasses practices through which workers and their associations challenge prevailing interpellative devices and adopt alternate identifications.

Precarity, the keyword catalyzing our research, exemplifies counter-interpellation. Before its adoption by critical scholars, precarity was a mobilizing term used by activist groups in Europe in the early 2000s bound up with an "alternative system of meaning ... about labour market flexibility" (Mattoni 2008: 108). By condensing in one word the social, financial, and existential undercurrent of the neoliberal pursuit of flexibiliza-tion, the idea of precarity helped to meet workers' need for "words to talk about what is happening to us," as the feminist collective Precarias a la Deriva (2004: 57) noted in a related context. More than describing conditions of labour and life marked by uncertainty and insecurity, the language of precarity circulated through activist inter-ventions, the term wielded not just to grieve collective marginalization but also to assert collective agency (Cosse 2008; Papadopoulos et al. 2008: 228). It is in the production of counter-publics that precarity came to function as a counter-interpellation: the concept sought to combat the individualizing effects of the conditions it named by encouraging the identification of common ground among disaggregated workers differentially affected by labour market instability. The activist origins of precarity affirm the autonomy of communicative capacities, with youthful militants turning the linguistic abilities, brand savvy, and media know-how that flexploitation thrives on, against itself.

While the concept of precarity was a general oppositional response to the neo-liberal doctrine of flexibility, struggles are also unfolding around dominant terms associated with specific forms of nonstandard work. One example comes by way of the Freelancers Union, which addresses its constituency as "independent workers." Recognizing workers' desire for autonomy vis-à-vis the standard employment rela-tionship, the independent worker label presents an alternative to the subject position of the entrepreneur while simultaneously appealing to a vague anti-government sensi-bility that potentially reinforces individual self-reliance. Underscoring the term's ambivalence, however, the process of hailing its members as independent workers is part of the Freelancers Union's bid to convert a source of marginalization (exclusion from state entitlements and employer-supported benefits) into a point of collective identification, in turn a prerequisite for fostering social relations of mutual aid.

Nowhere on the cultural labour landscape is the battle to identify and define work more pitched than around the figure of the intern, whose quasi-employers are densely clustered in creative industries. Dominant discourse on internships is littered with phrases that abet the process of "self-precarization" (Lorey 2009), including clichéd rationales ("paying your dues," "getting a foot in the door"), deprecating self-assessments ("But I have no experience"), and reluctant acquiescence ("This is the way to break in now"). Over the past two years, however, the intern label has become contentious, due largely to autonomous organizing and agitating by interns and their allies. Campaigns of intern activist initiatives, including Intern Aware in the UK, the Canadian Intern Association, and Intern Labor Rights in the US, are troubling the framework within which internships are normatively understood and the terminology deployed therein. Attracting considerable media attention, intern rights advocates have achieved some-thing quite striking: the politicization of the previously innocuous subject of the intern, by linking internships to "exploitation," an increasingly common word choice in mainstream media coverage of intern advocates (for example, Goodman 2014). Action on the internship issue, including internship policy reforms being floated by governments, the extra caution an employer might exercise before advertising an unpaid position, and the courage of young people to speak out against dubious internships, are fuelled by intersecting forces, including independently organized interns' practices of self-representation.

Other symbolic fronts are emerging in the fight against the naturalization of the performance of labour at a discount in creative industries. While the intern category is more or less accepted by intern rights activists, other cultural labour collectivities reject outright the legitimacy of prevailing terms. "Content provider," for example, is strongly resisted by freelance journalists and writers' unions. Their efforts overlap with campaigns such as the US National Writers Union's "Pay the Writer!" slogan. Similar campaigns have emerged in other sectors, including the UK Musicians' Union's Pay Not Play campaign, waged to erase the perception of working musicians as hobbyists. Discursively asserting the value of professional craft from below, as these and other initiatives do, is an attempt to protect workers' livelihoods from the material effects of industry-derived terms that devalue the labour of symbolic production. Responses based in professional identity are significant, yet potentially constrained politically to the extent that they skirt addressing a more universal subject, that of worker.

The artist is a prototype for the contemporary "do-what-you-love" ideology (Tokumitsu 2014). It is significant, then, that politicized artists are reviving efforts to ground artistic identity in labour, upsetting the reputation of the artist as a model of the de-alienated worker and bypassing individualized narratives of creative autonomy (for a historical study, see Bryan-Wilson 2009). The New York City-based group W.A.G.E. (Working Artists and the Greater Economy) formed in 2008 to challenge cultural institutions' habit of compensating artists merely in the "promise of exposure" (W.A.G.E. n.d.). Via teach-ins, conference presentations, and publications, W.A.G.E. has argued that the offer of exposure as remuneration "denies the value of our labor" (W.A.G.E. n.d.). Under such conditions, says W.A.G.E.'s Steiner (2008), artists "become market speculators rather than cultural workers." W.A.G.E.'s efforts to reject a market-based identification and instead frame the artist as an undercompensated worker performing value-generating labour for institutions was a preliminary step in an organizing process that has more recently focused on developing policy from below, specifically the W.A.G.E. certification programme, a proposal for minimum fee structures at galleries.

Singling out cultural workers risks reinforcing borders between groups of workers who otherwise share common structural conditions, and so it is notable that another artist-activist group, Arts & Labor, which emerged from Occupy Wall Street in New York, has also reclaimed the "art worker" category, inflected inclusively in an attempt to encourage solidarity across occupational strata. As Arts & Labor's (n.d.) mandate reads, "We are artists and interns, writers and educators, art handlers and designers, administrators, curators, assistants, and students. We are all art workers and members of the 99%." While there are unresolved political tensions in the "art worker" category (Bryan-Wilson 2009), groups like Arts & Labor and W.A.G.E. nonetheless engage cultural producers in a process of collective identification within a context of solidarity activism and a critique of structural inequality.

Inquiry into processes and practices of counter-interpellation in creative industries would explore livelihood struggles as also encompassing meaning struggles. Struggling over meaning is one of the principal activities of the collective initiatives we are researching. Activist aggregations are the political innovators of new semiotic means of self-understanding vis-à-vis the political economy of precarity. Access to counter-interpellations is, we argue, a condition of possibility for furthering labour politics in creative industries: resistance is enabled by terms for locating oneself differently in dominant relations of power. What the terminological contests we have described point to is a different kind of cultural work, that of producing new communicative devices for labour's critical self-awareness, self-activity, and collective organization.

Conclusion

Carrying out cultural labour research beginning from resistance and alternatives requires a revised conceptual lexicon that positions workers as agents directly confronting structural pressures on their work and lives. In this chapter, we have proposed three concepts that can serve as entry points for further investigation of how cultural workers organize, why they organize in certain formations, and what challenges their initiatives face. Mutual aid, we proposed, is a concept that can identify workers' collective efforts to resist the individualization and structural competitiveness of cultural labour. Through worker cooperatives, collective associations, and other institutions, cultural workers are engaging in cooperation to support one another in navigating precarious labour markets and developing collaborative practices that facilitate collectivity and solidarity, providing a counter to the enterprising ethos so ingrained in contemporary cultural work. Our second concept, policy from below, highlighted cultural workers' efforts to develop or push for bottom-up policy solutions that could mitigate the precarious nature of cultural work and which have potential to extend beyond the creative class. Our research points to a range of policy proposals emerging from cultural worker organizations, from a universal basic income to more specific initiatives such as labour protections for interns. Our third concept, counter-interpellation, identified the critical practice of struggling over meaning that underpins contemporary cultural worker organizing. By resisting being "hailed" into dominant subject positions, cultural workers are collectively proposing alternative meanings that attempt to interpellate cultural workers into a counter subjectivity, that of resistant, autonomous workers.

These conceptual entry points also begin to reveal some of the tensions marking and generated by workers' efforts, tensions arising from the political-economic conditions in which these activities occur. While mutual aid points to the spread of what have previously been marginal institutions and practices, the organizations we highlighted do not engage in collective bargaining, which is a serious limitation on their potential to democratize power relations in cultural production. And while policy from below reveals the development of innovative ideas from those who experience precarity firsthand, it will take serious collective power in the form of social movement backing to push for implementation and enforcement at the state level. Finally, while practices of counter-interpellation show promise for recoding discourses of cultural labour, it is still a minority of activist workers who are organizing and embracing a politicized worker identity – the majority of cultural workers tend to shrug off a labour-oriented identity.

Our proposed concepts nonetheless support a politicized understanding of labour autonomy in cultural and creative industries. The question facing further inquiry into emerging labour politics in creative industries is, ultimately, the same question facing all working people: how do you confront power? This includes the neoliberal forces seeking to individualize work and isolate workers, state power to impose austerity measures and scale back worker protections, and the aggressive power of corporations and capital. What cultural workers' collective initiatives show is the understanding that power cannot be effectively confronted individually, and that collective resistance under today's difficult conditions takes time to develop, mobilize, and sustain.

References

ACTRA (n.d.) "Income Tax Average" (accessed March 12, 2014: www.actra.ca/main/advocacy/issues/income-tax-averaging/).

Amman, J. (2002) "Union and the New Economy: Motion Picture and Television Unions Offer a Model for New Media Professionals," *WorkingUSA*, 6 (2): 111–31.

Arts & Labor (n.d.) "About" (accessed March 10, 2014: artsandlabor.org/about-al/).

Bailey, S. and Marcucci, M.E. (2013) "Legalizing the Occupation: The Teatro Valle as a Cultural Commons," *South Atlantic Quarterly*, 112 (2): 396–405.

Banks, M. (2007) *The Politics of Cultural Work*, London: Palgrave Macmillan.

Banks, M. (2010) "Autonomy Guaranteed? Cultural Work and the 'Art-Commerce Relation'," *Journal for Cultural Research*, 14 (3): 251–69.

Banks, M. and Hesmondhalgh, D. (2009) "Looking for Work in Creative Industries Policy," *International Journal of Cultural Policy*, 15 (4): 415–30.

Beito, D.T. (2000) *From Mutual Aid to the Welfare State: Fraternal Societies and Social Services, 1890–1967*, Chapel Hill, NC: The University of North Carolina Press.

Berardi, F. (Bifo) (2009) *The Soul at Work: From Alienation to Autonomy*, trans. F. Cadel and G. Mecchia, Los Angeles: Semiotext(e).

Birchall, J. (ed.) (2001) *The New Mutualism in Public Policy*, London: Routledge.

Boyle, D. (2012) *Good News: A Co-Operative Solution to the Media Crisis*, Manchester: Co-operatives UK.

Bryan-Wilson, J. (2009) *Art Workers: Radical Practice in the Vietnam War Era*, Berkeley, CA: University of California Press.

Cleaver, H. (1992) "Kropotkin, Self-valorization, and the Crisis of Marxism" (accessed March 10, 2014: libcom.org/library/kropotkin-self-valorization-crisis-marxism).

Cohen, N. and de Peuter, G. (2013) "The Politics of Precarity: Can the Urban Worker Strategy Address Precarious Employment for All?" Briarpatch, November/December: 6–9.

Coles, A. (2012) *Counting Canucks: Cultural Labour and Canadian Cultural Policy* (Ph.D. thesis), McMaster University.

Condé, C. and Beveridge, K. (forthcoming) "The Art of Collective Bargaining: An Interview with Carole Condé and Karl Beveridge" (interviewed by G. de Peuter and N. Cohen), *Canadian Journal of Communication*.

Cosse, E. (2008) "The Precarious Go Marching," *In the Middle of a Whirlwind* (accessed March 10, 2014: inthemiddleofthewhirlwind.wordpress.com).

Coulson, S. (2012) "Collaborating in a Competitive World: Musicians' Working Lives and Understandings of Entrepreneurship," *Work, Employment and Society*, 26 (2): 246–61.

Cultural Workers Organize (2013) "'Messages of Rupture': An Interview with Emanuele Braga on the Macao Occupation in Milan," trans. Roberta Buiani, *Scapegoat: Architecture, Landscape, Political Economy*, 04: 179–87.

Davies, A. and Ford, S. (2000) "Culture Clubs," *Mute* 1 (18): September 10 (accessed March 10, 2014: www.metamute.org/editorial/articles/culture-clubs).

DCMS (2008) *Creative Britain: New Talents for the New Economy*, London: Department for Culture, Media and Sport (accessed March 12, 2014: www.agcas.org.uk/assets/download?file=567& parent = 253).

de Peuter, G. (2014) "Confronting Precarity in the Warhol Economy: Notes from New York City," *Journal of Cultural Economy*, 7 (1): 31–47.

Detterer, G. and Nannucci, M. (2012) *Artist-Run Spaces*, Zurich: JRP| Ringier Kunstverlag AG.

Eidelson, J. (2013) "Will 'Alt-Labor' Replace Unions?" *Salon*, January 29 (accessed March 10, 2014: www.salon.com/2013/01/29/will_alt_labor_replace_unions_labor/).

Florida, R. (2012) *The Rise of the Creative Class-Revisited*, 10th Anniversary Edition, New York City: Basic Books.

Freelancers Union (2014) "Payment protection" (accessed March 12, 2014: https://www.freelancersunion.org/blog/2014/11/14/insurance/).

Fuchs, C. (2014) *Digital Labour and Karl Marx*, London: Routledge.

Gershman, J. (2013) "New Bill Would Outlaw Discrimination against Unpaid Interns," *The Wall Street Journal*, October 18 (accessed March 12, 2014: blogs.wsj.com/law/2013/10/18/new-bill-would-outlaw-discrimination-against-unpaid-interns/).

Gibson-Graham, J.K. (2006) *A Postcapitalist Politics*, Minneapolis, MN: University of Minnesota Press.

Goodman, L.-A. (2014) "Backlash Against Unpaid Internships in Canada, Called 'Exploitation'," *Calgary Herald*, March 2 (accessed March 10, 2014: www.calgaryherald.com/news/calgary/Backlash+growing+against+unpaid+internships+Canada+called+exploitation/9569271/story.html).

Hardt, M. (1999) "Affective Labour," *Boundary 2*, 26: 89–100.

Hesmondhalgh, D. and Baker, S. (2011) *Creative Labour: Media Work in Three Cultural Industries*, London: Routledge.

Holpuch, A. (2013) "New York Increases Protections for Young Models with Child Labour Laws," *Guardian*, October 22 (accessed March 12, 2014: www.theguardian.com/world/2013/oct/22/new-york-fashion-underage-model-law).

Horowitz, S. (2013) "What is New Mutualism?" *Huffington Post*, November 19 (accessed March 10, 2014: www.huffingtonpost.com/sara-horowitz/what-is-new-mutualism_b_4303316.html).

Huws, U. (2003) *The Making of a Cybertariat: Virtual Work in a Real World*, New York: Monthly Review Press.

Independent Artists Union (1986) "Social and Economic Status of the Artist in Canada," *FUSE*, 26 (142): 39–47.

Kennedy, H. (2012) *Net Work: Ethics and Values in Web Design*, London: Palgrave Macmillan.

Kropotkin, P. ([1902] 2006) *Mutual Aid: A Factor of Evolution*, Mineola, NY: Dover Publications.

Lazzarato, M. (1996) "Immaterial Labour," in P. Virno and M. Hardt (eds), *Radical Thought in Italy: A Potential Politics*, trans. P. Colilli and E. Emory, Minneapolis, MN: University of Minnesota Press.

Lorey, I. (2009) "Governmentality and Self-Precarization: On the Normalization of Cultural Producers," in G. Raunig and G. Ray (eds) *Art and Contemporary Critical Practice: Reinventing Institutional Critique*, trans. L. Rosenblatt and D. Fink, London: MayFly Books.

MACAO (2012) "Press release MACAO," May 5. Accessed March 10, 2014: www.teatrovalleoccupato.it/press-release-macao_may-5th-milan).

Martin, R. and Florida, R. (2009) *Ontario in the Creative Age*, Toronto: Martin Prosperity Institute.

Mattei, U. (2013) "Protecting the Commons: Water, Culture, and Nature: The Commons Movement in the Italian Struggle Against Neoliberal Governance," *South Atlantic Quarterly*, 112 (2): 366–76.

Mattoni, A. (2008) "ICTs in National and Transnational Mobilizations," *TripleC*, 6 (2): 105–24.

McKnight, Z. (2014) "Unpaid Interns: MPP Calls for New Protections," *Toronto Star*, March 4 (accessed March 12, 2014: http://www.thestar.com/news/gta/2014/03/04/unpaid_interns_mpp_calls_for_new_protections.html).

McRobbie, A. (2002) "Clubs to Companies: Notes on the Decline of Political Culture in Speeded Up Creative Worlds," *Cultural Studies*, 16 (4): 516–31.

Mosco, V. and McKercher, C. (2008) *The Laboring of Communication: Will Knowledge Workers of the World Unite?* Lanham, MD: Lexington Books.

Murray, C. and Gollmitzer, M. (2012) "Escaping the Precarity Trap: A Call For Creative Labour Policy," *International Journal of Cultural Policy*, 18 (4): 419–38.

Oakley, K. (2013) "Absentee Workers: Representation and Participation in the Cultural Industries," in M. Banks, R. Gill, and S. Taylor (eds), *Theorizing Cultural Work: Labour, Continuity and Change in the Cultural and Creative Industries*, London: Routledge.

Oakley, K. (2014) "Good Work? Rethinking Cultural Entrepreneurship," in C. Bilton and S. Cummings (eds), *Handbook of Management and Creativity*, Cheltenham: Edward Elgar.

Papadopoulos, D., Stephenson, N. and Tsianos, V. (2008) *Escape Routes: Control and Subversion in the 21st Century*, London: Pluto.

Pasquinelli, M. (2007) "ICW – Immaterial Civil War: Prototypes of Conflict Within Cognitive Capitalism," in G. Lovink and N. Rossiter (eds) *MyCreativity Reader: A Critique of Creative Industries*, Amsterdam: Institute of Network Cultures.

Pink, D. (2002) *Free Agent Nation: The Future of Working for Yourself*, New York: Business Plus.

Precarias a la Deriva (2004) "Adrift Through the Circuits of Feminized Precarious Work," *Feminist Review*, 77 (1):157–61.

Robertson, C. (2006) *Policy Matters: Administrations of Art and Culture*, Toronto: YYZ Artists' Outlet.

Rose, N. (1996) *Inventing Ourselves: Psychology, Power, and Personhood*, Cambridge: Cambridge University Press.

Ross, A. (2004) *No-Collar: The Humane Workplace and its Hidden Costs*, Philadelphia, PA: Temple University Press.

Ross, A. (2009) *Nice Work if You Can Get It: Life and Labour in Precarious Times*, New York: New York University Press.

Ryan, B. (1992) *Making Capital From Culture: The Corporate Form of Capitalist Cultural Production*, Berlin: Walter de Gruyter.

Steiner, A.L. (2008) "Presentation at Democracy in America, Creative Time in Association with Park Avenue Armory," New York City, September 27 (accessed October 4, 2010: www.wageforwork.com/WAGE_RAGE_08.pdf).

Throsby, D. (2010) *The Economics of Cultural Policy*, Cambridge: Cambridge University Press.

Tokumitsu, M. (2014) "In the Name of Love," *Jacobian*, 13 (accessed March 10, 2014: https://www.jacobinmag.com/2014/01/in-the-name-of-love).

United Nations Development Programme (2013) *Creative Economy Report 2013, Special Edition*, New York: United Nations Development Programme.

Vosko, L. (2010) *Managing the Margins: Gender, Citizenship, and the International Regulation of Precarious Employment*, Oxford: Oxford University Press.

W.A.G.E. (n.d.) "wo/manifesto" (accessed March 10, 2014: www.wageforwork.com/about/1/womanifesto).

Weeks, K. (2011) *The Problem with Work: Feminism, Marxism, Antiwork Politics and Postwork Imaginaries*, Durham, NC: Duke University Press.

Woddis, J. (2013) "Arts Practitioners in the Cultural Policy Process: Spear-Carriers or Speaking Parts?" *International Journal of Cultural Policy*, August: 1–17.

25
HOLLYWOOD COGNITARIANS

Toby Miller

Cultural labor is a complex term. Does "cultural" refer to the basic inputs and outcomes of an industry, or can it apply to an industry where cultural marks are epiphenomenal (Miller, 2009)? How much of the work done has to be cultural for it to characterize the overall *nature* of that work? Is a carpenter on a film set doing cultural labor? Is a designer in an automobile factory *not* doing cultural labor? Should we accept a distinction between workers "below" and "above" the mythic "line" that is drawn on a class basis by Hollywood accountants, where drivers, caterers, electricians, carpenters, secretaries, interns, and the like are placed in the lower category while writers, producers, executives, directors, actors, and managers reside in the upper? Is the cultural labor force divided along classic Taylorist lines of industrial work, distinguishing blue-collar workers who undertake tasks on the line from the white-collar workers who observe and time them (Scott, 1998a: 18)?

Epistemologically, is work a generative or descriptive category, a Marxist or Weberian one—is it about a relationship to the means of production, or one's position within a labor market? Must work be productive in capitalist terms in order to be counted as such? Or are moviegoers who buy tickets engaged in cultural work, given that they dress, drive, drink, smell, swear, inhale, and interpret in keeping with their idols? If people make YouTube videos for fun and free, are they working? And how far up- or downstream from Hollywood should we go when we speak of Hollywood workers—to enslaved people in Congo who mine the raw materials that go into cell phones that are used months later to communicate on a studio set, or artisans doing initial production work on animation in VietNam that is then "corrected" in LA? Finally, how do we study these workers, and what questions should we ask as we do so?

There is a voluminous scholarly literature about cultural labor, starting with ethnographies of newsrooms (Gans, 1979; Tunstall, 1971 and 2001; Boyd-Barrett, 1995; Ericson et al., 1989; Golding and Elliott, 1979; Fishman, 1980; Tracey, 1977; Tumber, 2000; Breed, 1955; Domingo and Paterson, 2008 and 2011; Cottle, 2003; Dickinson, 2008; Hannerz, 2004; Willig, 2013; "Worlds of Journalism," 2006; Tuchman, 1978; Riegert, 1998; Jacobs, 2009). Fictional and factual cinema and television have been anthropologically scrutinized since Hortense Powdermaker (1950) named Hollywood "the Dream Factory," on through John T. Caldwell's account of its "production cultures" (2008) to Sherry Ortner's investigation *Not Hollywood* (2013). Researchers have written about the proxemics and deictics of making horror movies, science fiction, documentary television, independent cinema, police procedurals, and soap opera (Buscombe, 1976; Alvarado and Buscombe, 1978; Elliott, 1979; Moran, 1982; Gitlin, 1994; Tulloch and Moran, 1986; Tulloch and Alvarado, 1983; Cantor, 1971; Espinosa, 1982; Silverstone, 1985; Dornfeld, 1998; Ginsburg *et al.*, 2002; Abu-Lughod, 2005; Gregory, 2007; Ytreberg, 2006; Mayer *et al.*, 2009; Mayer, 2011 and 2013; Kohn, 2006).

The primary emphasis of most of this work has been how meaning is encoded at the point of production. Like textual analysis and audience research, these studies generally seek the answer to a particular if endlessly recurring and seemingly universal riddle: why do screen texts matter and what makes them meaningful? The fundamental problematic animating such work is the question of consciousness—specifically, how consciousness is expressed and imbued in cultural production and experienced and interpreted in cultural reception.

This is both venerable and legitimate. But it is not the only means of studying cultural labor. What would happen if we sidestepped consciousness (just for a moment, between us) and loosened its hold on research? What if we accepted that worker consciousness matters, but no more in Hollywood than it does in Detroit? And what would we find if we looked beyond it?

Instead of exploring how cultural workers encode texts and spectators decode them, we might see cultural labor as a post-industrial exemplar that incarnates the latter-day loss of life-long employment and relative income security among the Global North's industrial-proletarian and, most recently, professional-managerial classes. For the truth is that a rarefied if exploitative mode of work—the artist and artisan—has become a shadow-setter for conditions of labor more generally.

Hollywood is a classic instance of this transformation. A car-assembly-like studio system of production (Fordism) applied to the industry between about 1920 and 1970, though it dramatically eroded from the late 1940s as a consequence of vertical disintegration, suburbanization, and televisualization (Miller *et al.*, 2012). A combination of trust-busting bureaucrats and judges leery of corporate power, returning white GIs clutching preferential housing deals, and the spread of TV across the nation turned urban moviegoers into suburban homebodies. That legal, demographic, and technological shift also transformed Hollywood labor from a regimented but reliable studio life, with longstanding relations of subordination and opportunity, into chaotically marketized, irregular employment.

One important *caveat* to the notion that the classical Hollywood studio system was truly Fordist is that while films were made *en masse*, the routinization, deskilling, and invigilation that manufacturing machinery forced on automotive and other factory workers rarely occurred. Many studio employees participated at various points in the labor process, and their work was not easily substituted. In addition, they had strong social interaction across class barriers (Powdermaker 1950: 169). Ironically, these differences from classic working-class *anomie* helped open the way to intense networking as a substitute for factory discipline.

The US film industry became a pioneer of the type of work beloved of contemporary management (post-Fordism). With jobs constantly starting, ending, and moving, it came to exemplify "flexible specialization"—a shift from life-long employment to casualized labor (Piore and Sabel, 1984). The pharmaceutical sector, for instance, looks to Hollywood's labor exploitation and avoidance of risk as a model for its own pernicious development (Franco, 2002; Surowiecki, 2004).

Hollywood workers and bosses strike complex, transitory arrangements on a project basis via temporary organizations, with small or large numbers of divers hands involved at different stages, sometimes functioning together and sometimes semi-autonomously. Networks are fluid:

> independent contractors coalesce for a relatively short period of time around one-off projects to contribute the organizational, creative, and technical talents that go into the production of a film. The inherent transience of this production system results in a high rate of tie formation and dissolution
>
> (Ferriani *et al.* 2009: 1548)

It's a bit like the hothouse of a conference or convention (Moorhouse, 1978). Places, times, and groups affect textual cues, contracts, technology, laws, insurance, policy incentives, educational support, finance, skills, costs, and marketing. Work may be subject to local, national, regional, and international fetishization of each component. This matches the way that the labor undertaken is largely fetishized away from the final text, rendered invisible other than to those dedicated credits watchers in theaters who peer around the bodies of the early rather than the dearly departed. Conventional organizational charts cannot adequately represent Hollywood, especially if one seeks to elude the conventions of hierarchy through capital whilst recognizing the eternal presence of managerial surveillance. Business leeches want flexibility in the numbers they employ, the technologies they use, the places where they produce, and the sums they pay—and *in*flexibility of ownership and control. The power and logic of domination by a small number of vast entities is achieved via a global network of subcontracted firms and individuals, in turn mediated through unions, employer associations, education, and the state.

This relates to wider shifts in the economics of labor in the Global North that were predicted, ideologized, and planned for over several decades. Fritz Machlup, a neo-classical prophet of the knowledge society, produced a 1962 bedside essential for true believers in doctrines of human capital. New and anticipated developments in the media and associated knowledge technologies were likened to a new Industrial Revolution or the Civil and Cold Wars, touted as a route to economic development as well as cultural and political expression/control. By the 1970s, "knowledge workers" were identified as vital to information-based industries that generate productivity gains and competitive markets (Bar with Simard, 2006). Cold War futurists like National Security Advisor Zbigniew Brzezinski (1969), cultural conservative Daniel Bell (1977), and professional anti-Marxist Ithiel de Sola Pool (1983) saw converged communications and information technologies moving grubby manufacturing from the Global North to the South and ramifying US textual and technical power, provided that the blandishments of socialism, and negativity toward global business, did not stimulate class struggle.

This suited the ideological, investment, and managerial agendas of policy makers and think tanks, but it occurred against a seemingly inimical backdrop—the statist project of mid-century liberal politics, to build a "Great Society," a term coined by the Edwardian Fabian Graham Wallas (1967). Wallas' student Walter Lippmann spoke of "a deep and intricate interdependence" that came with "living in a Great Society." He worked against militarism and other dehumanizing tendencies that emerged from "the incessant and indecisive struggle for domination and survival" (1943: 161, 376). This idea was picked up by Lyndon Johnson (minus the anti-militarism) and became a foundational argument for competent and comprehensive social justice through welfarism and other forms of state intervention.

Ronald Reagan launched his successful 1966 campaign for the governorship of California with a clear alternative, birthed from the idea of human capital: "I propose … 'A Creative Society' … to discover, enlist and mobilize the incredibly rich human resources of California [through] innumerable people of creative talent" (1966). Reagan's rhetoric publicly birthed today's idea of technology unlocking the creativity that is allegedly lurking, unbidden, in individuals, thereby permitting them to become happy, productive—and without full-time employment.

Much of the "Great Society" vision has been undermined by decades of neoliberalism, as per the influence of Reagan and his kind. That deregulatory revolution has ultimately disempowered the very people around whom it was built: the educated middle class. Hollywood showed that workers with abundant cultural capital could move from security to insecurity, certainty to uncertainty, salary to wage, firm to project, and profession to precarity with smiles on their faces. It's that theoretically bizarre but industrially apt moment when scientific management embraces human-relations management. Capital luxuriates in the disciplined and disciplining love-in that ensues.

Following this logic, US residents hone their education and vocation in the direction of "immaterial labor" (Hardt and Negri, 2000: 286, 290–92). As a consequence, many Hollywood workers come from highly educated, middle-class backgrounds and tailor their education to suit technological and economic change. But against the prevailing *nostra*, that has often resulted in proletarianization: "While capitalist labor has always been characterized by intermittency for lower-paid and lower-skilled workers, the recent departure is the addition of well-paid and high-status workers into this group of 'precarious workers'" (Gill and Pratt, 2008: 2).

A quarter of a century ago, the lapsed leftist Reaganite Alvin Toffler (1983) coined the concept of a cognitariat to describe the workers who would come to characterize this new age. Today, an autonomist, Antonio Negri (2007), applies the term to people mired in contingent media work who combine fulsome qualifications with marked expertise in cultural technologies and genres. This cognitariat plays key roles in the production and circulation of goods and services, through both creation and coordination.

Work is not defined in terms of location (factories), tasks (manufacturing), or politics (moderating ruling-class power and ideology). What used to be the fate of artists and musicians working on a casualized basis—where "making cool stuff" with relative autonomy was meant to outweigh the benefits of ongoing employment within a controlling corporation—has become a norm. The outcome is contingent labor as a way of life. The cognitariat is comprised of downwardly-mobile (yet hyper-mobile!) people whose immediate forebears, with similar or less cultural capital, were confident of secure health care and retirement income. Today's cognitariat lacks both the organization of the traditional working class and the political *entrée* of the middle class from which it sprang.

Needless to say, the prevailing ideology sees the situation quite differently from the critical perspective I adopt. In cybertarian fantasies of this new era, flowers bloom all around in a phantasmagoria of opportunity. New technologies supposedly allow us to be simultaneously cultural consumers and producers (prosumers)—no more factory conditions, no more factory emissions. The result is said to be a democratized media, higher skill levels, and powerful challenges to old patterns of expertise and institutional authority—hence the popularity of "disintermediation": the putative demise of gatekeepers patrolling the boundaries of meaning (Graham, 2008; Ritzer and Jurgenson, 2010).

Time magazine exemplified this love of a seemingly immaterial world when it chose "You" as 2006's "Person of the Year," because "You control the Information Age. Welcome to your world" (Grossman, 2006). On the liberal left, the *Guardian* is prey to the same touching warlockcraft: someone called "You" heads its 2013 list of the hundred most important folks in the media (www.theguardian.com/media/2013/sep/01/you-them-mediaguardian-100-2013). Rupert Murdoch was well behind, at number eight (www.theguardian.com/media/series/mediaguardian-100-2013-1-100).

The comparatively cheap and easy access to making and circulating meaning afforded by internet-based media and genres has allegedly eroded the one-way hold on culture that saw a small segment of the world as producers and the larger segment as consumers, while the economy glides into an ever greener, funkier, more flexible post-industrialism. As barriers to the culture industries crumble, hitherto unimaginable freedoms proliferate: readers become writers, listeners transform into speakers, viewers emerge as stars, fans are academics, and *vice versa*. Zine writers are screenwriters, vanity bloggers are citizen journalists, children are columnists, and bus riders are witnesses.

This pseudo-de-professionalization-and-democratization of the media takes many fancy forms. Think of the job prospects that follow! Coca-Cola hires African Americans to drive through the inner city, selling soda and incarnating hip-hop. AT&T pays San Francisco buskers to mention the company in their songs. Urban performance poets rhyme about Nissan cars for cash, simultaneously hawking, entertaining, and researching. Subway's sandwich commercials are marketed as made by teenagers. Cultural-studies majors become designers. Graduate students in New York and Los Angeles read scripts for producers, then pronounce on whether they tap into audience interests. Precariously employed part-timers spy on fellow-spectators in theaters to see how they respond to coming attractions. Opportunities to vote in the Eurovision Song Contest or a reality program disclose the profiles and practices of viewers to broadcasters and affiliated companies so they can be monitored and wooed. End-user licensing agreements ensure that players of corporate games on-line sign over their cultural moves and perspectives to the very firms they are paying in order to participate (Miller, 2012; www.theguardian.com/sustainable-business/big-data-sustainability-podcast?CMP=twt[_]gu). In other words, corporations are using discounted labor whenever and wherever they can and banking on hipsters and desperates alike colluding in their own exploitation.

The neoclassical economic *doxa* preached by neoliberal cultural chorines favor an economy where competition and opportunity cost are in the litany and dissent is unforgiveable, as crazed as collective industrial organization (you know—unions). In short, "decent and meaningful work opportunities are reducing at a phenomenal pace in the sense that, for a high proportion of low- and middle-skilled workers, full-time, lifelong employment is unlikely" (Orsi, 2009: 35). Even the US National Governors Association recognizes that many tasks that are historically characteristic of "middle class work have either been eliminated by technological change or are now conducted by low-wage but highly skilled workers" (Sparks and Watts, 2011: 6).

The way that marginal cultural labor, from the jazz musician to the street artist, has long survived *sans* regular compensation and security now models the expectations we are *all* supposed to have, displacing our parents' or grandparents' assumptions about steady employment (Ross, 2009). Hence the success of concerns such as Mindworks Global Media, a company outside New Delhi that provides Indian-based journalists and copyeditors who work long-distance for newspapers whose reporters are supposedly in the US and Europe. There are 35–40% cost savings (Lakshman, 2008; mindworksglobal.com). Or the US advertising agency Poptent, which undercuts big competitors in sales to major clients by exploiting prosumers' labor in the name of "empowerment." That empowerment takes the following form: Poptent pays the creators of homemade commercials US$7,500; it receives a management fee of US $40,000; and the buyer saves about US$300,000 on the usual price (Chmielewski, 2012; www.poptent.com/creativenetwork).

How does this work in Hollywood? People are employed on a precarious basis by thousands of small firms dotted across the hinterland of California that offer post-production services, DVD film commentaries, music for electronic games, reality TV shows, and the like (Banks and Seiter, 2007; Scott, 1998b). Highly-qualified graduates and experienced artists and artisans increasingly look for jobs in visual effects, animation, and game development (Cieply, 2011). Many currently ply their trade in wonderfully satisfying jobs at YouTube's hundred new channels, the fruit of Google's US$100 million production (and US$200 million marketing) bet that five-minute on-line shows will kill off TV. Explosions are routinely filmed for these channels near my old loft in downtown LA. The workers blowing things up are paid US$15 an hour (Thielman, 2012). Luxury, really. But they've all got smart phones … and not-so-smart loans.[1]

Those who come from Los Angeles or flock to it may not even obtain such precarious employment, let alone the fabulous spoils they anticipated, in part because of monetary incentives for film and television to move elsewhere. In 2010, 43 US states sought to "attract" Hollywood through US$1.5 billion in public subvention. Critics argue that regardless of where projects are shot, most of the key labor force is only temporarily transplanted from the north-east and south-west, specifically New York, traditional home of network TV, and LA, traditional home of film. So the plum jobs go to people who spend most of their income and pay most of their taxes outside the places where they briefly work. The locals, by contrast, get distinctly below-the-line positions, as caterers and hairdressers—non-unionized sectors that do not build careers (Tannenwald, 2010; Foster *et al.*, 2013).

Susan Christopherson sees things differently, suggesting that the impact on southern California has been dire:

> Entertainment media jobs in the Los Angeles metropolitan region declined by 7.7% between 2005 and 2010, manifesting the impact of the financial crisis. However, for Los Angeles, which has consistently maintained at least a 45% share of the US national film and television employment and is the single most important centre of film and television production in the USA ... , the crisis punctuated a longer-term decline in employment and production capacity ... on-location shooting of feature films reached a high of 13,980 days in 1996; by 2009, it was only 4976 days ... location activity for television productions reached a high of 25,277 days in 2008, reflecting the expansion of low-cost reality and dramatic productions for cable television. Demonstrating the impact of the recession, on-location television production days in Los Angeles dropped by almost 17% in 2009. So, the more-lucrative film production jobs were replaced during the decade by less-lucrative television jobs. These jobs then decreased as the recession took hold ... the number of workers employed in films, television programmes and commercials in 2010 in Los Angeles County was lower than that in any year since 2001. In addition, because of the supply chains that are connected to project-based production, California state employment numbers actually undercount employment losses in the entertainment industry agglomeration in Los Angeles: they do not include unemployment of part-time workers (nearly a quarter of the industry workforce) nor unemployment in ancillary business services such as property, houses and equipment rental shops, which depend on Los Angeles productions for their employment and profits
>
> (Christopherson, 2013: 142)

As well as the complex impact of runaway production on workers, the system is structured in gender inequality. Women are severely over-represented and disempowered in the Hollywood cognitariat. In 2012, they held 18% of above-the-line, off-camera positions in Hollywood's top-grossing 250 motion pictures—an increase of just 1% on 1998. Such iniquities are common in project-based industries because of a tendency towards parthenogenesis when looking for employees quickly, as opposed to hiring in more stable organizations that are governed by personnel policies inflected with equal opportunity or affirmative action (Lauzen, 2013; Klos, 2013; Skilton, 2008: 1749).

Conclusion

As Hollywood transmogrified from Fordism to post-Fordism, it modeled a new world of insecurity and uncertainty, an economy founded on risk and anxiety. The cognitariat that resulted has been in the forefront of vanguardist capitalism, enabled by cultural workers' cybertarian self-exploitation that colludes in their oppression. The ideology of cybertarianism delivers workers into college and grad school debt, followed by an existence lived from project to project, with lengthy liminal time and space occupied and colored by serving drinks and clearing tables. It's not a good look.

That said, social movements linked to precariousness have made large claims for new alliances of cultural workers and other, yet more marginal, subjects, via the notion of a shared experience of mobility, powerlessness, isolation, competition, and new forms of work founded in risk and responsibility (Gill and Pratt, 2008). Cognitarians unite. You have nothing to lose but your precariousness. But you'd best lose your cybertarianism along the way, dudes. Party on.

Note

1 In 1993, 45% of undergraduates nationwide borrowed to pay tuition. Today's figure is 94%. Almost 9% of debtors defaulted on student loans in 2010, up 2% in a year. Average debt in 2011 was $23,300. Across the country, people graduating with student loans confronted the highest unemployment levels for recent graduates in memory: 9.1% (Martin and Lehren, 2012).

Works cited

Abu-Lughod, Lila. (2005). *Dramas of Nationhood: The Politics of Television in Egypt*. Chicago: University of Chicago Press.

Alvarado, Manuel and Edward Buscombe. (1978). *Hazell: The Making of a TV Series*. London: British Film Institute/Latimer.

Banks, Miranda and Ellen Seiter. (2007, December 7). "Spoilers at the Digital Utopia Party: The WGA and Students Now." *Flow* 7, no. 4, flowtv.org/2007/12/spoilers-at-the-digital-utopia-party-the-wga-and-students-now/.

Bar, François with Caroline Simard. (2006). "From Hierarchies to Network Firms." *The Handbook of New Media: Updated Students Edition*. Ed. Leah Lievrouw and Sonia Livingstone. Thousand Oaks: Sage. 350–63.

Bell, Daniel. (1977). "The Future World Disorder: The Structural Context of Crises." *Foreign Policy* 27: 109–35.

Boyd-Barrett, Oliver. (1995). "The Analysis of Media Occupations and Professionals." *Approaches to Media*. Ed. Oliver Boyd-Barrett and Chris Newbold. London: Edward Arnold. 270–76.

Breed, Warren. (1955). "Social Control in the Newsroom: A Functional Analysis." *Social Forces* 33, no. 4: 326–35.

Brzezinski, Zbigniew. (1969). *Between Two Ages: America's Role in the Technotronic Era*. New York: Viking Press.

Buscombe, Edward. (1976). *Making Legend of the Werewolf*. London: British Film Institute.

Caldwell, John T. (2008). *Production Culture: Industrial Reflexivity and Critical Practice in Film and Television*. Durham: Duke University Press.

Cantor, Muriel G. (1971). *The Hollywood TV Producer: His Work and His Audience*. New York: Basic Books.

Chmielewski, Dawn C. (2012, May 8). "Poptent's Amateurs Sell Cheap Commercials to Big Brands." *Los Angeles Times*, articles.latimes.com/2012/may/08/business/la-fi-ct-poptent-20120508.

Christopherson, Susan. (2013). "Hollywood in Decline? US Film and Television Producers Beyond the Era of Fiscal Crisis." *Cambridge Journal of Regions, Economy and Society* 6, no. 1: 141–57.

Cieply, Michael. (2011, July 4). "For Film Graduates, an Altered Job Picture." *New York Times*: C1.

Cottle, Simon, ed. (2003). *Media Organisation and Production*. London: Sage.

de Sola Pool, Ithiel. (1983). *Technologies of Freedom*. Cambridge, Mass.: Harvard University Press.

Dickinson, Roger. (2008). "Studying the Sociology of Journalists: The Journalistic Field and the News World." *Sociology Compass* 2, no. 5: 1383–99.

Domingo, David and Chris Paterson, eds. (2008). *Making Online News: The Ethnography of New Media Production*. New York: Peter Lang.

Domingo, David and Chris Paterson, eds. (2011). *Making Online News Volume 2: Newsroom Ethnographies in the Second Decade of Internet Journalism*. New York: Peter Lang.

Dornfeld, Barry. (1998). *Producing Public Television, Producing Public Culture*. Princeton: Princeton University Press.

Elliott, Philip. (1979). *The Making of a Television Series: A Case Study in the Sociology of Culture*. London: Constable.

Ericson, Richard V., Patricia M. Baranek, and Janet B. L. Chan. (1989). *Negotiating Control: A Study of News Sources*. Buckingham: Open University Press.

Espinosa, Paul. (1982). "The Audience in the Text: Ethnographic Observation of a Hollywood Story Conference." *Media, Culture and Society* 4, no. 1: 77–86.

Ferriani, Simone, Gino Cattani, and Charles Baden-Fuller. (2009). "The Relational Antecedents of Project-Entrepreneurship: Network Centrality, Team Composition and Project Performance." *Research Policy* 38, no. 10: 1545–58.

Fishman, Mark. (1980). *Manufacturing the News*. Austin: University of Texas Press.

Foster, Pacey, Stephan Manning, and David Terkla. (2013). "The Rise of Hollywood East: Regional Film Offices as Intermediaries in Film and Television Clusters." *Regional Studies* 10.1080/00343404.2013.799765.

Franco, Robert J. (2002). "Beyond the Blockbuster." *Pharmaceutical Executive* 22, no. 11: 74–80.

Gans, Herbert J. (1979). *Deciding What's News: A Study of CBS Evening News, NBC Nightly News, Newsweek and Time*. New York: Vintage Books.

Gill, Rosalind and Andy Pratt. (2008). "Precarity and Cultural Work: In the Social Factory? Immaterial Labor, Precariousness and Cultural Work." *Theory, Culture and Society* 25, nos. 7–8: 1–30.

Ginsburg, Faye D., Lila Abu-Lughod, and Brian Larkin, eds. (2002). *Media Worlds: Anthropology on New Terrain*. Berkeley: University of California Press.

Gitlin, Todd. (1994). *Inside Prime Time*, 2nd ed. New York: Pantheon.

Golding, Peter and Philip Elliott. (1979). *Making the News*. London: Longman.

Graham, Mark. (2008). "Warped Geographies of Development: The Internet and Theories of Economic Development." *Geography Compass* 2, no. 3: 771–89.

Gregory, Steven. (2007). *The Devil Behind the Mirror: Globalization and Politics in the Dominican Republic*. Berkeley: University of California Press.

Grossman, L. (2006, December 13). "*Time*'s Person of the Year: You." *Time*, content.time.com/time/magazine/article/0,9171,1570810,00.html.

Hannerz, Ulf. (2004). *Foreign News: Exploring the World of Foreign Correspondents*. Chicago: University of Chicago Press.

Hardt, Michael and Antonio Negri. (2000). *Empire*. Cambridge, Mass.: Harvard University Press.

Jacobs, Ronald N. (2009). "Culture, the Public Sphere, and Media Sociology: A Search for a Classical Founder in the Work of Robert Park." *American Sociologist* 40, no. 3: 149–66.

Klos, Diana Mitsu. (2013). *The Status of Women in the U.S. Media 2013*. Women's Media Centre, www.womensmediacenter.com/pages/statistics.

Kohn, Nathaniel. (2006). *Pursuing Hollywood: Seduction, Obsession, Dread*. Lanham: AltaMira Press.

Lakshman, Nandini. (2008, July 8). "Copyediting? Ship the Work Out to India." *Business Week*, www.businessweek.com/stories/2008-07-08/copyediting-ship-the-work-out-to-indiabusinessweek-business-news-stock-market-and-financial-advice.

Lauzen, Martha M. (2013). *The Celluloid Ceiling: Behind-the-Scenes Employment of Women in the Top 250 Films of 2012*, womenintvfilm.sdsu.edu/files/2012_Celluloid_Ceiling_Exec_Summ.pdf.

Lippmann, Walter. (1943). *The Good Society*. New York: Grosset & Dunlap.

Machlup, Fritz. (1962). *The Production and Distribution of Knowledge in the United States*. Princeton: Princeton University Press.

Martin, Andrew and Andrew W. Lehren. (2012, May 13). "A Generation Hobbled by College Debt." *New York Times*: A1.

Mayer, Vicki. (2011). *Below the Line: Producers and Production Studies in the New Television Economy*. Durham: Duke University Press.

Mayer, Vicki, ed. (2013). *The International Encyclopedia of Media Studies. Vol. II. Media Production*. Malden: Blackwell.

Mayer, Vicki, Miranda J. Banks, and John Thornton Caldwell, eds. (2009). *Production Studies: Cultural Studies of Media Industries*. New York: Routledge.

Miller, Toby. (2009). "From Creative to Cultural Industries: Not All Industries Are Cultural, and No Industries Are Creative." *Cultural Studies* 23, no. 1: 88–99.

Miller, Toby. (2012). "The Shameful Trinity: Game Studies, Empire, and the Cognitariat." *Guns, Grenades, and Grunts: First-Person Shooter Games*. Ed. Gerald A. Voorhees, Josh Call, and Katie Whitlock. New York: Continuum. 113–30.

Miller, Toby, Nitin Govil, John McMurria, Richard Maxwell, and Ting Wang. (2012). *Küresel Hollywood: Ekonomi-Politik*. Istanbul: Doruk.

Moorhouse, Frank. (1978). *Conference-ville*. Sydney: Vintage Australia.

Moran, Albert. (1982). *Making a TV Series: The Bellamy Project*. Sydney: Currency Press.

Negri, Antonio. (2007). *Goodbye Mister Socialism*. Paris: Seuil.

Orsi, Cosma. (2009). "Knowledge-Based Society, Peer Production and the Common Good." *Capital and Class* 33: 31–51.

Ortner, Sherry B. (2013). *Not Hollywood: Independent Film at the Twilight of the American Dream*. Durham: Duke University Press.

Piore, Michael J. and Charles F. Sabel. (1984). *The Second Industrial Divide: Possibilities for Prosperity*. New York: Basic Books.

Powdermaker, Hortense. (1950). *Hollywood: The Dream Factory: An Anthropologist Looks at the Movie-Makers*. Boston: Little, Brown & Company.

Reagan, Ronald. (1966, April 19). "The Creative Society." Speech at the University of Southern California, www.freerepublic.com/focus/news/742041/posts.

Riegert, Kristina. (1998). *"Nationalising" Foreign Conflict: Foreign Policy Orientation as a Factor in Television News Reporting*. Edsbruk: Akademitryck.

Ritzer, George and Nathan Jurgenson. (2010). "Production, Consumption, Prosumption: The Nature of Capitalism in the Age of the Digital 'Prosumer'." *Journal of Consumer Culture* 10, no. 1: 13–36.

Ross, Andrew. (2009). *Nice Work if You Can Get It: Life and Labor in Precarious Times*. New York: New York University Press.

Scott, Allen J. (1998a). *Regions and the World Economy: The Coming Shape of Global Production, Competition, and Political Order.* Oxford: Oxford University Press.

Scott, Allen J. (1998b). "Multimedia and Digital Visual Effects: An Emerging Local Labor Market." *Monthly Labor Review* 121, no. 3: 30–38.

Silverstone, Roger. (1985). *Framing Science: The Making of a TV Documentary.* London: British Film Institute.

Skilton, Paul F. (2008). "Similarity, Familiarity and Access to Elite Work in Hollywood: Employer and Employee Characteristics in Breakthrough Employment." *Human Relations* 61, no. 12: 1743–73.

Sparks, Erin and Mary Jo Watts. (2011). *Degrees for What Jobs? Raising Expectations for Universities and Colleges in a Global Economy.* Washington: National Governors Association Center for Best Practices.

Surowiecki, James. (2004, February 16–23). "The Pipeline Problem." *New Yorker*: 72.

Tannenwald, Robert. (2010). *State Film Subsidies: Not Much Bang for Too Many Bucks.* Washington, DC: Center on Budget and Policy Priorities.

Thielman, Sam. (2012, May 3). "YouTube Commits $200 Million in Marketing Support to Channels." *AdWeek*, www.adweek.com/news/technology/youtube-commits-200-million-marketing-support-channels-140007.

Toffler, Alvin. (1983). *Previews and Premises.* New York: William Morrow.

Tracey, Michael. (1977). *The Production of Political Television.* London: Routledge & Kegan Paul.

Tuchman, Gaye. (1978). *Making News: A Study in the Construction of Reality.* New York: Free Press.

Tulloch, John and Manuel Alvarado. (1983). *Doctor Who: The Unfolding Text.* New York: St Martin's Press.

Tulloch, John and Albert Moran. (1986). *A Country Practice: "Quality" Soap.* Sydney: Currency Press.

Tumber, Howard, ed. (2000). *Media Power, Professionals and Policies.* London: Routledge.

Tunstall, Jeremy. (1971). *Journalists at Work: Specialist Correspondents: Their News Organisations, News Sources, and Competitor-Colleges.* London: Constable.

Tunstall, Jeremy, ed. (2001). *Media Occupations and Professions: A Reader.* Oxford: Oxford University Press.

Wallas, Graham. (1967). *The Great Society: A Psychological Analysis.* Lincoln: University of Nebraska Press.

Willig, Ida. (2013). "Newsroom Ethnography in a Field Perspective." *Journalism* 14, no. 3: 372–87.

"Worlds of Journalism." (2006). *Ethnography* 7, no. 1.

Ytreberg, Espen. (2006). "Premeditations of Performance in Recent Live Television: A Scripting Approach to Media Production Studies." *European Journal of Cultural Studies* 9, no. 4: 421–40.

26

CLASS AND EXCLUSION AT WORK

The case of UK film and television

Keith Randle

The creative industries: Young, white, male and middle-class

Policy makers applaud the growth of the creative and cultural industries (CCI) in the developed economies; indeed, it has been argued that these sectors have achieved global popularity as a plank of economic development strategy (Cunningham, 2007). Even in the context of the current recession Pratt (2009: 496) remarks on both 'the relative and absolute rise of the CCI'. In the United Kingdom they are held up for the potential they may have to create wealth and new jobs in the wake of declining secondary and tertiary sectors (DCMS, 2008, 2011; Bakhshi et al., 2013). In 2010 approximately 1.5 million people were employed in creative industries in the UK (DCMS, 2011) and the value of the sector has grown at an average of 5 per cent per annum against an average of 3 per cent across the economy more generally (Short-house, 2010). As part of this wider set of industries the UK film industry has been estimated to contribute around £5.3bn to the economy and provide 70,000 jobs, including 46,000 in production (BFI, 2013) while the television industry, which includes the British Broadcasting Corporation (BBC) – a semi-autonomous public service broadcaster (PSB) and not primarily profitmaking – provides around 80,000 jobs and £1bn to the export economy (House of Lords, 2010). Universities see the continued year-on-year growth of creative arts and mass communications degree programmes (HESA, 2013), and the cultural and creative industries remain popular as aspirational graduate destinations, with associations of glamour (Davies and Sigthorssen, 2013).

However, behind this 'good news story' is a more complex picture. These industries are uneven in their growth, employment potential or economic significance despite similarities in organisational and workforce structures. In contrast to their popularity and glamorous associations they have a collective history of nepotistic recruitment through informal networks (Holgate and McKay, 2007; Grugulis and Stoyanova, 2012); a very substantial proportion of freelance, casual, contingent, 'flexible' or precarious work (Hesmondhalgh and Baker, 2010, 2011; Skillset, 2011); an increasing expectation that entrants will be filtered through a system of unpaid or low-paid internships (Siebert and Wilson, 2013; Skillset, 2010; Holgate, 2006); and an employment profile that suggests that mechanisms are at work which exclude on the basis of gender, ethnicity, age, geography, disability and social class (Randle, Leung and Kurian, 2007; Grugulis and Stoyanova, 2012; Warhurst and Eikhof, 2011; Gill, 2011). One wide ranging review of creative and cultural industries (Pratt and Jeffcutt, 2009: 269) concludes:

> a careful examination of the socio-economic backgrounds of participants reveals a distinct bias to the mainly young, white, male, middle classes. In the UK, and it is likely in other nations for which we do not have direct data, the creative and cultural industries are particularly poorly representative of diversity.

UK broadcasters and industry support organisations have recognised the poor record of diversity and inclusion exhibited by the film and television industries for some time (BECTU, 2000; IES, 2004; UK Film Council, 2003; BFI, 2001; BSAC, 2001; NESTA, 2001; Skillset/UK Film Council, 2008; BFI, 2013) and have committed to improving this both in front of and behind the camera. However, initiatives to address under-representation have met with little significant success and Oakley (2013: 66) comments, 'in terms of gender, ethnicity or social class in the cultural industries … most of the data show the problem to be getting worse rather than improving'. This appears to be borne out by industry statistics which show that the proportion of women working in the creative industries as a whole fell from 38 per cent in 2006 to 27 per cent in 2009 (Skillset, 2009) and the proportion of BME workers fell from 7.4 per cent to 6.7 per cent. Against this there is a strong belief, argues Gill (2011: 258), that, despite clear underrepresentation by some groups, success in the media industries is based on merit, leading to the 'increasing unspeakability' of inequalities, both structural and those related to ethnicity.

Where industry initiatives have addressed underrepresentation they have generally focused on the most visible absences, with gender and ethnicity most frequently the subject of research, reports or action. There has been less concern with disability, age, region of origin or sexuality, though all have been raised as issues for these industries. However, research also suggests that an approach to organisational diversity that focuses on the underrepresentation of specific demographic groups overlooks an overarching mechanism of exclusion: that of social class (Acker, 2006; Randle et al., 2014). Class is one basis for disadvantage for which there is no UK legislative imperative to eradicate or control and is perhaps less visible and less easy for organisations to address should they wish to do so. In the following section I will provide a brief description of these industries.

UK film and television: Similar production processes, overlapping workforces

In a short chapter it is necessary to make some assumptions about familiarity with the sectors under discussion and therefore the following account is necessarily very brief. I have previously provided a fuller description of the production process in film and television (Randle, 2011). Across the creative industries more widely, while the product may be different, industry and employment structures have a great deal in common. In the case of film and television these commonalities go further and the sectors are characterised by a similar production process that, significant technological advances apart, changed little during the 20th century, and has three stages: pre-production, production and post-production. These stages are followed by distribution and exhibition (in film) and broadcast (in television). In the pre-production stage projects are conceived, ideas generated, written and developed, finance is secured and the cast and key creatives appointed. Production is probably the most familiar stage, where crews are brought together in the studio and/or on location, to capture a performance by actors or presenters on film, video or (increasingly) hard disk. In post-production content is edited, special effects credits and titles are added and music tracks are synchronised. The finished product is then duplicated before being distributed and consumed via a widening range of platforms including: broadcast television, cable or satellite, video/DVD, on board aircraft and, increasingly, mobile devices such as telephones or streamed via the internet onto, for example, laptop screens. In the case of animated films production and post-production are less separable.

In the United Kingdom, where there is a significant national film industry, those employed in the production process may find themselves working on content destined for cinema or for television. If we take TV drama productions, for example, companies may be competing to employ the same crew members (camera, lighting, sound, hair and make-up, set design or production assistants) as feature film production companies. However, in television news, crews may be permanently employed in-house, although many broadcasters do outsource news coverage to independent companies. In the most highly developed industries (e.g. in the United States), with an international market for their products, workforces tend to be more specialised and boundaries between the sectors may be less porous, especially at the higher levels. In these territories staff might work in, for example, feature film, documentary, music video, industrial films, commercials, pornography or television, more or less exclusively. In the United Kingdom, where the volume of film work expands and contracts, not least because of the need to attract foreign (mainly US) productions in competition with other locations, there is more overlap between these workforces. A study of one UK film crew demonstrated that individuals also worked in commercials and theatre and every member had worked in television during the previous year, though 49 per cent of their aggregate jobs had been in film (Blair et al., 2001).

One important development in the organisation of these industries is the fragmentation that has given rise to their 'hourglass' shape, with a large number of people employed, and a greater proportion full-time and permanent, by a small number of broadcasters, cable and satellite TV companies and film majors. A large number of others are employed by small or micro businesses in production or post-production, with a greater proportion of freelancers or temporary staff. The medium sized company represents a 'missing middle' (Pratt, 2008). The project-based nature of production in these industries means that many of those working in it are obliged to re-enter the labour market on a regular basis and search for new employment, with one study indicating an average work project of 7.4 weeks (Blair et al., 2001). This prompts the frequently heard saying in the industry, 'You're only as good as your last job' (Blair, 2001).

The labour markets for 'creative labour' as a whole have changed dramatically as cultural organisations have turned to a marketised and outsourced approach to managing their operations (McKinlay and Smith, 2009). However, there are exceptions (Haunschild, 2003) and we must be careful not to assume that the models described here of short-term, outsourced, freelance and network based approaches to employment are universal or inevitable across the creative and cultural industries, or that institutions operate free of state or cultural contexts. Reviews of this development in work organisations more generally point to permanent positions as enduring alongside models of flexible production (Doogan, 2009).

Social composition and employment patterns in film and television

A review of recent literature confirms that the UK film and television industries are increasingly characterised by a workforce with a high proportion of freelancers or independent contractors working on short-term contracts (Bhavnani, 2007; Holgate and McKay, 2007; Grugulis and Stoyanova, 2012; Patterson, 2012). In 2012 this was most prevalent in the film production sector (46 per cent against a UK average for all industries for self-employment of 15 per cent) while in distribution and exhibition most were employed (BFI, 2013). In television the movement towards flexibility of employment and industry fragmentation has gathered pace since the Broadcasting Act of 1990 (Dex et al., 1998; Saundry, 2001). Prior to 1979 nearly all jobs in the BBC and ITV were 'staff', but by 1979 some 39 per cent had become freelance, rising to 54 per cent by 1994, before falling again to 45 per cent where, for the moment at least, it appears to have stabilised.

In this project-based environment (Blair et al., 2001) word of mouth recruitment predominates (Skillset/UK Film Council, 2008; Lee, 2011) and consequently there is reliance by workers on both formal and informal networks as a means of finding work (Holgate and McKay, 2007; Lee, 2011). These characteristics are not unique and can be found in other creative industries (see Haunschild, 2003 on work in the theatre) and in other countries (see Randle and Culkin, 2009 on film and television in the United States).

However, earlier comments about commonalities notwithstanding, there are differences between the creative and cultural industries in management, work and employment relations and between different sectors where, for example, stable employment is more or less likely or skills are regarded as of a higher or lower order. Furthermore, there are notable differences *within* specific industries. Employment itself, for example, may be full-time and permanent (TV broadcast engineering), or freelance and project-based (TV content production), or part-time and low-paid (office cleaning). Experiences will be different at different levels: from entry level production assistant (often known as 'runner') to senior executive, or in different occupations and departments.

A recent text makes an important point that links these sectoral or occupational differences to patterns of underrepresentation. Not only are minorities underrepresented as a whole in the creative industries but the 'most visible and glamorous parts ... are also the most white middle-class and male' (Davies and Sigthorssen, 2013: 114). As well as further qualifying and reinforcing the earlier observation by Pratt and Jeffcutt (2009), this underlines the point above: that apparent overall similarities obscure the reality that there are indeed 'parts' to the creative industries where different demographic characteristics are represented to a greater or lesser extent.

This characteristic is most obvious if we follow what might be termed the 'value chain' of a film or TV product from conception through to consumption. At the 'conception' end of the process we generally find much of the 'thinking' or 'creative' work that is involved in writing or design. Some of the most high-profile occupations involved at this stage, screenwriting or directing, for example, are heavily male dominated. In 2012 the proportion of women screenwriters fell back from a five-year high of 19 per cent in 2011 to 13 per cent and directors from 15 per cent to 8 per cent, the lowest since 2007 at 6 per cent (BFI, 2013). As we move through the production stage we find more 'doing' and more involvement by craft workers. Here again there is a noticeable gender split between occupations, with associated differences in income expectations. Compare the composition of hair, make-up and wardrobe (predominantly female) with lighting (predominantly male) in film. Similarly, occupations may have a greater or lesser black and minority ethnic (BME) presence. Note the absolutely low proportion of BME workers in VFX (visual effects) at 1 per cent in 2012 against a creative industries average of 5.4 per cent and an all industry average of 9 per cent. In the final stages, for example the exhibition of a film in the cinema, we find more part-time low-skill work with the majority of staff either 'front of house' (ticket and confectionary sales) or in cleaning, with a young, often BME workforce. What explains these, sometimes startling, differences?

Working for free: The rise of the intern

For many prospective employees the only viable route into the sector is through 'internships', which often require them to work for free or for very little pay (National Union of Journalists, 2007; PACT, 2007). While internships exist in many sectors, they are particularly common in cultural and media work (Low Pay Commission, 2011), and increasingly so. Between 2005 and 2008 the proportion of the creative economy workforce reporting having done unpaid work grew from 38 to 45 per cent (Skillset/UK Film Council, 2008; Siebert and Wilson, 2013) with between 40 and 50 per cent of entrants spending some time in unpaid positions. Ball et al. (2010) found that 42 per cent of graduates from the creative sector had undertaken voluntary work since graduating. Twenty-nine per cent of companies studied in a survey of the independent production sector used or were made up of unpaid workers, with the practice of working for free being more common among those from minority ethnic backgrounds (IES, 2004). Around three-quarters of photographers, 58 per cent of radio freelancers and nearly half of the TV workforce had previously undertaken unpaid work in their sector (Skillset, 2010).

Siebert and Wilson (2013) found that graduates in creative industry related studies expected to have to work for free in order to find permanent work, but that this was not a guaranteed outcome for them and furthermore there were impacts on other stakeholders, such as undermining of the position of existing workers, leading to the replacement of paid workers on temporary contracts with unpaid staff. The result, they found, was an 'erosion of trust between unpaid workers motivated by a desire to enter the industry, freelance workers already in the sector and the employers' (2013: 8). Resistance to unpaid work, for instance by complaining, could make people unemployable consequently 'fear of victimization in the labour market normalized the expectation of unpaid work' (2013: 7). Watson (2008) provides considerable evidence that in the United Kingdom the extent of free working suggests significant illegal employment practices where minimum wage regulations are being flouted.

The Milburn Report (Milburn, 2009) highlighted unpaid internships as a major barrier to potential working class entrants to the professions, suggesting that their social base had narrowed rather than widened and recent work (Siebert and Wilson, 2013) has reinforced the exclusionary consequences of unpaid work in the creative media sector. Production centres of the media industry are concentrated in London and the South East, the most expensive parts of the United Kingdom for living accommodation, with 74 per cent of those working in film production living in those areas (Skillset/ UK Film Council, 2008). Hence, individuals from economically disadvantaged groups are likely to face financial challenges when attempting to enter the industry. For those from ethnic minority backgrounds this may be further exacerbated; people from ethnic minorities are more likely to belong to lower income households than the average white British household (Palmer and Kenway, 2007).

The nature of the employment system, which has resulted in new entrants often agreeing to work for free for up to a year, means that the social composition of the workforce is likely to be shaped by the ability of entrants to draw on financial support from family members, or their own resources, or to negotiate a portfolio of part-time, temporary and casual employment frequently in the service sectors (Randle et al., 2007; Randle and Culkin, 2009).

Networking: An exclusionary practice?

If workers in these sectors experience precariousness and uncertainty in their careers it is nevertheless experienced as a kind of 'precarious stability' (Blair, 2001) or 'structured uncertainty' (Randle and Culkin, 2009). While the conditions that cause uncertainty in employment are out of the control of individual workers, they are able employ a range of strategies in an attempt to ensure some continuity in employment and a steady income stream.

Individuals cope with the uncertainty in media work by: diversifying income sources, gathering intelligence, considering or actually leaving the sector and building informal networks. As the number of permanent staff has declined in television and casualisation increases, despite the lowered barriers to entry referred to earlier, it has become more difficult to gain a foothold in the industry. At the same time earnings have fallen, working terms and conditions have deteriorated (Ursell, 2000) and trade union organisation has been undermined (McKinlay and Quinn, 1999).

Blair (2003) describes how film workers form what she calls 'semi permanent work groups' (SPWGs), moving as a department or team from one project to the next with the onus being on the generally most experienced and, we may assume, best networked member to find a stream of projects to keep other members of the crew employed. Blair proposes the term 'active networking' as 'a means of capturing the dynamic and conscious, yet structured process of networking and the interpersonal webs that are reproduced by that process' (2009: 132). What this term implies is a strategic engagement in the networking process with wider social and economic structures both enabling and constraining actors.

Networking is an extremely important skill, process or behaviour in these sectors, where recruitment is often on the basis of who you know and your reputation (Blair, 2001). Trust is frequently mentioned as a vital intervening variable. When projects are 'green lit', have to be staffed quickly and may not last more than a few weeks, those responsible for production need to have a degree of certainty that a crew member will be technically competent and will also 'fit in' with others. Consequently, those in positions to make recommendations do not do so lightly as a recommendation that turns out to be ill-judged will rebound on them, diminishing their own reputation. The outcome is that while the networks mediating employment are a source of stability and decreasing uncertainty for some, they can be a source of exclusion for others.

Without the benefits of an internal labour market within the firm a key issue after 'getting in' is 'getting on', moving up the occupational ladder or making a career in industry (Randle and Culkin, 2009) where there are fewer opportunities to climb a corporate ladder. An example might be making the move from camera operator to director of photography (the head of the camera department). This can often mean returning to a previous, more precarious, stage of employment and working for free or for 'copy and credit' to gain experience, make new contacts and establish a new professional identity.

The increasing predominance of freelance working throws up a range of managerial issues, with that of training and skills development being key (Grugulis and Stoyanova, 2009). Historically in the UK, the system of permanent employment in major studios or public service broadcasters formed a robust system of apprenticeships and on-the-job training. This has largely gone and the onus is now on the individual to ensure that (s)he has the skills employers require in what can be seen as part of a wider societal move towards 'individualisation', which in turn has led the push towards a managerial emphasis on individual creative entrepreneurship (Storey et al., 2005) and what Castells (2000: 12) calls 'self-programmable labor' as one of the key elements of the contemporary network society. In most countries media training is now predominantly carried out by colleges, universities and a range of private sector training companies and equipment manufacturers, with the individual taking on the responsibility for seeking out appropriate training and arranging finance for initial training and often for professional development too.

Class and the creative industries

Discourses around class are familiar territory in film and media studies but it is more frequently representations of class within the product itself (e.g. Hill, 1986; Stead 1991; Richards, 1997), or its consumers (Hesmondhalgh and Baker, 2011) that are the subject of investigation, rather than the production workforce. Historically, where those working in film or television have been the subject of investigation, studies tend to focus on those higher up the industry hierarchy: the 'creatives' and 'talent': directors, actors, cinematographers and producers (see Powdermaker, 1950; Rosten, 1941). 'Below-the-line' occupations such as camera, wardrobe, hair and make-up, lighting or sound were largely overlooked, though recent work has begun to pay them more attention (Atkinson and Randle, 2013) and the newer 'production cultures' literature includes these less studied trades (Caldwell, 2008; Mayer, Banks and Caldwell, 2009) as a key part of the production system. Nevertheless, class, in the context of creative industries employment, still remains relatively understudied. A short chapter cannot rectify this anomaly nor do justice to the range of debates and theoretical perspectives in this field as it must necessarily be both selective and brief. The aim here is to give an outline of how key aspects of thinking on class can give us further insight into the social composition of the film and television industry workforce.

Much of the work on the sociology of class derives from the writings of two of the 'founding fathers' of sociology, Karl Marx and Max Weber, although more recently the work of the French sociologist Pierre Bourdieu has been drawn upon to provide an analysis of how people are positioned within society (for example see Atkinson, 2010; Randle et al., 2014; Mcleod et al., 2009). In the case of the creative media industries, analysis has, I suggest, been hampered by a tendency to reduce labour in these industries down to a 'creative class', albeit sometimes subdivided between, for example, a 'Super-Creative Core' and 'creative professionals' (Florida, 2002: 69). This characterisation of a relatively undifferentiated mass of creative workers, based on US data, provides us with little that is useful for explaining the structural position of the UK film and TV workforce. One criticism of Florida's definition, is that in covering such a broad swathe of the workforce we can identify no common identity or a 'class consciousness' within this group. Hartley et al. (2013: 49) speculate on the unlikely solidarity between the bohemian artist 'pushed out of her urban loft by the gentrifying tastes' of more highly paid 'creative professionals' and this latter group themselves. Their point, essentially, is that a 'class' must have some overriding commonality of interest to be of value either as an analytical device or a meaningful social category. Perhaps such a commonality of interest can be found in the reality of the labour of many of those whose experience of work has been glamourised by Florida's account. As authors have demonstrated (Gill and Pratt, 2008; Banks, 1999), the increasingly casual and freelance forms of labour adopted by these industries are 'often badly paid, insecure, and positively hostile to the kind of work–life balance that people need in order to make a living, raise families, and sustain their careers' (Davies and Sigthorssen, 2013: 19).

While the relationship between 'class' and 'employment' is very well established (Crompton, 2010), this association is probably most established as a way to determine the class location of particular groups of workers. A key motive for wishing to locate groups of workers in relation to the production process is derived from a 'liberation project' that emanates from Marx (1974) and identifies the driving force for social change in the classes formed by workers with a common relationship to the means of production. In the case of the media industries, this task of 'locating' the workforce is addressed in some detail by Wayne (2003) who, adopting a Marxist framework, concludes that most media workers are employed and are therefore part of the class that sells its capacity to work in order to survive – Labour. In this dichotomous (two class) model Labour is counterposed only to Capital. The two-class model has, however, been found to be of little value in understanding contemporary organisational arrangements. This was never its purpose, its aim being to demonstrate what objectively united otherwise apparently disparate occupational groups. However, taking into account the more contemporary arrangements that characterise the media industries, Wayne goes on to produce a synthesised model of class relations that incorporates the 'petit bourgeoisie' and a 'middle class' (2003: 14). A more complex formulation again is reflected in Eric Olin Wright's (1997) twelve class locations, a further attempt 'to move beyond crude Marxist class distinctions based purely on ownership of the means of production' (Hesmondhalgh and Baker, 2011: 67).

Weber (1964) defines social class in relation to the market rather than in relation to productive forces. People bring to the market different sorts and amounts of personal and material resources; skills, for example, or property of different values. This produces a class continuum that Weber converts to a usable classification system by aggregating 'class situations within which individual and generational mobility is easy and typical' (Weber, 1964). From this Weber derives a set of four social classes: entrepreneurial groups, the propertyless white-collar intelligentsia, the petty bourgeoisie and the manual working class, itself divided into skilled, semi skilled and unskilled (McKenzie, 1982: 65).

However, this chapter is predominantly concerned with examining the relatively less studied question of the impact of class-related phenomena in determining who is able and who is not able to *enter* a particular set of occupations, rather than how their membership of that occupation defines them and assessing their prospects of developing a common class identity. Here the most important association is between the employment available to other adults in their families and their own experience of entry into an occupation (Crompton, 2010). Citing Bourdieu, Crompton comments, 'Family relationships do not in and of themselves *create* classes and class relationships, but they play the major role in reproducing them and the family is the major transmission belt of social advantage and disadvantage' (2010: 20).

Bourdieu (1986, 1990) suggests that actors in the social space internalise objective structures and reproduce them over time through practice, drawing our attention to the mechanisms by which class positions are created and maintained and how this, in turn, impacts the life chances of individuals in particular contexts. At the heart of Bourdieu's theory are three important constructs – field, habitus and capitals. He sees individual social actors as initiators, consumers and re-producers of social practices based on their resources (capitals) and in accordance with particular logics of practice (habitus) within a given context (field) (Randle et al., 2014).

The various capitals available to individuals are of at least three kinds: economic, social and cultural; and might comprise, for example, access to financial resources (economic), access to networks or powerful people (social) and qualifications, language, attitudes and behaviour (cultural). Capitals can be acquired, exchanged or converted into other forms. When these forms of capital are valued in a given field – for example the UK film and television industry – they become 'symbolic capital'. The habitus, a way of thinking or behaving, that incorporates values, expectations, lifestyles and tastes acquired through experience, interacts with elements of the field (for example a sectoral structure that is characterised by project-based employment and informal recruitment methods), to favour particular symbolic resources which might include, for example, privileged educational backgrounds, professional reputations and networking ability. Without necessarily operating at a conscious level, the ownership of such symbolic capital, combined with the more tangible benefits associated with economic capital (the ability, for example, to undertake periods of unpaid work experience) or social capital (parents, perhaps, who offer ready made industry networks) could lead to the replication of the status quo, ensuring that individuals from some social class backgrounds are favoured in their efforts to either enter or progress through the film and television industries. This might help to explain the persistence of the young, white, male and middle class profile of these industries, against the continuing efforts to diversify them.

Conclusion

This chapter has examined the social composition of the UK film and television industry workforce, taking as its starting point the reality of underrepresentation in terms of both specific demographic minorities and of social class more widely. It links continuing underrepresentation to: the increasing use of freelance contracts and the project based nature of production work, the importance of social networks, informal recruitment methods and the consequent absence of formal equal opportunities procedures.

At the same time, this cannot tell the whole story. While there is ample evidence of important structural features that may aggravate underrepresentation, we currently only have the story from the perspective of those who have got a foothold in the industry or are currently trying to enter. What is missing is a robust account of the experiences of those who tried and failed, or those who entered and subsequently left. Perhaps unsurprisingly, we have no accounts from those who never tried in the first place. If an industry has an image of being 'white, male and middle class' then it may well deter prospective entrants who do not fit the model from even considering it as a career. It may also be the case that the parents of young people from some social groups, for example some ethnic minorities, will try to steer their children away from these less certain industries, or away from the programmes of higher education that are designed to prepare them for work in these industries. As the prospect of 'good jobs' in the creative industries declines with increasing casualisation, and the scale of graduate debt increases in the UK, it remains to be seen whether the stream of skilled graduates in creative arts and media subjects formed by those emerging from the universities will continue to flow. It also remains to be seen what will happen to the social composition of those who continue to choose to study these subjects.

The chapter has portrayed social class as an overarching but understudied determinant of inclusion/exclusion in film and TV labour markets. While there has been a long association between class and employment in social science, the focus of work sociology has been largely on trying to understand the class position of particular occupational groups. This chapter has had an altogether different concern: to try to understand how class has shaped the chances of 'getting in and getting on' in film and television. In order to make sense of the emerging occupational landscape, we need the tools to create a more finely grained analysis that takes some account of the heterogeneity of the creative industries, their workforces, of employment relationships, of life chances and of identity, and which acknowledge a number of competing contemporary discourses.

The writings of Marx and Weber, central characters in the development of theories of class, were argued to be of relatively limited use in this venture, but it is acknowleged that this was not their purpose. Of more help has been the work of Bourdieu and his focus on the acquisition of various capitals, the possession of which appears to provide insight into how certain social groups are more able to secure careers in film and television than others. While some work has been carried out using Bourdieusian analytical frameworks, scope remains to learn more about the ways in which economic, social and cultural capitals, individually or in tandem, operate to include some and exclude others from an increasingly important economic sector.

References

Acker, J. (2006) 'Inequality Regimes: Gender, Class and Race in Organizations', *Gender and Society* 20 (4): 441–64.

Atkinson, W. (2010) 'The Myth of the Reflexive Worker: Class and Work Histories in Neo-Liberal Times', *Work, Employment and Society* 24 (3): 413–29.

Atkinson, W. and Randle, K. (2013) *Working Below the Line in the Studio System: Exploring Labour Processes in the UK Film Industry 1927–50*, HBS Working Paper, hdl.handle.net/2299/10670 (retrieved 28 November 2013).

Bakhshi, H., Hargreaves, I. and Mateos Garcia, J. (2013) *A Manifesto for the Creative Economy*, London: NESTA.

Ball, L., Pollard, E., Stanley, N. and Oakley, J. (2010) *Creative Graduates, Creative Futures*, Brighton: Institute for Employment Studies.

Banks, M. (1999) 'Cultural Industries and the City: Findings and Future Prospects', paper presented at the *Cultural Industries and the City Conference*, Manchester Institute of Popular Culture, Manchester Metropolitan University, 13–14 December.

BECTU (2000) *Ethnic Minority Employment in Film and Television*, London: BECTU.

BFI (British Film Institute) (2001) *Towards Visibility: A Three-Year Cultural Diversity Strategy*, London: BFI.

BFI (2013) *Statistical Yearbook*, London: BFI.

Bhavnani, R. (2007) *Barriers to Diversity in Film: A Research Review*, London: UK Film Council.

Blair, H. (2001) '"You're Only as Good as Your Last Job": The Labour Process and Labour Market in the British Film Industry', *Work, Employment and Society* 15 (1): 149–69.

Blair, H. (2003) 'Winning and Losing in Flexible Labour Markets: The Formation and Operation of Networks of Interdependence in the UK Film Industry', *Sociology* 37 (4): 677–94.

Blair, H. (2009) 'Active Networking: Action, Social Structure and the Process of Networking', in A. McKinlay and C. Smith (eds), *Creative Labour: Working in the Creative Industries*, Basingstoke: Palgrave.

Blair, H., Grey, S. and Randle, K. (2001) 'Working in Film: Employment in a Project-Based Industry', *Personnel Review* 30 (1 and 2): 170–85.

Bourdieu, P. (1986) 'The Forms of Capital', in J.G. Richardson (ed.) *Handbook of Theory and Research for the Sociology of Education*, 241–58, New York: Greenwood Press.

Bourdieu, P. (1990) *The Logic of Practice*, Stanford: Stanford University Press.

BSAC (2001) *Achieving Diversity in the Film Industry* (Committee for Ethnic Minority Employment in Film, British Screen Advisory Council), London: BSAC.

Caldwell, J.T. (2008) *Production Culture: Industrial Reflexivity and Critical Practice in Film and Television*, Durham, NC: Duke University Press.

Castells, M. (2000) 'Materials for an Exploratory Theory of the Network Society', *British Journal of Sociology* 51 (1): 5–24.

Crompton, R. (2010) 'Class and Employment', *Work, Employment and Society* 24 (1): 9–26.

Cunningham, S.D. (2007) 'Creative Industries as Policy and Discourse Outside the United Kingdom', *Global Media and Communication* 3 (3): 347–52.

Davies, R. and Sigthorssen, G. (2013) *Introducing the Creative Industries*, Los Angeles: Sage.

DCMS (2008) *Creative Britain: New Talents for the New Economy*, London: Department for Culture, Media and Sport.

DCMS (2011) *Creative Industries Economic Estimates*, December 2011, London: Department for Culture, Media and Sport.

Dex, S., Willis, J., Paterson, R. and Shepherd, E. (1998) 'Freelance Workers and Contract Uncertainty: The Effects of Contractual Changes in the Television Industry', *Work, Employment and Society* 14 (2): 283–305.

Doogan, K. (2009) *New Capitalism?* Cambridge: Polity.

Florida, R. (2002) *The Rise of the Creative Class*, New York: Basic Books.

Gill, R. (2011) 'Sexism Reloaded, or, It's Time to Get Angry Again', *Feminist Media Studies* 11 (1): 61–71.

Gill, R. and Pratt, A.C. (2008) 'In the Social Factory? Immaterial Labour, Precariousness and Cultural Work', *Theory, Culture and Society* 25 (7–8) : 1–30.

Grugulis, I. and Stoyanova, D. (2009) '"I Don't Know Where You Learn Them": Skills in Film and TV', in A. McKinlay and C. Smith, *Creative Labour*, Basingstoke: Palgrave MacMillan.

Grugulis, I. and Stoyanova, D. (2012) 'Social Capital and Networks in Film and TV: Jobs for the Boys?' *Organisation Studies* 33 (10): 1311–31.

Hartley, J., Potts, J., Cunningham, S., Flew, T., Keane, M. and Banks, J. (2013) *Key Concepts in Creative Industries*, London: Sage.

Haunschild, A. (2003) 'Managing Employment Relationships in Flexible Labour Markets: The Case of German Repertory Theatres', *Human Relations* 56 (8): 899–929.

HESA (2013) 'Higher Education Statistics Agency', www.hesa.ac.uk/content/view/1897/239/ (retrieved 11 November 2013).

Hesmondhalgh, D. and Baker, S. (2010) ' "A Very Complicated Version of Freedom": Conditions and Experiences of Creative Labour in Three Cultural Industries', *Poetics* 38 (1): 4–20.

Hesmondhalgh, D. and Baker, S. (2011) *Creative Labour: Media Work in Three Cultural Industries*, Abingdon: Routledge.

Hill, J. (1986) *Sex, Class and Realism: British Cinema 1956–1963*, London: British Film Institute.

Holgate, J. (2006) *Making the Transition from College to Work: Experiences of Media, Film and Television Students, and Recent Graduates in London's Audio-Visual Industries*, London: Working Lives Research Institute.

Holgate, J. and McKay, S. (2007) *Institutional Barriers to Recruitment and Employment in the Audio Visual Industries: The Effect on Black and Minority Ethnic Workers*, London: Working Lives Research Institute.

House of Lords (2010) 'Communications Committee: First Report', London: The British Film and Television Industries.

IES (2004) *Research the Independent Production Sector: A Focus on Minority Ethnic Led Companies*, London: PACT and the UK Film Council.

Lee, D.J. (2011) 'Networks, Cultural Capital and Creative Labour in the British Independent Television Industry', *Media, Culture and Society* 33 (4): 549–65.

Low Pay Commission (2011) 'National Minimum Wage: Low Pay Commission Report', London: BIS.

Marx, K. (1974) *Capital*, Volume 3, Harmondsworth: Penguin.

Mayer, V., Banks, M.J. and Caldwell, J. (ed.) (2009) *Production Studies: Cultural Studies of Media Industries*, New York: Routledge.

McKenzie, G. (1982) 'Class Boundaries and the Labour Process', in A. Giddens and G. McKenzie, *Social Class and the Division of Labour*, Cambridge: Cambridge University Press.

McKinlay, A. and Quinn, B. (1999) 'Management, Technology and Work in Commercial Broadcasting, c. 1979–98', *New Technology, Work and Employment* 14 (1): 2–17.

McKinlay, A. and Smith, C. (2009) *Creative Labour*, Houndmills: Palgrave MacMillan.

McLeod, C., O'Donohoe, S. and Townley, B. (2009) 'The Elephant in the Room? Class and Creative Careers in British Advertising Agencies', *Human Relations* 62 (7): 1011–39.

Milburn, A. (2009) *Unleashing Aspiration: The Final Report on the Panel on Fair Access to the Professions*, London: Cabinet Office.

National Union of Journalists (2007) *Work Experience Guidelines*, London: NUJ.

NESTA (2001) *Beyond the Creative Industries: Mapping the Creative Economy in the United Kingdom*, London: NESTA.

Oakley, K. (2013) 'Absentee Workers: Representation and Participation in the Cultural Industries', in M. Banks, R. Gill and S. Taylor, *Theorizing Cultural Work*, Abingdon: Routledge.

PACT (2007) *Work Experience Guide*, London: PACT.

Palmer, G. and Kenway, P. (2007) *Poverty Among Ethnic Groups: How and Why Does it Differ?* London: Joseph Rowntree Foundation.

Patterson, R. (2012) 'Working as a Freelancer in UK Television', in A. Dawson and S.P. Holmes, *Working in the Global Film and Television Industries*, London: Bloomsbury.

Powdermaker, H. (1950), *Hollywood: The Dream Factory*, New York: Little, Brown and Company.

Pratt, A. (2008) 'Creative Industries: The Cultural Industries and the Creative Class', *Geografiska Annaler: Series B, Human Geography* 90 (2): 107–17.

Pratt, A. (2009) 'The Creative and Cultural Economy and the Recession', *Geoforum* 40: 495–96.

Pratt, A.C. and Jeffcutt, P. (2009) 'Conclusion', in A.C. Pratt and P. Jeffcutt, *Creativity, Innovation and the Cultural Economy*, Abingdon: Routledge.

Randle, K. (2011) 'The Organization of Film and Television Production', in M. Deuze (ed.), *Managing Media Work*, Los Angeles: Sage.

Randle, K. and Culkin, C. (2009) 'Getting In and Getting On in Hollywood: Freelance Careers in an Uncertain Industry', in A. McKinlay and C. Smith (eds), *Creative Labour: Working in the Creative Industries*, Basingstoke: Palgrave.

Randle, K., Leung, W.F. and Kurian, J. (2007) *Creating Difference: Overcoming Barriers to Diversity in UK Film and Television Employment*, Report to EU ESF/EQUAL Programme, Hatfield: University of Hertfordshire.

Randle, K., Forson, C. and Calveley, M. (2014) 'Towards a Bourdieusian Analysis of the Social Composition of the UK Film and Television Workforce', *Work, Employment and Society* (20 October), 0950017014542498.

Richards, J. (1997) *Films and British National Identity*, Manchester: Manchester University Press.

Rosten, L.C. (1941) *Hollywood: The Movie Colony, The Movie Makers*, New York: Harcourt Brace.

Saundry, R. (2001) 'Employee Relations in British Television: Regulation, Fragmentation and Flexibility', *Industrial Relations Journal* 32 (1, March): 22–36.

Shorthouse, R. (ed.) (2010) *Disconnected: Social Mobility and the Creative Industries*, London: Social Market Foundation.

Siebert, S. and Wilson, F. (2013) 'All Work and No Pay: Consequences of Unpaid Work in the Creative Industries', *Work, Employment and Society* 27 (4): 711–21.

Skillset (2009) *2009 Employment Census: The Results of the Seventh Census of the Creative Media Industries*, London: Skillset.

Skillset (2010) *2010 Creative Media Workforce Survey*, London: Skillset.

Skillset (2011) *Sector Skills Assessment for the Creative Media Industries in the UK*, London: Skillset, creativeskillset.org/assets/0000/6023/Sector_Skills_Assessment_for_the_Creative_Industries_-_Skillset_and_CCSkills_2011.pdf.

Skillset/UK Film Council (2008) *Feature Film Production Workforce Survey Report 2008*, London: Skillset/UK Film Council.

Stead, P. (1991) *Film and the Working Class*, London: Routledge.

Storey, J., Salaman, G. and Platman, K. (2005) 'Living with Enterprise in an Enterprise Economy: Freelance and Contract Workers in the Media', *Human Relations* 58 (8): 1033–54.

UK Film Council (2003) *Success Through Diversity and Inclusion*, London: UK Film Council.

Ursell, G. (2000) 'Television Production: Issues of Exploitation, Commodification and Subjectivity in UK Television Labour Markets', *Media, Culture and Society* 22: 805–25.

Warhurst, C. and Eikhof, D. (2011) 'You Don't Have To Be Male, White and Middle Class to Work Here – But it Helps: Explaining the Lack of Opportunity and Advancement in the Creative Industries', Creative Industries Workshop.

Watson, M. (2008) *Young Unpaid Workers in Popular Industries*, A submission to the Low Pay Commission consultation for the Annual Report on the National Minimum Wage, www.lowpay.gov.uk (retrieved 14 January 2015).

Wayne, M. (2003) *Marxism and Media Studies*, London: Pluto Press.

Weber, M. (1964) *The Theory of Social and Economic Organisation*, New York: Free Press.

Wright, E.O. (1997) 'Intellectuals and the Class Structure', in P. Walker (ed.), *Between Labour and Capital*, Hassocks: Harvester Press.

Part V
AUDIENCES, INTERMEDIARIES AND MARKETS

This section looks not only at audiences, fans and consumers but also at the organisation of markets for cultural consumption and the role of intermediaries such as
public relations (PR) professionals. The consumer has become a much-celebrated
figure in some cultural industry research, and indeed in the popular media, as Miller
points out (this volume). Relatively cheap and easy access to the technologies needed
for media-making has allegedly broken down the barriers between producers and
consumers, given consumers unprecedented power and access and seen not only the
demise of gate-keeping but also, according to some optimistic accounts, the rise of
people power in a wider political context. As this section makes clear, while there
have undoubtedly been shifts in the roles of producers and consumers and while
new market makers and intermediaries demand our attention, the situation is considerably more complex than the hype would have you believe and, as ever, clear
attention needs to be paid to the specifics of markets in transition.

Meier examines arguments about how the alleged 'democratization' of popular music
is in fact playing out in the working lives of musicians. Breaking free from 'the man' in
terms of traditional record labels has brought with it its own set of challenges and
musicians must become their own agents, promoters and bookers. This has implications not only for musicians but also for fans as time spent on self-promotion drains
away the time available for perfecting one's craft. Far from flattening hierarchies, as
Meier suggest, this simply establishes new ones.

Wright eloquently reminds us that the world of cultural consumers remains as
class-riven and uneven as ever, and that whether we describe them as fans, audiences
or participants, "such distinctions are as much a result of judgments about the
qualities of people as the qualities of culture, as much about who is doing the consuming as what is consumed". This is not just an issue for cultural policymakers,
wrestling as they do with the persistence of class and education as determinants of
consumption, but for any analysts of the commercial cultural industries tempted to
prematurely celebrate the collapse of cultural hierarchy.

Sandvoss builds on the extensive literature on fan cultures to probe the role of fans, not only as consumers, but also as agents within the cultural industries. He defines them in terms of their emotional and affective relationship with culture and while not minimising the problems – their ability to undermine the production of paid for content for example – reminds us that there is no better place to start understanding the cultural industries than with those to whom they matter most.

Rowe considers a particular kind of engaged fan – the sports fan (see also Redhead this volume) and considers the role of the media in particular in the changing nature of these fans – from the local crowd to the global audience. He considers the role of newspapers, television and now the internet in this 'media–sport nexus' and again draws attention to the way this produces different kinds of fans – those with 'authenticity' and physical connection to place (for example the home of a football team) being set against the potential for global audiences, while 'culturally significant' national sporting events battle desires for global revenues. The cultural significance of these questions, about identity, media power, gatekeeping and competition, as Rowe suggests, makes the notion that sport is not a 'cultural industry' a hard one to defend.

Maxwell brings another much-neglected aspect of cultural consumption to our attention – that of the waste and environmental damage – that mediated culture produces. The promise of digital technology to extend reach and create new audiences is one that is consistently driven home, not only by those with a direct financial stake in such adoption, but by policymakers and funders. Maxwell considers how arts organisations – keen to secure the legitimacy of new audiences and to lower costs – are becoming part of a relentless cycle of new technology adoption and increasing energy use and electronic waste. Far from standing outside this, cultural production is part and parcel of it, and only by a greater self-consciousness of this on the part of cultural producers and consumers can such processes be challenged.

Two chapters look at related or adjunct industries that, the authors argue, are crucial to the production of culture and thus can be seems as cultural industries. There are definitional questions here for sure, but perhaps more important is the question of what benefits a 'cultural industry' lens brings to the analyses of these activities. Kennedy argues compelling that the critical scrutiny of, for example, data visualisations would help us to move beyond naive assumptions of neutrality or objectivity that often accompany the presentation of 'the numbers'. Edwards argues that a cultural industry approach would bring a more sharply critical analysis to PR, an area of increasing importance and significance in terms of cultural consumption and distribution, but which often falls under the radar of our analysis of the cultural world.

27

IMAGINING THE CULTURAL CONSUMER

Class, cool and connoisseurship

David Wright

Introduction: Placing 'the cultural consumer' in context

This chapter considers the changing visions of the cultural consumer that emerge from historical and contemporary research into 'consumer societies'. These visions play out, the chapter will argue, through some perennial debates, stretching back to at least the sixteenth century and intensifying across the late twentieth, about the processes and meaning of the consumption of culture and the role of the cultural industries in shaping these meanings. The chapter will focus on the persistent and continuing role of *class* as a surprisingly hardy, underlying infrastructure for these processes and their accompanying images of the cultural consumer as a distinctive and distinguishing figure.

It is an accepted truism that, at least in the global North, we live in a 'consumer society'. The meaning of the term changes depending on the context of its use but it tends to refer to the relationships between the practice of consumption – that is, the buying and selling of consumer goods – and the broader social processes that stem from these practices, including the formation of individual forms of identity. Contemporary consumer goods are especially suited to be used in this kind of society, so this story goes, because they are inscribed with various forms of meaning, sign-values and symbolism that allow them to become resources in the construction of late-modern selves. Such resources help fill in the gaps vacated by older forms of identity work – including those connected with the class struggle – that have an apparently weakened grip on the imagination of contemporary subjects. The assumptions and the historical novelty of these relationships are clearly debatable, and doing so extensively is beyond the scope of this chapter, but the consumption of *culture*, i.e. of art, literature, music, film and similar goods that are explicitly concerned with the aesthetic and the symbolic has a distinct place in this story. Culture, unlike other commodities in the consumer market-place, is often thought of as *appreciated*, *experienced* or *engaged* with, rather than *produced*, *consumed*, bought or sold. The *popular* and commercial versions of these symbolic forms, by contrast, have an ambiguous role in the stories of the consumer society. Contemporary cultural genres or products, such as reality TV, blockbuster films, fast food and X-Factor-style music production exemplify what have been long established by critics of radical and conservative bents as the tendencies of a crude 'mass' culture towards inauthenticity and shallowness. In this version of the story the consumption of commercial culture is a form of exploitation of the leisure time of consumers, which mirrors, and ultimately enables, their exploitation in the capitalist workplace (Adorno and Horkheimer, 1997/ 1947). At the same time, the studied appreciation of other, 'higher' kinds of culture, art, literature and music, albeit that these forms are also increasingly distributed on commercial lines, provide resources for refuge from, or even creative resistance to, these same tendencies. Cultural consumption, then, can be seen to provide the resources for the *critique* of abiding social and political relationships in consumer society.

At the same time, as the French sociologist Pierre Bourdieu (1984) revealed in his study of the social patterns of taste in the France of the 1960s, cultural consumptions helps to *cement* these relationships by securing certain kinds of culture as the legitimate property of dominant classes and undermining other forms as the popular distractions for the subordinate. Traces of these class-inflected contrasts remain despite the considerable transformations in social life more generally in 'consumer societies' and in the cultural industries in particular. The labels attached to consumers of art and culture – whether historical ones such as 'flâneur' or 'bohemian' or more recent ones such as 'fan' or 'omnivore' draw on and evoke specific imaginaries about the characteristics of the activities of appreciation, experience and engagement and those who participate in them. By drawing on examples of these labels, I argue that such distinctions are as much a result of judgements about the qualities of people as the qualities of culture, as much about who is doing the consuming as what is consumed. The next section begins this process by sketching some of the changing relationships between social and cultural hierarchies revealed by empirical and historical perspectives on cultural consumption.

Class hierarchy and cultural authority

Relationships between class and cultural consumption have a long history, an important element of which is the recurrence of disquiet from those in positions of cultural authority over the extent of access to symbolic things within broader populations. Raymond Williams' account of the growth of the 'reading public' notes the deliberate attempts by English authorities to restrict access to printed material that had the potential for sedition, subversion or dangerous mis-interpretation by a newly literate mass as far back as the sixteenth century (Williams, 1961). More recent anxieties outlined by literary scholars and historians place struggles over access to and mastery of literature as the cultural manifestation of the class struggles of nineteenth century Britain. On one side were workers' self-education movements seeking mastery over the language of the powerful and a 'quest for singularity' from their labelling as merely the sum of their physical labour power (Rose, 2001). On the other were both conservative elites concerned about, in the case of mass literacy, the effects of the 'softening, demoralizing practice' of reading on the 'vigour of nations' (Arnold

Austin, 1880 quoted in Bratlinger, 1998: 23) and writers and intellectuals concerned about the effect of the spread of reading on minds not suited to the rarefied requirements of a literary sensibility and on their own cultural authority (Carey, 1992).

In more contemporary sociological debates, 'culture' remains a significant touchstone for understanding class relations. A crude summary of Bourdieu's position in *Distinction*, the most influential contribution to this debate, would be that in the 1960s in France, the object of his empirical study, there were clear relationships between hierarchies of culture and the social and occupational class structure. These relationships reflect how the establishment of tastes for legitimate culture, as determined by the education system, act as a form of capital that becomes central to the reproduction of class hierarchies. Towards the bottom of this hierarchy are the unrefined tastes of the labouring classes who prefer such things as simple plots in literature or film, mistrust experimentation in theatre or visual art and prefer hearty and filling forms of food. Towards the top are the *connoisseurs*, who not only know and like legitimate forms of culture, but are at ease with this knowledge in exhibiting a 'practical mastery' that 'presupposes a prolonged contact with cultured works and cultured people' (Bourdieu, 1984: 66). Such a summary – equivalents of which become something of a shibboleth in cultural analysis since the publication of these findings – does not quite capture some of the nuance of the fuller analysis. It specifically fails to recognize that these relationships between tastes and classes are *not* deterministic and that, importantly, in Bourdieu's analysis there were fractions of the dominant class – nominally 'cultural intermediaries' – for whom the selective pursuit of items and genres of popular culture was part of a struggle over the process of legitimizing culture itself – struggles that are significant in the shifting imaginary of cultural consumption and which have, as we'll see, arguably intensified in the years since *Distinction* was published. Cultural hierarchies are fluid things; the cultural industries and those who work in them are active in their reproduction and transformation and in their relationship to social hierarchies.

Importantly, the empirical snapshot of social and cultural hierarchies provided by *Distinction* in 1960s France was coterminous with some shifting of the tectonic plates of culture in France and elsewhere in this period, as the cultural industries expanded in size and influence. The empirical evidence provided by more recent studies of cultural consumption that share Bourdieu's concerns reveal some differences in the nature of these relationships. Whilst, for example, Bennett et al. (2009) on the United Kingdom in the early twenty-first century identify a persistent correspon-dence between participation in what might be identified as the high arts (visiting museums and galleries, regular attendance at the theatre, liking opera) and higher social and occupational groups, it is as interesting to note both the relative *un*popularity of these forms of culture within these groups, and that more educated and professional groups are also more likely to like a range of popular activities, including commercial genres of music, literature and film that historically they might have shunned. Indeed, most of the forms of cultural participation, be they popular and commercial or legitimate, that are asked about by Bennett et al., especially those that take place outside the home, are more associated with participants with higher levels of educa-tion and income. Such a finding resonates with the most substantive empirical development of Bourdieu's thesis, provided by Richard Peterson's notion of the *omnivore* (Peterson, 1992; Peterson and Kern, 1996). This analysis, based on large-scale survey data on cultural participation in the United States in the 1980s and 1990s, indicates an increasing tolerance amongst higher social classes for certain musical genres, including rock and jazz, which might have been shunned by the cultural elites of previous generations.

Such changes might be accounted for in relation to the broader social and cultural history of late-modern, Western societies. First, Peterson himself suggests a strong cohort effect in relation to omnivorousness, whereby the tastes of some elites in the 1990s reflect the tastes of some young people in the 1960s, when both rock music and jazz were becoming more established genres in social consciousness. Enthusiasts for these genres, which may have had the patina of rebellion or inter-generational struggle, have held onto their tastes as they have moved through their educational and professional careers and up the occupational and social structure, allowing rock music to become an entirely acceptable genre for higher social classes, despite its relative lack of formal consecration by the education system. Second, the latter part of the twentieth century also saw significant expansion in the volumes of people attending higher education institutions, including those from working class back-grounds, making the class-exclusivity of tastes, at least in the same ways that they had been established before such an expansion, more difficult for cultural elites to 'control'. Within the arts and humanities, Miller (2012) points to data indicating significant changes within higher education in the United States, including a relative decline in those traditional humanities subjects such as languages, philosophy and history most associated with cultural consecration ('Humanities 1' in his typology, the traditional repertoire of the elite US universities). Similarly, from the 1970s to the mid-noughties he notes significant increases – of over 600 per cent – in enrollments in communication and media studies ('Humanities 2' – the humanities of state education and of newer colleges). The latter is significant for both a more vocational approach to preparation for work in the expanding cultural industries themselves, but also because, for the last forty years at least, such disciplines have been central to the *legitimizing* of forms of popular commercial culture. This is evident in the rise of film and television as objects of academic analysis in their own right, rather than as a crude 'other' to literature or theatre. It is also evident in the ways in which cultural hierarchies, or at least some of the canons (Guillory, 1993) on which they are based, have been scrutinized as elitist and exclusionary, patriarchal and ethnocentric by scholars in the humanities and social sciences – meaning that critique of the dom-inating tendencies of legitimate culture is becoming written into the very processes of reproduction of new forms of institutionalized cultural capital.

Finally, developments in the technologies of cultural distribution have blurred the historically established institutional boundaries around the production of elite cultures. In his classic account of the emergence of elite culture in the United States, DiMaggio (1982) describes how in nineteenth century Boston public enter-tainments were as likely to contain a mixture of what would now be considered refined exhibits alongside more bawdy and base ones. It was a conscious attempt at separation by the emerging bourgeoisie that resulted in special places (theatres, museums, galleries) and institutions for special kinds of culture, increasing their rarity and scarcity and preserving them for special people. Successive technological developments, from film to television to the digital media, have challenged the coherence of these forms of separation. Film and television adaptations of literary works, for example, do more than bring such works to a broader audience. They also, as Collins (2010) argues, change the characteristics of the category of the 'literary' to be more inclusive and accessible and less the exclusive property of accredited experts. Such developments might be met with grumbling from established cultural authorities about 'dumbing-down', commodification and trivialization but they are also significant in challenging the exclusive distribution of culture within distinct class groups. The increased bandwith of digital television and the vast and expanding archives of *iTunes* or *Amazon*, or their illegal equivalents, mean that culture, and legitimate culture in particular, is not scarce in a way that makes it easily preserved and managed as DiMaggio's elites desired. Digital means of cultural distribution and circulation, such as You-Tube, make it as easy to access pornography or home-made videos of amusing pets as it is to access uploaded television productions of Beckett's *Waiting for Godot*, or even *Sesame Street's* pastiche of the same, 'Waiting for Elmo'.

In these contexts, the kinds of cultural authority that seemed irredeemably linked to the dominant class in Bourdieu's schema need to compete with other forms, which are more potentially diffuse in their class origins and aims. The next section examines this diffusion of cultural authority through exploring some further historical and contemporary labels attached to cultural consumption.

Cool, the cultural industries and 'critique'

The contemporary vision of the cultural consumer emerges alongside the development of the cultural industries themselves. Throughout their history, this has included, for the commercial media industries in particular, a classed conception of their audience. Taylor's (2012) account of the historical role of popular music in the development of consumer capitalism, for example, outlines how, in the early history of broadcast radio, types of music were selected for advertisements to specifically appeal to more refined and affluent consumers who were the preferred audience of sponsors. Moreover, the letters from listeners, which amounted to the principle forms of audience research and feedback in this period, were judged according to their quality (of language, of presentation, of stationery) as an indication of the relative levels of education and, by extension, affluence, of their correspondents. Subsequently the accurate measurement and classification of the media audience became a key source of competitive advantage in industries where the cultural consumer – the viewer or listener – was both the audience for products and a product to be 'sold' to advertisers and sponsors. More affluent middle-class consumers have always been more attractive to cultural producers than amorphous masses. By extension, the critique of mass culture has been a distinguishing strategy in the development of consumer culture. These are selective, safe forms of critique in terms of the underlying class structure of modern capitalism, but they are significant in understanding the ways in which class might operate through cultural consumption in the contexts of consumer societies in which the concept of social class itself appears a less evocative resource for identity work than individualized, symbolic consumer goods. The key insight, expressed succinctly by Boltanski and Chiapello, is that generating and responding to critique of various forms is a 'motor in the changes in the spirit of capitalism' (Boltanski and Chiapello, 2005: 27). The artistic critique, i.e. that which emerges from the experience of art and literature, is crucial to this story, as it 'presents itself as a radical challenge to the basic values and options of capitalism' (Boltanski and Chiapello, 2005: 39), specifically in relation to the real or perceived challenge to or loss of what is 'beautiful', 'valuable' or 'authentic' that is seen inevitably to accompany cultural standardization. Cultural consumption becomes constitutive of, rather than a refuge from, broader consumer societies in this story.

The imagined cultural consumer, their values and the social and cultural context in which they are situated change over time. A useful starting point for considering these changes is provided by the figures of the bomenian, the flâneur and the romantic artist as historical models of the contemporary consumer. The former, according to David Brooks' argument for the relevance of bohemia for understanding contemporary elites, 'celebrated creativity, rebellion, novelty, self-expression, anti-materialism and vivid experience' (Brooks, 2000: 69). With their emphasis on pleasure, excess and on the distinctive merits of the aesthetic and 'authentic' in artistic and everyday life, these figures provide the first prototype of the contemporary cultural consumer as rebel rather than conformist. The bohemian was also a figure for whom, as Bourdieu's account of the development of the field of cultural production suggests, the relationship between production and consumption became blurred, as bohemians were, if not artists themselves, then either workers in the supporting industries of the art or literary worlds or the 'celebrants and believers' (Bourdieu, 1996: 169) in the charismatic cult of the artist as genius – prototypes, in other words, for the cultural intermediaries who have subsequently become significant figures in the framing of the present-day economy for cultural things (Smith Maguire and Matthews, 2012). This vision of the nineteenth century cultural consumer as a seeker of new experiences who stands askance from the values of 'mainstream society' is also present in the other exemplary proto-consumer, the flâneur. At first an attempt to describe a new kind of orientation to the space of the city, as evidenced in the writings of Baudelaire (Benjamin, 1997), the flâneur is developed in theoretical accounts of consumer society as emblematic of a range of values that stand, if not quite in opposition to, then at least ambivalent to the mores of modern life – and to the unwashed herd that was one of the principal anxieties of nineteenth century intellectuals. The flâneur gains experience of the world through playful, voyeuristic window-shopping, seeking, in Bauman's terms, not only 'the crowd' but also 'the elbow room, which the man of the crowd does not have and does not want to have' (Bauman, 1994:139). Both figures share characteristics that might be familiar to the contemporary cultural consumer – including a disquiet with 'mass society' and, by extension, something of an ambivalence towards and a sense of distance from 'the masses' themselves.

A similar disquiet is present in the figure of the romantic artist, who shares these characteristics of detached contemplation, a commitment to self-development through experience and ambivalence to contemporary mores. For Colin Campbell (1987) it is these characteristics that make the Romantic Movement in art and literature of the late eighteenth and early nineteenth centuries a key influence on the formation of the contemporary version of consumerism. Its influence is not limited to artists or consumers as 'proto-producers', but is also more readily identifiable with more 'ordinary' participants in cultural life – albeit that this too has a class resonance. It was, for Campbell, the women of the new leisured classes, wives and daughters of the emerging bourgeoisie of the British Industrial Revolution who were, in this period, voraciously consuming that overtly symbolic good, the novel. Their detached contemplation of these commodities – enabled by their relative separation from the struggles for survival of the labouring classes – provided a refuge from the coming 'mass', urban, industrialized society about which writers and intellectuals of this period were so anxious. Consumption also provided a space for the kinds of reflection that serve as a model for consumer society in its late-modern experiential, hedonistic, self-actualizing mode. For these romantic consumers, according to Campbell, the experience of art was itself a source of moral renewal through which a relatively affluent audience could cleanse itself of the more rational, calculable and therefore vulgar machinations of the emerging modern world.

There are echoes of these same impulses in the rise of the counterculture normally associated with the 1960s in the United States and Europe and the emergence of 'cool' as a criterion of cultural value in the mid to late twentieth century. 'Cool' was characterized by ambivalence to 'mainstream' forms of culture, the privileging of *authentic* experience over mass produced artifice and the selective appropriation of the styles of oppressed groups, especially, in the United States, the music and language of African-Americans. These counter-cultural energies were integrated into the emerging cultural industries during the expansion of the consumer society in the post-war United States and its cultural imperial outposts. The familiar story here, exemplified by recurring motifs of radical artists or performers 'selling out', or the commercial exploitation of much loved works of counter-cultural expression, is that the impulse to escape mass society and to pursue experience, even to excess, is incorporated into the strategies of capitalism itself. 'Cool' shifts from being a defiant stance against prevailing orders to being, in Frank's (1997) analysis, the very epitome of late capitalist style. The kinds of close attention to these processes given by both McGuigan (2009) and Frank reveal that the story of the incorporation of rebellion is more nuanced – and that the counterculture itself emerges not simply as a cultural *opposition* to the prevailing capitalist social order but as part of a symbolic struggle *within* the dominant class. Frank argues that the values of the counterculture were welcomed by emergent voices in US business elites, for example, precisely because they resonated with a new vision of the consumer they were attempting to mould – individualist, thirsty for authentic experiences and dissatisfied with what 'mass culture' was offering. As a result, the apparently insurrectionist energies of the counterculture are, for Frank, 'more accurately understood as a stage in the development of the values of the middle-class, a colourful installment in the twentieth century drama of consumer subjectivity' (Frank, 1997: 29). A recent iteration of this is found in Michael's (2013) empirical study of a proto-cultural elite of hip young consumers exhibiting a complex and nimble tightrope walk between distance from the 'mainstream' and proximity to the 'authentic' in their consuming practices of fashion and music in the creative cities of Europe. Here 'cool' can be imagined as a form of capital, a form of 'insider knowledge' (Nancarrow and Nancorrow, 2007: 135) whereby, like the connoisseur's comfort with the conventions of fine dining or how to behave in a theatre, those who possess it exhibit a practical mastery over its codes. At the same time as requiring comfort with the codes of cool, though, the existentialist, cool, rootless, hedonistic individual thirsty for authentic experiences also needs access to the social networks or the financial means to sustain a lifestyle of anti-materialism.

Our final figure, the 'fan', is an interesting vision of the contemporary culture in the light of some of the characteristics of contradiction and critique outlined already. Unabashed enthusiasm might mean that the fan is, at least outside the circles of their fandom, decidedly *uncool* – given cool's associations with studied distance and detachment. This is perhaps except inasmuch as it is the focused dedication of the fan that allows her/him to do the work to be in the inner circle at concerts, or on the red carpet at premiers. The fan's association with almost pathological enthusiasm allows them to be seen as an inevitable extension of the critique of the 'mass' consumer. This is including by Bourdieu, for whom the forms of fandom mentioned in *Distinction* are presented as a taste position to which 'ordinary people' are reduced in relation to music or sports representing 'merely an illusory compensation for dispossession by experts' (Bourdieu, 1984: 386). Contemporary 'fans' are more complex than this rather peripheral part of Bourdieu's anlaysis allows, but scholars of fandom (Jenkins, 1992; Hills, 2002) have used Bourdieu's schema as a tool to think against, with the homologous relationships between class and cultural forms revealed by the empirical evidence in *Distinction*, envisaged as one structure that fan activity can be seen to subvert or undermine. The fan is also emblematic of the 'active audience' – beloved of media and cultural studies more generally, as revealing the extent to which critical accounts of 'mass' forms of consumption are classed and gendered, with audiences making creative uses of the products of mass entertainment in what might be interpreted as con-temporary versions of Rose's 'quest for singularity'. Although feminist scholars of popular culture have also revealed how class overlaps with gender in the activity of fan audiences, this 'active–passive' nexus is itself classed with the imaginary of 'excessive' television watching, for example, evoking imagery of worklessness and lack of discipline and the 'active' resonating far more with the 'totalitarian imperative' (Born, 2000: 417) to improve oneself that is characteristic of contemporary middle-class consumer culture. Fans do not sit easily into this categorization either, though, as fan activity is almost by default *univorous* – focusing on single artists or genres and therefore less open to the variety that has become the contemporary version of Bourdieu's aesthetic gaze as the default taste culture of the omnivorous middle-classes. Thornton (1997) develops the model of the creative and spectacular consuming practices of the cultural studies version of youth culture to develop 'sub-cultural capital' as the in-group means of distinguishing real enthusiasts from arrivistes within the study of dance music culture. However, the forms of capital generated within contemporary fan cultures are more transferable and translatable than even this model suggests. Within the commercial cultural industries, including TV and film, fans are increasingly powerful actors in the field of cultural production, acting, through organized and online forums that serve as important market information for producers, as, following Bourdieu, 'agents of consecration', according to Shefrin's analysis of their role in contemporary Hollywood (Shefrin, 2006: 91).

The class identity of this modern version of the fan is less immediately legible – and class has been less central to fan studies itself. They are clearly more than the duped mass consumer of Bourdieu's vision, though, and moreover they can increasingly point to academic critique from the cultural studies tradition as a form of consecration, be it of soap opera or genre forms of fiction in literature, television or film. We can imagine them, at least in their more activist mode, as contemporary iterations of Taylor's letter writers, applying their technical skills, their articulacy and their knowledge of the codes and conventions of their preferred forms to their own identity work as well as their interactions with producers. The fan, then, might well be the form of cultural consumer that does most to indicate how the relations between institutional forms of cultural capital and social hierarchies are unclear in the contemporary context in relation to how items and practices can be used as distinguishing forms of capital in class relations.

Conclusions: Class, consumers and the cultural industries

Boltanski and Chiapello's (2005) account of the shifting spirits of capitalism from the ascetic culture of deferred gratification to its more expressive contemporary, consumerist version points out that 'artistic critique' helped capitalism to transform its hierarchies, including it class hierarchies. Part of this process, as this chapter has attempted to demonstrate, has been a persistent dance between a conception of certain kinds of cultural consumption as indicative of 'rebellion' or 'critique' on the one hand, and narratives of cultural consumption as emblematic of 'incorporation' and 'commodification' on the other. Both these strands of cultural consumption can be seen as related to different forms of cultural authority, and, therefore, to on-going questions about the cultural aspects of class relations in contemporary social life.

Bourdieu still offers useful tools for exploring the persistently classed nature of contemporary forms of cultural consumption, but some modification to our understanding of the nature of cultural capital is also merited to reflect the altered empirical reality of the early twenty-first century. The codes of classification might be different, and less firmly associated than they once were with, for example, the consecrating strategies of the education system. Competing with these forms of institutional capital are a range of other forms of accreditation – including those from within fan cultures, and from the promotional strategies of the cultural industries themselves, for whom traditional academic or high cultural forms of authority are likely to be dismissed as stuffy or old-fashioned rather than embraced as distinguishing. Such developments are likely to reflect changes within classes, rather than an egalitarian opening up of the ability to produce and interpret cultural codes – and the persistent quest for affluent consumers by the cultural industries means that working class culture is only present in these processes as a resource to be selectively appropriated into the cool or authentic. But these changes – of inter-generational cohort effects, the expansion of university education and the prevalence over the last thirty years within the humanities and social sciences of a critical scepticism about the coherence of cultural canons and the potentially democratizing influence of new modes of distribution at least imply that the relationship between class and cultural consumption is in continuous flux, rather than ever settled, and that Williams' *Long Revolution* is on-going.

References

Adorno, T. and Horkheimer, M. (1997/1947) 'The culture industry: enlightenment as mass deception' in S. During (ed.) *The Cultural Studies Reader*, London: Routledge, pp 29–43.

Bauman, Z. (1994) 'Desert spectacular' in K. Tester (ed.) *The Flâneur*, London: Routledge, pp 138–57.

Benjamin, W. (1997) *Charles Baudelaire: A Lyric Poet in the Era of High Capitalism*, Verso: London.

Bennett, T., Savage, M., Silva, E.B., Warde, A., Gayo-Cal, M. and Wright, D. (2009) *Culture, Class, Distinction*, London: Routledge.

Boltanski, L. and Chiapello, E. (2005) *The New Spirit of Capitalism*, London: Verso.

Born, G. (2000) 'Inside television: Television studies and the sociology of culture', *Screen* 41(4): 404–24.

Bourdieu, P. (1984) *Distinction: A Social Critique of the Judgment of Taste*, London: Routledge.

Bourdieu, P. (1996) *The Rules of Art*, Cambridge: Polity.

Bratlinger, P. (1998) *The Reading Lesson: The Threat of Mass Literacy in Nineteenth Century British Fiction*, Bloomington: Indiana University Press.

Brooks, D. (2000) *Bobos in Paradise*, New York: Simon and Schuster.

Campbell, C. (1987) *The Romantic Ethic and the Spirit of Modern Consumerism*, Oxford: Blackwell.

Carey, J. (1992) *The Intellectuals and the Masses*, London: Faber.

Collins, J. (2010) *Bring on the Books for Everybody: How Literary Culture Became Popular Culture*, Durham: Duke University Press.

DiMaggio, P. (1982) 'Cultural entrepreneurship in 19th century Boston: The creation of an organizational basis for high culture in America', *Media, Culture and Society* 4: 33–50.

Frank, T. (1997) *The Conquest of Cool: Business Culture, Counter-Culture and the Rise of Hip Consumerism*, Chicago: University of Chicago Press.

Guillory, J. (1993) *Cultural Capital: The Problem of Literary Canon Formation*, London: University of Chicago Press.

Hills, M. (2002) *Fan Cultures*, London: Routledge.

Jenkins, H. (1992) *Textual Poachers*, London: Routledge.

McGuigan, J. (2009) *Cool Capitalism*, London: Pluto Press.

Michael, J. (2013) 'It's not really hip to be a hipster: Negotiating trends and authenticity in the cultural field', *Journal of Consumer Culture*. Published online before print June 25, 2013, doi: 10.1177/1469540513493206.

Miller, T. (2012) *Blow Up the Humanities*, Philadelphia: Temple University Press.

Nancarrow, C. and Nancarrow, P. (2007) 'Hunting for cool tribes' in B. Cova, R.V. Kozinets and A. Shankar (eds) *Consumer Tribes*, Oxford: Butterworth-Heinemann.

Peterson, R.A. (1992) 'Understanding audience segmentation: From elite and mass to omnivore and univore', *Poetics* 21(4): 243–58.

Peterson, R.A. and Kern, R.M. (1996) 'Changing highbrow taste: From snob to omnivore', *American Sociological Review* 61 (5): 900–9.

Rose, J. (2001) *The Intellectual Life of the British Working Classes*, New Haven and London: Yale University Press.

Shefrin, E. (2006) '*Lord of the Rings, Star Wars* and participatory fandom: Mapping new congruences between the internet and media entertainment culture' in E. Ezra and T. Rowden (eds) *The Transnational Cinema Reader*, London: Routledge, pp 81–96.

Smith Maguire, J. and Matthews, J. (2012) 'Are we all cultural intermediaries now? An introduction to cultural intermediaries in context', *European Journal of Cultural Studies* 15 (5): 551–62.

Taylor, T. (2012) *The Sounds of Capitalism*. Chicago and London: University of Chicago Press.

Thornton, S. (1997) *Club Cultures*, London: Routledge.

Williams, R. (1961) *The Long Revolution*, Harmondsworth: Penguin.

28
CHALLENGING BOUNDARIES
Fans and cultural industries

Cornel Sandvoss

The possibly most notable feature distinguishing cultural industries from other industry sectors is that they are confronted with a very particular type of customer: fans. In contrast to consumers operating by the sober rationale of the marketplace imagined in liberal economic theory, the consumption of the texts and goods produced by cultural industries can only be understood through the analysis of its emotional and affective underpinnings and associated forms of enjoyment. In turn the vast majority of fan objects are found within the textual and symbolic realm of contemporary, commercial popular culture.

The implications of the resulting interplay of fans and cultural industries are far reaching. The inadequacy of classic economic models to understand these implications is illustrated by two seemingly contrary observations: emotionally and affectively engaged consumers make investments in the form of financial capital, labour and curatorial activity that seem sparsely warranted by objects' use value; leading, for instance, to widely publicised occasions of fan memorabilia being sold for hundreds of thousands or even millions of pounds (Geraghty 2014; cf. Sandvoss 2005a). And yet, much of the cultural industries encounter difficulties in monetising their output. Indeed, much of it is accessed by users for free: the business model of the most popular forms of entertainment continues to be based on providing free content and services to audiences and users by selling advertisers access to these groups – a model that remains largely unchanged from commercial broadcasters to online services such as search engines, video portals and social media sites. When businesses seek to employ a traditional model in which content is being sold to customers the evasion of the intended payment mechanisms through the easy reproducibility of nonmaterial cultural objects, as in, for example, cases of audio and video file sharing, leads to the *de facto* though not *de jure* free accessibility of the products of cultural industries.

The question of value – monetary and otherwise – therefore requires very different approaches in the analysis of cultural industries. In simple numerical terms, the significance of cultural industries to the overall economy – and hence its wider significance to contemporary consumer capitalism – appears modest: possibly reflecting some of the monetisation issues mentioned above. According to a 2013 report by the Centre for Economics and Business Research, cultural industries account only for about 0.4 per cent of the gross domestic product in the United Kingdom. And yet, in our everyday experience cultural industries are at the heart of consumer culture: they evoke passion and loyalty among fans, providing a model of affective engagements that facilitate emotion, enjoyment and the integration of products into users' identity positions; a capacity sought to be emulated in other industry sectors, as both the extensive efforts of sponsorship in realms of popular culture from sports to music and film, and the wider role of popular media as carriers of advertisements, powerfully illustrate. In order to explore the particular relevance of fans to cultural industries, it is thus necessary to explore how affective attachments in fandom are constituted and which practices they give rise to.

Defining fans

As inescapable and omnipresent fans appear in (digital) landscapes of contemporary entertainment, as contested any definition of the term has remained. Two factors in particular have fuelled controversy over who and what constitutes fans and fandom. First, fans' investments are closely tied to particular identity positions. From music fans (Cavicchi 1997; Sandvoss 2008, 2014; Duffett 2014) to film (Brooker 2002), television (McClellan 2013; Hills 2014; Booth and Kelly 2013) and many further fields of cultural industry output and beyond,[1] choices of fan objects are worked and woven into everyday life identity practices and personal narratives underscoring individuals' identity in late modernity. Given the significance of fandom to many consumers' and indeed scholars' sense of self, it is unsurprising that definitions of who is regarded as a fan have remained contested. Seemingly too inclusive definitions have led to loud protestations from scholars/fans wishing to attribute the status of being a fan only to particular audience groups defined by a more narrow set of practices (for example, Coppa 2014; see also Fiske 1992 for a further normative, if less narrow approach).

In examining the interplay between cultural industries and fans, I instead propose a definition that is inclusive of all consumers and users who have developed a sustained meaningful affective relationship with cultural texts and objects, thus defining fandom as 'the regular, emotionally involved engagement with a given narrative or text' (Sandvoss 2005a). This wider definition, however, increasingly encompasses a large section of all practices of cultural consumption. The digitalisation of cultural industries' output has not only created unparalleled access to cultural texts and objects, but also necessitates selection in actively seeking out types of content. An affective disposition, or fan habitus, is thus a near inevitable premise for the engagement in digital cultural landscapes. Consequently, fandom also constitutes an ideal mode of engagement and use that cultural industries aim to facilitate. In Henry Jenkins' (2007: 361) words:

> Fandom represents the experimental prototype, the testing ground for the way media and culture industries are going to operate in the future. In the old days, the ideal consumer watched television, bought products, and

didn't talk back. Today, the ideal consumer talks up the program and spreads word about the brand. The old ideal might have been the couch potato; the new ideal is almost certainly a fan.

With such ubiquity, however, Jenkins (2007: 364) asserts,

> one starts to wonder – who isn't a fan? What doesn't constitute fan culture? When does grassroots culture end and commercial culture begin? […] Maybe there is no typical media consumer against which the cultural otherness of the fan can be located. Perhaps we are all fans or perhaps none of us is.

And to expand on Jenkins' line of thought, is fandom so ubiquitous that the figure of the fan has lost analytic relevance in exploring the particularities of cultural industries? I will argue here that 'fans' and 'fandom' remain important concepts in understanding cultural industries and production, although in doing so I will depart from Jenkins' assessment of the future of fandom in an important respect. We will return to this question below.

In the first instance the prominence of fandom in the digital age does require further differentiation between fan groups with different practices and levels of engagement. Following the influential audience continuum of Abercrombie and Longhurst (1998), fan typologies have commonly positioned fans and different subgroups in the borderlands between cultural consumption and production. Fans are not only emotionally engaged, but the closer we move towards the production end of the continuum also engage in a range of activities and practices that mimic, emulate, aspire to – but also challenge, critically question and place at risk of redundancy – the works and products of cultural industries. The fan as active consumer, or indeed user, thus, as Jenkins observes, already describes and encompasses a range of new terms and concepts that have been associated with consumers and audiences in the digital age: 'loyals', 'media-actives', 'connectors', influencers' and maybe most prominently 'prosumers' (see Bruns 2008). In Jenkins' words (2007: 359) 'none of these commentators on the new economy are using the terms "fan", "fandom" or "fan culture", yet their models rest on the same social behaviours and emotional commitments that fan scholars have been researching over the past several decades'. What is at stake in these reflections on the accuracy of labels given to participatory media users is more than a question of ownership over the analysis of audience practices by different conceptual and methodological traditions in media and cultural studies. Rather they point to the important continuities in cultural engagements that span from the pre-digital age of mass communication and mass consumption through to contemporary transformations of online cultural production, often overlooked in new media-centred accounts of prosumption. This is further illustrated as we turn to a brief examination of forms of fan productivity and labour.

Fan productivity and labour

While more narrow questions of the precise translation of models of offline fan productivity to online environments have attracted some debate,[2] it is the value of fan productivity itself that has been at the heart of the field's controversy. Hills (2013) has usefully summarised the polar ends of this prominent debate: on the one hand the outright and indiscriminate endorsement of user productivity in the work of Gauntlett (2011) and Shirky (2010) who in their flat celebratory approach lose the capacity to distinguish between the value of different types of fan-generated content, and the attempts to reassert traditional dividing lines between cultural industry professionals and fan amateurs in which the latter are *a priori* relegated to the realm of ineptitude (Keen 2008). In the last instance such approaches attribute value assumed to be constituted through authenticity and 'talent' only through the tauto-logical frame of institutional legitimacy (see, for example, Lanier 2010), rather than a coherent aesthetics of the creative process.

The discourse about the value of fans' enunciatve and textual productivity is not limited to scholarly debates. Rather, it is manifest in the judgements in and about fan-generated texts among fans, in fans' assessments of interactions with cultural industries and indeed in cultural industries' discourses about fans, as Derek Johnson (2007) illustrates in reference to *Buffy the Vampire Slayer* and its fans (see also Murray 2004, and Chin and Hills 2008). Such 'fantagonisms' (Johnson 2007), however, cannot, at least *per se*, be equated to forms of wider social, cultural and political empowerment and rejection of dominant ideologies and hegemonic structures by fans that much of the 'first wave' of fan studies (Gray et al. 2007) foregrounded. Fans, *pace* fan studies' 'second wave' of post-Bourdieuian approaches, 'operate dis-cursively to constitute a hegemony within fictionalised fan communities' as much as to 'attach and criticise media producers who they feel threatened their meta-textual interests' who in turn 'respond to these challenges, protecting their privilege by diffus-ing and marginalising fan activism' (Johnson 2007: 298). Fans' creative and reflexive engagements and their dissemination online hence impact on cultural industries by potentially challenging micro and meso levels (cultural industry workers and business models) yet rarely the macro regimes of contemporary cultural production. Costello and Moore (2008), for example, highlight the potential impact of fans on cultural industries: in contrast to the limited 'collective bargaining power' of pre-internet fandom, 'online fan communities have the potential to produce unified centres of resistance to influence the global industries of cultural production'. Yet, what is bargained for, as R.M. Milner's (2009, 2010) study of the interaction between gamers and software producer Bethesda in the production and design process of *Fallout 3* demonstrates, is – alongside intra-fandom related concerns over recognition and status within fan cultures – primarily a struggle over the correct textual form and meaning, or what Milner (2011) describes as 'text integrity', triggering four dominant approaches fans enacted when interacting with cultural industries (managerial, agnostic, cynical and deferential). Notably, in identifying the converse strategies employed by producers when interacting with fans, Milner can still apply Jenkins' (1992) pre-digital classification of 'support, contempt and supervision' to digital cultural industries–fan interactions with ease, indicating that changes to cultural industry workers' attitudes to fans have been largely incremental despite radical technological change. Moreover, the continuity of a tripart approach that seeks to endorse and manage fan productivity on the one hand and remains hostile on the other, reflects the opportunities and threats that arise from fans' productivity for cultural industries and their employees. Because fans share a concern over the cultural objects and texts – even if they disagree with creative and commercial choices made on behalf of producers – their productivity is system imminent and therefore constitutes a potential resource in the process of production, enabling cultural industries to harvest such productivity as a form of free labour or what Baym and Burnett (2009), drawing on Hardt and Negri (2000) and Terranova (2000), describe a 'immaterial labour'. Being system immanent, fans' productivity, even if antagonistic to individual cultural industry workers or companies, is therefore not contrary to principles of capitalist cultural production as it is aimed at 'the formal rational goal of improving the fan text – and hence of doing the job of the producer better and more efficiently' (Sandvoss 2011a: 56–57).

This highlights the simultaneous opportunity and threat that fan labour carries for existing cultural industries: one the one hand fans are enthusiastic and unpaid contributors. They willingly serve as content providers, focus groups and disseminators, thus being co-opted into production processes increasingly dominant in late consumer capitalism (cf. Ritzer 1996; Ritzer et al. 2012). On the other hand, such fan labour not only threatens the professional status of professional creative workers but also threatens to make their paid-for productivity uncompetitive and possibly redundant, explaining some of the hostility enunciatively and textually productive fans are confronted with. There is little doubt that transmedia auteurs need to 'treat audiences as their partner' (Scott 2013: 50) and that, as Artieri (2012) notes, corporations 'and the storytelling professionals – from journalists to novelists, from screenwriters to designers – are adapting their ways of producing and disseminating contents, developing ways that are more suitable to the new logic of circulation'. Unsurprisingly, it is comparatively small-scale companies, producers and artists, such as the Swedish independent musicians in Baym's (2011) study who rely on their fans to drive the international distribution of their work, and who have adopted strategies of flexible accumulation in response to the emergence of digital cultural landscapes, that have most successfully and harmoniously harnessed or, if you will, exploited fan labour; whereas larger corporations originating in, and relying on the business models of, the era of mass communication and consumption (such as major record labels and film studios seeking to guard their 'intellectual property' through legal action) have often failed to co-opt fans into the production process by aiming to maintain boundaries between production and consumption.

However, debates about the interplay of fan productivity/labour and cultural industries need to be contextualised in two important respects that in turn highlight their conceptual reach beyond the notion of 'prosumption'. First, textual and enunciative productivity remain a minority practice among fans and must not be misconstrued as the dominant mode of cultural consumption, albeit that fan-generated texts are of significance to fans who are not textually productive themselves. We will return to this theme in the following section. Second, attesting and mapping different forms of fan productivity – or prosumer activity – tells us little about the motivations that drive fans' productivity, nor their wider social, cultural and economic significance.

In this respect Jenkins curiously limits the conceptual contribution that fan studies can make to the understanding of processes consumer productivity and engagement by suggesting that recent studies of digital media, having revisited and reiterated central themes of fan studies such as the social, network and collaborative processes that mark fan productivity, affirm the centrality of such themes and thus stand in a paradoxical contrast to 'much of the recent work in fan studies [...] which has returned to focus on the individual fan' (Jenkins 2007: 361). However, it is in the focus on the affective relationship between self and fan objects, which has shaped the 'third wave of fan studies' (Gray et al. 2007), that the notion of the 'fan' offers greater analytical potential than the notion of prosumption, precisely because it has commonly focused on an exploration of the interplay between practices and technology, to explore the motivations and affective foundations that structure this interplay and thus fundamentally shape interactions and engagements between cultural industries and their users.

Affect and practise

In contrast to the narrower emphasis on the interplay between technology and practice in the notion of 'prosumption', fan theory offers a broader appreciation of the emotive basis of consumer loyalty, motivations for fan productivity and labour, as well as the forms of enjoyment and pleasure that drive the engagement with cultural objects; and thus by extension shape the (textual) form of cultural objects and the structures of the cultural industries producing them. Furthermore, it positions fans' contemporary engagements with cultural industries within the wider context of post-war consumption and communication systems. The continuities that Jenkins highlights between contemporary user practices and audience practices in the pre-digital age are equally evident when examining the motivational basis of the bond between fans and fan objects. In illustrating how the study of fans reveals cultural practices of media use that are a dual reflection of mass media *and* digital media, of distance *and* interaction, and of reception *and* participation, I thus turn first to the affective foundations of fandom.

Early work in fan studies, such as Grossberg (1992) or Fiske (1992), sought to explain the emotional rewards and pleasures of fandom through notions of subversion or 'affect', thus either attributing the emotional substance of fandom to existing power relations (and their evasion), or by attesting the fairly obvious without advancing the understanding of its causes, such as how and under what conditions affect is constituted. The past two decades in fan studies have thus witnessed a shift towards the exploration of the psychological and psychoanalytical foundations through which texts and objects gain the emotional significance that underscores the bond between fan and fan object (see Harrington and Bielby 1995; Stacey 1994; Elliott 1999; Hills 2002; Sandvoss 2003, 2005a; for a recent summary of such approaches, see Duffett 2014). Broadly psychoanalytical in their orientation, these studies draw on a range of post-Freudian theory from the work of object relations theorists such as Melanie Klein and Donald Woods Winnicott to the integration of Freudian and Marxist thought in the work of Herbert Marcuse. The comparative validity and accuracy of each of these theoretical models is of central significance in assessing the aesthetic, cultural, social and political consequences of fandom. However, in focusing on the aspects most relevant to the analysis of the interplay between cultural industries and fans, namely the technological, the textual and the symbolic, helpfully a common theme emerges. Whether the bond between fans and fan objects is grounded in identificatory fantasies that are maintained through processes of projection and introduction (Stacey 1994; Elliott 1999), fan objects serve as transitional objects between self and object world (Harrington and Bielby 1995; Hills 2002, 2007) or as a space of self-reflection in narcissistic enjoyment of the extension of self into the object world (Sandvoss 2003, 2005a), the affective basis of the bond between fan and fan objects is rooted in the far-reaching semiotic control of the fan object by the fan: it is because fans are able to radically appropriate cultural objects that these objects can function as spaces of projection, self-reflection and as a transitional object.

The levels of ideational autonomy upon which the affective qualities and pleasures of fandom rest are illustrated in fans' reading habitus, the semiotic condition of fan objects, and the interplay between fan practices and technologies, all three of which substantively shape interactions between fans and cultural industries. We will explore all three themes in turn.

First, fans' reading position is based upon clear and frequently rigid expectations. Given fans' interest and regular engagement with given cultural objects and texts, the degree of familiarity with their fan object is high, and commonly higher than that of any other audience members. Or, to put it in the terms of reception aesthetics, fans' 'horizon of experience' leads to a specific and detailed 'horizon of expectation' (Jauss 1982). Conversely, failing to meet fans' set expectations causes a rupture of the affective bond between fan and fan object as meanings upon which projective and self-reflective readings are based can no longer be maintained. In other words, once the fan object cannot be read in a fashion that meets fans' expectations, the bond between fan and fan object is eroded, giving rise to frustration and antagonism. The failure to meet fans' horizon of expectations is at the heart of the conflicts between fans and producers illustrated above as well as numerous further studies of fans in which such expectations are commonly met: fans of romance novels in Janice Radway's (1989) study have clear and narrow expectations of story lines firmly embedded in heteronormative and patriarchal articulations of happiness; fans of television shows (Harrington and Bielby 1995; Willis 2003; Scardaville 2005) or film franchises such as *Star Wars* (Brooker 2002, see also Proctor 2013; Davis et al. 2014) all have clearly defined and articulated expectations.[3] Similarly, fans, both individually and collectively as a member of interpretive communities, construct and critically examine the canon of their favoured genres and texts, a practice that in the digital era has become highly visible through fan blogs, social media activity, online evaluations and comment sections. Rather than being unreflective hyper-consumers, fans' love of the fan object is tied to a narrow, precise and subjective horizon of expectation that is grounded in the detailed knowledge of the fan object and its context, against which the outputs of cultural industries are continuously and critically assessed.[4] While fan expectations can thus constitute barriers against crass commercialism and exploitation, they can also be experienced as curtailing creative freedom, as many popular musicians seeking to evolve stylistically – and probably none more famously than Bob Dylan who in taking to the electric guitar left his folk roots behind to a public backlash culminating in his famous denunciation as 'Judas' at a concert in Manchester in 1966 – can give witness to.

Fandom, however, would be far from the near ubiquitous mode of cultural consumption if disappointment and antagonism were frequent occurrences in fans' engagements with the outputs of cultural industries. This leads us to the second point. Rather, cultural text and objects appear to have the remarkable capacity to accommodate a wide range of diverging, always in the last instance subjective readings and expectations. Elsewhere, I have suggested that the question of polysemy has been insufficiently explored in media and cultural studies as its particular relevance lies not in its existence (all texts are polysemic) but in its degree (Sandvoss 2005b, 2007, 2011b). Notably, those cultural texts and objects that are able to attract the largest and most diverse groups of fans appear to be those that are 'neutrosemic' – 'the semiotic condition in which a text allows for so many diverging readings that it intersubjectively does not have any meaning at all' (Sandvoss 2005a: 126). There is a shortage of studies of cultural production and cultural industries that have examined the degree to which considerations of textual openness and neutrosemy in an effort to attract the widest possible fan base enter the strategic planning and everyday life practices in cultural industries, but anecdotal evidence from as diverse realms as political marketing (in its effort to define political opponents rather than the political actor on whose behalf the campaign is conducted, in what has become widely known as 'negative campaigning'), football (in which clubs have actively sought to overcome particular social, cultural or religious affiliations that have defined but also limited their traditional supporter base [Sandvoss 2003]) or popular music as record labels seek to impose a stylistic direction, commonly aimed at the largest possible market, on artists.

Yet, to move to the third and final point on the impact of affective engagements on fans' ideational practices, neutrosemy is not solely a result of deliberate, unaware or inadvertent creative practices, but primarily constituted through means of distribution and dissemination that create the material conditions of processes of reading. If fan expectations have been as much a feature of the reception of popular culture in the age of analogue cultural industries, heightened degrees of polysemy have facilitated such expectations to be met in an ever greater number of reception contexts driven by technological change. The impact of the dissemination of means of production of mediated content to vast sections of users in digital culture is thus not only constituted through fan productivity as discussed above. What has been much less frequently considered is that digital media have also reshaped the process of reading itself. As fandom constitutes one of the most visible phenomena of the eroding boundaries of production and consumption, of industries and consumers, it has undermined taken-for-granted assumptions about the objects and texts that were previously constituted in the dichotomy between author and reader: in an environment of electronic and increasingly digital media, textual boundaries are no longer exclusively defined by cultural industries at the point of production. Instead they are negotiated through practices of selection necessitated by mode and form of dissemination and reception contexts (Sandvoss 2005a, 2005b, 2007, 2011b). Traditional forms of art and entertainment that require physical co-presence such as a painting or a theatre play enforce textual boundaries in both time and space – the frame of a classical painting against the gallery wall or the rituals and spatial organisation of a theatre visit all force modes of reception in which the text/object is received in its entirety and clearly demarcated from its setting.[5] While printed books are at a greater risk of selective reading – a mode of reception that might even be encouraged through a book's narrative and organisational structure as, say, an encyclopaedia, or as in our case here, a handbook – it is still possible to determine the intended textual boundaries at the point of production, albeit that they fail to be enforced at the point of reception. In the case of electronic and digital content, however, even the intended textual boundaries at the point of production can become increasingly unclear. The longitudinal seriality of much broadcasting content creates great difficulty in determining the start, let alone end point, of a given text – to the extent that watching all episodes of a long-running show such as *Dr Who* becomes a minor news event in itself.[6] Feature films are embedded within 'making-of-documentaries', DVD extras, promotional appearances by directors and actors and marketing campaigns – in addition to often being part of franchises, remakes, or literary adaptations in the first place. The hypertextuality of the internet or the multiple choice universe of offline and online gaming moves beyond singular, linear narration altogether. Hence, fans make both *a priori* selection of given genres and texts, and are required to draw textual boundaries at the point and in the process of reception.

Of yet greater significance to forms of cultural production is, however, that convergence culture further challenges notions of 'texts' and 'objects' through the rise of transmediation in which given narratives, or 'textual fields' (Sandvoss 2007), span across different platforms. If the painting we see at the gallery in the above example is Vincent van Gogh's *Sunflowers* at the National Gallery in London, its immediate boundaries might be obvious at the point of reception, but will, to the vast majority of recipients, be positioned within a firmly established meta-narrative composed of the wider 'van Gogh' brand, the frequent reproduction of the sunflower variations in and through everyday life objects from postcards to pens, mugs and t-shirts, discourses about impressionism, the physical experience of the museum and its positioning in central London and exchanges about the artwork with friends and family, though the particular narrative constructed will of course vary in each instance or reception. In other words, the (transmedia) narrative of van Gogh's *Sunflowers* exists far beyond the frame of the painting, thus heightening the plethora of texts and contexts from which the recipient constructs narrative fields. At this point the original work of art or creativity – the 'urtext' (Sandvoss 2007) – is constructed within and read through a selection of what Jonathan Gray (2003, 2010) has in reference to Gérard Gennette (1997) described as 'paratext': trailers, posters, blurbs, toys and other promotional material, but also user and fan-generated content such as blogs, comments, remixes, spoofs, spoilers, fan art and so on. Crucially, it is the resulting textual fields that serve as what I have described here as 'fan objects'. It is the ability to draw boundaries around these textual fields by selecting and discriminating between an array of paratexts and urtexts as the gravitational centre of these textual fields that enables fans to create the affective bonds through which the pleasures and emotional rewards of fandom are experienced. While, as I have suggested above, only a section of fans will engage in the creation of mediated user-generated content, the process of textual selection and discrimination in order to fulfil existing horizon of expectations is universal to all fans' readings (Sandvoss and Kearns 2014); and increasingly, as the example of Highfield et al.'s (2013) study of the use of twitter as a backchannel for live television events illustrate, the textual fields through which fan objects are constructed are hybrid fields spanning across industry- and fan-produced content. In turn, it is through this drawing of textual boundaries that polysemy is heightened to the degree of neutrosemy, and that textual fields can accommodate the projections and self-reflective needs of users, thus further proliferating fandom as the increasingly prevalent mode of cultural consumption in the digital age.

Conclusion

Assessing the economic and cultural consequences of the interplay between fans and cultural industries, a number of conflicting vectors emerge. In an environment of unprecedented choice of cultural texts and objects, fans' affective attachments and associated textual loyalties are of crucial importance to cultural industries. Cultural industries can benefit from harnessing fans' productivity and labour as fans in their affective foundations do not self-impose a logic of capitalist exchange on their pro-ductivity, yet remain vulnerable to the application of such principles by third parties in exploiting this productivity commercially. As fans review, share, critique, comment, remix, gossip, publicise, reflect and produce, they create texts, and paratexts and, ultimately, value; value that, as fan-generated texts are easily accessible online, can be readily utilised as resources in cultural production by commercial providers.

However, as the reception and the appropriation of cultural texts are increasingly freed of boundaries, structures and meanings imposed at the point of production, com-mercial creativity and artistic freedom are increasingly confined by fans' expectations that for the psychological basis of their affective bond with the fan object militates against aesthetic change and challenges – regardless, coincidentally, of whether the fan object in question is associated with popular entertainment or realms of artistic and creative production that proclaim higher cultural value.

In these respects the study of the impact of fandom on cultural industries concurs with the assessment of prosumption and its impact on contemporary capitalism in the work of Ritzer and Jurgenson (2010: 31) as the manifestation of 'a new form of capitalism' built on abundance rather than scarcity and that might lead to the emergence of a distinct economic system, although one that is rooted in long-term developments and continuities that preceded the notion of prosumption (Ritzer et al. 2012), much like the study of fandom highlights the origin of fan practices in pre-moderm systems of mass communication and production before the emergence of the notion of the prosumer in media studies and related dispciplines. Both approaches point towards the possible emergence of new economic relations that sit uneasily with established patterns of capitalist production. In creating content and drawing textual boundaries, fans transform the marketplace of cultural industries' output into a hybrid space in which meaning and value creation are inextricably linked with participation, affective engagements and the actualisation of meaning through fans/users. While the social, cultural, political and aesthetic consequences of (digital) fandom remain contested, the impact on cultural industries is less ambiguous: as fandom becomes an increasingly common and necessary mode of cultural engagement and reception in response to digital landscapes of unprecedented choice and abundance of both industry-created and fan/user-generated content, business models derived from an analogue age of cultural production aimed at the monetisation of a fixed 'product' whose boundaries and uses are sought to be enforced and limited through legal action, or which fail to endorse the significance of the affective basis of fan engagements in their interactions with fans, seem doomed to long-term decline.

These observations and conclusions thus further highlight the fuller appreciation of the relationship between users and cultural industries that fan studies enable. In explorations of how cultural industries matter, there is, I want to suggest, no better place to start than with those (fans) to whom they matter most.

Notes

1 Such as in the case of spectator sports (Sandvoss 2003, 2012b, 2012c; Crawford 2004) or even politics (Sandvoss 2012a, 2013).
2 Hills (2013) suggests that adaptations of these types of productivity to online environments partly misread Fiske, as the 'crucial distinction between enunciative and textual productivity is not "primarily one of form" (Sandvoss 2011a: 60), but rather one of mediation.' While Fiske does indeed note that enunciation occurs only in immediate social relationships, such immediacy and localisation now exists in online spaces such as social networks. Hence, to describe commenting, gossiping, debating and sharing online as enunciative, rather than textual productivity captures, to my mind, the essence of Fiske's notions of enunciative productivity as the generation and circulation of certain meanings about the object of fandom within a given community – albeit that the latter is a vague category in processes of cultural consumption in both online and offline contexts.
3 Beyond popular entertainment equally narrow expectations exist that tie enthusiasm in politics (Sandvoss 2012a) or sports (Sandvoss 2003) to the ability of the fan object to accommodate specific, pre-formulated meaning.
4 For a more detailed discussion of the interplay between love and expectation, see Sandvoss (2005a).
5 It should, however, be noted that textual boundaries are ultimately constituted in the interplay of form and content – modern visual arts and sculptures, such as Marcel Duchamp's 'Fountain', or branches of modern theatre such as epic theatre, have deliberately sought to blur the clear demarcation between text and context as well as the work of art and the recipient.
6 See, for example, BBC online's coverage headed '"Doctor Who fan's wife's epic labour of love' about Sue and Neil Perryman's viewing of all 697 Dr Who episodes in existence by November 2013 (www.bbc.co.uk/news/education-24914229).

References

Abercrombie, Nicholas and Longhurst, Brian (1998) *Audiences: A Sociological Theory of Performance and Imagination*, London: Sage.
Artieri, Giovanni Boccia (2012) 'Productive Publics and Transmedia Participation', in: *Participations: International Journal of Audience Research*, 9(2): 448–68.
Baym, Nancy K. (2011) 'The Swedish Model: Balancing Markets and Gifts in the Music Industry', in: *Popular Communication: The International Journal of Media and Culture*, 9(1): 22–38.
Baym, Nancy K. and Burnett, Robert (2009) 'Amateur Experts: International Fan Labor in Swedish Independent Music', in: *International Journal of Cultural Studies*, 12(5): 1–17.
Booth, Paul and Kelly, Peter (2013) 'The Changing Faces of Doctor Who Fandom: New Fans, New Technologies, Old Practices?', in: *Participations: International Journal of Audience Research*, 10(1): 56–72.

Brooker, Will (2002) *Using the Force: Creativity, Community and Star Wars Fans*, London: Continuum.

Bruns, Axel (2008) *Blogs, Wikipedia, Second Life, and Beyond: From Production to Produsage*, New York: Peter Lang.

Cavicchi, Daniel (1997) *Tramps Like Us: Music and Meaning Among Springsteen Fans*, New York and Oxford: Oxford University Press.

Centre for Economics and Business Research (2013) 'The Contribution of the Arts and Culture to the National Economy: An Analysis of the Macroeconomic Contribution of the Arts and Culture and of some of their Indirect Contributions Through Spillover Effects felt in the Wider Economy', Report for Arts Council England and the National Museums Directors' Council, May 2013.

Chin, Bertha and Hills, Matt (2008) 'Restricted Confessions? Blogging, Subcultural Celebrity and the Management of Producer–Fan Proximity', in: *Social Semiotics*, 18(2): 253–72.

Coppa, Francesca (2014) 'Fuck Yeah, Fandom is Beautiful', in: *Journal of Fandom Studies* 2(1): 73–82.

Costello, Victor and Moore, Barbara (2008) 'Cultural Outlaws: An Examination of Audience Activity and Online Television Fandom', in: *Television and New Media*, 8(2): 124–43.

Crawford, Garry (2004) *Consuming Sport*, London: Routledge.

Davis, Charles H., Michelle, Carolyn, Hardy, Ann and Hight, Craig (2014) 'Framing Audience Prefigurations of *The Hobbit: An Unexpected Journey*: The Roles of Fandom, Politics and Idealised Intertexts', in: *Participations: Journal of Audience and Reception Studies*, 11(1): 50–87.

Duffett, Mark (ed.) (2014) *Popular Music Fandom: Identities, Roles and Practices*, New York: Routledge.

Elliott, Anthony (1999) *The Mourning of John Lennon*, Berkley: University of California Press.

Fiske, John (1992) 'The Cultural Economy of Fandom', in: L. A. Lewis (ed.) *The Adoring Audience*, London: Routledge.

Gauntlett, David (2011) *Making is Connecting*, Cambridge: Polity Press.

Gennette, Gérard (1997) *Paratexts: The Thresholds of Interpretation*, Cambridge: Cambridge University Press.

Geraghty, Lincoln (2014) *Cult Collectors: Nostalgia, Fandom and Collecting Popular Culture*, Abingdon, Oxon: Routledge.

Gray, Jonathan (2003) 'New Audiences, New Textualities: Anti-fans and Non-fans', in: *International Journal of Cultural Studies*, 6(1).

Gray, Jonathan (2010) *Show Sold Separately: Promos, Spoilers, and Other Media Paratexts*, New York: NYU Press.

Gray, Jonathan, Sandvoss, Cornel, and Harrington, C. Lee (2007) 'Why Study Fans?', in: Jonathan Gray, Cornel Sandvoss and C. Lee Harrington (eds) *Fandom: Identities and Communities in a Mediated World*, New York: New York University Press.

Grossberg, Lawrence (1992) 'Is There a Fan in the House: The Affective Sensibility of Fandom', in: L. A. Lewis (ed.) *The Adoring Audience*, London: Routledge.

Hardt, Michael and Negri, Antonio (2000) *Empire*. Cambridge: Harvard University Press.

Harrington, C. Lee and Bielby, Denise (1995) *Soap Fans: Pursuing Pleasure and Making Meaning in Everyday Life*, Philadelphia: Temple University Press.

Highfield, Tim, Harrington, Stephen and Bruns, Axel (2013) 'Twitter as a Technology for Audiencing and Fandom', in: *Information, Communication and Society*, 16(3): 315–39.

Hills, Matt (2002) *Fan Cultures*, London: Routledge.

Hills, Matt (2007) 'Essential Tensions: Winnicottian Object-Relations in the Media Sociology of Roger Silverstone', in: *International Journal of Communication*, 1: 37–48.

Hills, Matt (2013) 'Fiske's "Textual Productivity" and Digital Fandom: Web 2.0 Democratization Versus Fan Distinction?', in: *Participations: International Journal of Audience Research*, 10(1): 130–53.

Hills, Matt (2014) '*Doctor Who*'s Textual Commentators: Fandom, Collective Memory and the Self-Commodification of Fanfac', in: *Journal of Fandom Studies*, 2(1): 31–51.

Jauss, Hans Robert (1982) *Toward an Aesthetic of Reception*. Minneapolis: University of Minnesota Press.

Jenkins, Henry (1992) *Textual Poachers: Television Fans and Participatory Culture*, New York: Routledge.

Jenkins, Henry (2007) 'Afterword: The Future of Fandom', in: Jonathan Gray, Cornel Sandvoss and C. Lee Harrington (eds) *Fandom: Identities and Communities in a Mediated World*, New York: New York University Press.

Johnson, Derek (2007) 'Fan-tagonism: Factions, Institutions and Constitutive Hegemonies of Fandom', in: Jonathan Gray, Cornel Sandvoss and C. Lee Harrington (eds) *Fandom: Identities and Communities in a Mediated World*, New York: New York University Press.

Keen, Andrew (2008) *The Cult of the Amateur*, London: Nicholas Brealey.

Lanier, Jaron (2010) *You Are Not a Gadget*, New York: Vintage.

McClellan, Ann (2013) 'A Case of Identity: Role Playing, Social Media, and BBC Sherlock', in: *Journal of Fandom Studies* 1(2): 139–57.

Milner, R.M. (2009) 'Working for the Text: Fan Labor and the New Organization', in: *International Journal of Cultural Studies*, 12(5): 491–508.

Milner, R.M. (2010) 'Negotiating Text Integrity', in: *Information, Communication and Society*, 13(5), 722–46.

Milner, R.M. (2011) 'Discourses on Text Integrity: Information and Interpretation in the Contested Fallout Knowledge Community', in: *Convergence: The International Journal of Research into New Media Technologies*, 17(2): 159–72.

Murray, Simone (2004) '"Celebrating the Story the Way It Is": Cultural Studies, Corporate Media and the Contested Utility of Fandom', *Continuum: Journal of Media and Cultural Studies*, 18(1): 7–25.

Proctor, William (2013) '"Holy Crap, More Star Wars! More Star Wars? What if They're Crap?": Disney, Lucasfilm and Star Wars Online Fandom in the 21st Century', in: *Participations: International Journal of Audience Research*, 10(1): 198–224.

Radway, Janice (1989) *Reading the Romance: Women, Patriarchy and Popular Literature*, London: Verso.

Ritzer, George (1996) *The McDonaldization of Society*, Newbury Park: Pine Forge Press.

Ritzer, George and Jurgenson, Nathan (2010) 'Production, Consumption, Prosumption: The Nature of Capitalism in the Age of the Digital "Prosumer"', in: *Journal of Consumer Culture*, 10(1): 13–36.

Ritzer, George, Dean, Paul and Jurgenson, Nathan (2012) 'The Coming of Age of the Prosumer', in: *American Behavioral Scientist*, 56(4): 379–98.

Sandvoss, Cornel (2003) *A Game of Two Halves: Football, Television and Globalization*, London: Routledge.

Sandvoss, Cornel (2005a) *Fans: The Mirror of Consumption*, Cambridge: Polity Press.

Sandvoss, Cornel (2005b) 'One Dimensional Fan: Toward an Aesthetic of Fan Texts', in: *American Behavioral Scientist*, 48(7): 822–39.

Sandvoss, Cornel (2007) 'The Death of the Reader? Literary Theory and the Study of Texts in Popular Culture', in: Jonathan Gray, Cornel Sandvoss and C. Lee Harrington (eds) *Fandom: Identities and Communities in a Mediated World*, New York: New York University Press.

Sandvoss, Cornel (2008) 'One the Couch with Europe: The Eurovision Song Contest, the European Broadcast Union and Belonging in Europe', in: *Popular Communication: The International Journal of Media and Communication*, 6(3): 253–89.

Sandvoss, Cornel (2011a) 'Fans Online: Affective Media Consumption and Production in the Age of Convergence', in: Miayse Christensen, Andre Jansson and Christian Christensen (eds) *Online Territories*, New York: Peter Lang.

Sandvoss, Cornel (2011b) 'Reception', in: Virginia Nightingale (ed.) *Handbook of Media Audiences*, Malden, MA and Oxford: Blackwell.

Sandvoss, Cornel (2012a) 'Enthusiasm, Trust, and its Erosion in Mediated Politics: On Fans of Obama and the Liberal Democrats', in: *European Journal of Communication*, 27(1): 68–81.

Sandvoss, Cornel (2012b) 'Jeux Sans Frontières: Europeanisation and the Erosion of National Categories in European Club Football Competition', in: *Politique Européenne*, 36: 76–101.

Sandvoss, Cornel (2012c) 'Liquid Stars, Liquid Identities: Political Discourse in Transnational Media Sport', in: Cornel Sandvoss, Alina Bernstein and Michael Real (eds) *Bodies of Discourse: Sports Stars, Media and the Global Public*, New York: Peter Lang.

Sandvoss, Cornel (2013) 'Toward an Understanding of Political Enthusiasm as Media Fandom: Blogging, Fan Productivity and Affect in American Politics', in *Participations: International Journal of Audience Research*, 10(1): 252–96.

Sandvoss, Cornel (2014) '"I ♥ Ibiza": Music, Place and Belonging', in: Mark Duffett (ed.) *Popular Music Fandom: Identities, Roles and Practices*, New York: Routledge.

Sandvoss, Cornel and Kearns, Laura (2014) 'From Interpretive Communities to Interpretative Fairs: Ordinary Fandom, Textual Selection and Digital Media', in: Linda Duits, Koos Zwaan and Stijn Reijnders (eds) *Ashgate Research Companion to Fan Cultures*, Farnham: Ashgate.

Scardaville, Melissa C. (2005) 'Accidental Activists: Fans Activism in the Soap Opera Community', in: *American Behavioural Scientist*, 48(7): 881–902.

Scott, Suzanne (2013) 'Who's Steering the Mothership? The Role of the Fanboy Auteur in Transmedia Storytelling', in: Aaron Delwiche and Jennifer Jacobs Henderson (eds) *The Participatory Cultures Handbook*, New York: Routledge.

Shirky, Clay (2010) *Cognitive Surplus*, London: Allen Lane.

Stacey, Jackie (1994) *Stargazing: Hollywood Cinema and Female Spectatorship*, London: Routledge.

Terranova, Tiziana (2000) 'Free Labour: Producing Culture in the Digital Economy', in: *Social Text*, 63, 18(2): 33–58.

Willis, A. (2003) 'Martial Law and the Changing Face of Martial Arts on US Television', in: Mark Jancovich and J. Lyons (eds) *Quality Popular Television*, London: British Film Institute.

29

UNDERSTANDING PUBLIC RELATIONS AS A CULTURAL INDUSTRY

Lee Edwards

This chapter deals with the question of how one might categorise the work done by one important distribution mechanism in the cultural industries: public relations (PR). PR has grown rapidly over the last three decades, due in large part to the increased need for promotional communication in the context of neoliberal markets (Davis, 2013). It continues to be a growth industry despite the lingering effects of the global recession, as evidenced by the healthy growth rates of the largest global PR firms (Holmes, 2013). Hesmondhalgh (2013: 19) suggests that PR, alongside other promotional functions, can be considered a cultural industry because it is concerned primarily with the production of symbolic meaning through a range of different texts. However, other than Hesmondhalgh's book, very little attention has been paid to the claim that PR constitutes a cultural industry in itself. Throsby's (2008) comparison of cultural industry models shows that PR receives no mention as a stand-alone industry in any model. It is simply noted as an advertising-related industry in the first DCMS creative industries mapping document (DCMS, 1998), but this reference subsequently disappears and PR campaigns transform into an 'output' of the advertising industry in the revised mapping document, three years later (DCMS, 2001). In fact, Hesmondhalgh's 'symbolic texts' approach is the only model that explicitly recognises advertising and public relations as core cultural industries based on their actual output as well as their contribution to other cultural industries. Indeed, even in Hesmondhalgh's approach, PR is categorised alongside marketing and advertising, but little attention is paid to the differences between the occupations; for the latter, their cultural industry status seems to be considered largely on the basis of their roles within the core cultural industries (broadcasting, film, music and print), rather than as equivalent industries (see Hesmondhalgh, 2013, Chapters 7 and 11).

Despite the lack of detailed attention to the specificities of PR, it is reasonable to argue that PR's contribution to the cultural industries is made in the context of its role as a promotional industry, contributing to the creation of demand for cultural artefacts among specific audiences, without which cultural industries cannot succeed. As Miège and Garnham note:

> The cultural industry is not, in the end, a response to pre-existing demand. Rather, basing itself on the dominant conceptions of culture, it must, as a first stage, at the same time as it puts new products onto the market, create a social demand, give it a consistency, in other words, lead certain social groups selected as commercial targets to prepare themselves to respond to the producers' offer.
>
> (Miège and Garnham, 1979: 300)

PR occupies an 'editorial' role, deploying promotional initiatives that help companies mitigate risk and maximise the probability of success in a world of high production costs and relatively unpredictable markets, by matching the costs of production to the spending power of consumers for the product (Garnham, 1987). It is also a supporting factor in the 'star' system that characterises cultural industries (Hesmondhalgh, 2013), because most PR investment is likely to be made in texts that have the greatest chance of success. At the same time, it contributes to the communication of novelty, part of the 'flow' production that requires new products to be always available for consumption as social and cultural trends alter patterns of consumer demand (Miège, 1987). Finally, and not infrequently, PR practitioners working outside the cultural industries make reference to different forms of cultural output (e.g. popular TV series, celebrities, popular music) in non-cultural campaigns as a means of increasing the symbolic appeal of their texts. At the same time, the meaning of the cultural work itself is changed by its association with a new context. For example, in 2013 global consumer goods company Reckitt Benckiser employed Frank PR (Australia) for the summer promotion of its anti-mosquito spray, Aerogard. Frank PR structured the campaign around a parody of the TV series Baywatch, with David Hasselhoff lookalikes patrolling Australian beaches as 'mozzie guards', and an online video echoing the opening sequences of the series (mUmBRELLA, 2013). In the UK, Freshwater (Wales), used celebrity endorsement to promote candy brand PEZ's Red Nose Day fundraising initiative. One-off PEZ dispensers featuring Red Nose ambassadors One Direction, Jesse J, Ricky Gervais and Keith Lemon were auctioned on eBay and the celebrities themselves tweeted about the dispensers and the auction during the campaign (Freshwater, 2013). Through this kind of work, PR practitioners outside the cultural industries both contribute to the indirect productivity of culture, and extend the visibility and consumption of cultural artefacts across space and time, embedding them in non-cultural areas of material production (Miège and Garnham, 1979).

Alongside its role in cultural distribution, PR is integral to the structures of the cultural industries. Like other multinational corporations, the conglomerates that dominate the field use PR practitioners to communicate with specialist and general media, policymakers and politicians as a way of protecting their interests and maintaining their commercial superiority. Smaller and mid-sized companies, on the other hand, may use PR to try and access influence and power within the industry – in other words, to move from the periphery towards the core of the cultural industries – by strengthening their corporate presence and visibility. In these roles, PR work becomes more distant from the distribution processes for actual cultural arte-facts and more focused on commercial operations such as mergers, takeovers and shareholder communications, as well as policy-directed initiatives such as lobbying. The press page on Vivendi's corporate website, for example, features a company diary, corporate news releases, quarterly results and a downloadable copy of the latest annual report (www.vivendi.com/press/). Practitioners working on such activ-ities are dealing less with culture and creativity, than with commerce. They are also more remote from consumers; audiences for their work will comprise financial journalists, analysts, investors, policymakers and competitors – the media and policy elites identified by Davis (2003) – rather than the average film buff or music fan. While their work is central to the cultural industries, it is substantively different to that of colleagues promoting cultural artefacts: in providing support for organisa-tional objectives, the corporate PR practitioner in the cultural industries mediates processes of production rather than consumption, and the distribution of capital rather than culture.

Taking these roles into account, the categorisation of PR as a cultural industry *within* the cultural industries sector can be understood to be based on both symbolic and commercial grounds: PR, like other promotional industries, produces texts that do symbolic work, but is also fundamentally commercial in that the symbolism it communicates is designed to generate concrete material benefits for cultural industry organisations.

As far as they go, then, Hesmondhalgh's grounds for the inclusion of PR as a core cultural industry are sound in that PR work in the cultural industries does involve the production of symbolic texts. However, in this chapter I argue that the claim that PR is a cultural industry *per se* requires further attention, for two reasons. First, it seems to me to be insufficient to accept the claim based on an understanding of PR's role in cultural industries contexts. I am not suggesting that PR's role within the cultural industries should be set aside; as Garnham (1987) has argued, the importance of distribution mechanisms like PR to the cultural industries cannot be over-estimated: 'It is cultural distribution, not cultural production, that is the key locus of power and profit' (31). However, PR as an industry in its own right is more extensive, covering all sectors of the economy, government and the third sector. Much of this work is in the service of non-cultural industries, political parties and social causes, but the substance of the actual PR activity – the construction of symbolic texts in order to persuade someone to adopt a particular view or action – remains the same. Cate-gorising PR as a cultural industry based only on the contexts in which it addresses cultural objects, would make sense if PR work in other industries was fundamentally different. This is not the case; it is the objects that PR promotes that differ and shape the way that PR is used, not the nature or techniques of PR itself. Second, while there are some structural similarities between PR and other cultural industries, important characteristics that shape cultural industry work, including the nature and management of risk, production and reproduction costs, and the semi-public status of cultural 'goods', do not directly translate to PR.

Given these differences, I suggest that any definition of PR as a cultural industry has to take the majority of PR work seriously and find a way of making sense of its unique characteristics within a cultural industries analytical framework. In addition, the specificity of the PR industry, its structures and processes, have to be taken into account and accommodated if the claim that PR is a cultural industry is to be robust. Such challenges cannot be met through pure theoretical analysis; they require investigations of PR work both within and outside the cultural industries. To date, very little work has been done in this area, by either cultural industry or PR scholars. However, some existing research on PR does provide a starting point for discussion and in this chapter I combine these insights with cultural industries analyses to explore how an understanding of PR as a cultural industry might develop.

The remainder of the chapter is structured in two parts. First, I consider research that informs the question of whether PR does actually do cultural work, to establish what we know already about the cultural dimensions of PR activity, and what bearing these might have on its status as a cultural industry. I then reflect on the important ways in which PR differs from other cultural industries, before concluding with some thoughts about future research.

Does PR do cultural work?

PR practitioners represent, advocate and prompt action on behalf of the organisations they serve (Wernick, 1991). They work across all sectors of the economy, but PR has most often been analysed as a means through which commercial corporations and government achieve their objectives (sales of products or services, or political support), since these are the economic sectors that have the largest resource to devote to PR and are the industries most likely to use it in dubious ways (Moloney, 2006, Davis, 2013, McKie and Munshi, 2007). Functional PR research has examined the processes and practices of PR within organisations that facilitate these goals, including modelling communications processes, campaigns and tactics such as media relations, sponsorship, online campaigns, events and other interventions. Functional approaches categorise practitioners as either managerial or technical workers, depending on the level of strategic knowledge and skills required of them in their role (Broom and Dozier, 1986). Managerial work includes tasks such as liaising with senior management teams about communications strategies, providing a communications perspective on business decisions, managing crises, and developing long-term strategic communications plans. Their role incorporates a 'boundary-spanning' function, bringing information about the environment to bear on organisational decisions and requiring a strong grounding in generalist knowledge and skills related to business functions, markets and organisational leadership, alongside specialist communications knowledge (Tench et al., 2013, Gregory, 2008). Technicians do the 'legwork' associated with the execution of PR tactics: organising and running events, monitoring media coverage, responding to information requests, managing online communication, writing press releases and compiling press materials for distribution (Tench et al., 2009).

The division between managerial and technical work is largely heuristic; in practice, managers frequently cover technical tasks as well, while technicians cannot execute their tasks effectively without some kind of strategic understanding of the purpose of communication. For example, in the cultural industries, PR managers and technicians work together to develop and run campaigns supporting films, books, bands and TV series, generating media coverage and prompting consumer interest through online and offline events. Their work may involve placing books or albums with appropriate media outlets, setting up early screenings to generate film reviews, arranging launch parties, scheduling media interviews with 'stars', organising stunts, or seeding social media campaigns. Alongside the media relations work that remains at the heart of much PR activity (Chartered Institute of Public Relations, 2013, PR Week/PRCA, 2011), the opportunities afforded by digital technology mean that PR texts are frequently multi-media and interactive. In 2012, for example, for the launch of *The Muppets* movie, Disney's UK PR team sent Muppet character cupcakes to prolific tweeters, who then tweeted pictures of the cakes, generating much more visibility and awareness for the movie (prexamples.com/2012/02/muppets-cupcakes-sent-to-stephen-fry/). In the same year, new Belgian TV channel TNT employed communications agency Duval Guillaume Modem to support the channel's launch in April 2012. The agency set up a stunt in a quiet town square, where the public were invited to push a large red button 'to add drama'. Once pushed, a sequence of dramatic events unfurled, including an ambulance racing to the square, a police chase, a shoot-out, and several accidents and 'deaths'. The sequence ended with a large banner unfurling 'TNT: Your Daily Dose of Drama' (prexamples.com/2012/04/push-to-add-drama-brilliant-belgian-tv-stunt-footage-released/).

Functional research is useful in providing an understanding of the day-to-day practices of PR, but from the perspective of PR as cultural work, the categories of manager and technician are less constructive because they engage with processes of making and distributing PR texts, rather than with the symbolic nature of their content. More recently, a 'socio-cultural turn' in PR research (Edwards and Hodges, 2011) has paid more attention to the symbolic dimensions of PR texts. The approach is encapsulated in its broadest form in the definition offered by Edwards (2012: 21), where PR constitutes 'the flow of purposive communication produced on behalf of individuals, formally constituted and informally constituted groups, through their continuous trans-actions with other social entities. It has social, cultural, political and economic effects at local, national and global levels.' PR is understood as a strategy to increase the voice, visibility and appeal of organisations and their products in the rhetorical 'marketplace' (Heath, 2006) that is central to societies infused by promotional culture (Lash and Urry, 1994, Davis, 2013). At the heart of these, mostly critical, approaches is recognition that the substance of PR work is the production and circulation of various kinds of texts (visual, verbal, written) that communicate ideological discourses across a wide variety of contexts (Motion and Leitch, 1996, Curtin, 2011). It is conceived as both an aggregate (a continuous flow of communication connected across space and time) and a particular set of practices, producing meaning about the world we live in and our place within it, but also prompting particular configurations of material resources (for example, the distribution of capital, goods and production) across local, national and global contexts.

The recognition of PR as both aggregate flow and specific practice helps to explain the connection between the semiosis PR constructs in the context of a specific campaign, and the bigger contribution it makes to society. It opens the way to understanding PR as cultural work, fundamentally symbolic and ideological, producing meaning even when it is executed for goods and services that are more utilitarian than cultural. The approach reflects Negus' (2002) understanding of cultural intermediation as a continuous process of meaning production that shapes 'both use values and exchange values, and seeks to manage how those values are connected with people's lives' (505). Cultural intermediation by the promotional industries is increasingly important as 'the effort to shape mass taste, and specifically to use the mass media and various cultural categories to do so, has become more central to late-capitalist economies' (Moor, 2008: 412). Put another way, PR work incorporates the production of 'expressive value', grounded in culture but with an economic impact (O'Connor, 2010).

Like branding and advertising, PR uses texts and symbols to define individual goods and services (Moor, 2007, Lury, 2004, Arvidsson, 2006, Nixon and du Gay, 2002); these individual symbolic interventions also contribute to the 'economy of qualities' (Callon et al., 2002), where 'the modalities of the establishment of supply and demand, and forms of competition, are all shaped by the organized strategies deployed by the different actors to qualify goods' (202). Designers, producers, marketers and distributors all attempt to align the symbolic and material qualifications of their goods with what consumers want and expect based on their experience, their knowledge of similar products and the norms and values associated with the good's position in hierarchies of distinction (Bourdieu, 1984). The process is dialectical and ongoing: each initiative from an actor engaged in the process calls out a response from the others, and each new product must build on existing markets and qualifications to establish its unique appeal (Callon et al., 2002).

A more detailed understanding of the forms of cultural intermediation enacted by PR is revealed by applying the prism of the circuit of culture to PR work (Du Gay et al., 1997; Negus, 2002). PR can be understood as a cultural intervention because of its effects on meaning production in all five 'moments' of the circuit. Practitioners draw on normative identities, representations and modes of consumption, in symbolic ways that make campaigns more easily understood by relevant audiences. They work within the boundaries of existing regulatory environments and norms, and use existing modes of production to construct their texts, but may also challenge and change regulation and production through their work (for example, when they engage with policymakers or industry associations). Each moment of the circuit articulates with the others, such that the meaning of PR interventions is never fixed but is dependent on how they shape the articulations within the circuit (Curtin and Gaither, 2007) and how those articulations in turn change the manifestation of identity, representation, consumption, production and regulation. From this perspective, the importance of PR as a cultural industry is grounded in the ways in which its symbolic texts constitute and are constitutive of social reality (Fairclough, 2003), a locus of cultural change and continuity (Hesmondhalgh, 2013) with symbolic *and* material effects on each moment of the circuit.

Based on the discussion above, it seems fair to argue that PR is a recognisable source of symbolic meaning both within and outside the cultural industries, and its outputs may be fairly described as 'cultural', in that they have an important symbolic element, even when the object of promotion is not a cultural artefact. However, commerce and culture are never too far apart in PR work. PR outputs are utilitarian, in that they persuade people to engage with markets, organisations and ideas in particular ways; as forms of commercially useful expressive value, they reflect 'the extension of "cultural" inputs into the wider economy of goods and services' (O'Connor, 2010: 55–6). PR work is cultural, in so far as its texts constitute culture in the act of communicating meaning *about other things*. This is not the same as the work done by the artefacts produced by the broadcast, film, media and publishing industries, where the texts are the objects to be marketed, not the vehicle for persuasion.

Is PR a cultural industry?

A socio-cultural understanding of PR helps to explain the cultural dimensions of PR work and the importance of PR campaigns as sources of meaning embedded in many different areas of life. Equally, recognising the role PR plays in supporting the indirect productivity of culture, where cultural products are used to promote other goods and services (Miège and Garnham, 1979), is an important part of the 'picture' of cultural work that takes place across the whole of the industry. In fact, based on the terms that Hesmondhalgh (2013) proscribes, a socio-cultural perspective of PR admits it to the cultural industries 'family': it constructs texts for circulation; the 'use-value' of PR 'products' themselves is primarily symbolic in that they generate meaning, although they have an important functional component; and they are designed to influence our understanding of the world and our place within it (Hesmondhalgh, 2013: 4). However, as noted above, while recognising PR as cultural work is required for its classification as a cultural industry, it is not necessarily sufficient. Claiming PR as a cultural industry demands a more in-depth consideration of PR in relation to existing research on cultural industries.

In fact, there are important ways in which PR work differs from industries that are more commonly designated as 'cultural'. In this section, I review the differences in relation to PR texts, production, and risk.

PR texts, production and risk

PR texts can take a wide variety of forms: film, video, songs, websites, books and pamphlets, material artefacts, stunts and the more widely recognised media releases and press information. With the exception of the latter, PR work borrows formats from cultural industries to communicate its messages. However, unlike the music, film, broadcast or publishing industries, PR does not produce products for paid consumption; its outputs are not, generally, commercial or cultural 'goods' with a specific use or exchange value for their audience. While they are designed to be consumed (read, viewed, heard), they are not marketed in and of themselves[1] (one does not buy a Youtube video, a PR twitter campaign, a press release, press conference, or a speech by a CEO). Moreover, the audiences for PR texts – a group of consumers, journalists, investors or policymakers, for example – do not purchase the PR work that is directed towards them; rather, it is the organisations aiming to persuade them of a particular point of view that make the financial investment.

PR texts also differ from those normally associated with the cultural industries in that they do not inevitably incur high costs of production and distribution; one of PR's competitive selling points vis-à-vis other promotional industries, is that it is cheaper to use a PR campaign than to invest in expensive advertising or other forms of direct marketing. The company PR for Books, for example, offers an 'all-in package' for £195, 'which includes a professionally written press release, strategic targeting and distribution to all relevant media in the UK'. It also offers a low-price video trailer (www.prforbooks.co.uk/). Thus, while many companies do invest a great deal in PR, individual campaigns need not be expensive, particularly given the opportunities for customer-driven, viral PR opened up by social media.

PR also differs from other cultural industries in the nature of risk that it is faced with. While intellectual property rights pertain to PR work, they are not the basis for the income generated by PR companies, and in this sense they differ from other cultural outputs such as film, TV or music. Copyright enforcement has little relevance to daily PR practice. In fact, rather than worrying about audiences picking up and passing on their work without acknowledgement, practitioners focus on crafting texts such as viral videos or twitter trends, which will prompt exactly that kind of behaviour. They are *designed* to be public goods, since the more PR outputs are talked about and shared, the greater the publicity generated for the object they promote. The consumption and circulation of PR outputs by a target audience is a mark of PR's success, evidence that the PR message has been taken up and the persuasion process is underway. There is no risk of losing income as a result of audiences sharing PR work; rather, the risk exists in PR work *not* being shared, and the symbolic value of the texts never being fulfilled. The latter possibility is normally mitigated by extensive market and audience research before campaigns are constructed (Gregory, 2006).

A final important difference between PR and other cultural industries is in its employment structures. The core cultural industries are concentrated in the global north and west, and tend to cluster around large cities (Oakley, 2009, Hesmond-halgh, 2013). They usually have a small core of secure labour and a larger, more precarious reserve labour market of freelancers (Hesmondhalgh and Pratt, 2005). In PR, patterns of industry concentration are similar (Holmes, 2013), but while there is a market for freelance workers, research suggests that practitioners move into free-lance work after a career working in organisations in in-house or consultancy roles (Chartered Institute of Public Relations, 2013). This suggests freelance work in PR may be a question of choice as much as, if not more than, an issue of the precarity of the work available[2].

Conclusion: Understanding PR as a cultural industry

PR is an important component of the cultural industries. Its work is central to cultural production and distribution processes, both in the form of promotional campaigns, and through its work promoting the companies that participate in the cultural industries, which contributes to global movements of capital, labour and technology. In this sense, PR contributes to the 'social logics' (Miège, 1987) that help to organise the cultural industries and, given that its role is under-researched, it is worthy of attention on this basis alone.

The discussion in this chapter shows that the status of PR as a cultural industry per se, however, is more complex than it might first appear, and is inextricably linked to the organisations that deploy it. PR works symbolically through texts that attempt to influence attitudes, values and beliefs more often than they do behaviours, and in this sense it is eminently cultural. However, its texts cannot be separated from the interests of those who pay for them. PR *as* a cultural industry, then, must be conceptualised as an industry that facilitates links between symbolic and material worlds in a wide range of contexts. Its cultural 'contribution' varies and should be interpreted with reference to the specific social, economic and political circumstances that give rise to PR. Exploring the social logics of the industry in more detail would help to illuminate the particular nature of its work.

The fact that PR differs in many ways from other cultural industries is not, in itself, a problem. What matters more is that we understand what the differences are, and attempt to make sense of them within a cultural industries framework. For example, as an industry that produces symbolic texts, PR is correctly categorised as a cultural industry in Hesmondhalgh's (2013) model; however, its texts have a particular character, and are not the same as the TV and radio programmes, films, books or music that are normally associated with the cultural industries. Questions then arise about how we might accommodate these differences using and potentially extending the lens of existing scholarship.

As O'Connor (2010) notes, we need to engage with the complexity of the cultural industries if we are to adequately theorise them. The problems associated with identifying PR *as* a cultural industry cannot be fully answered theoretically. Rather, they require concrete empirical investigations of the industry, its structures, its output, the means by which that output circulates, and its effects. As I hope to have illustrated here, considering the status of PR as a cultural industry opens up new and interesting research areas that are worthy of greater attention from both cultural industry and PR scholars.

Notes

1 There are rare exceptions to this: most recently, the British Airports Authority employed Alain de Botton to write a book about Heathrow Airport which sold widely, but this is the exception rather than the rule (Milmo, 2009, De Botton, 2010).
2 The same pattern may apply to advertising and marketing, of course, although this needs to be empirically explored.

References

Arvidsson, A. (2006) *Brands: Meaning and value in media culture*, London: Routledge.
Bourdieu, P. (1984) *Distinction: A social critique of the judgement of taste*, London: Routledge & Kegan Paul.
Broom, G. M. and Dozier, D. M. (1986) Advancement for public relations role models, *Public Relations Review*, 12(1): 37–56.
Callon, M., Méadel, C. & Rabeharisoa, V. (2002) The economy of qualities, *Economy and Society*, 31(2): 194–217.
Chartered Institute of Public Relations (2013) *State of the profession 2013*, London: Chartered Institute of Public Relations.

Curtin, P. A. (2011) Discourses of American Indian racial identity in the public relations materials of the Fred Harvey company, 1902–1936, *Journal of Public Relations Research*, 23(4): 368–96.

Curtin, P. A. and Gaither, T. K. (2007) *International public relations: Negotiating culture, identity and power*, Thousand Oaks, CA: Sage.

Davis, A. (2003) Whither mass media and power? Evidence for a critical elite theory alternative, *Media, Culture and Society*, 25(5): 669–90.

Davis, A. (2013) *Promotional cultures: The rise and spread of advertising, public relations, marketing and branding*, Cambridge: Polity Press.

DCMS (1998) *Creative industries mapping documents 1998*, London: Department for Culture, Media and Sport.

DCMS (2001) *The creative industries mapping document 2001*, London: Department for Culture, Media and Sport.

De Botton, A. (2010) *A week at the airport: A Heathrow diary*, London: Profile Books.

Du Gay, P., Hall, S., Janes, L., MacKay, H. and Negus, K. (1997) *Doing cultural studies: The story of the Sony Walkman*, London: Sage/The Open University.

Edwards, L. (2012) Defining the 'object' of public relations research: A new starting point, *Public Relations Inquiry*, 1(1): 7–30.

Edwards, L. and Hodges, C. E. M. (2011) Introduction: Implications of a radical socio-cultural 'turn' in public relations scholarship, In: Edwards, L. and Hodges, C. E. M. (eds) *Public relations, society and culture: Theoretical and empirical explorations*, London: Routledge, pp. 1–14.

Fairclough, N. (2003) *Analysing discourse: Textual analysis for social research*, London: Routledge.

Freshwater. (2013) *Sweet PR campaign to support PEZ's fun-raising challenge*, London: Chartered Institute of Public Relations. Available at: www.cipr.co.uk/sites/default/files/28173150%20OKAY%20TO%20PUBLISH.pdf (Accessed 8 January 2014).

Garnham, N. (1987) Concepts of culture: Public policy and the cultural industries, *Cultural studies*, 1(1): 23–8.

Gregory, A. (2006) Public relations as planned communication, In: Tench, R. and Yeomans, L. (eds) *Exploring Public Relations*, Harlow: Pearson, pp. 182–207.

Gregory, A. (2008) Competencies of senior practitioners in the UK: An initial study, *Public Relations Review*, 34(3): 215–223.

Heath, R. (2006) Onward into more fog: Thoughts on public relations' research directions, *Journal of Public Relations Research*, 18(2): 93–114.

Hesmondhalgh, D. (2013) *The cultural industries (3rd edition)*, London: Sage.

Hesmondhalgh, D. and Pratt, A. (2005) Cultural industries and cultural policy, *International Journal of Cultural Policy*, 11(1): 1–13.

Holmes, P. (2013) *The Global 250 Agency Ranking 2013*, The Holmes Report, International Communications Consultancy Organisations.

Lash, S. and Urry, J. (1994) *Economies of Signs and Space*, London: Sage.

Lury, C. (2004) *Brands: The logos of global economy*, London: Routledge.

McKie, D. and Munshi, D. (2007) *Reconfiguring public relations: Ecology, equity and enterprise*, Abingdon, Oxon: Routledge.

Miège, B. (1987) The logics at work in the new cultural industries, *Media, Culture and Society*, 9(3): 273–89.

Miège, B. and Garnham, N. (1979) The cultural commodity, *Media, Culture and Society*, 1(1): 297–311.

Milmo, D. (2009) Heathrow airport hires Alain de Botton: Philosophical author begins work as airport's writer-in-residence, 18 August, *The Guardian*. Available at: www.theguardian.com/uk/2009/aug/18/alain-de-botton-heathrow-airport.

Moloney, K. (2006) *Rethinking public relations: PR propaganda and democracy*, Oxon: Routledge.

Moor, L. (2007) *The Rise of Brands*, London: Berg.

Moor, L. (2008) Branding consultants as cultural intermediaries, *The Sociological Review*, 56(3): 408–28.

Motion, J. and Leitch, S. (1996) A discursive perspective from New Zealand: Another world view, *Public Relations Review*, 22(3): 297–310.

mUmBRELLA (2013) *PR agency Frank creates Baywatch spoof for Aerogard*, Chippendale, NSW: Focal Attractions. Available at: mumbrella.com.au/hoff-lookalikes-in-online-and-experiential-oz-day-campaign-for-aeroguard-135808 (accessed 8 January 2014).

Negus, K. (2002) The work of cultural intermediaries and the enduring distance between production and consumption, *Cultural Studies*, 16(4): 501–15.

Nixon, S. and Du Gay, P. (2002) Who needs cultural intermediaries? *Cultural Studies*, 16(4): 495–500.

O'Connor, J. (2010) The cultural and creative industries: A literature review (2nd ed.), *Creativity, Culture and Education Series*, Newcastle Upon Tyne: Creativity, Culture and Education.

Oakley, K. (2009) 'Art works' – cultural labour markets: A literature review, *Creativity, Culture and Education Series*, London: Creativity, Culture and Education.

PR Week/PRCA (2011) *PR Census*, London: Public Relations Consultants' Association.

Tench, R., D'Artrey, M. and Fawkes, J. (2009) Role of the public relations practitioner. In: Tench, R. and Yeomans, L. (eds) *Exploring public relations*, Harlow: Pearson Education, pp. 35–67.

Tench, R., Zerfass, A., Verhoeven, P., Vercic, D., Moreno, A. and Okay, A. (2013) *Communication Management Competencies for European Practitioners*, Leeds, UK: Leeds Metropolitan University.

Throsby, D. (2008) Modelling the cultural industries, *International Journal of Cultural Policy*, 14(3): 217–232.

Wernick, A. (1991) *Promotional culture: Advertising, ideology and symbolic expression*, London: Sage.

30
IS DATA CULTURE?
Data analytics and the cultural industries

Helen Kennedy

Introduction: Data work as cultural production

Everyone is doing data analytics, it seems. Multinational corporations, small and medium-sized enterprises (SMEs), governments, public sector organizations, community groups, charities and social movements, and media, arts and cultural organizations can all engage in data mining and benefit from the resulting insights, it is claimed. High-profile examples of the increasing ubiquity of such practices circulate online, such as the example of the young woman whose father became aware that she was pregnant when the online department store Target directed advertisements for pregnancy-related products to her based on her online behaviour (Duhigg 2012). Much of the data that is subjected to monitoring, mining and analytics comes from social media, as more and more social activities take place online, social media data is increasingly available and the cost of storing that data is falling. Social media data is sometimes merged with data from different sources and used for more ominous purposes than advertising, as seen in recent high-profile cases such as "PRISM-gate" (Rushe 2013). Consequently, the results of data analytics permeate more and more of our daily lives: personalized online advertisements, journalism that is increasingly dependent on and driven by data, and digital reputations measured by systems that quantify social media activity, such as Klout and PeerIndex, are just some examples.

The purpose of this chapter is to propose that the analysis of data (sometimes big, sometimes not) plays an increasingly important role within the cultural industries, as within society at large. Or, to put it simply, this chapter argues that data matters to the cultural industries. Indeed, as its title suggests, the chapter considers whether data and its representations might be thought of as cultural. I reference phenomena that draw attention to the convergence of data and culture, and so to the significance of data analytics for the cultural industries. First, I highlight the growth of the social media monitoring sector, which might be seen as an emergent cultural industry, evolving as it does from behavioural advertising and other forms of digital and non-digital marketing. Second, I discuss data journalism, an example of a cultural industry increasingly compelled to deal in data. More often than not, social media monitoring and data journalism communicate analysed data through visualizations, which are the main means through which the public gets access to data. Visualizations draw attention to the fact that data is frequently consumed in aesthetic and symbolic form. This is the third phenomenon indicative of the changing data/culture relationship that I discuss here. Finally, I point to the various ways in which data is constitutive of culture, such that we could start to think of data *as* culture.

Thus, as with other industries about which it is argued that these *are* in fact cultural and that what they produce *is* in fact culture (see Edwards on public relations, this volume), in this chapter, I argue that we need to consider "data work" as a contemporary form of cultural production and to attend to the role that data plays in the production of culture. The data/culture relationship is mutating and, because of this, cultural industries research needs to engage with current debates about the possibilities, problems and limitations of data and its analysis.

Social media data as monetizable cultural asset: The growth of intermediary social media monitoring industries

Within cultural industries scholarship, there has been a great deal of interest in the ways in which related policy constructs culture as a primarily monetizable asset. The rise of social media monitoring is a spectacular manifestation of the monetization of culture, as social media platforms and monitoring companies cash in on the sharing, viewing and reviewing of users' vernacular creativity (Burgess 2006) and the metadata that these practices produce, through the mining and analysis of social media data. Whatever the initial aims of social media platforms, their content is now monetized.

Van Dijck's book *The Culture of Connectivity: A critical history of social media* (2013) provides an excellent account of the business models and political economy of social media platforms. Despite their origins as informal spaces for communication and creative exchange, van Dijck argues that today, social media sites have become international information and data mining sources. In this context, argues van Dijck, human connectedness obscures the automated connectivity that is taking place beneath the tip of the iceberg; Facebook founder Mark Zuckerberg's emphasis on making the web social is a coded way of talking about "making sociality technical" (van Dijck 2013: 12). This means that relationships can be commoditized, connectedness can be converted into connectivity through code, and both can be mined, analysed and sold for profit.

Such activities are not only undertaken by the social media mega-platforms, but also by emergent social media monitoring companies, which mediate and analyse social media data for paying clients. In *The Daily You*, Turow (2012) locates such companies in the context of the digital advertising industries, which have long used similar techniques to monitor, measure and understand target audience psychographics (such as values, attitudes, interests, lifestyles). Similarly, Arvidsson (2011) argues that social media monitoring practices like sentiment analysis have historical precedents not only in the use of pyschographic variables in advertising, but also in the rise of value attached to ephemeral phenomena like "the brand". These authors identify continuities between social media monitoring and other forms of persuasive communication like advertising, marketing and PR, whose workers have come to be seen as cultural intermediaries (Edwards 2012).

According to Francesco D'Orazio (2013), Chief Innovation Officer at Face, which develops the social media monitoring platform Pulsar, at the end of 2013 there were "more than 480 platforms currently available on the market". It is hard to know which social media monitoring companies might be included here as D'Orazio does not specify, but other reviews identify important players in the field. The website Social Media Biz (2011) produced a comparison of the top twenty social media monitoring platforms in January 2011 and the website Social Media Today (2013) produced a similar list in May 2013, this time with a top fifty rather than a top twenty, reflecting a growth in the numbers of companies operating in this sphere. Companies dominating the English speaking market that are widely acknowledged as key players include: Sysomos; Radian6 (now part of SalesForce Cloud); Alterian SM2; Lithium and Attensity360, most of which are US-based, and Brandwatch in the United Kingdom.

Companies refer to themselves in different ways, which can make it difficult to recognize this as a cohesive sector. In 2012 global marketing research company Forrester produced a number of reports that aimed to map out this market, in which they primarily refer to companies as "listening platforms" (Forrester 2012a, 2012b). In an article focusing specifically on sentiment analysis, Andrejevic (2011) points out that the companies themselves use the language of "listening" to describe the services that they offer (he then provides a much more critical account of what these companies actually do). Some companies use the phrase social media monitoring to describe their services, such as Brandwatch. But Brandwatch, like other companies offering similar services, also refer to what they do as social media analytics or insights. Some companies such as BrandsEye in South Africa prefer the latter term, perhaps because "insights" has a less surveillant connotation than "monitoring". Still others differentiate themselves from their competition by describing themselves as "intelligence" platforms, such as Pulsar, mentioned above. The implication here is that intelligence is superior to insights: insights are simply data, whereas intelligence is empowering and actionable.

The services these companies offer go beyond just listening, despite the widespread use of this term, to include: tracking how many people are talking about a particular topic or brand across social media; identifying key influencers; identifying where key conversations are taking place; identifying "share of voice" or how much conversation in a particular area is dedicated to a product or brand; identifying strength of feelings about particular topics and brands; and identifying the demographics of people engaged in social media conversations, such as geographical location, gender, income, interests. Social media monitoring companies often promise, directly or indirectly, that these actions can help clients to increase efficiency, effectiveness and profits. Many companies emphasize the fact that the social media conversations that they are able to track are both real-time and high volume. For example, "Sysomos lets you listen to millions of conversations about your brand and products in real-time" (Sysomos 2012). Andrejevic (2011) confirms this, arguing that claims made about services refer not to what he calls "referential accuracy" (that is, that the data can actually be taken to represent what it is assumed to represent, or that it comes from target demographic populations), but rather to the huge quantities of synchronous data analysed. Size and immediacy make up for the roughness of the data, he claims. The gathering, monitoring and analysing of social media chatter make it possible to "create authentic conversations" (BazaarVoice 2012), claim many companies, and, through this, insights into what customers are thinking are developed, which serve to enhance the experience of the customer, who can then do word-of-mouth advertising on behalf of businesses. For example, Lithium claims to "build brand advocates, and deliver better traffic, conversation and sales results than other vehicles" (Lithium 2012).

Social media monitoring companies achieve their stated aims through the automated monitoring of core social media platforms, most notably Twitter, but also public content on Facebook, YouTube, Instagram, Tumblr, blogs, forums and conversations from elsewhere on the web designated "social" because they are user-generated, such as the comments sections of newspapers' websites. And companies use a range of technologies and methods to deliver their services. Boolean search (a type of search that combines keywords with operators such as AND, NOT and OR) is commonly used. Some tools map networks, either of connected people or connected content. Methods like sentiment analysis use complex systems such as Natural Language Processing to instruct computers to make sense of word use, word combination and word order and so identify expressed sentiments. The Associated Press used machine learning in the development of its freely available conversation analysis tool Overview, designed to enable journalists to assess vast swathes of data as part of their efforts to identify relevant stories. In contrast to this free platform, commercial services do not come cheap, with prices from around £500 per month for restricted licenses to more than £20,000 a year at the time of writing.

Social media monitoring companies provide their services to a range of actors including those operating within the cultural industries. Alongside specialist social media monitoring companies, digital marketing agencies increasingly offer social media insights amongst their services. Hesmondhalgh (2007) has highlighted how marketing plays an increasingly significant role within the cultural industries, and the growth of social media monitoring forms part of that trend. The social media monitoring sector is a marketing sector and, at the same time, the fruits of its labour impact upon the ways in which cultural industries produce meanings (Edwards, this volume). Therefore, scrutinizing how this sector functions and subjecting its claims and impacts to critical scrutiny needs to form part of the cultural industries research agenda. As boyd and Crawford argue in relation to data analytics more generally, questions need to be asked about how data is gathered and constructed, what data can be taken to mean, to what ends it is deployed, who gets access to it, how its analysis should be regulated and what new digital divides emerge in relation to big data practices (boyd and Crawford 2012). These questions are important in the context of cultural industries research, not only because new cultural industries like social media monitoring are emerging out of the big data gold rush, but also because more and more traditional cultural industries are undertaking their own data work, as I outline in the next section.

Data mining in the cultural industries: Data journalism and data visualization

Data analytics techniques such as those discussed in the previous section are increasingly used across a wide range of cultural industries, not just within social media monitoring and digital marketing companies. Such methods often extend beyond the realms of social media, to draw on other data sources. The growth of data journalism is a good example of how one cultural industry concerned with the production of symbolic goods is increasingly compelled to deal in data.

Although there is a long history of journalists working with data of all kinds, data journalism as it exists today is widely seen to have started in the United Kingdom with the launch of the *Guardian* newspaper's DataBlog in 2009. Simon Rogers, DataBlog editor and author of *Facts Are Sacred* (Rogers 2013), a book about data journalism at the *Guardian*, argues that data journalism represents a shift from journalism based on words to journalism that builds on the power of data (*Guardian* 2013a). Meyer (2012) argues that when data was scarce, journalists concentrated on hunting and gathering it in order to build stories out of it. Now it is abundant, journalism involves not just obtaining but also processing and analysing data. Some commentators see data journalism as a necessity in the context of a contemporary data deluge, in order to counter information asymmetry, as data-aware journalists can use their data literacy to make sense of data circulated by the digital and social media marketing companies discussed in the previous section (Fries 2012). Matsunami (2012) highlights the continuities between data journalists and traditional journalists, in that both provide independent interpretations of information, but now that information looks a lot like data. Data journalist and visualizer David McCandless describes data journalism as simultaneously applying the techniques of data analysis to telling stories and applying story-telling techniques to data: scraping, mining, and analysing data to find a story, and using story-telling to reveal patterns and trends in data (*Guardian* 2013a).

The *Guardian*'s DataBlog is replete with examples of data journalism. At the time of writing, the blog shared data about: the world gender gap index; how people have died in the twenty-first century; happiness and well-being indices in the United Kingdom; what the 2011 Census tells us about language diversity in England and Wales; the distribution of redheads across the world; and Dr Who (*Guardian* 2013b). Thus the DataBlog not only shares stories based on data, but also aims to open up the news gathering process, sharing data and allowing it to be analysed and scrutinized by readers who can arrive at their own conclusions about shared data. Rogers claims that in a context in which journalists are increasingly distrusted, this approach allows them to provide the workings behind their stories, to be open and transparent and so to attempt to rebuild trust.

One example of data journalism in action is the work done by the *Guardian* in collaboration with academic researchers on the *Reading The Riots* project, which analysed data about the riots that took place in the United Kingdom in the summer of 2011. The project aimed to identify why looting took place, in response to the absence of a government enquiry into why the riots had occurred. Combining data about where the riots were located with deprivation data allowed the project collaborators to question the government narrative that asserted that there was no link between the riots and poverty. A parallel analysis of the role social media played in the riots found that Twitter was not used to organize people to go looting, as was widely believed, but rather to respond to the riots: #riotcleanup, used to mobilize people to clean up the streets after the riots, was one of the most popular hashtags during the period (Vis 2012). In this example, data journalism fulfilled journalism's traditional watchdog function, thus confirming Rogers' assertion that data journalism is simultaneously "just journalism" and "a new way of seeing things" (*Guardian* 2013a).

An important means of communicating analysed data on the *Guardian*'s DataBlog, within data journalism more broadly, and within the social media monitoring and other cultural industries engaging in data analytics, is through data visualizations. Indeed, the main way that the public gets access to big data is through visualizations, which, like the big data on which they are based, are increasingly widely circulated, online, in the mainstream media, and elsewhere. As Gitelman and Jackson (2013: 12) assert, "data are mobilized graphically". In this context, data visualizers have been described as new information intermediaries and visualizations themselves as a new form of story-telling, or story-showing (Kirk 2013).

Widely circulated examples of data visualizations include David McCandless's (2009) Billion Dollar Gram, a visualization that compares quantities of money relating to apparently disparate things from the Iraq War to governmental bailout, stimulus and debt packages to Walmart revenues. Hans Rosling's (2006–12) use of visualizations in his TED talks is another well-known example. These are drawn from Gapminder, an organization he co-founded to use data to promote sustainable global development. Other well-known examples include an animated visualization of years lost due to US gun deaths by Periscopic (2013), and the website We Feel Fine by Jonathan Harris and Sep Kamvar (2005), which captures sentiment expressed online to paint a picture of national and international moods. Thus visualizations draw our attention to the fact that data is mostly consumed in aesthetic form.

Discussion of data journalism and data visualization by practitioners in these fields reveal some commitment to the belief that data is objective and factual. The mobilization of the term "facts are sacred" as a byline on the *Guardian*'s DataBlog and as the title of the associated book, is one example of this. So are numerous assertions about the power of data in a promotional online video accompanying the blog and the book, such as motion and interactive designer Mariana Santos' assertion that data can be understood as "what's really there" (*Guardian* 2013a). In contrast, a number of academic commentators have contested such beliefs. Gitelman and Jackson (2013) counter the ubiquity of the term "raw data" (and its underlying assumptions of neutrality and objectivity) by referring to Geoffrey Bowker's claim that "raw data is both an oxymoron and a bad idea; to the contrary, data should be cooked with care" (Bowker 2005: 184). Data does not simply exist, argue Gitelman and Jackson. Rather, it is generated by human actors, in particular contexts, using particular methods, and so cannot be assumed to be raw, or "really there". Examining the etymology of the term "data," Rosenberg (2013) proposes that, historically, the function of data was primarily rhetorical. Thus data could not be taken to be true or real; it was simply rhetorically useful. In contrast, a fact is "that which is done, occurred, or exists". Rosenberg argues that, therefore, "facts are ontological, evidence is epistemological, data is rhetorical" (2013: 18). This is important because it shows that data and facts are not the same, despite the *Guardian*'s suggestion that they might be. As suggested above, the growing dependence of cultural industries like journalism on data compels cultural industries researchers to unpack such elisions and to interrogate the assumptions about what data can do on which such assertions are premised.

Data visualizations need to be subjected to the same critical scrutiny that boyd and Crawford (2012) suggest we apply to the data on which they are based because, like data, visualizations are not neutral. Taking one of the examples cited above, a different visualization of lives lived to completion would make gun deaths seem much less significant. The Billion Dollar Gram is not a mathematically accurate illustration of global capital; rather, it is designed to tell a certain story and to evoke a certain visceral response. Crawford (2013) uses a geographical metaphor to highlight the constructedness of visualizations, pointing out that "the map is not the territory". Understanding data visualizers as cultural producers, seeing data work as cultural production and exploring what factors in the production process influence the resulting visualizations would make a significant contribution to developing our understanding data and its visualization. Here, then, cultural industries approaches could be productive in enhancing understanding of these new cultural forms.

The convergence of data and culture

Not only is data consumed in visual form but, as Beer and Burrows (2013) convincingly argue, data is increasingly constitutive of culture. Data does not just capture popular culture, they argue. Rather, "data feeds back into popular culture and thus begins to have a constitutive shaping effect […] popular culture is constituted by data about popular culture" (2013: 56). They use the consumption of popular music as an example to illustrate this point. Services like iTunes generate back-end archive data about users which is created and harvested through users' musical consumption. The use of mobile devices like iPods creates detailed logs not only of what kinds of music are consumed, how frequently and for how long, but also of the geographical locations of consumption practices. Such data might end up in a range of locations: with the developers of music consumption software and hardware; with music download retailers; or with streaming sites which offer free access to music that is delivered alongside advertising. Ratings and reviews on music websites and elsewhere on the social web simultaneously serve as cultural artifacts and as data about culture.

This data then feeds back into popular culture and begins to shape it. In each of the locations in which it ends up, the data plays a role in constituting the hardware, software and commerce of music consumption in different ways. Thus data about music consumption informs and shapes music provision services. Last.fm, for example, serves music to its listeners based on data about what listeners have previously listened to, predicting musical preferences from aggregate data. So does the Apple iTunes' Genius software. Music consumption is thus constituted by data about music consumption; such data forms part of the circuit of culture. Beer and Burrows suggest that data about listening practices might not only constitute listening practices, but might also "feed into the production of large-scale national geodemographic systems that in turn provide postcode-level analysis of people's tastes and preferences" (2013: 59). As such, data constitutes much more than culture, serving also to shape regimes of governance and control. Lash describes this as algorithmic power. Algorithms become actors; they are "virtuals that generate a whole variety of actuals" (Lash 2007: 71).

There are other ways in which data constitute cultural life. Writing about the data generated through behavioural advertising, Turow argues that such data leads to social discrimination, as "individual profiles" are turned into "individual evaluations" (2012: 6). Individuals' marketing value is calculated based on behavioural and other data, and each individual is categorized as target or waste. This data defines our identity and our worth, suggests Turow, determining not only what marketing firms do, but how we see ourselves. This is because those of us who are considered to be waste receive narrowed options through the advertising messages that are targeted at us, and, according to Turow, these messages constitute a form of social discrimination that impacts upon our sense of self. Writing about a broader range of data gathering practices, Pariser (2012) outlines the impacts of the personalized filters that are constructed for us by our data. These include the undermining of civic discourse and of creativity, both of which are dependent on exposure to the unfamiliar, or to ideas that do not sit comfortably with our own.

Thus data's power to constitute our cultural world has political implications. But it is not only data that functions in this way; the methods used to generate data also have their consequences. Law and Urry (2004) argue that methods have social effects, not only representing aspects of social life but also helping to constitute the things that they claim to represent. What, then, are the effects of the methods of social media monitoring, data-dependent journalism and data visualization? What absences and inequalities result from the methods that these sectors use? Understanding the effects of particular methods has long been a concern of cultural industries research, as its focus on production processes aims to illuminate the ways in which the methods used to produce cultural artifacts shape those artifacts. Again, cultural industries approaches can contribute to developing our understanding of the effects of the methods of data analytics on culture.

Data constitutes culture: Cultural industries researchers, take heed!

This chapter has attempted to put data analytics on the agenda of cultural industries scholarship, proposing that data and culture are converging. As such, cultural industries research needs to engage with contemporary debates about the analysis of data both big and small (and a companion to the cultural industries needs a chapter about data mining and analytics).

In order to make this argument, I first highlighted the growth of the social media monitoring sector, which might be seen as an emergent cultural industry whose activities impact on circulating cultural meanings. The second example of the merging of data mining and cultural production that I discussed is data journalism, a new form of journalism based not only on the analysis and processing of data, but also on sharing the data that underlies journalistic stories. Another way in which data mining and the production of cultural goods merge is in the visual forms that much analysed data takes when it is presented back to the people from whom it is often generated. Data visualizations are fundamentally cultural, I suggest, because they are aesthetic. The increasing ubiquity of data visualizations is another example of the convergence of data and culture. These various examples point to ways in which data is increasingly constitutive of culture.

Throughout this chapter I have highlighted some political considerations relating to the growing dependence of culture on data. These include the non-neutrality of data and its visualizations, and of the methods used to generate data that then serves to constitute culture. The increasing ubiquity of data analytics across a range of cultural spheres raises other political questions too, about power and control, regulation and transparency, and citizen agency. These questions also vex scholars of other cultural industries, although of course they manifest in particular ways in the specific context of data analytics. In the chapter I have suggested that cultural industries approaches that focus on production practices can contribute to addressing these questions and to developing our understanding of data analytics. Understanding data work in terms of cultural production opens it up to the kind of scrutiny that has served to enhance our knowledge of other, more traditional cultural industries. Social media monitoring, data journalism, data visualization and other forms of data mining increasingly are cultural industries, in that they contribute to the flows of cultural meanings, they mediate culture, their products are aesthetic and they constitute culture. In this sense, they have a place in cultural industries research.

References

Andrejevic, M. (2011) "The Work That Affective Economics Does", *Cultural Studies*, 25(4–5): 604–20.

Arvidsson, A. (2011) "General Sentiment: How Value and Affect Converge in the Information Economy", *Social Science Research Network* (accessed 4 May 2011: dx.doi.org/10.2139/ssrn.1815031).

BazaarVoice (2012) *BazaarVoice Website* (accessed 31 July 2012: www.bazaarvoice.com/ products).

Beer, D. and Burrows, R. (2013) "Popular Culture, Digital Archives and the New Social Life of Data", *Theory, Culture and Society*, 30(4): 47–71.

Bowker, G. (2005) *Memory Practices in the Sciences*, Cambridge, MA: MIT Press.

boyd, D. and Crawford, K. (2012) "Critical Questions For Big Data: Provocations for a Cultural, Technological and Scholarly Phenomenon", *Information, Communication and Society*, 15(5): 662–79.

Burgess, J. (2006) "Hearing Ordinary Voices: Cultural Studies, Vernacular Creativity and Digital Storytelling", *Continuum: Journal of Media and Cultural Studies*, 20(2): 201–14.

Crawford, K. (2013) "Algorithmic Illusions: Hidden Biases of Big Data", paper presented at Strata Conference, Santa Clara, CA, February (accessed 1 October 2013: www.youtube.com/watch?v=irP5RCdpilc).

D'Orazio, F. (2013) "The Future of Social Media Research: Or How to Re-Invent Social Listening in 10 Steps" (accessed 6 November 2013: abc3d.tumblr.com/post/62887759854/social-data-intelligence).

Duhigg, C. (2012) "How Companies Learn Your Secrets", *New York Times*, 16 February (accessed 4 October 2013: www.nytimes.com/2012/02/19/magazine/shopping-habits.html).

Edwards, L. (2012) "Exploring the Role of Public Relations as a Cultural Intermediary", *Cultural Sociology*, 6(4): 438–54.

Edwards, L. (2015) "Understanding Public Relations as a Cultural Industry", in K. Oakley and J. O'Connor (eds) *Routledge Companion to the Cultural Industries*, Abingdon and New York: Routledge.

Forrester (2012a) "It's Time For Listening Platforms to Grow Up", January (accessed 31 October 2013: www.forrester.com/home/).

Forrester (2012b) "Listening Metrics That Matter" (accessed 31 October 2013: www.forrester.com/home/).

Fries, T. (2012) "A Remedy for Information Aymmetry", in J. Gray, L. Bounegru and L. Chambers (eds) *The Data Journalism Handbook* (accessed 12 November 2013: datajournalismhandbook.org/1.0/en/index.html).

Gitelman, L. and Jackson, V. (2013) "Introduction", in L. Gitleman (ed.) *Raw Data is an Oxymoron*, Cambridge, MA: MIT Press.

Guardian (2013a) "What Is Data Journalism?" April 4 (accessed 11 November 2013: www.theguardian.com/news/datablog/video/2013/apr/04/what-is-data-journalism-video).

Guardian (2013b) *DataBlog* (accessed 23 November 2013: www.theguardian.com/data).

Harris, J. and Kamvar, S. (2005) "We Feel Fine" (accessed 4 June 2010: www.wefeelfine.org/index.html).

Hesmondhalgh, D. (2007) *The Cultural Industries*, 2nd edition, London and New York: Sage.

Kirk, A. (2013) "Introduction to Data Visualization" (course), August 15, University of London.

Lash, S. (2007) "Power after Hegemony: Cultural Studies in Mutation", *Theory, Culture and Society*, 24(3): 55–78.

Law, J. and Urry, J. (2004) "Enacting the Social", *Economy and Society*, 33(3): 390–410.

Lithium (2012) *Lithium Website* (accessed 2 March 2013: www.lithium.com/solutions).

McCandless, D. (2009) "The Billion Dollar Gram" (accessed 2 March 2013: www.informationisbeautiful.net/visualizations/the-billion-dollar-gram/).

Matsunami, I. (2012) "Providing Independent Interpretations of Official Information", in J. Gray, L. Bounegru, and L. Chambers (eds) *The Data Journalism Handbook* (accessed 12 November 2013: datajournalismhandbook.org/1.0/en/index.html).

Meyer, P. (2012) "Filtering the Flow of Data", in J. Gray, L. Bounegru, and L. Chambers (eds) *The Data Journalism Handbook* (accessed 12 November 2013: datajournalismhandbook.org/1.0/en/index.html).

Pariser, E. (2012) *The Filter Bubble: What the Internet is Hiding From You*, London and New York: Viking.

Periscopic (2013) *US Gun Deaths Visualization* (accessed 2 March 2013: guns.periscopic.com/?year=2013).

Rogers, S. (2013) *Facts Are Sacred*, London: Faber and Faber.

Rosenberg, D. (2013) "Data Before the Fact", in L. Gitleman (ed.) *Raw Data is an Oxymoron*, Cambridge, MA: MIT Press.

Rosling, H. (2006–12) "TED Talks" (accessed 31 October 2013: www.ted.com/speakers/hans_rosling.html).

Rushe, D. (2013) "Facebook Reveals Government Asked for Data on 38,000 Users in 2013", *Guardian*, 28 August (accessed 25 September 2013: www.theguardian.com/technology/2013/aug/27/facebook-government-user-requests).

Social Media Biz (2011) "Top 20 Social Media Monitoring Vendors for Business", 12 January (accessed 31 October 2013: socialmedia.biz/2011/01/12/top-20-social-media-monitoring-vendors-for-business/).

Social Media Today (2013) "50 Top Tools for Social Media Monitoring, Analytics and Management", 13 May (accessed 31 October 2013: socialmediatoday.com/pamdyer/1458746/50-top-tools-social-media-monitoring-analytics-and-management-2013).

Sysomos (2012) *Sysomos Website* (accessed 31 July 2012: www.sysomos.com/solutions/).

Turow, J. (2012) *The Daily You: How the New Advertising Industry is Defining Your Identity and Your Worth*, New Haven and London: Yale University Press.

van Dijck, J. (2013) *The Culture of Connectivity: A Critical History of Social Media*, Oxford: Oxford University Press.

Vis, F. (2012) "*The Guardian* DataBlog's Coverage of the UK riots", in J. Gray, L. Bounegru, and L. Chambers (eds) *The Data Journalism Handbook* (accessed 12 November 2013: datajournalismhandbook.org/1.0/en/index.html).

31
SOCIAL LIABILITIES OF DIGITIZING CULTURAL INSTITUTIONS
Environment, labour, waste

Richard Maxwell

This chapter offers an eco-materialist analysis of the digital turn in the administration of arts and cultural organizations. The digital turn in this sector can be understood as another instance in the sixty year process of political-economic transformation that has wired information and communication technology (ICT) into the heart of the capitalist system. In this context, digitization is supposed to be a driver of more efficient, more productive, and more relevant cultural provision derived mostly from so-called audience development (that is, marketing). I argue that arts and cultural groups might want to revisit their fulsome love of high-tech solutions, especially if they truly want to live up to promises of sustainable operations. As the novelist, Philip Pullman says, "it would be strange if the best work being produced didn't take some account, in some way, of what's happening to our climate. Art is not only about beauty: sometimes it has to warn" (IMAGINE 2020, n.d.). The chapter begins with a brief introduction on the digital turn in arts/cultural administration, placing it in a political-economic context of digital capitalism. The subsequent sections focus on digitization's impact on the environment, on labour involved in the global supply chain of digital technologies, and on electronic waste (e-waste).

Digital capitalism and the arts

In the United States, digital online media are now at the centre of operations within three-quarters of the most established non-profit arts organizations (Thom et al. 2013). To some, making this change was a matter of survival in a world where the public's cultural affections had become increasingly focused on commercial electronic screen content. Others have integrated digital technology into the way they make their art or design experiences, adding a video spectacle to live events or interactive electronic sidebars to supplement content of on-site museum collections. Behind the rhetoric justifying digital schemes are external pressures, including diminishing benefactor support and rising electronic consumption/participation relative to on-site arts programming. These rationales are shaded with slightly uncomfortable and vaguely populist acknowledgments that the challenges from electronic media should more productively be seen as opportunities to entice the masses to experience history, heritage and opera, while also reimagining the arts to engage with audience expectations that are more readily addressed by popular forms in commercial media (for example, by including the act of emailing a photograph as a form of arts participation) (National Endowment for the Arts 2013).

The situation in Britain is somewhat similar. Cultural institutions report that digital systems mostly enhance marketing activities, but with perceptible increases in revenue for only about one-third of these groups. The same flurry of excitement about digitization can be found in the way arts and cultural groups are promoting these technologies as enhancements of on-site exhibition and performance (interactivity being the keyword), online distribution, promotion, and, tautologically, as catalysts for enlarging stand-alone digital art collections and exhibitions. But success is not simply achieved by launching websites and social media marketing. Successful cultural institutions are distinguished by their ability to, among other things, "crowdfund" and sell digital commodities – apps, e-books, music, recorded performances, games, etc. – as well as physical goods via online retail. Those lacking income, or a tangible "product," that would enable them to become involved in these activities face barriers of entry similar to those in the US – little money to invest in digital technology or skilled staff, little existing internal experience to manage digital systems on a shoestring budget, and shrinking public investment. Yet despite this apparent digital divide, virtually all arts and cultural organizations report high levels of confidence in digital systems as drivers of growth, innovation, and consumer outreach. And that means continued investment and deployment of more and more digital technology, with a vanguard of "cultural digerati" leading the laggards into the future (Digital R&D Fund for the Arts 2013).

Perhaps the most significant change from digitization is the "mission creep" that follows the shift of emphasis from the social mission of art (art-for-art's-sake, for uplift, for national identity, etc.) to the economic mission of aspiring to a healthy return on investment in exchange for the time and money that arts organizations devote to audience development via research, data analytics, and advertising. Obviously, it's vital for these institutions to increase attendance and participation, but it's expensive to do this with digital systems, which are not simply installed and forgotten. Online marketing schemes using social media, for example, must be well-designed, maintained, and scaled up as needed. This requires ongoing spending for new hardware and software as well as investing in technical training of existing staff or hiring employees adept at operating these systems. As digitization consumes more of these cultural institutions' revenue, the potential for market criteria to overtake public interest principles grows as well.

To be fair, these organizations lack options to help them remain relevant within digital capitalism, an age in which value creation has been indexed to the growth of ICT as a portion of overall investment. They are under a number of other structural constraints, from the drop in leisure time available for on-site arts and cultural consumption and the gutting of the middle class, to the rising costs of doing business that affect all such activities, performing arts in particular (Baumol's cost disease) (Baumol and Bowen 1966; cf. Ross 2000). In an existential sense, if the surveys are to be believed, they link their survival to the growing share of cultural consumption that takes place via high-tech digital electronics. This shift has indeed been breathtaking: mobile devices – tablets, smartphones, notebooks, and laptops – are contributing the lion's share of global spending on consumer electronics, which reached $1 trillion for the first time in 2012, a whopping 5 percent increase over 2011. When this occurs in the wake of the worst economic crisis since the 1930s, it reinforces the idea that digital investments are immune to recession, offering a lifeline to cultural institutions who have few alternatives to engage with consumers entranced by digital entertainments. Forecasts for 2013 predicted annual spending increases of 3.5 percent in all information technology to total about $3.7 trillion (Gartner 2013).

Absent a revolution, it looks like these cultural institutions will continue to be integrated into the commercial system, which is now a thoroughly digital system. But commericalization runs deeper than having to rely on corporate sponsorship to fill the vacuum of old-time patronage and state support for the arts; and while it's possible, it probably won't mean blockbuster museum exhibits tapping into the advertising revenue generated by media events like the Super Bowl or World Cup (though you never know). Digital technology will hammer cultural and arts provision into the same shape we've seen in businesses, and in non-profits like universities, as they deploy ICT throughout their operations. This includes, among other probable characteristics, a greater share of administration controlled by enterprise resource planning (ERP) systems with locked-in partnerships for database management and performance audits – only a handful of ERP systems offer services that address non-profit operations (mostly education and government) though all are hungry for this business (FindTheBest 2014). In most cases, this will foist institutional roles and functions designed for businesses upon staff whose work has traditionally been organized and assessed by non-business criteria. This shift also entails a greater monetization of audience value where size of attendance, internet views and click-throughs become more important than measuring the social significance of arts organizations as, for example, public goods.

Finally, digitization encourages arts and cultural administrators and digerati to endorse upstream educational curricular reform to meet demands for skilled high-tech workers downstream inside digitized organizations. It's an obvious solution to the so-called staffing problem in digital arts administration, but it also exemplifies one of the latest instances of a sixty-year trend of "corporate educational provision" of workers "suitably trained" for digital capitalism and all that this brings with it: a back door allowing training of "human capital" inside public institutions, with "vocational objectives," precarity, with work routines and performance outcomes measured by how well they serve the status quo (Schiller 1999: 204–5). This education/employment dimension is critical: just as digitization via online sales, marketing, and audience analytics is perceived as the most worthwhile means of raising revenue from arts and cultural activities, the digitization of training in the arts and cultural sector – increasingly in university programs of digital humanities and the like – proposes dramatic, untested changes in the way we are asked to teach, interpret, and measure the value of artistic and cultural resources.

While it is not preordained that digital technology will distort the mission of arts institutions, those who want to preserve non-market goals must be vigilant. (Reportedly, many smaller, community-based groups are finding it hard to participate in high-tech arts administration [Thom et al. 2013].) As we'll see, digital technology is not a neutral set of tools that benignly build up arts and culture. They come with ideological baggage and a toxic record of harms to the environment and workers.

Ecological effects of digitization[1]

While digitization has been positioned and embraced as the best defence of arts institutions – and it does hold the potential to relieve some existing and worrisome ecological problems – its expansion raises additional environmental concerns, in particular its relation to energy consumption, to the international division of labour in the ICT and consumer electronics sector, and to e-waste. Museums, for example, tend to be electricity hogs and terrible partners in recycling efforts (Museum Association 2008: 4). Digital technologies can help reduce energy consumption through LED lighting and "smart" air quality and temperature controls, but audience development through ICT adds additional energy use, waste and other long-term environmental effects.

The performing arts range in size and complexity, but many scenarios require lots of energy and produce lots of waste, neglecting reuse and recycling routines – problems that multiply with touring. Of course, there are green artists keen to change these dirty practices, but sustainability seems easier to foster in small-scale productions (Beer 2012). Scaling up efforts to green these activities at a national level has shown some success, but bureaucrats in charge of these programs still tend to enter digital solutions on the plus side as purportedly sustainable practices (Arts Council England 2012; Bottrill and Tsiarta 2011). Environmental harms that occur beyond the confines of these organizations' immediate operations are easy to ignore or treat as peripheral to such greening strategies. The following sections shed a bit of light on these ecological contexts.

Energy

As long as we don't see the smokestacks and pollution that accompany the electricity needed for digitization, high-wattage operations of digital networks, office equipment, and video displays can be sold as clean, environmentally benign technologies ('Managing Energy Costs'). But these systems are plugged into the utility grid, which makes them part of a global problem of climate change.

With over ten billion high-tech devices needing electricity today, 15 percent of global residential energy is now spent on powering domestic digital technology. If energy demand continues to grow at this rate, the residential electricity needed to power electronics will rise to 30 percent of global consumption by 2022, and 45 percent by 2030 (International Energy Agency 2009). When residential use is added to the electricity it takes to make and distribute these goods, the total energy consumed translates into carbon emissions that are about the same as current levels from aviation – and this does not account for the energy it takes to make chemicals and gases that go into the production of semiconductors or the energy used to dispose or recycle the devices.

RICHARD MAXWELL

There's more. Enormous amounts of data pass daily through massive networks and data centres – "the cloud" – now scattered across the globe. Data centres' energy demand continues to rise at a steady pace, with business practices that range from serious plans to reduce reliance on coal-fired energy to widespread examples of waste and thoughtless energy management. At current levels, cloud computing eats up energy at a rate somewhere between what Japan and India consume (Greenpeace International 2012). The environmental impact of this networked culture will depend on the type of energy production used to power the grids – coal-fired power being the biggest menace.

Arts organizations that increase content provision to mobile devices have joined another unsustainable trend. There are nearly seven billion mobile phones in use worldwide today. But we're not just talking about people following map directions to the theatre or museum. Wireless connectivity consumes a tremendous amount of electricity – up to 90 percent of the total energy consumed by mobile connections (CEET 2013).

In sum, a more realistic price tag for digitized audience development would factor in these environmental liabilities. But, as in most business accounting practices, such negative outcomes are treated as external to the cost of operations – making environmental harms the price society pays for its industriousness.

Labour

While energy consumption is rising in the electronic core of networked systems, increasingly in mobile and cloud computing operations, these systems are built out of rough labour conditions in the global supply chains where the essential technologies are manufactured. The proliferation of high-tech supply chains combines with their geographical dispersion to pose uncertainties for anyone interested in gathering comprehensive data about workplace hazards and exploitation in the global assembly line. This makes it hard to present cultural workers in developed countries with a clear understanding of the ties that bind them to labourers who assemble their digital tools in the developing world. Stories from the shop floor help make this connection more palpable. A young woman in a circuit board factory tells of her estrangement from her body: "I work like a machine and my brain is rusted" (quoted in Chan and Ho 2008: 22). At an electronics factory in Chihuahua, Mexico, where circuit boards were assembled for the American contract manufacturer, Jabil, 21-year-old Rosa recounted a searing story of loss:

> I was three months pregnant. ... I asked my facilitator to move me, but she said no, not until they had found someone else. I worked from 3.30 a.m. to 12 p.m. On November 17th, when I arrived at work, I started to feel unwell. I went to the lavatory and noticed I was bleeding. I went straight to the infirmary and the doctor told me it was nothing ... that it was normal. I went back to the production line and told my supervisor I was feeling quite sick, and asked him for permission to leave. He talked with the doctor over the phone and then told me "I'm not letting you out, don't be a wimp". ... [T]he baby wasn't growing properly. [The doctors] told me it was because of the lead, and I believe that; that's why I wanted to be moved when I found out I was

pregnant, but I wasn't allowed [and] I lost my baby. I got very depressed and spent all those days crying. I was only given two days sick leave.

(quoted in CEREAL 2006: 23)

This episode occurred far from the major cultural and arts centres described above, both in geographical and moral terms. It's hard to imagine this part of our digital culture having anything to do with the progressive, clean digital technologies promoted as the key to survival of arts and cultural institutions. The circuit board that Rosa was assembling is not the only physical connection that can be made with the digitization of cultural and arts institutions; her $10 a day wage and harsh working conditions are fundamental to a system that elevates ICT and electronics consumption to its acclaimed status (Patterson 2012). For her and other ICT assembly workers in the global supply chain, health risks are a fact of life that cannot be simply remedied by ferreting out the bad managers or corrupt owners and punishing them.

Structural conditions in the global political economy – including lax regulation, low levels of independent union membership, and multinational corporate domination – have given free rein to contract manufacturers like Jabil, Foxconn and others around the globe to exploit workers in high-stress, hazardous, and precarious jobs. Most of these workers are just kids – teenagers, mostly girls, looking for a way out of subsistence economies. Weak workplace protections have historically been the bread and butter of this system.

One of the most vexing obstacles to understanding high-tech supply chain conditions is the lack of information on the number of workers making ICT and consumer electronics – it's just hard to get accurate information about far-flung and often high-security factories, not to mention data on the millions who potentially work as in-home component assemblers. Estimates on the high end delineate this labour very broadly to include IT professionals, software and services, assembly workers, and jobs enabled by skilled use of information technology, suggesting that there are over 200 million people in Organisation for Economic Co-operation and Development (OECD) countries and the Asia-Pacific region alone who work in some kind of digital technology job (Raina 2007: 18–25). Add another 200 million for mining and related jobs, and some additional millions for transport, distribution, retail sales, and end of life management, disposal, and destruction. While these are rough numbers – there could be millions more or millions less – they represent the scale and variety of work involved in the digitization process. Such uncertainty is not just an effect of the geographically dispersed labour involved in the global supply chain; union membership density in ICT manufacturing is very low, which adds to the difficulty of finding reliable and representative information on workers' exposure to toxic materials and other workplace hazards.[2]

This distancing reinforces unthinking technophilia by making it easy to forget the industrial origins of so-called post-industrial goods. They come to us all shiny and new – so clean you could eat off of them. The true story is that they're born from a toxic and unsustainable process that begins in mines around the world – primarily Africa and Latin America – where the copper, gold, tin, coltan, lithium, and other elements that go into smartphones and computers come from. Component and final assembly work reaches around the globe with most of the contract manufacturers concentrated in Asia and Mexico.

All this limits the ability of workers and bureaucrats in arts organizations in the United States and United Kingdom to comprehend, let alone sympathize with, the vast numbers of workers and their plight. Academic research on cultural and creative industries provides little help in this regard. In contrast, studies on the impact of bio-physical risks faced by workers have been generated by labour and human rights activists, independent unionists, health and environmental researchers and advocates, and workers like Rosa who are willing to speak up about the conditions inside the electronic sweatshops. If arts and cultural workers in the Global North care about connecting the dots across the global supply chain, those are the folks they must turn to for information.

Electronic waste

Digitization of arts and cultural organizations will increase waste associated with routine upgrades and the discards of downgraded electronics. These dead, broken, incompatible or unfashionable high-tech goods are generated at a rate of 20 to 50 million tons worldwide – last year, 184 countries generated about 49 million metric tons of electric and electronic waste (Duan et al. 2013). Some time in the last decade or so, e-waste became the fastest growing part of global waste streams. E-waste is full of toxins that, if not properly removed, reused or recycled, can poison the land, air, water, and bodies of people exposed to the hazardous contents.

Waste is a problem throughout the life cycle of any electronic device, from water over-used and contaminated in semi-conductor production to discarded solvents and other materials. While such waste is presently designed into high-tech goods, there exist promising alternatives of green design that could today be put into production. But the pernicious business strategy of planned obsolescence still dominates corporate thinking in the high-tech sector, its destructiveness a stark reality for those working in mostly informal, low-tech e-waste dump sites around the world.

Where does all the e-waste go? Wealthy high-tech nations export 80 to 85 percent of the e-waste that they do not recycle themselves to Latin America, Eastern Europe, Africa, Asia, United Arab, and Lebanon. Recent estimates from the United Nations suggest that China now receives 70 percent of all e-waste imports, though Chinese law prohibits this. China is also the third biggest generator of e-waste after the European Union and United States (Watson 2013).

It's notoriously difficult to estimate the precise scale of illegal e-waste flowing into China because of problems with measurement and the way loopholes in existing regulations can be exploited. This confounds tracking and mapping of e-waste flows, interceptions of hazardous materials, and enforcement of laws. Much of the research ignores e-waste that is dumped into landfills or misidentified after collection, tracking "for the record" only retrieved discards that are categorized and labelled explicitly as e-waste. Most studies based on trade statistics only count intact items, not component parts or scrap. Studies in the European Union show that only a third of all e-waste is identified as such and "separately collected and appropriately treated." Unidentified portions of the rest of this junk are "going to landfills and to sub-standard treatment sites in or outside the European Union" (European Commission 2012). This is the fount of a huge and growing, and mostly illegal, international scavenger business.

While China has banned the import of e-waste, making direct imports increasingly rare, smugglers have figured out ways to get the junk across the border by indirect means (in 2001, a year after the ban was implemented, estimates put the volume of imports at 1.5 million tonnes). Some of it is smuggled in with shipments of otherwise legal scrap metal. But the bulk of the junk travels into China thanks to scoundrels who figured out ways to exploit legal loopholes. For example, because of legislative differences with mainland China, Hong Kong can import vast amounts of e-waste, which is legal if the items are intact and identified as second-hand electronics and electric equipment. But then there are no permits required in Hong Kong for re-exporting this material to China. A similar loophole allows second-hand devices to be imported into Vietnam for the stated purpose of re-export to China and elsewhere. While items refurbished in China cannot legally be exported back into Vietnam, a black market for these second-hand goods is thriving anyway. Since there are few effective protocols for distinguishing reusable e-waste from scrap, a great deal of illegal transportation of hazardous e-waste takes place. Interceptions of these shipments produce post-facto data on existing flows and entry points of the illegal waste, though this doesn't stop smugglers from finding alternatives (Wang et al. 2013: 13–16).

While it's hard to create accurate world maps of the digital junk's destinations, there is abundant research on the health and ecosystem risks associated with exposure to burned, dismantled, and open-pit disposal of e-waste in low-skilled, low-tech salvage yards. Health and safety risks include: brain damage, headaches, vertigo, nausea, birth defects, diseases of the bones, stomach, lungs, and other vital organs, and disrupted biological development in children. These conditions result from exposure to heavy metals (lead, cadmium, chromium, and mercury), and to burned plastics, and poisonous fumes emitted when melting components in search of precious metals. To understand the ecosystem impact, consider Guiyu in Guangdong Province, China. Once a farming town, 80 percent of local families have left farming for recycling; contaminants from recycling saturate the human food chain; and persistent organic pollutants in the soil and water prohibit the safe return of affected agricultural lands to future generations. Even if people wanted to return to a mixed economy that included agriculture, they could only produce poisoned crops (Maxwell and Miller 2012: 104–5).

Conclusion: Environmental accounting, sustainability, and solidarity

In their mission statement, IMAGINE 2020, a network of eleven European arts organizations, calls on the cultural industries to stand up to the challenges of the ecological crisis, asking how the arts and cultural sector can make "changes necessary to stabilise the climate and secure a sustainable future" (IMAGINE 2020). Funded by the European Union, IMAGINE 2020 seeks to play a role in raising environmental awareness through the arts and by sharing information about green practices in the cultural sphere. This chapter has endeavoured to bring attention to some key problems on which these green institutional initiatives must focus: energy consumption and conservation, ICT design and manufacturing processes, working conditions throughout the global supply chain, and e-waste. The bulk of these problems reside outside of the cultural sector, but they are not disconnected. If arts administrators perceived upstream and downstream environmental and labour liabilities connected to their digitized organizations as costs to their operations, they might identify unexpected ways to incorporate environmental accounting into management protocols and contribute to sustainable cultural production and consumption.

There's a growing list of organizations working to stop digital devices from poisoning ecosystems in their place of manufacture; who have pushed for more extensive and thorough forms of end-of-life management of e-waste; who are pressing for ecologically sound design for high-tech goods and manufacturing processes that protect biophysical rights of workers who today fall sick from exposure to poisons and deadly factory operations. These are the untapped partners for arts and cultural institutions making the digital turn. All of us, through our teaching, activism, and research, can contribute in some way to these efforts to press for a culture of sustainability over the prevailing one of consumerism – to advocate for a way of thinking and acting that is based on the idea that the Earth has limited resources to support human activities and limited capabilities to absorb and recycle our excesses. A culture of sustainability is also built on an ethics of intergenerational care with the enduring solidarity that binds our destinies to those of workers like Rosa.

Notes

1 Parts of this section draw on and update research from Maxwell and Miller (2012).
2 Without widespread union representation and improved associational rights, ICT production workers lack independent institutional sources of information about their rights, safety risks, and health protections. And even where you find electronics workers signed up in a union, there's a good chance that this is not an independent union but a business-friendly one. It's likely that Rosa was a member of such a union in Mexico, and was probably enrolled when one of the scores of employment agencies working for the factory owners signed her up for the job.

References

Arts Council England. (2012) *Environmental Sustainability Report*. January 31 (www.artscouncil. org.uk/media/uploads/pdf/environmental_sustainability_reportv2_final210212.pdf).

Baumol, W. and Bowen, W. (1966) *Performing Arts – The Economic Dilemma: A study of problems common to theater, opera, music, and dance*, New York: Twentieth-Century Fund.

Beer, T. (2012) "An Introduction to Ecological Design for the Performing Arts," *Proceedings of the Cultural Ecology Symposium*, Deakin University, Australia (accessed: January 23, 2014: www. academia.edu/4974188/An_Introduction_to_Ecological_Design_for_the_Performing_Arts).

Bottrill, C. and Tsiarta, C. (2011) "Green Mobility: A guide to environmentally sustainable mobility for performing arts," Julie's Bicycle/On the Move (on-the-move.org/files/Green-Mobility-Guide.pdf).

CEET (2013) *The Power of Wireless Cloud: An analysis of the energy consumption of wireless cloud,*' Melbourne: University of Melbourne (accessed January 23, 2014: www.ceet.unimelb.edu.au/ publications/downloads/ceet-white-paper-wireless-cloud.pdf).

CEREAL (Centre for Reflection and Action on Labour Issues) (2006) "New Technology Workers: Report on working conditions in the Mexican electronics industry," Guadalajara, Mexico: Centro de Reflexión y Acción Laboral (accessed January 23, 2014: cerealgdl.org/ images/informes/cereal-informe-2006.pdf).

Chan, J. and Ho, C. (2008) *The Dark Side of Cyberspace: Inside the sweatshops of China's com-puter hardware production*, Berlin: World Economy, Ecology and Development.

Digital R&D Fund for the Arts (2013) *Digital Culture: How arts and cultural organizations in England use technology* (accessed January 23, 2014: artsdigitalrnd.org.uk/wp-content/uploads/2013/11/DigitalCulture_FullReport.pdf).

Duan, H., Miller, T. Reed, Gregory, J. and Kirchain, R. (2013) *Quantitative Characterization of Domestic and Transboundary Flows of Used Electronics: Analysis of generation, collection, and export in the United States*, Cambridge, MA: MIT/StEP Initiative.

European Commission (2012) "Waste Electrical and Electronic Equipment (WEEE)" (accessed January 23, 2014: ec.europa.eu/environment/waste/weee/index_en.htm).

FindTheBest (2014) "Compare Enterprise Resource Planning Software" (accessed January 23, 2014: erp-software.findthebest.com/).

Gartner (2013) "Gartner Says Worldwide IT Spending on Pace to Reach $3.7 Trillion in 2013," *Gartner*, July 2 (accessed January 23, 2014: www.gartner.com/newsroom/id/2537815).

Greenpeace International (2012) *How Green is Your Cloud?* (accessed January 23, 2014: www.greenpeace.org/international/Global/international/publications/climate/2012/iCoal/HowCleanisYourCloud.pdf).

IMAGINE 2020 (n.d.) *Art and Climate Change Network* (accessed March 30, 2014: www.imagine 2020.eu/).

International Energy Agency (2009) *Gadgets and Gigawatts: Policies for energy efficient electronics – executive summary*, Paris: Organization for Economic Cooperation and Development.

Maxwell, R. and Miller, T. (2012) *Greening the Media*, New York: Oxford University Press, 2012.

Museum Association (2008) *Sustainability and Museums: Your chance to make a difference* (accessed January 23, 2014: www.museumsassociation.org/campaigns/sustainability/sustainability-report).

National Endowment for the Arts (2013) *How a Nation Engages with Art*, Washington, DC: NEA (accessed January 23, 2014: arts.gov/sites/default/files/highlights-from-2012-sppa-revised-jan2015.pdf).

Patterson, K. (2012) "Mexican High-Tech Workers Demand Justice and Dignity," *New American Media: Science and technology*, March 12 (accessed January 23, 2014: newamericamedia.org/2012/03/mexican-high-tech-workers-demand-justice-and-dignity.php).

Raina, R. (2007) *ICT Human Resource Development in Asia and the Pacific*, Incheon: United Nations Asian and Pacific Training Centre for Information and Communication Technology for Development.

Ross, A. (2000) "The Mental Labour Problem," *Social Text* 18(2 63): 1–31.

Schiller, D. (1999) *Digital Capitalism: Networking the global market system*, Cambridge, MA: MIT Press.

Thom, K., Purcell, K. and Rainie, L. (2013) *Arts Organizations and Digital Technologies*, Pew Research Center's Internet and American Life Project (accessed January 23, 2014: www.pewinternet.org/~/media/Files/Reports/2013/PIP_ArtsandTechnology_PDF.pdf).

Wang, F., Kuehr, R., Ahlquist, D. and Li, J. (2013) *E-waste in China: A Country Report*, Tokyo: United Nations University Institute for Sustainability and Peace (accessed October 12, 2014: isp.unu.edu/publications/scycle/files/ewaste-in-china.pdf).

Watson, I. (2013) "China: The electronic wastebasket of the world," CNN.com, May 30 (accessed January 23, 2014: www.cnn.com/2013/05/30/world/asia/china-electronic-waste-e-waste).

32

POPULAR MUSIC MAKING AND PROMOTIONAL WORK INSIDE THE 'NEW' MUSIC INDUSTRY

Leslie M. Meier

For music fans, the idea of creating popular music can seem so alluring and removed from the world of work that there can be a tendency to overlook the fact that professional music makers are cultural *workers* – that making music requires considerable time, financial commitment, and labor. In the digital age, the commercial realities faced by popular music makers are marked by complexity, overwhelming competitiveness, and continual change. In many ways, working musicians do the same things they always have done: write, record, and perform popular music. Yet their careers are shaped by decidedly different working conditions. Aspiring and emerging music makers have unprecedented access to the technological means of producing, distributing, and marketing music. The ability to self-produce and self-release music has allowed for remarkable autonomy in creative expression. The popularization of internet radio and music recommendation services (e.g., Pandora), on-demand music streaming sites (e.g., Spotify), and digital download retailers (e.g., iTunes) has provided new or alternative sites for the promotion and (albeit to varying degrees) 'monetization' of sound recordings. The wide availability of direct-to-fan sales and marketing platforms (e.g., Topspin), crowdfunding and fundraising services (e.g., Kickstarter, PledgeMusic), and social media sites (e.g., Facebook, Twitter) has enabled 'unsigned' music makers to assume greater control over the ways they choose to finance, market, and generate revenue from their music.

Understandably, these developments have been received with much excitement. After all, on the surface, this 'new' music industry bears little resemblance to the 'old' music industry, whose gatekeepers – the major record companies – limited access to the music marketplace and maintained 'artificial scarcity' in a systematic way (see Garnham 1990: 38–40, 161; Hesmondhalgh 2013: 31). With the shift from compact discs (CDs) to digital audio files (MP3s) and (often unauthorized) downloading, this ceased to be possible in the same way. However, the attendant explosion of new popular music has produced a number of challenges for working artists. Digital delivery has produced a grimmer reality than straightforward arguments regarding popular music's 'democratization' suggest. This chapter sheds light on issues tied to the shifting contours of music-related work – including the expansion of new forms of promotional labor performed by artists – that have accompanied new music industry models.

Musicians who decide to work around the established record label system must juggle the roles of creator, self-promoter, and entrepreneur, taking on jobs in the spheres of marketing and promotion on top of performing tasks more directly linked to songwriting, recording, and live performance. As we shall see, the new music industry model is oriented around monetizing 'artist-brands' rather than just selling records – a shift that is shaping the ways that music makers ranging from stars to the little known are obliged to see and sell themselves. Significantly, against a backdrop of considerable change remains an abiding continuity with the 'old' music industry: extraordinary financial rewards continue to accrue to a select few whilst staggering commercial failure rates remain the norm. This examination draws on trade press and newspaper coverage and music industry guidebooks, podcasts, and reports.

Delineating job descriptions, allotting pay

The term 'music industry' is routinely employed as shorthand for the range of activities, sectors, and enterprises involved in the commercial production of popular music. Whether the industry involved in the production of sound recordings, songs, and live performances is better conceptualized as the music industry (singular) or the music industries (plural) is the subject of debate. John Williamson and Martin Cloonan (2007: 305) point out that the notion of a music industry in the singular is routinely – and problematically – used as a synonym for the *recording* industry; these authors stress that the term obscures the complexity, plurality, and diversity of the range of sectors involved in the production and circulation of popular music. Music publishing, live performance, artist management, and music merchandising sectors exist alongside the recording industry. According to Dave Laing, however, the core music-producing sectors nevertheless can be understood as 'a unitary business sector, albeit one in which sub-sectors have a relatively autonomous relationship to each other' (Laing 2009: 15). This is especially so in a context that has seen deepening consolidation, with the major music companies – Universal, Sony, and Warner – not only maintaining a firm grip over recording and music publishing revenues but also expanding their interests in artist management, merchandising, and promotion (Billboard 2009). Important for the purposes of a discussion of musical labor is the fact that music makers routinely perform work tied to the recording, music publishing, and live performance sectors.

Within industry circles, professional music makers are typically (though not exclusively) referred to as 'recording artists' – a designation that speaks to the legacy of record sales as the foundation of music industry profits. The idea of the recording *artist* also evokes romantic notions of inspired cultural creation. David Hesmondhalgh

(2013: 6) supports the use of the terms 'symbol creators' and 'symbol makers' over the term 'artists' (which summons 'connotations of individual genius and a higher calling') to describe creative cultural industry workers. In a similar vein, as an analytic term, I prefer 'music makers'. The idea of the gifted, as opposed to hard working, artist actually serves to mask the labor that goes into the creation of popular music texts and performances and, as such, the specific ways that music industry business models are premised on the extraction of surplus value from this labor. Nonetheless, in practice, I find it useful to draw on the terms that have currency among music industry executives in addition.

Indeed, industry definitions signal distinct forms of work and produce real effects for how music makers are (or are not) remunerated. Record companies sign recording contracts with recording artists (i.e., featured performers on master recordings) who are compensated through advances and royalties. Music publishers, on the other hand, work with songwriters (i.e., composers of lyrics and music, understood by the music publishing industry as the 'notes'). Music publishers are in the business of exploiting (i.e., converting into revenue) rights associated with these compositions, including: mechanical reproduction rights, performance rights, and synchronization (sync) rights (for the use of compositions in audiovisual media), among others. Songwriters receive a share of the revenues generated. In the live music sector, meanwhile, music makers are positioned as performers and they may receive 'guarantees' from venues and/or a percentage of concert ticket sales. These three sectors require very different sets of skills. While different genres of music involve varying divisions of labor across these areas, many music makers work as recording artists, songwriters, *and* performers. What is more, this wider commercial apparatus and the copyright system at its foundation also influence do-it-yourself (DIY) music makers who attempt to operate outside the formal record label system – a point to which I will return.

Though based on distinct profit generation models, each of these music sectors metes out financial rewards unevenly. The royalty rates and sync license fees received by superstars are (often considerably) higher than those paid to new artists, and the concert ticket prices and fees paid to top-tier acts bear little resemblance to those received by lesser known artists, some of whom even pay for prime opening slots on major tours (see Passman 2012: 88–89, 248–53, 372–77). The music industry is characterized by 'winner-take-all' economies – a fact that has not been disrupted by online distribution and promotion.

New commercial realities, persistent industrial logics

Today, independent and unsigned artists are able to circumvent the major label system in notable ways. DIY artists can use increasingly affordable and accessible digital technologies and social media to bypass the music industry's traditional 'middlemen' in order to reach audiences (Young and Collins 2010). This ready availability of digital recording and distribution tools, however, has produced an inconvenient truth: the corresponding flood of new releases has translated into tremendous competition for audience attention. Furthermore, reaching an audience and building a (paying) fan base remain two very different things. As a result, the deep power asymmetries that have long marked the music industry persist.

Far more music is released today than was the case prior to the institutionalization of digital delivery. According to Nielsen SoundScan figures, the number of new albums released in the United States jumped from 36,000 in the year 2000 to 106,000 in 2008, before dipping to 75,000 in 2010 (Digital Music News 2011). Although this market is in flux, competition for record-buying customers is high. What remains stable is the fact that the major music companies – now just three corporations – continue to control an overwhelming share of the global market for recorded music. Universal Music Group, Sony Music Entertainment, and Warner Music Group reportedly captured 38.9 percent, 29.5 percent, and 18.7 percent of U.S. album sales in 2013, respectively – figures that include CDs, vinyl, digital albums, and 'track equivalent albums' (Christman 2014). Industry analyst Mark Mulligan characterizes the music industry as a 'superstar economy'; his analysis of 2013 global sales data reveals that 1 percent of artists accounted for 77 percent of all recorded music income (in Resnikoff 2014). According to *Billboard*'s Glenn Peoples, in 2010, 60,000 new titles released in the United States sold 100 units or fewer, averaging 'just 13.3 units per title' (Peoples 2011). These figures tell a very different story than optimistic claims regarding 'disruptive' new music models would suggest.

Hopes regarding the emergence of a more egalitarian music industry, however, typically do not hinge on rosy record sales forecasts. Instead, they center on the viability of live performance. Unfortunately, the concert business is likewise marked by what legal scholar Mark F. Schultz (2009) characterizes as a 'superstar problem'. Just 25 tours (the top 0.76 percent) accounted for 53.25 percent of all gross touring earnings reported to *Billboard* for 2007 (Schultz 2009: 734–35). It is difficult to paint a precise picture of performers' shares of live music income, especially given the tendency to report gross and not net figures; considerable costs can be incurred when touring. Top stars may hire musicians, dancers, set and costume designers, engineers, and so forth, but even more modest tours must absorb expenses associated with transportation, accommodations, and crew wages. Artists are typically the last to get paid and income is shared among group members and any other members of 'the team'. Thus, it remains difficult for little known artists to generate substantial profits from live performance.

Amid declining sound recording revenues, the viability of music streaming services has been a subject of ongoing debate. While U.S. major record companies received $500 million in advances from Spotify, the income generated for recording artists from such services has been paltry thus far, prompting criticism from David Byrne, Radiohead, Aimee Mann, David Lowery, and others (Byrne 2013). Pandora reportedly pays record labels and artists 0.12 cents total per stream, whereas Spotify's rate has been estimated at half a cent per stream (Sisario 2013). While these digital services may constitute valuable revenue streams for record companies, which are able to aggregate revenues from entire catalogs of music, and perhaps a handful of star artists whose hits are streamed in extremely high volumes, the income potential for the vast majority of artists remains very much in doubt.

Crowdfunding sites, meanwhile, work best for those who are already able to draw a crowd. This is not a viable way of *developing* an audience but rather of communicating with an already dedicated group of fans. What is more, these approaches are often project-based; this intermittent funding is typically earmarked for specific outputs and not artist salaries.

The music industry's profit generation models reflect a response to the distinctive economics of the cultural industries: high production costs and low reproduction costs mean that profits are most efficiently generated through audience maximization – through the production of star artists and hit songs (Garnham 1990: 160–61; Hesmondhalgh 2013: 29–32). Despite decreasing production costs, these industrial logics have not been fundamentally altered in the digital age. In fact, the second portion of an oft-cited passage by Nicholas Garnham has assumed renewed importance: '*It is cultural distribution, not cultural production, that is the key locus of power and profit*. ... The cultural process is as much, if not more, about creating audiences or publics as it is about producing cultural artefacts and performances' (Garnham 1990: 161–62; emphasis in original). In this era of musical abundance, the ability to create and *monetize* audiences – the work of market-making and marketing – is paramount. Marketing to mass audiences remains a costly but nevertheless effective approach and is still mastered by major music companies. What is noteworthy in the contemporary context is the growing assumption of financial risk by aspiring music makers.

While star artists continue to trade in hit records and international tours, they also generate substantial revenues from branded merchandise, music licensing, sponsorship, and endorsement deals. Although working on a totally different scale and lacking the apparatus of major label support, unsigned and lesser known music makers also are expected to rely on merchandising and brand-related products in addition to concert ticket sales amid shrinking recorded music income. These starkly different realities are united by a common idea: the monetization of the 'artist-brand'.

The 'artist-brand' paradigm

The idea that music makers can be likened to – and paired with – brands has been adopted as the new common sense across the music industry. Record companies now aggregate multiple revenue streams connected to artist-brands, including monies derived from new digital music products, expanding business-to-business markets for the licensing of music and artist personae, and more traditional music businesses (see Meier 2013). 'The concept of "band as brand" is an economic cornerstone for musicians today,' explains Catherine Fitterman Radbill, Director of New York University's music business program (2013: 19) – echoing industry opinion across the United States and Canada. In the United Kingdom, too, the 'artist him or herself (as a brand, reputation or image)' is positioned as a core 'commercial asset' (alongside the master recording, musical composition, and live performance) (UK Music 2013: 16). The idea that record company personnel are interested in marketing the recording artist as an 'entire entertainment package' whose creative output extends well beyond music is not new (Negus 1992: 5). However, the destabilization of recorded music revenues has hastened the formalization of this line of business thinking. Significantly, the artist-brand paradigm affects signed and unsigned artists.

The origins of this approach can be located within record company contracting conventions and the shift toward the multiple rights contract or '360 deal'. It is now standard practice for record companies to request 'participation' in a broad range of revenue streams, such as music publishing, live performance, merchandising, licensing, branding, and sponsorship revenues, by way of these encircling contracts (see Stahl and Meier 2012; Marshall 2013). Record companies have used this diversification strategy to dampen the impact of declining record sales and 'to recast themselves as music – rather than just recording – companies' (Goodman 2008). Entertainment attorney Donald S. Passman sums up the recording industry's argument as follows:

> In this new world, we are no longer just a record company … We are now an artist brand-building company. Of all the players in your life, we are the only ones who spend substantial money to make you a household name. Then, thanks to our rocket launch, you make tons of money by touring, song-writing, selling your face to teenagers on T-shirts, etc. This isn't right. We should share in all the business we help build for you. … Oh, and one other thing. We won't sign you if you don't agree.
>
> (Passman 2012: 97)

A thorough treatment of 360 deals and the dynamics of artist stratification and vulnerability they promise to produce lies outside the scope of this chapter (see Stahl and Meier 2012). Important here is how the influence of this branding logic has reached well beyond the major record companies.

The idea of the artist-brand has informed approaches adopted by DIY music makers who ultimately want to secure a contract with a music company as well as those who intend to operate outside this corporate system for the long term. For the former group, music makers are tasked with the work of 'building their brand' well in advance of securing any such support from record companies, artist managers, agents, or other music businesses. As artist manager Marcus Grant advised recording artists interested in courting representation, 'If you're not selling tickets and T-shirts, you don't even matter' (Herstand 2014). Those music makers who seek to build sustainable careers on their own likewise are tasked with leveraging their brand – their reputation, image, and 'personality' – as a source of revenue. Some may develop relatively hands-off partnerships with 'lifestyle brands' (see Sisario 2010; Meier 2013). Others may attempt to generate revenue from artist branded merchandise and mementos independently. Overall, as Damian Kulash of independent band OK Go explains, 'making a living in music isn't just about selling studio recordings anymore. It's about selling the whole package: themselves' (Kulash 2010).

Such an approach can produce vexing or alienating effects. In an interview with Chris Ruen, Andrew Falkous of independent rock band Future of the Left expressed frustration with the situation faced by music makers:

> So, you're telling me that I spent years learning an instrument, writing songs and putting my heart and soul into this music to become a fucking T-shirt salesman? Because that is so contrary to the 'all music is made for free' crowd's stated goal. 'Free music' pushes bands that are genuinely in it for

the love of music ... towards a more explicit commercial understanding of their music. And I'm not just talking about careerist bands, I'm talking about any band that wants to tour.

(Ruen 2012: 83)

The time, effort, and financial commitment that goes into practicing, writing, rehearsing, and recording music – the unglamorous, the everyday, and perhaps even the mundane – frequently goes unseen or unrecognized as work. Such a dynamic contributes to the prevalence of un- or under-compensated musical labor.

As a result, music makers are compelled to participate in branding and merchandising opportunities if they are to build careers that do not rely on recorded music income. Selling T-shirts is hardly novel, of course. In a marketplace in which independent artists are coached to use their unique 'personalities' as differentiation devices, creativity has extended into the realm of artist-branded merchandise. For instance, British recording artist CJ Wildheart has partnered with a chili sauce company to concoct a custom hot sauce, as he explains on his PledgeMusic page: 'a new album and a hot sauce ... what's not to love!' (PledgeMusic 2014).

Unsigned and independent music makers are now expected to harness the potential of social media and digital distribution and marketing services in order to build their careers on their own. This new requirement demands the development of skills in and the investment of considerable time to the areas of publicity, target marketing, and even data analytics. The new paradigm requires music makers to take on new forms of promotional labor – to act as both product and salesperson.

Drumming up business: The DIY bottom line

About 5% of my time goes to actually making music sadly. ... The rest is promo, technical, planning, running around, schedules ... blah.

Imogen Heap, singer-songwriter (Morris 2014: 284)

Emerging and smaller-scale music makers are now expected to take on a range of promotional tasks that formerly were handled by record companies, artist managers, and marketing departments (Morris 2014: 275). The 'old' record label system involved 'loose' control over the creative process and 'tight' control over circulation (Hesmondhalgh 2013: 32–33). In other words, recording artists were granted considerable autonomy in the creation of music but record labels took control of marketing and distribution. The new system affords unsigned music makers control over production *and* circulation. The flipside of this new freedom is a marked increase in work tied to publicity and a corresponding decline in time available to make music: 'DIY (do-it-yourself) artists take charge of their own writing, recording, publishing, touring, licensing, sales, fan development, and marketing. It's a lot of work, and it's not for everyone' (Fitterman Radbill 2013: 6).

Initially, the novel luster of social media meant that clever use of these platforms could allow music makers to set themselves apart in the cluttered music marketplace. This is no longer the case. Instead, promotional work of this sort is the price of admission to the music industry; it is expected. Discussing the case of DIY independent artists, one music industry executive characterizes the new requirement to self-market and self-promote as 'the dark downside to all the … potential that the internet … brings. … There's nobody else to help you project yourself' (in CIRAA 2008). Those interested in securing financial backing or help with promotion from record labels or other business partners are tasked with leveraging online platforms as a way of tracking and quantifying their popularity and, hence, pitching their potential commercial viability (Morris 2014: 276). Effective use of these tools is not simply a matter of publicizing tours and music releases: 'artists are finding that there are potentially new demands on what they must do to keep their fan base animated and connected, requiring much more than just making good music' (Powers 2013: 320). While continual 'interaction' and 'engagement' with fans may be a rewarding experience, it can also be very time consuming. Time is at a premium in an industry where many independent artists support their creative endeavors by working part-time jobs. This reflects the fact that music income remains scarce for most.

As a study conducted by the Future of Music Coalition (2012) demonstrates, the widespread assumption that 'musicians are rich' is entirely inaccurate. The organization's online survey of over 5,000 American musicians and composers suggests an average gross music income of $34,455 USD (Future of Music Coalition 2012). What must be considered when interpreting these figures is that this survey included classical and salaried musicians and, again, the figures cited are gross and as such do not account for expenses incurred. A report commissioned by the Canadian Independent Music Association (CIMA) yielded bleaker findings. It revealed average individual artist earnings of $7,228 CAD for 'music-related activities' in 2011 – a sum derived from an estimate of 29 hours of music-related work per week and based on a study that involved the participation of over 1,000 Canadian independent artists (Nordicity 2013: 29). While key details remain somewhat opaque (What are the net income figures? What constitutes a music-related activity?), it is apparent that fair remuneration remains a problem for non-star music makers.

Overall, widespread excitement over falling costs of technology has overshadowed a primary source of cost savings under digital DIY models: unpaid labor. In fact, many of these approaches seem to entail what Kathleen Kuehn and Thomas F. Corrigan term 'hope labor': 'un- or under-compensated work carried out in the present, often for experience or exposure, in the hope that future employment opportunities may follow' (Kuehn and Corrigan 2013: 10). While their analysis focuses on web-based companies Yelp and SB Nation, their conclusions strike a chord more widely. There is a temporal dimension to hope labor – people are willing to work for very little in the short term in the hope that it will pay off in the long term – but in so doing, 'hope laborers undermine the very labor market that they aspire to enter by continually supplying it with individuals who are willing to work for nothing' (Kuehn and Corrigan 2013: 20). Pay-to-play schemes, plummeting music licensing fees, encircling contracts, shrinking advances, and negligible streaming revenues render the idea that anyone can 'make it' in the new music industry problematic. Who can afford to work for free and for how long? What does it even mean to make it? What are the consequences of this situation for the diversity of creative expression?

Concluding thoughts

This chapter has outlined a distinct set of challenges faced by unsigned and independent music makers today. Work inside the music industry has always been complex. It involves three distinct sectors – recording, music publishing, and live performance – which monetize music in different ways and place different expectations on music makers. The emergence of the artist-brand paradigm, however, has required major label and DIY music makers alike to experiment with new ways to make a living from making music, leveraging their image as a core 'asset'. The popular notion that 'new technologies are driving a mesh-like networking model with flattened hierarchies' (Young and Collins 2010: 340) is complicated by the continued dominance of the major record companies, which have effectively shored up interests across the various music sectors. Financial rewards continue to be distributed in a profoundly uneven way, with a handful of superstars achieving incredible wealth and the majority of working artists struggling for fair remuneration.

The changing contours of music-related work and new forms of promotional work warrant more in-depth empirical investigation. Future research might flesh out details regarding artist income and expenses, contracts and licensing agreement terms, time allocated to making music versus promoting music and performing administrative tasks, and the potential for artist collectives and unions to help counter the race to the bottom that many new music business models encourage. It also ought to consider the relationship between professional opportunities and gender, ethnicity, social class, sexual orientation, and age. The diversity of musical sounds and ideas surely is contingent on the diversity of those afforded a voice. Media coverage of the empowering potential of the new music industry tends to focus on the success stories – on those who take full advantage of new tools and opportunities and rise above the rest against the odds. While lessons regarding how to achieve career longevity might be gleaned from such cases, many more lessons could be learned from the experiences of those who do not make it and instead remain at the music industry's periphery. Only through developing a more nuanced understanding of the various hurdles facing music makers might we begin to forge workable strategies for overcoming those obstacles.

References

Billboard (2009) 'The Decade in Music: Top 10 Trends of the Last Ten Years', *Billboard*, December 19.

Byrne, D. (2013) 'David Byrne: The Internet Will Suck All Creative Content out of the World', *Guardian*, October 11, available at www.theguardian.com/music/2013/oct/11/david-byrne-internet-content-world (accessed January 19, 2014).

Christman, E. (2014) 'Digital Music Sales Decrease for First Time in 2013', *Billboard.biz*, January 3, available at www.billboard.com/biz/articles/news/digital-and-mobile/5855162/digital-music-sales-decrease-for-first-time-in-2013 (accessed April 2, 2014).

CIRAA (Canadian Independent Recording Artists Association) (2008) 'Introduction', *The New Indie: Making a Living Making Music* (podcast on CD).

Digital Music News (2011) 'The Number of New Releases is Suddenly Nosediving ... ', *Digital Music News*, February 18.

Fitterman Radbill, C. (2013) *Introduction to the Music Industry: An Entrepreneurial Approach*, London: Routledge.

Future of Music Coalition (2012) 'Mythbusting: Data Driven Answers to Four Common Assumptions About How Musicians Make Money', *Future of Music Coalition*, available at money.futureofmusic.org/mythbusting/2/ (accessed October 13, 2013).

Garnham, N. (1990) *Capitalism and Communication: Global Culture and the Economics of Information*, London: Sage.

Goodman, F. (2008) 'Rock's New Economy: Making Money When CDs Don't Sell', *Rolling Stone*, May 29.

Herstand, A. (2014) 'Want to Know What a Big Time Manager Says to Indie Bands?' *Digital Music News*, April 30, available at www.digitalmusicnews.com/permalink/2014/04/30/youre-selling-tickets-t-shirts-dont-even-matter (accessed May 3, 2014).

Hesmondhalgh, D. (2013) *The Cultural Industries* (3rd edn), London: Sage.

Kuehn, K. and Corrigan, T. F. (2013) 'Hope Labor: The Role of Employment Prospects in Online Social Production', *The Political Economy of Communication* 1 (1): 9–25.

Kulash, D. (2010) 'The New Rock-Star Paradigm', *Wall Street Journal*, December 17, available at online.wsj.com/news/articles/SB10001424052748703727804576017592259031536 (accessed April 15, 2014).

Laing, D. (2009) 'World Music and the Global Music Industry: Flows, Corporations and Networks', *Collegium* 6: 14–33, available at https://helda.helsinki.fi/bitstream/handle/10138/25811/006_03_Laing.pdf?sequence=1 (accessed April 15, 2014).

Marshall, L. (2013) 'The 360 Deal and the "New" Music Industry', *European Journal of Cultural Studies* 16 (1): 77–99.

Meier, L. M. (2013) *Promotional Ubiquitous Musics: New Identities and Emerging Markets in the Digitalizing Music Industry*, unpublished Ph.D. thesis, University of Western Ontario.

Morris, J. W. (2014) 'Artists as Entrepreneurs, Fans as Workers', *Popular Music and Society* 37 (3): 273–90.

Negus, K. (1992) *Producing Pop: Culture and Conflict in the Popular Music Industry*, London: Edward Arnold.

Nordicity. (2013) *Sound Analysis: An Examination of the Canadian Independent Music Industry*, Report Commissioned by Canadian Independent Music Association, available at www.nordicity.com/media/201336fjtnrdeunp.pdf (accessed April 20, 2014).

Passman, D. S. (2012) *All You Need to Know about the Music Business* (8th edn), New York: Free Press.

Peoples, G. (2011) 'Business Matters: 75,000 Albums Released in U.S. in 2010 – Down 22% From 2009,' *Billboard.biz*, February 18, available at http://www.billboard.com/biz/articles/news/1179201/business-matters-75000-albums-released-in-us-in-2010-down-22-from-2009 (accessed April 2, 2014).

PledgeMusic (2014) *CJ Wildheart PledgeMusic Profile*, available at www.pledgemusic.com/artists/cjwildheart (accessed May 3, 2014).

Powers, D. (2013) 'Now Hear This: The Promotion of Music', in M. McAllister and E. West (eds) *The Routledge Companion to Advertising and Promotional Culture*, New York: Routledge, 313–25.

Resnikoff, P. (2014) 'The Top 1% of Artists Earn 77% of Recorded Music Income, Study Finds … ', *Digital Music News*, March 5, available at www.digitalmusicnews.com/permalink/2014/03/05/toponepercent (accessed April 8, 2014).

Ruen, C. (2012) *Freeloading: How Our Insatiable Hunger for Free Content Starves Creativity* (Kindle e-book), New York: OR Books.

Schultz, M. F. (2009) 'Live Performance, Copyright, and the Future of the Music Business', *University of Richmond Law Review* 43 (2): 685–764.

Sisario, B. (2010) 'Looking to a Sneaker for a Band's Big Break', *New York Times*, October 10, available at www.nytimes.com/2010/10/10/arts/music/10brand.html?pagewanted=all (accessed April 4, 2014).

Sisario, B. (2013) 'Defining and Demanding a Musician's Fair Shake in the Internet Age', *New York Times*, September 30, available at www.nytimes.com/2013/10/01/business/media/defining-and-demanding-a-musicians-fair-shake-in-the-internet-age.html?_r=0&pagewanted=print (accessed April 19, 2014).

Stahl, M. and Meier, L. M. (2012) 'The Firm Foundation of Organizational Flexibility: The 360 Contract in the Digitalizing Music Industry', *Canadian Journal of Communication* 37 (3): 441–58.

UK Music (2013) *The Economic Contribution of the Core UK Music Industry*, London: UK Music, available at http://www.ukmusic.org/assets/general/Summary_Document_-_The_Economic_Contribution_of_the_Core_UK_Music_Industry.pdf (accessed April 20, 2014).

Williamson, J. and Cloonan, M. (2007) 'Rethinking the Music Industry', *Popular Music* 26 (2): 306–22.

Young, S. and Collins, S. (2010) 'A View from the Trenches of Music 2.0', *Popular Music and Society* 33 (3): 339–55.

33
SPORT, MEDIA AND AUDIENCES

David Rowe

Introduction: The sporting and the cultural

There is important but well-trodden ground that this *Companion* has necessarily addressed – how does an industry qualify as cultural? The debate will not be rehearsed here (cf. Redhead, this volume), except in so far as it is necessary to introduce the specific cultural form of sport and to situate it within debates about culture and the cultural industries. It has been historically common for some, especially artists and their advocates, to criticize the influence of sport on culture and creativity, complaining that it is anti-intellectual, unaesthetic, aggressive and instrumental, and that it tends to crowd out more deserving cultural pursuits both in public culture and in competition over state and corporate sponsorship (see, for example, Atherden, 2009; Thurman, 2010). This debate is part of a larger one on culture and entertainment that must be set aside here in favour of more directly relevant concerns with sport as a 'borderline and problem case', according to Hesmondhalgh (2013: 19–20), who singles out sport for particular attention in a manner that is worth pursuing in this context:

> Sport industries such as football (soccer) and baseball arrange for the per-
> formance of live spectacles that are, in many respects, very like the live
> entertainment sector of the cultural industries. People pay to be entertained
> in real time in the co-presence of talented or not-that-talented performers.
> But there are notable differences, even from live entertainment in the cultural
> industries. Sport is fundamentally competitive, whereas symbol making
> isn't. Texts (in the sense in which I use the term in this book) tend to be
> more scripted or scored than in sports, which are essentially improvised
> around a set of competitive rules.

This division of sport from 'core cultural industries' can be continuously canvassed, but it should be noted that football, baseball and other sport forms are not so much industries in themselves as sub sets of something that is much larger and more diverse. This industry is inseparable from the 'media sports cultural complex' (a concept developed out of earlier formulations by Jhally, 1984 and Maguire, 1993) that 'embraces all the *media* and sports organizations, processes, personnel, services, products and *texts* which combine in the creation of the broad, dynamic field of contemporary sports culture' (Rowe, 2004: 216). The synthetic notion of a complex is more appropriate than the singular concept of a sport industry because, since the second half of the twentieth century and, especially, following the widespread installation of television in the domestic sphere, it has been increasingly difficult to isolate the sport industry from the media (especially its broadcasting sub set) industry.

Wenner (1998: xiii), in an influential eponymous anthology, has proposed that the 'cultural fusing of sport with communication has resulted in a new genetic strain called *MediaSport*'. Crucially, this cultural fusing is also an industrial interpenetration through which sport, 'both as content and as medium of communication' (p. xiii), has become inextricably intertwined with the media, creating a hybridic cultural industrial phenomenon in which it is increasingly difficult to establish where sport begins and its mediation ends. The most striking – compulsively referred to as 'spectacular' – exemplification of the media sports cultural complex in action is witnessed during events such as the opening ceremony of the Summer Olympic Games, the FIFA World Cup Final or the Super Bowl. At such moments, as Dayan and Katz (1992: 25) conceive it, sport events can be defined as 'media events' with predictably and carefully constructed scripts and narratives involving 'contest', 'conquest' or 'coronation'. The most important mediated sport text involves live competition, which combines essential competitive outcome uncertainty with semi-improvised interpretive commentary scripts. A well-known example of this phenomenon is the sending off for violent conduct of the French captain Zinedine Zidane in the FIFA World Cup Final against Italy in Germany in 2006 (an incident that is photographically captured on the cover of Young, 2012). The live audience for the match exceeded a billion although, ironically, it only saw the famous headbutt on replay because it occurred when the gaze of the cameras was directed to the moving ball. This was not 'just a sport story' as, following accusations that Zidane was reacting to racist abuse, it became a global front-page, lead-news item inquisition as to what was said to him by opponent Marco Materazzi, even involving the enlistment of teams of multilingual lip readers (Rowe, 2010). This intimate involvement of the media – both as carrier of live mediated sport and conductor of the ensuing *post mortem* – inevitably meant that the 'sport audience' expanded to include many more people who did not watch the match in real time or, indeed, had even heard of Zinedine Zidane before he became notorious in the non-sport news.

The widescale cultural reach of sport through the media means that, far from the field of play, even a scripted live press conference such as golfer Tiger Woods' apology for serial philandering or the 2010 announcement (grandly dubbed 'The Decision') by basketballer LeBron James of his chosen new team, can become the biggest news item of the day in some countries (Griffin and Phillips, 2014; Rowe, 2011a). At such moments, the sport industry becomes rather more than merely content for the media industry, and the media's role is greater than that of vehicle for the symbolic diffusion of sport. Their interpenetration – which in some cases is accentuated by media corporations (such as Disney, Liberty Media, Mediaset and News Corporation) owning sport clubs, and competitions and governing bodies operating their own substantial media operations (including Manchester United, Real Madrid, Australian

Football League, National Football League, Indian Premier League and the International Olympic Committee) – suggests the progressive hybridization of mediasport. This trend is evident at many levels and in diverse forms because unmediated sport is now almost unimaginable, to the degree that it is subject to *mediatization* – that is, the shaping of sport by the demands of the media – as well as a corresponding *sportization* of media, whereby some forms of media, such as competitive 'reality TV', take on many of the characteristics of live sport contests (*pace* Hesmondhalgh's 'fundamental' distinction between competition and symbol making).

In focusing on the most commercially saleable aspect of mediasport, the live contest performed in a specific space and time and relayed audio-visually to large, dispersed and heterogeneous audiences (a conventional definition of mass communication), the audience's role in the mediasport text is a pivotal one. This is because the audience is a significant component of the text that it is consuming – the co-present audience is performing both for those in the stadium and for those who are watching on a range of media devices, supplying essential atmosphere, ambience, drama and colour in the creation of vibrant mediasport spectacle. Thus, the co-present sport audience is inscribed into the text and contributes significantly to its exchange value as something that, quite apart from the performance of athletes in the stadium, offers its own pleasurable spectacle and communicates, through mass, noise, movement and visual signification, that what is being represented on screen is important and, indeed, part of the 'live broadcasting of history' (the sub-title of Dayan and Katz's aforementioned work). Thus, a key element of the media sports cultural complex is the involvement of fans as co-producers as well as consumers (as is also discussed by Cornell Sandvoss in this volume). But the audience of a relatively small number of co-present sport spectators is part of a much larger and dynamic mixtures of 'active fans', dedicated sport media consumers and 'incidental' viewers and readers temporarily attracted by high-profile media coverage. This complex interaction of sport, media and audiences most resembles, among cultural industries, music (especially rock and pop – McLeod, 2011; Rowe, 1995), but the live moment is not as dominant in that field. Sport has no equivalent of the music studio, its locker rooms, training grounds and gymnasia preparing athletes for performance of the live text in public rather than operating as the spaces of technology that produce a key text in its own right (the recorded work). As competitive physical culture, sport does not need media technology in order to be practised, but as noted above it is essential if it is to transcend the limits of space and time in being communicated to distant others. The mass-scale industrial development of sport relied, therefore, on the simultaneous development of another institutional product of modernity – the media.

The sport–media nexus

It is important to understand the historical underpinning of sport and media's co-dependency and progressive interpenetration as a synthetic cultural industry. What we now recognize as sport developed out of the rationalization of folk physical play, which was usually intermittent, informal, and non- or lowly remunerated. Sport contests gradually industrialized, with competitive spaces becoming enclosed so that there could be a charge for entry, and the provision of ancillary services, notably gambling on outcomes and hospitality, in and around sport stadia. As a result, professional athletic careers became more common, involving tours by paid sport performers who played the locals at various sports and also exhibited their athletic skills. As more interaction took place between sportspeople from different areas, and more money was wagered on the outcomes of contests, rules and procedures need to be rationalized and standardized. Sport governing bodies were established to set these rules, taking on an international character in the late nineteenth and early twentieth centuries, thereby enabling standardized sporting competition between nations as well as within them (Guttmann, 2004). The industrialization of sport advanced through a range of developments: regular competitions (leagues and cups), paid performers, paying spectators, sport apparel, equipment and merchandising manufacture, and so on. In many countries, the state played a stimulating role in the growth of the sport industry through compulsory sport and physical education in schools (Hargreaves, 1986), as well as in early expressions of what came to be known as 'sport[s] diplomacy' (Murray, 2013).

Audiences at embodied sport contests, generally known as 'crowds', congregated in home venues or travelled, along with the sport players and their support staff, to away venues, or to the spaces designated for intermittent multi-sport events like the Olympics. In these respects it can be seen that sport, like live theatre and music, was limited by its formative reliance on embodiment and physical practice. But sport, like those other cultural forms, has never been confined entirely within the moment, and 'intelligence' about it has been communicated for centuries in newspapers that reported results and described sport contests that had already happened (Harris, 1998). As sport contests became more organized and frequent, they took up increasing space in newspapers and developed their own sections, and specialist sport newspapers and magazines also emerged. Simple sport event reportage became much more extensive, with a range of hard and soft news about sport responding to the growing scale of industry and audience. Successive new media technologies, such as radio and news-reels, made this mediation of sport more diverse, while still sport photography enhanced written text and sport became the subject of drama and documentary film, novels, digital games, and so on (Rowe, 2004). Of all media technologies, television, with its flexible capacity to show sport events live to far away spectators, carry sport news and current affairs, and broadcast sport-based quiz shows, discussion programmes and documentaries, has been most significant in insinuating sport into multiple cultural spaces. Television also became crucial to the economics of sport not merely by publicizing it but by directly funding it through the increasingly inflated purchase of broadcast rights to popular sport contests. This 'marriage made in heaven' consummates the union that is mediasport and shows no sign of waning – in fact, the reverse is the case (Hutchins and Rowe, 2012). That the cost of premium sport broadcast rights has steadily escalated in the last three decades could suggest the very opposite of a union – that the sport industry is instrumentally exacting a price for its service from the media. But although ownership structures and share registries are by no means irrelevant, the sport–media nexus, set within the larger media sports cultural complex, is much greater than the sum of its constituent parts. In this sense the relationship can be represented as one of co-dependency.

The most important professional sports (various forms of football, tennis, golf, cricket, motor racing, and so on) and the major multi-sport competitions (like the Olympic, Commonwealth and Asian Games) all rely heavily on sport broadcast rights and media exposure. Yet, as in most areas of investment and representation, those who supply the capital are unlikely to be 'sleeping partners' and their textual product will not be 'innocent'. If corporations are to inject large amounts of capital into a sport, they will necessarily seek to reduce risk in the task environment of finding audiences and maximizing return on investment. The resultant *mediatization* of sport mentioned above takes many forms. At its most obvious there is the television-inspired re-drafting of the rules and routines of sport. Among the best known of these are tennis tie-breaks that help prevent disruption to television schedules because of very lengthy matches; television timeouts of variable duration that impose a mandatory pause in play in order to enable advertising to occur; and scheduling of sports such as boxing, cricket, football and athletics so that contests occur in pri-metime for the largest, most commercially important audiences. But there are many other clear examples of the influence of television on sport, from the privileging of 'telegenic' contact sports in which collisions can be replayed at multiple speeds, constant rule changes (such as in the rugby codes) that speed up play to avoid action 'dead spots' that could negatively affect viewer decisions, and visual innovations in sporting dress codes to make them more attractive to the casual viewer (here the sexualization of sportswomen in particular is a pressing issue). While there may be resistance among sport organizations and individuals to pressure to be as television-friendly as possible, they operate in internal and external competitive environments that make it difficult to accept lower or no broadcast rights funding because of commercial media calculations of value. It should also be pointed out that the nation-state, which has underwritten sport in most cases and has championed it in almost all of them, makes its own demands on sport, in particular by requiring that national sport teams encourage appropriately positive representations of their nation in global media (Rowe, 2011b).

The physical moving text that is a sport contest is, in the hands of the media, inevitably changed and even transformed by its sustained mediation. Indeed, in cases where in-stadium atmosphere is not viewed as being as important as a viewing audience and ancillary activity (such as sport betting), made-for-television sport programming can be found within the schedules of, especially, digital multi-channels. This does not mean that sports without a high media profile will disappear and, indeed, what appears consistently on screen is only the tip of a much larger sporting iceberg where play from junior to adult lower grade levels is likely to receive little mediation beyond rudimentary uploaded YouTube footage and a results announcement in local or community media. But without a high-end showcase, such sports are likely to move back in the direction of their origins as place-dependent physical activity, in contrast to the global drift and diffusion of the most conspicuous sports.

However, while in the final analysis sport needs the media to survive more than the other way round, sport content has never been so important to the media, and especially to television. As is well known, the digitization of media and the rise of online, social and mobile media have precipitated a fragmentation of audiences. At the peak of analogue media, large audiences could be routinely attracted to a small number of mastheads and broadcast networks, but digitization greatly expanded content choices and permitted unprecedented multiple-media platform use and time shifting. Again, this does not mean that established media brands and technologies are disappearing (indeed, their enduring power and advantage is much underestimated), but they have had to work much harder at audience building and retention (Hutchins and Rowe, 2012). Sport functions as a crucial readymade assembly point for substantial media audiences. As discussed above, the live mediated sport event constitutes a rare form of 'appointment' or 'event' television (and radio) that reliably draws large, sometimes vast audiences to it in a manner that was formerly much more common across television genres when viewing choice was limited and viewing schedules predetermined. Observing how television can create its own live events by mimicking the competitive dimensions of sport, it has created forms of 'reality' programme which, sometimes in front of a live audience, adopt much of the grammar of sport television, from the constructions of heroes and villains to the cutaways and close-ups that show the contestant under duress (Rowe, 2011a). These signs of *sportization* of the media are manifest in the increasing physicality of television, with even newsreaders now commonly shown on their feet and in motion.

Newspapers have retained substantial pages that offer sport analysis, gossip and photography, and in their web-based versions can be supplemented by audio-visual sport action. The Internet, which is the site of media convergence, is also the space where sport generates vast traffic that runs through and between institutional and social media. It is hardly surprising, therefore, that among the organizations that have helped to inflate not only sport media rights – that is, those pertaining to sport across multiple platforms, not just broadcasting – are telecommunications companies and Internet service providers (Hutchins and Rowe, 2012). So, just as sport would find it difficult to thrive without the media, how could the latter find predictably large and reliable audiences for exposure to advertisers, subscribers to pay-TV, consumers to sign up for applications for 4G mobile devices, enthusiastic and loyal readers for dedicated newspaper sections, radio listeners for talk stations, and so on, without sport? The audiences that they would assemble without sport would likely be more elusive, less numerous and, in many cases, less affluent and/or willing to part with their disposable income. This point turns the discussion more directly towards the anatomy of the mediasport audience, the subject of considerable perturbation among the cultural industries that rely on them while being anxious about their practices and intentions in uncertain times.

Sport and its many audiences

Audiences are conventionally corralled as singular entities despite the evidence of media research that they are, to a considerable degree, a construct of the process on interpellation rather than of taxonomy (see various contributions to Nightingale, 2011). As noted, the sport audience is both unstable and consists of people with wildly different orientations, ranging from the fanatically engaged to the enjoined detached, the latter being the everyday citizen who at times such as sharing a city/ country with a mega media sport event, could only avoid sport via a coma-like condition or media blackout. Mediasport audiences are not only divided by their orientation to sport and use of media, but also stratified by both their commercial value and fan status (the latter qualities often in conflict). This shifting landscape of mediated sport and those who attend to it requires a fuller appreciation, beginning from the originating space of sport spectatorship.

As observed earlier, sport as professional, rationalized competitive physical practice emerged out of highly localized environments, first in rural folk life and then in industrialized urban environments. The territoriality that first marked competitive sport has not been entirely destroyed by its mass mediation. In particular, fans of the various football codes value place of origin and propinquity – that is, 'real' fans claim privilege by coming from the same place as their team (in terms of home stadium, club headquarters and principal identifying catchment area). This topophilia is highly mythologized, often evoking nostalgia for very different times when, for example, football stadia were in densely packed urban environments alongside their mainly working-class fans rather than in green field purpose-built sites accessed by car; when players earned modest wages, lived alongside the people who watched them, and were neither socially nor geographically mobile to any major degree; when – with more than a tinge of racism or ethnocentrism – players, club officials and fans were socially and culturally homogeneous; and, finally, when sport fans were less media dependent and access to sport events via television more difficult. For obvious practical reasons, the fans who pay to enter the stadium regularly (and, as noted, form a crucial part of the audio-visual sport text) are valuable club assets, especially through season tickets and merchandising. But they are also major consumers and users of sport media of all kinds – newspapers, subscription television, fan websites and so on. This 'captive' market, while important in anchoring sport to place and history, is nonetheless insufficient to allow the development of a global sport industry.

Hence, important national sport league competitions (including the English Premier League and Spain's La Liga in association football, and the USA's National Basketball Association, National Football League, Major League Soccer and Baseball), bolstered by international competitions such as the European Champions League and the FIFA World Cup, are carried via television and the Internet to new markets, especially in the growing Asia-Pacific region, seeking to stimulate fan bases in parts of the world far distant from the cities and countries with which they are identified. This practice sets up a tension between 'authentic' fans who were 'born' to support a team or particular players, and those regarded as 'inauthentic' or 'fickle' by exercising consumer choices prompted by slick sport marketing. From a commercial perspective, however, global sport brand development is highly desirable, although it requires a careful negotiation between continuity and novelty. Longstanding fans must be reassured and new fans welcomed, with the former expected to relinquish some of their proprietorial rights for the good of the club, and accepting foreign ownership, players and fans. In franchise-based leagues such as those that predominate in North America, these fans may also be asked to continue supporting teams that have not only moved to other cities and regions, but may have crossed national boundaries (such as National Hockey League teams in Canada and the United States).

The mobility of the mediasport industry, therefore, is both physical and symbolic, with teams moving to and visiting markets, and mediasport texts finding audiences irrespective of their physical location. 'Travelling circuits' in tennis, golf, motor racing, cycling, athletics and so on most obviously represent this material and symbolic mobility, while the development of a global/transnational athletic labour force under what has been called the New International Division of Cultural Labour (Miller et al., 2001) has provoked disputes about, for example, what is English about an English Premier League dominated by non-English owners, managers, coaches and players, or questioned the national credentials of the 'Plastic Brits' who represented Team GB during the London 2012 Olympic Games without being born in that country. Such flows of capital and labour have, in Giddens's terms (1990), a disembedding effect (as Rumford (2011) has argued of Twenty20 cricket), but also with a range of re-embedding permutations. In cases where sport clubs have financially collapsed, been taken over or relocated, fans may as members own (in whole or in part) and administer sport clubs (member ownership is an integral part of organizational history in cases such as Barcelona Football Club). The most audacious – though failed – instance of 'executive fandom' (Rowe, 2011b), and one that sought to combine club emplacement with Internet-based organizational model, is that of MyFootballClub in Britain, which garnered a worldwide group of members to buy a football club (the semi-professional club Ebbsfleet United in southern England) under the motto 'Own the Club, Pick the Team' as part of the 'world's first web community owned club'. Although this sport club arrangement did not achieve its original aim of deciding team composition and tactics through an online vote of members, it did make collective online decisions on such matters as team colours, sponsors and ticket prices. Because of its dependence on the Internet with, at its peak, 32,000 members across all continents (although with the majority in Britain), MyFootballClub pointed to a deeper intrication of sport, communication and media. That it also foundered because of local disputation, unrealistic expectations and significant member attrition after the novelty of running a football club online had worn off should not be taken as a conclusive end to sport initiatives that seek to combine spatial grounding with mobile identity and operation (Hutchins and Rowe, 2012).

Although this discussion necessarily began with the most dedicated forms of sport fandom, it cannot stop there. There are many more in the notional audience for sport who have neither the capacity nor the interest to help run it, and are content to treat sport as a part of the suite of cultural fare available to them and engaged with according to taste. They may be interested in only one or a limited number of sports, or be heavy consumers of a multitude of sports made available to them through dedicated TV sport channels and websites. Most of the audience available for sport is necessarily culturally omnivorous or opportunistic. For example, during the Olympic Games or other mega media sport events, audiences are likely to be drawn to sport in very large numbers for reasons of saturation media coverage and nationalism. Sport mega events create the impressive numbers that prompt intimations of the global village, but they are intermittent occasions and their audience typically segmented by nation (Rowe, 2011b). At such times, and more generally with regard to major national sport events, a familiar debate arises over whether sport audiences should be construed as consumers exercising consumptive choices or citizens exercising their rights to national public culture.

These questions concerning national cultural citizenship have their origins in the development of national broadcasting systems that in many parts of the world (notably Europe, Asia, Africa and South America) were once dominated by public service broadcasters responsible for the development of televised sport (the USA is a signal exception to this history). Live broadcast sport events became one of the pivotal nation-building features on the media landscape, showing the nation united in common cultural pursuit in an enhancement of socio-cultural solidarity. As televised sport became clearly lucrative, the public service monopoly was lost, and advertising-based commercial free-to-air television networks permitted to monopolise it on the grounds of universal availability (which was already largely the case in the United States). However, as the economic potency of sport television became even more obvious, premium live sport began to migrate further to subscription television platforms, which immediately installed a barrier to access for those of insufficient means (such as the substantial capture of broadcasting the English Premier League by the Murdoch-controlled BSkyB, a highly profitable arrangement that saved the company). Public anxiety about the disappearance behind a paywall of what in Australia, for example, are called 'events of national importance and cultural significance', has been allayed in many countries by the use of legislated anti-siphoning lists that prevent the capture of some major sport events by subscription television, or by the implied threat of anti-trust intervention to break up sporting monopolies (see various contributions to Scherer and Rowe, 2014). During the often-heated debates about sport, media and cultural citizenship, the crucial importance of the media–sport nexus is starkly illuminated, and the familiar tensions over citizen-consumers and the cultural industries replayed in an unfamiliar context for many cultural policy researchers.

Conclusion: Mediasport industrial futures

Sport occupies a rather awkward (if not anomalous) place in considerations of culture, as is evident in the UK's Department for Culture, Media and Sport, where it is both co-located in governmental terms but also distinguished through nomination and internal organization. Conflicts over the positioning of the Cultural Olympiad that accompany each Olympic Games (Collins and Palmer, 2012) highlight such tensions of cultural positioning not evident in the 1896 revival of the Modern Games by Baron Pierre de Coubertin, with its integration of athletic and aesthetic competition. In contrast, the Harvard business academic Anita Elberse (2013) includes sport among film, television, music and book publishing conceived as entertainment sectors rather than as cultural industries, with the business models of Hollywood studios and football clubs like Real Madrid shown to have many similarities. Elberse, though, sets aside the questions of cultural value and symbol making that permeate cultural industries discourse.

This chapter has argued that the convergence of media and sport as mediasport is so advanced it has substantially decentred matters of primary symbol making and functionality. This does not mean that these are entirely smooth synergies or unproblematic alliances. The separate histories of the institutions and mostly distinct ownership and operational structures continue to produce tensions. This dynamism is exacerbated by the development of 'networked media sport' (Hutchins and Rowe,

2012), which has problematized the hegemony of broadcast television in the media-sports cultural complex while witnessing the incorporation of proprietorial social media services, such as Twitter and Facebook, as agencies feeding the parasocial 'buzz' that has helped to create record television audiences for major sport events. In turn, this continual audience expansion and deepened communication–mediasport engagement has both raised the value of broadcast sport rights and encouraged large tele-communication companies like BT and Internet companies such as Google to move into the guaranteed meeting place of mediated sport. At the same time, sport organiza-tions have expanded their media operations and foreshadowed the vertical integration of the production of sport events and their mediation. Ironically, this sport material will pass through the 'pipes', including Internet Protocol Television (IPTV), that will ensure the remuneration of the Internet companies that supply them. This arrange-ment, just as it has done previously with broadcasters, will encourage another form of vertical integration – the mediator owning the content producer (otherwise known as a sport club or company) and disseminating its content. Either way – sport organizations becoming mediasport producers or mediasport producers taking over sport organizations – the relationship between media and sport will inevitably intensify. The only likely check on this industrial convergence will be the state (both national and supranational), in the name of competitive markets and also cultural citizenship, and the citizen-consumers who constitute the mediasport audience, some-times in the capacity of co-producers. The mediasports cultural complex, therefore, remains a dynamic site of contemporary culture that continues to confound the more orthodox analyses and taxonomies of the cultural industries.

References

Atherden, G. (2009) 'Art versus Sport – Oh Yes, and Money', *Griffith Review* 23, https://griffith review.com/articles/art-and-sport-oh-yes-and-money/.

Collins, S. and Palmer, C. (2012) 'Taste, Ambiguity and the Cultural Olympiad', in J. Sugden and A. Tomlinson (eds) *Watching the Games: Politics, Power and Representation in the London Olympiad*. London and New York: Routledge, 138–50.

Dayan, D. and Katz, E. (1992) *Media Events: The Live Broadcasting of History*. Cambridge, MA: Harvard University Press.

Elberse, A. (2013) *Blockbusters: Hit-making, Risk-taking, and the Big Business of Entertainment*. New York: Henry Holt.

Giddens, A. (1990) *The Consequences of Modernity*. Cambridge: Polity.

Griffin, R.A. and Phillips, J.D. (2014) 'Lebron James as Cybercolonized Spectacle: A Critical Race Reading of Whiteness in Sport', in B. Brummett and A.W. Ishak (eds) *Sport and Identity*. New York: Routledge, 60–82.

Guttmann, A. (2004) *From Ritual to Record: The Nature of Modern Sports*. New York: Columbia University Press.

Hargreaves, J. (1986) *Sport, Power and Culture: A Social and Historical Analysis of Popular Sports in Britain*. Cambridge: Polity.

Harris, M. (1998) 'Sport in the Newspapers before 1750: Representations of Cricket, Class and Commerce in the London Press', *Media History*, 4(1): 19–28.

Hesmondhalgh, D. (2013) *The Cultural Industries* (third edition). London: Sage.

Hutchins, B. and Rowe, D. (2012) *Sport Beyond Television: The Internet, Digital Media and the Rise of Networked Media Sport*. New York: Routledge.

Jhally, S. (1984) 'The Spectacle of Accumulation: Material and Cultural Factors in the Evolution of the Sports/Media Complex', *The Insurgent Sociologist*, 12(3): 41–57.

Maguire, J. (1993) 'Globalization, Sport Development, and the Media/Sport Production Complex', *Sport Science Review*, 2(1): 29–47.

McLeod, K. (2011) *We Are the Champions: The Politics of Sports and Popular Music*. Burlington, VT: Ashgate.

Miller, T., Lawrence, G., McKay, J. and Rowe, D. (2001) *Globalization and Sport: Playing the World*. London: Sage.

Murray, S. (2013) 'Sports Diplomacy in the Australian Context: A Case Study of the Department of Foreign Affairs and Trade', *Sports Law eJournal*, ISSN 1836–1129, epublications. bond.edu.au/slej/18/.

Nightingale, V. (ed.) (2011) *Handbook of Media Audiences*. Oxford: Wiley-Blackwell.

Rowe, D. (1995) *Popular Cultures: Rock Music, Sport and the Politics of Pleasure*. London: Sage.

Rowe, D. (2004) *Sport, Culture and the Media: The Unruly Trinity*. Maidenhead, UK: Open University Press.

Rowe, D. (2010) 'Stages of the Global: Media, Sport, Racialization and the Last Temptation of Zinedine Zidane', *International Review for the Sociology of Sport*, 45(3): 355–71.

Rowe, D. (2011a) 'Sports Media: Beyond Broadcasting, Beyond Sports, Beyond Societies?', in A. Billings (ed.) *Sports Media: Transformation, Integration, Consumption*. New York: Routledge, 94–113.

Rowe, D. (2011b) *Global Media Sport: Flows, Forms and Futures*. London and New York: Bloomsbury Academic.

Rumford, C. (2011) 'Twenty20, Global Disembedding and the Rise of the "Portfolio Player"', *Sport in Society*, 14(10): 1369–82.

Scherer, J. and Rowe, D. (eds) (2014) *Sport, Public Broadcasting, and Cultural Citizenship: Signal Lost?* New York: Routledge.

Thurman, C. (ed.) (2010) *Sport versus Art: A South African Contest*. Johannesburg: Wits University Press.

Wenner, L.A. (ed.) (1998) *MediaSport*. London: Routledge.

Young, K. (2012). Sport, Violence and Society. New York: Routledge.

Part VI

POLICY AND THE CULTURAL INDUSTRIES

Most of the chapters in this volume have implicit or explicit policy consequences and concerns; in this section we have chapters that directly address some of the changing policy structures and issues that directly affect the cultural industries. Following on from Part IV on cultural labour, Catherine Murray attempts to outline a framework within which social welfare rights can be made applicable to those working in the cultural industries. Whilst not denying the specificity of cultural labour she also tries to find ways in which their interests might intersect and join with other groups in calling for appropriate social welfare legislation.

Caitriona Noonan explores another crucial element of policies for the cultural (and creative) industries – higher education. The importance of higher education to these highly skilled sectors is so obvious that it often goes without closer examination. What Noonan finds is a higher education sector that has adopted a completely instrumentalised version of its links to the cultural sector. Organised under the rubric of industry engagement, it has often ignored the complex, multi-levelled connections between staff and students and the cultural sector. Noonan charts the changing relation between these two sectors over the last three decades and suggests that the possibilities and potential for dialogue in these areas have been sacrificed to a higher education sector increasingly given over to the market and a cultural/creative industries policy exclusively focused on innovation and economic growth.

Dave O'Brien, by contrast, focuses on the changing outline of the British State and how this is related to the adoption of the creative industries agenda in the late 1990s. Rather than seeing the instrumentalisation of the creative industries as a retreat from a more rounded cultural policy, O'Brien suggests that this is a British State returning to form. He suggests it is social democracy in Britain that needs to be explained as exemption – rather than as some inevitable trajectory of the State. The adoption of the creative industries represented that State's concern with technological innovation as a source of economic competitiveness going beyond the more recent era of neoliberalism. Echoing Gibson et al. (Chapter 5 this volume), O'Brien points to the British State's concern to promote the service sector ahead of manufacturing, and how the embracing of the creative industries as a service sector by the higher echelons of that State has long roots.

By contrast Philip Schlesinger looks at the cultural policy process in very close detail via the United Kingdom's current coalition government's abolition of the British Film Council. This chapter takes us into the heart of how cultural industries policies are framed and implemented, and how opaque this process can be even amongst those directly affected by it. It reminds us how ambiguous that policy process can be and how rapidly a change of government can alter the landscape. At bottom, the volatility and opacity of the political process reflect a wider loss of legitimacy and a shared language within which such cultural policy matters can be framed.

Yudhishthir Raj Isar end this section with a more optimistic and outward-looking account of the global field of cultural policy making. Building on UNESCO's 2013 Creative Economy Report (of which he was lead author), Isar gives us an account of what is at stake for global cultural policy in the current debates around culture and development, cultural/creative economy and the role of culture in the millennium development goals. Whilst the cultural and certainly the creative industries were usually seen as an option for developed and, latterly, newly developed countries the possibilities they open out for 'developing countries' have important lessons for cultural policy as a whole. That is, the reality and specificity of cultural industries policy on the ground in developing countries highlight not only some key contradictions and blind spots of the global creative economy agenda but help us rework that agenda in progressive ways for the Global North as well as the Global South.

34

A FRAMEWORK FOR CULTURAL LABOUR[1]

Shoring up the good jobs, well done

Catherine Murray

The proposition that there is a moral and material diversity in cultural work quite apart from aesthetic dimensions (Banks, 2006; Ross, 2009) continues to require socio-economic alternatives to the current winner-take-all neoliberal economic formation.[2] As the rocky start to the 21st century continues, the 1980s restructuring of the welfare state across many countries has produced a dramatic U-turn into inequality, which is higher in Canada than in all but one other Organisation for Economic Co-operation and Development (OECD) country. Such income distributions – not seen since the Depression (Fortin et al., 2012; Smith, 2006; Banting and Myles, 2013; McKenna, 2013) – feature a stagnant or hollowing-out middle class and emerging 'labour apartheid' or class polarization (Ross, 2009). Contemporary austerity politics after billions in bank bailouts in 2008 feature pitched battles over cuts in social and cultural programs, taxes, and redistribution. While any return to the Keynesian era of big general social welfare programs is unlikely in many OECD countries, there is a revival in elite and popular opinion of policy debates over fairness and equity (Steeves, 2013; Grant, 2013; Battle and Torjman, 2012). It is timely to explore how discursive differences in framing a renewed or 3.0[3] version of the social investment state defined below may or may not advance more egalitarian and inclusive visions of cultural work and collectivist action.

One consequence of the broadening of the cultural field to include new digital media, design, and other craft sectors is that structural policy levers to improve the condition of cultural work have migrated to economic (especially tax), labour, and social policy portfolios. Progressive discourses around cultural/creative labour must now manoeuvre within a wholly new multilevel complexity and devolution in cultural industry labour policy governance. Far from opposing any slide into 'soft economic sociology' (Peck, 2005), I argue that it is incumbent upon cultural scholars to reason more systematically through the social-economies-as-varieties imaginary (O'Connor, 2013; Vinodrai, 2013). With reference to experience in Canada, a mixed neoliberal social welfare regime in the context of OECD member states, this chapter introduces a fuller framework for cultural labour policy and calls for further debate over policy options facing the sector and coordinated strategies to supply missing empirical evidence and decide how to mobilize.

The social relations of cultural work

In all but the Nordic countries, the macro picture of distribution of income suggests income polarization, declining social mobility, a persistent poverty trap, and increase in the health costs associated with the stress of economic and psychic precarity in everyday life (Standing, 2011; Vosko, 2004; McKenna, 2013). Employment and output in the creative industries continue to seemingly outperform other aspects of the economy in many countries (De Propris, 2013) while masking some upward mobility as well as sharp and growing income disparities among certain cultural workers, widespread casualization, declining unionization, loss of mid-wage cultural jobs (Christopherson, 2008), and persistent patterns of social exclusion (Donald et al., 2013; Bain and McLean, 2013; Newbery, 2012).

Before realistic assessment of the prospects for a politics of progressive cultural labour reform, it is important to ask: what is the relative level of poverty among cultural workers compared to other workers? How do wages in the cultural sector compare, and are they as prone as the general economy to the trend to unacceptable income ratios between managers and workers? What is the relative level of non-standard employment risk encountered and how does this affect social mobility over time?

Not surprisingly, answers are not empirically straightforward and little comparative work has been done.[4] The numbers game is not without consequence: by overstating the precarious situation of cultural work, unwitting analysts may end up weakening workers' political bargaining clout (Tweedie, 2013). By blurring the story of selective middle class mobility, on the other hand, we may avoid grappling with key redistributive issues within the cultural sector.

Given the rise of a new cultural digitirati, arguably *not* as aligned with a new global elite (Higgs and Cunningham, 2008) as much as supposed (O'Connor, 2013), the following discussion examines the room for different distributive welfare politics.

Data on the relative poverty of cultural workers in other countries are not easily accessible on policy websites, but in Canada they have a higher poverty rate than the general workforce.[5] The social distribution of income for cultural workers shows a similar significant structural wage discount among OECD member countries, confirmed by Hans Abbing and others.[6] Comparatively, this earnings gap is significantly *smaller* than disadvantages accruing by gender and immigrant status in the general labour force, but can compound. However, full-time wages in many subsectors have now achieved parity with the general workforce (excluding music, performing and visual arts: Cultural Human Resources Council, 2010). Indeed, over 20 years, the full-time cultural workforce in Canada shows significant income mobility.

The casualization thesis in non-standard work, and by implication the need to mitigate insecurity, is thus by no means uncontested among economists. Doogan and Fevre, for example, disputed the macro structural shift in their attack on Richard Sennett (cited in Tweedie, 2013: 95). The 2011 survey of the Canadian Cultural

Human Resources Council (CHRC) actually found that the rate of part-time versus full-time employment among cultural professionals was no different from that of the overall employed Canadian labour force at 20 per cent.[7] Feminist analysts argue that this ignores the impacts on already marginalized social groups. Nonetheless, cultural unemployment tends to be lower than for the general workforce.[8]

Canadian cultural workers are twice as likely to be self-employed (44 per cent and higher among musicians, performing and visual artists). A substantial proportion are self-employed by default.[9] Of these, more than two-thirds did not have access to benefits or pensions (Conference Board of Canada, 2009).

Progressive policy discourses

Most early creative economy policies fell into a fairly narrow neoliberal range of instruments to support the cultural sector: education and training (Crouch and Keune, 2012), awards and trade assistance, business and new venture stimulus (Gollmitzer and Murray, 2009). However, it is a mistake to frame the policy efforts of the last decade solely as uncoupling from traditional welfare state politics and entirely away from semi-skilled or unskilled workers (O'Connor, 2013; Christopherson, 2008). A re-articulation is underway.

The noted institutional comparative welfare analyst Gota Esping-Anderson reminds us that the tidy-taxonomy of corporatist, liberal, and democratic socialist social welfare regimes was collapsing by 2000 (White, 2012). There is undeniable convergence in the new micro policy playbook across these historic welfare systems, and, arguably, a piecemeal, ad hoc, disaggregated set of activities under the term social investment state (SIS) that together provide a degree of adaptation to cultural work conditions that is impressive, if undocumented and as yet not evaluated (Jenson, 2012; Bonoli and Natali, 2012; Mazur, 2002).

Paradoxically, the struggle to forge the new SIS on the ashes of the neoliberal retrenchment has taken place *with a relative absence* of the politics of recognition and representation associated with the social movements and labour of the post-World War II period! However, it is characterized by active 'think tankery',[10] more international policy networks, and even bureaucratic politics of stealth.

The social investment state

A label coined by the OECD in the mid-1990s and picked up by the European Union and World Bank, the social investment state designs economic and social policies to be mutually reinforcing (Jenson, 2012: 251; Ross, 2009). While interpretations vary widely, new SIS policy design is based on proactive and preventive social spending, reflective of a concern with future orientation rather than present 'social protection'. This shift from universal social services to selective transfer payments, from insurance to assistance, appears to be here to stay. SIS policies tend to focus on children and especially early childhood education,[11] promotion of human capital, and 'making work pay' with supplements rather than income replacements (effected with in-work tax benefits and tax credits for children, especially for families at risk of poverty).[12] Much of SIS falls under the jurisdiction of Treasury, Tax or Finance ministries.

In SIS labour policy, the metaphor shifts from social safety net to trampoline, actively bouncing people back into the labour market by fostering a resilient base of cognitive capacities for lifelong learning to adapt to recurrent job seeking, support adjustment, and mobility. SIS 'plus' prescriptions focus additionally on the need for parental/compassionate and eldercare leaves and access to child care to better balance the work/life nexus (Florida, 2013; Banting and Myles, 2013; Jenson, 2010). They are the next overlay to the usual Canadian safety net of universal public education, health, and pension law (not without problems in the current austerity era with a rapidly aging population).

Rights-based frames: The right to work

Full employment or the right to a job has apparently ended in contemporary politics and among social movement union platforms. Post-Keynsians are struggling to revive the concept (Zannoni and McKenna, 2007). Admittedly, liberal human rights have done little to explain why people act as citizens, failed to address inequalities of wealth and power that polarize rich and poor, and pandered to the free rider problem that undercuts trust in government (Fainstein, 2010). A rights-based focus can also undermine collectivism if it becomes an elite-driven court strategy (Savage, 2009).

Since the UNESCO drive for status of the artist legislation in the 1980s, critical cultural policy talk has omitted the discussion of economic rights of cultural workers entirely (Stevenson, 2003), located them as an outcome of Marshall's concept of social rights (Hackworth, 2007), or asserted an exceptionalist framework based on the right to cultural expression (Murray and Gollmitzer, 2012; Neil, 2010). The Status of the Artist approach (SoA) has not diffused widely among United Nations Educational, Scientific and Cultural Organization (UNESCO) countries and, aside from Quebec, lost traction in Canada (Gollmitzer and Murray, 2009). The root problem is that rather than authority based in labour law, SoA approaches base it in contract law, avoiding certification and collective bargaining and leaving voluntary associations in a grey zone of enforceability – and without the properly constituted rights to represent their members (Coles, 2012). They also inhibit efforts to reach out to the broader formal union movement. A summative policy evaluation done federally in 2002 concluded that the (SoA) era launched some 22 or more subsectoral private 'associations' after the first wave of public sector unionization but failed to improve the overall economic status of artists, and called for other measures.

The last decade has seen rights to intellectual property dominate the cultural agenda in many countries. To protect those with little market power, coalitions from the cultural sector pushed a new voluntary floor approach that suggests minimum terms for intellectual property agreements on royalties, advances, and for other resale rights for creators (see the Federation of Canadian Artists, artists.ca), including the recognition of artists as secured creditors in the event of bankruptcy.[13] More positive SoA recommendations call for exemption of annual copyright income for artists to median income levels.

Moral frames: Decent work

A new moral discourse around decent work with a living wage favoured by the International Labour Organization tends to focus on salary and push standards of employment conditions, not right to work (full employment) or conditions in non-standard work (Peccoud, 2004). Decent living wage is variously defined as keeping pace with inflation, meeting a certain threshold of viability, and carrying basic benefits. The living wage movement in Canada, although stalled, is relevant to cultural workers who can't afford to give up their day jobs. In a stronger form, decent work platforms can push for equal pay scales between full- and part-time workers for work of equal value. The Communications, Energy and Paperworkers Union joined in the summer of 2013 with the Canadian Auto Workers Union under the name Unifor in Canada and pushed for a 'Join the Good Jobs' revolution and policy summit in 2014. One of Unifor's best-known economists is also pushing persuasively for the need to standardize international employment figures to cover those underemployed, in forced part-time work, or who have left the work force (Stanford and Hennessy, 2013).

Flexicurity

Originally attributed to the Dutch, flexicurity is often treated as a European Union Trojan horse for neoliberalism (Heyes, 2011) for its expansion of the employer's right to use fixed-term contracts, outsource, or downsize, but the term is all too easily ceded. It is intended to balance both employer and employee needs and explicitly rejects involuntary job assignment. The conceptual breakthrough in labour regulation is that flexicurity attaches access to security benefits to the individual, not the employment relationship, switching focus to the worker rather than the employee (Langille, 2002).[14] A ceiling on the time in a temporary position is important.

Flexicurity has the virtue of low-stakes bureaucratic enactment: after it is set up, costs to administer such programs have been found to diminish, ostensibly fitting demands for 'less government' (Nichols, 2012) and reducing the political costs of enforcing a sector-by-sector specific approach. But it is opposed by those like Guy Standing (2011) who reject its lack of attention to systemic inequality or failure to banish the remnants of the male breadwinner precedent (McDowell, 2004). All-too-rare studies like Vinodrai's (2013) make the case that the response of the design industry to the crash in a liberal labour market regime in Toronto versus a coordinated flexicurity one in Copenhagen illustrates the resilience of the Danish flexicurity model – providing a stronger context for increased entrepreneurship, innovation, and risk-taking.

The deeply seated preference among young cultural workers for freedom and autonomy, while individualistic, introduces both predisposition to 'venture labour', as Gina Neff argues (2012), and social networking. While not inimical to collectivist labour impulses, it is not yet friendly (Tailby and Pollert, 2011). On the whole, venture labour requires favourable terms for access to capital and recording tax losses during start-up, support for the gestation of not-for-profit associations, and tax credits for hiring young workers. Inasmuch as start-ups depend solely on net worth, the class basis of cultural work is more exclusive, despite Kickstart or Indiegogo crowdsourcing sites for financing. DIY – do it yourself – can become DIO – do it ourselves – in new cooperative or social enterprise models, but this is still marginal in the contemporary cultural policy portfolio.

Nonetheless, high acceptance of the individualization of risk in 'cool jobs' or 'good work' can prevent stabilization of norms and regulation of workplace behaviour and rewards (Neff, 2012), which can perpetuate discrimination (Newbery, 2012). Women's efforts to organize for more positions of creative control or against harassment in video game workplaces have failed, yet opposition to free internships is building.[15]

An ethic of care

Feminist theorists of a philosophy of care have sought to draw attention to the 'chains of care' in transnational migration, revalue menial work, and value unpaid work in the name of equity or social justice (McDowell, 2004; Kershaw, 2005; Sayer, 2003; Couldry, 2012) in the private and family realms. Rejecting the autonomy of the individual, care theorists look at trust, responsibility, and relationships in labour relations in a new way. Indirect family support for artistic practice requires a value to be placed on it: so does voluntary work supporting cultural production and important to community arts and local heritage,[16] which requires costly volunteer training and coordination. A care lens raises a whole set of questions about how to foster hybrid social enterprise or patient, socially responsible capital that are beyond the scope of this chapter.

All approaches to these ideas and actually embedded politics of social investment (Jenson, 2010, 2012: 26) are historically contingent, and dependent on effective mobilization of cultural workers in current political opportunity structures.

A framework to shore up the good jobs

Clearly, the complexity of cultural practice in daily life requires a more holistic/coordinated SIS policy framework. I have argued that this framework must be grounded in empirical mapping of the material circumstances of cultural workers and their work practices, be cognizant of general welfare, and then interrogate the needed policy repertoires emerging in progressive labour discourse. The demand side of cultural labour movement in the context of social policy reform weighs heavily in assessing realistic prospects for policy reform and is explored elsewhere (see DePeuter and Cohen; Randle, Saha and Milestone in this volume). 'Puzzling' about public policies occurs amid uncertainty about the effectiveness of interventions and instruments (Jenson, 2012: 23). In view of the new modes of employment, the progressive policy maker has to construct a complex matrix; Crouch and Keune (2012) call it a grammar of uncertainty management. Andrew Sayer (2003) suggests the fundamental questions of the moral economy might include: whose keeper are we? Who is ours? What are our responsibilities? What standards of care? What standard of living should people expect? What things cannot be commodified? To what extent should we be reliant on wages? Cultural workers must join these public dialogues.

A sensible review of labour policy would weigh the variety of social policies emerging in the SIS against the wide variety of new work relationships in and outside of employment relationships to see if original welfare goals can be achieved through existing strategies or require new ones (Langille, 2002; Crouch and Keune, 2012: 54–55). It would also accommodate sectoral and associational labour strategies in voluntary regulation. In the view of cultural and creative labour organizers interviewed from Canada after the crash, strategies for mobilization include exceptionalist or specialist ones, and subsectoral, sectoral, and coalition/generalist ones (Murray and Gollmitzer, 2012). The progressives' dilemma is the tension between solidarity with other workers and diversity, or asserting differentiated rights in competitive politics internal to the cultural and creative industries (Banting, 2010, Murray and Gollmitzer, 2012).

The goal is to have such multi-dimensional analysis open up opportunities for new actors defending certain interests and values to obtain inclusion, and for new coalition formation (Bonoli and Natali, 2012:291; Mazur, 2002; Tailby and Pollert, 2011).

Notwithstanding the need in all OECD countries for an orientation to youth unemployment and under-employment (good jobs to build a life on), a policy framework for cultural labour begins by mapping the intersections among the following policy fields.

Anti-poverty strategies (generalist)

Cultural workers are more at risk of poverty than the general population and obviously potential agents in such coalition building. Canada has ranked 18th in the OECD on poverty for more than 20 years. After a small local pilot study was discontinued in the 1970s, the guaranteed annual income is deemed too archaic in parlance today, but even Canadian reformers from the progressive right are calling now for a refundable anti-poverty tax credit (see Oakley, forthcoming; Segal, 2013) that avoids top-down needs-based testing.[17] Yet coalitions of artists and cultural workers are difficult to sustain and have suffered with the collapse of the Canadian Conference of the Arts and loss of federal support for the sectoral labour council. The biggest problem is whether the cultural sector will go it alone – hoping to push anti-poverty strategies for the arts under the political radar – or join a coalition.[18] The time is overdue to answer the question posed by Hans Abbing, David Throsby and others: are general income policy, social security, and tax measures to help the poor a more effective way to achieve sustainable incomes amongst the more disadvantaged of cultural workers, since more direct sectoral subsidy has not helped (Abbing, 2002: 136)?

Income (flex)security (generalist)

We can no longer rely on the standard employment relationships in cultural work to provide access to pension or special health benefits (Steeves, 2013). Our ideas about who we protect, what we protect against, and how best to do so must change (Langille, 2002). Cultural work policy and income security fields crosscut to the extent that minimum wage, income security provisions for non-standard workers, or recognition of dual status are enacted.

Some economists (Corak, 2013) argue for refundable working income tax credits, which can be broadened more aggressively to reduce income inequality by raising all workers to a floor income at least a quarter of the way up the median income ladder (Battle and Torjman, 2013).

Are employment insurance payments just? Allegations that payments made by employees and employers are in surplus in Canada and directed to other areas of government revenue should be studied and a strategy of asserting redirection to general redistribution to those out of work examined.[19]

Active labour policy (sectoral)

Active labour market instruments to foster job transitions, job searches, or networking are obviously relevant to cultural work and expanding with new urban players in the SIS era. Unfortunately, self-employed entrepreneurs do not have access to public retraining programs, and the allowable expenses for professional development under self-employment are not elastic enough to recognize that cultural workers spend more than twice the time on such education and training as their counterparts. Such oversights merit attention. Since children are used regularly in the performing arts and recorded media, they require special protections. In countries like Canada where civil human rights enforcers in the workplace are weak, seeking to end systemic or particular racism or sexism or ableism in the legacy or new digital workplaces is extra difficult. If active labour expands to include affirmative labour measures, consideration must be given to revisiting ideas of voluntary or imposed quotas or other approaches to a range of issues: representation in professional associations, industry boards, and allocation of state subsidy investment to screen productions could be redirected at equity-seeking groups in the progressives' agenda.

Immigration policy (subsectoral)

Immigration policy involves either investor or skilled worker classes of immigrants or temporary worker exemptions requested by employers. Hidden barriers to immigrant inclusion in professional credentials must be addressed. In Canada, only interactive digital media workers are eligible under the skilled program and often exceed their quotas, prompting high employer demand for temporary work permits. Sectoral dialogues are needed. The digital game industry is now contested by the Writer's Union, which seeks more job mobility in adaptation of the narrative craft. Intra-sectoral politics are complicated.

Economic and tax policy (general and sectoral)

Important dimensions of tax policy for self-employed workers (McAndrew, 2002) need to be examined for their post-recession changes. The problem with a tax approach is that the self-employed are often isolated and powerless against arbitrary rulings, unaware of the frequent changes in tax law, and unable to maximize their positions. Tax intermediaries available pro bono to the self-employed are scarce. The lack of continuous research and advocacy assessing these options and their impact on the cultural sector are marked.

Debates go on over what constitutes more or less progressiveness among these policy instruments and programs, but the crux of the tax tests is to see how the reasonable expectation of profit test is applied to the self-employed worker over time – and given the radical fluctuations of this global economy, how they benefit the lost generation. What is a just lifecycle model of taxation?

The policy problem is whether tax-based instruments are advisable or efficient. The Canadian tax system is a mishmash of credits and deductions that defies analysis, is moving away from consumption-based taxes, and is becoming more unacceptably regressive in cases of child arts tax credits, for example, something opportunistically lauded by the cultural sector on introduction (Tedds, 2013).

Canada is coping with a populist right-wing tax backlash. Like all countries, its citizens are reevaluating a system that sets up tax avoidance as a game, rewards the professionals who administer it and benefits the rich, and has forgotten the value behind what we need to pay for together. Taste for redistribution is derived from personal values, education, and experience. If gains are lopsided, public support for state intervention wanes.

Yet progressives must fight for fuller disclosure of the enormity of such ad hoc concessions (estimated to be half the entire cost of universal health spending in Canada: Tedds, 2013). They must also fight against the right's call for ever-lower taxes. If one in three tax filers in Canada pays no tax, there is limited room to further lower individual tax rates, so the politics of austerity must: a) argue for increased consumption taxes as more progressive; b) look at the top 1 per cent and/or rebalance corporate taxes; c) enhance refundable tax credits, like child or working benefits for all; or d) address social assistance in another way (adapted from Fortin et al., 2012).

Some economists argue that the hollowing out of the middle class cannot be handled through the tax system, and creative/cultural policy analysts need to respond.

The political subject positions of cultural workers are unstable on commitment to redistribution, and rent-seeking has ruled all too often in early cultural industry labour politics. In the audio-visual industries, a Canadian labour tax credit is calculated on total labour costs for foreign service and domestic productions, returning between 16 and 33 per cent. It is generous, has over time supported rising median incomes in full-time work, and become a source of competition between provinces. To what social effect? Is this kind of public spending better redirected to the needed working tax credit to lift more workers (Ross, 2009; Corak, 2013; Abbing, 2002)?

Multi-level governance (subsectoral)

Unquestionably, the reworking of the welfare state to a punitive and competitive model in the 1990s recentred the role of cities in the provision of public services – in practice, if not in legal jurisdiction (MacDonald, 2011). Since, as Lily Kong (2011) argues, creative labour markets continue to be predominantly local, cities have a great role to play in negotiating active labour market policies and providing important enhancements to live/work and other spatial policies that enable the enjoyment of a good job, well done.

Consistent with devolutionary trends in a range of policy areas, cultural work intersects with urban policies including tools like zoning for affordable public housing, effective public transit, adequate supplies of live/work space, mixed-use development to restrain displacement through gentrification, and, finally, deployment of new (urban) taxes that are reinvested to aid local cultural production. Cities may also introduce living wage campaigns. Ironically, a philosophy of care or nurturance of lively cultural ecologies in the city may turn the responsibility for affirmative active labour policies on its head compared to the Keynesian era.

Conclusion

Such intersectionality usefully probes for policy overlaps, identifies disparate paradigmatic worldviews, and compels consideration of how to ameliorate the material conditions produced by marginality and labour segregation in cultural work by gender, age, race, and space. The intent of this chapter has been to reject TINA thinking (there is no alternative to the market: Jenson, 2010). But the work ahead in sorting out alternative progressive policy demands, renovating the social investment state, choosing areas with higher probability of success in the current climate, and forging coalitions is daunting.

The SIS merits deeper exploration for how its policies may mitigate poverty, redistribute incomes, ameliorate stress and time out of paid work (Burchell, 2009) while seamlessly integrating good unpaid work, or creative growth free for a moment from the tyranny of the clock. They must enable cultural workers, like all workers, to live if not well at least adequately and enjoy class mobility over time. Indeed, creative decent work can be seen as a basic right or entitlement of the entire workforce (Massey, 2013). Cultural workers share with all workers the need to find the modest luxury of good jobs, well done, and this surely does not have to depend on carpetbagging, free riding, or self-abnegation.

Notes

1 This paper builds upon an earlier one published in the *International Journal of Cultural Policy* (18: 4, September 2012) called 'Escaping the Precarity Trap', coauthored with Mirjam Gollmitzer. It is in small tribute to the now-defunct 50-year-old Canadian Conference of the Art's historical commitment to keep coalition politics alive for cultural workers.
2 Based on the postulate that many aspects of work are not reducible to the market, such diversity includes: the 'creative' working poor, those who work for subsistence, work for free, work another job to support themselves, do not have to work thanks to family or angel support, those who work alone, run sole proprietorships, or work for others for pay, those who barter or donate time for volunteer motives or work for financial reward in simple or complex production entities.

3 This designation assumes 1.0 refers to the postwar welfare expansionism, 2.0 the neo-conservative reshaping after the 1972 economic collapse. It posits the 3.0 version works as more than a 'flanking mechanism' to blunt the worst effects of neoliberalism (White, 2012).

4 In Canada, analysis is much more difficult since the Conservative government in power since the 2008 recession has ended the mandatory long-form census, abolished the cultural sector council for labour, and cut grants to Statistics Canada, leading to the closure of its cultural statistics branch. Relative social mobility of cultural workers over time is now virtually impossible to establish. The costs of holding policy makers to account have risen.

5 One in four cultural workers make $20,000 or less, compared to one in six in the general population. Source: The Conference Board of Canada, 2010. See page 27 Table 11; see also Statistics Canada, 2012, www.statcan.gc.ca/search-recherche/bb/info/low-faible-eng.htm.

6 See Gary Neil, 2010; Hill Strategies, 2009. Caves (2000), Abbing (2002), Menger (2014), and Towse (2011) confirm these findings of hardship. Nonetheless, recent works dispute the relative discount thesis. See Kamil Zawadzki, 2012. In Canada, salary gaps range between 7–25 per cent for the sector. Is this a big gap? Not compared to the unconscionably high (50 per cent) one between temporary and full-time workers in the Greater Toronto Area (Grant, 2013).

7 Canada has still not examined the situation of cultural workers outside of the sector: Cunningham and Higgs, 2008: 5.

8 See www.povnet.org/node/4702 (accessed January 14, 2015).

9 Nearly a third (31 per cent) of self-employed workers had been unable to find full-time employment in an organization. Another 5 per cent had either been fired or laid off from their last job (Cultural Human Resources Council, 2010: 29).

10 In Canada, these progressive think tanks include the Tamarack Institute, Caledon Institute, Canadian Centre for Policy Alternatives and McConnell Foundation.

11 Canada has no universal child care, but is exploring earlier universal access to education in some provinces, and has introduced a child tax benefit. It has not yet been proven to help low-income families. A tax deduction for child arts and sports activities capped at $500 is purely regressive.

12 Such top-ups have the downside of subsidizing employers to offer low wages, and encourage parents to stay in any job, including low-income, poor-quality work. See Peck, 2001.

13 An *Ottawa Citizen* story on Annie Pootoogook, the Sobey Art Award-winning artist who has recently been living on the streets of Ottawa, reported her selling drawings on the streets for $25, but her earlier work was selling in a gallery for $2,500. See more at: www.canadianart.ca/news/2013/06/24/mps-push-for-artists-resale-right-in-canada/#sthash.1UJgcI8J.dpuf.

14 Canada has recently extended employment insurance benefits to the self-employed, but dual status workers are exempt (Neil, 2010) and the eligible time periods exclude too many of the working poor. Yet this represents a significant concession from the existing Conservative regime, and opens an advantage that now may be widened incrementally.

15 See www.cbc.ca/news/business/21-year-old-s-death-focuses-attention-on-u-k-interns-1.1332837. This case mimics one for an unpaid intern at a radio station in Canada in 2011 still working its way through the courts (www.cbc.ca/news/canada/british-columbia/intern-s-death-after-overnight-shift-sparks-outcry-1.1704532, accessed January 15, 2015). In Canada, Hootsuite, a West Coast social media company rising like a meteor, recently reversed its policy on free interns.

16 Volunteers do 64 per cent of the work overall in cultural establishments in Canada, and the time they donated in 2006 is valued at $3.6 billion (Statistics Canada, June 2006). See www.statcan.gc.ca/daily-quotidien/060605/dq060605a-eng.htm.

17 A National Council of Welfare Report on the Dollars and Sense of Poverty estimated that it would cost $12.6 billion to top up the 3.5 million Canadians beneath the poverty line. That is less than 5 per cent of the federal budget, and less than half the cost imposed on the economy by poverty and its effects. See Segal, 2013. By contrast, it can be argued the banks got $114 billion in housing loan liquidity guarantees – or bailouts totalling 7 per cent of the gross domestic product. See www.cbc.ca/news/business/banks-got-114b-from-govern ments-during-recession-1.1145997.

18 Artists are on record arguing a 'mere' $1.9 billion (more than is allocated to Canada's national public broadcaster on a per capita basis) would bring poor cultural workers up to liveable levels, under SoA exceptional status claims (Neil, 2010).

19 Estimates suggest, at a $3.5 billion surplus in 2013, this might cover a quarter annually of the actual cost of working tax top-ups. Despite the office of the Auditor General and the new Parliamentary Budget Office, transparency of budgeting under the Conservative government has declined, and opposition parties and policy analysts find it much harder to assess real redistribution strategies. As a proponent with Pierre Juneau and Peter Herrndorf of the now-failed communications distribution tax idea as a means for funding our cultural institutions in a public review (Juneau et al., 1996), I am hardly a reliable predictor of tax trends. However, the principle of proportionality in taxes would assert that a reasonable proportion of funds raised through goods and services taxes on the sector in fact be reinvested in it, not mostly payable to institutions or companies as in earlier eras, but to cultural workers.

References

Abbing, H. (2002) *Why are artists poor? The exceptional economy of the arts*, Amsterdam: Amsterdam University Press.

Bain, A. and McLean, H. (2013) 'The artistic precariat', *Cambridge Journal of Regions, Economy and Society*, 6: 93–111.

Banks, M. (2006) 'Moral economy and cultural work', *Sociology*, 40 (3): 455–72.

Banting, K. (2010) 'Is there a progressive's dilemma in Canada? Immigration, multiculturalism and the welfare state', *Canadian Journal of Political Science*, 43 (3), December: 797–820.

Banting, K. and Myles, J. (2013) *Inequality and the Fading of Redistributive Politics*, Vancouver: UBC Press.

Battle, K. and Torjman, S. (2012) 'Enhancing the working income tax benefit', Caledon Institute of Social Policy, December, for the All party Anti Poverty Caucus, www.caledoninst.org/Publications/PDF/1001ENG.pdf.

Battle, K. and Torjman, S. (2013) 'As the fiscal chill thaws: Social policy ideas for the medium term', Caledon Institute of Social Policy, January, www.caledoninst.org/Publications/PDF/1003ENG.pdf.

Bonoli, G. and Natali, D. (eds) (2012) 'Multidimensional transformations in the early 21st century welfare states', in *The Politics of the New Welfare State*, Oxford: Oxford University Press, 287–306.

Burchell, B. (2009) 'Flexicurity as a moderator of the relationship between job insecurity and psychological well-being', *Cambridge Journal of Regions, Economy and Society*, 2: 365–78.

Caves, R. (2000) *Creative Industries: Contracts Between Art and Commerce*, Cambridge: Harvard University Press.

Christopherson, S. (2008) 'Beyond the self-expressive creative worker: An industry perspective on entertainment media', *Theory, Culture and Society*, 25 (7–8): 73–95.

Coles, A. (2012) 'Counting Canucks: Cultural labour and Canadian cultural policy', dissertation presented for the degree of political studies, Hamilton: McMaster University.

Conference Board of Canada. (2009) 'The effect of the global economic recession on Canada's creative economy', produced for the Cultural Human Resources Council, Ottawa: Author, October.

Corak, M. (2013) 'This refundable tax credit could reduce income inequality', *The Globe and Mail*, November 8, www.theglobeandmail.com/report-on-business/economy/this-refundable-tax-credit-could-reduce-income-inequality/article15358155/.

Couldry, N. (2012) *Media, Society, World: Social Theory and Digital Media Practice*, London: Polity Press.

Crouch, C. and Keune, M. (2012) 'The governance of economic uncertainty: Beyond "new social risks" analysis', in Bonoli, G. and Natali, D. (eds) *The Politics of the New Welfare State*, Oxford: Oxford University Press, 45–65.

Cultural Human Resources Council. (2010) *Cultural HR Study 2010: Labour Market Information for Canada's Cultural Sector Report*, December, Ottawa: Cultural Human Resources Council.

Cunningham, S. and Higgs, P. (2008) 'Embedded creatives: Revealing the extent and contribution of creative professionals working throughout the economy', in *The Compendium of Research Papers for the International Forum on the Creative Economy*, Conference Board of Canada, August.

De Propris, L. (2013) 'How are creative industries weathering the crisis?' *Cambridge Journal of Regions, Economy and Society*, 6: 159–76.

Donald, B., Gertler, M.S., and Tyler, P. (2013) 'Creatives after the crash', *Cambridge Journal of Regions, Economy and Society*, 6: 3–21.

Esping-Andersen, G. and Gallie, D. (2002) *Why We Need a New Welfare State*, New York: Oxford University Press.

Fainstein, S. (2010) *The Just City*, Ithaca, NY: Cornell University Press.

Florida, R. (2013) 'More losers than winners in America's new economic geography', *The Atlantic Cities*, January 30, www.theatlanticcities.com/jobs-and-economy/2013/01/more-losers-winners-americas-new-economic-geography/4465/.

Fortin, N., Green, D.A., Lemieux, T., and Milligan, K. (2012) 'Canadian inequality: Recent developments and policy options', *Canadian Public Policy*, 38 (2), June: 121–45.

Gollmitzer, M. and Murray, C. (2009) *Workflows and Flexicurity: Canadian Cultural Labour in the Era of the Creative Economy*, Report for the Canadian Conference of the Arts and the Cultural Human Resources Council, Centre for Policy Studies on Culture and Communities, Burnaby, BC: Simon Fraser University, May.

Grant, T. (2013) 'Why temp workers are here to stay', *The Globe and Mail*, May 6, B1.

Hackworth, J. (2007) *The Neoliberal City: Governance, Ideology and the Development in American Urbanism*, Ithaca, NY: Cornell University Press.

Heyes, J. (2011) 'Flexicurity, employment protection and the jobs crisis', *Work, Employment and Society*, 25 (4): 642–657.

Higgs, P. and Cunningham, S. (2008) 'Embedded creative: Revealing the extent and contribution of creative professionals working throughout the economy', in Academic Papers for the International Forum on the Creative Economy, Ottawa: Conference Board of Canada, 19–21.

Hill Strategies. (2009) *A Statistical Profile of Artists in Canada: Based on the 2006 Census*, prepared for the Canada Council, Canadian Heritage and Ontario Arts Council, www.hillstrategies.com/content/statistical-profile-artists-canada.

Jenson, J. (2010) 'Diffusing ideas after neoliberalism: The social investment perspective in Europe and Latin America', in *Global Social Policy*, 10 (1): 59–84.

Jenson, J. (2012) 'A new politics for the social investment perspective', in Bonoli, G. and Natali, D. (eds) *The Politics of the New Welfare State*, Oxford: Oxford University Press, 21–44.

Juneau, P., Herrndorf, P. and Murray, C. (1996) *Making Our Voices Heard: Report of the Mandate Review Committee on the Future of the CBC, NFB and Telefilm*, Ottawa: Supply and Services.

Kershaw, P. (2005) *Carefair: Rethinking the Responsibilities and Rights of Citizenship*, Vancouver: UBC Press.

Kong, L. (2011) 'From precarious labor to precarious economy? Planning for precarity in Singapore's creative economy', *City, Culture and Society*, 2 (2), June: 55–64.

Langille, B.A. (2002) 'Labour policy in Canada: New platform, new paradigm', *Canadian Public Policy*, 28 (1): 132–42.

MacDonald, I.T. (2011) 'Bargaining rights in luxury city: The strategic dilemmas of organized labor's urban turn', *Labor Studies Journal*, 36 (2): 197–220.

Massey, D. (2013) 'Neoliberalism has hijacked our vocabulary', *Guardian*, June 11.

Mazur, A. (2002) *Theorizing Feminist Policy*, Oxford: Oxford University Press.

McAndrew, C. (2002) *Artists, Taxes and Benefits: An International Review*, Research Report 28, December, for the Arts Council of England.

McDowell, L. (2004) 'Work, workfare, work/life balance and an ethic of care', *Progress in Human Geography*, 28 (2): 145–63.

McKenna, B. (2013) 'Mind the gap: The wealth paradox', *The Globe and Mail*, November 9, F1.

Menger, P.-M. (2014) *The Economics of Uncertainty: Art and Achievement Under Uncertainty*, translated by Steven Randall et al., London: Harvard University Press.

Murray, C. and Gollmitzer, M. (2012) 'Escaping the precarity trap: A call for creative labour policy', *International Journal on Cultural Policy*, 18 (4): 419–38.

Neff, G. (2012) *Venture Labor: Work and the Burden of Risk in Innovative Industries*, Boston: MIT Press.

Neil, G. (2010) *Status of the Artist in Canada: An update on the 30th Anniversary of the UNESCO Recommendation Concerning the Status of the Artist*, report for the Canadian Conference of the Arts, Ottawa, supported by the Canadian Artists and Producers Professional Relations Tribunal.

Newbery, M. (2012) 'Gender and the games industry: The experiences of female games workers', thesis for the degree of Master of Arts, School of Communication, Simon Fraser University, Spring.

Nichols, L.J. (2012) 'Labour market policies in Denmark and Canada: Could flexicurity be the answer for Canadian workers?', *Socialist Studies*, 8:2, 163–188.

Oakley, K. (forthcoming) 'Good work? Rethinking cultural entrepreneurship', in Bilton, C. and Cummings, S. (eds) *The Handbook of Management and Creativity*.

O'Connor, J. (2013) 'Intermediaries and imaginaries in the cultural and creative industries', *Regional Studies*, DOI:10.1080/00343404.2012.74892.

Peccoud, D. (ed.) (2004) *Philosophical and Spiritual Perspectives on Decent Work*, Geneva: International Labour Office.

Peck, J. (2001) *Workfare States*, New York: Guildford Press.

Peck, J. (2005) 'Economic sociologies in space', *Economic Geography*, 81 (2): 129–76.

Ross, A. (2009) *Nice Work if You Can Get It: Life and Labour in Precarious Times*, New York: New York University Press.

Savage, L. (2009) 'Workers' rights as human rights: Organized labour and rights discourse in Canada', *Labour Studies Journal*, 34 (1), March: 8–20.

Sayer, A. (2003) '(De)commodification, consumer culture and moral economy', *Environment and Planning D: Society and Space*, 21 (3): 341–57.

Segal, H. (2013) 'Why guaranteeing the poor an income will save us all in the end', 04/08, www.huffingtonpost.ca/hugh-segal/guaranteed-annual-income_b_3037347.html.

Smith, S.J. (2006) 'States, markets and an ethic of care', *Political Geography*, 24 (1): 1–20.

Standing, G. (2011) *The Precariat: The New Dangerous Class*, London: Bloomsbury.

Stanford, J. and Hennessy, T. (2013) *More Harm Than Good: Austerity's Impact on Ontario*, Toronto: Centre for Policy Alternatives.

Steeves, J. (2013) 'Benefits and pensions for all: Why Canada needs a new social contract', *The Globe and Mail*, November 8, www.theglobe andmail.com/news/national/time-to-lead/bene fits-and-pensions-for-all-why-canada-needs-a-new-social-contract/article15348751/.

Stevenson, N. (2003) *Citizenship: Cosmopolitan Questions*, London: Open University Press.

Tailby, S. and Pollert, A. (2011) 'Non unionized young workers and organizing the unorganized', *Economic and Industrial Democracy*, 32(3): 499–522.

Tedds, L. (2013) 'It's time to restore fairness to Canada's tax system', *The Globe and Mail*, November 8, www.theglobeandmail.com/news/national/time-to-lead/its-time-to-restore-fairness-in-canadas-tax-system/article15348157/.

Towse, R. (2011) *A Handbook of Cultural Economics*, Northhampton MA: Edward Elgar. 2nd edition.

Tweedie, D. (2013) 'Making sense of insecurity: A defence of Richard Sennett's sociology of work', *Work, Employment and Society*, 27 (1): 94–104.

Vinodrai, T. (2013) 'Design in a downturn? Creative work, labour market dynamics and institutions in comparative perspective', *Cambridge Journal of Regions, Economy and Society*, 6: 159–76.

Vosko, L.F. (2004) 'Standard-setting at the ILO: The case of precarious employment', in Kirton, J. and Trebilcock, M.J. (eds) *Hard Choices, Soft Law: Combining Trade, Environment, and Social Cohesion in Global Governance*, New York: Ashgate.

White, L.A. (2012) 'Must we all be paradigmatic? Social investment policies and liberal welfare states', *Canadian Journal of Political Science*, 45 (3): 657–83.

Zannoni, D.C. and McKenna, E.J. (2007) 'The right to a job: A post Keynsian perspective', *Journal of Post Keynsian Economics*, 29 (4), Summer: 555–71.

Zawadzki, K. (2012) 'Bringing up the rear? Wages in cultural industries in Poland: empirical evidence', https://www.yumpu.com/en/document/view/23620914/culture-brings-up-the-rear-wages-in-the-cultural-industries-in-poland (accessed January 14, 2015).

35
CONSTRUCTING CREATIVITIES

Higher education and the cultural
industries workforce

Caitriona Noonan

Over the past decades the spheres of higher education (HE) and cultural industries have evolved considerably. Globalization, massification, economic instability, technological innovation and neoliberal policy agendas have impacted considerably on both sectors, opening them up to greater competition, creating a downward pressure on costs and leading them to have very different relationships with their publics. Like never before, questions about what university education is, and indeed should be, are emerging along with threats to the economic viability of some of its institutions and academic disciplines as a result of new relationships between the HE system and the governments that largely fund and regulate it. Historically education in culture and the arts has enjoyed a social significance linked to values like creativity, inclusion and community; however, these subjects are increasingly positioned within a pervasive economic agenda. At the same time, the cultural industries are endorsed as part of the knowledge economy contributing to "UK PLC" and offered as a remedy to numerous financial and social ills, a logic that is critically discussed throughout this volume.

The relationship *between* these two sectors has also evolved over the last three decades with the well-established links between HE and the cultural industries developing to become "more formal, more directed and more calculating" (Oakley 2013: 26), characterized by points of both co-operation and tension. This chapter examines this relationship, focusing on how the expectations, attitudes and conditions of education linked to creative work has changed in response to an evolving policy landscape, and it discusses HE's role in (re)producing some of the structural conditions of labour in the cultural sector, particularly around mechanisms of exclusion in response to internal and external demands.

Higher education and the cultural industries:
A mutual dependence?

The complex entanglement of higher education and the cultural sector is not a new phenomenon. Higher education has long nurtured creative practitioners in all fields of cultural production and has been an important site of cultural production in itself. As Frith and Horne (1987) identify, particularly in the milieu of the art school, the role of the institution was as much about the social development of a cultural practice and "scene", as about vocational education. Rather than through the implementation of discrete public policy (Oakley 2013), this context was nurtured through increased personal freedom and greater cultural experimentation associated with youth culture. While this mutual dependence remains, today the relationship between HE and cultural industries is far more strategic and instrumental, and the balance of power is shifting.

Higher education remains a popular route for prospective workers to the cultural industries, with graduates making up more than two-thirds of the workforce in interactive media, literature, computer games, TV and radio, with this figure increasing to 80 per cent in animation (Catchside 2012). These graduates are seen as bringing the higher-level skills demanded by knowledge economy policies and strategies.

While Frith and Horne (1987) highlight how historically universities have played a vital role in nurturing creative and cultural projects, these activities are gradually being framed as commercial opportunities. Along with teaching and research activities, universities are increasingly called on to perform a further role in the interplay between regional industry and society, particularly around regional development, local regeneration and the development of creative cities (Wilson 2012; Lazzeroni and Piccaluga 2003). Over the last few decades, the creative and cultural regeneration agenda has been married with the provision of higher education in UK regions, particularly in peripheral areas, as a way of distributing resources and addressing inequalities (to mixed success). By providing public spaces for networking, a forum for industry/user debate and access to resources as part of their knowledge transfer initiatives, universities are framed as spaces through which stakeholders can realize their economic goals.

While this supports the view that "without higher education, there would be no creative economy" (Crosswick cited in Catchside 2012), the direction of traffic is certainly not one way. Increasingly higher education institutions (HEIs) are dependent on the cultural industries for expertise, indirect revenue and collaboration. The *Looking Out* report surveyed 108 art, design and media departments in the UK and found that 85 per cent employed teacher-practitioners in a "deliberate effort to maintain the currency of practice-based knowledge in the curriculum" (ADM-HEA 2010). This form of practical knowledge has contributed directly to the curriculum with work simulations and live industry projects a key feature (and thus selling point) for many creative and cultural degrees. Demand for these courses continues to grow and since 1999/2000 there have been above-average increases in enrolments in "mass communications" and "creative arts and design" degrees (Universities UK 2010), highlighting this as a lucrative market for UK universities who are dealing with falling enrolments in other subjects such as electrical engineering and computer science (Grove 2012). Creative and media courses, therefore, have become a significant source of revenue for universities in a new era of austerity, private funding models and market-driven agendas.

This relationship, however, extends beyond teaching and course enrolments. In England 81 per cent of universities identified the creative industries as a target sector for outward activities through external engagements such as knowledge transfer, commercialization of intellectual property and the marketization of creative works (Catchside 2012). Universities have always maintained relationships with external stakeholders but this has transitioned from relational to functional (Boden and Nedeva 2010). On one level, we can see this as a practical response to declining resources and as an attempt by universities to become more entrepreneurial and aggressive by extending revenue streams (Lazzeroni and Piccaluga 2003), something that is relatively easy to deliver in the context of cultural production. However, on another level this also resonates with a "policy trajectory that is preoccupied with the construction of a knowledge economy and a learning society" (Ozga and Jones 2006: 2). In this system universities become instruments for furthering economic growth, a process which has accelerated since the 1980s, and within which university research in particular is expected to become "more responsive, rhetorically and substantively, to commercial and political agendas" (Willmott 2003: 2). Universities must now pursue "direct, immediate and demonstrable economic utility" (Boden and Nedeva 2010: 41) through many of their activities.

The Wilson Review (Wilson 2012), which appraised business–university collaboration, highlighted the positioning of universities as an integral part of the supply chain to business – "a supply chain that has the capability to support business growth and therefore economic prosperity" (Wilson 2012: 1).[1] The opportunities for creative disciplines within the framework of business–university interaction is clear, enacted at a macro level through government interventions and employer-led demands for industry-ready talent; and at a micro level in the work placements, internships and professional accreditations that shape and condition the everyday experiences of students, academic staff and management (Ashton and Noonan 2013). However, some question the marriage of business and university goals, and the ways in which "business involvement is bound to regulate and limit cultural productivity" (Buckingham and Jones 2001: 12). Differences in motivations and purposes mean that partnerships can become problematic and education is increasingly seen as the weaker partner due to its positioning in the policy system (Buckingham and Jones 2001). To that policy framework, and the inequalities it is claimed to perpetuate, we now turn our attention.

Historical Cultivation of the Creative Student-Professional

The historical coupling of education and work-related policy has a long lineage and can be traced back to the mid-nineteenth century. The Select Committee on Arts and Manufactures, convened in 1836 in response to the fear that Britain was losing the export race to low-cost competition from abroad, investigated the "best means of extending a knowledge of the arts and of the principles of design among the people (especially the manufacturing population) of the country" (Report from Select Committee on Arts and Manufactures cited in Romans 2007: 217).[2] The report concluded that countries that were successful at exporting were also funding design education for their manufacturing industries and so this led to the foundation of the Government School of Design (now the Royal College of Art) (Sproll 1994).

Over the next century education policy continued to develop with the focus on both social- and work-related goals. For instance, the Robbins Report (Committee on Higher Education 1963: 6) sought to expand and democratize university provision, arguing that university places should be available to all who were qualified for them by ability and attainment. It outlined a number of objectives for the university; the first, a utilitarian one, was "instruction in skills"; but, second, universities must also promote the "general powers of the mind", to produce "not mere specialists but rather cultivated men and women". This was followed by the Dearing Review (Dearing 1997), which stated that, alongside contributions to society and personal fulfilment, a key aim for HE should be to ensure individuals are well-equipped for the workplace.

However, in the last decades of the previous century and the first decades of this one, a significant shift has occurred in policy, a shift that is in line with neoliberal agendas for public service provision more widely. First, under the Conservative government (1979–97) universities were progressively "corporatized, massified and marketized" (Boden and Nedeva 2010: 39). Then, as part of a New Labour agenda, universities were positioned as working in partnership with the private sector. This neoliberal agenda had at its core a number of characteristics that legitimized it as "moral and democratic" (Boden and Nedeva 2010: 39). These characteristics included the concept of individual "choice" and the exercise of agency, while at the same time performance management regimes and audits were deemed necessary under the auspices of transparency and accountability. Consequently, universities became the site of much government intervention, activity and the central exercise of power usually related to public funding systems and "narrowly established performance indicators and norms" (Buckingham and Jones 2001: 5).

The most recent evidence of the ever-increasing overlap between work and HE is the growing embeddedness of an employability agenda within policy circles (Boden and Nedeva 2010; Thornham and O'Sullivan 2004). In the Department for Business, Innovation and Skills' (BIS) *Students at the Heart of the System* (2011) White Paper the government's intention was clear: "to create the conditions to encourage greater collaboration between HEIs and employers to ensure that students gain the knowledge and skills they need to embark on rewarding careers" (BIS 2011: 33). The prevalence of economic discourses can also be seen in the government-commissioned Browne Review (Browne 2010) and its changes to HE funding and student finance, which have shifted the cost to the individual student, creating greater pressure on young people to subsidize their own tertiary education.[3] Within these discourses students are positioned as "self-investing customers" (Boden and Nedeva 2010: 41), and "[a] major role of universities today is the production of an appropriately trained workforce that fits employers' needs. In many contemporary neoliberal states the long-standing contributions of universities to the development of citizens' knowledges and skills have been re-badged as 'employability'" (Boden and Nedeva 2010: 38). In this context HE is seen as "surrendering" to the logic of the market (Collini 2012). The importance of competitiveness, employability and training becomes firmly embedded within education and business policy discourses (Wilson 2012), and has become increasingly difficult to move against within the context of academic disciplines like media (Thornham and O'Sullivan 2004).

Within this general employability agenda a sector-specific one also prevails. This emerges directly from creative industries policy that foregrounds skills development but with little critical consideration of the impact. The role of education to foster marketable creative skills at all levels can be traced to New Labour strategies. Both the *Creative Industries Mapping Document* (DCMS 2001) and *Creative Britain: New talents for the new economy* (DCMS 2008) can be seen as further blueprints for how to develop human capital and how it may be put to work in the creative economy. "Creativity" and the "cultural productivity of young people" (Buckingham and Jones 2001: 11) is celebrated in generalized terms, as a social good that should be cultivated and commercialized; and, despite the emphasis on diversity, there is little recognition of the politics of culture and exclusion (Buckingham and Jones 2001). The report goes on to signal the approach to helping this creative talent "flourish", and states that, "having unlocked creativity, the vital stage is to ensure that young people have real opportunities to develop, and that they can see clearly the directions in which their talent can take them" (DCMS 2008: 7). Therefore, the education system becomes an important partner in the discovery of talents, and subsequently directs these to become commercially exploitable resources.

Such discursive and political framing of the creative economy and its relationship to an education framework is significant. By positioning the cultural industries under the umbrella of the creative economy, the *Creative Britain* report indicates "a concerted drive to develop workplace skills, stimulate business-orientated education and improve competitive advantage across the creative industry sector" (Banks and Hesmondhalgh 2009: 426). HEIs are "encouraged" to prioritize the development of certain skills (that is, those that have economic value in the market). Contemporary employability discourses emphasize the development or "banking" of narrow job-related skills in preference to capacity-building education and the acquisition of social and cultural capital (Boden and Nedeva 2010) with little or no reference made in any of these documents to career difficulties or issues faced by graduates from creative disciplines.

HEIs have certainly responded to this employability agenda through their curricula and pedagogical practices. Academic faculties have been rebranded, restructured or initiated to service this industry. Increasingly work placements, live simulations (such as television or radio broadcasts) and assessments mimicking the experience of cultural work are a visible part of the curriculum. Industry input also comes directly in the form of course accreditation (from organizations such as Creative Skillset)[4] and the inflow of teacher-practitioners to the HE system. While all of these are often important and attractive aspects of the curriculum, shaping both its graduates and its public image, it affirms the lure of vocationalism and the artificial framing of a theory/practice dichotomy (Corner 1995) with potentially serious implications for the nature and role of universities in developing "critical citizenship and civic courage" (Giroux 2000).

However, while HE has evolved to accommodate this neoliberal agenda and the demands of the knowledge economy, concerns also remain that HEIs are still not delivering effectively for the creative industries. For example, Creative Skillset (2009), the skills council responsible for the creative sector, has warned that despite an oversupply of willing graduates competing for jobs in the sector, the industry is reporting that HE is failing to deliver the *right* kind of skills needed. Reports indicate serious skills shortages in areas like digital technology and multiplatform capability, broadcast engineering, business and commercial know-how, visual effects and craft-orientated jobs (see Creative & Cultural Skills and Creative Skillset 2011).

Furthermore, while there are claims of gaps in specific occupational and sectoral roles, the curriculum itself comes under fire (for example in the NESTA commissioned report *Next Gen.* (2011), which is uncompromising in its criticism: "There are already many university courses purporting to provide specialist training for video games and visual effects. But most of these courses are flawed, leaving those graduating from them with poor job prospects" (Livingstone and Hope 2011: 5)). Guile (2010: 470) argues, "despite universities' close links with this sector, studying for a C&C-related [creative and cultural] degree rarely provides an expectation or understanding of what is required in vocational contexts." Again, the pressure is on the HE sector to remedy this – for example, through ensuring a "greater uptake of Skillset-backed courses and accreditation services, such as Skillset Academies [...] strongly supported by employers" (Creative Skillset 2009).

Under the ideologies of neoliberalism and the knowledge economy, two policy movements have come together to direct the relationship between higher education and the creative industries. The result has been that individual creative talents are now framed as economic resources and employability has become central to the role of the university. This has been managed by a plethora of economic metrics (for example, monitoring and measuring graduate destinations) and changes to the funding structures. However, while many continue to voice their reservations about this development (Collini 2012; Comunian et al 2011; Thornham and O'Sullivan 2004; Buckingham and Jones 2001), it is likely to continue apace in the future.

Governance and labour structures

This policy landscape, and the evolutions therein, have had a direct impact on curriculum content and the ways in which the expectations of a cultural education and subsequent work are shaped. As outlined, creative industries discourse has been very influential in policy circles as it merges innovation, creativity and economic growth. However, while policy purports to nurture many of the central ingredients of the knowledge economy, the "dynamics of policy formation in the UK impose a straightjacket on the education and training system" (Guile 2010: 466) as universities are caught between two systems of governance. On the one hand there are "supply-side measures" from policymakers imposing targets, merging funding with targets and taking a one size fits all sectors approach to education policy development (Guile 2010: 468). On the other hand are the demand-led pressures of industry for specific work-based skills with massification ensuring a ready and cheap supply of labour. For example, the evolution of the employability agenda ensures a reframing of the role of the universities, marking a transition of authority over the definition of what constitutes employability away from HE to industry and the state (Boden and Nedeva 2010). These converging forces mean that universities have had their strategic capacity to act on the basis of their "professional judgement severely circumscribed" (Boden and Nedeva 2010: 47). "Failure to comply with the demands of the purchaser – to 'play the game' according to its rules – risks a loss of funding, with consequences for employment as well as the continuation of funded activities" (Willmott 2003: 3).

Structural data on the labour market also reveals the impact of HE on the creative ecology and how its own agenda for growth feeds some of the labour issues encountered by creative workers. From their research Comunian et al. (2011: 305) conclude that the growth in scale of creative disciplines in HE has "expanded the provision of those skills without real corresponding opportunities". The result is an oversupply of graduate labour, which contributes directly to the continuing cycle of lower economic prospects and precarious working conditions. Oversupply results in earning capacity falling (the scarcity of skills/talent that drives wages up is dissipated by more graduates entering the market annually). Wages are dampened with competition continuing in the form of "prolonged entry tournaments" (Marsden 2007: 965) and work placements often involve free labour under the rubric of "gaining experience". This pressure to professionalize through demonstrable experience becomes a mechanism of exclusion in itself for those from certain socio-economic backgrounds. Comunian et al.'s (2011: 292) research questions the current policy framework and whether it has really benefited prospective creative workers or if it has done the opposite, "blurring economic and structural differences across the creative industries in a positive portrait" that is experienced only by a few.

With this expansion and massification of HE, greater scrutiny has been put on institutional structures, discourses and practices. The impact of these forces on access has become a key theme in educational policy both in the UK and internationally. Burke and McManus's (2011) research examines admission practices on a number of art and design courses, concluding that such practices are often tied to the complex operation of power, exclusion and subjective constructions of value and potential that "unwittingly reproduce deeply embedded inequalities" (700). This is particularly significant in the context of the creative sector, where judgements of quality and value are often subjective and cultural work itself is often cited as gendered, classed and racialized with substantial inequalities existing around access, development and pay (Oakley 2013; Comunian et al. 2011; Guile 2010). Furthermore, micro level initiatives within the curriculum, which are endorsed by reports such as *Creative Britain* (for example, industry collaborations, work placements and project simulations), can reproduce rather than challenge current structural conditions around exclusions (Allen 2013; Oakley 2013; Siebert and Wilson 2013), though some see these simulated work environments not just as naive reproductions but where the critical issues and politics of cultural work can be rendered visible, debated and contested (Ashton 2013).

Further, staff in HE are caught in their own precarious labour market and expected to behave as strategic actors in a research and degree market as alternative providers enter the market. One of the greatest threats to the sustainability of the current HE system comes from intermediary organizations that create new spaces for aspiring entrants to enter industry (Guile 2010). The emergence of corporate, for-profit and virtual universities – along with private universities and colleges, poly-technical institutes and specialist institutions – challenges the privileged position of universities on the higher education landscape, and this trend is unlikely to be reversed as HE becomes increasingly subject to consumer sovereignty and existing media companies look for new revenue streams.

Finally, the transfer of responsibility for financing research, which has shifted from higher education institutions to research councils, foundations and sectoral agencies means that academic staff engaged in research increasingly rely on external sources of finance. Allocation of public funding for research (through systems like the Research Excellence Framework)[5] is selective, legitimized through a system of peer review (Willmott 2003), and governed by centralized assessments of performance; thus deepening and widening government management of the research process (Couldry 2011). Critics argue that these allocation systems do not encourage autonomy or risk-taking but rather conformity (Collini 2012; Couldry 2011) requiring academics to act as intermediaries between policy and industry. Universities are measured on their responsiveness to commercial, industrial and political agendas with industry engagement often encouraged and used directly as a measure of academic effectiveness. As researchers become increasingly reliant on external resources, partnerships and knowledge exchanges, their ability to be critical of practices and enthusiasm for engaging in such exchanges is uncertain.

In many ways HE may be complicit in (re)producing many of the structural issues within cultural labour. The convergence of policy, admission practices, occupational pressures and current models of governance render universities largely powerless, marginalizing their voice, and rendering them seemingly impotent in current policy decision-making. The focus of this chapter has been predominantly on the UK context. However in an era of globalization, policy often travels and such monitoring and management of teaching and research is likely to be attractive to other governments looking to further their development of the knowledge economy, to make the work of academics more responsive to industrial and policy priorities, while reducing costs and competing internationally for prestige and talent. However, while such conditions seem impermeable, strategies for resistance are discernible both within and outside HE; how HEIs engage with social enterprises, co-operatives, trade unions and activist organizations will be vital to ensuring that conversations about exploitation, access and what constitutes "good work" remain part of the curriculum for vocational and theoretical degrees, thus helping to recover a debate lost to mainstream economic thought (Oakley 2013).

Notes

1 In 2011 Sir Tim Wilson was commissioned by the UK government to review university–business collaboration. Recommendations made by the report included strengthening graduate employability through subsidized internships, enhancing the structure for knowledge transfer partnerships and making employment data for postgraduate courses available.
2 The Select Committee on Arts and Manufactures is regarded as a significant milestone in the development of British art education as "it was the first occasion when key questions regarding the relationship between art, commerce, and art education were the subject of parliamentary debate" (Sproll 1994: 108).
3 The Department for Business, Innovation and Skills (BIS) is a UK ministerial department created in 2009 by the merger of the Department for Innovation, Universities and Skills (DIUS) and the Department for Business, Enterprise and Regulatory Reform (BERR). BIS is responsible for areas such as business regulation and support, further education and higher education, intellectual property, regional and local economic development, science and research, skills and training. Due to devolution some policies apply to England alone (such as further and higher education policy), while others are not devolved (see Court

2004 for further discussion of the impact of devolution on HE policy). The Department for Education (DfE) is a separate department of the UK government responsible for education (up to secondary level).

4 Creative Skillset is the industry body supporting training for the UK creative industries. It accredits practice-based degrees, offering "an invaluable signpost for potential students, apprentices and employers to indicate those programmes that provide the most up-to-date and relevant industry training and education" (Creative Skillset 2013).

5 The Research Excellence Framework (REF) is the national system for assessing the quality of research in UK HEIs. It allocates funding for research based on measures of "excellence"; provides accountability for public investment in research; and provides benchmarking information to establish reputational yardsticks (REF 2012).

References

ADM-HEA (2010) "Looking Out 2009–10". (accessed 29 April 2014: www.adm.heacademy.ac.uk/projects/adm-hea-projects/looking-out/).

Allen, K. (2013) "'What Do You Need to Make it as a Woman in this Industry? Balls!': Work Placements, Gender AND THE Cultural Industries", in D. Ashton and C. Noonan (eds) Cultural Work and Higher Education, Hampshire: Palgrave Macmillan.

Ashton, D. (2013) "Cultural Workers in the Making", European Journal of Cultural Studies 16(4): 468–88.

Ashton, D. and Noonan, C. (eds) (2013) Cultural Work and Higher Education, Hampshire: Palgrave Macmillan.

Banks, M. and Hesmondhalgh, D. (2009) "Looking for Work in Creative Industries Policy", International Journal of Cultural Policy 15(4): 415–30.

BIS (2011) Students at the Heart of the System, London: Department for Business, Innovation and Skills.

Boden, R. and Nedeva, M. (2010) "Employing Discourse: Universities and Graduate 'Employability'", Journal of Education Policy 25(1): 37–54.

Browne, J. (2010) Independent Review of Higher Education Funding and Student Finance, London: Department for Business, Innovation and Skills.

Buckingham, D. and Jones, K. (2001) "New Labour's Cultural Turn: Some Tension in Contemporary Educational and Cultural Policy", Journal of Education Policy 16(1): 1–14.

Burke, P. J. and McManus, J. (2011) "Art for a Few: Exclusions and Misrecognitions in Higher Education Admissions Practices", Discourse: Studies in the Cultural Politics of Education 32(5): 699–712.

Catchside, K. (2012) "Lack of Higher Education Funding Could Stifle UK's Creative Industries", Guardian: Higher Education Network, February 27 (accessed 25 March 2013: www.guardian.co.uk/higher-education-network/blog/2012/feb/27/funding-creative-disciplines-in-higher-education).

Collini, S. (2012) What Are Universities For? London: Penguin.

Committee on Higher Education (1963) Higher Education: Report of the Committee Appointed by the Prime Minister under the Chairmanship of Lord Robbins 1961–63, Cmnd. 2154, London: HMSO.

Comunian, R., Faggian, A. and Jewell, S. (2011) "Winning and Losing in the Creative Industries: An Analysis of Creative Graduate's Career Opportunities Across Creative Disciplines", Cultural Trends 20(3–4): 291–308.

Corner, J. (1995) "Media Studies and the 'Knowledge Problem'", Screen 36(2): 147–55.

Couldry, N. (2011) "Post-neoliberal Academic Values: Notes From the UK Higher Education Sector", in B. Zelizer (ed.) Making the University Matter, London: Routledge.

Court, S. (2004) "Government Getting Closer: Higher Education and Devolution in the UK", Higher Education Quarterly 58(2–3): 151–75.

Creative & Cultural Skills and Creative Skillset (2011) "Sector Skills Assessment for the Creative Industries of the UK" (accessed 14 November 2012: creativeskillset.org/assets/0000/6023/Sector_Skills_Assessment_for_the_Creative_Industries_-_Skillset_and_CCSkills_2011.pdf).

Creative Skillset (2009) "Strategic Skills Assessment for the Creative Media Industry" (accessed 5 July 2012: creativeskillset.org/assets/0000/6044/Strategic_Skills_Assessment_for_the_Creative_Media_Industries_North_of_England_2010.pdf).

Creative Skillset (2013) "Apply for Creative Skillset Degree Accreditation" (accessed 14 August 2013: creativeskillset.org/who_we_help/training_educators/tick_course_accreditation).

DCMS (Department of Culture, Media and Sport) (2001) *Creative Industries Mapping Document*, London: DCMS.

DCMS (2008) *Creative Britain: New Talents for the New Economy*, London: DCMS.

Dearing, R. (1997) *National Committee of Inquiry into Higher Education*, London: Department for Education and Employment.

Frith, S. and Horne, H. (1987) *Art into Pop*, London: Methuen.

Giroux, H. (2000) "Cultural Politics and the Crisis of the University", *CultureMachine*, 2 (accessed 16 June 2011: www.culturemachine.net/index.php/cm/article/viewArticle/309/294).

Grove, J. (2012) "Spanner in the Industrial Works as Engineering Degrees Lose Traction", 15 November (accessed 2 July 2013: www.timeshighereducation.co.uk/news/spanner-in-the-industrial-works-as-engineering-degrees-lose-traction/421834.article).

Guile, D. (2010) "Learning to Work in the Creative and Cultural Sector: News Spaces, Pedagogies and Expertise", *Journal of Education Policy* 25(4): 465–84.

Lazzeroni, M. and Piccaluga, A. (2003) "Towards the Entrepreneurial University", *Local Economy* 18(1): 38–48.

Livingstone, I. and Hope, A. (2011) "Next Gen.", *NESTA* (accessed 20 August 2013: www.nesta.org.uk/publications/next-gen).

Marsden, D. (2007) "Labour Market Segmentation in Britain: The Decline of Occupational Labour Markets and the Spread of 'Entry Tournaments'", *Economies and Societies* 28: 965–98.

Oakley, K. (2013) "Making Workers: Higher Education and the Cultural Industries Workplace", in D. Ashton and C. Noonan (eds) *Cultural Work and Higher Education*, Hampshire: Palgrave Macmillan.

Ozga, J. and Jones, R. (2006) "Travelling and Embedded Policy: The Case of Knowledge Transfer", *Journal of Education Policy* 21(1): 1–17.

REF (2012) *Research Excellence Framework* (accessed 14 February 2013: www.ref.ac.uk/).

Romans, M. (2007) 'An Analysis of the Political Complexion of the 1835/6 Select Committee on Arts and Manufactures', *International Journal of Art and Design Education* 26(2): 215–24.

Siebert, S. and Wilson, F. (2013) "All Work and No Pay: Consequences of Unpaid Work in the Creative Industries", *Work Employment and Society* 27(4): 711–21.

Sproll, P. (1994) "Matter of Taste and Matters of Commerce: British Government Intervention in Art Education in 1835", *Studies in Art Education* 35(2): 105–13.

Thornham, S. and O'Sullivan, T. (2004) "Chasing the Real: 'Employability' and the Media Studies Curriculum", *Media, Culture and Society* 26(5): 717–36.

Universities UK (2010) "Patterns of Higher Education Institutions in the UK", *Universities UK* (accessed 19 August 2013: www.universitiesuk.ac.uk/highereducation/Documents/2010/Patterns10.pdf).

Willmott, H. (2003) "Commercializing Higher Education in the UK: The State, Industry and Peer Review", *Studies in Higher Education* 28(2): 129–41.

Wilson, T. (2012) "A Review of Business-University Collaboration: The Wilson Review" (accessed 8 August 2013: www.gov.uk/government/publications/business-university-collaboration-the-wilson-review).

36
BUSINESS AS USUAL
Creative industries and the specificity of the
British state

Dave O'Brien

Introduction

The concept of creative industries has a close relationship to the British state. As a result of this it is important to follow Vernon's argument that:

> We must ... remember that the brevity of social democracy was not confined to Britain. We need better ways of explaining why and how Britain shares much of its twentieth-century history with others across the globe and yet why and how they assumed a specifically British character.
>
> (Vernon 2012: 418)

The UK government did much to develop the idea of creative industries by moving it beyond the more arts focused cultural industries and linking cultural activity with technology, for example software design (Garnham 2005, Campbell 2013). However, the 'Britishness' of the concept has been underexplored. This chapter uses the close relationship between the concept of creative industries and the British state to open up a new research agenda for the study of creative industries, one that is closely attentive to the parochial aspects of that concept and its related practices. It argues for a new research agenda in two ways. In the first instance it draws on the 'social life of methods' approach developed in British sociology by John Law, Evelyn Rupert and Mike Savage (Law et al. 2011) and applied to cultural policy by O'Brien (2014). Second the chapter links the need to see measurement methods as having a 'social life' to emerging trends in the historiography and analysis of the British state, suggesting an important supplemental narrative to understanding the creative industries. The chapter argues that the emergence of specific forms of measurement is intertwined with the specific form of the British state. This underpins the argument made in the second half of the chapter that the creative industries are inseparable from the way the British state has been configured since the rise of British modernity in the eighteenth century. Thus the chapter offers an important new area of research in the comparative study of creative industries, building on the work of Ross (2007) and

Flew (2013), but one that pays more attention to the role of national specificity in shaping this now global phenomenon.

Redefining creative industries: The search for methods and policy

In a 2013 newspaper article the then British Chancellor George Osborne outlined a range of schemes to make Britain competitive within the current economic context, whereby government would be: 'making sure this country is the best place in the world to learn digital skills, engage with the digital economy and set up the next Wikipedia' (Osborne, G. 2013).

Alongside education programmes and changes to the computing curriculum (framed, of course, within the requirements of rigour and toughness favoured by British Department for Education discourses), Osborne wrote of generous tax breaks for tech start ups, helping companies to list on the London Stock Exchange and offering government contracts to small firms.

In Osborne's rhetoric the digital economy was a key site for British growth and British competitiveness. This is a distillation of the United Kingdom's Department for Business, Innovation and Skills' industrial strategy (BIS 2014), where there is a focus on what it calls the information economy. Here it echoes Osborne's comments, albeit with the additional focus of developing information and communication technology (ICT) use by existing businesses and promoting citizens' engagement with ICT.

It would seem, therefore, that the position outlined by McRobbie captures a key idea in creative industries discourses: 'We will soon begin to see the "creative industry" phenomenon as something specifically linked with the Blair and post-Blair years, starting 1997 and in effect lasting for just more than a decade' (McRobbie 2011: 32).

The creative industries were, in the original conception of the Department for Culture, Media and Sport (DCMS), supposed to take in much of the industrial activity that is now badged as ICT, information and digital economy. Indeed, 2011 saw the beginning (or perhaps the end) of a battle over the status of ICT within the DCMS definition of creative industries. As Campbell (2013) has shown, much of the creative industries claims on growth and impact were dependent on linking the complex, but perhaps not entirely cultural or artistic, activities of database designers and software engineers to computer games and then on into all manner of cultural and creative sectors, including performance, visual arts and fashion. In 2011 DCMS removed this form of ICT activity from its estimates of creative industries economic activity, causing a clear reduction in the economic impact and thus the ability of creative industries to attract the interest of policy makers from beyond DCMS and the broader cultural sector with which they were associated (DCMS 2011).

This redefinition has seen something of a counter-revolution with the latest DCMS consultation on what will and what will not be seen as a creative industry (DCMS 2013). There has been considerable discussion (perhaps fallout would be a more appropriate term) of the proposals, which focus on the idea of 'creative intensity', which sees any industry in which over 30 per cent of people do 'creative' jobs as potentially included in the creative industries classification. So far, so circular, as the definition of 'creative' jobs is not addressed in the consultation document, but rather the reader is directed to the work of Creative Skillset (2013), an organisation tasked with developing skills in the creative industries and co-funded by the UK government and industry.

The Creative Skillset document illustrates one of the issues with the 30 per cent threshold, as well as attempting to clarify the new definition of creative industries. The 30 per cent threshold rules out library and museum activities, not because they are un-creative, but because the institutional organisation of these areas, which depend on relatively high levels of support staff, gives figures of only around 22 per cent creative intensity. This new way of understanding creative intensity is at the root of the removal of craft and arts and antiques, the latter as it is defined as more of a retail than a creative industry, the former for reasons of data collection, in essence that much craft activity is too small to be captured by Standard Industrial Classification (SIC) codes that underpin the DCMS's survey devices.

The debates over measurement can be understood through the lens of a perspective that is developing in the study of cultural policy that suggests methods and methodological choices have a social purpose and position (O'Brien 2014). There is, therefore, a social life of methods story to be told here as, although the subsequent protests by organisations such as the Crafts Council[1] focused on the potential marginalisation of craft from government policy (and thereby risking the loss of resources), the real issue was one of data collection devices and their imprecisions.

The role of methods and methodological choices runs throughout the consultation document. It is, after all, a consultation on methods. What is most interesting is the marginalisation of intellectual property (IP) as the basis for creative industries. The original DCMS definition focused very closely on IP as the core of creative industries: 'Those industries which have their origin in individual creativity, skill and talent which have a potential for job and wealth creation through the generation and exploitation of intellectual property' (DCMS 2001).

That focus generated a whole range of criticism, not the least of which was identified by Skillset's consultation document, which argued the definition: 'could actually apply to all economic activities as nearly all activities do involve some degree of creativity, either in the creation of new products and services or when innovating in the production of goods and provision of services' (Creative Skillset 2013: 6).

The new DCMS definition, which aims to move beyond these issues, will run thus: 'in essence a creative industry is defined as being one which employs a significant proportion of creative people, as identified by those being employed in a creative occupation' (Creative Skillset 2013: 11).

The contested idea of creativity is given clarification by NESTA: 'A role within the creative process that brings cognitive skills to bear to bring about a differentiation to yield either novel, or significantly enhanced products whose final form is not fully specified in advance' (NESTA 2013: 24).

More detailed criteria demand that there be a novel process, that the occupation be resistant to mechanisation, that the effect of the occupation is non-repetitive or non-uniform and that there is a creative contribution to the value chain associated with the product. This last element is especially problematic given the contested nature of creativity detailed above. Skillset's own reading of these detailed criteria admits to their lack of coherence and contestability. It is difficult not to be reminded of Thomas Osborne's (2003) self-described 'rant' against creativity as both a misunderstanding of inventiveness and innovation and as a new form of capital to be deployed in both economic and bureaucratic contexts.

Locating creative industries

The problem of how to measure cultural and creative activity has taken place against the backdrop of both the financial crisis and the longer-term conflicts over the funding of arts and cultural activity in the United Kingdom. The contested status of software is related to the way in which the creative industries agenda emerged from that of the cultural industries, one that in turn had a relationship with the transformations of the role and purpose of culture spurred on by work in the cultural studies tradition. In turn, cultural studies has tried to make a contribution to the debates over the global financial crisis and potential post-crisis economy and society (Hayward 2011). For these critical voices the financial crisis and the responses to it are continuations of a project of inequality that has seen elites, both economic and social, attempt to 're-establish and fortify an economic and social order that was on the brink of collapse and discredit' (Hayward 2011: 3). The critiques of this attempt are framed within the tripartite tradition of cultural studies' engagement with the economic: as critics of the social relations generated by economic systems, whilst seeking to avoid crude economic determinism; as critics of the governmentality of economy and economics; and as post-colonial and feminist critics of political economy (Hayward 2011).

Harney (2012) writes from this tradition in an attempt to assess the creative industries in the post-crash era. He argues that creative industries discussions have been drawn too narrowly (although he draws on an argument with a potentially debatable historical narrative). Harney's position is worth focusing on as it gives clues as to where a productive development may occur in terms of a new research agenda for the creative industries. Whilst Garnham (2005) points to the European Union's innovation agenda and discourses of information society and knowledge economy as the backdrop to creative industries, McRobbie (2011) founds their rise in the transformations of night-time and subcultural economies and Hesmondhalgh (2013) offers a narrative that demands attention is paid to the aesthetic and symbolic elements of economic practice, Harney locates creative industries in the rise and conquest of culture by management, alongside the culturalisation of management itself: 'On the one had, the arts as the object of management and, on the other hand, the arts as the objective of management' (Harney 2012: 153).

Eschewing a story of the absorption of cultural activity by capital, which has been a critical position since aestheticist and art for art's sake discourses of the nineteenth century, Harney offers a position in which 'a broad view of the creative industries is established by tracking the arts not through their own commodification, but through the commodification of those whom produce them' (2012: 150). Echoing Gill (2010) and the grander narratives of Boltanski and Chiapello (2007), Harney sees a long-term trend whereby the arts are conceived of as work, as a form of labour, which can be subject to debates over hours, pay and conditions, but can also be granted a position within governmental industrial and economic policies. If art is to be work, if it has moved from 'the workshop to the workplace' (Harney 2012: 150) then it will need a form of analysis commensurate to how workplaces have been previously understood across academic disciplines. It will also need analysis of the role and position of work within the societies that have embraced cultural activity as creative industries.

For sure, some of this work is being, and has been, done by a range of scholarship from both cultural studies and areas such as economic geography and the sociology of work. However, as Harney points out, why are the processes he identifies happening and why now? Why has culture been subject to management and why has management taken up culture? Why is it that governmental discourses still perform the sorts of doublethink identified by Campbell (2013) to make claims for the role and impor-tance of creative industries? And why is it that specific forms of creative industries, so roundly eviscerated by academic discussion, still hold sway in governmental visions of new forms of economy and society able to respond to the challenges of financial crisis and global competition?

Creative industries and the British state: Elite debacles, elite identities

One way of answering Harney's potentially rhetorical questions is to try to link creative industries discussions to areas of academic research where they have been peripheral or have not seen a disciplinary tradition emerge around them. It is in these areas that the sort of scholarship needed to supplement cultural studies' engagement with creative industries can be found. For example, recent work (O'Brien 2014) has attempted to do this in terms of political science, but in this instance the following discussion will drawn on a combination of history, political economy and sociology. For sure there have been historical (McRobbie 2011), political economy and sociological (Campbell 2013) perspectives on creative industries. But casting the intellectual net more widely can be useful for two reasons. In the first instance there is an opportunity to suggest why, rather than just being a New Labour phenomenon, the creative industries relate directly to the longstanding configuration of the British state. Indeed the combination of primarily service and intellectual property driven forms of economic activity, alongside class based elite social groups, may be a further explanatory factor for the traction the creative industries have, and seemingly continue, to have in the United Kingdom. Second there is a chance to use creative industries to comment on the nature of the British state, adding detail and depth to the sort of work that will be discussed below.

The place to start with this approach is how best to narrate the British state. Here there are four main sources; Colin Hay's work (1996 and 2007), which is part of a larger state theoretical tradition in British Political Economy (e.g. Jessop 1990 and Kerr 2001); The extensive work of Engelen et al. (2011) on the financial crisis, parti-cularly its UK aspects; recent historical work on the nature of identities within the British state by Edgerton (2006) and Savage (2010) and finally a much larger historical tradition that has attempted to understand the dynamics of finance, institutions and individuals that are the basis for the narratives contained in the previous three sets of work (Cain and Hopkins 2001, Kynaston 2012).

To deal with the latter and former first. There is a historical tradition that unites Marxist political economy and histories of institutions such as the City, whereby both sets of authors proclaim the importance and, indeed, dominance of the needs of finance over other areas of British economy and society. This is for a wide variety of reasons, as:

> From the middle of the nineteenth century the major area of growth was the service sector and the most rapidly developing region was the south-east. The City was at the heart of both. London stood at the centre of a well-developed network of international services, and these were destined to expand rapidly as world trade increased in the second half of the nineteenth century. Even before 1850, financial flows from the City were a major determinant of the rhythm of development in the colonies. Beyond formal empire, London's influence as the main source of long-term international finance had begun to spread to Europe and North America after 1815 and was poised to increase dramatically after 1850, as the age of the steamship and railway began. The service sector and the City supported the introduction of free trade and proved, during the next seventy years, to be its chief beneficiaries. They also carried into free-trade Britain many of the cultural values acquired in the course of their long apprentice to the landed aristocracy. After 1850, as one form of gentlemanly capitalism began to fail, another rose to take its place (Cain and Hopkins 1986:525).

Cain and Hopkins (1986) narrate the British state as one dominated, from the late 1600s up until 1850, by a landed aristocracy, which, as a result of transformations in British capitalism, lost direct influence over policy to a newer form of gentlemanly capitalism driven by the 'new men' of the financial service sector up to 1945. This is not to marginalise manufacturing and industry, but rather to stress the importance of the emerging institution of the City as a key driver for state policy. Indeed, at the beginning of the twentieth century City, government and public administration were closely intertwined with the nexus of City, Treasury and Bank of England focusing policy in promoting a narrow view of the British national interest (Hay 1996, Cain and Hopkins 1987). This conception of the national interest placed the non-industrial, financial services forms of economic activity at its heart:

> in particular, recognition needs to be given to the fact that economic development was not synonymous with the industrial revolution, that non-industrial activities were far more important, progressive and independent than has been allowed, and that these employments were associated with high status and gave access to political influence. (Cain and Hopkins 1987:18)

The importance of finance to the development of the modern British state had profound influence on how industrial policy was, or more accurately was not, made. Decisions to privilege the City over and above Britain's manufacturers form the basis of much of Cain and Hopkins' *British Imperialism* (2001) but are also important to the wider debate around the role and function of material forms of labour in the Britain that followed the Industrial Revolution (Weiner 1981, Rubenstein 1981).

These policy decisions are also reflected in the identities of elites governing the British state, whereby the identities of those seeking to foreground finance whilst marginalising manufacturing were dependent on their lack of connection to the wealthy manufacturing classes emerging from provincial England in the nineteenth century (Cain and Hopkins 2001, Joyce 2013). The English gentleman of landed aristocracy dominant in the eighteenth century became the 'gentlemanly capitalist' of the nineteenth and twentieth, dependent on the 'invisible' (Cain and Hopkins 2001:15) earnings of finance.

What is most interesting about this line of historical analysis is the way that it intersects with recent work focusing on the relationship between culture, creativity and management. The previous section discussed Harney's (2012) interest in the way arts and culture has been co-opted into the language of management to run the modern economy. This is supported by Boltanski and Chiapello's (2007) work on how management of the corporation is now expected to be creative and even, in the post 1968 tradition, critical. Boltanski and Chiapello were writing in the French context, with a global perspective.

The co-option of the language of the cultural and artistic fits well, in the British context, with a narrative of the state that is keen to deny the artisan and the manufacturer as a key force in the economy. Rather it is the financier, the gentlemanly capitalist whose hands are never sullied, who is the ideal type worker in the British economy since the industrial revolution. This is, of course, notwithstanding the range of different forms and class compositions to which this ideal type has been subject (Cain and Hopkins 2001). This sort of historical research points towards a view of both the artistic critique, as it has been co-opted into present day British management of all varieties, and the preponderance of financial capitalism being fertile ground for the transformation of cultural into creative industries within contemporary British industrial and cultural policy.

The rise of the creative industries, where software is yoked with more traditionally cultural labour, such as visual arts or dance, was thus an easy fit to take a place at the vanguard of British policy to develop economic activity following the culmination, during the 1980s, of the longstanding marginalisation of manufacturing and heavier industry. This is because the vision of cultural labour that became associated with the ownership and exploitation of intellectual property, in the 2001 DCMS definition of the creative industries, owed more to the longstanding trope of the financier and the broader activity of the City, than to the artist actually *making* culture, as opposed to merely deriving rents from the ownership of it. Indeed, in the British economy of the housing boom as opposed to the car manufacturing plant (Engelen et al. 2011), the rentier of the creative industries is much more appropriate than the artisan of the cultural industries.

This perspective adds depth to comparisons of the rise (or irrelevance) of creative industries discourses in the global setting, going some way to deepening the explanations of Ross (2007) and Miller (2009) as to the uneven take up of the idea around the world. This is not to deny the particulars of other national narratives of cultural and then creative industries. Nor is it to entirely assert a colonial narrative at the root of the globalisation of this set of ideas. Indeed the question remains as to how these discourses are popular in, say, China, but not in the USA. Rather it gestures towards the need for national, historical work to help explain and thus critique ideas of both cultural and creative industry.

This historical work suggests that struggles over creative industries policy can certainly be considered from a national perspective. To focus on this point and to provide a transition to the second part of this nationally specific analysis, it is worth considering how the turn to an economy based on immaterial forms of labour requires an understanding of the role of this form of labour and how the associated identities were present over time in the United Kingdom and were unrelated to culture and creativity. Whilst many narratives of the emergence of creative industries discourses and policy often, rightly, focus on the political project of left wing local authorities in the United Kingdom as a crucial influence on New Labour's conception of creative industries (Hesmondhalgh and Pratt 2005, Garnham 2005), the above discussion suggests that by the time cultural industries had become embedded within central government discourses in the form of creative industries, they were able to take a place within a British governmental context still bearing the imprint of the gentlemanly capitalist (Cain and Hopkins 2001).

The previous paragraph may be used to bridge the history of British government to work that has attempted to understand the inequalities of labour markets for cultural and creative industries. There are important elements of the class composition of creative work and the assumptions about what forms of labour, particularly those associated with finance, are legitimate and those which are not, for example more traditional manual and industrial occupations. Indeed this point may be of direct benefit to those grappling with questions surrounding the stratification of creative employment (e.g. Oakley 2009, Gill 2010).

It would be inaccurate to focus solely on the idea of gentlemanly capitalists as the dominant actors in public policy, something which, as any review of the creative industries literature shows, has remained a peripheral concern within cultural studies' attempts to frame creative industries as an epiphenomenon of the supposed neo-liberal turn in Britain. In actual fact the identity of those at the heart of the state, since the 1940s, has been as much technical as it has been gentlemanly and amateur. This dual identity in the twentieth century raises questions for the historical research agenda suggested by the discussion of work such as *British Imperialism*. At the same time it points to a further mechanism by which culture and creativity were embraced in the United Kingdom whilst the challenging or radical elements of those ideas were largely ignored in favour of rents from the control of intellectual property and database design.

This position, held by two differing authors in the form of historical sociologist Savage (2010) and historian of science and technology Edgerton, is captured by the latter's frustration that: 'in many accounts the British state is all welfare, administrators, civilians, arts graduates, Keynesianism and nationalisation' (Edgerton 2006: 7). The vision of a British state staffed by those with specifically technical identities adds depth to discussions of non-industrial identities within the British state. Edgerton's position takes issue both with the two cultures thesis of C.P. Snow, which railed against the marginalisation of scientific knowledge by the seemingly dominant strands of gentlemanly humanities scholarship and the assumption that British 'declinist' scholarship (a tradition that Edgerton seeks to refute) and discourses is correct in its laments about the collapse of British technological capacity from the heights of the nineteenth century. Rather, Edgerton insists that well into the 1960s Britain was 'without doubt, the scientific and technological powerhouse of Western Europe' whilst at the same time a range of writers, from left and right, were denouncing Britain's controlling elites as 'traditional, backward and anti-scientific' (Edgerton 1996:54). This insistence is backed by a wealth of information on research and development (R&D) spending (much of which is defence spending seen as R&D), narratives of civil servants' identities and reflections on the formal organisation of the British state. However, the focus on defence spending is important, as just as Kynaston and Cain and Hopkins point us to the demands of finance in shaping the British state, Edgerton insists on the influence of military concerns, the 'warfare state' (2006), on determining the character of *a profoundly technological nation* (Edgerton 1996: 82).

If Edgerton is arguing that there is an incorrect narrative about the marginal position of science within the British state, when science is understood in terms of war and military development, what implications are there for our present position? This chapter is in no way arguing that Britain is at the leading edge of innovation, indeed Osborne's comments in the opening section of this chapter, Engelen et al.'s (2011) work and recent discussions of British industrial policy Mazucatto (2011) all agree on the highly problematic position of British science and technological development in the context of a government (and a wider political class) that, at best, is deeply suspicious of anything that might really be seen as an interventionist industrial strategy. However, it does help to explain how aspects of creative industries that linked to narratives of new forms of economy (Garnham 2005) and innovation (Oakley 2012) were able to gain traction and, in the estimation of this chapter, continue to do so. The need for Britain to be competitive in areas that are related to technological advancement and the prevailing fear amongst policy makers, backed by political and media discourses is, as Edgerton shows, part of the cultural memory of Whitehall, as much as the City of London is influential on policy.

Conclusion: Can there be a new research agenda for creative industries?

By way of conclusion, it is worth returning to the quote from Vernon that opened this chapter. For sure, creative industries are a global phenomenon. However, the narrative of creative industries may be usefully retold as part of the wider story of the British state, one focused on the service sector, in particular on financial services. Most specifically these discussions all suggest the need for a research agenda that takes the Britishness of creative industries seriously. This is not a call for a myopic parochialism. Rather that the emergence and continued traction for conceptions such as creative industries need to be placed into the proper social and economic context. This is, of course, a context of cultural studies, the Greater London Council, the rise of sub-cultural capital and of night-time economies. These are all essential part of explaining the creative industries. However, there is a further relationship to the specificity of the British state that is under-developed when writers connect creative industries directly to narratives of the political economy of whichever version – post, reflexive, late – of modernity they are happy to adopt.

Recent work exploring creative industries as part of cultural policy more generally (e.g. Stevenson et al. 2010, Hesmondhalgh et al. 2014) has done much to contribute to developing a perspective that takes seriously the 'Britishness' of creative industries policy in the United Kingdom and its subsequent global career. In the case of Stevenson et al. (2010) the analysis is still dependent on the standard narrative of New Labour's struggle to come to terms with the rupture of the 'post war consensus' by Thatcherism. However, they do offer the important dimension of the role and influence of the European Union in shaping British cultural policy's regional dimensions. Hesmondhalgh et al. (2014) have done much to correct the simplistic elision between an ill defined conception of neo-liberalism and New Labour's cultural policy. However, more work is needed to re-interrogate the standard narratives of creative industries using developments in other disciplines. The current author has attempted this in a recent book, suggesting the explanation for creative industries' importance lies in political actors' responses to modernity (O'Brien 2014), particularly how phenomena such as globalisation are constructed and then acted upon by politicians, public administration and the state. The previous three sets of work give examples as to how thinking specifically about the British state can challenge narratives of creative industries. The next step may be to explore how a more fully developed historical research agenda could connect the disparate but interrelated historical and political economy work described in this chapter to those writers who have their basis in cultural and communications studies. The essential point of this chapter is, therefore, to develop new insights into seemingly settled questions for the now established research community around creative industries.

Note

1 The Crafts Council is the national development and support agency for crafts in the UK.

References

BIS (2014) *Industrial Strategy: Government and Business in Partnership*, London: BIS.

Boltanksi, L. and Chiapello, E. (2007) *The New Spirit of Capitalism*, London: Verso.

Cain, P. and Hopkins, A. (1986) 'Gentlemanly Capitalism and British Expansion Overseas: I. The Old Colonial System, 1688–1850', *Economic History Review* 39(4): 501–25.

Cain, P. and Hopkins, A. (1987) ' Gentlemanly Capitalism and British Expansion Overseas, II. New Imperialism, 1850–1945' *Economic History Review* 40(1): 1–26.

Cain, P. and Hopkins, A. (2001) *British Imperialism*, London: Pearson.

Campbell, P. (2013) 'Imaginary Success? The Contentious Ascendance Of Creativity', *European Planning Studies*, DOI: 10.1080/09654313.2012.753993.

Creative Skillset (2013) *Classifying and Measuring the Creative Industries*, London: Creative Skillset.

DCMS (2001) *Creative Industries Mapping Document*, London: DCMS.

DCMS (2011) *Creative Industries Economic Estimates*, London: DCMS.

DCMS (2013) *Classifying and Measuring the Creative Industries: Consultation on Proposed Changes*, London: DCMS.

Edgerton, D. (1996) 'The White Heat Revisited: The British Government and Technology in the 1960s', *Twentieth Century British History* 7(1): 53–82.

Edgerton, D. (2006) *Warfare State*, Cambridge: CUP.

Engelen, E., Erturk, I., Froud, J., Johal, S., Leaver, A., Moran, M., Nilsson, A. and Williams, K. (2011) *After the Great Complacence: Financial Crisis and the Politics of Reform*, Oxford: OUP.

Flew, T. (2013) *Global Creative Industries*, London: Polity Press.

Garnham, N. (2005) 'From Cultural to Creative Industries', *International Journal of Cultural Policy* 11(1): 15–29.

Gill, R. (2010). 'Life is a Pitch: Managing the Self in New Media Work', in Deuze, M. (ed.) *Managing Media Work*, Indiana: Indiana University Press.

Harney, S. (2012) 'Unfinished Business: Labour, Management, and the creative Industries', in Hayward, M. (ed.) *Cultural Studies and Finance Capitalism*, London: Routledge.

Hay, C. (1996) *Re-Stating Social and Political Change*, London: OUP.

Hay, C. (2007) *Why We Hate Politics*, Cambridge: Polity.

Hayward, M. (ed.) (2011) *Cultural Studies and Finance Capitalism: The Economic Crisis and After*, London: Routledge.

Hesmondhalgh, D. (2013) *The Cultural Industries*, London: Sage.

Hesmondhalgh, D. and Pratt, A. (2005) 'Cultural Industries and Cultural Policy', *International Journal of Cultural Policy* 11(1): 1–13.

Hesmondhalgh, D., Nisbett, M., Oakley, K.and Lee, D.J. (2014) 'Were New Labour's Cultural Policies Neo-Liberal?' *International Journal of Cultural Policy*, available from www.tandfon-line.com/doi/abs/10.1080/10286632.2013.879126?af=R#.U1Vj4xbtJUQ (accessed 1 February 2014).

Jessop, B. (1990) *State Theory*, Philadelphia: Penn State Press.

Joyce, P. (2013) *The State of Freedom*, Cambridge: CUP.

Kerr, P. (2001) *Postwar British Politics: From Conflict to Consensus*, London: Routledge.

Kynaston, D. (2012) *City of London: The History*, London: Vintage Press.

Law, J., Ruppert, E. and Savage, M. (2011) 'The Double Social Life of Methods', *CRESC Working Paper* No.95.

Mazucatto, M. (2011) *The Entrepreneurial State*, London: Demos.

McRobbie, A. (2011) 'Rethinking Creative Economy as Radical Social Enterprise', *Variant* 41: 33–4.

Miller, T. (2009) 'From Creative to Cultural Industries', *Cultural Studies* 23(1): 88–99.

NESTA (2013) *A Manifesto for the Creative Industries*, London: NESTA.

Oakley, K. (2009) *Art Works*, London: CCE.

Oakley, K. (2012) "Not the New, New Thing: Innovation and Cultural Policy in the EU", in Elam, I. (eds) *Artists and the Arts Industries*, Stockholm: Konstnarsnamnden, 56–66.

O'Brien, D. (2014) *Cultural Policy*, London: Routledge.

Osborne, G. (2013) 'Technology: Let's Make this Country the Best', *The Observer*, 1 September.

Osborne, T. (2003) 'Against "Creativity": A Philistine Rant', *Economy and Society* 32(4): 507–25.

Ross, A. (2007) 'Nice Work If You Can Get It', in Lovink, G. and Rossiter, N. (eds) *My Creativity Reader*, Amsterdam: Institute of Network Cultures.

Rubenstein, W. (1981) *Men of Property: The Very Wealthy in Britain Since the Industrial Revolution*, New Jersey: Rutgers University Press.

Savage, M. (2010) *Identities and Social Change in Britain Since 1940: the Politics of Method*, Oxford: Oxford University Press.

Stevenson, D., McKay, K. and Rowe, D. 2010, 'Tracing British Cultural Policy Domains: Contexts, Collaborations and Constituencies', *International Journal of Cultural Policy* 16(2): 159–72.

Vernon, J. (2012) 'The Local, the Imperial and the Global: Repositioning Twentieth-century Britain and the Brief Life of its Social Democracy', *Twentieth Century British History* 21(3): 404–18.

Weiner, M. (1981) *English Culture and the Decline of the Industrial Spirit 1850–1980*, Cambridge: CUP.

37

THE CREATION AND DESTRUCTION OF THE UK FILM COUNCIL

Philip Schlesinger

Introduction

Established by a Labour government in April 2000 and wound up at the end of March 2011 by a Conservative-led coalition, the UK Film Council (UKFC) was the key strategic body responsible for supporting the film industry and film culture in Britain for over a decade. Cultural agencies such as the UKFC may be conjured into life by governments of one colour and unceremoniously interred by those of another. Such decisions are of considerable interest to all those who wish to understand the nature and exercise of political power in the cultural field.

The UKFC's creation owed much to the personal commitment of Chris Smith, Secretary of State for Culture, Media and Sport in the 'new' Labour government that took office in May 1997.[1] Another Culture Secretary – the Conservative Jeremy Hunt – was responsible for its peremptory demise, as a member of the Conservative-Liberal Democrat cabinet installed in May 2010.[2] These individuals' actions need to be set in the wider context of the history of British film policy and also the particular conjunctures in which they took their decisions.

The present chapter is a fragment of a wider study that addresses the UKFC's performance in the round, ranging from the quest to develop a 'sustainable' film industry to facing the challenge of digital distribution (Doyle et al. 2015).[3] By focusing here on two key moments – the creation and the destruction of a public agency – I intend to explore a largely unexamined aspect of cultural policy-making. In doing so, I wish to underline the role of elites and the uses of favoured forms of expertise in film policy-making, which exemplifies an approach to creative industries policy-making I have developed elsewhere (Schlesinger 2009). The UKFC's creation was decided on and implemented by a coterie around Chris Smith. Its closure ignored standard governmental processes.

My account exposes discontinuous, irrational and asymmetrical features of the policy process. Anthony King and Ivor Crewe (2013: 6), in an overview of 'blunders' in British government, describe these as 'occasions on which ministers and officials failed to achieve their declared objectives'. As we shall see, Labour did not achieve its goal of rationalizing the film agencies, and the Coalition's cut had little to do with the official account given.

We might count the closure of the UKFC as a minor governmental blunder, contributed to – in no small measure – by a lack of clarity in its original construction.

A neat history?

The UKFC's decade-long lifespan makes it an ideal case for policy analysis, although there is both a pre-history and an aftermath to be taken into account. British governments have devised one or other form of state aid for film production since the early twentieth century in line with two persistent governing assumptions: first, an emphasis on promoting national identity through cultural expression; and second, a need to keep inventing new forms of economic intervention to keep the film industry alive (Magor and Schlesinger 2009).

In the formative decade prior to the UKFC's creation, tax incentives for film production returned to the policy agenda. In 1992, under Conservative Prime Minister John Major, key moves took place. Fiscal support for the film industry was reintroduced and the Department for National Heritage (DNH) was established. The DNH began to administer the UK's new National Lottery in 1992. Arts Council England allocated £96m of Lottery funding to support three 'film franchises', in effect mini-studios set up in May 1997, as well as supporting individual projects. The incoming Labour government therefore inherited a Conservative policy initiative in the shape of Lottery support for film (Caterer 2011). Dissatisfied with how this was working, Labour decided to pursue institutional change.

Creating the UKFC

It rebadged the DNH as the Department for Culture, Media and Sport (DCMS). In May 1997 Culture Secretary Chris Smith set up the Film Policy Review Group (FPRG). This was co-chaired by Film Minister Tom Clarke, and – significantly – by Stewart Till, President of International, PolyGram Filmed Entertainment, whose appointment reflected the special status that global trade and distributor interests were given in the review (Magor and Schlesinger 2009: 306).

The creation of the FPRG was a crucial step in establishing the Film Council. Published in March 1998, its report *A Bigger Picture* set the scene for future change:

> In the longer term, the Government will review the machinery for providing Government support to film in light of the recommendations of the British Screen Advisory Council[4] and other bodies. Its aim will be to establish structures which:
>
> - provide strategic leadership for the film industry and a clearer focus on its development;
> - achieve greater coherence by ensuring that the allocation of resources reflects priorities and that gaps and areas of overlap in provision are eliminated;
> - ensure that discretionary funding decisions are not all taken by one person or group of people.

It will look at how the roles of all the national and regional publicly funded bodies fit together and will consider whether any changes are needed in order to maximize the benefits for the UK as a whole.

(DCMS 1998: 50)

The Film Council was launched on 2 May 2000 as a non-departmental public body, working at 'arm's length' from government, with the status of a company limited by guarantee. It absorbed other public and semi-public bodies concerned with film, including the Lottery Film Department of the Arts Council, British Screen Finance, the British Film Commission, and the production and regional funding roles of the British Film Institute (BFI). All remaining activities in the BFI came under the Film Council's control. Although the BFI retained its formal autonomy, it now received funding through the Film Council, which also appointed the chair of its board. According to one well-placed source, interviewed in 2013, who wished to remain off the record, Chris Smith had wanted from the start to fold the BFI into the new body but was persuaded not to by some of its highly influential defenders. The rationalization, therefore, was incomplete as devolution of political powers to the United Kingdom's 'nations' meant that, along with the BFI, separate screen support agencies existed in Scotland, Wales and Northern Ireland.

An idea whose time had come

The idea of a unitary film body had been discussed in Labour Party circles in the 1970s. A committee chaired by John Terry, managing director of the National Film Finance Corporation – appointed by Labour Prime Minister Harold Wilson – recommended the creation of a British Film Authority in 1976. But despite further work pursued under his successor James Callaghan, the opportunity to reshape the support landscape disappeared when Labour lost the 1979 general election. The Labour-supporting Director of the BFI, Wilf Stevenson,[5] revived the idea again in 1996, shortly before the FPRG's report. Richard Attenborough, then Chairman of the BFI, prepared the ground for the meeting on the future of the film convened on 15 June 1990 by Conservative Prime Minister, Margaret Thatcher (Puttnam 2010). Stevenson then thought that government needed to devolve decision-making by creating a body like France's Centre national de la cinématographie (CNC). In his view, there were too many film bodies and more coherence was needed to represent the industry. Stevenson thought the unitary body's time had finally come, that civil servants in the DNH shared his frustrations, and that the ground was being prepared for a policy shift (Interview 2013).

Our research has uncovered other behind-the-scenes initiatives. One involved John Woodward who, after being appointed director of the BFI in February 1998, became the Film Council's first chief executive officer (CEO) in October 1999. He had moved there from the BFI to join the new chairman, the leading film director, Alan Parker, who had been chairman of the BFI's board. These new appointments came at the initiative of Culture Secretary Chris Smith. Prior to running the BFI, Woodward was already a key player as CEO of the Producers Alliance for Cinema and Television, PACT, when he had a 'conversation with Chris Smith ... about all these different bodies ... and [Smith] said, "Well, wouldn't it make more sense to pool all the stuff together? ... Could you write me a paper about how you might rationalize it all?" Which I did' (Interview 2013).

Woodward commissioned a consultancy report (Hydra Associates 1997) that he said 'was a model for one overarching film organization for the industry' but which would exclude the BFI as 'the cultural institution' (Interview 2013). Woodward had been 'amused' to find the idea resurfacing in the FPRG's report. His account provides an insight into how decisions seemingly taken as a result of recommendations after a due process of inquiry may be pre-decided:

> When this [A *Bigger Picture*] was published, there was a page at the back which basically, literally in the small print, that said, by the way, we are going to rationalize [the] machinery – which was never discussed at any point in the Film Policy Review by anyone. And that was a decision that had clearly been made privately.
>
> (Interview 2013)

Woodward believed that the rationalization of existing structures was Smith's pitch to the Treasury to show that there would be 'efficiency savings' in government (Interview 2013). His account suggests that Smith had – or was advised – to rationalize. He then asked Woodward to figure out how to do it, used the idea informally as a justification for change, and with the proposal now firmly lodged in his private circle, had something to drop into the FPRG's recommendations via his appointees. Setting up the FPRG, therefore, did not so much instigate a process of discovery but rather endorsed a policy position already privately established. However, this certainly is *not* Smith's own retrospective account:

> We didn't come into government with the idea of creating a Film Council – it emerged out of the work of the *Bigger Picture* group, my response to the rather chaotic landscape of support for film, and the need to bring some coherence to it.
>
> (Interview 2013)

Smith's emphasis is on his pursuit of a rational process to arrive at a conclusion. This was the official view taken by the DCMS, where civil servants were tasked with following up the Film Policy Review Group's recommendation to create a new leading body – which became the Film Council.[6] Inside government, it was maintained that the drive towards creating such a new institution offering strategic leadership had been the outcome of discussion and debate, and had emerged as a result of this process.

It was evident, nonetheless, that a strong lead had come from Smith's special advisor in the DCMS, John Newbigin, as well as from Neil Watson, a very close associate of the prominent film producer, David Puttnam, who (as a life peer) later occupied a multifaceted policy-related role in the 'new' Labour project.[7]

John Newbigin said that what came out of A *Bigger Picture* was the idea of 'one big organization', that Chris Smith knew what he was looking for and the Film Policy

Review Group was set up with that in mind (Interview 2013). Prior to this, there had been 'high-level involvement' in the rethinking of structures by key film industry figures such as David Puttnam and also Richard Attenborough, then chairman of the BFI board of governors, which underlines the importance of private conversations outside the formal review process. We may conclude, therefore, that the direction of travel was set well before the FPRG's deliberations occurred.

The logic of rationalization

Reflecting on the UKFC's origins, just as Jeremy Hunt, his eventual Conservative successor was dismantling that body, Chris Smith remarked:

> I felt there was a need for two things. One was much greater coherence – hence the idea of bringing everything together under one roof. Second, I wanted to make sure that we brought what one might call the artistic side of British film-making together with the more commercial side so that each could usefully feed off the other.
>
> (Macnab 2010: 3)

This encapsulates the logic of rationalization. It is based on the belief that one agency is better than many because it may concentrate resources and pursue more effective strategic action. This logic also involves a process of disavowal and taking distance from superseded bodies judged to be ineffective.

The pursuit of 'coherence' meant that the existing patchwork funding arrangement was found wanting. But the goal of creating a single agency was not achieved because, as noted, the creation of the Film Council – while sweeping up some smaller bodies – left the BFI reduced and weakened, with much of the cultural remit of film policy sub-contracted by the Film Council to the older body. This affected the achievement of Smith's second goal: that of making the industrial and the cultural wings of the film sector interact. This proved difficult, Geoffrey Nowell-Smith (2012a: 300, 298) has suggested, because New Labour strategy 'really was about the creative industries', putting 'film culture firmly in second place', removing 'production from the BFI's brief' and leading to 'the subordination of the BFI to a new organisation of a totally different type'.

Woodward, who became director of the BFI in February 1998, recalled that he and Alan Parker had met Chris Smith at the DCMS some six or seven months later. It was made clear at this meeting that a new organization would 'have oversight of all the film funding. ... At which point, the BFI would not be getting its money direct from government. ... It was a fundamental shift in the power relationship' (Interview 2013) and this was hard for the BFI to accept. In fact, the creation of the Film Council was a tremendous blow to the BFI, which both lost its chairman, Alan Parker, and its director, John Woodward, to the new body. During the 'shadow' period from October 1999 to April 2000, when the Film Council was finally established, the BFI's top leadership was very ill-prepared for the coming change in status, according to one key insider (Interview 2013).

The logic of expertise

A second logic also informed the new arrangements. The role of expertise in government was central to the Labour project, not least as so many of its leading lights either came from or relied heavily on think-tanks or policy advising. The creation of the Film Council was of a piece with Labour's drive to develop the creative industries, with think tanks and input by leading industry figures mobilized to that end (Schlesinger 2007; 2009).

Applying the logic of expertise entailed, first, finding fault with (and disavowing) the know-how and practice of existing agencies. Second, it set a value on specific kinds of expertise as especially credible and effective, thus legitimizing them. The next task was to find the right exemplars of embodied knowledge by choosing particular individuals to undertake the necessary task of transformation.

Mid-way through the UK Film Council's life, Margaret Dickinson and Sylvia Harvey (2005: 425) criticized the closed process whereby the UKFC was established and noted the 'relatively limited range of interests represented on its governing body'. This stricture is borne out by our research.

Smith has described how he set about creating the framework for change:

> [When] I became Secretary of State – one of the very first engagements I had was to go to the Cannes Film Festival [in May 1997] and I hosted a reception for the British film industry and I met with a lot of the key players at that time. And, sort of, on the spur of the moment – it wasn't quite on the spur of the moment, but it was only, sort of, 2 or 3 days in the gestation – I decided to establish the Film Policy Review Group and to ask Stewart Till to chair it. And I announced that at the Film Festival.
>
> (Interview 2013)

Stewart Till, who after his stint co-chairing the FPRG became deputy-chairman, and subsequently the second chairman of the Film Council, described his recruitment thus:

> It was … 1997 and Chris Smith was the Secretary of State for the Department for Culture, Media and Sport and he went to David Puttnam and said, 'Look, I want to review the British film industry and I want to have the Film Minister, Tom Clarke, to co-chair with someone from the industry.' And Puttnam put me forward. I had a thirty-second interview with Chris Smith on the beach in Cannes. And Chris said, would I chair it with Tom.
>
> (Interview 2008)

Producer, amongst numerous other films, of *Chariots of Fire* (1981) and *The Killing Fields* (1984), and former CEO of Columbia Pictures (1986–88), David Puttnam's advice was evidently crucial in identifying the required experts. Puttnam had a complex and contradictory relationship with Hollywood. He was marked by the immense influence of what – following Pierre Bourdieu (1984: 101) – I have labelled the 'Hollywood entertainment habitus'. This was shared in distinct ways by several of the UKFC's board members, and certainly by all three of its chairmen

(Schlesinger 2013). Till – with his PolyGram Filmed Entertainment role (until the company folded in 1999) – represented a European attempt to create a quasi studio system. His deputy chairmanship of the Film Council, along with the appointment of Alan Parker as chairman, gave a strong inflection to major production house and distributor values.

Within the DCMS, civil servants worked with Chris Smith and his special adviser, John Newbigin, who led much of the input from senior officials. A key move was to produce clear role specifications for the Film Council's Chairman and CEO posts, so that the new incumbents would have ample scope to develop their strategy and produce their first business plan (Interview 2013).

However, those seen as the men for the job, Alan Parker, the new Chairman, and John Woodward, the new CEO, were initially in the wrong place: doing precisely those jobs at the BFI. Once their services had been secured for the new body, the DCMS needed to find the right board members. Inside government, those selected to join the board were seen as embodiments of the best available expertise and as complementing the skills possessed by the new Chairman and CEO.

Whereas inside the DCMS, it was the careful pursuit of the appointments process that was invoked, thus legitimizing those selected for their expertise in terms of explicit criteria, Stewart Till emphasized the role of personal connections: 'I mean from the get-go, Chris Smith recruited, put together the first board almost, well, totally himself, taking some members of the Film Policy Review Group and just people he'd come across' (Interview 2008).

Intimations of mortality

We now shift from a tale of creation to one of destruction, preceded by an indeterminate interim phase. From early 2009, over a period of eighteen months, merger talks between the UKFC and the BFI were in train. The key question during that period, in the run-up to the general election of May 2010, was which body would survive. Geoffrey Nowell-Smith (2012b) has given the best available bare bones account to date.[8] John Woodward made the first key move, it appears, in May 2009, when – mindful of economic stringency ahead, whichever government might be elected in May 2010 – he commissioned a legal analysis from which two main options emerged:

> Either the BFI might be absorbed into the UKFC through the creation of a BFI Trust of which the UKFC would be sole trustee, or the UKFC could be folded into the BFI. The former model, which was the preferred one, would leave the UKFC in control; the BFI would retain its charitable status but probably have to lose its Royal Charter.[9]
>
> (Nowell-Smith 2012b: 307)

This initiated a complex series of negotiations, with the DCMS apparently determined to effect a merger before the next general election, but – in part, through ministerial indecision – failing to bring this about. Both organizations' boards and

CEOs were involved in the merger talks, as well as ministers and civil servants at the DCMS. The dialogue was conducted in a wary and mutually mistrustful atmosphere. The UKFC's chairman, Tim Bevan, later remarked that the talks were 'not what would be called a smooth road' (Bevan 2011). Senior figures inside the BFI believed that its values were not respected by the UKFC. In the acerbic view of one insider, the BFI, which sought its own contrary legal advice to that of the UKFC, and which played both its charitable status and the Royal Charter as obstacles to take-over, had successfully deflected attack.

> The BFI kept putting up the Royal Charter and kept putting up Charity Commissioner's blocks. ... They say, 'Oh, we are an independent charity'. Well, of course you are not, you're totally dependent on government funding for your sustainability. ... Your Royal Charter is governed by the Privy Council, which is, in effect, the Cabinet. ... The BFI did, from time to time, put up these alleged roadblocks to structural reform.
>
> (Interview, 2013)

The process reached an inconclusive stage, as Nowell-Smith (2012b: 308) recounts:

> an outline agreement was reached before the end of March [2010], leaving the BFI and its Charter formally intact but with crucial questions about the form the new organisation would take and it would pursue still very much up in the air.

However, this still half-baked solution was soon overtaken by events.

Death of the UKFC

The UKFC's abolition followed the May 2010 general elections, which had resulted in the formation of a Conservative–Liberal Democrat coalition government. The Conservative wing of the coalition came into power determined to axe at least some quangos strongly associated with Labour. In opposition, the new Conservative prime minister, David Cameron, had identified the communications regulator, Ofcom, as a target. After the general election that body experienced a deep cut and a rolling back of its policy role rather than annihilation.[10] The BBC had also been fingered, with evidence of collusive attacks by the Murdoch media camp and the Tories. It too faced cuts and a redefined use of the licence fee.[11] But well before those actions were taken, it was on the UKFC – never publicly in the frame for closure – that the ultimate blow fell.

On 21 June the new government announced that the merger talks were on hold. Because he had considered the two bodies to be incompatible, Ed Vaizey, the Conservative Minister for Culture, Communications and Creative Industries, told John Woodward (Interview 2013) that he wanted the UKFC to concentrate on the film industry (perhaps becoming the core of a new creative industries council), with the BFI continuing to support film culture. Both Woodward and the UKFC's chairman, film producer Tim Bevan, disagreed with this position.

A month later, therefore, the decision to abolish the UKFC, announced in the House of Commons on 26 July 2010 by Jeremy Hunt, the Secretary of State for Culture, Media and Sport, came as a huge shock to the UKFC. As Woodward (Interview 2013) put it:

> One Saturday morning, Tim [Bevan] got a ... call from Ed Vaizey when he was in LA, I think, just saying, 'I am terribly sorry, but we decided yesterday we have to abolish the Film Council and we are announcing it on Monday.'

Why was the UKFC abolished? The official reason given to the House of Commons on 26 July 2010 by Culture Secretary Jeremy Hunt was that: 'abolishing the UK Film Council and establishing a direct and less bureaucratic relationship with the British Film Institute [...] would support front-line services while ensuring greater value for money. Government and Lottery support for film will continue' (Hunt 2010).

But at that time, no decision had yet been taken as to which body would administer Lottery support and replace the UKFC as lead body for film. Still on the attack, in September 2010, Hunt subsequently told the House of Commons Culture, Media and Sport (CMS) Committee:

> The Film Council spent 24% of the grant that it received on its own admininstration and we asked ourselves if there was a better way to support the UK film industry than having a large number of executives paid more than £100,000 and an office in LA.
>
> (cited in CMS Committee 2011: par. 116)[12]

Tim Bevan responded that the government had taken

> a bad decision, imposed without any consultation or evaluation. People will rightly look back on today's announcement and say it was a big mistake, driven by short-term thinking and political expediency. British film, which is one of the UK's more successful growth industries, deserves better.[13]

He also later disputed Hunt's calculations in his own evidence to the CMS Committee in November 2010. Although Vaizey delivered the blow, Bevan (2011) told the Committee: 'He was the bearer of the tidings. I don't know whether he fired the bullet or not.' Less equivocally, he told us: 'I entirely blame Jeremy Hunt, actually, because he made the policy decision and then got somebody else to go and execute it' (Interview 2013). Both he and Woodward were furious at the lack of planning behind the decision, which the latter publicly described as a 'blitzkrieg'.[14]

Beyond the official account of making efficiency savings, political ambition is the recurrent explanation given for the cut. According to John Newbigin, 'Jeremy Hunt wanted to be best boy' by demonstrating he could undertake cuts as part of the coalition's austerity drive. This was also Woodward's view and that of most informants. In off the record comments, moreover, some key players have said that there were divisions between Hunt and Vaizey over the decision and that the latter believed that the government had axed the wrong body. If so, Vaizey certainly held to the official line in later evidence to the CMS Committee. He observed: 'I think the merger of the Film Council with the BFI is an achievement and a renewed policy for British film' (Vaizey 2011). He acknowledged that the decision had come as a 'bolt from the blue' and said the Friday phone call to Tim Bevan had been intended to minimize leaks before the parliamentary announcement the following Monday. The CMS Committee found the decision 'surprising' and was 'critical of the Government's lack of dialogue' with those affected. It did, however, endorse the eventual decision taken on 29 November 2010, namely that the BFI would become the 'flagship body for film policy in the UK' from 1 April 2011 (Vaizey 2010).

On 7 March 2011, the Labour peer Wilf Stevenson raised questions about the closure process in the House of Lords, where he accused the government of 'abolishing the UK Film Council by press release'.[15] He explained his intervention as follows:

> The reason I went on about this is because we were talking about the proper processes that should exist for closing down a public body ... We [Labour] could hardly argue against because we had asked the BFI and the Film Council to consider merging themselves. So we weren't very far apart on it.
>
> (Interview 2013)

For its part, the National Audit Office drew attention to other procedural failings. It reported that the DCMS's decision to close the UKFC 'was not informed by a financial analysis of the costs and benefits of the decision ... such as lease cancellation, redundancy and pension crystallization costs.' Nor had the Department planned for the transfer of functions to the BFI on 1 April 2011 (National Audit Office 2011: 7, 31).

All of these criticisms underline King and Crewe's (2013: 386–87) point that there is a 'deficit of deliberation' in British politics. They characterize a deliberative approach as involving careful consideration, not being over-hasty, and conferring and taking counsel. None of these criteria was met when the UKFC was axed.

In fact, the key shifts following the UKFC's closure involved yet another redrawing of the institutional map. Most of the UKFC's functions (and 44 of its 73 posts) were transferred to the BFI on 1 April 2011. The Regional Screen Agencies were closed and replaced by a new body intended to work alongside the BFI, Creative England. Film London took over the role of attracting inward investment. In the end, the BFI was the principal beneficiary of the closure, although in ways that would come deeply to challenge its existing cultural norms. In a paper written after the abolition had been decided, the BFI welcomed the restoration of its direct reporting to the DCMS which would allow it 'to have a conversation at a departmental level alongside other national cultural bodies and collections, giving a much needed direct voice for film as an art form' (BFI 2010: par.7.2). However, given its newly expanded remit, major adjustments – not least absorbing former UKFC staff and their ethos – would lie ahead.

Conclusions

By focusing on a striking case, this brief account reveals much about how cultural policy is made in the UK. The UKFC's creation was preceded by a considerable backroom preparatory phase involving a small 'new' Labour policy-forming nexus. The creation of the FPRG – handpicked on advice given to Chris Smith – provided the framework for endorsing a key policy already decided on, as opposed to actually discovering the need for a new agency through a deliberative process. The selection of the duo to head the new venture – Alan Parker and John Woodward – emerged from the same network of connections, based on a shared diagnosis of the ills of the UK film industry and what was needed to cure them. So did the appointment of the rest of the Film Council's first board.

Two logics legitimized the creation of the UKFC: rationalization and expertise. Rationalization involves a critique of the existing landscape coupled with a proposal to simplify its workings, whereas the expertise that matters is seen as possessed by those who agree with the new project. This picture is consistent with my earlier analysis of creative industries policy, which involved the preferred sourcing of ideas by a small number of key players with a broadly shared worldview (Schlesinger 2009).

'New' Labour's innovation hardly came about in a transparent manner, appearances to the contrary. But by comparison, complete opacity prevailed when the Film Council was axed. Jeremy Hunt's zealous desire to kill a quango was acted on so rapidly and ruthlessly that the UKFC's decision-makers were taken totally by surprise and there was no wider consultation to assess the consequences. After a period of indecision following the closure announcement, Conservative ministers hit upon precisely the rationalization that they had earlier rejected: a merger that meant shifting surviving UKFC expertise into the BFI. The lack of due process – commented on both in Parliament and by the National Audit Office, not to speak of across the film industry – left an institutional succession problem for which urgent solutions had to be found.

The creation of the UKFC was the outcome of strategic calculation by a coterie committed to a broader conception of creative industries policy. However, when under the successor government the axe unexpectedly fell, the implications of the Film Council's expedient demise had not been thought through at all. Will any lessons be learned?

Notes

1 Created Baron Smith of Finsbury in June 2005, he was Secretary of State from May 1997 to June 2001.
2 He was Secretary of State from May 2010 to September 2012.
3 'The UK Film Council: A Study of Film Policy in Transition' was funded by the UK Arts and Humanities Research Council, grant ref. no. AH/J000457X/1. The project team's members were Gillian Doyle (PI), Philip Schlesinger and Raymond Boyle (CIs) and Lisa Kelly (Research Associate). Thanks to my colleagues for their comments and to Richard Paterson and his eye for the nuance.
4 The British Screen Advisory Council is 'an independent industry-funded body' that represents 'the audiovisual sector in the UK' – in effect, a lobby (www.bsac.uk.com/about-us.html, accessed 29 November 2013). It was set up under a Labour government in 1975.
5 Created Baron Stevenson of Balmacara in 2010.
6 One civil servant tasked with implementing the FPRG's recommendations later joined the Film Council as Senior Executive Government Relations.

7 Created Baron Puttnam of Queensgate in 1997. Neil Watson became a key strategy adviser to the UKFC and subsequently the BFI.
8 For further detail about these negotiations, see Doyle et al, chapter 9.
9 A royal charter is a formal document issued by the monarch, granting a right or power to an individual or a body corporate. The BFI's royal charter was originally granted in 1983 and amended in 2000.
10 www.theguardian.com/media/2010/oct/21/ofcom-job-losses-spending-review, accessed 3 January 2014.
11 www.bbc.co.uk/news/entertainment-arts-11572171.
12 The costs of the UKFC were heavily disputed in evidence to the CMS Committee. There is no space to deal with this here.
13 www.guardian.co.uk/film/2010/jul/26/uk-film-council, accessed 3 January 2014.
14 www.guardian.co.uk/film/2010/jul/26/john-woodward-film-council, accessed 3 January 2014.
15 www.publications.parliament.uk/pa/ld201011/ldhansrd/text/110307-0002. htm#11030728000052, Col. 1413T, accessed 3 January 2014.

References

Bevan, T. (2011) 'Examination of Witnesses, Response to Q150', *Culture, Media and Sport Committee – Third Report. Funding of the Arts and Heritage*, Printed 22 March 2011, www.publications.parliament.uk/pa/cm201011/cmselect/cmcumeds/464/46402.htm, accessed 3 January 2014.

BFI (2010) 'Written Evidence Submitted by the British Film Institute (BFI) (Arts 211)', *Culture, Media and Sport Committee – Third Report. Funding of the Arts and Heritage*, Printed 22 March 2011, www.publications.parliament.uk/pa/cm201011/cmselect/cmcumeds/464/46402.htm, accessed 3 January 2014.

Bourdieu, P. (1984) *Distinction: A Social Critique of the Judgement of Taste*, London: Routledge & Kegan Paul Ltd.

Caterer, J. (2011) *The People's Pictures: National Lottery Funding and British Cinema*, Newcastle upon Tyne: Cambridge Scholars Publishing.

CMS Committee (2011) *Culture, Media and Sport Committee – Third Report. Funding of the Arts and Heritage*, Printed 22 March 2011, www.publications.parliament.uk/pa/cm201011/cmselect/cmcumeds/464/46402.htm, accessed 3 January 2014.

DCMS (1998) *A Bigger Picture: The Report of the Film Policy Review Group. Department for Culture, Media and Sport*, DCMSJO285NJ, March.

Dickinson, M. and Harvey, S. (2005) 'Film Policy in the United Kingdom: New Labour at the Movies', *The Political Quarterly*, 76(3), 420–29.

Doyle, G., Schlesinger, P., Boyle, R. and Kelly, L. W. (2015) *The Rise and Fall of the UK Film Council*, Edinburgh: Edinburgh University Press.

Hunt, J. (2010) 'DCMS Improves Efficiency and Cuts Costs with Review of Arms Length Bodies', DCMS press release 081/10, 26 July.

Hydra Associates (1997) *A Review of Potential Structures of Government Support for the Film Industry in the United Kingdom*, London: Hydra Associates.

King, A. and Crewe, I. (2013) *The Blunders of our Governments*, London: Oneworld Publications.

Magor, M. and Schlesinger, P. (2009) '"For This Relief Much Thanks": Taxation, Film Policy and the UK Government', *Screen*, 50(3), 1–19.

Macnab, G. (2010) 'The life and death of the UK Film Council', *Sight and Sound*, October, old. bfi.org.uk/sightandsound/feature/49647, accessed 3 January 2014.

National Audit Office (2011) *Department for Culture, Media and Sport: Financial Management. Report by the Comptroller and Auditor General HC821 Session 2010–2011*, 10 March 2011, www.nao.org.uk/wp-content/uploads/2011/03/1011821.pdf, accessed 3 January 2014.

Nowell-Smith, G. (2012a) 'Towards the Millennium', pp. 272–303 in G. Nowell-Smith and C. Dupin (eds), *The British Film Institute, the Government and Film Culture, 1933–2000*, Manchester and New York: Manchester University Press.

Nowell-Smith, G. (2012b) 'Epilogue 2011', pp. 304–9 in G. Nowell-Smith and C. Dupin (eds), *The British Film Institute, the Government and Film Culture, 1933–2000*, Manchester and New York: Manchester University Press.

Puttnam, D. (2010) 'Directors' Cut: The End of the UKFC', *New Statesman*, 14 October, www.newstatesman.com/film/2010/10/british-nffc-government.

Schlesinger, P. (2007) 'Creativity: From Discourse to Doctrine?' *Screen*, 48(3), 377–87.

Schlesinger, P. (2009) 'Creativity and the Experts: New Labour, Think Tanks and the Policy Process', *International Journal of Press Politics*, 14(3), 3–20.

Schlesinger, P. (2015) 'Transnational framings of UK film policy: the case of the UK Film Council', in Astrid Böger and Christof Decker (eds), *Transnational Mediations: Negotiating Popular Culture between Europe and United States*, Heidelberg: Winter Verlag.

Vaizey, E. (2010) 'The Future of the UK Film Industry', Speech, 29 November, BAFTA, London, www.gov.uk/government/speeches/the-future-of-the-uk-film-industry, accessed December 2014.

Vaizey, E. (2011) 'Examination of Witnesses, Ed Vaizey, Minister for Culture, Communications and Creative Industries, Response to Q399', *Culture, Media and Sport Committee – Third Report. Funding of the Arts and Heritage*, Printed 22 March 2011, www.publications.parliament.uk/pa/cm201011/cmselect/cmcumeds/464/46402.htm, accessed 3 January 2014.

38
WIDENING LOCAL DEVELOPMENT PATHWAYS

Transformative visions of cultural economy

Yudhishthir Raj Isar

Introduction

Soon after the November 2013 launch of the *United Nations Creative Economy Report 2013*, subtitled *Widening Local Development Pathways*, Justin O'Connor posted a blog in *The Conversation* that made significant claims on the publication's behalf. He thought it would free international cultural policy from the reigning 'creative industries/creative economy' approach, whose advocates 'stand accused of over-emphasizing the commercial aspects of culture, reducing creativity to intellectual property rights, ignoring the growing exploitation of creative labour, and becoming narrowly economistic, reducing cultural value to the bottom line' (O'Connor 2013). He also thought the report could counter 'the uncritical adoption of creative industry policy nostrums from the Global North, [that] wrapped in promises of a dynamic new source of economic growth, has become increasingly counter-productive.'

Countering those nostrums was among the purposes that I brought to the task of serving on behalf of the United Nations Educational, Scientific and Cultural Organization (UNESCO) as the principal investigator and lead writer of the report, a task it assigned to me after having taken over responsibility for the new edition. The United Nations Conference on Trade and Development (UNCTAD) had prepared the 2008 and 2010 editions. The subtitle *Special Edition* suited both, since the idea was that it would take a markedly different approach. Although UNESCO chose prudently to stick with the existing 'creative economy' brand, my conceptual preference went to the more inclusive notion of 'cultural economy'. That is the term I would have used and is the one I shall therefore employ throughout this chapter, whose main aim is to give the reader a sense of how the report might justify O'Connor's claims. In order to do so, I shall paraphrase or cite passages from the text.

Any analyst in my position, however, who has laboured on behalf of an institutional position (and cause), needs also to understand the nature of the discursive artefact that has been produced. From this position, it would be useful to begin by alluding to an important issue of global knowledge production implied by O'Connor's remarks and also trace the evolution of the 'cultural and creative industries' discourse within UNESCO.

As regards the first point, many national and local cultural policy frameworks are deeply influenced by forms of knowledge articulated by international agencies such as UNESCO: ideas, methods, goals, motives and values that, combined, form what are presumed to be universally valid principles, constituting a kind of 'global doctrine' or even an inchoate form of 'institutionalized cosmopolitanism' (Beck 2006). These master narratives include 'world heritage', 'intangible cultural heritage', 'cultural diversity' (or at least a particular reading thereof), as well as the terms 'creative industries' and 'creative economy'. All of these originated in the global North, whose 'universalist' patterns of understanding still dominate thinking within UNESCO. Yet as these ideas have travelled, many of them have been received, adapted, connoted and interpreted in different ways. In place of the conceptual imperialism of earlier years, the growing economic and political strength of non-western nations in a multi-polar world has helped reinforce these shifts of understanding and usage. In some domains, such as heritage, the shifts have been significant. In others, such as the 'creative industries/ creative economy', much less so, and hence the need for the report in question.

The story at UNESCO

As shown in accounts of the etiology of the 'creative industries' paradigm, UNESCO played no role in its initial elaboration (O'Connor 2007). In the 1980s, however, the Organization did take up the 'cultural industries', understood in the French perspective of those years, when it organized a meeting of experts, mostly from the global North, to discuss 'The Place and Role of Cultural Industries in the Cultural Development of Societies'.[1] The discussions revealed a somewhat uneasy marriage 'between those whose feelings towards cultural industries are those of fundamental and outright distrust, and those for whom cultural industries are the key to cultural democracy and the vehicle for putting it effectively into practice' (UNESCO 1982a: 22). This duality meshed into two of the international tropes of that period. The first was the 'New International Economic Order', originating in proposals put forward by developing countries with a view to recasting the international economic system in favour of the 'Third World' and jettison the Bretton Woods-based framework. The second was the 'New World Information and Communication Order', an idea elaborated at UNESCO with a view to correcting the North–South media divide that impaired the 'independent cultural development of the Third World Nations' (Hamelink 1994: 198).

Both sets of positions were sub-texts at the World Conference on Cultural Policies of 1982, which stressed inter alia the importance of the cultural industries 'in the distribution of cultural goods' and observed that 'the absence of national cultural industries may, particularly in developing countries, constitute a source of cultural dependence and give rise to alienation' (UNESCO 1982b: 44). Yet UNESCO was unprepared to engage with the marketplace. As Pratt has observed, the cultural industries 'sit uneasily within the public policy framework' (2005: 31), which generally concerns the provision of 'high' culture forms supported and funded as public goods. In the Cold War environment, it was impossible for any intergovernmental body to reconcile a deep mistrust of the commercial sector, in particular the multi-national corporations, with the practical imperative of building cultural productive capacity. Hence UNESCO's work in this domain remained limited, focusing on awareness building.

In 1990, UNESCO's Third Medium Term Plan recognized the importance of 'the industrial production of cultural goods' yet envisaged only a boilerplate agenda under a 'culture for development' programme of 'encouragement … to domestic production, particularly in developing countries' (UNESCO 1990: 87). That said, in certain fields such as book development direct support was provided to international networks of publishers and advice was provided on regional book development strategies, notably in Latin America. In the neo-liberal post-Cold War atmosphere of the 1990s, however, market forces gradually became more reputable. Thus, although the medium-term strategy for 1996–2001 (note the semantic shift from a 'plan', with its statist connotations, to the term 'strategy') stated that 'UNESCO cannot provide direct support to cultural industries, which generally come under the private sector', it saw merit in encouraging 'those States which so wish, the developing countries in particular, to design national or regional policies conducive to the development of those industries' (UNESCO 1995: 32).

At this juncture, the 'cultural exception' agenda that France and Canada had been negotiating for since the end of the Uruguay Round discussions was taking on political salience. When the United States attempted in the General Agreement on Tariffs and Trade–World Trade Organization (GATT–WTO) context to make free trade principles apply to all 'cultural goods', principally their own audio-visual exports, France countered that a 'cultural exception' was necessary. By the time of the 1998 Inter-governmental Conference on Cultural Policies for Development, the question had become a global issue and the Action Plan the Conference adopted included the fostering of the cultural industries (UNESCO 1998).

By this time also, the British government's 'creative industry' rhetoric was beginning to acquire considerable purchase in Europe and beyond. As we now know, Richard Florida's *The Rise of the Creative Class* (2002) gave a worldwide push to the broader 'creativity' trope, which began to be deployed by city activists, officials and politicians everywhere. The idea of the 'creative' became a siren song in the United Nations (UN) agencies, including in particular UNESCO. But at the end of the 20th century, another global discourse began to emerge. French diplomacy, allied with that of Canada, shifted from 'cultural exception' to 'cultural diversity', using the latter as the master concept in an international campaign of influence that led to UNESCO's *Universal Declaration on Cultural Diversity*, whose Article 8, was entitled 'Cultural goods and services: Commodities of a unique kind'. This in turn informed the drafting of a new medium-term strategy, which affirmed that 'cultural enterprises and creative industries are privileged channels of creativity as well as increasingly important sources of employment and wealth creation' (UNESCO 2002: 41). The goal was also to attain 'enlarged and diversified cultural offer, in particular from developing countries, contributing to a deceleration of asymmetries at the global level'. The strategy envisaged activities 'demonstrating the solidarity of companies in industrialized countries with developing countries, and highlighting the concept of social responsibility by corporations' (UNESCO 2002: 41). This was to be achieved through a 'global alliance for cultural diversity' in which developed country actors would help foster and/or open up markets for cultural goods and services from developing countries. This was the spirit in which UNESCO's General Conference adopted the *Convention on the Protection and Promotion of the Diversity of Cultural Expressions* in 2005. Article 14, 'Cooperation for Development', states that 'Parties shall endeavour to support cooperation for sustainable development and poverty reduction, especially in relation to the specific needs of developing countries ... ' and listed means by which this might be done.

The 2005 Convention provided the conceptual template from which the idea emerged that a different kind of report was needed, one that would focus on the developing countries. The 2008 and 2010 editions of the *UN Creative Economy Report* had clearly set out the key justifications for nation-states to invest in the cultural and creative industries, while drawing principally upon experience in the global North. The two editions also necessarily stressed the relevant international trade statistics. For the 2013 report, UNESCO made the reasoned choice of a perspective that would analyse *the potential of the cultural economy at the local level in developing countries* and locate it squarely within a less economistic paradigm, that of human development.

Diversity and contingency

I shall now provide a brief review of some salient arguments of *Widening Development Pathways*.[2]

The first is that cultural creativity both marketable and non-marketable exists in many different places and forms. In the global South these forms are not mirror images of those in the North, nor do they need to be. Everywhere they are contingent and path-dependent, with structures and modes of functioning that vary considerably. The gigantic Indian film industry is a good example, for unlike 'the global film industry which has an oligopolistic structure, the Indian film industry is informal, highly fragmented and characterized by investment forms of proprietorship and partnership' (Mukherjee 2008: 177). Its specificity reflects contingent structural, cultural and geographic conditions. In a similar vein, the Asian landscape is characterized by the rise in production and consumption of purely Asian cultural products, such as those of Bollywood, the Hong Kong and Korean film industries, Cantopop and Mandarin pop, Japanese manga and *anime* productions, and the animation and digital media industry.

The report also argues that today, in even the poorest or most remote places, cultural production can be a viable path to sustainable human development. Yet many internal obstacles exist. The main challenge is financing. Governments have few subsidy mechanisms in place, including tax credits for creators as well as entrepreneurs. Cultural producers or managers of creative enterprises find it very difficult to obtain loans or access other types of bank services. In many places the cultural economy has grown without the resources required for extensive marketing campaigns, the capital to fund significant new investments, or the trans-national network connections to ensure that outlets across the entire planet feature creative products from everywhere on their shelves and in their programming. It remains largely low-key and informal, intricately connected with community life and social networks. Strategies to foster it will therefore need to integrate awareness of such specificities and pay due attention to systemic challenges of inequality and poverty. Other important obstacles include lack of entrepreneurial skills or infrastructure. Upstream from these are ignorance of the workings of contemporary cultural markets, both national and international; inadequate organizational and management skills within the cultural sector, or underdeveloped professional skills; and finally, often but not always, a degree of political interference that hinders true creativity. However, these on-the-ground conditions cannot mask the operation of power and the centripetal forces at work in the global economy, which are among the root causes of North–South disparities in the cultural economy, as they are in many other domains. These forces have also led to the sharp decrease in State funding through 'structural adjustment' and similar programmes.

Another key point is that not all forms of cultural economy are successful or beneficial, that is to say consonant with the broader aims of human and sustainable development. Developing the sector is not intrinsically or universally an unalloyed 'good'. Yet much policy in this field is still driven largely by economic agendas alone, often in the search for a 'quick fix'. Other policy stances are inspired by a narrow city marketing or place branding agenda, using culture merely as a symbolic asset. Some developments are clearly better than others, notably when they are deployed in balance with the goals of preserving and renewing existing cultural forms, or with a view to reducing inequalities rather than exacerbating them, or to providing sustainable livelihoods for the many rather than inordinate profits for the very few.

For all these reasons, the report foregrounds *cultural creativity*, envisioning it as an embodied, lived quality that informs a diverse range of industries and activities. Some creative activities are not heavily commercialized; many spring from vernacular pastimes and activities, with little relation or functional connection to globalized entities. Accelerated diffusion of mobile and social media technologies across the developing world, and the possibilities for user-content generated forms of vernacular creativity to emerge through them, make the prospects especially strong. Moreover, the creative industries can play to existing local strengths, taking advantage of skills and forms of expression – all in abundant supply – that are intrinsic to each specific place and often unique to it. The dynamics that generate creative places are not exclusive to key centres, and recent history is replete with examples of how new material, products or expressions from diverse places – in music alone for instance, reggae, zouk, rai, salsa, samba, tango, flamenco, bhangra, fado, gamelan, juju, or qawwali – have entered the space of global flows. Other creative pursuits have emerged endogenously simply to meet demand locally, where they can be constrained in their scope and influence – such as urban, regional and national media, broadcasting and publishing industries. Examples abound: Tanzanian hip-hop; West African community radio; Taiwanese publishing; television production in Mexico; and film industries around the world from Lebanon to Brazil to Burkina Faso. The common outcome across the developing world is that consumers have access to a mixture of imported content, persistent local expressions and hybrids of outside influence with vernacular traditions. The key is to ensure that local culture remains viable (which is not the same thing as requiring it to be 'frozen' in an effort to preserve heritage or tradition).

The report also warns of the danger that an increasingly formulaic imported 'creative-city' agenda will be imposed on places in a damaging and/or unrealistic manner, ignoring local needs, and missing opportunities to galvanize already-existing or vernacular cultural expressions. The much desired cultural capital in whose name policies are put in place may have little meaning for many local people; megaprojects in would-be 'world cities' can disenfranchise local populations or remain oblivious to the real needs of local communities. As the report puts its, 'A more productive way to think about policy development in diverse developing world settings is to consider the manner in which policy ideas about the potential of creativity elaborated in the developed world can be fruitfully and critically hybridized with local aspirations, assets, constraints and energies' (United Nations/UNDP/UNESCO 2013: 85).

In praise of cultural creativity

In other words, there is far more to culture-led development than the purely economic benefits generated by the production, distribution and consumption of cultural goods and services. By the same token, the kinds of creativity the cultural and creative industries require and mobilize are not the only kinds. The *Creative Economy Report 2010* distinguished between *artistic creativity* (which is located at the core of the various concentric circle diagrams); *scientific creativity* involving curiosity and a willingness to experiment and make new connections; and *economic creativity* as a process leading towards innovation in technology, business practices, marketing, etc. Over a decade earlier, the World Commission on Culture and Development had envisaged creativity as the attribute of better problem-solving in every field – including politics and governance – and pointed out that 'in our climate of rapid change, individuals, communities and societies can adapt to the new and transform their reality only through creative imagination and initiative' (World Commission on Culture and Development 1996: 78). Following such reasoning, the notion of creativity could refer in a very general way to the processes or attributes bound up in imagining and generating new ideas, products, or ways of interpreting the world.

On deeper reflection, however, this is far too broad a view to be useful in arguing the case for culture as such or for the cultural economy. For this reason, the report focuses upon the contributions *cultural* resources can make to drive processes of sustainable development as a whole. It argues that culturally driven ways of imagining, making and innovating, both individual and collective, generate many human development 'goods'.

For this purpose, the report explores three domains. The first is *cultural expression (or artistic practice)*, both individual and collective, which energizes and empowers individuals and groups, particularly the marginal and the downtrodden, and provides platforms for their social and political agency; the second is *cultural heritage both tangible and intangible*, which, in addition to the income it affords, provides people with the cultural memories, knowledges and skills vital for the forging of sustainable relationships with natural resources and ecosystems; and the third is *urban planning and architecture*, for the quality of the built environment enables and nurtures not just individual and group well-being, but the capacity to create and innovate. Being able to either generate or access all three – in addition to the opportunities that people are given to produce, distribute and consume cultural goods and services – must be counted among the instrumental freedoms that are integral to human development.

Cultural expression

Cultural expression in developing countries often takes small-scale vernacular forms that generate various kinds of 'cultural energy'. These in turn are able to mobilize individuals, groups, and communities to transformative action (Kleymeyer 1994). This cultural energy can move people to lock arms and join in group efforts; it can stir their imaginations and drive their aspirations to transform their lives; it can shore up their confidence and give them resilience in the face of hardship, helping them to find strength and resolve they were not sure they had. Group practice such as singing (whether in choirs in the West or in many other collective modes in different cultural traditions) or dance, for example, increases social capital, creating stronger bonds between participants, increasing individual self-esteem, improving their physical and mental wellbeing and enabling new creative outlets. Such group practice also depends on emotional engagement – it simply is not meaningful (or commercially viable) without connecting with listeners or spectators in this fashion. Such engagement also implies that dissonant voices may be heard, but these are aspects of culture that policy-makers are not always prepared to accommodate. Indeed cultural expression has informed or inspired many recent democracy movements, as people recognize that freedom of artistic expression is constitutive of a free society – of its diversity, of its liberties, of its openness and of its flexibility. Such a society must also have a place for those who raise embarrassing questions, confront orthodoxy and dogma and cannot be easily co-opted by either governments or corporations. Cultural actors – artists as well as arts-producing or arts delivering organizations and networks – generate ideas, art works, art forms, projects and spaces that support and enrich the engagement with democratic governance and fundamental rights in many different societies. This was graphically evident during the 'Arab Spring' of 2011 and in subsequent developments in that region (and indeed elsewhere), where artists and artistic forms have expressed and/or bolstered the values and aspirations that underpin the energies of civil society and the indignation to which it gives voice. Across the global South, similar manifestations are emerging. Many of them are still fragile. Yet they demonstrate clearly that cultural practitioners are among the citizen actors who are acting independently to bring about change, for example in favour of ethnic pluralism and minority rights, which go hand in hand with the democratic ethos. Citing the 'Arab Spring' also reminds us that today a considerable amount of cultural expression is produced, distributed or consumed in digital forms. Hence the report does not recommend an emphasis on traditional arts and cultural practices at the expense of contemporary forms. Nor does it seek to pit inherited values and practices against the dissonant and disruptive spirit that exists in so much of the cultural life of today, in particular among young people.

Heritage as memory and energy

Community energy and inspiration is also provided by the living practices that make up the *intangible cultural heritage* (ICH), described by UNESCO's eponymous 2003 Convention as 'the practices, representations, expressions, knowledge, skills – as well as the instruments, objects, artefacts and cultural spaces associated therewith – that communities, groups and, in some cases, individuals, recognize as part of their cultural heritage' (UNESCO 2003). To be sure, these heritage assets are now being preserved and presented as marketable assets and have become an integral part of the marketized tourism–heritage nexus. Yet they also have an additional human development impact on community awareness and identity affirmation that is akin to that of cultural expression and brings many of the same kinds of benefits to bear. What is more, the knowledge embodied in the ICH is valuable also to the 'green economy', in other words to enable environmental sustainability through reduced use of resources that are growing ever scarcer (such as forests, minerals or fossil fuels). Indeed many of the indigenous and local communities who maintain, transmit and recreate ICH live in areas where the vast majority of the world's genetic resources are found. Many of them have carefully cultivated and used biological diversity in sustainable ways for thousands of years. They are recognized to be brilliant trustees of the biodiversity of their own environments (Appadurai 2002). Their contributions to the conservation of this 'natural capital' offer precious information to the global community and often serve as useful models for biodiversity policies that drive development

Urban planning and architecture

The urban landscape is a defining feature of every city, a value to be understood, preserved and enhanced through attentive policies and public participation. Historic fabric and new development can interact and mutually reinforce their role and meaning. Conservation of the built environment therefore has a plurality of meanings: the preservation of memory, the conservation of artistic and architectural achievements, the valuing of places of significance and collective meaning. Conservation is not the only issue, however, for it is also the urban planning imagination of today that contributes to the sense of belonging and identity of each local population. In this sense, city form is as much an idea as it is an artefact, for it helps answer the questions 'who are we?' and 'where do we want to go?' Hence the importance for the human development perspective of *urban planning and architecture*.

Contemporary architecture figures prominently in the standard creative economy paradigm, notably in 'creative cities' thinking that relies on the provision of large-scale cultural infrastructure – new 'flagship' museums, theatres, libraries, etc., often designed by star architects, and the economic benefits they generate. These benefits are thought to underpin the 'cultural ballast that in turn sustains global flows by attracting capital investment and drawing tourists and skilled migrants (the "creative class") through contributing to an urban image befitting a global city, and supporting a culturally enriched lifestyle' (Kong 2010: 167). Yet the investment in such 'hardware' may well take place at the cost of the 'software', in other words of the capacity of local arts practitioners to actually create new work or produce cultural goods and services. And even more important perhaps is to recognize and build upon the ways in which architecture 'structures the human experience of the city, how it sets the terms on which people are brought together in urban space' (Brook 2013: 310). In this spirit, it is also important to remember that in most developing countries, the design of the built environment is largely informal and often unplanned, often a matter of 'architecture without architects'. In all cases, the connection between every community and the built environment in which it lives and works is crucial.

Key conclusions

Notwithstanding the importance of global and national scale policy interventions, the cultural economy is not a single superhighway, but a multitude of different local trajectories found at the sub-national level – in cities and regions in developing countries. The next frontier of knowledge generation therefore rests on understanding interactions, specificities and policies at the local level. In the absence, however, of systematically gathered data at the local level in developing countries how to capture the vibrancy and scale of creative economies? Hence the need for a broader-based examination of the relationships between the economic and the non-economic benefits of local creative economies and the factors contributing to transformative change. This was the challenge also issued by the UN System Task Team on the Post-2015 UN Development Agenda in its 2012 Report, *Realising the Future We Want for All*, in the following terms (UN System Task Team on the Post-2015 UN Development Agenda 2012, paras 50 and 71):

> Business as usual cannot be an option and transformative change is needed ... It is crucial to promote equitable change that ensures people's ability to choose their value systems in peace, thereby allowing for full participation and empowerment. ... There is therefore an urgent need to find new development pathways that encourage creativity and innovation in the pursuit of inclusive, equitable and sustainable growth and development.

Local cultural economies are highly diverse and multi-faceted. They are emerging across the world from many distinct path-dependent and situated contexts, where different institutions, actors and flows of people and resources shape a range of different opportunities. There is no 'one size fits all' solution. The report argues that successful cultural and creative industries are not necessarily those that maximize exports, or generate significant royalties or wages. They may and should do both, but neither of these outcomes is either a necessary or a sufficient condition for human wellbeing, for achieving people-centred, sustainable development. Central, however, is the continuous search for the most appropriate strategies and pathways to develop the cultural and creative industries across the entire cultural production value chain, for the most suitable forms of expertise to help do this and for the most culturally sensitive ways of ascertaining value and reward.

The cultural economy has important empowering dimensions as well. Much successful cultural production emerges from localities and contexts where access to infrastructure and mainstream employment opportunities are highly constrained – but where tradition and cultural values remain strong. Although precariousness is ever-present, cultural occupations offer valuable flexibility in community contexts where cultural work can complement, rather than disrupt, other daily responsibilities and obligations (such as the maintenance of traditions, on-going land management activities and participation in community decision-making). The cultural and creative industries can also deliver flexible environments for engagement with formal spheres of work, while substantially enhancing prospects for expression, wellbeing and intercultural dialogue in both rural and rapidly urbanizing parts of the developing world. Moreover, widespread local control and accessibility to cultural production enables people to represent themselves through a mix of images, sounds and words.

In these ways, then, the value of promoting the cultural and creative industries extends far beyond, and is independent from, the generation of purely economic benefits. These include enhanced social energy, trust, confidence and engagement, enabling both individuals and groups to aspire to and imagine alternative futures. These are arguments that remind us, returning to O'Connor, that 'a new approach to cultural economy would not just ask what kind of culture we want to produce – but what kind of economy we want to help us do this'. The report leads us to ask that very question.

Notes

1 This section is based on an earlier account of mine (Isar 2008).
2 This section is based entirely on the 2013 Report, which may be downloaded at: www.unesco.org/culture/pdf/creative-economy-report-2013.pdf. The author would like to acknowledge the key contribution of Chris Gibson to the formulation of several of the key ideas of the Report.

References

Appadurai, A. (2002) 'Diversity and Sustainable Development', in *Cultural Diversity and Biodiversity for Sustainable Development*. Nairobi: UNESCO and UNEP.

Beck, U. (2006) *Cosmopolitan Vision*. Cambridge: Polity Press.

Brook, D. (2013) *A History of Future Cities*. New York: W.W. Norton & Company.

Florida, R. (2002) *The Rise of the Creative Class*. New York: Basic Books.

Hamelink, C. (1994) *The Politics of World Communication*. London, Thousand Oaks, New Delhi: Sage.

Isar, Y.R. (2008) 'The International Policy Actors', in *The Cultural Economy: The Culture and Globalization Series, 2*, Helmut Anheier and Y.R. Isar (eds). London: Sage.

Kleymeyer, C. (1994) *Cultural Expression and Grassroots Development: Cases from Latin America and the Caribbean*. Boulder: Lynne Reiner Publishers.

Kong, L. (2010) 'Creative Economy, Global City: Globalizing Discourses and the Implications for Local Arts', in *Cultural Expression, Creativity and Innovation: The Cultures and Globalization Series, 3*, Helmut Anheier and Y.R. Isar (eds). London: Sage.

Mukherjee, A. (2008) 'The Audio-Visual Sector in India', in *Creative Industries and Developing Countries: Voice, Choice and Economic Growth*, D. Barrowclough and Z. Kozul-Wright (eds). London and New York: Routledge.

O'Connor, J. (2007) *The Cultural and Creative Industries: A Review of the Literature*. London: Creative Partnerships.

O'Connor, J. (2013) 'UNESCO Leads the Way on a Truly Global Approach to Cultural Economy', *The Conversation*, theconversation.com/unesco-leads-the-way-on-a-truly-global-approach-to-cultural-economy-19595 (accessed 14 January 2015).

Pratt, A. (2005) 'Cultural Industries and Public Policy: An Oxymoron?', *The International Journal of Cultural Policy*, Vol. 11, Number 1.

UNESCO (1982a) *Cultural Industries: A Challenge for the Future of Culture*. Paris: UNESCO.

UNESCO (1982b) *Final Report of the World Conference on Cultural Policies* (document CLT/MD/1). Paris: UNESCO.

UNESCO (1990) *Third Medium-Term Plan, 1990–1995*. Document 25 C/4 Approved. Paris: UNESCO.

UNESCO (1995) *Medium-Term Strategy for 1996–2001*. Document 28 C/4 Approved. Paris: UNESCO.

UNESCO (1998) *Final Report of the Intergovernmental Conference on Cultural Policies for Development*. Document CLT-98/Conf.210/CLD.19. Paris: UNESCO.

UNESCO (2002) *Medium-Term Strategy 2002–2007*. Document 31 C/4 Approved. Paris: UNESCO.

UNESCO (2003) *Convention for the Safeguarding of the Intangible Cultural Heritage*. Paris: UNESCO.

United Nations/UNDP/UNESCO (2013) *Creative Economy Report 2013: Special Edition. Widening Local Development Pathways*. New York: United Nations.

UN System Task Team on the Post-2015 UN Development Agenda (2012) *Realising the Future We Want for All* (Report to the UN Secretary-General). New York: United Nations.

World Commission on Culture and Development (1996) *Our Creative Diversity*. Paris: UNESCO Publishing.

Part VII

THE POLITICS OF THE CULTURAL INDUSTRIES

If Part VI on policy certainly involves politics, this last section focused more directly on some of the directly political implications of the cultural industries. These connect both with cultural studies concerns with the politics of representation and identification, and with political economy's concern with the wider role of the media in contemporary society.

However, one aspect that is relatively new in this field is the use of cultural industries – both the content and the fact of their reach and influence – to project political power. If cities have used cultural industries as part of 'global branding' then states have also used them to project their idealised identities and aspirations. The United Kingdom's 'Cool Britannia' was one such; the United States itself is more self-conscious about its preeminent cultural industries sector. In contrast Kingsley Edney looks at the use of the cultural industries by China. Though embracing the creative industries as a new high-value-added sector, the Chinese Communist Party has also held on to the role of culture as national projection. The economic weight of China and its ambitions to become a(nother) global hegemon has meant that the kinds of cultural competition not seen since the end of the Cold War have begun to make their re-appearance. This time it is the cultural industries not so much 'the arts' that are involved. Edney's chapter looks at how this has unfolded and the prospects for the future.

In contrast Katie Milestone looks at the role of gender in the cultural industries. Increasingly highlighted in the work around cultural labour (see Part IV), gender issues have been flagged since the 1990s as an area in which 'creative' and 'digital' work are rehashing some very old exclusions – and some new ones. By looking in-depth at practices and attitudes held by employers and creative industry workers, it argues that recruitment strategies, organisational cultures and behaviours prevalent within the sector directly and indirectly discriminate against women. Only through exposing and making visible these subtle yet ubiquitous, powerful and essentialised social constructions of ideal creative workers, can a dialogue be entered into about how to bring about change.

Anamik Saha looks at the issue of 'race' and the cultural industries, using the particular perspective of British South Asians. The chapter identifies issues around the representation of South Asians in the cultural industries as workers, and around their representation in the products of these industries. That there are more South Asians working in the cultural industries and yet representations of race remain narrow and stereotyped requires explanation – something Saha sets out to provide in this detailed study.

Andy Ruddock takes us back to audiences and intermediaries (Part V) but asks questions about the relationship between 'content' and wider social behaviour and beliefs (or even ideologies) which have been unfashionable in cultural studies for some time. Examining Gerbner's 'cultivation analysis', Ruddock suggests that it remains entirely relevant for an understanding of the ways in which the content of the cultural industries operate in society. His final concerns with 'profit-driven storytelling' take us back to some of the core concerns of the political economy of the media and culture.

Graeme Turner closes this volume with some reflections on the ways in which the creative industries have taken attention away from why the cultural industries matter socially, culturally and politically. He calls for a return for a more critical approach to the production of culture afforded by the notion of cultural industries.

39
BETWEEN CULTURAL CONFIDENCE AND IDEOLOGICAL INSECURITY

China's soft power strategy for the cultural industries

Kingsley Edney

There is a clear gap between the expectations of the Chinese Communist Party (CCP) that the country's rich and deep cultural tradition should be a source of cultural influence for China and the reality of an international marketplace in which contemporary Chinese cultural products, particularly books, music and television shows, often struggle to attract a global audience. As O'Connor and Gu (2006: 279) have pointed out, China's global cultural profile 'lacks real weight'. The CCP has attempted to remedy this discrepancy between China's rich cultural heritage and its weak international cultural presence by investing in a strategy to promote Chinese culture internationally. Heavily influenced by the concept of 'soft power' (Nye 2004), the Party has encouraged Chinese cultural industries to 'go out' (*zou chu qu*) and compete to win over international audiences (Zhang 2010).

Despite this growing emphasis on an international orientation, the cultural industries remain embedded in a domestic policy environment in which the propaganda system plays a strong role in promoting and restricting certain cultural expression. While the Chinese cultural industries have shifted away from politically driven cultural production and towards more market-oriented cultural industries (Tong and Hung 2012), and culture is no longer the focal point of open ideological struggle to the extent it was during either the Cultural Revolution or the 'culture fever' period of the 1980s, ideology still plays a key part in shaping official cultural policies. To understand the CCP's soft power strategy for the cultural industries therefore requires consideration of the complex and often subtle relationship between culture and ideology in contemporary China.

This chapter will investigate the CCP's push to develop China's cultural industries for international audiences by examining the official and semi-official discourse of culture in China. I draw on the statements of senior officials, CCP policy documents and written regulations and I also examine the semi-official discourse that can be found in the editorials and opinion pieces in state-run media outlets. The intention here is to use this official and semi-official discourse to gain insight into the CCP's strategy for the cultural industries, not to provide an overview of the various contested approaches to culture that find expression in the range of popular discourses within China, so I do not look at the ways in which individual artists or others who are outside or on the fringes of the formal power structure talk about culture. Despite the complexity generated by the wide range of policy pronouncements, by the variations in local implementation and by the proliferation of ideological jargon in the cultural sector, through looking at the official and semi-official discourses it is possible to begin to tease out some of the challenges facing the CCP in its attempts to develop a soft power strategy for the cultural industries.

Looking at how the official and semi-official discourse links culture with soft power, nationalism and the market reveals the heavy and sometimes contradictory ideological burden that the Party places on the cultural industries in contemporary China. An unusual combination of cultural confidence and ideological insecurity emerges from these discourses. The CCP expects the cultural industries simultaneously to generate domestic cohesion (*ningju li*), remain within the politically correct boundaries of 'socialism with Chinese characteristics' and attract international audiences. The propaganda authorities aim to protect China from ideological challenges that arrive in the guise of foreign cultural imports and at the same time promote Chinese culture internationally as part of an ongoing struggle to increase China's global power.

During the more than 35 years of the reform era the cultural policy landscape in China has continued to evolve. Prior to the beginning of reform in 1978 the CCP did not need to develop cultural policies because there was not enough civil autonomy to require them (Tong and Hung 2012: 265); it instead exercised specific and prescriptive control over all aspects of cultural activity. From 1978 onward, however, the Party developed a broad strategic plan for the cultural sphere. This plan was still issued from the top but was more of an indication of a general direction than a tool for prescriptive control (Tong and Hung 2012). Further cultural reform policies were introduced in the late 1990s to make cultural units profitable in order to enhance the authorities' position vis-à-vis private actors in the cultural sphere, to build China's knowledge economy as a step to greater international economic competitiveness, and so that cultural units would not drain the financial resources of the state but instead generate revenue for local governments and propaganda organs (Volland 2012: 108–9). A Culture Industry Bureau was established within the Ministry of Culture in 1998 and a Cultural Reform Office was set up within the CCP's Propaganda Department in 2004 (Volland 2012: 109–10).

The international discourse of the cultural industries arrived in China in the early 2000s (Ren and Sun 2012: 507) and the CCP has clearly recognized that the sector requires further state intervention and support. Local authorities have pursued policies designed to promote the cultural industries in their areas, often in the form of 'creative clusters' or art districts, although these initiatives may be motivated more by factors related to economic competitiveness or property development than the actual cultural output of such endeavours (Keane 2009; Ren and Sun 2012). At the national level the official media has published commentaries on China's 'cultural trade imbalance' with the rest of the world (e.g. Jin and Zhang 2007) and in 2006 the National Bureau of Statistics released information on the cultural industries for the first time (Xinhua 2006).

The CCP's contemporary reform agenda, which is represented as the building of 'socialism with Chinese characteristics', includes culture as one of its key components alongside the economy, politics and society. Over time, the Party's policies to modernize the cultural sphere have become known collectively as 'cultural systems reform' (*wenhua tizhi gaige*). This official focus on cultural systems reform reached a high point in late 2011, when the Sixth Plenum of the Seventeenth Central Committee took the issue of cultural system reform as its major theme. The plenum referred to the need to 'protect national cultural security' and claimed that this important task is becoming more difficult. The plenum also noted that the need to increase the influence of Chinese culture overseas was becoming more pressing. The Party's statement linked reform of the cultural system with achieving the goal of 'the great rejuvenation of the Chinese nation', which has since become one of Chinese President and CCP General Secretary Xi Jinping's key ideological phrases. The CCP also linked cultural reform with the socialist system and national cohesion when it discussed the need to build a 'strong nation of socialist culture' (*shehui zhuyi wenhua qiangguo*) and to make use of the shared ideals of socialism with Chinese characteristics in order to 'coalesce power' (*ningju liliang*) (*Zhongguo Fayuan Wang* 2011).

Cultural industries and soft power

This growth in the official focus on cultural systems reform has coincided with a period in which the concept of soft power has received an increasing amount of attention in the upper echelons of the CCP. The concept of soft power was originally developed by Joseph Nye, who described it as the ability to influence others through agenda setting, attraction or cooption (Nye 2004: 8). Distinct from 'hard power', which involves inducements or threats, soft power involves 'getting others to want the outcomes that you want' (5) and is based on a country's 'culture (in places where it is attractive to others), its political values (when it lives up to them at home and abroad), and its foreign policies (when they are seen as legitimate and having moral authority)' (11).

The soft power concept first came to China in 1993 via an article by Wang Huning, who at the time was the dean of Fudan University's International Politics Department (Wang 1993). Wang, who has been a key policy adviser to past leaders Jiang Zemin and Hu Jintao as well as current leader Xi Jinping, is now a member of the CCP's Politburo and the most senior member of the Party with foreign affairs expertise. As he has risen through the ranks of the Party the soft power concept has become absorbed into the official policy language of the CCP. After a period in which academic discussions of soft power increased dramatically in China (Li 2009), in 2007 the concept of soft power made an appearance in Hu Jintao's report to the Seventeenth Party Congress. China's strategy for developing its cultural industries and the issue of soft power were both topics that were included in the Politburo study sessions attended by top leaders in the lead-up to the Congress (Zhang 2010: 388–89). This inclusion signalled that the idea of soft power had become part of the CCP's official policy discourse. Since 2007 the concept of soft power has been included in many more high-level statements.

The cultural industries are closely linked with soft power in the official discourse because the CCP views culture as the key component of Chinese soft power. The concept of soft power has been reinterpreted in China to make it more compatible with the objectives and principles of the Party's existing propaganda system (Edney 2012). This has meant that the Party has mainly focused on the cultural aspects of soft power while Nye's two other components – foreign policy and political values – have not generally been mentioned in official policy statements and remain largely limited to the realm of academic debate. An editorial in *People's Daily* titled 'How to Improve China's Soft Power?' argued that although soft power 'includes factors in fields such as culture, political system, and media ... culture is the core, for it fully reflects a country's influence, cohesion, and popularity' (*People's Daily* 2010). When in his previous position as head of the State Council Information Office, which is the organ that coordinates China's foreign propaganda efforts, Culture Minister Cai Wu stated that culture is soft power's 'core element' (Cai 2006). This link between culture and soft power is so strong that the term 'cultural soft power' (*wenhua ruan shi li*) is often employed in official statements. In mid-2007, for example, members of the Chinese People's Political Consultative Conference held a discussion where they identified the need for greater government support to develop China's cultural soft power (Ye 2007). The Party's 2011 plenum on cultural systems reform observed that the need to increase the country's cultural soft power was becoming more pressing and stated that one of the goals of reforming of the cultural system was to increase China's cultural soft power. In August 2013 at the national propaganda and thought work conference the head of the Central Propaganda Department, Liu Qibao, referred to the need to raise China's cultural soft power by promoting the 'going out' of Chinese culture into the world (*People's Daily* 2013). In late 2013 Xi Jinping told a Politburo study session that deepening the reform of the cultural system, promoting socialist core values and advancing the cultural industries would provide a solid platform for the building of China's soft power (Xinhua 2014).

Cultural nationalism

China's official discourse also reveals the high expectations placed on culture as a national resource and a source of national cohesion. In Hu Jintao's report to the Eighteenth Party Congress in 2012 he called culture the 'lifeblood of a nation' and spoke of the need to 'enable culture to guide social trends, educate the people, serve society, and boost development' (Xinhua 2012b). In this discourse China's historical cultural legacy is a source of both responsibility and opportunity. In 2012 the government's annual work report stated that Chinese people today must 'shoulder the historic duty' of advancing Chinese culture (Wen 2012). At the same time, China's rich civilization and long continuous history grants it a wealth of traditional cultural resources that the contemporary cultural industries can draw on. The Party is acutely aware, however, that this traditional culture does not necessarily generate contemporary cultural influence. An opinion piece by a member of the CCP Central Committee published in the overseas edition of the *People's Daily* pointed out that although China is an ancient country with great cultural resources it is still not a 'cultural great power' (Ye 2011). The author noted that the combined income of all of China's more than five hundred book publishers is less than that of the multi-national German media corporation Bertelsmann. Although this cultural legacy is a great resource, it is possible that too much reverence for traditional cultural icons can stifle contemporary creativity. This particular worry came to prominence following the global success of the American movie *Kung Fu Panda* – a Hollywood film that combined two classic icons of Chinese culture – as Chinese commentators asked why their own country had not been able to produce such a film.

For the CCP the success (or lack of success) of the cultural industries internationally represents a marker of China's global status. Hu Jintao claimed in his 2012 speech to the Party Congress that the 'strength and international competitiveness of Chinese culture are an important indicator of China's power and prosperity and the renewal of the Chinese nation' (Xinhua 2012b). The link between culture and status is not one-way, however, and the Party views China's increasing global power as providing an opportunity for the country's cultural industries to succeed internationally. The cultural document for the CCP's Twelfth Five-Year Plan (hereafter referred to as the Plan) claims that 'China's international status and attractiveness is increasing, creating an important juncture for Chinese culture to go out into the world' (Xinhua 2012a).

The desire for China to become a 'cultural great power' (*wenhua qiangguo*) is an idea that appears frequently in the official discourse. An article in *People's Daily* in late 2011, written by a highly influential commentary team known as Ren Zhongping, focused on the topic of a 'Chinese way' to becoming a cultural great power and key leaders such as Xi Jinping and Cai Wu have also referred to the concept, often in terms of a 'socialist cultural great power' (*shehui zhuyi wenhua qiangguo*) (Cai 2013; *People's Daily* 2013). Party documents consistently emphasize that the status and function of culture as a component of international competition for 'comprehensive national power' is becoming increasingly clear.

CCP statements on developing the international competitiveness of Chinese culture reflect not only the desire to return Chinese culture to its rightful place on the world stage, but also the need for 'cultural security'. At times culture is described as a kind of ideological weapon or armour that can be used in an international battle for cultural supremacy. For example, the cultural component of the Plan states: 'Facing increasing global ideological and cultural struggle, it is increasingly urgent to strengthen national cultural capabilities and international competitiveness, to resist the cultural infiltration of foreign hostile forces, and to protect national cultural security' (Xinhua 2012a).

Official statements also point to culture as a source of national cohesion. For example, the Plan identifies culture as an increasingly important wellspring of national cohesion while the 2012 government work report refers to Chinese culture as 'highly cohesive'. Similarly, investing in culture can be a way to improve the level of cohesion in China. In 2010 the Fifth Plenum of the Seventeenth CCP Central Committee identified the need to develop the cultural industries in order to boost national cohesion (*The Beijing Review* 2010). The concept of the 'Chinese dream', which has formed the core of Xi Jinping's ideological innovation since he assumed leadership of the Party in 2012, has merged smoothly with this existing rhetoric of culture as a source of national cohesion. Propaganda chief and member of the Politburo Standing Committee, Liu Yunshan, stated in June 2013 that 'culture provides strong spiritual support and a cohesive force for the realization of the Chinese dream' (Xinhua 2013).

Cultural industries and the market

The language of competition links the cultural nationalism discourse with the discourse of international markets and commercial competitiveness. If the international influence of Chinese culture is an important marker of China's soft power and international status, then the most straightforward way for the Party to assess the level of influence is to examine the commercial success of the cultural industries in the international market. The international success of the cultural products of other countries is held up as an example of China's relative lack of competitiveness. For example, official media commentary has pointed out that even though American films make up only 10 per cent of the world's total, they occupy half of global screen time (Ren Zhongping 2011).

Alongside culture's role in the international marketplace, it also has an important role to play in the domestic economy. In Hu Jintao's 2007 report to the National Party Congress he identified three major ways in which culture was becoming more important: as a source of national cohesion and creativity, as a component of comprehensive national power competition, and as an important element of the Chinese people's desire for an abundant life (Hu 2007). More recently, official documents have expanded this list to include culture as an increasingly important pillar for social and economic development (Xinhua 2012a). The 2011 and 2012 government work reports referred specifically to the goal of making the cultural industries a pillar of the national economy (Wen 2011, 2012). During the CCP plenum on cultural reform in October 2011 the influential commercial newspaper *Xin Jing Bao* (*Beijing News*) published an editorial, which was later reproduced on the website of the official *People's Daily*, extolling the virtues of the market and arguing that giving the market a greater role to play in the cultural realm through further reform would stimulate those in the cultural sector to produce more work, which would lead to social and economic benefits (*Xin Jing Bao* 2011).

Following the Third Plenum of the Eighteenth CCP Central Committee in late 2013 the official Party documents stated that the market would now play a 'decisive' role in allocating resources, rather than its previous 'basic' role. In relation to culture the meeting referred to the need to perfect the cultural management system, build a robust modern cultural market system, construct a modern public cultural service system and raise the level of cultural openness (Sina 2013). Although whether this shift in terminology will lead to major increases in the market's role in the cultural sphere remains to be seen, the report released following the Plenum indicates that cultural development will still be subject to strong political control. The report stated that building a 'socialist cultural great power' and strengthening 'national cultural soft power' requires maintaining the direction of advanced socialist culture, maintaining the cultural development path of socialism with Chinese characteristics, maintaining 'people-centric' work guidance (*yi renmin wei zhongxin de gongzuo daoxiang*) and, lastly, taking steps forward in deepening cultural systems reform (Sina 2013). Although the overall document stresses the need to improve the functioning of markets, in relation to culture it emphasizes maintaining and upholding the existing approach rather than overhauling it.

A primary social function of culture in the official discourse is to meet the cultural needs of domestic consumers. According to the Plan, even though China's cultural production is increasing it is still not enough to meet the people's needs. Despite the commercialization process that has occurred in the cultural industries and the CCP's stated desire to build a 'robust modern cultural market system', in the official discourse the state still has a responsibility for creating the supply to meet public demand in the cultural realm. The 2012 government work report claims that the state 'will provide a large quantity of high-quality cultural products to meet people's demand for culture' (Wen 2012). In the terminology of the 2013 Third Plenum the goal is to construct a modern public cultural service system. One objective that the government's work report for 2013 says has already been achieved is making all museums, libraries and cultural centres free to the public. The government also emphasizes that rural areas, which traditionally have less access to cultural activities and resources, should also be included in the nationwide network of state cultural provision.

The ideological burden

It is clear from these official discourses that the cultural industries in China carry a heavy ideological burden. Although there has been a general shift away from overt political contestation over the content of cultural production, official talk of cultural soft power and the top level discussions of cultural systems reform indicate that as a political project the development of the cultural industries in China remains high on the policy agenda. Even absent the desire to direct the specific content of cultural production, the CCP's expectations that the cultural industries should be a unifying force for national cohesion and that the international success of Chinese cultural products is a matter of national pride that reflects China's international status combine to create clear limits to the Party's willingness to tolerate pluralism and creativity in the cultural industries, particularly where international audiences are involved. It is very difficult for the Party to support cultural enterprises that are iconoclastic, divisive or that can be seen as disrespectful of official ideology or the nation, even when they are popular internationally.

The CCP's view of the cultural industries is encapsulated by the phrase '*yi shou zhua fanrong, yi shou zhua guanli*' (one hand grasps flourishing, one hand grasps management). The Party is trying simultaneously to promote creativity and growth through market-based reforms while also maintaining its ability to control the cultural industries to ensure that China becomes not just a 'cultural great power' but a 'socialist cultural great power'. The language of cultural markets and economies can sometimes disguise underlying concerns about political control. For example, although statements about meeting the cultural needs of domestic Chinese consumers can be interpreted through the economic terminology of supply and demand, if domestic cultural products fail to meet the demands of their potential Chinese consumers there are wider implications for what the CCP refers to as cultural security. If China cannot meet the demand from its own people for cultural products then those people will look to fulfil their cultural needs by looking outside the country, thereby limiting the influence of the propaganda system to its ability to censor cultural imports.

Although at times the language of friendship and cultural exchange does appear in the official discourse, in the international context the Party views the cultural industries largely in terms of power and competition. The growth of the cultural soft power concept has coincided with the Party's emphasis on the increasing urgency of global cultural and ideological competition. The CCP's desire to improve the international competitiveness of the cultural industries is not simply about transforming China's rich cultural heritage into a modern, profitable global business; it is part of a broader strategy designed to tackle what the Party sees as a global ideological struggle and the success or failure of these efforts has important domestic repercussions for cultural security.

At the regional level the ideological threat from China's cultural competitors is somewhat less acute than it is from the West but there is still anxiety in China about the comparative status of the country's cultural industries within East Asia. The global success of the South Korean pop song 'Gangnam Style' in 2012 prompted a new round of introspection about the lack of creativity in China. The mainland has been making gains in areas such as art and fashion, but it is the pop culture products of Hong Kong and Taiwan that have been the driving force behind the export of Chinese culture to East Asia markets. While it would be inaccurate to claim that the cultural industries in Hong Kong and Taiwan have been completely free from political constraints, their success throughout the region demonstrates that Chinese cultural products with strong international appeal can be generated when the ideological burden and propaganda restrictions are lifted. The mainland, with its significant resources, has the potential to have major international cultural influence. Despite more than 30 years of reform and opening, however, the current priorities of the CCP in the area of cultural reform have led the Party to take a conservative and defensive approach in designing its soft power strategy for the cultural industries. This indicates that the process of catching up with established regional competitors such as Japan will likely be a slow one. The building of international cultural influence is a long-term objective for the CCP, whereas domestic ideological vulnerability is of much more urgent concern.

For the CCP the development of the cultural industries as part of a soft power strategy is not just a matter of dedicating more resources to promoting Chinese culture on the world stage. Instead, it requires carefully directing the domestic cultural industries so that they simultaneously help to generate national cohesion and cultural security, do not undermine the official political project of socialism with Chinese characteristics and successfully compete in the global cultural marketplace.

References

Cai, Wu (2006) 'Guowuyuan Xinwen Ban zhuren Cai Wu wei "kua wenhua chuanbo luntan" zhici [State Council Information Office director Cai Wu addresses the 'cross-cultural broadcasting forum]', 31 August, www.chinanews.com/other/news/2006/08-31/782661.shtml, accessed 19 January 2015.

Cai, Wu (2013) 'Zai Zhonghua wenhua de chuancheng chuangxin zhong shixian "Zhongguo meng" [Realize the "Chinese dream" through Chinese culture's tradition and creativity]', *People's Daily*, 5 August, theory.people.com.cn/n/2013/0805/c40531-22440725.html, accessed 20 August 2013.

Edney, Kingsley (2012) 'Soft Power and the Chinese Propaganda System', *Journal of Contemporary China* 21(78): 899–914.

Hu, Jintao (2007) 'Gaoju Zhongguo tese shehui zhuyi weida qizhi, wei duoqu quanmian jianshe xiaokang shehui xin shengli er fendou [Hold high the great banner of socialism with Chinese characteristics, strive for the new victory of comprehensively building a moderately prosperous society]', cpc.people.com.cn/GB/104019/104099/6429414.html, accessed 20 August 2013.

Jin, Yuanpu and Zhang, Jiangang (2007) 'Miandui "wenhua maoyi nicha" Zhongguo gai dang he wei? [Facing the "cultural trade gap": what should China do?]', *China Daily*, 4 March 2007, www.chinadaily.com.cn/2007npc/2007-03/04/content_819107.htm, accessed 19 January 2015.

Keane, Michael (2009) 'The Capital Complex: Beijing's New Creative Clusters', in Lily Kong and Justin O'Connor (eds) *Creative Economies, Creative Cities: Asian-European Perspectives* (Dordrecht: Springer), pp. 77–95.

Li, Mingjiang (2009) 'Soft Power in Chinese Discourse: Popularity and Prospect', in Mingjiang Li (ed.) *Soft Power: China's Emerging Strategy in International Politics* (Lanham, MD: Rowman and Littlefield), pp. 21–43.

Nye, Joseph S., Jr. (2004) *Soft Power: The Means to Success in World Politics* (New York: Public Affairs).

O'Connor, Justin and Gu Xin (2006) 'A New Modernity? The Arrival of "Creative Industries" in China', *International Journal of Cultural Studies* 9(3): 271–83.

People's Daily (2010) 'How to Improve China's Soft Power?', *People's Daily*, 11 March, english. peopledaily.com.cn/90001/90776/90785/6916487.html, accessed on 26 August 2010.

People's Daily (2013) 'Xionghuai daju bawo dashi zhuoyan dashi, nuli ba xuanchuan sixiang gongzuo zuo de geng hao [Open one's mind to the general situation, grasp the general trends, concentrate on major events, work hard to conduct even better propaganda and thought work]', *People's Daily*, 21 August, cpc.people.com.cn/n/2013/0821/c64094-22636876. html, accessed 15 November 2013.

Ren, Xuefei and Meng Sun (2012) 'Artistic Urbanization: Creative Industries and Creative Control in Beijing', *International Journal of Urban and Regional Research* 36(3): 504–21.

Ren Zhongping (2011) 'Wenhua qiangguo de "Zhongguo daolu" ["Chinese path" of a cultural great power]', *People's Daily*, 15 October, opinion.people.com.cn/GB/15904150.html, accessed 1 July 2013.

Sina (2013) 'Zhongguo gongchandang shiba jie san zhong quanhui gongbao fabu (quanwen) [Chinese Communist Party releases communique of the third plenum of the eighteenth (full text)]' *Sina*, 12 November, news.sina.com.cn/c/2013-11-12/191828691069.shtml, accessed 18 March 2015.

The Beijing Review (2010) 'Communique of the Fifth Plenum of the 17th CPC Central Committee', *The Beijing Review*, 25 October, www.bjreview.com/Cover_Story_Series_2010/2010-10/25/content_305968.htm, accessed 15 August 2011.

Tong, Q.S. and Ruth Y.Y. Hung (2012) 'Cultural Policy between the State and the Market: Regulation, Creativity and Contradiction', *International Journal of Cultural Policy* 18(3): 265–78.

Volland, Nicolai (2012) 'From Control to Management: The CCP's "Reforms of the Cultural Structure"', in Anne-Marie Brady (ed.) *China's Thought Management* (Abingdon, Oxon: Routledge), pp. 107–21.

Wang, Huning (1993) 'Zuowei guojia shili de wenhua: ruan quanli [Culture as national strength: soft power]' *Fudan xuebao (shehui kexue ban)* [*Fudan Journal (Social Science Edition)*] 3.

Wen, Jiabao (2011) 'Report on the Work of the Government', www.npc.gov.cn/englishnpc/Special_11_4/2011-03/15/content_1647416.htm, accessed 19 January 2015.

Wen, Jiabao (2012) 'Report on the Work of the Government (2012)', www.npc.gov.cn/englishnpc/news/Supervision/2012-03/14/content_1713983.htm, accessed 19 January 2015.

Wen, Jiabao (2013) ' Report on the Work of the Government', *Xinhua*, news.xinhuanet.com/english/china/2013-03/18/c_132242798.htm, accessed 28 June 2013.

Xin Jing Bao (2011) 'Shichang shi tongwang wenhua da fanrong de biyou zhi lu [The market is an essential path to a flourishing culture]', 16 October, epaper.bjnews.com.cn/html/2011-10/16/content_284841.htm?div = -1.

Xinhua (2006) 'Cultural Industry Potential', *Xinhua*, 25 May, news.xinhuanet.com/english/2006-05/25/content_4598537.htm, accessed 17 September 2009.

Xinhua (2012a) 'Guojia "shier wu" shiqi wenhua gaige fazhan guihua gangyao [Outline of the national "twelve-five" period culture reform and development plan]', 15 February, www.gov.cn/jrzg/2012-02/15/content_2067781.htm, accessed 20 August 2013.

Xinhua (2012b) 'Full Text of Hu Jintao's Report at 18th Party Congress' *Xinhua*, 17 November, news.xinhuanet.com/english/special/18cpcnc/2012-11/17/c_131981259.htm, accessed 15 November 2013.

Xinhua (2013) 'Senior CPC Leader Urges Cultural Reform Efforts', *Xinhua*, 17 June, news.xinhuanet.com/english/china/2013-06/08/c_132442405.htm.

Xinhua (2014) 'Xi: China to Promote Cultural Soft Power', *Xinhua*, 1 January, www.china.org.cn/china/2014-01/01/content_31059390.htm, accessed 2 January 2014.

Ye, Xiaonan (2007) 'Zhengxie weiyuan huyu: jiaqiang guojia wenhua ruanshili jianshe [Political Consultative Conference members call for strengthening the building of national cultural soft power]', *Xinhua*, 25 July, news.xinhuanet.com/politics/2007-07/25/content_6425793.htm, accessed 14 October 2010.

Ye, Xiaowen (2011) 'Wenming guguo daguo geng dai wenhua qiangguo [Ancient and great civilization still waiting to be a cultural great power]', *People's Daily* [Overseas edition], 17 October, paper.people.com.cn/rmrbhwb/html/2011-10/17/content_942389.htm.

Zhang, Weihong (2010) 'China's Cultural Future: From Soft Power to Comprehensive National Power', *International Journal of Cultural Policy* 16(4): 383–402.

Zhongguo Fayuan Wang (2011) 'Zhonggong zhongying guanyu shenhua wenhua tizhi gaige, tuidong shehui zhuyi wenhua da fazhan da fanrong ruogan zhongda wenti de jueding [Central Party decision on some questions of deepening cultural system reform and pushing forward the great development and great flourishing of socialist culture]', 26 October, www.chinacourt.org/html/article/201110/26/467709.shtml, accessed 27 October 2011.

40
GENDER AND THE CULTURAL INDUSTRIES

Katie Milestone

Introduction

This chapter examines gender dynamics in cultural industries. In particular the focus is on gender and cultural producers. In almost all the subsections of the cultural industries, from the audio-visual industry through to digital design, women are underrepresented in the most prestigious and creative roles (see for example Gill 2002). In the main women are consigned to lower paid roles and struggle to access roles with prestige and respect attached to them. This is certainly the case in the United Kingdom, as many sector and university research projects have emphasised (Skillset[1] 2010a, Richards and Milestone 2000, Haines 2004). These trends are found elsewhere such as in the USA (Christopherson 2008) and Australia (Akuma and Barnes 2009). There are other intersectional inequalities in terms of access to the cultural industries that are based on ethnicity, class, sexuality and disability. However, for the purpose of this chapter we keep our focus solely on gender.

It is uncomfortable to confront the statistics that point to cultural industries as places where 'the typical creative industry workforce is white, male, young and highly qualified' (Skillset 2010b). Neo-liberal and post-feminist discourses allege that we have moved away from dichotomies of what constitute 'men's work' and 'women's work'. To get hung up on old classifications is deemed outmoded and irrelevant in a new meritocratic world where the individual is responsible for their own success or failure. On the face of it there should be no reason why cultural industries are not composed of a diverse workforce. Cultural industries tend to be located in cities and are frequently connected with popular, rather than high culture. Richard Florida (2002) champions creative cities as bohemian places that thrive on diversity and difference. But, as Gill has noted, although media representations of cultural industries tend to emphasise the presence of a diverse workforce, research findings repeatedly reveal that this is not the case.

Let us explore how to account for this troubling situation. In 1975 Laura Mulvey wrote a highly influential article that highlighted the gender and power dichotomies at play in the film industry. Using Hitchcock films as a case study, Mulvey highlighted the problematic impact of the male domination of film director roles. As most films are produced from the standpoint of the 'male gaze', when women feature in films their role is predominantly 'to be looked at'. Women are passive, decorative and powerless because they are excluded from key cultural production roles (notably in film direction). As Judith Williamson (1978) also noted, this gendered power relationship is also overwhelmingly pervasive in the realm of advertising. A glance at contemporary media products reveals that little has changed in terms of how women are represented in the media. Indeed many argue that the situation is now far worse than in the 1970s. Concerns have recently been raised in reports such as the 2010 report of the American Psychological Association Task Force on the Sexualisation of Girls and UK Government Home Office commissioned research (Papadopoulos 2010) on the same subject. The media doesn't encourage girls and women to imagine themselves in charge of the means of cultural production. Instead women continue to be bombarded with messages and images that infer that a woman's role is to conform to the regulations of the 'male gaze'.

It is undeniably depressing that we seem to have a tidal wave of 'retrosexism' (Whelehan 2000) dominate the output of the cultural industries. However if we take the view that these ascribed roles (of men as creators and women as malleable, voiceless objects) are cultural constructions then the possibility of change is present. Judith Butler (1990) argues that all gendered behaviour is a performance. It is the work of ideology to render what is learned, socially constructed behaviour as natural and therefore unchangeable. Taking a cue from Butler's ideas let's consider this idea of gender and performance with an example from the cultural industries. In a recently unearthed BBC documentary from 1967[2], Mick Jagger describes how, in this period, British audiences of live performances given by The Rolling Stones were overwhelmingly female, whilst in continental Europe the opposite was the case. Importantly here Jagger observed that the male fans in Europe behaved in ways typically associated with female fans. This response to pop music in its infancy appears yet to have been constrained by ideals about masculine and feminine fan behaviour (Sandvoss 2005). There had already been high-profile circulation of images of 'spectacular' female fandom in response to acts such as Elvis and The Beatles. But, in some parts of Europe at least, some young men felt that a highly emotional expression of fandom was available to them. This example supports claims that masculinity is a cultural construct as gender identities can manifest themselves in variable ways depending on context. The case of these young music fans provides an example of why gendered behaviour should not be regarded as being fixed and 'natural'.

Having briefly highlighted some key research about gender and popular culture, let us now examine gender in a contemporary case study from the cultural industries workplace. The case study is of new media businesses in Manchester (United Kingdom) and serves as an illustrative case study of gendered inequalities and creative labour. Cultural industries that are centred on new media or digital technologies are considered to be increasingly important to both the UK and Manchester economy (Künster et al. 2013). Evidence from labour market research and academic research projects have both highlighted that new media businesses are particularly problematic sub-sectors of the creative industries in terms of providing employment opportunities for women (Skillset 2010a, Gill 2002, Perrons 2003, Tams 2002, Banks and Milestone 2011). Data from interviews with owner-managers and key decision makers in 20 small to medium sized enterprises (SMEs) in the field of web design, interactive gaming, digital marketing and advertising are discussed. This research explores cultural industries workplace cultures at close range to consider why women are finding it difficult to gain recognition and reward for their cultural work. We provide some contextual information before looking at the research findings in detail.

The promotion of the creative industries in the UK context was accompanied by a sense of optimism in the early years of the New Labour government's term of office. Cultural industries (as they were initially termed in the Greater London Council's (GLC) influential cultural industries policies) were seen as offering employment possibilities that could tap into the creativity and enthusiasm of diverse groups of young people (O'Connor 2007, Mulgan and Worpole 1986). The GLC project prioritised the promotion of diversity as a key criterion for funding. There was an optimism that unlike the hierarchical business models and elite 'old boy networks' of the old economy, the creative sector could offer an attractive new alternative to groups who had previously been marginalised from the workplace. There was optimism about the apparent low barriers to entry and the modest start-up costs made possible by the falling price of new creative technologies. As Kate Oakley observes, '[t]raditions of popular culture from music to videogames, the strength of subcultural identity, the informal skills associated with creativity and in some cases the low capital entry that digital technology opened up, all combined to suggest that the growth of a "creative economy" was one in which everyone could play' (2007: 262). Oakley concurs that this inclusivity has yet to materialise.

Contemporaneously to the development of cultural/creative industries was the emergence of new information and communication technologies (ICTs) and the internet. This had a profound impact and spawned a plethora of novel career options in areas such as web design, internet marketing, interactive gaming and digital music production – to name but a few. As Kennedy notes, the new economy – and new media work in particular – was a sphere that was frequently held up as being particularly progressive for women (2009: 179). However when researchers began to investigate these new businesses an unpalatable pattern began to emerge that contradicted the arguments about the openness of this industry and the diverse make-up of the workforce (Richards and Milestone 2000, Ursell 2000, Gill 2002). The creative industries are also not as accessible to those from working class backgrounds as had been assumed (Oakley 2007, Allen and Holligworth 2013). In addition to class barriers, research also points to the exclusion of ethnic minorities from creative industries (Bose 2005, Tatli and Özbilgin 2012). Whilst it would be highly valuable to examine intersecting inequalities there is not space to do this now.

Disappointingly, 30 years after the GLC project and with a far more developed creative industries landscape, there remain some uncomfortable questions about why these new, 'informal', anti-hierarchical businesses that rely on 'light' technology and creativity have not delivered a diverse workforce. As Adkins argues, there is a 'deep rooted exclusion of women from these reflexivized occupations' (1999: 126). The creative industries have emerged concurrently with a 'post feminist' (Aronson 2003, McRobbie 2004) landscape where feminism is represented as outmoded and unnecessary, and the rise of neo-liberalism (Prasad 2006), where equal opportunities

policies are held to be excessively bureaucratic. Recent research about student placements in creative industries reiterates earlier arguments made in the work of Gill (2002)
and McRobbie (2002) and reveals that a lack of acknowledgement of the inequalities
dominates because of an assumed meritocracy; 'privilege and disadvantage is reproduced by the gatekeepers in the sector through unspoken assumptions and resistance
to acknowledge discrimination' (Tatli and Özbilgin 2012: 259). Within the sector its
workers and advocates do not routinely acknowledge that creative industries are
difficult for many people to access.

The products of the cultural industries often exacerbate, reinforce and solidify
cultural expectations about the type of person that is 'naturally' suited to working in
the new media sector. There has been little evidence of culture change across the
creative sector and this inhibits the career development of women. This trend is
clearly not unique to Manchester. A recent Skillset census, the largest gender-specific
research on the creative industries in England, concludes that there is 'widespread
under-representation across the board and enormous variance between sectors and
occupations in levels of employment of women' (2010a: 2). The authors note that
women are most heavily represented in sectors with large employers who are able to
offer more stable and long-term employment prospects (television, radio and book
publishing are cited as the largest employers of women). Their research recorded a
massive drop of women in interactive content design (dropping from 32 per cent to
5 per cent from 2006 to 2009).

The local context: Manchester – creative city

The creative industries in Manchester are highlighted by the city council as an
important growth area. Research commissioned by the city council predicts that
over the next ten years 'the creative industries could bring an estimated 23,000 new
jobs to Greater Manchester' (New Economy 2013). Within the creative industries in
Manchester businesses that focus on the creative use of digital technology are seen
as strategically important. Recent policy documents state that Manchester has the
largest cluster of digital and creative businesses outside London and the south-east
(New Economy 2013) and claims are made that Manchester has the potential to be 'a
truly global digital content hub by 2025' (Oliver and Ohlbaum Associates 2012).
Recent research about UK geographical distribution of cultural industries shows that
Manchester is a strong centre in terms of 'advertising, architecture, software, computer games and electronic publishing, and radio and TV' (De Propris et al. 2009:
23). The report highlights that Manchester is also notable in terms of 'Designer
fashion/photography, film and video/music and the visual and performing arts' and
that Manchester is one of the few places outside of London to have a notable presence in terms of 'software, computer games and electronic publishing'. The authors
of this report acknowledge how atypical Manchester is compared to other cities
outside of London.

Having provided a brief overview of the emergence of and importance to the local
economy provided by creative industries I now seek to highlight one explanation as
to why the new media sector in Manchester does not currently have a diverse

workforce by focusing on interview data from research of 'creative new media' companies in Manchester. The interview questions were focused on recruitment and retention strategies; new patterns of working; contracts of employment; organisational cultures and behaviours. Interviewees were asked to talk about the roles that men and women typically work in and to give their explanations for the absence of women in the frontline creative and technical roles. Of the key decision makers of the 20 companies we interviewed, 17 were men and three were women. 12 of the companies had an all-male workforce. Only six of the companies had women working in key roles. The businesses focused on were involved with design work that relied on the use of ICT/new media in the design and dissemination process – mainly interactive games design, web design, internet marketing and advertising.

This research takes an approach that is comparable with research carried out by Perrons (2003) about the new media sector in Brighton and Hove, UK. In Perrons' work she focused on a specific geographic locale that, like Manchester, emerged as a new media hub. Perrons critically examined issues around work–life balance and the new economy potentially creating new opportunities for people with caring responsibilities. Perrons concluded that as the new media had been shoehorned into existing social structures a marked gender imbalance remained in the new media sector. Perrons' work is highly informative and provides valuable insights into the problems and opportunities for women in this developing sector.

Men, women and creative new media work in Manchester

In this section I will highlight and discuss a number of quotes from interviews with key decision makers (often owner-managers) of Manchester's new media companies. As noted above, these were small and micro businesses in the area of games design, web design, graphic design, advertising and marketing. Quotes have been selected where gender was explicitly or implicitly discussed. The analysis of these interviews focused on comments and inferences made about men's and women's skills and aptitudes towards certain types of work. It came through very strongly in the interviews that there are dominant ideas about the type of work that men and women are apparently 'naturally' suited to. Crucially these ideas result in women being significantly over-represented in lower paid, lower status jobs that are distanced from frontline creative production. I argue that there are deeply entrenched ideas about 'men's skills' and 'women's skills' which rely on values that are often claimed to be outmoded or redundant in the new economy. In short there is a disjuncture between theory and practice. As authors such as Angela McRobbie (2004) and Rosalind Gill (2007) have argued, post-feminist discourses about apparent gender equality render this problem 'unspeakable' and often unacknowledged. This in turn inhibits debate about how to effect cultural change.

Awareness of the male dominated workforce

When mapping out the workforce of new media workplaces in this research project it became very clear that hardly any women were working in frontline creative/

technical roles. Hesmondhalgh uses the term 'symbol creator' to describe frontline cultural producers and identifies these as including 'those who make up, interpret or rework stories, songs, images and so on' (2007: 5). In the 20 companies we identified six women who were part of the creative teams. Indeed in some companies there were no women at all; 'I'll come right out and say it, we don't have any women working for us, not by design, it's just worked out that way' (Miles, company 4, interactive products mainly for education sector).

Like many other of the interviewees, Miles says there wasn't a conscious decision not to employ women. To him it was a 'coincidence'. We heard similar stories from many of our interviewees. There were women working in some of the new media companies we interviewed but there were clear signs of a gendered division of labour. In the majority of the new media companies that were researched, the male employees were the designers and content producers and women were the administrators and project managers:

> Interviewer: 'Do you often get women sending their CVs in?'
> Seth, company 10 (advertising): 'Yeah, quite a lot. And quite a lot of the stuff that I've seen is really good but some blokes are really good and there's rubbish of each. So you know, I've not noticed any polarisation except that curiously here, some of, well only two girls work here out of fifteen, sixteen.'
> Interviewer: 'But do they do technical things as well?'
> Seth, company 10 (advertising): 'No actually, interestingly.'

These comments suggest that Seth hasn't noticed the gender make-up of his workforce and when he reflects on this he seems to find it a curious coincidence that women are absent. A spokesperson for a company of 11 men (and no women) said that they are a 'gender neutral' company – in spite of having an all male workforce. Seth refers to women as 'girls' and this was a common occurrence during our interviews.

Here there are signs of a post-feminist sensibility (Gill 2007) pervading the discourse and the sense that equal opportunities policies are no longer necessary because the work of feminism is complete. None of the companies we interviewed had looked at strategies to recruit a more diverse workforce. Indeed if we look at the dominant patterns these SMEs use for recruitment it becomes clear that a practice of 'appointing in their own image' is endemic.

Recruitment through closed networks

With few exceptions, recruitment appeared to be always based upon informal and business networks, word of mouth recommendations and hiring of friends. Going through formal recruitment procedures involving job advertisements, application forms and interviews were eschewed on the grounds that they were overly bureaucratic and ultimately ineffectual in getting the right person for the job. 'It all began with knowing them socially, which is the case very much in our industry' (Charles, company 16, creative agency/brand management).

This replacement of human resources management and equal opportunities policies with informal networking is problematic for anyone on the outside trying to get in.

The importance of 'fitting in' was a recurring theme in the majority of companies that were interviewed and seemed to be a euphemism for recruiting 'people like us'. This attitude makes the prospect of a diverse workforce unattainable. Here we can see evidence of the homophily identified by Grugulis and Stoyanova in their research into social capital and networks in film and TV. As they argue, 'relationships do not occur in a vacuum and social networks are likely to be composed of similar people' (2012: 1315).

Furthermore, although skills (high-end technical or graphic design skills) were central to the work involved in these companies, many respondents expressed a view that formal qualifications were not important. When asked about skills and qualifications one responded said, 'Irrelevant. You know, a certificate on a wall, great. You know, I want to know how quickly they can come up with a really nice logo or a clever piece of code' (Seth, company 10, advertising).

This disregard for externally gained qualifications (in favour of self-training and learning on the job) was a sentiment expressed by a number of the people we interviewed. Skillset data shows that women in creative industries are likely to have received more training than men (63 per cent compared with 55 per cent (2010a)). Even women who gained industry specific training found it hard to break into the industry. In a sector where technology changes quickly workers who experience a gap between receiving training and gaining work are likely to be at a disadvantage.

Masculine 'ideal type'

When employers were asked about what sort of people, skills, attributes they were looking for, a masculine 'ideal type' (Acker 1992) was frequently and powerfully alluded to. The interview data highlighted a model of a new media worker who is expected to display new forms of machismo that rely on 'fire and energy', 'adrenaline', 'stamina' and 'being obsessively driven'. Managers, although rarely specific, were consistent in their description of the distinctiveness of the organisational culture and working environment, and argued that a key consideration at recruitment was how the individual would fit within this culture. The ability to 'fit in' was often closely aligned with being flexible in terms of working hours and being available to work as and when the projects demanded.

New patterns of working rarely seemed to be translated into good practice in terms of work-life balance, enabling more flexible working, and allowing some employees to reduce hours spent in the workplace or to work from home. On the contrary, flexible work was often defined in terms of employees showing 'commitment to their work' in that they were willing to work long hours and ensure project deadlines were met.

When asked of a company with an all-male workforce if anyone had children it was clear that workers' private lives did not 'bleed' into workplace identities: 'I think there are one, two, three other guys with families that are here with small children and stuff. And I think the wives tend to stay at home'. Domestic life seems to be rendered almost invisible in these new media companies. Adkins challenges theories of risk society when she argues that individualisation is a gender process, and thereby links individualisation to the reproduction of a traditional division of labour: 'Individualization in terms of the labour market – becoming an individualized worker – may [therefore] be said to be a gendered process which relied on, or is founded upon the appropriation of women's labour in the private sphere' (1999: 128).

These male workers rely on their partners to cover all aspects of domestic life. It would be difficult for those facing the expectation of being ever available in the new economy to request flexible, family-friendly working conditions.

Perceptions of women's skills (and implied explanation for their absence from the new media workplace)

Some employers did articulate ideas about what women could bring to the new media workplace. It was widely held that women were good as project managers and in client-facing roles. These are clearly intermediary roles and roles where the women are distanced from the creative process: 'In my personal experience of multimedia, in terms of the nitty gritty end you don't tend to see women … you do see a lot of female project managers, more organisational than hands dirty' (Gus, company 11, multimedia development company).

Women are not perceived to be suited to getting their 'hands dirty' even in the realm of the new media industry with its clean, weightless technology. Women are perceived to have skills in organisation, project management and customer facing roles. These roles are less valued than the 'nitty gritty' creative roles and women's financial remuneration reflects this.

The explanation for the limited opportunities for women to work in high status, creative roles in new media companies is clearly linked to the following factors. First, there is a powerfully vivid social construction of the ideal new media worker amongst the gate keepers of the sector. This ideal worker is routinely characterised as being young, male, and not involved caring roles outside of the workplace. Masculinity is linked to qualities such as obsessiveness, heroic commitment to working long hours and being in possession of social capital that involves an interest in extreme sports, club culture and music. Women are never described in these terms. Instead, attributes such as being balanced, being able to multi-task and not allowing work to consume them were attached to women and these qualities did not work in their favour. Second, recruitment practices clearly worked against women. Employers frequently stated that they were not interested in formal qualifications and training and instead favour word of mouth recommendations. This is clearly linked to the first explanation of appointing from a clearly defined paradigm from which women are routinely excluded. Third, it was claimed that that women 'don't apply'. However as it was reported by the interviewees that jobs were rarely advertised it would be difficult for women to identify potential opportunities. Fourth, there was no expression of interest in developing strategies to recruit more women and similarly no debate about how to make working practices more flexible for all employees. Within the sector there is scant evidence of reflection on the gendered division of labour and no evidence of the development and implementation of strategies to recruit women. Our research findings are consistent with other research into women and creative work elsewhere (Perrons 2003, Gill 2002 and Christopherson 2008).

Conclusion

This chapter sought to highlight why cultural industries have thus far failed to attract a diverse workforce in terms of gender. By looking in-depth at practices and attitudes held by employers and creative industry workers, we argue that recruitment strategies, organisational cultures and behaviours prevalent within the sector directly and indirectly discriminate against women. Only through exposing and making visible these subtle yet ubiquitous, powerful and essentialised social constructions of ideal creative workers, can a dialogue be entered in to about how to bring about change. The images and cultural values that are circulated by the cultural industries themselves perpetuate retrograde ideas about men's and women's roles in society. These essentialised ideas about gender have been questioned in this chapter and some hope can be drawn from the recognition that displays of gender are socially constructed. These displays are therefore fluid, not fixed, and the potential for change is possible.

Notes

1 Skillset is the UK industry body for the creative industries.
2 *The Look of the Week*, originally broadcast on BBC television in May 1967. Available at www.youtube.com/watch?v=4bhBpuM9Pz0.

Reports/magazine articles

Manchester City Council (2012) 'Manchester economic factsheet', February.
New Economy (2013) 'Financial and creative industries forecast to drive Manchester's growth in 2013', neweconomymanchester.com/stories/1719-financial_and_creative_industries_forecast_to_drive_manchesters_growth_in_2013.
Skillset (2010a) *Women in the Creative Media Industries*, London: Skillset.
Skillset (2010b) *Northern Strategic Skills Assessment: Executive Summary*, London: Skillset.
Skillset (2010c) *Strategic Skills Assessment for the Creative Industries*, London: Skillset.
Oliver and Ohlbaum Associates (2012) 'Manchester: A truly global digital content hub by 2025', October, London: Oliver and Ohlbaum Associates.
American Psychological Association, Task Force on the Sexualisation of Girls (2010) 'Report of the APA Task Force on the Sexualisation of Girls', Washington, DC: APA, www.apa.org/pi/women/programs/girls/report-full.pdf.

References

Acker, J. (1992) 'Gendering organizational theory', in Mills, A.J. and Tancred, P. (eds) *Gendering Organizational Analysis*, Newbury Park, CA: Sage.
Adkins, L. (1999) 'Community and economy: A retraditionalization of gender?' *Theory, Culture and Society* 16 (1): 117–37.
Akuma, Y. and Barnes, C. (2009) 'Where is our diversity? Questions of visibility and representation in Australian graphic design', *Visual Design Scholarship* 4 (1): 29–40.
Allen, K. and Hollingworth, S. (2013) '"Sticky subjects" or "cosmopolitan creatives"? Social class, place and urban young people's aspirations for work in the knowledge economy', *Urban Studies* 50 (3): 499–517.

Aronson, P. (2003) '"Feminists" or "post feminists"? Young women's attitudes towards feminism and gender relations', *Gender and Society* 17 (6): 902–22.

Banks, M. and Milestone, K. (2011) 'Individualization, gender and cultural work', *Gender, Work and Organization* 18 (1): 73–89.

Bose, M. (2005) 'Difference and exclusion at work in the club culture economy', *International Journal of Cultural Studies* 8 (4): 427–44.

Butler, J. (1990) *Gender Trouble*, Abingdon: Routledge.

Christopherson, S. (2008) 'Beyond the self-expressive creative worker: An industry perspective on entertainment media', *Theory, Culture and Society* 25 (7/8): 73–95.

De Propris, L., Chapain, C., Cooke, P., MacNeill, S. and Mateos-Garcia, J. (2009) *The Geography of Creativity*, London: NESTA.

Florida, R. (2002) *The Rise of the Creative Class and how it's Transforming Work, Leisure, Community and Everyday Life*, New York: Perseus Book Group.

Gill, R. (2002) 'Cool, creative and egalitarian? Exploring gender in project based new media work', *Information and Communication Studies* 5 (1): 70–89.

Gill, R. (2007) *Gender and the Media*, Cambridge: Polity Press.

Grugulis, I. and Stoyanova, D. (2012) 'Social capital and networks in Film and TV: Jobs for the Boys?', *Organization Studies* 33 (10): 1311–31.

Haines, L. (2004) *Why are there so few women in games?* Report for Media Training North West, archives.igda.org/women/MTNW_Women-in-Games_Sep04.pdf.

Hesmondhalgh, D. (2007) *The Cultural Industries*, London: Sage.

Kennedy, H. (2009) 'Going the extra mile: Emotional and commercial imperatives in new media work' *Convergence* 15 (2): 177–96.

Kunstner, T., Le Merle, M., Gmelin, H. and Dietsche, C. (2013) *The Digital Future of Creative UK: The Economic Impact of Digitization and the Internet on the Creative Sector in the U. and Europe*, London: Booz and Co for Creative England.

McRobbie, A. (2002) 'Clubs to companies: Notes on the decline of political culture in speeded up creative worlds', *Cultural Studies* 16 (4): 516–31.

McRobbie, A. (2004) 'Postfeminism and popular culture', *Feminist Media Studies* 4 (3): 255–64.

Mulgan, G. and Worpole, K. (1986) *Saturday Night or Sunday Morning? From Arts to Industry – New Forms of Cultural Policy*, London: Comedia.

Mulvey, L. (1975) 'Visual pleasure and narrative cinema', *Screen* 16 (3): 6–18.

Oakley, K. (2007) 'Include us out: Economic development and social policy in the creative industries', *Cultural Trends* 15 (4): 255–73.

O'Connor, J. (2007) *The Cultural and Creative Industries: A Review of the Literature*, Report for Creative Partnerships, Arts Council of England.

Papadopoulos, L. (2010) 'Sexualisation of young girls: Report for the UK Government Home Office', https://shareweb.kent.gov.uk/Documents/health-and-wellbeing/teenpregnancy/Sexualisation_young_people.pdf.

Perrons, D. (2003) 'The new economy and the work–life balance: A case study of new media in Brighton and Hove', *Gender, Work and Organization* 10 (1): 65–93.

Prasad, M. (2006) *The Politics of Free Markets: The Rise of Neoliberal Economic Policies in Britain, France, Germany and the United States*, Chicago: University of Chicago Press.

Richards, N. and Milestone, K. (2000) 'What difference does it make? Women's pop cultural production and consumption in Manchester', *Sociological Research Online* 5 (1): www.socresonline.org.uk/5/1/richards.html.

Sandvoss, C. (2005) *Fans: The Mirror of Consumption*, Cambridge: Polity Press.

Tams, E. (2002) 'Creating divisions: Creativity, entrepreneurship and gendered inequality', *City* 6 (3): 393–402.

Tatli, A. and Özbilgin, M. (2012) 'Surprising intersectionalities of inequality and privilege: The case of the arts and cultural sector', *Equality, Diversity and Inclusion: An International Journal*, 31 (3): 249–65.

Ursell, G. (2000) 'Television production: Issues of exploitation, commodification and subjectivity in UK television labour markets', *Media, Culture and Society* 22 (6): 805–25.

Whelehan, I. (2000) Overloaded: Popular Culture and the Future of Feminism, London: The Women's Press.

Williamson, J. (1978) *Decoding Advertisments*, London: Marion Boyars.

41

THE MARKETING OF RACE IN CULTURAL PRODUCTION

Anamik Saha

Research into cultural industries has generally focused on what makes cultural industries distinct from other industries. Scholars working in the cultural industries tradition draw attention to its commerce/creativity tensions, the relative autonomy of creative workers and loose/tight control in industrialized cultural production (see Hesmondhalgh 2013). Conversely, there is a focus as well on how, in the shift toward neoliberal market models, the cultural industries behave like other industries where production is rationalized to counter the inherent risk involved in producing cultural commodities (Ryan 1991). Where cultural industries research has been lacking is in issues to do with the nature of the text itself. While praxis in this field of research is discussed in terms of media regulation and cultural policy (Garnham 1990; Oakley 2004) or workers' rights (Banks 2007; Ross 2007), there has been very little attention paid to what structural changes (and continuities) in the cultural industries mean for the nature of media representation, particularly for marginalized groups (see Hesmondhalgh and Saha 2013). This is surprising because, as I aim to demonstrate in this chapter, a cultural industries approach has much to offer in deepening our understanding of the governance of race under capitalism. Within the Western media racialized minorities are either left out of discourse entirely or represented in a way that that reinforces racial stereotypes. Unpacking these neo-colonial processes from a cultural industries perspective exposes us to the operations and mechanisms through which the media work to reproduce ethnic and racial stereotype, while pointing us to ways in which these processes can be disrupted and subverted.

This chapter is based on an empirical study of British South Asian cultural producers working in three cultural industries – television, publishing and theatre – and consisted of interviews and ethnographic fieldwork. The main protagonists of the research were British Asian creative workers who foreground issues of Asian identity and culture in their productions. Such individuals were often motivated by a desire to challenge what they saw as the persistent, regressive and stereotypical representation of Asian cultures and identities in the media. Dwyer and Crang (2002) in their research on British Asian fashion designers work with the term 'ethnicized commodities'. While I have slight misgivings about this term, it has a useful application in this context as it helps distinguish those British cultural producers who are explicitly working with issues of culture and identity from those who are not (of which there are many). It also stresses the 'transruptive' (Hesse 2000) potential of these texts in challenging normative and stereotypical versions of race and ethnicity, and at the same time producing more progressive accounts of multiculture.

The particular focus of this chapter is on the *tight control* stage of cultural production, and the marketing of ethnicized cultural commodities. As Nicholas Garnham (1990: 161–62) states, it is the 'cultural distribution' stage of production, which includes marketing, '*that is the key locus of power and profit* […] [i]t is access to distribution which is the key to cultural plurality'. Indeed, my research found that marketing and promotion was a particularly fraught stage of production for my respondents. Ethnicized cultural commodities generally receive very little (if any) marketing attention from the cultural industries. In those instances where they were the recipients of marketing campaigns I found two very different strategies at play: either they were promoted and aestheticized in a way that attempts to appeal to the biggest audience, or designed to target specific niches. In this chapter I want to demonstrate how both of these strategies are underwritten with neo-colonial ideology that produces racializing effects, where the producer's attempt to present a counter-narrative of difference is perversely transformed into racial stereotype.

Ethnicity as unique selling point (USP)

Within the core cultural industries (i.e. those that deal with mass audiences), the challenge for minority cultural producers is not just in creating a marketable product that convinces executives that it can attract an audience, but also in convincing executives to allocate sufficient resources to promote it. The scale of the marketing campaign – if media owners do decide it's worthy of promotion – will be determined by how the product is prioritized against other cultural goods in the company's repertoire. This is particularly the case in television. When I spoke to British Asian producers working in broadcasting, the common grievance was that even though they might receive a commission for a programme dealing with (multi)cultural issues, it would be considered a low priority for the broadcaster, denoting little, if any, publicity. Compounded by the allocation of a slot outside of primetime, this can severely limit the size of the potential audience. To quote a British Asian television director I interviewed, 'You can make the best thing in the world, but if people don't know about it they're not going to watch it. So you're kind of dead in the water'. The British Broadcasting Corporation (BBC) employs a colour-coding system that ranks television programmes/series in terms of whether they are high, mid or low priority, which determines the scale of the marketing drive. The higher the ranking the greater the marketing push, usually reserved for big-budget, high profile, prime-time programmes such as *The Apprentice*, or a popular soap opera's Christmas special. The task of ranking programming falls under the jurisdiction of the schedulers, the controller, commissioners and the head of marketing, which at the BBC is a centralized department. It is worth noting as well that the marketing of the good is often taken out of the producer's hands to become the responsibility of either an in-house marketing department (as is the case in television) or an external agency – part of the 'tight control' of industrial cultural production.

Inevitably, this has particular ramifications for programmes produced by British Asians, as the following account from a respondent working in programme development at the BBC suggests:

> The impression I get is you hand [the programme] over and the channel – according to their needs and who they want to attract, and what's big for the audiences – will decide whether they are likely to promote say, a one hour show on multiculturalism versus a ten-part series with Alan Sugar. What goes first is fairly obvious. And don't forget it costs a lot of money making trailers and so on. So there's no point spending a lot of your budget on a one-off documentary that might get only one and a half million people at 9pm when you can attract 10 million people for *The Apprentice*.

The respondent narrates the process of choosing what to market as following a logic where it is only the big budget production that can potentially get the largest audiences (relative to the channel) that will have a marketing campaign to promote it. According to this narrative, those programmes that are expected to garner lower ratings – such as a 'one-off documentary on multicultural issues' – will not get publicity, certainly not in any of the mainstream outlets. Again, this is described in normative terms, as though it is 'obvious' common sense (though the respondent in this quote was being sarcastic about the attitudes of the executives). It is also interesting to note that she provides her opinion based on 'the impression' she gets; it was a recurrent theme that those respondents who actually work on the shows have little grasp of the decision-making process behind what gets marketed and how.

Interestingly, at the time of my research one 'Asian' themed programme – or rather, set of programmes – did receive a promotional campaign. The BBC was broadcasting an India/Pakistan season to mark the 60th anniversary of the partition of India, which included productions commissioned not just by the BBC's Asian Programming Unit (now defunct) but also by other BBC regional centres, such as *India with Sanjeev Bhaskar* produced by BBC Bristol, and *Michael Wood: The Story of India* produced by the independent television company Maya Vision. A short trailer was produced, consisting of a montage of scenes from the programmes making up the season, though mostly taken from the bigger 'mainstream' productions, inter-spersed with animations, and specially produced scenes with four Asian actors and actresses who introduce the season. Their lines are almost poetic. I quote them here in order to convey the mood of the trailer:

> How do you tell a story
> That stretches from Kolkata to Karachi?
> That tells of ancient cultures and modern societies
> Of two ever changing societies?

As the lines suggest, this trailer is based upon very familiar tropes of India – amongst the images of modern India, we still see Bengal tigers, old Hindu sages, ancient Moghul palaces and clouds of brightly coloured power hanging over crowded streets during the festival of Holi. With regard to why and how this season of programming on South Asian histories and cultures did receive publicity treatment in the first place, it can be explained in fairly common sense economic terms: the BBC had spent a lot of money on this series so, as a public service broadcaster, it had to ensure it generated ratings that justified the amount of money spent. But also there was a clear press angle or hook – that is, the season was to commemorate the 60th anniversary of the partition of India. As such, according to these intertwining editorial and commercial rationales the India/Pakistan season was *naturally* going to receive a fairly significant marketing push. In some ways, this represents a progressive cultural political moment, where a formerly disavowed culture is placed at the heart of British broadcasting.

Yet such a normative rationale conceals an ideological dimension. With regard to 'multicultural programming', what gets commissioned, scheduled at primetime, and significant marketing attention are generally those representations of difference that neatly slot into the imagined geographies of the dominant nationalist ideology. With the case of the BBC's Indian/Pakistan season we see a particular narrative of Indianness, framed through the lens of the British Raj, that lends itself to a tried and tested Orientalist formula and allows for certain nationalist fantasies to be played out, regardless of the actual content of the season. It is in this way that the rationalized processes and mechanics of marketing in the cultural industries act as a form of racial governance. As one British Asian woman who works at the BBC told me, 'If it's got that colonial veneer it will get attention […] it's about showing these stories through that prism'. Consequently, those narratives of difference that help ease the nation's postcolonial melancholia (Gilroy 2004) get foregrounded in discourse thanks to a sustained marketing drive that crystallizes rather than explodes existing perceptions of difference.

Asian audiences for Asian work?

Within the mainstream television industries we find that, through standardized market-ing practices, ethnicized cultural commodities are either marginalized and excluded (i.e. are not publicized), or aestheticized in the publicity material such as to squeeze the text into well-known (and racialized) tropes in order to appeal to the largest amount of people. What is troubling is how this reductive effect is produced through a discourse of common sense economic rationale that increasingly characterizes production in the cultural industries. In other forms of cultural production where it is understood that the cultural commodities of British Asian producers are not going to attract the biggest audience, we see a different rationale at play, one based upon niche marketing. In this part of the chapter I want to demonstrate how, despite once again appearing as sensible, common sense commercial practice, it in fact produces similar racializing effects.

When I asked the in-house press officer of a London theatre venue about which sections of the press she was targeting for a play produced by a British Asian theatre company, she replied, 'Well, for that you'd be obviously targeting Asian press, because it's an Asian-based theatre production'. The matter-of-fact way in which this was expressed was such that it went unnoticed at first. After speaking to British Asian cultural producers, it became clear that such a discourse constituted what they saw as the biggest challenge to their work: the assumption that Asian work is only for Asian people. As Hardt and Negri (2000: 151–52) discuss, the new hybrid forms of difference that characterize the new global order benefit postmodern forms of marketing that thrive on differentiated 'target markets' that can each be addressed by specific marketing strategies. Effectively, under neoliberalism, diasporic communities are not only racialized but reduced to niche markets as well.

This is troubling for cultural producers from racialized minorities who define their work in terms of challenging ethnic absolutist ideology that sustains the distinctions with racial and ethnic groups. In the following account, the (white) producer of the theatre company mentioned above unpacks the implications of the assumption that *Asian plays are for Asian audiences*:

> I think that is the thing that people have had to try and accept with us – that we're looking for an audience in everybody. As I was saying before, that whole kind of thing of *ok this is brown, we can get the brown people in* or all of that kind of marketing cynicism … the amount of times I have had a phone conversation with a marketing manager or press person saying, *right ok this is a piece about Asians* … But [our play] will work with your core drama audience, it will work with people who like this kind of show, it'll work with your black audience; you need to be telling everybody about it and focusing on everybody. It's amazing the amount of black women who like [our] work but you try getting that across to some marketing departments and they don't quite comprehend that.

In this quote, the producer describes the struggle in convincing venues and their marketing staff that their productions can work with its 'core drama audience', that is the mainstream audience, rather than just Asians who are assumed to be the natural audience for their plays. This narrative underlines niche marketing strategies as a form of racial governance and the corporeal management of the Other, where the supposed core Asian audience is reduced to 'brown' bodies to be counted; that is, '*ok this is brown, we can get the brown people in*' (in order to meet certain diversity quotas, as is the case in the subsidized arts sector). According to this quote, the theatre company is trying to do something universal, but this is impeded by the in-house marketing team; the producers lament that while black women enjoy their work marketing departments are incapable of *comprehending* this and will only target 'brown people'. This is what the theatre producer describes as 'marketing cynicism' – the lack of faith accorded to British Asian productions in terms of their ability to resonate with the 'outside', that is the wider 'white, mainstream' (or even black female) audience.

I asked the (Asian) playwright who also works at this theatre company to reflect further upon what she saw as the implications of the practice of specifically targeting Asian audiences for what is construed as 'Asian work':

> It's to do with what you're allowed to be. Are you above your station? Sometimes I have got that. I have got that from Asian publicity people who only

will address the Asian press because that is [seen to be] my audience. [But] my potential audience [is] people who are Radio 4, who read more, who have travelled more, who know all these references I have made and are not frightened by literariness.

In this quote the respondent believes the particular marketing strategies adopted for her plays immediately foreclose her work from addressing a wider audience – or to be more precise, a very middle-class, and implicitly white, audience. The fear from the establishment that she may be *above her station* refers specifically to the racial and social hierarchies that she finds herself placed in. So in this instance from theatre and the examples from television described above, we see how particular cultural commodities come to be defined and marketed in terms of the ethnic identity of the producer that can limit their ability to reach and speak beyond their supposed (ethnic) constituency.

But what I find particularly interesting in both this quote and the one before it is that they implicitly suggest that the causal factor for the reductive approach in marketing is due to the individual attitudes of marketing personnel. This would suggest that change could be imposed at the micro level, through modifying the behaviour and values (and perhaps even the ethnic and racial make up) of creative managers. How-ever, such a view fails to acknowledge the structural context against which social actions occur. It is interesting to note that the playwright highlights how 'Asian publicity people' are also 'guilty' of only addressing the Asian press. Rather than using this to suggest that fellow Asians *should know better*, I argue that this observation is in fact evidence of how it standardized practice (rationalized through a notion of niche) that comes to have racialized effects, regardless of the culture and values of the social actors involved. It is this chapter's contention that it is the increasingly commercialized cultures of production within the cultural industries – even in a heavily subsidized culture industry such as theatre – through which marketing practices (re)produce the reification of difference. Such standardized marketing processes act as a form of racialized governance that structure the social hierarchical forms of racialized inclu-sions, where the playwright above is not 'allowed' to be what she wants to be. In other words, there is a danger in according perhaps *too much* agency to marketing personnel, as it fails to acknowledge the structural context of the cultural industries through which marketing practice is formed and enacted.

The contradiction of marketing Asianness

According to a 2003 report published by The Institute of Practitioners in Advertising, Asian communities in Britain have a spending power worth £32 billion. The report argued that advertising agencies should be doing more to target the 'brown pound', including improving representation within adverts, and diversity amongst their employees (Cozens 2004). However, Pedro Carvalho, chief executive officer of the public relations firm F-NIK PR (which represents British Asian musician Rishi Rich amongst others) argues that Asians prefer not to be targeted as an ethnic commu-nity, and would rather be regarded as having the same consumer aspirations as their 'white', 'mainstream' counterparts (Carvalho 2004).

ANAMIK SAHA

Even though Carvalho is speaking from a commercial point of view, it nonetheless evokes a cultural political concern that questions the separation of racialized minorities from a mainstream, British national identity – what Stuart Hall (1996: 468) calls 'segregated visibility'. The question of reach is what informs this concluding section on what I consider to be the paradox of marketing Asianness in the cultural industries. Despite attempts to attract Asian audiences to 'Asian work', it is disputable whether the Asian audience is large enough to sustain an Asian production by itself. This is particularly the case with mass produced goods. Indeed, a marketing memo I saw for a novel written by a British Asian author stressed how the 'Asian subgroup is an important but relatively small subsection'. In light of this, one would expect that media companies involved in the production of ethnicized cultural commodities would be targeting the largest, mainstream audience. Yet standardized marketing practice dictates carving up the audience into segments and targeting specific niches. The current trend in the cultural industries is towards employing increasingly rationalized methods for predicting success. This is true of the marketing stage of production in both the commercial *and* subsidized sector. For instance, an issue of the publishing trade magazine *The Bookseller* contained a column by a marketing consultant who argues that the adoption of quantitative and qualitative research methods to inform marketing strategy is central to publishers gaining 'a distinct competitive advantage in a crowded market place', ominously suggesting that 'it won't be long before every publisher employs a strategic research planner as a key member of the editorial team' (Horner 2005). Despite the contrasting political economies, a handbook on marketing in theatre echoes Horner's sentiment, emphasizing the centrality of box office data to successful marketing campaigns, arguing that 'Strategic marketing management is nothing if not about segmentation and positioning' (Fraser 2004: 48). This is indicative of the forms of rationalization that have spread into and throughout the cultural industries as part of a shift towards neoliberal market models. It is through this context that the discourse of 'Asian audiences for Asian work' is normalized and practised, despite at times contradicting the cultural industries focus on audience maximization. Hence, highlighting the paradox of marketing Asianness exposes the ideological dimension to the commodification of British Asian cultural production. The chapter's focus on the intersections between the cultural industries and the postcolonial brings to the forefront the issue of niche-focused marketing as the material manifestation of cultural essentialism and ethnic absolutist ideology.

The stress of the chapter is on how this racializing process is hidden within common sense, normative economic/commercial rationale. In addition, it hides the contradictory and *ambivalent* character of neocolonial ideology. Encapsulating this is an exchange with the owner of an imprint of a major publishing house that specializes in fiction written by people of colour:

AS: Who do you see as your audience?
  Respondent: I think, from the time I set up, the only difference between [my publishing imprint] and, say, Penguin and Bloomsbury and any of those big houses, is that most of the writers I published are non-white. I see the reader as anybody who wants to have a good read, so I'm not targeting any ... I'm targeting a book-buyer. And the whole point of publishing that book is

518

because I feel it's a good enough book for everybody to read. You can't segregate yourself, not in this industry or any industry. You shouldn't do that.

AS: Have you ever segmented your market in terms of ethnicity? For instance, this is a Chinese writer so I'll target the Chinese community ...

Respondent: No you don't do that. But if you do have a Chinese writer, when you are promoting the book you would go for those Chinese magazines, you do promote it that way. If there's any kind of Chinese event happening you make sure you are in there, making that community aware. You don't ignore the community the writer is from – it's like a white writer who comes from Liverpool, and the book is published in London. That publisher would go to Liverpool to tell everybody you have a local writer who has done something wonderful. You cannot ignore the community the writer has come from. That's just the promotion. But the buyers are going to be anybody you can get.

This is what I regard as the contradiction of marketing Asianness. In the first half of the quote the respondent stresses how even though the books she publishes are mostly written by non-white authors, she is not targeting a specific audience – instead, she is targeting 'anybody who wants to have a good read'. This no doubt emerges from a genuine belief that the novels have universal appeal, but there is also an economic rationale that dictates that targeting a relatively small niche is not sustainable. Yet when asked if she would hypothetically target a Chinese audience for a book written by a Chinese author, she immediately replies in the negative. But then she somewhat contradicts this by outlining the various techniques she would employ that target the Chinese community, through what are perceived as 'its' media and institutions. Her justification that 'you cannot ignore the community the writer has come from' (and her example of a Liverpudlian author is presumably designed to quash the racial dimension of this response) is not particularly controversial, and it is implied that such niche-marketing strategies would be coupled with efforts to entice the mainstream book-buying audience as well. Yet there is still nonetheless a persistent ideology of *Asian audiences for Asian work* at play. There is nothing wrong in targeting these audiences per se, but designing a marketing campaign on the product's brand based upon ethnic or racial difference reifies that difference in the process. According to this logic, despite the respondent's warning of the dangers of segregation, Asians will forever be contained within the peripheral spaces. According to Paul Gilroy (2004), national identity is dependent on the concept of fixity in the ideological construction of Otherness, as the Other must not pollute the Self. As I have argued in this chapter, it is through the tight control phase of production in the cultural industries, in this case under the guise of common sense marketing practice, that such an ideology persists.

Conclusion

To reiterate, the practices that typify the marketing of British Asian cultural products in the cultural industries result in two related outcomes. One produces a discourse of Asian audiences for Asian work, whereby a combination of a niche logic and a perception of Asian cultural production as having little appeal beyond the Asian community determines a marketing strategy that is designed and aestheticized so as to appeal to a particular Asian audience, whilst in fact confirming to the values of the white bourgeoisie who run the institutions that fund and mount this work. This is particularly the case with theatre. A second outcome is produced in a more industrialized setting, where the cultural commodity is mass-produced. In this scenario, 'Asianness' still remains the product's USP, but is marketed in a way that is believed to appeal to the largest (white) mainstream audience, as is typical in television and publishing. In both instances, the Asianness of the cultural commodity is overdetermined, and reduced to a stereotype. In more general terms, minority cultures are stressed as absolutely different to (white) national identity, and their difference reified. Subsequently, the unsettling potential of the diasporic text as a 'cultural translation' (Bhabha 1997), an agnostic, anxious, ambivalent counter-discourse, is subsumed by cultural commodification, and reduced to a more stable state that can be safely contained. It is in this way that the rationalized processes of cultural production in the cultural industries amount to a form of racialized governance.

Moreover, the chapter argues that the marketing of ethnicized cultural commodities in the cultural industries contains a contradiction: if capitalism was only concerned with profit, then it would be in the best interests of the cultural industries to stress the universal qualities of the minority-produced cultural commodity, rather than foregrounding its ethnic particularity. Yet through niche strategies, USPs, market research, audience segmentation and subsequent aestheticization techniques, the cultural commodity is racialized in a deeply problematic manner, framed as it is through the Orientalist gaze of the status quo. The perverse effect is that the conflation of the producer's ethnic identity with the commodity's brand identity can actually limit the appeal of these particular cultural commodities, which, when not fetishized, are considered repulsive, or at least alien and different. Thus, the contradiction is that stressing the essential difference of the ethnicized cultural commodity through rationalized marketing strategies is actually at odds with the cultural industries focus on audience maximization and capitalism's profit motive, since its ability to crossover is immediately foreclosed, resulting in fewer unit sales, ratings or 'bums-on-seats'. Marxist critical political economy accounts argue that a critique of commodification needs to be based upon exposing commodity fetishism and the exploitation of the worker (see Mosco 1996; Garnham 2001), yet I argue this underplays the ideological, neocolonial dimension to cultural commodification. Commodification in the context of the creative management of minority cultural production in the cultural industries is the means by which racialized difference is governed in very specific ways, designed to maintain a pure, national identity, and the necessary hierarchies of race. The marketing of the ethnicized cultural commodity as outlined in this chapter suggests that the cultural industries' key role is in sustaining the regulatory practices of racialized governmentalities, rather than accumulating surplus value.

References

Banks, M. 2007. *The Politics of Cultural Work*. Basingstoke: Palgrave Macmillan.
Bhabha, H.K. 1997. Minority Culture and Creative Anxiety. London: British Council Available at: www.britishcouncil.org/studies/reinventing_britain/bhabha_1.htm (accessed 29 June 2007).

Carvalho, P. 2004. Minorities Look to the Mainstream. *The Guardian*. Available at: www.the guardian.com/media/2004/jan/16/advertising.comment.

Cozens, C. 2004. Advertisers Wake Up to the 'Brown Pound'. *The Guardian*. Available at: www.theguardian.com/media/2004/jan/12/advertising.marketingandpr (accessed 13 January 2015).

Dwyer, C. and Crang, P. 2002. Fashioning Ethnicities: The Commercial Spaces of Multiculture. *Ethnicities* 2(3): 410–30.

Fraser, I. 2004. The Marketing of Theatre. In F. Kerrigan, P. Fraser and M. Özbiligin (eds) *Arts Marketing*, London: Elsevier Butterworth Heinemann.

Garnham, N. 1990. *Capitalism and Communication: Global Culture and the Economics of Information*. London: Newbury Park; New Delhi: Sage Publications Ltd.

Garnham, N. 2001. Contribution to a Political Economy of Mass-Communication. In M.G. Durham and D.M. Kellner (eds) *Media and Cultural Studies: KeyWorks*, Malden; Massachusetts: Blackwell Publishing.

Gilroy, P. 2004 *After Empire*. Oxon and New York: Routledge.

Hall, S. 1996. New Ethnicities. In D. Morley and K.H. Chen (eds) *Stuart Hall: Critical Dialogues in Cultural Studies*, 441–49. London: Routledge.

Hardt, M. and Negri, A. 2000. *Empire*. Cambridge, Massachusetts and London, England: Harvard University Press.

Hesmondhalgh, D. 2013. *The Cultural Industries*, third edition. London; Thousand Oaks, Calif.; New Delhi: Sage Publications Ltd.

Hesmondhalgh, D. and Saha, A. 2013. Race, Ethnicity, and Cultural Production. *Popular Communication* 11(3): 179–95.

Hesse, B. 2000. Introduction. In *Un/settled Multiculturalisms: Diasporas, Entanglements, 'Transruptions'*, London; New York: Zed Books.

Horner, D. 2005. Research Methods. *The Bookseller*: 22.

Mosco, V. 1996. *The Political Economy of Communication*. London: Sage.

Oakley, K. 2004. Not So Cool Britannia: The Role of Creative Industries in Economic Development. *International Journal of Cultural Studies* 7(5–7).

Ross, A. 2007. Nice Work If You Can Get It: The Mercurial Career of Creative Industries Policy. *Work, Organisation, Labour and Globalisation* 1(1): 13–30.

Ryan, B. 1991. *Making Capital from Culture:The Corporate Form of Capitalst Cultural Production*. Berlin and New York: Walter de Gruyter.

42

CULTURAL INDUSTRIES AND A MASS COMMUNICATION RESEARCH

A cultivation analysis view

Andy Ruddock

Introduction

Cultural industries research acknowledges the marketization of popular culture as a political challenge (Hesmondhalgh, 2009, 2004; Lewis, 1990). Hard questions follow. Can media industries limit social inclusion and participation with the social realities that they create? If so, how can such "effects" be conceived and examined without misrepresenting the diversity of media industries and audiences?

One topic where such academic curiosities have vividly captured public imaginations is around the role of media in rampage shootings. The association of media consumption and mass murder has been a perennial feature of these events (Scharrer et al., 2003). Recently, the effects of gaming have taken the spotlight. Some mass communication researchers think that quantitative surveys and experiments have delivered convincing evidence that the consumption of videogame violence leads to socially significant, long-term increases in aggression among those who play them (Anderson et al., 2010). Others demur; dubious experimental methods, exaggerated claims about findings, and the tendency to ignore studies that find no "effects" offer few compelling reasons to believe that gaming is bad (Ferguson and Ivory, 2012; Tear and Neilson, 2013). The gaming effects question only endures, in this view, for political reasons.

Such controversies beg the question of how cultural industries research might "fit" with contemporary mass communications research. Historically, experimental studies and surveys on the relation between screen violence and the real thing have not questioned how those images are produced and circulated. However, there is one branch of that tradition that does think these matters are relevant to the effects question; cultivation analysis.

Cultivation analysis made its name by shifting the debate on media violence from the actions of individuals to the ideologies of societies. Starting in the 1960s, cultivation analysts used quantitative content analysis and surveys to argue that screened murders and assaults mattered as agents of political socialization. Together, these acts drip-fed audiences with ideas about what the world was like, how it worked, who had power, and who needed protection. These messages became persuasive, by ubiquity and repetition (Gerbner, 1998; Gerbner et al., 1980; Gross, 2009; Morgan et al., 2012). Contemporary cultivation analysis embraces "research variables" that scrutinize the relationship between the structures of media industries and audiences. This is in keeping with founding figure George Gerbner's conception of media texts as "cultural indicators", and as links in chains of social communication (1969, 1976).

Looking at school shootings as a case study, it is possible to see relationships between the cultivation and cultural industries paradigms. These intersections open new research panoramas from which to contemplate a world where media industries organize audiences as political publics (Livingstone, 2012).

This argument will be made in relation to the reactions from gamers to debates about the effects of media violence that erupted after the Sandy Hook tragedy. In particular, it will examine how gaming bloggers – key cultural intermediaries in gaming cultures – implicitly used ideas about cultivation in their critical reactions to this event, and how this reaction provided a meaningful platform for gamers to enter into political debates about the causes of crime. Through this case study, it is possible to see how multi-method analysis of the production and consumption of media can empower audiences and users to speak on matters of international significance.

On the effects of violent games

School shootings have been related to a number of ideas about media influence; myths and moral panics (Muschert, 2007), media rituals (Sumiala and Tikka, 2010), agenda setting (Muschert, 2009), and the "effects" of media consumption (Ferguson and Ivory, 2012). According to some, school shootings are icons par excellence of mediatization in action; what they are, and what they do as social events cannot be separated from how they are represented and even enacted through media resources (Muschert and Sumiala, 2012; Ruddock, 2013). For this reason, school shootings arrange audiences as publics in heated political debates about the causes of real violence.

In recent years, the focus has fallen on video games. In 2013 a 20-year-old gunman murdered 26 people – 20 of them children – with an AR 15 Bushman assault rifle at the Sandy Hook primary school in Connecticut. The massacre prompted renewed Federal efforts to institute more stringent gun control laws *and* more research on the effects of playing violent games on young people. Gamers were castigated alongside gun enthusiasts; both accused as hobbyists who sustained cultures of real violence.

This isn't surprising; ever since school shootings became an unwelcome blemish on the cultural landscape, the fear that they are encouraged by consuming screen violence has been loudly voiced (Scharrer et al., 2003). This accusation has considerable support from the effects community; perhaps most notably, Anderson et al.'s 2010 meta analysis, which claims that international experimental and survey data confirms that gaming is a significant risk factor for real aggression.

Qualitative researchers have been critical of the idea that media consumption exercises general behavioural effects across "exposed" populations for some time. The very idea, so the argument goes, underestimates the complexity of culture, both in terms of the way that it is produced and how it is consumed (for example Gauntlett, 2011; Newcomb, 1978). But it's important to recognize that many effects researchers are equally dubious.

In fact, the main lesson of effects research is that direct behavioural effects do not come from media consumption alone. On the topic of violence, the relationship between seeing and repeating an action is mediated by all kinds of factors; how the viewer or player understands what s/he sees or does onscreen, whether or not that person has the desire to be violent, and whether or not they have the opportunity and motivation to act out (Bandura, 2009). Added to that, negative effects, where they can be found, tend to congregate within social disenfranchised groups (Comstock, 2008). Then, there are the acknowledged problems with this "evidence", which is often based on dubious experimental proxies for real violence, or else correlations between the co-presence of media and real aggression, where no causal link between the two can be established (Gunter, 2008). Even determined advocates of social learning theory, which holds that screens do model behaviour, concede that the real problem, and research issue, is how media content exacerbates a world of inequality. Actually, the most powerful effect that media have is to prompt *no* behaviour, by encouraging a fatalistic, passive outlook on the prospects for social change (Bandura, 1978). In other words, effects researchers are sceptical about the idea that media violence makes people violent, and have long doubted whether that is the right question to ask in the first place.

Unsurprisingly, this scepticism has carried over into studies on gaming and school shootings. In *School Shootings: Mediatized Violence in a Global Age* (2012) Ferguson and Ivory argued the inherent limitations of effects methods noted above are exacerbated by publication bias toward studies that do claim to show evidence of effects, exaggerated claims about the size of effects, and the deeply conservative politics of effects studies.

Ferguson and Ivory observed that questions about effects tend to only be asked when guns are turned on the affluent. Then, the main effect of effects research is to propel a moral panic and moral regulation based on cultural prejudices rather than evidence. One of the most damaging effects of media violence is that it has created an academic wild goose chase – albeit a well-funded one – where the main outcome is to distract public attention from a proper consideration of what causes social violence, and where media fit into this, if at all. This ignores the positive potential of mediatized violence. As the authors put it, "Video games form a media outlet in which individuals may experience, explore and consider violent behavior which occurs naturally within our species" (Ferguson and Ivory, 2012; 60).

Ferguson and Ivory's intervention sits neatly in a history of effects research that has positioned media consumption as a political and collective as opposed to a behavioral and individual issue. This came to matter significantly in the wake of the Sandy Hook shooting, as Ferguson organized a petition of scholars who urged the

American Psychological Association to be more circumspect in its public announcements on-media effects; part of a broader campaign to resist a federally funded, disproportionate focus on the damage that gaming causes.

But this may not be as welcome in gaming circles as one might imagine. After Sandy Hook, the American National Rifle Association's President, Wayne Lapierre, blamed games for an escalation in social violence (Tassi, 2013), and Barack Obama commissioned more research on the dangers of playing them. Then something unexpected happened; some gamers began to wonder if they *were* involved.

On the gaming website *Rock, Paper, Shotgun*, journalist Nathan Grayson wrote an op-ed where he reasoned that the vast consumption of this violence by gamers must have some sort of social relevance. He then challenged his readers to participate in a discussion on ways of conceiving screen brutality as something that does affect how people live in the world.

The move was partly based on the feeling that gamers and the gaming industry could no longer dissociate from the gun violence issue. Given the product placement of actual guns in games (Meier and Martin, 2012), at the very least it seemed that the industry could be doing more to protect its consumers from political attack. At any rate, what was clear was that some gamers were looking for a new, political language to talk about the screen brutality that so many of them enjoy. Why did they enjoy it? What might playing it over long periods "do" in the lives of the millions who never act out, but might be influenced in other ways? And, how might this knowledge empower gamers to demand change in the industry (Grayson, 2012)?

The cultural indicators project

Media research has been here before. In the 1960s, a research team at the University of Pennsylvania, led by George Gerbner received funding from the US Surgeon General to investigate the effects of television violence. Over a decade, the team compiled eleven violence profiles; annual content analyses enumerating the amount of violence on prime time US television. They also conducted a number of surveys, examining differences in the social attitudes of "heavy" and "light" television viewers. This data became the basis for cultivation analysis, one of the most frequently cited models of mass communication studies (Morgan et al., 2012).

The Penn team's findings revolutionized how the politics of media consumption was understood. Their innovation was to reframe violence as a "cultural indicator" of what happens to cultures that surrender their storytelling modes to commercial interests (Gerbner, 1998; Gerbner et al., 1980; Morgan, 2012; Morgan et al., 2012). Content analysis of primetime TV showed two things. First, television audiences were indeed exposed to a great deal of violence; far more than happens in the real world. But second, there was a marked political pattern at play. Women, people of colour, the young and the old were far more likely to be the victims of violence than were affluent white male professionals. These were not simply exhilarating images about how to be violent; they were also lessons about who runs the world (Gerbner, 1996).

So, screen violence told stories of power; and supporting survey evidence suggested that the main outcome of exposure was that it made people scared and suspicious

(Gerbner et al., 1979). Heavy viewers were significantly more likely than light viewers to overestimate the prevalence of assault and murder in society, exaggerate their chances of falling victim to this brutality, and hold the view that other people cannot be trusted. The researchers termed this the "mean world syndrome" (Gerbner et al., 1980).

This radically different view of why the consumption of media violence might be a social problem was grounded in Gerbner's work on commercial popular culture in the 1950s. Early on, Gerbner came to see popular culture as a potent source of social communication that bore a simple message: consume. He developed this view very clearly in research on confession magazines. Confession magazines of the 1950s, directed at women who worked in the home, contained lurid tales about "bad girls" who suffered terrible fates because they broke gender norms. Alongside the tales, the magazines also provided copious advertising, guiding readers through the bewildering world of consumer goods that increased industrial wages obliged them to negotiate. Gerbner argued that these "texts", stories and advertisements together, told a simple story: stay at home, stay married, and buy stuff. His argument was based not just on a content analysis of the stories, but also interviews with magazine editors, who were only too happy to confirm that this was exactly what they meant to do (Gerbner, 1958; Morgan, 2012).

What mattered most to Gerbner were the common stories – scenarios, heroes, villains, and victims – that commonly featured across genres. His "effects" question was how these stories affected ordinary people, by limiting the social imagination on what could be done about social problems. Violence proliferated in media culture because it was an easy means of attracting audiences to easily understood stories – and advertising. The fallout from this commercial imperative was that the more audiences consumed, the more likely they were to believe that the world was a dangerous place that they could do little to change, other than immerse themselves in consumer culture (Gerbner, 1998).

Blunt as these conclusions sound, they describe post-Newtown effects quite well. The rush of privatized solutions to Newtown – where individuals bought guns, or schools hired private security firms to teach teachers how to use weapons – was precisely the sort of individualized, consumerist response that corporate media have ever encouraged, and was again a diversion from the sort of root and branch social investigations that such tragedies clearly demand.

Cultivation and cultural industries

In its heyday, cultivation analysis was criticized for being little more than a nuanced version of an old idea. The position that television told basically the same story, over and over again, and that the more you watched, the more you were persuaded by the veracity of the medium's world view, seemed at odds with the complexities of culture. In particular, the cultivation concept did not seem to account for the diversity of meanings and interpretations that abound in popular culture (Newcomb, 1978). Certainly, differences within cultural industries and variations in audience interpretations of particular stories were deemed irrelevant to the overall processes of the mean world syndrome (Morgan et al., 2012). At face value, this clashes with the experience of video gamers who, as we shall see, make distinctions between "good" and "bad" screen violence.

However, this obstacle can be negotiated because the cultivation concept depends on understanding the structure and functions of media industries. The violence profiles emerged from extensive analysis of broadcast television, reaching the conclusion that, in the face of the domination of behaviourist effects studies and the absence of a political alternative, it was vital to focus on the role the medium played as a dominant "storyteller", tied to the ambitions of the corporate sector. That said, the release of an online Gerbner archive shows that the cultivation founder maintained a life-long correspondence with media producers, actors and screen writers, and was deeply committed to understanding how they did their work, and indeed how his research might provide evidence to lobby for more creative freedom (Morgan, 2012). The notion of television violence as a homogenizing force was very much tied to a situation where the medium addressed national audiences who consumed the same fare.

Consequently, contemporary cultivation analysis acknowledges that as media industries change, and with it the relationship with audiences, so too must views of how communication works. Gerbner saw media communication as a social process, comprising a series of "encoding and decoding" moments from the real world to the interpretation of media realities by its audiences (1976).

Gerbner was convinced that these effects could only be understood by looking at the circuit of cultural production. Resolute as he was about the notion that media violence served patriarchal interests, *how* this came to be was another matter. For example, in the confession magazine study, he noted a disparity between content and covers. Where the stories warned of the fate that lay in store for women who wouldn't stay at home and buy stuff, the covers always featured happy women. This, he discovered, was an editorial compromise designed to assuage shopkeepers. The magazine industry discovered that shopkeepers were happy to sell lurid stories, but not lurid covers that would disrupt the happy consumer flow of their shops. Shop-keepers therefore became key cultural intermediaries linking media and consumer, and texts, or their effects, couldn't be understood without taking their role into account (Gerbner, 1958; Morgan, 2012).

This early, small-scale study helps explain developments in contemporary cultivation studies. Changing media industries have brought new questions about how cultivation works. The concern with the political effects of storytelling remains. But cultivation scholars no longer think these effects are the products of a single media message, which, the more it is seen or heard, the more beguiling it becomes. Today, cultivation analysts are open to the possibility that cultivation processes can work in many directions (sometimes media violence seems to reassure viewers that crime will be punished), different genres might cultivate different ideas, media events might exist as distinct "cultivating" forces and audiences might mediate cultivation effects (Morgan et al., 2012). School shootings and gaming are events and a genre that have been identified as possibly showing how these different forms of cultivation take place (Oliver et al., 2012).

What remains is the idea that screen violence is a "cultural indicator" of the industrial processes that create powerful images of social reality. These images become ingrained in how audiences think about the world, and are therefore an index of the media's political power. Perhaps more importantly, looking at reactions of gamers to the Newtown murders, it also appears that cultivation is an idea that can help media users find a voice within cultural industries. Looking at their reactions, it is possible to see how some developed an organic cultivation perspective in expressing their discomfort with the gaming industry,

Rock, Paper, Shotgun

Two weeks after Sandy Hook, Nathan Grayson of the pc gaming site *Rock, Paper, Shotgun* wrote an editorial imploring readers and gamers to think about their place in cultures of violence. Grayson argued that gamers should demand more responsibility and creativity from the gaming industry. Fallacious as the argument that gaming causes murder is, its longevity, in Grayson's view, was helped by a flood of poorly designed games that relied on repetitive violence for violence's sake. Moreover, it was time for gamers to stop pretending that this violence was nothing but meaningless fun; the play of pixels:

> Forget the nutty politicians. Forget the "studies" that have been tailored to say whatever people want them to say. Just breathe, count to ten, and look inward. We take tremendous joy in virtual violence. We squeal with glee when life-giving liquid squirts out of men's necks. Does that *cause* violence? Probably not. I don't have any concrete reason to believe so, anyway. But it gives violence an active, constant role in our day-to-day lives ... it would be *impossible* for frequent immersion in violent scenarios – fictional or not – to not have some kind of effect on us.
>
> (Grayson, 2012)

Grayson then invited readers to discuss how gaming is involved in cultures of violence, and to think about how they might act *against* these cultures *as* gamers. The article attracted 703 replies, of which 156 addressed the point raised in the article itself (as opposed to being comments on comments).

Grayson's intervention was academically significant. The idea that media violence "cultivates" audiences has been characterized as an "elitist" argument that neither respects nor helps audiences (Gauntlett, 2005). Here, however, was a gaming insider using the language of cultivation – the idea that immersion in media violence must "do" something – as a means of turning gamers into a political community. So, what did his readers make of this?

Reader responses to this article represent a purposive sample (Babbie, 1989) to test the idea that a) cultivation is an idea that connects with the experience of media users, b) their reactions indicate how audiences serve as key mediators of cultivation effects and c) this identifies common ground held between the cultivation and cultural industries positions on the politics of popular culture.

These questions were pursued by coding responses, using the method of theoretically informed, grounded constant comparison analysis (Mayring, 2000; Schatzman and Strauss, 1973). The article and its responses represented a discourse, the use of language that sought to construct competing "realities" in the wake of a particular context (Gray, 2003). In this case, the discussion had significance as a linguistic construction of the place of gaming in a post-Sandy Hook world. Placing this conversation into a thematic order involves moving between what was said and what is significant in terms of scholarly knowledge about the meaning of media violence. The coding process – reading every response and categorizing segments according to key themes on this topic – involved looking for places where cultivation ideas were used. Were the views that violence expresses the limited creativity afforded by commercial media industries, and that this lack of creativity creates the overall perception that some people count more than others in social life, ones that gamers found useful? Alternatively, did participants think gaming was simply pleasure that had nothing to do with crime or politics?

The majority of respondents (91) maintained that violence in video games is not a problem, and has nothing to do with anything that happens in the world. Various reasons were given for this thinking:

- "Gaming is gaming" (31 people); it is a fantasy involving the play of pixels, where violence is simply a narrative device, and not a lesson about how to act in the real world ("there is something preposterous about the idea of video games aficionado 'discussing' violence in videogames, as if both were important things – they aren't – and personally I want to just have fun with my games" Very Real Talker, 2012).
- "Society is the problem"(25) "I felt fine playing videogames after the shooting. It was a terrible, pointless, tragic event that highlights how awful our world can be, but shit like it or equally pointless and terrible happens every day somewhere. Nobody seems to give a shit because they aren't little white children in a familiar environment. I honestly have found my media's and my fellow citizens' hysterical reactions to the shooting kind of disgusting given that they seem to be perfectly fine funding illegal drone strikes on civilians overseas" Finjy, 2012).
- Some readers (20) criticized Grayson for perpetuating a "moral panic". The mainstream press, Washington and the National Rifle Association had worked to create a diversion, talking about games instead of poverty and gun control, and this article simply fanned these flames ("Steps of journalist evolution: 1. Talented writers passionate about hobby start a blog. 2. Blog becomes successful. 3. Writers are invited to annual cocktail parties w/ Jezebel gawker and Kotaku for 'real journalists'. 4. Writers' social milieu changes to journalist cocktail party. 5. Writers start writing for their cocktail party audience." DrGhostman, 2012).
- In a related reaction, 13 people observed that if any media were to blame, it was other genres such as news, which sought to simplify and sensationalize rampage murders ("video game violence isn't the problem, guns (and quite possibly the US news media and mental health system) are" Bigjig, 2012).

On the other hand, 68 readers did agree with the idea that there was too much violence in video games. Moreover, it was this creative failure that "created" the political storm around the industry:

> I do not think there is any issue with gore or killing in games as a subject matter. But as long as violence is considered the only activity which can be

"fun" to play – and by extension, we keep seeing games composed of 5–10 straight hours of non-stop killing padded by brief non-interactive cut scenes – games will continue to offer an incredibly warped view of the worlds they place us in.

(Brise, 2012)

Notably, the anti-Grayson response was grounded in a rhetoric of pleasure and individual responsibilities. In one instance, this made for strange bedfellows:

[J]ust as we as gamers are frustrated when our passion is blamed from those who do not understand what we love, so too are millions of firearms owners who are constantly blamed for the actions of others. If you can, try to make it to a range and experience responsible firearm use before expressing your opinion, just as you would like reviewers to play a game before writing a review.

(Narnold, 2012).

In other words, gamers and the NRA should make peace and unite against a common foe – people who want to stop law-abiding consumers from doing what they want to do.

Gerbner's early views on what mass culture does therefore rang through both sets of responses. For naysayers, faced with Sandy Hook, the only thing you can do as a consumer is keep on doing what you are doing. Games or guns; whatever keeps you from trouble, and the people who cause it.

For the others who thought that there was too much violence in games, this was not all that they could do. The rhetoric of individual pleasure broke down in these reactions, because it seemed that to these gamers, gaming was actually quite unpleasant, as it involved wading through waves of unimaginative violence.

You know what effect violence in games has on gamers? None. Do you know what effect the game itself has on gamers? Rage induction. Why? Because games are terribly designed. Play *Battlefield 3*, on normal, on a daily basis or semi-weekly basis. Shoot someone 15 times in the face at pointblank with any gun in the game. Get killed when they shoot you once in the stomach with a less powerful gun. Then, try, just try not to get pissed off.

(Grenade, 2012)

Here, then, there was a desire to affect an industry that was letting its players down as audiences who want meaningful experiences that create the space to think about the world.

From this point of view, as important as Ferguson and Ivory's dissection of the "gaming violence equals real violence" case is, in the views of the Grayson camp, video games do not "form a media outlet in which individuals may experience, explore and consider violent behavior which occurs naturally within our species" (2012: 60). They should, and sometimes they do, but in the main they do not. In this regard, a cultural indicators project that enumerates how and how much violence players routinely encounter would be a useful tool in efforts to make gaming cultures richer.

In this small-scale pilot study, the data found a gaming community that was divided on the nature and significance of gaming violence. This suggests a number of valuable research questions; what patterns of media violence do gamers encounter? How are their reactions shaped by cultural intermediaries, such as games journalists and other gamers? How do insights on the gaming industry affect experiences of media violence, and the positions that gamers take in long-running media violence debates?

Discussion

These questions are important when contemplating the relationship between cultural industries research, mass communications research on the influence of consumption, as represented by cultivation analysis, and indeed broader developments in audience studies. All share interests in how media equate healthy citizenship with consumer choice – and the problems that this "common sense" produces (Bird, 2011; Livingstone and Lunt, 2011; Turner, 2010). Key figures in the latter model argue that far too much attention has been paid to the diversity of creativity of media reception and use in the last 20 years (Bird, 2011; Couldry and Hepp, 2013). Media industries congregate audiences, and in a mediatized world it is often *as* audiences that people enter public life (Livingstone, 2012). There is a general sort of media power, found in the reality that very often people have *no* choice other than to engage with the political as audiences for commercially driven media genres and events (Hepp, 2013). This is amplified by the tendency to address audiences as consumers rather than citizens in policy deliberations (Livingstone and Lunt, 2011). Additionally, many of the imaginative/creative ways of participations in media cultures that can be seen as sorts of "performances" (Abercrombie and Longhurst, 1999) can just as easily be understood as "habits" that synchronize well with industrial needs (Ruddock, 2013).

These are arguably the most important questions in media research, and the need to pursue them with vigour has intensified alongside the forces of mediatization. The synthesis of social, cultural, individual, and media life makes methods for conceiving the general rhythms of living in commercial public cultures more pressing. Nowhere has this been more poignantly dramatized than in the tragic topic of school shootings as media events.

Within this topic, one of the "effects" of consuming video games is to make people think of their "leisure" as something that is connected to the politics of violence. Here, complaints about creativity are not just related to pleasure but also politicized ideas about the good life, and to speak of these images is to address the industries and creative processes that make them. On the other hand, this is an activity that is hard to sustain, because of either the political venom that has been directed at gamers, or the absence of a well-defined language to articulate concerns.

Cultivation analysis is useful here. The goal of the paradigm was to encourage popular pressure for a richer public culture, by outlining the political problems caused by profit-driven storytelling. The investigation of how cultural industries work was a feature of early cultivation research, and so the case that cultural industries scholarship should inform contemporary cultivation analysis is clear. Moreover, the concept of cultivation can usefully inform the political dimensions of cultural industries research. Understanding patterns of representations in games, and attitudes about social reality that may form among gamers, is a useful baseline to start a conversation about why gaming matters politically. On the other hand, changing media industries demand a cultivation project that is truer to Gerbner's original interests. The logic of the model, with its focus on mass communication as a social process affected by structures and intermediaries, means that questions about what gaming does, politically, must be informed by understanding the "variables" that constitute it as an industry and a meaningful experience.

It's around matters like this that cultural industries research can productively interact with the mass communication approach to the politics of media consumption.

References

Abercrombie, N. and Longhurst, B. (1999) *Audiences*, London: Sage.

Anderson, C., Shibuya, A., Ihori, N., Swing, E., Bushman, B., Sakamoto, A., Rothstein, H., and Saleem, M. (2010) "Violent Video Game Effects on Aggression, Empathy, and Prosocial Behavior in Eastern and Western Countries: A Meta-Analytic Review", *Psychological Bulletin*, 136: 151–73.

Babbie, E. (1989) *The Practice of Social Research*, New York: Lawrence Earlbaum.

Bandura, A. (1978) "Social Learning Theory of Aggression", *Journal of Communication*, 28: 12–29.

Bandura, A. (2009) "Social Cognitive Theory of Mass Communication", in Bryant, J. and Oliver, M.B. (eds) *Media Effects: Advances in Theory and Research*, 3rd ed., New York: Lawrence Earlbaum.

Bigjig. (2012) *Comment*, www.rockpapershotgun.com/2012/12/28/why-arent-we-discussing-video game-violence/ (accessed November 1, 2013).

Bird, E. (2011) "Are We All Produsers Now?" *Cultural Studies*, 25: 502–16.

Brise. 2012. *Comment*, www.rockpapershotgun.com/2012/12/28/why-arent-we-discussing-video game-violence/ (accessed November 1, 2013).

Comstock, G. (2008) "A Sociological Perspective on Television Violence and Aggression", *American Behavioral Scientist*, 51: 1184–211.

Couldry, N. and Hepp, A. (2013) "Conceptualizing Mediatization: Contexts, Traditions, Arguments", *Communication Theory*, 23: 191–202.

DrGhostman (2012) *Comment*, www.rockpapershotgun.com/2012/12/28/why-arent-we-discussing-videogame-violence/ (accessed November 1, 2013).

Ferguson, C. and Ivory, J. (2012) "A Futile Game: On the Prevalence and Causes of Misguided Speculation About the Role of Violence Video Games in Mass School Shootings", in Muschert, G. and Sumiala, J. (eds) *School Shootings: Mediatized Violence in a Global Age*, Chicago: Emerald.

Finjy (2012) *Comment*, www.rockpapershotgun.com/2012/12/28/why-arent-we-discussing-video game-violence/ (accessed November 1, 2013).

Gauntlett, D. (2005) *Moving Images*, London: Routledge.

Gauntlett, D. (2011) "Media Studies 2.0, and Other Battles Around the Future of Audience Research", www.theory.org.uk/david/kindle.htm.

Gerbner, G. (1958) "The Social Anatomy of the Romance-Confession Cover Girl", *Journalism and Mass Communication Quarterly*, 35: 299–306.

Gerbner, G. (1969) "Toward 'Cultural Indicators': The Analysis of Mass Mediated Public Message", *AV Communication Review*, 17: 137–48.

Gerbner, G. (1976) 'Studies in Mass Communication', unpublished manuscript.

Gerbner, G. (1996) "Fred Rogers and the Significance of Story", *Current*, www.asc.upenn.edu/gerbner/Asset.aspx?assetID=1631.

Gerbner, G. (1998) "Cultivation Analysis: An Overview", *Mass Communication and Society*, 1: 175–95.

Gerbner, G., Gross, L., Jackson-Beck, M., Jackson-Fox, S., and Signorielli, N. (1979) "Cultural Indicators: Violence Profile #9", *Journal of Communication*, 28: 176–207.

Gerbner, G., Gross, L., Morgan, M., and Signorelli, N. (1980) "The Mainstreaming of America: Violence Profile #11", *Journal of Communication*, 30: 10–29.

Gray, A. (2003) *Research Practice*, London: Sage.

Grayson, N. (2012) "Why Aren't We Discussing Videogame Violence?" *Rock, Paper, Shotgun*, www.rockpapershotgun.com/2012/12/28/why-arent-we-discussing-videogame-violence/ (accessed January 6, 2013).

Grenade (2012) *Comment*, www.rockpapershotgun.com/2012/12/28/why-arent-we-discussing-videogame-violence/ (accessed November 1, 2013).

Gross, L. (2009) "My Media Studies: Cultivation to Participation", *Television and New Media*, 10: 66–68.

Gunter, B. (2008) "Media Violence: Is There a Case for Causality?" *American Behavioral Scientist*, 51: 1061–122.

Hepp, A. (2013) *Cultures of Mediatization*, Cambridge: Polity.

Hesmondhalgh, D. (2004) *Cultural Industries*, London: Sage.

Hesmondhalgh, D. (2009) "Politics, Theory and Method in Media Industries Research", in Holt, J. and Perren, A. (eds) *Media Industries: History, Theory and Method*, Chicester: Wiley-Blackwell.

Lewis, J. (1990) *Art, Culture and Enterprise*, London: Routledge.

Livingstone, S. (2012) "Exciting Moments in Audience Research: Past, Present and Future", in Bilandzic, H., Patriarche, G.F., and Traudt, P.J. (eds) *The Social Use of Media: Cultural and Social Scientific Perspectives on Audience Research*, Chicago: Intellect.

Livingstone, S. and Lunt, P. (2011) "The Implied Audience of Communications Policy Making: Regulating Media in the Interests of Citizens and Consumers", in Nightingale, V. (ed.) *The Handbook of Media Audiences*, Chicester: Wiley-Blackwell.

Mayring, P. (2000) "Qualitative Content Analysis", *Forum: Qualitative Social Research*, 1, nbn-resolving.de/urn:nbn:de:0114-fqs0002204.

Meier, B. and Martin, A. (2012) "Real and Virtual Firearms Nurture a Marketing Link", *New York Times*, www.nytimes.com/2012/12/25/business/real-and-virtual-firearms-nurture-marketing-link.html?ref=technology&_r=1& (accessed January 6, 2013).

Morgan, M. (2012) *George Gerbner: A Critical Introduction to Media and Communication Theory*, New York: Peter Lang.

Morgan, M., Shanahan, J., and Signorelli, N. (eds) (2012) *Living with Television Now: Advances in Cultivation Theory and Research*, New York: Peter Lang.

Muschert, G. (2007) "The Columbine Victims and the Myth of the Juvenile Superpredator", *Youth Violence and Juvenile Justice*, 5: 351–66.

Muschert, G. (2009) "Frame-Changing in the Media Coverage of a School Shooting: The Rise of Columbine as a National Concern", *Social Science Journal*, 46: 164–70.

Muschert, G. and Sumiala, J. (eds) (2012) *School Shootings: Mediatized Violence in a Global Age*, Chicago: Emerald.

Narnold (2012) *Comment*, www.rockpapershotgun.com/2012/12/28/why-arent-we-discussing-videogame-violence/ (accessed November 1, 2013).

Newcomb, H. (1978) "Assessing the Violence Profile Studies of Gerbner and Gross: A Humanistic Critique and Suggestion", *Communication Research*, 5: 264–82.

Oliver, M., Bae, K., Ash, E., and Chung, M. (2012) "New Developments in Analysis of Crime and Fear", in Morgan, M., Shanahan, J., and Signorielli, N. (eds) *Living with Television Now: Advances in Cultivation Theory and Research*, New York: Peter Lang.

Ruddock, A. (2013) *Youth and Media*, London: Sage.

Scharrer, E., Weidman, L., and Bissell, K. (2003) "Pointing the Finger of Blame: News Media Coverage of Popular-Culture Culpability", *Journalism and Communication Monographs*, 5: 277–94.

Schatzman, L. and Strauss, A. (1973) *Field Research: Strategies for a Natural Sociology*, New York: Prentice-Hall.

Sumiala, J. and Tikka, M. (2010) "Web First to Death: The Media Logic of the School Shootings in the Era of Uncertainty", *Nordicom Review*, 31: 17–29.

Tassi, P. (2013) "NRA Press Conference: Blame Video Games and Movies, Not Guns", *Forbes*, www.forbes.com/sites/insertcoin/2012/12/21/nra-press-conference-blame-video-games-and-movies-not-guns/ (accessed November 28, 2013).

Tear, M. and Neilson, M. (2013) "Failure to Demonstrate That Playing Violent Video Games Diminishes Prosocial Behavior", *PLOS ONE*, www.plosone.org/article/info%3Adoi%2F10.1371%2Fjournal.pone.0068382 (accessed July 3, 2013).

Turner, G. (2010) "Approaching Celebrity Studies", *Celebrity Studies*, 1: 11–20.

Very Real Talker (2012) *Comment* www.rockpapershotgun.com/2012/12/28/why-arent-we-discussing-videogame-violence/ (accessed November 1, 2013).

43
CULTURE, POLITICS AND THE CULTURAL INDUSTRIES
Reviving a critical agenda

Graeme Turner

It is possible to present a narrative that can trace the genealogy of the study of the cultural industries back to the beginnings of cultural policy studies in the late 1980s and early 1990s, a period when cultural policy occupied centre stage for reformist governments in (at least) the United Kingdom, Australia, and much of western Europe. Cultural policy studies established itself within the university as a field of teaching and research, and the level of pragmatism it displayed in engaging with policy-makers helped it to secure credibility within government. The manner in which it approached the production of culture reflected its Foucauldian theoretical orientation (Bennett, 1998) in that it was mostly, but not exclusively, interested in the role that government played in producing culture; hence its most important interventions concerned heritage-based cultural institutions such as museums and arts funding bodies as well as media regulation and film policy. In the United Kingdom these interests diversified, eventually leading to, among other things, a strand of research that engaged directly with political economy and thus with the industrial production of culture. The second chapter in our narrative, then, would deal with the emergence of the cultural industries paradigm in the United Kingdom from the late 1990s to the present. While just as interested in issues of policy and regulation as those in cultural policy studies, it had a far greater interest in political economy and what actually counted as the cultural industries in this paradigm was also significantly different. It concentrated its attention upon the expanding media and popular entertainment industries, what David Hesmondhalgh describes as industries that 'deal primarily with the industrial production and circulation of texts' (2013: 16), and in recent years it has been particularly concerned with examining the emergence of the digital media industries. If we turn to the third and most recent chapter in our story, we find traces of aspects of each of these preceding models in the development of the concept of the creative industries from the early 2000s (see Flew, 2012). The creative industries model understands the necessity of engaging with policy, it has concentrated upon the commercial and industrial response to digital technologies, and it is determined to find points of alignment between both government and industry but, rather than pursuing a fundamental concern with culture, it frames its interest as participating in a commercial and political agenda of innovation and enterprise (Cunningham, 2013).

One observation to make about that narrative would be to note that over the course of those three decades its central characters, the cultural industries, were asked to play significantly different roles. Crudely put, where the central focus of cultural policy studies was upon a broadly defined notion of culture and the politics of its construction, the focus of creative industries was upon a narrowly defined notion of the economy and the instruments of enterprise. I need to stress, however, that this has not been anything like a single or straightforward evolutionary trajectory. Significantly, for my purposes here, while the political and critical character of the original interest in the cultural industries may have been maintained in many locations within the academy and government, in many more locations it has been displaced, or at least compromised, by the successive variations of interest and position that have in effect fragmented the field. Among the casualties of this fragmentation has been what was once central: the critical examination of the cultural, social and political function and potential of the cultural industries.

Important, here, are the implications of some shifts in terminology, of categories and therefore of focus, in both the policy domain and in the academic fields concerned with understanding and informing that domain. I am referring, first, to the shift from the 'cultural' to the 'creative' in the framing of so much of the most recent work on the cultural industries, but also to the manner in which forecasts of the potential of a 'creative economy' have been taken up as a policy opportunity that has allowed a narrow conception of the economic to displace cultural or political categories. These shifts, I suggest, have contributed to a trend which, in certain configurations, takes us away from a focus on the cultural industries' participation in the construction and maintenance of forms of culture and community (those of the locality, the region or the nation), and towards a focus upon investment in the individual – the entrepreneur, the artist or the consumer. The concept of the creative economy has been influential and now constitutes one of the more common aspirations to appear in policy documents produced by contemporary government agencies dealing with the cultural industries – from transnational bodies such as the United Nations Educational, Scientific and Cultural Organization (UNESCO), to national cultural and regulatory bodies, and all the way down to the local council. The creative economy is an attractive proposition to these agencies: rather than having to reluctantly accept the fact that cultural initiatives will cost rather than raise money, for such agencies the creative economy holds out the prospect of serving both cultural and economic objectives simultaneously. By articulating a new rationale for prioritising the economic considerations that have become so fundamental for policy-makers, the complex of formations I am summarising under the term of the creative economy promises to develop cultural industries that are comprised of viable enterprises that do not require subvention or financial assistance. That possibility is made more likely as a result of the post-2000s broadening of the definitions of the cultural industries – moving from the traditional domains of the arts, culture and heritage towards embracing emerging technologies and their applications: multimedia arts, digital design and entertainment products as well as the cohort of online entrepreneurs developing social media platforms, retailing 'apps' and so on. These newly expanded boundaries have created fertile ground for the ideas of creative economy pundits such as Richard Florida (2002), informing policy approaches to, for instance, developing 'creative cities' (Landry, 2000) through planning projects aimed at seeding clusters of 'creatives' as a cultural component within enterprises in urban renewal.

This chapter argues that these developments have taken us quite some distance from what might once have been regarded as the key critical arguments about why the cultural industries might matter – socially, politically, culturally and ethically. It is time, I suggest, to respond by insisting that, the creative economy notwithstanding, the cultural industries can do much more for us than merely support small business enterprises run by 'creatives', or provide the cultural rationale for certain aspects of urban development projects. The approaches to the study and analysis of the cultural industries that underpinned earlier versions of the field, such as cultural policy studies, can remind us of that potential.

From cultural policy studies to creative industries

Beginning in the late 1980s and prospering through the early 1990s in the United Kingdom and Australia, the cultural policy studies moment lasted quite a while in both locations, although (it must be admitted) not much longer than the governments under whom it developed in the first place. As a field of teaching and research it has, of course, survived, but it has lost its place in the forefront of this kind of work as subsequent developments have superseded it. In the United Kingdom the cultural industries tradition has been the dominant model for quite some time. The key challenges to that position now come from the creative industries paradigm – a concept articulated in the United Kingdom by the Blair government's Creative Industries Taskforce (DCMS, 1998), but which was most actively developed as a research field in Australia – and from sections of new media studies that have focused on the expanding policy domain that has of necessity accompanied the emergence of digital and social media and e-commerce, and increasingly interested itself in telecommunications policy. Within the university sector in Australia, the creative industries idea was used to develop a more industry-friendly model for undergraduate programs in media and creative arts; as such, it exemplifies the Australian tertiary education system's instrumentalist agenda over the last decade or so. While proving attractive to university administrators because of its promise of vocational outcomes, the creative industries paradigm was also attractive to governments, especially in Asia. Connecting, as it did, with the popularisation of the notion of the creative class and projections of a new economy organised around their potential, the creative industries agenda offered governments a persuasive case for the economic benefits of forms of cultural entrepreneurship that were linked to the expansion of the domain of media, arts and entertainment which was in turn structured around clusters of small to medium sized businesses.

In Australia, cultural policy studies had developed at a time when there was significant public and government interest in the nation- and community-building capacities of cultural institutions. At that stage, from the mid-1980s through to the mid-1990s, the leading platforms were the institutions supporting Australian feature film production, public broadcasting, and the arts, broadly conceived (that is, all the way from literature to community arts). Cultural policy studies was interested not only in critical analysis of the policy structures established in order to support the organisations and industries involved, but also in their outcomes – in terms of the politics of the cultural imaginaries they represented, and also in terms of socio-democratic considerations such as equity and access. While there was certainly incidental interest in the possible economic benefits that might flow to the nation, the key concerns were not about the flow-on effects to the rest of the economy. Since these activities were understood as intrinsically worthwhile, the primary economic consideration was how to ensure their viability by instituting the appropriate funding and operational settings. It is difficult, in the current context, to imagine a time when economic considerations played such a subordinated role in generating the policy settings, and this emphasises just how comprehensive and categorical was the subsequent change in attitude towards the cultural economy.

There is an important transitional moment. Although this could not have been in anyone's mind at the time, one can see in retrospect that the process that took us from cultural policy studies to creative industries began with the publication of Stuart Cunningham's *Framing Culture* (1992). In this book, Cunningham asks, 'what relations do, and should, exist between cultural criticism and cultural policy?' In framing his answer, he points to Elizabeth Jacka's comment on the 'ever widening gap between cultural critique and cultural policy', and to the significant role played in widening that gap by the critical tradition he names as cultural studies – a 'neo-Marxist' formation aligned with the interests of the audience and unevenly informed about, as well as ideologically antagonistic to, the industries concerned (Cunningham, 1992: 3). While clearly arguing for an alternative model of cultural studies, one that was more pragma-tically aligned with the interests of the industries in question and less readily inclined to move straight into the practice of politically motivated critique, Cunningham does not at this juncture locate his primary interest in the development of these industries. Indeed, his primary objective is clear in his advocacy of what he describes as a 'renewed concept of citizenship', which he argues 'should be central to cultural studies as it moves into the 1990s' (10).

It is possible with the benefit of hindsight, however, to see this as the beginning of the more radical shift that eventually led Cunningham, among others identified with the creative industries project, to distance himself from the prevailing cultural studies practices of analysis and critique in favour of a commitment to the primary objective of informing industry development in the creative industries. The path towards out-lining an academic rationale for that commitment is a long one, with many participants, and marked by a series of opportunistic alignments within what was otherwise an inhospitable climate for government investment in humanities and social science research over the course of the 2000s. The success of that process of development and negotiation, however, is evident in the establishment of a perception within some quarters of the Australian government that the creative industries represented *the* key location from which the humanities and social sciences might most usefully participate in what had come to be called the 'national innovation system' (a phrase aimed at marrying industry and academic research). The alignment with a new economy agenda that rhetorically synonymised creativity, enterprise and innovation imagined the successful commercialisation of the cultural or creative industries by thinking of them as embedded within an enterprise culture romanticised by its links with new media and a cottage industry start-up model that effectively cleansed these industries of their association with business.

Among the considerable attractions of this new agenda was its definitive contemporariness. Creative industries categorically broke with the high culture/popular culture divide that still haunted this policy space and took us enthusiastically into a brave new world of digital technologies, multimedia arts, new telecommunication platforms, social media and new forms of entertainment such as computer games – enterprises that would eventually be described as contributing to a 'services' rather than a 'cultural' economy (Cunningham, 2002). Drawing on notions of, variously, the knowledge economy, the digital economy, the new economy or the creative economy, and notwithstanding the questionable evidence base for virtually all the predictions associated with them, this looked like what the cultural industries were set to become in the 21st century.

I have addressed what I see as the implications of this history at some length in *What's Become of Cultural Studies?* (Turner, 2012). To briefly reiterate the position outlined there, I argued that the cultural policy studies agenda was 'largely in accord with the core activity of cultural studies, what Jim McGuigan has called "critique in the public interest", in that it had its eyes firmly fixed on the public good' – this, 'understood as distinct from the political objectives of governments or the commercial objectives of the cultural industries'. I went on to suggest that the transition from cultural policy to creative industries takes us towards quite different objectives: 'for instance, the focus moves from the nation-state – the location of regulatory and developmental interests in the culture industries – to the global market, the desired location of commercializable convergent enterprises'. The beneficiary of the earlier project is the nation, the community and the citizen, typically through the state's subsidisation of the not-for-profit cultural organisation. The beneficiary of the latter project is the entrepreneur, the commercial industry, and the individual consumer, through the range of services or products offered for sale. The move from cultural policy studies to creative industries is, then, most definitively, 'a retreat from a commitment to the public good and its replacement by a belief in the social utility of a market outcome, reflecting the classic neo-liberal view that commercial success or "wealth creation" for the enterprises concerned in itself constitutes a public good'. Therefore, 'where the former was directly engaged with developing its potential as a social, political, cultural and theoretical project, the latter is primarily focused upon economic and market development objectives as themselves facilitators of other, but unspecified, kinds of social progress' (Turner, 2012: 112–13).

Nation, community, economy

What I have been describing above, of course, is not simply a story about research into the cultural industries. It is, as well, distressingly representative of the jostling for position and relevance required of disciplinary formations within the context of a higher education system subject to repeated changes of policy, each of them less committed than the last to the idea of the university as a public good. There is, however, a much broader and more familiar context than this: across a range of sectors in our societies – education, health, immigration, corporate regulation – the concepts of the 'nation' and, to a lesser extent, 'culture' have lost purchase as they are increasingly contrasted with the importance attached to the projection of 'the economy'. It would not be implausible to suggest that when policy-makers now talk of the context in which they wish their decisions to have impact, it is more common for this to be described as 'the economy' than as 'the nation' or 'the culture'. 'Community', another term that has the political potential to compete with economistic preferences, has, on the other hand, continued to turn up in policy documents as well as in academic analysis – albeit often in a particular way. There is a tendency for community to be co-opted as a proxy for the social or the cultural content usually contained with these other two terms. There is a reason for this. In the contexts I have in mind, this is not about developing, protecting, or respecting existing communities; rather, newly constructed communities are proposed as among the outcomes of policy initiatives. In a typical example, for instance, an urban planning initiative will aspire to create a community through the design of its built environment. In another genre of deployment, in policy documents as much as in academic debate, community is paired with the global in order to provide an alternative frame of reference that together operates as a means of making the nation, and indeed the political, irrelevant.

While we might argue about the extent to which such a generalisation is true across the political sector, the more fundamental point I wish to make here is not at all a contentious one. Few could deny that over the last decade or so the management of just about every policy domain has been reoriented around the primacy of the economy (it would be hard to imagine anyone who has worked in a university over the last decade disagreeing with this!). Simply, and as noted in my earlier discussion of the history of cultural policy studies, this constitutes a significant shift; where once the idea of the nation was right at the heart of cultural policy, now it is not.

There is no space, nor need, to rehearse here all the familiar arguments that usually accompany an account of the rise of neoliberalism within Western democracies, the customary explanation of the ascendancy of the economy in political and public discourse. In any case, my interest lies in making a quite specific secondary observation – which is, that when cultural policy was designed to deliver national, rather than economic, benefits, the door was open to a wider range of political and ethical critiques than is available today. This raises the question: why did we discard such a productive mode of critique? We have already noted one of the reasons: that the cultural objectives customarily implicated in the idea of the nation lost their purchase in the increasingly economistic context of political debate over the 1990s and 2000s. However, there were also significant theoretical shifts within the humanities and social science disciplines in the academy – in interdisciplinary formations such as postmodernism, post-colonialism and cosmopolitanism – which discredited the category of the nation. It became orthodox to argue that, because the nation carried so much conservative and nationalist baggage, it could no longer serve as a legitimate vehicle for progressive political critique. In the United Kingdom, in particular, the category had been thoroughly captured by the political right during the Thatcher era. Furthermore, less compromised alternative vehicles were available: globalism and cosmopolitanism, among them. For those to whom the concept of the creative economy was attractive, there seemed little need to hang on to a concept that had become so politically untenable. What's more, there was the possibility that the creative economy could productively modify standard conceptions of the economy, from within. For these and other reasons, it became extremely unfashionable for critical theorists to interest themselves in the nation (Morley, 2004: 317), and within media policy contexts it was seen as an almost reactionary position to take in the context of media globalisation. All of that said, it should also be acknowledged that in many domains of cultural policy – particularly within the creative arts – we continue to hear about the capacities of the nation; what has changed, however, is that these are now framed as economic rather than cultural capacities.

If we step outside the academic and policy arenas into broader arenas of public debate, the picture is quite different; discomfort with the idea of the nation is far from an orthodox position. To the contrary, the nation still constitutes a well understood and popularly endorsed platform from which to mount criticism of the social, political and cultural consequences of cultural policies of all kinds – that is, it mobilises widely accepted expectations about what policy should do for the nation, and not just for the economy. By not exploiting this potential – by allowing the category of the nation to be set aside, or colonised by the economy, in policy debates – we squander a valuable asset that can serve as a rallying point for the advocacy for investment in cultural activities, and as a basis from which to critique and analyse cultural policy initiatives that have been proposed or implemented. I would make a similar point about too readily accepting the cynical use of the category of community as a feel-good legitimating device for policy initiatives; in this case, it is important not so much to retrieve, as to renovate, the category of community so that it refers to an established formation with social and historical roots, rather than merely, say, the projected effect of the organisation of space in the planning of urban design.

We can see just what has been lost by the surrendering of such terms in the face of the hegemony of the economy, if we ask exactly how we might go about evaluating how well our current policy frameworks are serving us now. Could we do this adequately if we only think of 'us' as an economy, rather than as a community or a nation? To set these notions aside, and not to replace them with concepts of comparable power and provenance, is precisely to surrender the opportunity to appeal to values other than the economic.

New priorities for the cultural economy

Labels matter, and the construction of the term 'creative industries' has its own role to play here. It displaces a concern with cultural politics and constructs in its place an opportunistic pragmatism that is legitimated by its discursive connection to the projected potential of the digital economy. The label's exploitation of the apparent contradiction between the creative and the industrial has generated some trenchant responses, such as Jim McGuigan's dismissal of the project as 'cool capitalism'

(2006). Among the things accomplished by 'cool capitalism' is the displacement of any serious consideration of what actually goes on in the cultural economy. For instance, we would not look to the creative industries literature if we wanted to find an empirical examination of the conditions of work within these creative industries; that is found elsewhere, such as in cultural studies (see Ross, 2004; Gregg, 2011). Instead, precarity is romanticised as the grassroots democratisation of production, and the actual rewards for workers in these industries (let alone those who contribute their content for nothing) are ignored. The perspective from which the creative industries are viewed is largely that of the entrepreneur. This is true, even when it seems as if we are talking about the consumer. The much cited notion of 'produsage' (Bruns, 2008) and the excitement about the power shift implied by the explosion of user-generated content (UGC) online, certainly points to a significant change in the patterns of media consumption and production. However, it is also built upon a blurring of the structural, political and economic differences between the categories of paid and unpaid labour. Optimistic projections of the economic and 'democratising' potential of UGC are not only misleading because they elide these differences, but they also serve to legitimate and promote labour relations that might be 'cool' but are nonetheless exploitative.

One of the more worrying consequences of a lack of political and ethical scrutiny of the industries and commercial formations at the centre of the creative industries can be seen in its enthusiastic take-up as a policy orientation in developing countries – where creative industries has indeed been seen as a useful and productive strategy to explore as a means of finding innovative ways to participate in the global economy. It is now becoming clear that this strategy has not necessarily served these nations well. As Justin O'Connor has noted, commenting on the release of the 2013 UNESCO report on the creative economy, 'the focus on high value creative industries such as digital marketing and communication design in developing countries has led to widening imbalances between educated elites and the rest, and between metropolitan centres and poorer regions' (2013: np). The UNESCO report is particularly significant for its retreat from unqualified support for the creative industries model, arguing that policies informed by this approach may have in fact been implicated in 'increasing inequality, in eroding cultural diversity, and in overlooking the human and social consequences of such a strongly market-oriented approach to national development' (O'Connor, 2013: np).

It has to be recognised that creative industries explicitly displaces and implicitly devalues the cultural precisely because it operates through principles of analysis that are extrinsic to the industries themselves. Cut free from such principles, what mostly passes for analysis in the creative industries literature is the aggregation of anecdotal accounts of individual experiences leading to projections of how widespread such experiences will be in the future (for example, Shirky, 2008). More structured empirical analysis, or indeed the production of substantial evidence of how the creative sector actually informs or produces desirable cultural change – let alone economically viable career opportunities – is not a feature of this tradition. Most fundamentally for my purposes here, the contradiction at the heart of the creative industries model denies the distinctiveness of the cultural economy – that is, its capacity to do more than simply produce a commercial output. The cultural industries can do more for us than simply support small business enterprises, or participate in the project of wealth creation, and the approaches to their study and analysis that underpinned earlier versions of the field remind us of that potential: their focus was upon the capacity of these industries to improve the cultural and political conditions – in the broadest sense – in which communities live.

However, I am not suggesting we merely return to those earlier settings. Not only has the makeup of the cultural industries changed dramatically and thus there are now substantially new elements to deal with, but these earlier settings did little to demythologise the operations of a market economy, and were uncritically accepting of the notion of market failure. They routinely supported state subvention as a means of filling the gaps left by the market in order to prosecute a complementary agenda of national or community cultural development – fine as far as it goes, but it does mean that there was very little critical attention to the operation of actual markets. There is an opportunity to do better than this – to see the cultural economy as a means of not only incorporating the new elements that have come with the digital era, but also of dealing directly with the wider, political and ethical, consequences of the operation of the market across the cultural industries.

In a telling moment in Orson Welles' classic film, *Citizen Kane*, Kane's financial mentor assures him, 'there's no trick to making money, if that's all you want to do'. In order to construct a positive agenda for the next generation of work on the cultural economy, we need to focus on some of the *other* things we might want to do, explore the ways in which the cultural economy might enable us to do them, and evaluate how well the cultural economy is doing them now – that is, effectively to reverse the priorities that have shaped the transition from cultural policy studies to creative industries. The UNESCO report (2013) gives us some pointers to what this might look like in its call for global cultural policy to develop a more inclusive and sustainable cultural economy that emphasises the wider ecology of commercial and not for profit enter-prises across the sector; asserts and enacts the principle that cultural values are as important as economic values in framing policy; and argues that in fact these values should be shaping how we organise the economy to produce progressive and equitable cultural outcomes.

References

Bennett, T. (1998) *Culture: A Reformer's Science*, Allen and Unwin, St Leonards.

Bruns, A. (2008) *Blogs, Wikipedia, Second Life and Beyond: From Production to Produsage*, Peter Lang, New York.

Cunningham, S. (1992) *Framing Culture: Criticism and Policy in Australia*, Allen and Unwin, St Leonards.

Cunningham, S. (2002) 'From Cultural to Creative Industries: Theory, Industry and Policy Implications', *Media International Australia*, 102: 54–65.

Cunningham, S. (2013) *Hidden Innovation: Policy, Industry and the Creative Sector*, University of Queensland Press, St Lucia.

Department for Culture, Media and Sport (DCMS) (1998) *Creative Industries Mapping Document*, UK Government, London.

Flew, T. (2012) *Creative Industries: Culture and Policy*, Sage, London.

Florida, R. (2002) *The Rise of the Creative Class*, Basic Books, New York.

Gregg, M. (2011) *Work's Intimacy*, Polity, London.

Hesmondhalgh, D. (2013) *The Cultural Industries*, 3rd edition, Sage, London.

Landry, C. (2000) *The Creative City*, London, Earthscan.

McGuigan, J. (2006) 'The Politics of Cultural Studies and Cool Capitalism', *Cultural Politics*, 2 (2): 137–58.

Morley, D. (2004) 'At Home With Television', in L. Spigel and J. Olsson (eds) *Television After TV: Essays on a Medium in Transition*, 303–23, Durham, NC, Duke University Press.

O'Connor, J. (2013) 'UNESCO Leads the Way on a Truly Global Approach to Cultural Economy', *The Conversation*, 22 November, theconversation.com/unesco-leads-the-way-on-a-truly-global-approach-to-cultural-economy-19595 (accessed 28 November 2013).

Ross, A. (2004) *No-Collar: The Humane Workplace and its Hidden Costs*, Temple University Press, Philadelphia.

Shirky. C. (2008) *Here Comes Everybody: The Power of Organizing Without Organizations*, Penguin, New York.

Turner, G. (2012) *What's Become of Cultural Studies?* Sage, London.

UNESCO (2013) *United Nations Creative Economy Report 2013 Special Edition: Widening Local Development Pathways*, UNESCO, Paris.

INDEX

Note: Page numbers in **bold** are for figures, those in *italics* are for tables.

Cooke, P. 21
cool capitalism 541–2
cool/coolness 218, 353–4, 355
cooperation *see* mutual aid
cooperatives, worker 309, 315
Coppa, F. 358
copyright 79, 80, 111, 291, 292; and
  globalization of TV formats 134, 136;
  income 430; music industry 144–5,
  146, 147–8, 149n3 and 4, 404; and
  PR work 378
Corak, M. 434, 435
core cultural industries 63
Corner, J. 446
corporations 33, 34, 70–84, 289, 316;
  advertising 180–1; music industry 142;
  sports ownership 414; video games
  publishing 152, 153–4
Corrigan, T.F. 409
Corus Entertainment 276–7
Corwin, N. 190
cosmopolitanism 134, 168, 248, 540, 541;
  Shanghai 247, 249, 252
cosmopolitics 168
Cosse, E. 313
Costello, V. 360
Cottle, S. 319
Coubertin, Baron P. de 421
Couldry, N. 11, 432, 449, 531
Coulson, S. 307
Council for the Encouragement of Music
  and the Arts (CEMA) 286
counter-culture 11, 353
counter-interpellation 306, 312–15, 315
country music 229–30
Cow Clicker (videogame) 157
coworking 308
Cox, S. 78, 81
Cozens, C. 517
craft 454
craft-based manufacturing 92–3
craftivism 224, 229
Crafts Council (UK) 229, 454, 461n
Crang, P. 512–13
Crawford, G. 367n1
Crawford, K. 385, 387, 388
Creative Britain report (DCMA) 446, 448
creative capital 167
creative city concept 23, 24, 88, 166, 197,
  216, 248, 484, 537; China 254; and
  consumption 198, 212, 213–14; and
  developing countries 482; and economic
  growth 203
creative class 3, 4, 88, 197, 207, 248–9, 269,
  312, 337, 484, 537; and the country 224–5

creative clusters 52, 88, 198, 201, 224, 248,
  537; China 198, 246, 250–2, 254, 255, 492
creative consumer 12
creative core 63
creative destruction 11, 80, 109
creative economy 2, 4, 8, 9–10, 11, 24, 36,
  37, 42, 43, 57, 78, 503, 536–7, 539, 541;
  and developing countries 426, 477–87;
  and education system 446; and material
  production 87–9; UK 39, 57, 59, 446
Creative Economy Reports (UN) 57, 426, 477,
  480, 482, 542, 543
Creative England 473
creative industries 2–3, 6–10, 11, 26, 27n3,
  36, 57, 79–80, 86–7, 93–4, 208, 222, 229,
  478, 535–6, 537–9, 541, 542–3; and
  advertising 176–8; Australia 537, 538–9;
  China 249, 250, 252; defining 6–8, 60;
  developing countries 5, 542; East Asia 4,
  6, 537; economic value 37–40, 43; end of
  167–70; and Internet 79–80; UK agenda
  for 35, 37–40, 56, 90, 166–7, 425, 446,
  452–63, 468, 469, 479, 503, 537
Creative Industries Journal 165
Creative Industries Mapping Document
  (DCMS) (UK) 446
Creative Industries Task Force (UK) 56, 537
creative intensity 453–4
creative labour *see* labour
Creative Nation (1994) report, Australia
  56, 91
creative placemaking 206
Creative Skillset 446, 447, 450n4, 454–5
creative vocations 299–300
creativity 4, 5, 9, 25, 34, 35, 42, 46, 56, 59,
  89, 281, 454, 455, 482–5, 539; as an input
  2–3, 6, 8, 26; commodification of 213;
  economic 482; and manufacture,
  separation of 89–90; scientific 482
Crewe, I. 464, 473
Critical Distance website 160
critical media studies 13
critical self-reflection 33, 50
critical urban studies 22
critique 351–2, 355
Crompton, R. 337, 338
Cronin, A. 177
Crouch, C. 258, 429, 432, 433
crowdfunding 145, 393, 402, 405–6
crowdsourcing 156, 179, 293, 431–2
Cuccia, T. 65
Culkin, C. 333, 335, 336
cultivation analysis 490, 522–3, 525, 526–32
cultural activism 207–8
cultural animation 219

Writers Guild of Canada 308
Wu, T. 291
Wynne, D. 1, 220

Xi Jinping 493, 494, 495, 496
Xin Jing Bao (Beijing News) 496
Xinhua 493, 494, 495, 496
Xintiandi complex, Shanghai 253–4

Yahoo 113, 144, 178
Ye, X. 495
Yeh, W. 249
Yelp 409
Yo Soy Betty, La Fea (TV show) 133, 138
Young, C. 202, 207
Young, K. 414
Young, S. 404, 410
Young & Rubicam 181
YouTube 82, 178, 293, 319, 324, 351, 385

Ytreberg, E. 320
Yúdice, G. 25, 50, 176

Zacny, R. 154
Zannoni, D.C. 430
Zawadzki, K. 437n6
ZenithOptimedia 181
Zero Dark Thirty (film) 236–42, 243
Zhang, J. 493
Zhang, W. 491, 494
Zhong, S. 251
Zidane, Z. 414
Zimmerman, E. 160
Zizek, S. 163, 164, 168
zoning 206, 436
Zuberi, N. 141
Zuckerberg, M. 383
Zukin, S. 22, 24, 203, 204, 205, 215, 268
Zynga 157

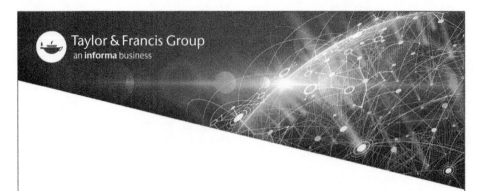